Lecture Notes in Artificial Intelligence   10791

Subseries of Lecture Notes in Computer Science

LNAI Series Editors

Randy Goebel
   University of Alberta, Edmonton, Canada
Yuzuru Tanaka
   Hokkaido University, Sapporo, Japan
Wolfgang Wahlster
   DFKI and Saarland University, Saarbrücken, Germany

LNAI Founding Series Editor

Joerg Siekmann
   DFKI and Saarland University, Saarbrücken, Germany

More information about this series at http://www.springer.com/series/1244

Ugo Pagallo · Monica Palmirani
Pompeu Casanovas · Giovanni Sartor
Serena Villata (Eds.)

AI Approaches
to the Complexity
of Legal Systems

AICOL International Workshops 2015–2017:
AICOL-VI@JURIX 2015, AICOL-VII@EKAW 2016,
AICOL-VIII@JURIX 2016, AICOL-IX@ICAIL 2017,
and AICOL-X@JURIX 2017
Revised Selected Papers

 Springer

Editors
Ugo Pagallo (iD)
University of Turin
Turin, Italy

Monica Palmirani (iD)
University of Bologna
Bologna, Italy

Pompeu Casanovas (iD)
La Trobe University
Melbourne, VIC, Australia

Giovanni Sartor (iD)
University of Bologna
Bologna, Italy

Serena Villata (iD)
Inria - Sophia Antipolis-Méditerranée
Sophia Antipolis, France

ISSN 0302-9743   ISSN 1611-3349   (electronic)
Lecture Notes in Artificial Intelligence
ISBN 978-3-030-00177-3   ISBN 978-3-030-00178-0   (eBook)
https://doi.org/10.1007/978-3-030-00178-0

Library of Congress Control Number: 2018953366

LNCS Sublibrary: SL7 – Artificial Intelligence

This Springer imprint is published by the registered company Springer Nature Switzerland AG
The registered company address is: Gewerbestrasse 11, 6330 Cham, Switzerland

Preface

AICOL stands for Artificial Intelligence Approaches to the Complexity of Legal Systems. This volume presents the revised selected papers of the five different AICOL Workshops during 2015–2017. The first took place as part of the JURIX 2015 conference at the Universidade do Minho in Braga, Portugal, on December 9, 2015. The second took place in Bologna, Italy, on November 19, 2016, in conjunction with the 20th International Conference on Knowledge Engineering and Knowledge Management (EKAW 2016). The third was held at the JURIX 2016 conference at the Inria Sophia Antipolis Mediterranée in Sophia Antipolis, France, on December 14, 2016, as an AICOL Workshop. The fourth was the Workshop on MIning and REasoning with Legal texts, held on June 16th, 2017, in London (UK) which was connected with the MIREL (MIning and REasoning with Legal texts) project, H2020 Marie Skłodowska-Curie grant agreement No 690974 (http://www.mirelproject.eu). It was organized in conjunction with ICAIL 2017, the 16th International Conference on Artificial Intelligence and Law. The fifth was held on December 13, 2017, at the JURIX 2017 conference in Luxembourg. All these workshops had the common rational to combine different disciplines for managing legal systems complexity, both in the foundations and in the applications aspects. Two workshops in particular investigated the Semantic Web techniques (EKAW 2016) and Natural Processing and Legal Reasoning models (MIREL 2016). The 37 selected papers, including the introduction, represent a comprehensive picture of the state of the art in legal informatics.

The present volume follows the previous AICOL volumes: AICOL I-II, published in 2010, include papers from the first AICOL conference in Beijing (24th IVR Congress in September 15–20, 2009, China) and the follow-up in Rotterdam (JURIX-09, November 16–18, The Netherlands); AICOL III, published in 2012, resulting from the third AICOL conference, held in Frankfurt a. M. (25th IVR, August 15–20, 2011, Germany); AICOL-IV@IVR in Belo Horizonte Brazil, July 21–27, 2013, and AICOL-V@SINTELNET-JURIX in Bologna, Italy, December 11, 2013.

Like its predecessors, this volume embodies the philosophy of the AICOL conferences, which is to provide a meeting point for various researchers, such as legal theorists, political scientists, linguists, logicians, and computational and cognitive scientists, eager to discuss and share their findings and proposals. In this sense, the keywords "complexity" and "complex systems" sum up the perspective chosen to describe recent developments in AI and law, legal theory, argumentation, the Semantic Web, and multi-agent systems.

AICOL incorporates in its VI edition the perspective of social intelligence, the intertwined human–machine perspective on cognition, agency, and institutions. This promising approach brings together the analytical and empirical perspectives of society. Stemming from this starting point, the volume is divided into six main sections: (i) Legal Philosophy, Conceptual Analysis, and Epistemic Approaches; (ii) Rules and Norms Analysis and Representation; (iii) Rules and Norms Analysis and

Representation; (iv) Legal Ontologies and Semantic Annotation; (v) Legal Argumentation; and (vi) Courts, Adjudication and Dispute Resolution. New entry topics need a particular spotlight like Legal Design or Legal Data Analytics.

Finally, a special thanks is due to the excellent Program Committee for their hard work in reviewing the submitted papers. Their criticism and very useful comments and suggestions were instrumental in achieving a high quality of publication. We also thank the authors for submitting good papers, responding to the reviewers' comments, and abiding by our production schedule.

July 2018

Ugo Pagallo
Monica Palmirani
Pompeu Casanovas
Giovanni Sartor
Serena Villata

Organization

Organizing Committee

Danièle Bourcier	Université de Paris II, France
Pompeu Casanovas	Autonomous University of Barcelona, La Trobe University
Monica Palmirani	University of Bologna, Italy
Ugo Pagallo	University of Turin, Italy
Giovanni Sartor	European University Institute and University of Bologna, Italy
Serena Villata	Inria Sophia Antipolis, France

Program Committee

Laura Alonso Alemany	Universidad Nacional de Córdoba
Michał Araszkiewicz	Jagiellonian University
Guido Boella	University of Torino
Daniele Bourcier	Centre d'Etudes et de Recherches de Science Administrative et Politique, Universite de Paris II
Pompeu Casanovas	Autonomous University of Barcelona, La Trobe University
Marcello Ceci	GRCTC - Governance, Risk and Compliance Technology Center
Pilar Dellunde	Autonomous University of Barcelona
Luigi Di Caro	University of Torino
Angelo Di Iorio	University of Bologna
Enrico Francesconi	ITTIG-CNR
Michael Genesereth	Stanford University
Jorge Gonzalez-Conejero	UAB Institute of Law and Technology
Guido Governatori	Data61, CSIRO
Davide Grossi	University of Groningen
John Hall	Model Systems
Renato Iannella	Queensland Health
Beishui Liao	Zhejiang University
Arno R. Lodder	Vrije Universiteit Amsterdam
Marco Manna	University of Calabria
Martin Moguillansky	Universidad Nacional del Sur
Paulo Novais	University of Minho
Ugo Pagallo	University of Torino
Marco Pagliani	Senate of Italian Republic
Monica Palmirani	University of Bologna
Adrian Paschke	Freie Universität Berlin

Contents

X   Contents

Courts, Adjudication and Dispute Resolution

Introduction: Legal and Ethical Dimensions of AI, NorMAS, and the Web of Data

Ugo Pagallo[1](✉) , Monica Palmirani[2] , Pompeu Casanovas[3,4] ,
Giovanni Sartor[2] , and Serena Villata[5]

[1] Torino Law School, University of Torino, Lungo Dora Siena 100, 10153
Turin, Italy
ugo.pagallo@unito.it
[2] CIRSFID, University of Bologna, via Zamboni 33, 40126 Bologna, Italy
{monica.palmirani,giovanni.sartor}@unibo.it
[3] CRC D2D, La Trobe Law School, Bundoora Campus, Melbourne, Australia
pompeu.casanovas@uab.cat
[4] IDT, Autonomous University of Barcelona, Bellaterra, Spain
[5] INRIA Sophia Antipolis, Sophia Antipolis Cedex, France
serena.villata@inria.fr

Abstract. AICOL workshops aim to bridge the multiple ways of understanding legal systems and legal reasoning in the field of AI and Law. Moreover, they pay special attention to the complexity of both legal systems and legal studies, on one hand, and the expanding power of the internet and engineering applications, on the other. Along with a fruitful interaction and exchange of methodologies and knowledge between some of the most relevant contributions to AI work on contemporary legal systems, the goal is to integrate such a discussion with legal theory, political philosophy, and empirical legal approaches. More particularly, we focus on four subjects, namely, (i) language and complex systems in law; (ii) ontologies and the representation of legal knowledge; (iii) argumentation and logics; (iv) dialogue and legal multimedia.

Keywords: AI & law · Legal theory · Complex systems · Semantic web
Legal ontologies · Legal semantic web services · Argumentation

1 Introduction

The first volume of this workshop series on Artificial Intelligence approaches to the complexity of legal systems (AICOL) was released at the very beginning of this decade (2010). In the meanwhile, the field of Artificial Intelligence ("AI") has known a new renaissance: for instance, according to the tally Google provided to *MIT Technology Review* in March 2017, the company published 218 journal or conference papers on machine learning in 2016 alone, nearly twice as many as it did two years before [1]. Google's AI explosion illustrates a more general trend that has to do with the improvement of more sophisticated statistical and probabilistic methods, the increasing availability of large amount of data and of cheap, enormous computational power, up to the transformation of places and spaces into AI-friendly environments, e.g. smart cities

U. Pagallo et al. (Eds.): AICOL VI–X 2015–2017, LNAI 10791, pp. 1–20, 2018.
https://doi.org/10.1007/978-3-030-00178-0_1

and domotics. All these factors have propelled a new 'summer' for AI. After the military and business sectors, AI applications have entered into people's lives. From getting insurance to landing credit, from going to college to finding a job, even down to the use of GPS for navigation and interaction with the voice recognition features on our smartphones, AI is transforming and reshaping people's daily interaction with others and their environment. Whereas AI apps and systems often go hand-in-hand with the breath-taking advancements in the field of robotics, the internet of things, and more, we can grasp what is going on in this field in different ways [2]. Suffice it to mention in this context two of them.

First, according to the Director of the Information Innovation Office (I2O) at the Defense Advanced Research Projects Agency (DARPA) in the U.S. Department of Defense, John Launchbury, there would have been so far two waves of research in AI.[1] The first wave concerns systems based on "handcrafted knowledge," such as programs for logistics scheduling, programs that play chess, and in the legal domain, TurboTax. Here, experts turn the complexity of the law into certain rules, and "the computer then is able to work through these rules." Although such AI systems excel at complex reasoning, they were inadequate at perception and learning. In order to overcome these limits, we thus had to wait for the second wave of AI, that is, systems based on "statistical learning" and the "manifold hypothesis." As shown by systems for voice recognition and face recognition, the overall idea is that "natural data forms lower-dimensional structures (manifolds) in the embedding space" and that the task for a learning system is to separate these manifolds by "stretching" and "squashing" the space.[2]

Along these lines, Richard and Daniel Susskind similarly propose to distinguish between a first generation and a second generation of AI systems, namely, between expert systems technologies and systems characterized by major progress in Big Data and search [3]. What this new wave of AI entails has to do more with the impact of AI on society and the law, than the law as a rich test bed and important application field for logic-based AI research. Whether or not the first wave aimed to replicate knowledge and reasoning processes that underpin human intelligence as a form of deductive logic, the second wave of AI brings about "two possible futures for the professions," that is, either a more efficient version of the current state of affairs, or a profound transformation that will displace much of the work of traditional professionals. According to this stance, we can thus expect that "in the short and medium terms, these two futures will be realized in parallel." Yet, the thesis of Richard and Daniel Susskind is that the second future will prevail: in their phrasing, "we will find new and better ways to share expertise in society, and our professions will steadily be dismantled" [3].

Against this highly problematical backdrop, three different levels of analysis should be however differentiated. They concern the normative challenges of the second wave of AI from a political, theoretical, and technical viewpoint, namely (i) the political decisions that should be—or have already been—taken vis-à-vis current developments

---

[1] See the video entitled "A DARPA Perspective on Artificial Intelligence," available online at https://youtube/-O01G3tSYpU.
[2] *Ibid.*

of e.g. self-driving cars, or autonomous lethal weapons; (ii) the profound transformations that affect today's legal systems vis-à-vis the employment of e.g. machine learning techniques; and, (iii) the advancements in the state-of-the-art that regard such areas, as semantic web applications and language knowledge management in the legal domain, or ejustice advanced applications. Each one of these levels of analysis is deepening in the following sections.

2 Architectural Challenges

The political stance on current developments of AI hinges on a basic fact: the more the second wave of AI advances, the more AI impacts on current pillars of society and the law, so that political decisions will have to be taken as regards some AI applications, such as lethal autonomous weapons, or self-driving cars. Over the past years, scholars, non-profit organizations, and institutions alike have increasingly stressed the ethical concerns and normative challenges brought about by many autonomous and intelligent system designs [4–6]. The aim of the law to govern this field of technological innovation suggests that we should distinguish between two different levels of political intervention, that is, either through the primary rules of the law, or through its secondary rules [7].

According to the primary rules of the law, the goal is to directly govern social and individual behaviour through the menace of legal sanctions. Legislators have so far aimed to attain this end through methods of accident control that either cut back on the scale of the activity via, e.g., strict liability rules, or intend to prevent such activities through bans, or the precautionary principle. Regulations can be divided into four different categories, that is, (a) the regulation of human producers and designers of AI systems through law, e.g. either through ISO standards or liability norms for users of AI; (b) the regulation of user behaviour through the design of AI, that is, by designing AI systems in such a way that unlawful actions of humans are not allowed; (c) the regulation of the legal effects of AI behaviour through the norms set up by lawmakers, e.g. the effects of contracts and negotiations through AI applications; and, (d) the regulation of AI behaviour through design, that is, by embedding normative constraints into the design of the AI system [8].

Current default norms of legal responsibility can entail however a vicious circle, since e.g. strict liability rules—let aside bans, or the precautionary principle—may end up hindering research and development in this field. The recent wave of extremely detailed regulations on the use of drones by the Italian Civil Aviation Authority, i.e. "ENAC," illustrates this deadlock. The paradox stressed in the field of web security decades ago, could indeed be extended with a pinch of salt to the Italian regulation on the use of drones as well: the only legal drone would be "one that is powered off, cast in a block of concrete and sealed in a lead-lined room with armed guards – and even then I have my doubts." [9] As a result, we often lack enough data on the probability of events, their consequences and costs, to determine the levels of risk and thus, the amount of insurance premiums and further mechanisms, on which new forms of accountability for the behaviour of such systems may hinge. How, then, can we prevent legislations that may hinder the research in AI? How should we deal with the peculiar unpredictability and risky behaviour of some AI systems? How should we legally regulate the future?

A feasible way out can be given by the secondary rules of the law, namely, the rules of the law that create, modify, or suppress the primary rules of the system. Among the multiple legal techniques with which we can properly address the normative challenges of the second wave of AI, suffice it to mention here three of them. First, focus should be on Justice Brandeis's doctrine of experimental federalism, as espoused in *New State Ice Co. v Leibmann* (285 US 262 (1932)). The idea is to flesh out the content of the rules that shall govern individual behaviour through a beneficial competition among legal systems. This is what occurs nowadays in the field of self-driving cars in the US, where several states have enacted their own laws for this kind of technology. At its best possible light, the same policy will be at work with the EU regulation in the field of data protection [10, 11].

Second, attention should be drawn to the principle of implementation neutrality, according to which regulations are by definition specific to that technology and yet do not favour one or more of its possible implementations. The 2016 *Federal Automated Vehicles Policy* of the U.S. Department of Transportation illustrates this legal technique. Although regulations are by definition specific to that technology, e.g. autonomous vehicles, there is no favouritism for one or more of its possible implementations. Even when the law sets up a particular attribute of that technology, lawmakers can draft the legal requirement in such a way that non-compliant implementations can be modified to become compliant.

Third, legislators can adopt forms of legal experimentation. For example, over the past decade and a half, the Japanese government has worked out a way to address the normative challenges of robotics through the creation of special zones for their empirical testing and development, namely, a form of living lab, or *Tokku* [12]. Likewise, in the field of autonomous vehicles, several EU countries have endorsed this kind of approach: Sweden has sponsored the world's first large-scale autonomous driving pilot project, in which self-driving cars use public roads in everyday driving conditions; Germany has allowed a number of tests with various levels of automation on highways, e.g. Audi's tests with an autonomously driving car on highway A9 between Ingolstadt and Nuremberg.

In general terms, these forms of experimentation through lawfully de-regulated special zones represent the legal basis on which to collect empirical data and sufficient knowledge to make rational decisions for a number of critical issues. We can improve our understanding of how AI systems may react in various contexts and satisfy human needs. We can better appreciate risks and threats brought on by possible losses of control of AI systems, so as to keep them in check. We can further develop theoretical frameworks that allow us to better appreciate the space of potential systems that avoid undesirable behaviours. In addition, we can rationally address the legal aspects of this experimentation, covering many potential issues raised by the next-generation AI systems and managing such requirements, which often represent a formidable obstacle for this kind of research, as public authorizations for security reasons, formal consent for the processing and use of personal data, mechanisms of distributing risks through insurance models and authentication systems, and more. The different legal techniques and types of rules that lawmakers may employ, on the one hand, should not overlook the importance of the goals and values that are at stake with choices of technological dependence, delegation and trust, in order to determine the good mix between legal automation and public deliberation [13]. On the other hand, such choices of techno-logical dependence, delegation and trust, through AI systems and procedures of legal automation are affecting pillars and tenets of today's law. As stressed above in this introduction, AI technology profoundly affects both the requirements and functions of the law, namely, what the law is supposed to be (requirements), and what it is called to do (functions). This profound transformation has to be examined separately in the next section.

3   Ethical and Legal Challenges: Device and Linked Democracy

In one of the most celebrated 2014 John Klossner's cartoons on the Internet of Things the husband resignedly says to his wife: "We have to go out for dinner. The refrigerator isn't speaking to the stove."[3] This is not a joke anymore, and neither is the possibility of connecting thousands of billions of devices that can literally speak to each other.

A world of *smart* objects shreds new challenges into the interconnected world of humans and machines. The 2015 IBM Institute for Business Value Report [14] has pointed out five major challenges: (i) the *cost* of connectivity (prohibitively high), (ii) the Internet *after trust* (in the after-Snowden era "trust is over" and "IoT solutions built as centralized systems with trusted partners is now something of a fantasy"), (iii) *not-future proof* (many companies are quick to enter the market but it is very hard to exit: the cost of software updates and fixes in products long obsolete and discon-tinued), (iv) a lack of *functional* value (lack of meaningful value creation), (v) broken *business models* (in information markets, the marginal cost of additional capacity—advertising—or incremental supply—user data—is zero).

This is setting the conditions for "Device Democracy", in which "devices are empowered to autonomously execute digital contracts such as agreements, payments and barters with peer devices by searching for their own software updates, verifying trustworthiness with peers, and paying for and exchanging resources and services. This allows them to function as self-maintaining, self-servicing devices" [14].

IBM suggests three new methodological trends for a scalable, secure, and efficient IoT regarding: (i) architecture (private-by-design), (ii) business and economic insights (key vectors of disruption), (iii) and *product and user experience design* (the trans-formation of physical products into meaningful digital experiences).

The keyword here is the emergence of "meaningful experiences" in between relationships, properties, and objects. Interestingly this has been also enhanced by 2016 and 2017 Gartner Hype Cycle of Emerging Technologies: (i) transparently immersive experiences (such as human augmentation), (ii) perceptual smart machines (such as

---

[3] https://www.computerworld.com/article/2858429/enterprise-applications/2014-the-tech-year-in-cartoons.html#slide5.

personal analytics), and (iii) digital platforms (including blockchain technologies).[4] "AI everywhere" and blockchain are especially highlighted.

Our contention is that meaning is created, distributed, and framed through a complex and dynamic world in which ethics and law cannot be set apart or let alone to regulate processes, actions, and outcomes. Thus, regulations are entrenched and evolve dynamically according to the network and the specific ecosystems they are contributing to create. Meaningful experiences and smart devices entail smart regulations.

This is a feature already stressed for many years now by all attempts to frame new developments in norMAS [15], non-standard deontic logic [16] and law and the semantic web [17]. What is new is the attention brought to encompass innovation, semantic developments and blockchain technologies with ethical, democratic (political), and legal values alike.

In a recent Nexxus Whitepaper,[5] Gavin Andresen, the leader of Blockchain Foundation, equates crypto-currencies with empowering people: "an unstoppable grass-roots movement that won't be trampled on by any government or bank. It's all about the people's freedom and reclaiming it" [18].

The first generation produced blockchain-based network protocols, such as Bitcoin, Ethereum, Litecoin, and Zerocash. The second one can take this same idea of creating encrypted blocks further: it uses distributed ledger databases along with user-programmable smart contracts[6] to create a number of social contracts in many fields—universal basic income schemes, birth and death certificates, business licenses, property titles, educational qualifications, marriage etc. This actually is the original dream of the semantic web. MIT Digital Currency Initiative furnishes good examples in the public domain, as they have launched the identity based services offered by BitNation, a project aimed at decentralising governance at a global scale, e.g. a World Citizenship ID based on blockchain, and a Refugee Emergency Response project. Ideally, when applied to social or economic institutions, the result would be Decentralized Autonomous Organizations (DAO): self-running organisations in which users can become part of the chain performing things that computers cannot do [19].[7]

However, there is still a long road ahead before implementing DAO properly, as complexity does not only lie on regulations, and transactions fuel a mixed, hybrid social and economic reality that displays its own problems and conflicts. The recent Ethereum crisis has shown security vulnerabilities [20]. Although preventive mechanisms such as distributed consensus, cryptography, and anonymity are put in place, iblockchain technologies remain vulnerable to many types of risks—mainly: the 51% attack, account takeover, digital identity theft, money laundering, and hacking [21].

---

[4] https://www.gartner.com/smarterwithgartner/.

[5] Nexxus Partners was established in January 2016 in Texas, USA as a services company for the bitcoin and cryptocurrency industry.

[6] "Smart contracts are computer programs that can be correctly executed by a network of mutually distrusting nodes, without the need of an external trusted authority" [20].

[7] See the first Decentralized Autonomous Organization (DAO) code to automate organizational governance and decision-making at [19].

There are problems regarding the legal dimension as well. Some criticisms have already stated that "cryptocurrencies cannot solve the problem of incomplete [relational] contracts, and as long as contracts are incomplete, humans will need to resolve ambiguities" [22]. The same diffidence has been shown from a public legal standpoint, as crypto-currencies cannot build up by their own a new public space [23].

The other way around, there are economic interpretations that highlight its positive aspects. Ethereum and blockchain platforms have been received "as *a new type of economy*: a 'spontaneous organization', which is a self-governing organization with the coordination properties of a market (Hayek), the governance properties of a commons (Ostrom), and the constitutional properties of a nation state (Brenan and Buchanan)" [24].

Perhaps this syncretic view is too over-confident, equating different dimensions (economic, social, and legal) but, be as it may, law and the definition of law—what it counts for—are at stake: "the legal status of DAOs remains the subject of active and vigorous debate and discussion. Not everyone shares the same definition. [...] Ultimately, how a DAO functions and its legal status will depend on many factors, including how DAO code is used, where it is used, and who uses it." [19]

It is our contention that the synergy between different kinds of complementary technologies can help to solve these regulatory puzzles and tensions, i.e. Blockchain is the result of assembling two software paradigms (peer-to-peer applications and distributed hash tables). They are not the only ones. Semantic technologies and linked data can be used to ease the tensions and create the shared scenarios in which crypto-currencies and smart contracts can be safely and effectively used in a personalised manner by a vast plurality of users. "Similarly as block chain technology can facilitate distributed currency, trust and contracts application, Linked Data facilitated distributed data management without central authorities" [25].

But for this to happen, to cross jurisdictions and different types of legal obstacles, smart regulations and values are essential and should be similarly linked and harmonised. Traditional legal tools at national, European and international levels, are important, but they still fall short to cope with the complexity of algorithm governance to reach metadata regulatory dimensions and layers [26]. This is why law, governance, and ethics are at the same time being embedded into design, and re-enacted again as contextually-driven to shape sustainable regulatory ecosystems. Beyond epistemic and deliberative democracy, one of the concepts that have recently coined to describe this new situation is *linked democracy*, i.e. the endorsement of (embedded) democratic values to preserve rights and protect people on the web of data [27]. It is worth noticing that these common trends are related to the combination of political crowdsourcing, legal and ethical argumentation, and expert knowledge [28]. Innovation is deemed to be a crucial component of democracy [29]. Thus, what the law is supposed to be and what it is called to do are related not only to its architecture and tools (e.g. normative systems, laws and rights) but to the many ways of balancing citizens' compliance and participation.

4   Web of Data and Legal Analytics

Over the last two decades we have witnessed a remarkable volume of legal documents and legal big data being put out in open format (e.g., the *legal XML* movement). The information was represented using specific technical standards capable of modelling legal knowledge, norms, and concepts [17, 30] in machine-readable format.

NormInRete [31] is an XML standard the Italian government issued in 2001 as the official XML vocabulary for the country's legislative documents. *MetaLex* was created in 2002 in the Netherlands, and it evolved into *CEN-MetaLex* as a general format for the interoperability of legal documents across Europe, this thanks to the EU Project *ESTRELLA* [32]. Another significant outcome of the *ESTRELLA* project was the Legal Knowledge Interchange Format-LKIF, composed of two main pillars: (i) a core legal ontology [33] and (ii) a legal-rule language [34]. Even if these outcomes are encouraging, they lack a common-framework technical design making it possible to easily integrate all the Semantic Web layers (e.g., text, norms, ontology). For this reason, the Akoma Ntoso project [35] (an UNDESA-based African initiative)[8] took the best practices from those experiences and in 2006 designed a unique XSD schema for all legal documents (e.g., including caselaw and UN resolutions [39]) and lawmaking traditions (e.g., common law and civil law). In 2012, LegalDocML TC,[9] of OASIS, expanded the Akoma Ntoso XML vocabulary to embrace an international vision of legal-document annotation. OASIS's LegalCiteM[10] TC provides semantic representation of legal references so as to foster a convergence of many existing syntaxes for legal and legislative identifiers, including ELI [37], ECLI [36], URN-LEX,[11] and the Akoma Ntoso Naming Convention [40], making sure that legal document collections can unambiguously be referred to and are also connectable to Linked Data assertions. OASIS's LegalRuleML TC [38] provides a standard for modelling constitutive and prescriptive norms using formal language for rules. LegalDocML, LegalRuleML, and LegalCiteM provide a common framework for modelling legal documents and for fostering contextual metadata. The CLOUD4EU [41, 42] project offers a rare example of a platform where those standards can act in an integrated manner: it is designed for the General Data Protection Regulation (GDPR), making it possible to provide compliance reports for this regulation.

LegalRuleML also provides an RDFS meta-model for modelling the deontic and defeasible logic operators applied in the legal domain in order to export metadata in RDF format. LegalDocML makes it possible to extract legal metadata and to convert it into RDF. In the web of data paradigm, RDF triples produce a distributed and networked legal knowledge repository that can be useful in enhancing the searchability of relevant legal concepts, the semantic classification of documents, a light legal-reasoning approach, and the integration of metadata with other nonlegal sources (e.g.,

---

[8] United Nations Department of Economic and Social Affairs https://www.un.org/development/desa/en/.

[9] https://www.oasis-open.org/committees/legaldocml/.

[10] https://www.oasis-open.org/committees/tc_home.php?wg_abbrev=legalcitem.

[11] https://datatracker.ietf.org/doc/draft-spinosa-urn-lex/.

DBpedia). However, the RDF technique is based on a collection of triples (assertions composed of a subject, a predicate, and an object), often not validated, and the underlying theory of inferential logic only approximates reality, like a map. In the complex nonmonotonic legal system, RDF reasoning is quite risky, especially in situations where antecedents are rebutted (e.g., retroactivity, modifications of modifications, exceptions to exceptions, suspensions of the application of norms, annulment, etc.). For this reason, the legal XML community is inclined to extract RDF assertions as a subproduct of legal XML documents that are authentically, officially validated by experts (e.g., principle of self-contained and self-explained assertions in a unique XML file validated by the expert).

In the meantime, this large web of legal data connected with official digital legal documents (often available from official-journal portals) in open format provides a rare opportunity to apply artificial intelligence (AI) techniques in order to rethink the legal theory and their institutions. In particular, *legal analytics* (LA)—combining data science, artificial intelligence, machine learning (ML), natural language processing techniques, and statistical methods—can reuse that vast and varied body of legal big data, even if approximate, to infer new patterns and legal knowledge, so as to then predict new models and bring out hidden correlations, often providing unexpected insights into the relation between legal phenomena [43].

The automated application of learning methods to vast sets of examples makes it possible to reproduce human behaviour and improve upon it, exploiting their computational power to learn from successes and failures and thus improve performance. Thanks to these new techniques and the sheer volume of the legal web of data now available on the Internet, artificial intelligence has been able to advance from mock examples to a host of real-life applications: conceptual retrieval and ranking, speech and image recognition, question-answering, recommendations, translation, planning, autonomous mobile robots, etc. Machine learning has been extensively applied to text analytics, which refers to the use of multiple technologies—such as linguistic, statistical, and machine learning techniques—to capture the information content of textual sources. Considering that legal sources of all kinds are recorded in textual form (this is true of statutes, regulations, judicial and other types of decisions and opinions, legal doctrines, contracts), the application of text analytics to the law has huge potentials. And indeed a number of applications are emerging, making it possible to automatically classify and extract documents, identify principles in judicial decisions, and predict the outcome of judicial cases.

Legal analytics (LA) has the potential to contribute to different aspects of legal scholarship and practice. LA can advance legal informatics, making for a vast range of successful new legal applications in the public and private sectors alike. In particular, it supports the provision of AI applications, but overcoming the knowledge-acquisition bottleneck. LA can support legal research, in particular, through its ability to unveil hidden patterns in data and documents, revealing unseen features of the structure and the functioning of legal institutions. The insights provided by LA, in combination with computable models of the law, support the development of a new, empirically based understanding of the law. LA can improve the efficiency and effectiveness of legal institutions, while providing all legal actors with better knowledge of the law and of its application. However, the use of big-data analytics has also raised a number of ethical issues that are already being discussed in several domains (targeted deceptive commercial and noncommercial communication, discrimination, manipulation of public opinion, etc.). Also already emerging in the law are some questionable practices, particularly where law enforcement tries to predict illegal or otherwise unwanted behaviour (e.g., a tendency to offend or reoffend). More generally, the knowledge provided by analytics brings new ways to assess, influence, and control behaviour, and these aspects have yet to be fully analysed. For instance, no study exists so far on how the ability to predict court decisions, even those of specific judges, could influence judicial decision-making.

The combination of LA and legal XML techniques improve our interpretation of the AI inferences. XML nodes provide structural information and contextual metadata that, in combination with the predictive assertions of LA, could be used to mitigate two important negative side effects of LA techniques: (i) the introduction of bias from the past experiences and mistakes (e.g., negative case-law, bad legal drafting practices in legislation, influences due to socio-historical conditions) that can reinforce a tendency to reiterate incorrect models and may impair the ability to creatively find brilliant new solutions in the future (e.g., through filter-bubble effects); (ii) the fragmentation of legal knowledge into separate sentences or isolated data without a logical connection making it possible to achieve a consistent legal and logical narrative flow (e.g., contextless prediction). XML nodes could provide the skeleton needed to reassemble the huge amount of unexpected insights produced by the LA layer.

Finally, also crucial is the usability and the easy access to legal knowledge produced by LA. It is essential that the outcome of LA and legal XML sources in web applications and new devices (e.g., *augmented reality*) be also understandable by people who are not legal experts, without reframing the message; and, at any event, it is also essential to provide clear mechanisms for explaining the algorithm decision-making process and outcome. In this effort to achieve transparent communication we can turn to human-computer interaction techniques, making it possible to create a fair environment in which to better communicate the legal concepts and principles extracted by LA. The *legal design* community is working to create new design patterns, looking to provide better ways of displaying content, in such a way that the legal community and end users (e.g., citizens) can place greater trust in LA and legal XML [44–46].

5   On the Content of This Volume

This new AICOL volume is divided into six parts. They concern (i) legal philosophy, conceptual analysis, and epistemic approaches; (ii) rules and norms analysis and representation; (iii) legal vocabularies and natural language processing; (iv) legal ontologies and semantic annotation; (v) legal argumentation; and, (vi) courts, adjudication and dispute resolution.

5.1   Legal Philosophy, Conceptual Analysis, and Epistemic Approaches

In the first part of this volume, four papers deal with matters of legal philosophy, conceptual analysis, and epistemic approaches. In *RoboPrivacy and the Law as "Meta-technology"*, Ugo Pagallo examines how a particular class of robotic applications, i.e. service robots, or consumer robots, may affect current legal frameworks of privacy and data protection. Instead of a one-way movement of social evolution from technology to law, a key component of the analysis concerns the aim of the law to govern techno-logical innovation as well as human and artificial behaviour through the regulatory tools of technology. By distinguishing between the primary rules of the law and its secondary rules, e.g. forms of legal experimentation, the chapter illustrates some of the ways in which the secondary rules of the law may allow us to understand what kind of primary rules we may want for our robots. In *Revisiting Constitutive Rules*, Giovanni Sileno, Alexander Boer and Tom Van Engers investigate how behaviour relates to norms, i.e. how a certain conduct acquires meaning in institutional terms. By addressing the double function of the 'count-as' relation, generally associated to constitutive rules and mostly accounted for its classificatory functions, the chapter reconsiders the relation between constitutive rules and regulative rules, and introduces a preliminary account on the ontological status of constitution. In *The Truth in Law and Its Explication*, Hajime Yoshino discusses what types of truth play their role in law and in what way such types of truth can be explicated. Whereas the concept of truth in law is classified into three types of truth, i.e. truth as fact, truth as validity and truth as justice, the chapter provides their formal semantic foundation, and analyses both the ways to explicate truth as validity and truth as justice in terms of intensional and extensional explication, and how to grasp the reasoning of justification and of creation. In *From Words to Images Through Legal Visualization*, Arianna Rossi and Monica Palmirani discuss the process of sense-making and interpretation of visual legal con-cepts that have been introduced in legal documents to make their meaning clearer and more intelligible. Whilst visualizations have also been automatically generated from semantically-enriched legal data, the analysis of current approaches to this subject represents the starting point to propose an empirical methodology that is inspired by the interaction with design practices and that will be tested in the future stages of the research.

5.2   Rules and Norms Analysis and Representation

The second part of the volume, which has to do with rules and norms analysis and representation, comprises seven contributions. In *A Petri Net-based Notation for Normative Modelling: Evaluation on Deontic Paradoxes*, Giovanni Sileno, Alexander Boer and Tom Van Engers focus on some of the problems that derive from the development of systems operating in alignment with norms, e.g. the continuous flow of events that modifies the normative directives under scrutiny. The chapter presents an alternative approach to some of these problems, by extending the Petri net notation to Logic Programming Petri Nets, so that the resulting visual formalism represents in an integrated, yet distinct fashion, procedural and declarative aspects of the system. In *Legal Patterns for Different Constitutive Rules*, Marcello Ceci, Tom Butler, Leona

O'Brien and Firas Al Khalil illustrate a heuristic approach for the representation of alethic statements as part of a methodology aimed at ensuring effective translation of the regulatory text into a machine-readable language. The methodology includes an intermediate language, accompanied by an XML persistence model, and introduces a set of "legal concept patterns" to specifically represent the different constitutive statements that can be found in e.g. financial regulations. In *An Architecture for Establishing Legal Semantic Workflows in the Context of Integrated Law Enforcement*, Markus Stumpner, Wolfgang Mayer, Pompeu Casanovas and Louis de Koker develop a federated data platform that aims to enable the execution of integrated analytics on data accessed from different external and internal sources, and to enable effective support of an investigator or analyst working to evaluate evidence and manage investigation structure. By preventing the shortcomings of traditional approaches, e.g. high costs and silos-effects, the chapter also aims to show how this integration can be compliant. In *Contributions to Modelling Patent Claims when Representing Patent Knowledge*, Simone Reis, Andre Reis, Jordi Carrabina and Pompeu Casanovas examine the modelling of patent claims in ontology based representation of patent information. They relate to the internal structure of the claims and the use of the all-element rule for patent coverage, in order to offer the general template for the structure of the claim, and provide the visualization of the claims, the storage of claim information in a web semantics framework, and the evaluation of claim coverage using Description Logic. In *Execution and Analysis of Formalized Legal Norms in Model Based Decision Structures*, Bernhard Waltl, Thomas Reschenhofer and Florian Matthes describe a decision support system to represent the semantics of legal norms, whereas a model based expression language (MxL) has been developed to coherently support the formalization of logical and arithmetical operations. Such legal expert system is built upon model based decision structures and three different components, namely a model store, a model execution component, and an interaction component, have been worked out, so as to finally test the execution and analysis of such structured legal norms vis-à-vis the German child benefit regulations. In *Causal Models of Legal Cases*, Ruta Liepina, Giovanni Sartor and Adam Wyner draw the attention to the requirements for establishing and reasoning with causal links. In light of a semi-formal framework for reasoning with causation that uses strict and defeasible rules for modelling factual causation in legal cases, the chapter takes into account the complex relation between formal, common sense, norm and policy based considerations of causation in legal decision making with particular focus on their role in comparing alternative causal explanations. In *Developing Rule-Based Expert System for People with Disabilities*, Michał Araszkiewicz and Maciej Klodawski present the features of a moderately simple legal expert system devoted to solving the most frequent legal problems of disabled persons in Poland. By casting light on the structure of the expert system and its methodology, the succession law of Poland and its procedures delivers sufficient material to reveal the most important issues concerning such a project on a rule-based expert system.

5.3 Legal Vocabularies and Natural Language Processing

The third part of the volume regards legal vocabularies and natural language processing. The eight contributions include *EuroVoc-based Summarization of European Case Law*, in which Florian Schmedding illustrates the on-going development of a multilingual pipeline for the summarization of European case law. By applying the TextRank algorithm on concepts of the EuroVoc thesaurus, so as to extract summarizing keywords and sentences, the intent is to demonstrate the feasibility and usefulness of the presented approach for five different languages and 18 document sources. In *Aligning Legivoc Legal Vocabularies by Crowdsourcing*, Hughes-Jehan Vibert, Benoit Pin and Pierre Jouvelot present the first Internet-based platform dedicated to the diffusion, edition and alignment of legal vocabularies across countries. As a seamless path for governments to disseminate their legal foundations and specify semantic bridges between them, the chapter describes the general principles behind the legivoc framework while providing some ideas about its implementation, e.g. crowdsourcing the alignment of legal corpora together. In *Data Protection in Elderly Health Care Platforms*, Ângelo Costa, Aliaksandra Yelshyna, Teresa C. Moreira, Francisco Andrade, Vicente Julián and Paulo Novais deal with solutions to the increasing cognitive problems that affect the elderly population in light of the iGenda project, which aims to build safe environments that adapt themselves to one's individual needs through a Cognitive Assistant inserted in the Ambient Assisted Living area. Whereas one of the main issues concerns the protection of the data flowing within the system and the protection of the user's fundamental rights, the chapter clarifies the principles and legal guarantees of data protection, embracing appropriate solutions for technological features that may be a threat. In *Assigning Creative Commons Licenses to Research Metadata: Issues and Cases*, Marta Poblet, Amir Aryani, Paolo Manghi, Kathryn Unsworth, Jingbo Wang, Brigitte Hausstein, Sunje Dallmeier-Tiessen, Claus-Peter Klas, Pompeu Casanovas and Víctor Rodriguez-Doncel tackle the problem of lack of clear licensing and transparency of usage terms and conditions for research metadata. Making research data connected, discoverable and reusable are the key enablers of the new data revolution in research. Accordingly, the chapter does not only discuss how the lack of transparency can hinder discovery of research data and make it disconnected from publication and other trusted research outcomes. In addition, the chapter suggests the application of Creative Commons licenses for research metadata, and provides some examples of the applicability of this approach to internationally known data infrastructures. In *Dataset Alignment and Lexicalization to Support Multilingual Analysis of Legal Documents*, Armando Stellato, Manuel Fiorelli, Andrea Turbati, Tiziano Lorenzetti, Peter Schmitz, Enrico Francesconi, Najeh Hajlaoui and Brahim Batouche tackle the complexity of the EU legal system, in which both the linguistic and the conceptual aspects mutually interweave into a knowledge barrier that is hard to break. In order to create a platform for multilingual cross-jurisdiction accessibility to legal content in the EU, the chapter addresses the challenge of Semantic Interoperability at both the conceptual and lexical level, by developing a coordinated set of instruments for advanced lexicalization of RDF resources (be them ontologies, thesauri and datasets in general) and for alignment of their content. In *A Multilingual Access Module to Legal Texts*, Kiril Simov, Petya Osenova, Iliana Simova, Hristo

Konstantinov and Tenyo Tyankov introduce a Multilingual Access Module, which translates the user's legislation query from its source language into the target language, and retrieves the detected texts that match the query. More particularly, the unit consists of two sub modules, i.e. an Ontology-based and a Statistical Machine Translation units, which have their own drawbacks, so that both are used in an integrated architecture, in order to profiting from each other. In *Combining Natural Language Processing Approaches for Rule Extraction from Legal Documents*, Mauro Dragoni, Serena Villata, Williams Rizzi and Guido Governatori address the problem of moving from a natural language legal text to the respective set of machine-readable conditions, by combining the linguistic information provided by WordNet and a syntax-based extraction of rules from legal texts, with a logic-based extraction of dependencies between chunks of such texts. Such a combined approach leads to a powerful solution towards the extraction of machine-readable rules from legal documents, which is evaluated over the Australian "Telecommunications consumer protections code". In *Analysis of Legal References in an Emergency Legislative Setting*, Monica Palmirani, Luca Cervone, Ilaria Bianchi and Francesco Draicchio provide for a taxonomy of legal citations that set up an interesting apparatus for analysing a country's legislative approach. By investigating the references of a legal corpus of ordinances issued by the Regional Commissioner for Emergency and Reconstruction over the first eighteen months after the 2012 earthquake in Emilia-Romagna, the chapter scrutinizes the critical issues arising in the regulative strategy for emergency situations. By distinguishing groupings based on lexical-textual analysis and groupings based on structural element, the aim is to help lawmakers act better in future disasters, to extract information concerning the number and the types of modifications produced, and to support the debate on emergency national laws that deal with natural disasters.

5.4 Legal Ontologies and Semantic Annotation

As to the fourth part of this volume on legal ontologies and semantic annotation, it comprises eight chapters. In *Using Legal Ontologies with Rules for Legal Textual Entailment*, Biralatei James Fawei, Adam Wyner, Martin Kollingbaum and Jeff Z. Pan describe an initial attempt to model and implement the automatic application of legal knowledge using a rule-based approach. Whilst an NLP tool extracts information to instantiate an ontology relative to concepts and relations, ontological elements are associated with legal rules written in SWRL to draw inferences to an exam question. Although further development of the methodology and identification of key issues require future analysis, the preliminary results on a small sample are promising. In *KR4IPLaw Judgment Miner- Case-Law Mining for Legal Norm Annotation*, Shashishekar Ramakrishna, Łukasz Górski and Adrian Paschke offer a proof-of-concept implementation for automatizing the process of identifying the most relevant judgments pertaining to a legal field and further transforming them into a formal representation format. On this basis, the annotated legal section and its related judgments can be mapped into a decision model for further down the line processing. In *Conceptual Annotation of Legal Documents with Ontology Concepts*, Kolawole John Adebayo, Luigi Di Caro and Guido Boella illustrate a novel task of semantic labelling, which exploits ontology in providing a fine-grained conceptual document segmentation and annotation. By dividing documents into semantically-coherent blocks and performing conceptual tagging for efficient information filtering, the chapter presents a promising solution, since the proposed task has several applications, such as granular information filtering of legal texts, text summarization and information extraction among others. In *Reuse and Reengineering of Non-ontological Resources in the Legal Domain*, Cristiana Santos, Pompeu Casanovas, Víctor Rodríguez Doncel and Leon van der Torre explain the processes of reusing and reengineering available non-ontological resources in the legal domain into ontologies, taking into account their specificities, as they are highly heterogeneous in their data model and contents. The description of these processes is further clarified by using a case-study in the consumer law domain. In *Ontology Modelling for Criminal Law*, Chiseung Soh, Seungtak Lim, Kihyun Hong and Young-Yik Rhim propose a general methodology for designing criminal law ontologies and rules. The chapter illustrates the super-domain ontology that contains the common characteristics of criminal law, in order to explain the rule design method of criminal law and present the application of the anti-graft act in Korea as an example. In *Con-trattiPubblici.org, a Semantic Knowledge Graph on Public Procurement Information*, Giuseppe Futia, Federico Morando, Alessio Melandri, Lorenzo Canova and Francesco Ruggiero present the ContrattiPubblici.org project, which aims to develop a semantic knowledge graph based on linked data principles in order to overcome the fragmentation of existent datasets, to allow easy analysis, and to enable the reuse of information. The objectives are to increase public awareness about public spending, to improve transparency on the public procurement chain, and to help companies retrieving useful knowledge for their business activities. In *Application of Ontology Modularization for Building a Criminal Domain Ontology*, Mirna El Ghosh and Habib Abdulrab carry out a survey on ontology modularization and present a modular approach to build a criminal modular domain ontology (CriMOnto) for modelling the legal norms of the Lebanese criminal system. CriMOnto, which will also be used for a legal reasoning system, is composed of four independent modules that will be combined together to compose the whole ontology. In *A Linked Data Terminology for Copyright Based on Ontolex-Lemon*, Víctor Rodriguez-Doncel, Cristiana Santos, Pompeu Casanovas, Asunción Gómez Pérez and Jorge Gracia discuss Ontolex-lemon, namely, the de facto standard to represent lexica relative to ontologies that can be used to encode term banks as RDF. A multi-lingual, multi-jurisdictional term bank of copyright-related concepts has been published as linked data based on the ontolex-lemon model. The terminology links information from several sources and the terms have been hierarchically arranged, spanning multiple languages and targeting different jurisdictions. Whilst the term bank has been published as a TBX dump file and is publicly accessible as linked data, it has been used to annotate common licenses in the RDFLicense dataset.

5.5 Legal Argumentation

Five chapters compose the fifth part of this volume on legal argumentation. In *Abstract Agent Argumentation (Triple-A)*, Ryuta Arisaka, Ken Satoh and Leon van der Torre introduce a Dung style theory of abstract argumentation, which they call triple-A, in which each agent decides autonomously whether to accept or reject her own arguments.

By distinguishing between trusted arguments, selfish agents, and social agents, the extensions of globally accepted arguments are defined using a game theoretic equilibrium definition. In *A Machine Learning Approach to Argument Mining in Legal Documents*, Prakash Poudyal analyzes and evaluates the natural language arguments present in the European Court of Human Right (ECHR) Corpus. By dividing the research into four modules, work on argumentative sentences vs. non-argumentative sentences in narrative legal texts, is accomplished, so as to flesh out the features of this module and conduct an experiment in Sequential Optimization Algorithm and Random Forest Algorithm, which can be used as the basis of a general argument mining framework. In *Answering Complex Queries on Legal Networks: a Direct and a Structured IR Approaches*, Nada Mimouni, Adeline Nazarenko and Sylvie Salotti compare two methods of search in legal collection networks, so as to present new functionalities of search and browsing. Relying on a structured representation of the collection graph, the first approach allows for approximate answers and knowledge discovery, whilst the second one supports richer semantics and scalability but offers fewer search functionalities. As a result, the chapter indicates how those approaches could be combined to get the best of both. In *Inducing Predictive Models for Decision Support in Administrative Adjudicati*, Karl Branting, Alexander Yeh and Brandy Weiss explore the hypothesis that predictive models induced from previous administrative decisions can improve subsequent decision-making processes. In light of three different datasets, three different approaches for prediction in their domains were tested, showing that each approach was capable of predicting outcomes. By exploring several approaches that use predictive models to identify salient phrases in the predictive texts, the chapter proposes a design for incorporating this information into a decision-support tool. In *Arguments on the Correct Interpretation of Sources of Law*, Robert van Doesburg and Tom van Engers deal with the formalization of legal reasoning and the representation of law through computational models of argumentation. Whereas most examples presented in literature can be characterized as post-hoc theory construction, the chapter aims to provide an instrument that can be used to inform legal experts on relevant issues in the process of solving current cases, i.e. using the interpretations of legal sources ex-ante. An actual case that is in discussion in the Dutch Tax Administration, in court as well as in Parliament, helps to further clarify this approach.

5.6   Courts, Adjudication and Dispute Resolution

The sixth part of the volume is devoted to courts, adjudication and dispute resolution, which are the subject matter of five chapters. In *Dynamics of the Judicial Process by Defeater Activation*, Martin Moguillansky and Guillermo Simari illustrate a novel activating approach to Argument Theory Change (ATC) for the study of the dynamics of the judicial process. By considering the sentences of two different real criminal procedures, the aim is to contribute to the discussion of how to deal with circumstances of the judicial process like hypothetical reasoning for conducting investigations of a legal case, and for handling the dynamics of the judicial process. In *Claim Detection in Judgments of the EU Court of Justice*, Marco Lippi, Francesca Lagioia, Giuseppe Contissa, Giovanni Sartor and Paolo Torroni address recent approaches to argumentation mining in juridical documents, so as to present two distinct contributions. The first one is a novel annotated corpus for argumentation mining in the legal domain, together with a set of annotation guidelines. The second one is the empirical evaluation of a recent machine learning method for claim detection in judgments. Whereas the latter method has been applied to context-independent claim detection in other genres such as Wikipedia articles and essays, the chapter shows that this method also provides a useful instrument in the legal domain, especially when used in combination with domain-specific information. In *A Non-intrusive Approach to Measuring Trust in Opponents in a Negotiation Scenario*, Marco Gomes, John Zeleznikow and Paulo Novais propose a threefold approach to trust, that regards the possibility of measuring trust based on quantifiable behaviour, the use of Ambient Intelligence techniques that use a trust data model to collect and evaluate relevant information based on the assumption that observable trust between two entities (parties) results in certain typical behaviours and, finally, relational aspects of trust and parties' conflict styles based on cooperativeness and assertiveness. The main contribution of this chapter is the identification of situations in which trust relationships influence the negotiation performance. In *Network, Visualization, Analytics. A Tool Allowing Legal Scholars to Experimentally Investigate EU Case Law*, Nicola Lettieri, Sebastiano Faro, Delfina Malandrino, Margherita Vestoso and Armando Faggiano dwell on the intersection between Network Analysis (NA), visualization techniques and legal science research questions. Their aim is to bring the network approach into "genuinely legal" research questions, and to create tools that allow legal scholars with no technical skills to make experiments with NA and push new ideas both in legal and NA science, so as to use NA and visualization in their daily activities. In *Electronic Evidence Semantic Structure: Exchanging Evidence across Europe in a Coherent and Consistent Way*, Maria Angela Biasiotti and Fabrizio Turchi provide for a seminal work on a common and shared understanding of what Electronic Evidence is and how it should be treated in the EU context and in the EU member states. The chapter develops a tailor-made categorization of relevant concepts which provides a starting analysis for the exchange of Electronic Evidence and data between judicial actors and LEAs, with a specific focus on issues of the criminal field and criminal procedures. This semantic structure might represent a good starting point for the alignment of electronic evidence concepts all over Europe in a cross border dimension.

Acknowledgments. Law and Policy Program of the Australian government funded Data to Decisions Cooperative Research Centre (http://www.d2dcrc.com.au/); Meta-Rule of Law DER2016-78108-P, Research of Excellence, Spain. This work was also partially supported by the European Union's Horizon 2020 research and innovation programme under the Marie Skłodowska-Curie grant agreement No 690974 "MIREL: MIning and REasoning with Legal texts".

References

1. Regalado, A.: Google's AI explosion in one chart. MIT technology review, 25 March 2017. https://www.technologyreview.com/s/603984/googles-ai-explosion-in-one-chart/
2. Pagallo, U., Massimo Durante, M., Monteleone, S.: What is new with the internet of things in privacy and data protection? Four legal challenges on sharing and control in IoT. In: Leenes, R., van Brakel, R., Gutwirth, S., de Hert, P. (eds.) Data Protection and Privacy: (In)visibilities and Infrastructures. LGTS, pp. 59–78. Springer, Dordrecht (2017)
3. Susskind, R., Susskind, D.: The Future of the Professions. Oxford University Press, Oxford (2015)
4. Abelson, H., et al.: Keys under the doormat: mandating insecurity by requiring government access to all data and communications. MIT Computer Science and AI Laboratory Technical report, 6 July 2015
5. Abelson, H., et al.: The future of life institute, an open letter: research priorities for robust and beneficial artificial intelligence (2015). http://futureoflife.org/ai-open-letter/. Accessed 18 Oct 2016
6. IEEE Standards Association: The Global Initiative for Ethical Considerations in the Design of Autonomous Systems, Forthcoming (2017)
7. Hart, H.L.A.: The Concept of Law. Clarendon, Oxford (1961)
8. Leenes, R., Lucivero, F.: Laws on robots, laws by robots, laws in robots: regulating robot behaviour by design. Law Innov. Technol. 6(2), 193–220 (2014)
9. Garfinkel, S., Spafford, G.: Web Security and Commerce. O'Reilly, Sebastopol (1997)
10. Pagallo, U.: The legal challenges of big data: putting secondary rules first in the field of EU data protection. Eur. Data Protect. Law Rev. 3(1), 34–46 (2017)
11. Pagallo, U.: LegalAIze: tackling the normative challenges of artificial intelligence and robotics through the secondary rules of law. In: Corrales, M., Fenwick, M., Forgó, N. (eds.) New Technology, Big Data and the Law. Perspectives in Law, Business and Innovation. PLBI, pp. 281–300. Springer, Singapore (2017)
12. Weng, Y.H., Sugahara, Y., Hashimoto, K., Takanishi, A.: Intersection of "Tokku" special zone, robots, and the law: a case study on legal impacts to humanoid robots. Int. J. Soc. Robot. 7(5), 841–857 (2015)
13. Pagallo, U., Durante, M.: The pros and cons of legal automation and its governance. Eur. J. Risk Regul. 7(2), 323–334 (2016)
14. Brody, P., Pureswaran, V.. Device democracy: saving the future of the internet of things. IBM, September 2014
15. Boella, G., Van Der Torre, L., Verhagen, H.: Ten challenges for normative multiagent systems. In: Dagstuhl Seminar Proceedings. Schloss Dagstuhl-Leibniz-Zentrum für Informatik (2008)
16. Hansen, J., Pigozzi, G., Van Der Torre, L.: Ten philosophical problems in deontic logic. In: Dagstuhl Seminar Proceedings. Schloss Dagstuhl-Leibniz-Zentrum für Informatik (2007)
17. Casanovas, P., Palmirani, M., Peroni, S., van Engers, T., Vitali, F.: Semantic web for the legal domain: the next step. Semant. Web 7(3), 213–227 (2016)
18. Andresen, G.: Nexxus Whitepaper (2017). http://nexxusuniversity.com
19. Jentzsch, C.: Decentralized autonomous organization to automate governance (2016). https://download.slock.it/public/DAO/WhitePaper.pdf. Asseced 23 June 2016
20. Atzei, N., Bartoletti, M., Cimoli, T.: A survey of attacks on ethereum smart contracts (SoK). In: Maffei, M., Ryan, M. (eds.) POST 2017. LNCS, vol. 10204, pp. 164–186. Springer, Heidelberg (2017). https://doi.org/10.1007/978-3-662-54455-6_8
21. Xu, J.J.: Are blockchains immune to all malicious attacks? Financ. Innov. 2(1), 25 (2016)

22. Arruñada, B.: Property as sequential exchange: the forgotten limits of private contract. J. Inst. Econ. **13**(4), 753–783 (2017)
23. DuPont, Q., Maurer, B.: Ledgers and Law in the Blockchain. Kings Review, 23 June 2015. http://kingsreview.co.uk/magazine/blog/2015/06/23/ledgers-and-law-in-the-blockchain
24. Davidson, S., De Filippi, P., Potts, J.: Economics of blockchain. In: Proceedings of Public Choice Conference Public Choice, Conference, May 2016, Fort Lauderdale, United States (2016). https://doi.org/10.2139/ssrn.2744751. HAL Id. hal-01382002
25. English, M., Auer, S., Domingue, J.: Block chain technologies and the semantic web: a framework for symbiotic development. In: Lehmann, J., Thakkar, H., Halilaj, L., Asmat, R. (eds.) Computer Science Conference for University of Bonn Students, pp. 47–61 (2016)
26. Rodríguez-Doncel, V., Santos, C., Casanovas, P., Gómez-Pérez, A.: Legal aspects of linked data—the European framework. Comput. Law Secur. Rev. **32**(6), 799–813 (2016)
27. Casanovas, P., Mendelson, D., Poblet, M.: A linked democracy approach for regulating public health data. Health Technol. **7**(4), 519–537 (2017)
28. Poblet, M., Casanovas, P., Plaza, E. (ed.) Linked Democracy: Artificial Intelligence for Democratic Innovation. http://ceur-ws.org/Vol-1897/
29. Poblet, M., Casanovas, P., Rodríguez-Doncel, V.: Linked Democracy. Springer Briefs, Cham: Springer Nature (2018, forthcoming)
30. Sartor, G., Palmirani, M., Francesconi, E., Biasiotti, M.A.: Legislative XML for the Semantic Web: Principles, Models, standards for Document Management. Springer, New York (2011)
31. Giovannini, M.P., Palmirani, M., Francesconi, E.: Linee guida per la marcatura dei documenti normativi secondo gli standard Normainrete, p. 200. European Press Academic Publishing, Firenze (2012)
32. Boer, A., de Maat, E., Francesconi, E., Lupo, C., Palmirani M.,, Winkels R.: General XML Format(s) for Legal Sources, Deliverable 3.1, Estrella Project - European project for Standardized Transparent Representations in order to Extend LegaL Accessibility, Proposal/Contract no.: 027655, European Commission (2007)
33. Breuker, J.A.P.J., et al.: OWL ontology of basic legal concepts (LKIF-Core). Estrella: Deliverable 1.4., AMSTERDAM, UVA 2007, pp. 138 (2007)
34. Gordon, Thomas F.: Constructing legal arguments with rules in the legal knowledge interchange format (LKIF). In: Casanovas, P., Sartor, G., Casellas, N., Rubino, R. (eds.) Computable Models of the Law. LNCS (LNAI), vol. 4884, pp. 162–184. Springer, Heidelberg (2008). https://doi.org/10.1007/978-3-540-85569-9_11
35. Vitali F., Palmirani M.: Akoma Ntoso Release Notes. Accessed 5 April 2018
36. Opijnen, M., Palmirani, M., Vitali, F., Agnoloni, T.: Towards ECLI 2.0. In: 2017 International Conference for E-Democracy and Open Government, Los Alamitos, CA, IEEE, 2017, P6082, pp. 1–9 (2017)
37. ELI Task Force: Technical ELI implementation guide citations, Publications Office of the European Union, Luxembourg (2015). https://doi.org/10.2830/74251
38. Athan, T., Governatori, G., Palmirani, M., Paschke, A., Wyner, A.: LegalRuleML: design principles and foundations. In: Faber, W., Paschke, A. (eds.) Reasoning Web 2015. LNCS, vol. 9203, pp. 151–188. Springer, Cham (2015). https://doi.org/10.1007/978-3-319-21768-0_6
39. Peroni, S., Palmirani, M., Vitali, F.: UNDO: the united nations system document ontology. In: d'Amato, C., Fernandez, M., Tamma, V., Lecue, F., Cudré-Mauroux, P., Sequeda, J., Lange, C., Heflin, J. (eds.) ISWC 2017. LNCS, vol. 10588, pp. 175–183. Springer, Cham (2017). https://doi.org/10.1007/978-3-319-68204-4_18

40. Barabucci, G., Cervone, L., Palmirani, M., Peroni, S., Vitali, F.: Multi-layer markup and ontological structures in Akoma Ntoso. In: Casanovas, P., Pagallo, U., Sartor, G., Ajani, G. (eds.) AICOL - 2009. LNCS (LNAI), vol. 6237, pp. 133–149. Springer, Heidelberg (2010). https://doi.org/10.1007/978-3-642-16524-5_9
41. Casalicchio, E., Cardellini, V., Interino, G., Palmirani, M.: Research challenges in legal-rule and QoS-aware cloud service brokerage. Future Gen. Comput. Syst. **78**, 211–223 (2016)
42. Governatori, G., Hashmi, M., Lam, H.-P., Villata, S., Palmirani, M.: Semantic business process regulatory compliance checking using LegalRuleML. In: Blomqvist, E., Ciancarini, P., Poggi, F., Vitali, F. (eds.) EKAW 2016. LNCS (LNAI), vol. 10024, pp. 746–761. Springer, Cham (2016). https://doi.org/10.1007/978-3-319-49004-5_48
43. Ashley, K.D.: Artificial Intelligence and Legal Analytics: New Tools for Law Practice in the Digital Age, p. 446. Cambridge University Press, Cambridge (2017)
44. Palmirani, M., Vitali, F.: Legislative drafting systems. In: Usability in Government Systems. Morgan Kaufmann, New York, pp. 133–151 (2012)
45. Rossi, A., Palmirani, M.: A visualization approach for adaptive consent in the European data protection framework. In: 2017 International Conference for E-Democracy and Open Government, Los Alamitos, CA, IEEE, 2017, pp. 1–12 (2017)
46. Haapio, H., Hagan, M., Palmirani, M., Rossi, A.,: Legal design patterns for privacy. In: Data Protection/LegalTech Proceedings of the 21st International Legal Informatics Symposium IRIS 2018, II, pp. 445–450. Editions Weblaw, Bern (2018)

Legal Philosophy, Conceptual Analysis, and Epistemic Approaches

RoboPrivacy and the Law
as "Meta-Technology"

Ugo Pagallo[(⊠)]

Law School, University of Torino, Lungo Dora Siena 100 A, 10153 Turin, Italy
ugo.pagallo@unito.it

Abstract. The paper examines how a particular class of robotic applications, i.e. service robots, or consumer robots, may affect current legal frameworks of privacy and data protection. More particularly, the focus is on (i) a new expectation of privacy brought about by these robotic applications; (ii) the realignment of the traditional distinction between data processors and data controllers; and, (iii) a novel set of challenges to the principle of privacy by design. Instead of a one-way movement of social evolution from technology to law, however, a key component of the analysis concerns the aim of the law to govern technological innovation as well as human and artificial behaviour through the regulatory tools of technology. Since most domestic and service robots are not a sort of "out-of-the-box" machine and moreover, their behaviour and decisions can be unpredictable and risky, special attention is drawn to the experiment of the Japanese government that has worked out a way to address (some of) the legal issues, which are at stake in this paper, through the creation of special zones for robotics empirical testing and development, namely a form of living lab, or *Tokku*. Interestingly, some EU member states have already followed suit.

Keywords: Data protection · Design · General theory of law
Level of abstraction · Philosophy of technology · Privacy
Robot · Special zone · Techno-regulation

1 Introduction

The level of abstraction (LoA) of this paper has to do with the impact of robotics technology in the fields of privacy and data protection, vis-à-vis the representation of the law as a "meta-technology." From a methodological viewpoint, a LoA sets the proper level of analysis as a sort of interface that defines the features representing the observables and variables of the research, the result of which provides a model for the field under exam [5, 19]. This methodological approach can be illustrated with a figure on the interface of the model, its observables and variables (see Fig. 1).

The next step is to determine the LoA concerning the law as a meta-technology, namely the aim of the law to govern the process of technological innovation, e.g., in the field of robotics. This stance corresponds to a glorious philosophical tradition, at least from Kant to Kelsen, according to which the law can conveniently be understood as a technique. In the phrasing of the *General Theory of the Law and the State* [9, at 26],

© Springer Nature Switzerland AG 2018
U. Pagallo et al. (Eds.): AICOL VI-X 2015–2017, LNAI 10791, pp. 23–38, 2018.
https://doi.org/10.1007/978-3-030-00178-0_2

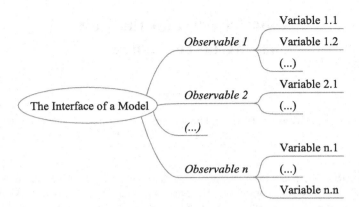

Fig. 1. Levels of abstraction of a model.

"what distinguishes the legal order from all other social orders is the fact that it regulates human behaviour by means of a specific technique," that hinges on the threat of physical coercion: "if A, then B." Therefore, once such technique regulates other techniques and moreover, the process of technological innovation, we may accordingly conceive the law as a meta-technology.

From this LoA, however, it does not follow that we have to buy any of Kelsen's ontological commitments: the stance this paper adopts on the law as meta-technology does not imply either that the law is merely a means of social control, or that no other meta-technological mechanisms exist. Rather, by insisting on the intent of the law to govern the process of technological innovation, we should recall that the latter, pace Kelsen, is affecting pillars of current legal systems. This has been, after all, a *fil rouge* of the AICOL series throughout the past years (2009–2017). Contrary to previous human societies that have used information and communication technology ("ICT"), but have been mainly dependent on technologies that revolve around energy and basic resources, today's societies are increasingly dependent on ICT and furthermore, on information as a vital resource [6, 20]. The processing of well formed and meaningful data is reshaping essential functions of current societies, such as governmental services, transportation and communication systems, business processes, or energy production and distribution networks, up to our understanding about the world and about ourselves. In a nutshell, after the revolutions of Copernicus, Darwin, and Freud, we are dealing with the "fourth revolution" [6].

The observables of the analysis set up by the LoA on the interplay between law and technology, are illustrated with a new figure (Fig. 2). The latter sheds light on both the impact of e.g. robotic technology on the law and the aforementioned intent the law has to govern the race of technological innovation, by further distinguishing the purposes that law-making can have and the aim of legal systems to regulate human and artificial behaviour.

The first observable of Fig. 2 suggests that the focus should be on how the fourth revolution is affecting the tenets of the law. In addition to transforming the approach of experts to legal information, e.g. the development of such fields as AI and the law,

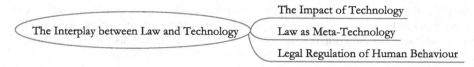

Fig. 2. Law as a meta-technology in context.

technology has induced new types of lawsuits, or modified existing ones. Consider new offences such as computer crimes (e.g. identity theft) that would be unconceivable once deprived of the technology upon which they depend. Moreover, reflect on traditional rights such as copyright and privacy, both turned into a matter of access to, and control and protection over, information in digital environments. By examining the legal challenges of technology, we thus have to specify those concepts and principles of legal reasoning that are at stake. Then, we can begin to determine whether the information revolution: (a) affects such concepts and principles; (b) creates new principles and concepts; or, (c) does not concern them at all, the latter being the view of traditional legal scholars [16].

The second observable of Fig. 2 has to do with the old, Kelsenian account of the law as a social technique of a coercive order enforced through the threat of physical sanctions: "if A, then B." As previously stressed, we can grasp the law as a form of meta-technology without buying any of Kelsen's ontological commitments. Rather, we should pay attention to the impact of technology on the formalisms of the law, much as how legal systems deal with the process of technological innovation, through such a complex network of concepts, as agency, accountability, liability, burdens of proofs, clauses of immunity, or unjust damages. In this latter case, the aim of the law to govern the field of technological innovation comprises several different techniques, so as to attain: (a) particular effects; (b) functional equivalence between online and offline activities; (c) non-discrimination between technologies with equivalent effects; and, (d) future-proofing of the law that should neither hinder the advance of technology, nor require over-frequent revision to tackle such a progress [11].

The third observable of Fig. 2 regards both the traditional aim of the law to regulate human behaviour, and the field of techno-regulation, or legal regulation by design. Since current advancements of technology have increasingly obliged legislators and policy makers to forge more sophisticated ways to think about legal enforcement, the focus is here on how national and international lawmakers have complemented the traditional hard tools of the law through the mechanisms of design, codes, and IT architectures. Although some of these architectural measures are not necessarily digital, e.g. the installation of speed bumps in roads as a means to reduce the velocity of cars, many impasses of today's legal and political systems are progressively tackled, by embedding normative constraints and constitutional safeguards into ICTs [20].

Against this backdrop, the paper adopts a further stance: the legal impact of domestic, or service, robots is illustrated in accordance with the different fields with which we are dealing, i.e. privacy and data protection, vis-à-vis the intent of the law to govern the process of robotic innovation. This perspective partially overlaps with the previous observables of Fig. 2 and yet, it allows us to pinpoint the new observables and variables of the analysis, i.e. what issues ought to be questioned, prioritized and made relevant, so as to stress the legal impact of domestic and/or service robots. Admittedly, we could have chosen a different interface for our analysis, such as the legal issues of liability and security, compulsory insurance and copyright, consumer law and environmental regulation, that robots brought about by in the fields of criminal law, civil law, administrative law, etc. However, matters of roboprivacy and data protection clarify how the traditional aim of the law to govern innovation and to regulate human behaviour is crucially changing nowadays. A new figure introduces the LoA of this paper, with its observables and variables (Fig. 3).

Next Section introduces the technology under scrutiny, namely robotics and the next generation of consumer and service robot applications. Then, in Sects. 3 and 4 respectively, the analysis dwells on the first two variants of Fig. 3, namely a new expectation of privacy triggered by this novel generation of robots, and the realignment of the traditional distinction between data processors and data controllers. As to the second observable of Fig. 3, Sect. 5 draws the attention to a novel set of challenges in the field of techno-regulation and especially, in connection with the principle of privacy by design. On this basis, the conclusions of the analysis will bring us back to the aim of the law to govern the process of technological innovation and consequently, the different purposes that the law can have. Since robots are here to stay, it seems fair to affirm that the aim of the law should be to wisely govern our mutual relationships.

2   The Charge of Consumer and Service Robots

Since the early 1960s and for more than three decades, the field of robotics mostly appeared as an automobile industry-dependent sector. A crucial point in this process occurred in the early 1980s, when Japanese industry first began to implement this technology on a large scale in their factories, acquiring strategic competitiveness by decreasing costs and increasing the quality of their products. Western car producers learned a hard lesson and followed Japanese thinking, installing robots in their factories a few years later. This trend expanded so much that, according to the UN World 2005 Robotics Report, the automotive industry in Europe still received around 60%–70% of all new robot installations in the period 1997–2003 [24].

Yet, in the same years as covered by the UN World report, things began to rapidly change. The traditional dependence of robotics on the automobile industry dramatically opened up to diversification, first with water-surface and underwater unmanned vehicles, or "UUVs," used for remote exploration work and the repairs of pipelines, oil rigs and so on, developing at an amazing pace since the mid-1990s. Ten years later, unmanned aerial vehicles ("UAVs"), or systems ("UAS"), upset the military field [16]. Over the past decade, robots have spread in both the industrial and service fields. Together with robots used in the manufacture of textiles and beverages, refining petroleum products and nuclear fuel, producing electrical machinery and domestic appliances, we also have a panoply of robot surgeons and robot servants, robot nannies and robot scientists, and even divabots, e.g. the Japanese pop star robot singer HRP-4C. The old idea of making machines (e.g. cars) through further machines (e.g. robots), has thus been joined – and increasingly replaced – by the aim to build fully autonomous

Fig. 3. The interface of this paper.

robots, namely AI machines that "sense," "think," and "act," in the engineering meaning of these words [1, 25]. In a nutshell, this means that robots can respond to stimuli by changing the values of their properties or inner states and, furthermore, they can improve the rules through which those properties change without external stimuli. As a result, we are progressively dealing with agents, rather than simple tools of human interaction [19].

The more robots become interactive, self-sufficient, and adaptable, however, the more attention should be drawn to the normative challenges of this technology, i.e. the reasons why such AI machines should, or should not, be deployed at our homes, in the market, or on the battlefield. Consider current debate on whether lethal force can be fully automated, or whether the intent to create robots that people bond with is ethically justifiable. The complexity of the subject-matter, i.e. the normative challenges of robotics, can be grasped with a new figure (Fig. 4).

Leaving aside the aim of the moral, political and economic fields, in governing the process of technological innovation, what matters here is the normative side of the law. As mentioned above in the introduction, the challenges of robotics may concern pillars of current international law, criminal law, civil law, both in contracts and tort law, administrative law, and so forth. Think of tiny robotic helicopters employed in a jewellery heist vis-à-vis other robotic applications trading in auction markets and how the random-bidding strategy of these apps clarifies, or even has provoked, real life bubbles and crisis, e.g. the financial troubles of late 2009 that may have been triggered by the involvement of such artificial agents. Since the "bad nature" of robots vary in accordance with the field under examination, we thus have to pinpoint the specific legal challenges of this technology. A thematic, rather than field-dependent, LoA seems fruitful, in order to flesh out some of the most urgent and trickier challenges of robotics. The last variable of Fig. 4 brings us back to the observables and variables of Fig. 3: the normative challenges of robotics are here grasped in connection with a particular class of robotic applications, i.e. "service robots" [24], or "consumer robots" [4], in order to determine whether, and to what extent, they may affect current legal frameworks of privacy and data protection. In the wording of the EU Agenda, "these robots will be bought or leased and used to provide services to individuals. They will be operated by, or interact with, untrained, or minimally trained people in everyday environments. Applications range from helping the elderly stay safely mobile in their own homes to the automation of everyday household chores and the provision of remote monitoring and security for home" [4, at 34].

In accordance with the LoA of this paper on the law as a meta-technology, the analysis follows a twofold approach. On the one hand, the attention should be drawn to the aim of the law to govern the process of technological innovation: this intent has to

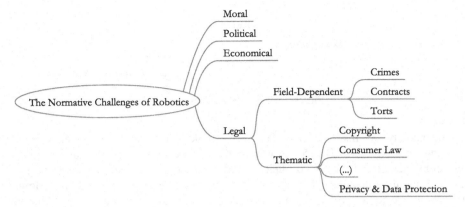

Fig. 4. The complexity of the field.

do, in this context, with the regulation of producers and designers of robots through specific sets of norms, or the regulation of user behaviour through the design of their robots. On the other hand, over the past years, scholars have increasingly stressed the many issues fated to remain open with the protection of people's privacy and the transparency with which service, or consumer, robots will increasingly collect, process, and make use of personal data [13, 19, 21, 23]. Remarkably, in *The Right to Privacy* (1890), Samuel Warren and Louis Brandeis claimed that "instantaneous photographs and newspaper enterprise have invaded the sacred precincts of private and domestic life; and numerous mechanical devices threaten to make good the prediction that 'what is whispered in the closet shall be proclaimed from the house-tops'" [26, at 195]. By taking into account current trends of robotics, should we expect a new invasion of the sacred precincts of our private life?

3   Private Expectations

Many readers of this paper may not have met a consumer robot so far and yet, they are familiar with some privacy challenges that will be brought about by these applications. Reflect on how a number of mobile devices, such as your smartphone, collect a myriad of different data, e.g. images and video through cameras, motion and activities through gyroscopes and accelerometers, fingerprints through biometric sensors, geo-location data through GPS techniques, and so forth. Likewise, consider such fitness applications, as Nike+ or Adidas miCoach, that track route, pace and time activities of users through GPS and sensors. Moreover, contemplate the real time facial recognition app NameTage for Google Glasses. Risks for user's informational privacy have been stressed time and again: for instance, as to the threats raised by sensors, consider how personal information can be inferred from such data, as occurs with information on mobility patterns, activity and face recognition, health information, and so on. In light of current risks for user's privacy, what is new about consumer robots is that sensors, cameras, GPS, facial recognition apps, Wi-Fi, microphones and more, will be assembled in a single piece of high-tech that will likely affect what US legal scholars dub as a "reasonable expectation of privacy."

In a nutshell, the formula means that individuals have the right to be protected against unreasonable searches and seizures under the Fourth Amendment. Pursuant to the jurisprudence of the US Supreme Court from the 1967 *Katz v. United States* case (389 U.S. 347), onwards, the overall idea is that the opinion of a person that a certain situation or location is private, must go hand in hand with the fact that society at large would recognize this expectation, so as to protect the latter as a fundamental right. Scholars and also justices of the Supreme Court, however, have emphasised that such twofold dimension of this reasonable expectation, both social and individual, can entail a vicious circle, much as "the chicken or the egg" causality dilemma. Moreover, the right to a reasonable expectation of privacy rests on the assumption that both individuals and society have developed a stable set of privacy expectations, whereas technology can dramatically change these very expectations. As Justice Alito emphasizes in his concurring opinion in *United States v. Jones* from 23 January 2012 (565 U. S. __), "dramatic technological change may lead to periods in which popular expectations are in flux and may ultimately produce significant changes in popular attitudes."

The legal framework is different in Europe. According to the EU legal rules and principles of privacy and data protection, the opinion of individuals does not play any normative role, in order to determine the legitimacy of the acts and statutes laid down by the public institutions. On the contrary, what individuals and society can reasonably expect, is that public organizations, multinational corporations, and other private parties, abide by the set of rules and principles established by the EU, or national, legislators. Notwithstanding this approach, it does not follow that social and individual expectations of privacy are totally irrelevant in Europe. Consider the proposal for a new data protection regulation in the EU legal system, presented by the Commission in January 2012. The same day in which the Parliament approved the new set of rules, the Commission was keen to inform us with a press release on 12 March 2014, that the intent to update and modernize the principles enshrined in the 1995 data protection directive is strictly connected with "a clear need to close the growing rift between individuals and the companies that process their data."[1] The source of this "clear need" was provided by the Flash Eurobarometer 359 from June 2011, on the attitudes concerning data protection and electronic identity in the EU. According to this source, 9 out of 10 Europeans (92%) said they are worried about mobile apps collecting their data without their consent, 7 out of 10 are concerned about the potential use that companies may make of the information disclosed, etc. Whether the new EU regulation n. 679 from 2016, the so called GDPR, will close the rift between individual and companies is, of course, an open issue and yet, it is highly likely that consumer and service robots will add new worries about radars, sensors or laser scanners of artificial agents collecting data of their human masters, much as companies that may infer personal information from such data on mobility patterns, user's preferences, lifestyles, and the like.

---

[1] See the press release at http://europa.eu/rapid/press-release_MEMO-14-186_it.htm.

A common expectation of privacy should thus be expected (not only, but also) in Europe and US, in the basic sense that users of robots will likely assume that some "degree of friction," restraining the flow of personal information, should be respected. Clearly, this is not to say that personal choices will have no role in determining different levels of access to, and control over, information. Rather, from a legal point of view, there are two ways in which we can appreciate the role of these personal choices in keeping firm distinctions between individuals and society, agents and the system. On the one hand, the different types of information which robots may properly reveal, share, or transfer, will often hinge on personal preferences of the human master on whether it is appropriate to trace back information to an individual, and how information should be distributed according to different standards in different contexts. Depending on how humans have taken care of their artificial agents, specimens of the same model of robot will accordingly behave in different ways. On the other hand, personal choices on both norms of appropriateness and flow will further hinge on the type of robot under scrutiny. The type of information that makes sense to communicate and share with an artificial personal assistant, would be irrelevant or unnecessary to impart to a robot toy. It is thus likely that individuals will modulate different levels of access to, and control over, information, depending on the kind of the artificial interlocutor, the context of their interaction, and the circumstances of the case.

The impact of domestic and service robots on current expectations of privacy, however, not only regards problems of reliability, traceability, identifiability, trustfulness and generally speaking, how the interaction with such robots and their presence in "the sacred precincts of private and domestic life" may realign both norms of appropriateness and of informational flow [15]. In addition, we should expect psychological problems related to the interaction with robots as matters of attachment and feelings of subordination, deviations in human emotions, etc. [25]. This scenario suggests that we should go back to the general intent of the law to govern the process of technological innovation through the four different categories stressed by Ronald Leenes and Federica Lucivero in *Laws on Robots, Laws by Robots, Laws in Robots* (2014). Accordingly, the focus should be on (a) the regulation of human producers and designers of robots through law, e.g. either through ISO standards or liability norms for users of robots; (b) the regulation of user behaviour through the design of robots, that is, by designing robots in such a way that unlawful actions of humans are not allowed; (c) the regulation of the legal effects of robot behaviour through the norms set up by lawmakers, e.g. the effects of robotic contracts and negotiations; and, (d) the regulation of robot behaviour through design, that is, by embedding normative constraints into the design of the artificial agent. This differentiation can be complemented with further work on the regulation of the environment of the human-robot interaction and the legal challenges of "ambient law" [7, 8]. We should thus take into account the set of values, principles, and norms that constitute the normative context in which the consequences of such regulations have to be evaluated. In addition, we have to consider issues of data protection that mostly revolve around the transparency with which personal data are collected, processed, and used.

In the EU legal system, for example, individuals have the right to know the purposes for which their data are processed, much as the right to access that data and to have it rectified. In the wording of Article 8(2) of the EU Charter of fundamental rights, "such data must be processed fairly... and on the basis of the consent of the person concerned or some other legitimate basis laid down by law." This type of protection through the principles of minimization and quality of the data, its controllability and confidentiality, may of course overlap with the protection of the individual privacy. In such cases, the aim is to constraint the flow of information, and keep firm distinctions between individuals and society, in order to protect what the German Constitutional Court has framed in terms of "informational self-determination" since its *Volkszählungs-Urteil* ("census decision") from 15 December 1983. Yet, there are several cases in which the norms of data protection do not entail the safeguard of any privacy. Together with the mechanism of "notice and consent," laid down by Article 7 of the EU directive 46 from 1995, reflect on how the processing of personal data can – and at times should – go hand in hand with the strengthening of further rights and interests of individuals, such as freedom of information and the right to knowledge, freedom of expression and access to public documents, up to participatory democracy and the functioning of the internal market with the free circulation of services and information pursuant to the EU directive on the reuse of public sector information, i.e. D-37/2013/EC [22].

As a result of this differentiation between privacy and data protection, how should we strike a fair balance in the case of domestic and service robots?

4 Holders of Personal Data

The reference point for today's state-of-art in roboprivacy is given by the guidelines that a EU-sponsored project, namely "RoboLaw," presented in September 2014. According to this document, the principle of privacy by design can play a key role in making and keeping robots data protection-compliant [23, at 19]. For example, some legal safeguards, such as data security through encryption and data access control, can be embedded into the software and interface of the robot. Likewise, "requirements such as informed consent can be implemented in system design, for example through interaction with users displays and input devices" (*ibid*). After all, this is what already occurs with some operating systems, such as Android, that require user's consent whenever an application intends to access personal data. Furthermore, robots could be designed in a privacy-friendly way, so that the amount of data to be collected and processed is reduced to a minimum and in compliance with the finality principle. This means that, pursuant to Article 6(1)(b) of the EU data protection directive 46 from 1995 and now, Article 5(1)(b) of the GDPR, robots should collect data only insofar as it is necessary to achieve a specified and legitimate purpose.

In addition, this set of legal safeguards on data minimization, finality principle, informed consent, etc., shall be pre-emptively checked through control mechanisms and data protection impact assessments, so as to ensure that privacy safeguards are at work even before a single bit of information has been collected. More particularly, in the words of the RoboLaw Guidelines, "as a corollary of a privacy impact assessment, a control mechanism should be established that checks whether technologies are constructed in the most privacy-friendly way compatible with other requirements (such as information needs and security)" [23, at 190]. Leaving aside specific security measures for particular classes of service robots, such as health robots, personal care robots, or automated cars examined by the EU project, the latter suggests that "the adoption of updated security measures should not be considered only as a user's choice, but also as a specific legal duty. It is clear that the illicit treatment of the data is unlikely to be considered a responsibility of the manufacturer of the robot, but rather a liability of its user, who is the 'holder' of the personal data" [23, at 190].

Whether the end-user, or "human master," of the robot should be deemed as the data controller and hence, liable for any illicit treatment of personal data, is however debatable. As stressed above in the previous sections, we may admit cases in which the role of personal choices suggests that end-users should be conceived as data controllers and thus, liable for how their artificial agents collect, process, and make use of personal data. But, as occurs today with issues of internet connectivity, or sensors and mobile computing applications, several other cases indicate that the illicit treatment of personal data may depend on designers and manufacturers of robots, internet providers, applications developers, and so forth. After all, the illicit treatment of personal data may be traced back to the malfunctioning of the robot, or to HTTP headers in packets of network traffic data that can be used to determine interests and other personal information about the master of the robot, along with applications that leak identifiable data, such as device ID, GPS, and more. What all these cases make clear is not only hypotheses of illicit treatment of data that do not depend on end-users or masters of robots as data controllers. Additionally, the liability of designers and manufacturers of robots, internet providers, etc., can be problematic in connection with different interpretations of current rules and principles of the data protection legal framework, e.g. the EU 2016 norms on the protection of individuals with regard to the processing of personal data and on the free movement of such data. As stressed by Art. 29 Working Party in the opinion 1/2010 (WP 169), "the concept of controller is a functional concept, intended to allocate responsibility where the factual influence is, and thus based on a factual, rather than a formal analysis," which "may sometimes require an in-depth and lengthy investigation" (*op. cit.*, 9).

However, even admitting the conclusions of the Working Party, so that liability of data controllers "can be easily and clearly identified in most situations" (*ibid.*), we still have to face a major problem. Although normative safeguards can be embedded into the software and interface of domestic robots, significant differences between multiple data protection jurisdictions, e.g. between US and EU, remain. Whereas, in the US, privacy policies of the industry and the agreement between parties mostly regulate matters of data protection in the private sector, we already stressed that the EU has adopted a comprehensive legislation since its 1995 data protection directive, up to the current provisions of the GDPR. Principles and rules of this legal framework on data minimization, finality principle, informed consent, etc., set limits to the contractual power of individuals and companies. This divergence between US and EU will likely increase with the GDPR. Even the RoboLaw Guidelines concede that these "significant differences... could make it difficult for manufacturers catering for the international market to design in specific data protection rules" [23, at 19]. As a matter of legal fact, which norms and rules should designers and manufactures of domestic robots embed into their products? Should such norms and rules vary according to the specific market (and jurisdiction)? Would this latter option be technically and economically sustainable?

A feasible way-out is pragmatic. Following Anu Bradford's thesis on "the Brussels effect" and how Europe's regulatory model wields unilateral influence across such legal fields, as data protection, antitrust, or health and environmental legislation [2], we may envisage a similar effect in the case of domestic robots. The non-divisibility of data and the compliance costs of multinational corporations dealing with multiple regulatory regimes, may prompt most robot manufacturers to adopt and adapt themselves to the strictest international standards across the board, that is, the EU data protection framework, much as occurred in the case of internet companies vis-à-vis data protection issues. However, compared with traditional privacy regulation, we should not overlook some peculiarities of domestic and service robots. By affecting what US lawyers dub as a reasonable expectation of privacy, as explored above in the previous section, it is highly likely that such expectation, both individual and social, will be "in flux" for a while. Some insist on this flux to stress that lawmakers, rather than judges or data protection authorities, are in the best position to determine the rules of the game and guide social and individual behaviour [10]. But, even in light of the strictest international standards of the EU legislation, it is still vague how we should interpret some of its key assumptions, e.g. the principle of privacy by design. Neither the Commission's proposal for a new data protection regulation in January 2012, nor the amendments of the EU Parliament in March 2014, nor the final 2016 text of the general data protection regulation (GDPR), clarify how to design robots that abide by the law. All in all, we lack a regulatory model that may represent a reference point for international standards on the design, production and commercialization of domestic robots. The aim of next section is thus to deepen current uncertainties on the principle of privacy by design, by fleshing out how such uncertainties are intertwined with the aim of the law to govern the process of technological innovation.

5 How to Design Robots that Abide by the Law

Legal design has different and even opposite aims. Think about the latter according to a spectrum: at one end, the purpose is to determine and control both social and individual behaviour through the use of self-enforcing technologies and such automatic techniques, as filtering systems and digital rights management (DRM)-tools, that intend to restrict any form of access, use, copy, replacement, reproduction, etc., of informational resources in the environment. At the other end of the spectrum, design may aim to encourage the change of people's behaviour by widening the range of the choices through incentives based on trust (e.g. reputation mechanisms), or trade (e.g. services in return). In between the ends of the spectrum, design may aim to decrease the impact of harm-generating behaviour through security measures, default settings, user friendly interfaces, and the like. Notwithstanding these different ends, it is noteworthy that legislators and scholars alike often refer to the aim to embed legal constraints into technology, e.g. privacy by design, in a neutral manner, that is, as if the intent of this legal embedding could be impartial and value-free. Consider articles 23 and 30 of the EU Commission's proposal for a new data protection regulation, much as § 3.4.4.1 of the document with which the Commission illustrated the proposal. Here, the formula of "privacy by design" is so broad, or vague, that it can include whatever end design may have. Although, in the amendment 118 of the EU Parliament, the latter refers to "comprehensive procedural safeguards regarding the accuracy, confidentiality, integrity, physical security and deletion of personal data," it is still unclear vis-à-vis Article 25 of the GDPR whether the aim should be to decrease the impact of harm-generating conducts or rather, to widen the range of individual options, or both. In light of these uncertainties, how about the design of consumer and service robots and the environment of human-robot interaction through sensors, GPS, facial recognition apps, Wi-Fi, RFID, NFC, or QC code-based environment interaction?

First of all, the principle of privacy by design and the EU Parliament's "comprehensive procedural safeguards" can be grasped in terms of security measures, e.g. data access control and encryption, much as user-friendly default configurations of robotic interfaces. Robots can indeed be designed in such a way that values of design are appropriate even for novice users and still, the robot improves efficiency. Furthermore, the intent can be to seamlessly integrate robots into domestic workflows and IT systems of smart houses via compliant motion control systems and situation awareness technologies, much as flexible and modular systems for the measurement of physical, physiological and electro-physiological variables, that should make the user experience an integral and even natural part of the process. In addition, we should take into account the set of legal safeguards on data minimization, finality principle, or informed consent, that were mentioned in the previous section, so as to tackle the convergence of robotic data processing and the internet (of things, of everything, etc.).

However, a number of further cases suggest that domestic robots could alternatively be designed with the aim to prevent any harm-generating behaviour from occurring. This is not only a popular stance among Western lawmakers in such fields as intellectual property ("IP") protection, data retention, or online security [19]. Moreover, in the field of robotics, two further reasons may reinforce this design policy. On the one hand, in the phrasing of the EU Parliament, "the accuracy, confidentiality, integrity, physical security and deletion of personal data," processed by domestic robots, will more often concern data of third parties. On the other hand, we must reflect on both the psychological problems related to the very interactions with robots, and the case of human masters that do not properly fulfill their role of caretakers. Lawmakers, data protection authorities and courts may thus adopt a stricter version of the principle of privacy by design, in order to preclude any data protection infringement through the use of self-enforcing technologies, e.g. filtering systems, in the name of security reasons. This scenario is not only compatible with the new EU regulation, but has been endorsed by some popular versions of the principle. In Ann Cavoukian's account of privacy by design, for example, personal data should be automatically protected in every IT system as its default position, so that a cradle-to-grave, start-to-finish, or end-to-end lifecycle protection ensures that privacy safeguards are automatically at work even before a single bit of information has been collected [3]. But, is this automatic version of privacy by design technically feasible and even desirable?

There are several ethical, legal, and technical reasons why we should resist the aim of some lawmakers to protect citizens even against themselves. First, the use of self-enforcing technologies risks to curtail freedom and individual autonomy severely, because people's behaviour and their interaction with robots would be determined on the basis of design rather than by individual choices [14, 28]. Once the normative side of the law is transferred from the traditional "ought to" of rules and norms to what actually is in automatic terms, a modeling of individual conduct follows as a result, namely, that which Kant used to stigmatize as "paternalism" [17].

Second, specific design choices (not only, but also) in robotics may result in conflicts between values and furthermore, conflicts between values may impact on the features of design. Since both privacy and data protection may be conceived in terms of human dignity or property rights, of contextual integrity or total control, it follows that privacy by design acquires many different features. In the case of self-enforcing technologies, their use would make conflicts between values even worse, due to specific design choices, e.g. the opt-in vs. opt-out diatribe over the setting of information systems [17].

Third, attention should be drawn to the technical difficulty of applying to a robot concepts traditionally employed by lawyers, through the formalization of norms, rights, or duties. As stressed by Bert-Jaap Koops and Ronald Leenes, "the idea of encoding legal norms at the start of information processing systems is at odds with the dynamic and fluid nature of many legal norms, which need a breathing space that is typically not something that can be embedded in software" [12, at 7]. All in all, informational protection safeguards present highly context-dependent notions that raise several relevant problems when reducing the complexity of a legal system where concepts and relations are subject to evolution [18].

At the end of the day, it should be clear that the use of self-enforcing technologies would not only prevent robotic behaviour from occurring. By unilaterally determining how the artificial agent should act when collecting, for example, the information they need for human-robot interaction and task completion from networked repositories, such design policies do impinge on individual rights and freedom. If there is no need to humanize our robotic applications, we should not robotize human life either. The time is ripe for the conclusions of this paper.

6 Conclusions

Most service and consumer robots are not a mere "out of the box" machine. Rather, as a sort of prolonged epigenetic developmental process, robots increasingly gain knowledge or skills from their own interaction with the living beings inhabiting the surrounding environment, so that more complex cognitive structures emerge in the state-transition system of the artificial agent. Simply put, specimens of the same model will behave in quite different ways, according to how humans train, treat, or manage their robots. Correspondingly, both the behaviour and decisions of these artificial agents can be unpredictable and risky, thus affecting traditional tenets of the law, such as a "reasonable expectation" of privacy, which was mentioned above in Sect. 3, together with matters of data protection (Sect. 4), and the troubles with legal design (Sect. 5). How, then, should legal systems proceed? What purposes should the law have? What lessons did the LoA of this paper on the law as a meta-technology learn?

All in all, the conclusion is "pragmatic." Over the past 15 years, the Japanese government has worked out a way to address most of the issues examined in this paper, through the creation of special zones for robotics empirical testing and development, namely, a form of living lab, or *Tokku*. Whereas the world's first special zone was approved by the Cabinet Office in November 2003, covering the prefecture of Fukuoka and the city of Kitakyushu, further special zones have been established in Osaka and Gifu, Kanagawa and Tsukuba. The overall aim of these special zones is to set up a sort of interface for robots and society, in which scientists and common people can test whether robots fulfil their task specifications in ways that are acceptable and comfortable to humans, vis-à-vis the uncertainty of machine safety and legal liabilities that concern, e.g., the protection for the processing of personal data through sensors, GPS, facial recognition apps, Wi-Fi, RFID, NFC, or QC code-based environment interaction. Although the Japanese typically are perceived as conservative and inclined to a formalistic and at times, pedantic interpretation of the law, it is remarkable that such special zones are highly deregulated from a legal point of view. "Without deregulation, the current overruled Japanese legal system will be a major obstacle to the realization of its RT [Robot Tokku] business competitiveness as well as the new safety for human-robot co-existence" [27]. Furthermore, the intent is "to cover many potential legal disputes derived from the next-generation robots when they are deployed in the real world" (*ibid.*).

So far, the legal issues addressed in the RT special zones regard road traffic laws (at Fukuoka in 2003), radio law (Kansai 2005), privacy protection (Kyoto 2008), safety governance and tax regulation (Tsukuba 2011), up to road traffic law in highways (Sagami 2013). These experiments could obviously be extended, so as to strengthen our understanding of how the future of the human-robot interaction could turn out. Consider again some of the problems mentioned above in the previous sections, such as the realignment of the traditional distinction between data processors and data controllers, or the aim of the law to design robots that abide by the law. By testing these scenarios in open, unstructured environments, the Japanese approach shows a pragmatic way to tackle the challenges brought about by possible losses of control of AI systems. Significantly, in the field of autonomous vehicles, several EU countries have endorsed this kind of approach: Sweden has sponsored the world's first large-scale autonomous driving pilot project, in which self-driving cars use public roads in everyday driving conditions; Germany has allowed a number of tests with various levels of automation on highways, e.g. Audi's tests with an autonomously driving car on highway A9 between Ingolstadt and Nuremberg. Whereas the Japanese automotive sector acquired a strategic competitiveness in the early 1980s through the use of robots, the aim of Western producers and some of its lawmakers is to follow suit and prevent on this basis another hard lesson.

References

1. Bekey, G.A.: Autonomous Robots: From Biological Inspiration to Implementation and Control. The MIT Press, Cambridge (2005)
2. Bradford, A.: The Brussels effect. Northwest. Univ. Law Rev. **107**(1), 1–68 (2012)

3. Cavoukian, A.: Privacy by design: the definitive workshop. Identity Inf. Soc. **3**(2), 247–251 (2010)
4. EU Robotics: Robotics 2020 Strategic Research Agenda for Robotics in Europe, draft 0v42, 11 October 2013
5. Floridi, L.: The method of levels of abstraction. Mind. Mach. **18**(3), 303–329 (2008)
6. Floridi, L.: The Fourth Revolution. Oxford University Press, Oxford (2014)
7. Hildebrandt, M.: Legal protection by design: objections and refutations. Legisprudence **5**(2), 223–248 (2011)
8. Hildebrandt, M., Koops, B.-J.: The challenges of ambient law and legal protection in the profiling era. Mod. Law Rev. **73**(3), 428–460 (2010)
9. Kelsen, H.: General Theory of the Law and the State (trans: A. Wedberg). Harvard University Press, Cambridge, Mass (1945/1949)
10. Kerr, O.: The fourth amendment and new technologies: constitutional myths and the case for caution. Mich. Law Rev. **102**, 801–888 (2004)
11. Koops, B.J.: Should ICT regulation be technology-neutral? In: Koops, B.J., et al. (eds.) Starting Points for ICT Regulation: Deconstructing Prevalent Policy One-Liners, pp. 77–108. TMC Asser, The Hague (2006)
12. Koops, B.-J., Leenes, R.: Privacy regulation cannot be hardcoded: a critical comment on the "privacy by design" provision in data protection law. Int. Rev. Law Comput. Technol. **28**, 159–171 (2014)
13. Leenes, R., Lucivero, F.: Laws on Robots, laws by robots, laws in robots: regulating robot behaviour by design. Law Innov. Technol. **6**(2), 193–220 (2014)
14. Lessig, L.: Free Culture: The Nature and Future of Creativity. Penguin Press, New York (2004)
15. Nissenbaum, H.: Privacy as contextual integrity. Wash. Law Rev. **79**(1), 119–158 (2004)
16. Pagallo, U.: Robots of just war: a legal perspective. Philos. Technol. **24**(3), 307–323 (2011)
17. Pagallo, U.: On the principle of privacy by design and its limits: technology, ethics, and the rule of law. In: Gutwirth, S., Leenes, R., De Hert, P., Poullet, Y. (eds.) European Data Protection: In Good Health?, pp. 331–346. Springer, Dordrecht (2012). https://doi.org/10.1007/978-94-007-2903-2_16
18. Pagallo, U.: Three roads to complexity, AI and the law of robots: on crimes, contracts, and torts. In: Palmirani, M., Pagallo, U., Casanovas, P., Sartor, G. (eds.) AICOL 2011. LNCS (LNAI), vol. 7639, pp. 48–60. Springer, Heidelberg (2012). https://doi.org/10.1007/978-3-642-35731-2_3
19. Pagallo, U.: The Laws of Robots: Crimes, Contracts, and Torts. Springer, Dordrecht (2013). https://doi.org/10.1007/978-94-007-6564-1
20. Pagallo, U.: Good onlife governance: on law, spontaneous orders, and design. In: Floridi, L. (ed.) The Onlife Manifesto: Being Human in a Hyperconnected Era, pp. 161–177. Springer, Dordrecht (2015). https://doi.org/10.1007/978-3-319-04093-6_18
21. Pagallo, U.: Teaching "consumer robots" respect for informational privacy: a legal stance on HRI. In: Coleman, D. (ed.) Human-Robot Interactions. Principles, Technologies and Challenges, pp. 35–55. Nova, New York (2015)
22. Pagallo, U., Bassi, E.: Open data protection: challenges, perspectives, and tools for the reuse of PSI. In: Hildebrand, M., O'Hara, K., Waidner, M. (eds.) Digital Enlightenment Yearbook 2013, pp. 179–189. IOS Press, Amsterdam (2013)
23. RoboLaw: Guidelines on Regulating Robotics. EU Project on Regulating Emerging Robotic Technologies in Europe: Robotics facing Law and Ethics, 22 September 2014
24. UN World Robotics: Statistics, Market Analysis, Forecasts, Case Studies and Profitability of Robot Investment, edited by the UN Economic Commission for Europe and co-authored by the International Federation of Robotics, UN Publication, Geneva (Switzerland) (2005)

25. Veruggio, G.: Euron roboethics roadmap. In: Proceedings Euron Roboethics Atelier, 27th February–3rd March, Genoa, Italy (2006)
26. Warren, S., Brandeis, L.: The right to privacy. Harv. Law Rev. **14**, 193–220 (1890)
27. Weng, Y.-H., Sugahara, Y., Hashimoto, K., Takanishi, A.: Intersection of "Tokku" special zone, robots, and the law: a case study on legal impacts to humanoid robots. Int. J. Soc. Robot. **7**(5), 841–857 (2015)
28. Zittrain, J.: Perfect enforcement on tomorrow's internet. In: Brownsword, R., Yeung, K. (eds.) Regulating Technologies: Legal Futures, Regulatory Frames and Technological Fixes, pp. 125–156. Hart, London (2007)

Revisiting Constitutive Rules

Giovanni Sileno[(✉)], Alexander Boer, and Tom van Engers

Leibniz Center for Law, University of Amsterdam, Amsterdam, Netherlands
{g.sileno,aboer,vanengers}@uva.nl

Abstract. The paper is an investigation on how behaviour relates to norms, i.e. how a certain conduct acquires *meaning* in institutional terms. The simplest mechanism determining this phenomenon is given by the 'count-as' relation, generally associated with constitutive rules, through which an agent has the legal capacity, via performing a certain action, to create, modify or destroy a certain institutional fact. In the analytic literature, however, the 'count-as' relation is mostly approached for its classificatory functions, mapping entities to categories whose members carry institutional properties. Besides making explicit this double function, the paper reconsiders the relation between constitutive rules and regulative rules, and introduces a proposal on the ontological status of constitution.

Keywords: Constitutive rules · Institutional rules · Regulative rules
Connotation · Import · Institutional power · Behaviour · Norms
Supervenience

1 Introduction

An important question, still unresolved in legal theory and in analytic literature, concerns the nature (and for certain authors, the very existence) of *constitutive rules*, and their distinction from *regulative rules*. The best known (and discussed) account is the one developed by Searle [1–3]. As their name suggests, regulative rules regulate pre-existing forms of behaviour. For example, eating is an activity introduced well before that any rule of polite table behaviour was introduced. On the contrary, the rules of playing chess are constitutive: actions in accordance with them constitute the very activity of playing chess. Searle then argues that institutions like marriage, money or promise are not different from games such as baseball or chess, in the sense that they are all systems of constitutive rules.

Despite this simple and intuitive presentation, however, many authors have attempted to better define the two types of rules, without reaching a definitive agreement. Understanding *institutional constitution* is in effect a crucial part of the study of *social ontology*, and for this reason it is addressed in linguistics, social sciences, developmental psychology, economics, and information science, as well as in philosophy.

While ontology is the general philosophical study about existence, social ontology focuses on the social reality (distinguished from the physical reality,

© Springer Nature Switzerland AG 2018
U. Pagallo et al. (Eds.): AICOL VI-X 2015–2017, LNAI 10791, pp. 39–55, 2018.
https://doi.org/10.1007/978-3-030-00178-0_3

and from the individual mental reality), normally by tracking the understanding of properties and functions of *institutions*. As convincingly observed by Roversi in [4] this type of investigation usually takes a *rule-realist view*: "rules constitutive of an institution can exist only as part of the causal (mental or behavioural) process through which the institutional activity they constitute is practiced". This is the most natural perspective that we could take by reflecting on our experience as social participants: if mankind disappeared from the world, so would its institutions. At the same time, Roversi observes that social ontology is not (yet) a major field of interest for contemporary legal philosophy. Most legal scholars embrace with more ease a *rule-positivist view*: "rules constitutive of an institution can exist before and independently of the causal process through which the institutional activity they constitute is practiced". This preference can be explained: the rule-realist view undermines a general *tenet* of legal positivism, i.e. the independence of the treatment of elements belonging to the legal-institutional domain from considerations about their effectiveness (in economic, social or psychological terms) in the actual world.

Are the rule-positivist and the rule-realist views irredeemably incompatible? Works on *legal institutions* as those of [5,6] attempt this quest from a legal philosophical standpoint. From a knowledge engineering point of view, the problem can be put differently: *can a system of norms be aligned—representation-wise— with a system of practices guided by norms?* The investigation of constitutive rules is a necessary requirement to answer to this question. In the present paper, for reasons of space, we will overlook technical details, preferring to give a more exhaustive presentation of the problems at stake and of the solutions presented in the literature (Sect. 2). Exploiting this analysis, we will introduce an integrated account on constitution (Sect. 3), and utilize this to dissect institutional power (Sect. 4). Additionally, we will set up the basis for an investigation of the ontological status of constitution (Sect. 5), preparatory to check the alignment of representational models.

2   Relevant Literature

Searle: Constitutive and Regulative Rules. Searle's account on constitutive and regulative rules can be plausibly taken as the starting reference on this topic today. Elaborating on considerations by Anscombe and Rawls, he proposes (e.g. in [1, p. 34]) that the underlying structure of *constitutive rules* is in the form of:

$$\text{X counts as Y in context C.} \tag{1}$$

where X and Y are acts. Instead, *regulative* rules can be paraphrased as:

$$\text{Do X.} \tag{2}$$

or in a conditional form:

$$\text{If Y do X.} \tag{3}$$

Acts of type X are 'brute', i.e. they may occur independently of the rules regulating them, whereas acts of type Y are institutional: they cannot occur if no definite constitutive rule is applicable.

Conte: *Ludus* vs *Lusus*. Revisiting Wittgenstein, Conte [7] starts by observing that there is an ontological difference between the rules *eidetic-constitutive* of a 'game' (*ludus*) and the rules perceived from the 'play' (*lusus*). The former are necessary for the game to occur.[1] He then identifies different and incongruous uses of the term constitutive rules in Searle's work:

- X-type of rule: e.g. *"to make a promise is to undertake an obligation"*, which can be rewritten as "a promise counts as the undertaking of an obligation", with *'promise'* occupying the position X according to the template (1);
- Y-type of rule: e.g. *"a checkmate is made when the king is attacked in such a way that no move will leave it unattacked"*, which can be rewritten to "checks in which the king cannot meet the attack counts as checkmate", with *'checkmate'* occupying the position Y;
- rules as *"one ought not to steal"*, which seem to fall more under the definition of regulative rules;[2]
- rules related to (linguistic) performance: e.g. promises should be about future behaviour.

According to Conte, Y-type rules are the only proper *eidetic-constitutive* rules. The issues with the third and fourth case are evident. The argument against the X-type is that the rule given in the example is not necessary to make a promise, either ontologically (i.e. it is not necessary for the conception, the actual possibility or the perception of the promise) or semantically, as it makes only explicit an intension already present in the *speech act* of promising.

Jones and Sergot: "Count-As" as Conditional. According to Jones and Sergot [8], a 'count-as' relation establishes that a certain state of affairs or an action of an agent "is a sufficient condition to guarantee that the institution creates some (usually normative) state of affairs". They start by characterizing this connection as a *logic conditional* calibrated to avoid unsound effects. Consider, for example, a case in which x's declaration 'I pronounce you man and wife' "counts in the institution s as a means of guaranteeing that s sees to it that a and b are married." In classic propositional logic, the introduction of an inclusive *or* in the consequent does not change the validity of the rule: if $a \to b$ holds, then $a \to b \lor c$ also holds. However, Jones and Sergot correctly observe that it would "be bizarre to conclude that x's utterance act would also count in

---

[1] We may read the perspective of the legal scholar in this claim. In an actual social setting, this is often not the case: players may play even without knowing any rule, just mirroring what others are doing (*mimesis*) or, more rationally, fabricating their own models of the rules in place.

[2] In Searle's words, the prohibition of stealing is "a constitutive rule of the institution of private property", [1, p. 168].

s as a means of guaranteeing that either Nixon is impeached or s sees to it that a and b are married".

Going further, they acknowledge that there "will surely be conditionals which describe relations of logical consequence, of causal consequence and of deontic consequence". Rather than further defining the different types, they propose to translate the conditional underlying the count-as relation as a constraint 'if A then B' operative in the institution, or, via the *material implication*[3], as the incompatibility with the constraints operative in the institution such that 'A and not B'.

Boella and Van der Torre: Normative Goals and Belief Rules. Trying to analyze the relation between regulative and constitutive norms, Boella and Van der Torre [9] interpret the normative system via an agent metaphor, applying the *intentional stance* [10]. A normative system promotes *interests* as goals or values shared by some, most or all agents. These *normative goals*, delegated by the individual agents at the collective level, are expressed by regulative rules (obligation, prohibitions, etc.). What, then, are the 'beliefs' of the normative system? Boella and Van der Torre identify them as 'brute' and institutional facts. The creation of institutional facts (and therefore constitution) is obtained through *belief rules*, which introduce institutional categories abstracting actual situations or other institutional categories.

Grossi: Constitutive, Classificatory, Proper Classificatory Rules. Grossi starts by observing how several authors in the analytic literature have highlighted the classificatory character of non-regulative elements of norms, calling these *determinative rules* [11], *conceptual rules* [12], *qualification norms* [13] and *definitional norms* [14]. This aligns with Searle's argument about the definitional nature of constitutive rules.[4] Thus, acknowledging that 'counts-as' statements function in practice as classifications, [15] concludes that they could ultimately be modeled as *subsumption* relations.[5] Constitutive rules would then define an internal ontology, a conceptualization of the domain under regulation, crucial for the operationalization of the regulative components, as in the famous example: "vehicles are not admitted in public parks" (*general norm*), "bicycles are vehicles" (*classification rule*), therefore "bicycles are not admitted in public parks" (*specific norm*). Grossi proposes to discriminate three different components:

- *constitutive rules*: making explicit the extra-institutional conditions under which an institutional term applies, e.g. "In normative system N, conveyances transporting people or goods count as vehicles"

---

[3] The material implication allows to convert a logic conditional into a composition of disjunction and negation: $(a \rightarrow b) \leftrightarrow (\neg a \vee b)$. It makes explicit the 'constraint' nature of the operator of implication, rather than (epistemic) 'production' aspects.

[4] "The rules for checkmate or touchdown must 'define' checkmate in chess or touchdown in American Football [...]", [1, p. 34].

[5] Informally, given two concepts X and Y, 'X subsumes Y', or 'Y is subsumed by X', means that X (e.g. animal) is an abstraction of Y (e.g. whale).

- *classificatory rules*: making explicit the extra-institutional conditions that specifies an extra-institutional term, e.g. "It is always the case that bikes count as conveyances transporting people or goods"
- *proper classificatory rules*: connecting an extra-institutional term with an institutional term, e.g. "In normative system N, bikes count as vehicles"

The classificatory rule is completely extra-institutional and can be seen as given, while the others follow the XYC pattern proposed by Searle: the constitutive rule is at a more abstract level and the proper classificatory rule *contextualizes* the general constitutive rule in more specific terms, but they both refer to a 'middle term' [16] or 'intermediate concept' [17]—*vehicle*, in our example.

Additionally, Grossi observes that, beyond rules constituting institutional facts (i.e. new classificatory rules), there are rules which "constitute" in the sense that they "define the normative system, or institution, to which they pertain". These rules can be connected to the third type identified by Conte.

Hindriks: Connotation and Import. Following [18], Hindriks [19] distinguishes two aspects of constitutive rules:

- *connotation* defines the conditions which have to be satisfied in order to apply a certain institutional term: it is a descriptive component;
- *import* specifies the institutional consequences which occur once those conditions are satisfied.

He proposes therefore to refine constitutive rules under a XYZ scheme. The first part (XY) corresponds to connotation, which, including context (CXY), takes the form proposed by Searle. Such *constitutive rules* (in a strict sense) link the satisfaction of certain conditions to the applicability of an institutional term. For instance, "In the United States, bills issued by the Federal Reserve (X) count as money (Y)". The second part (YZ) is a *status rule*, specifying the practical significance of the institutional status constituted by the first. The status rule defines the *function* of the institutional concept. For instance, "one of the functions of money is that it can be used as a means of exchange, which means that it facilitates or enables actions, in particular exchange of goods and services without the use of barter. However, the same idea can be expressed using the term 'power': money can be said to give people the power to perform the action mentioned." Hindriks's convincing argument for this extension is that without the import, the constitutive rule would not have any concrete role in the institution.

Boer: Institutional Rules, Constituting, Constitutive Acts. All constitutive rules require at least a 'brute' fact to create institutional facts. Boer [20, p. 93] proposes that we also consider *institutional rules*: rules that operate on institutional facts, on the basis of other institutional facts. Status rules can be therefore seen as a sub-set of institutional rules. Furthermore, he correctly highlights that 'brute' and 'institutional' respectively correspond not to physical and social referents, but to extra-institutional and intra-institutional entities. A 'brute' fact may be a fact that belongs to another institution.

Additionally, he suggests distinguishing *constitutive acts*, i.e. the acts *intended* to constitute an institutional act, within the more general class of *constituting acts*. This serves as a reminder that "the operative principle behind constitutive rules and institutional facts is that people to a large extent have control over what institutional facts they bring about". An example of a constituting act is theft: thieves have no intent to be qualified as such. Interestingly, a similar intentional/non-intentional characterization may specified distinguishing *regulative* from *regulating* rules. The second would refer to side-effects that were not intended by the legislator.

Hage: Regulative Rules are Constitutive Rules. A recent article presented by Hage [21] contends that regulative rules *are* constitutive rules. Hage first identifies three types of constitutive rules:

- *dynamic rules*, which create, modify, or remove facts as the consequence of an event, e.g. "making a promise generates an obligation for the promisor"; they may be conditional, e.g. "if it is dark, the occurrence of a car accident obligates the drivers to place a light on the road next to the cars".
- *fact-to-fact rules*, which (defeasibly) attach a fact to another fact in a *timeless* fashion (not accounting change); e.g. "if P owns O, P is competent to alienate O"; they may also be conditional, e.g. "in case of emergency, the mayor of a city is competent to invoke the state of emergency".
- *count-as rules*, rules of the type "individuals of type 1 count-as individuals of type 2", where individuals may be *persons* (e.g. "the parents of a minor count-as the minor's legal representatives"), or *events* (e.g. "under suitable circumstances, causing a car accident counts-as committing a tort").

Building upon on these categories, he argues that *constitutive rules* consist in a more general class than count-as rules, and their general characterization is that of rules that eventually affect facts of the world, but that also exhibit some correspondence between their propositional content and what is in the world. If we say, e.g. "criminals are liable to enforcement", this means that any criminal *is* liable to enforcement. For completeness, Hage includes a categorization of regulative rules:

- *prescriptive rules*, which make a specific conduct obligatory, e.g. "car drivers must drive on the right hand side of the road";
- *proscriptive rules*, prohibiting a specific conduct, e.g. "it is forbidden to torture sentient beings";
- rules that specify what should be done, e.g. "if the king is in chess, the threat should immediately be removed";
- rules about "how something should be done, without imposing a duty or an obligation to do so", as e.g. rules of *etiquette*.

but argues that they belong to the constitutive category as well, if, in addition to (descriptive) facts, we take into account *deontic facts*. In the traditional sense, a fact is associated with an objective, mind-independent description of what is the case. However, social reality is a domain for which the ontological realist stance is not (directly) appropriate, as it mostly depends on what people accept or recognize about it. Nevertheless, we do say "He is the owner of...", just as "It is raining". Thus, as these (descriptive) institutional facts depend on standards, and are produced by rules, nothing forbids us from considering facts that describe normative directives (e.g. "He has the duty to...") as deontic facts, also produced by rules.

3 An Integrated Model for Constitutive Rules

3.1 Distinguishing Constitutive-Of and Constitutive-For

We acknowledge two meanings for *constitutive* elements:

(a) as characteristic regulative drivers (*constitutive-of* the institution),
(b) as part of an interpretative system (*constitutive-for* the institution).

The former category deals with *what constitutes the institution*, considered as a 'subject' acting in the world. As agents are primarily defined—in terms of the impact they are disposed to produce on the world—by their desires, institutions can thus be primarily defined by the requirements they put on the social system.[6] The latter deals with *how meaning is constituted for the institution*, that is, with the selection of what makes sense for the institution of what occurs in the social environment, and with the processing of such selection. Interestingly, the two components are inseparable, although for different reasons.

Let us imagine an institution consisting only of regulative rules. The operational minimal structure of an obligation consists of two recognition rules, one for violation and one for satisfaction. Therefore, each regulative rule *implicitly* brings at least two constitutive (more precisely, constituting) rules, namely those defining what generates 'violation' and 'satisfaction' institutional facts related to the given prescription. Thus, extending this observation, we unveil the first function of constitutive rules: they serve to explicitly specify the operating terms of regulative rules, defining not only satisfaction or violation conditions, but also the classes of beneficiaries, of addressees, the initiating conditions, etc. In this sense, they are *participatory to the commitment-related structure* implemented by the institution.

On the other hand, games like chess for instance do not have standardized regulative rules[7]: they are in practice mere systems of constitutive rules used to interpret what counts-as a *valid* move. Therefore, the second function of constitutive rules is at the level of competences or abilities of the social participants. Interestingly, some of these rules may be expressed by referring to deontic

---

[6] Considering that regulative norms can be interpreted as goals associated to the normative system [9], they are constitutive in the same sense in which maintenance goals are the *policy* or, in cybernetic terms, the *identity* of an autonomous system, cf. the *viable system model* (VSM) [22].

[7] Bulygin [12] suggests the following: "a player must make a given number of moves in a given period of time on pain of losing the game", where losing can be seen as a sort of *punishment*, considering the pragmatics around games.

notions, e.g. "one must play with the piece which has been touched", or "if the king is in check, the threat should immediately be removed", but despite what is observed in the literature (e.g. [12,21]) these rules are not regulative as in the previous sense. Invalidity entails nullity of the move, but not 'breach', nor 'violation', nor 'offense' (on these lines, see [23, p. 28]). Interpreting the game as *a system of conditional abilities*, players follow the rules to acquire new *abilities* with the purpose of being able to approaching the winning state, also defined within the rules of the game. The 'must' made manifest in these rules is a derivation from this individual interest: if you want to win (or at least to play), you need to make valid moves, and to make valid moves, you must follow the procedures.[8] The regulation of behaviour of two persons playing chess is a consequence of this practical reasoning mechanism and not of regulative rules. Interestingly, this *ability-related structure* can be interpreted as a *soft form of control*, because it is constructed without any reference to coercion.

Thus, if we include the creation, modification, and destruction of potestative positions as a form of regulation (just as Hohfeld brought forward the second potestative square of fundamental legal concepts), we have completed the circle: *Regulative rules always consist of constitutive rules. Constitutive rules always contribute to regulation.* This circularity may explain the analytical difficulty encountered in the literature to come up with consistent definitions of regulative and constitutive rules.

3.2 Constitutive Elements

All constitutive elements play a role in the interplay between institutional and extra-institutional domains. Elements *constitutive-for* the institution map facts, actions, or events from the extra-institutional to the institutional domain. Elements *constitutive-of* the institution are obligative and potestative dispositions that (supposedly) influence the behaviour of the agents, occurring in the extra-institutional domain. Reusing part of the terminology used in the literature we recognize the following elements:

constitutive rule rule mapping extra-institutional facts to institutional facts;
constitutive fact fact captured by the antecedent of a constitutive rule;
institutional rule rule relating institutional facts to other institutional facts;
status rule institutional rule mapping institutional facts (e.g. about roles) to normative positions;

---

[8] To reiterate, the 'must' that is used in certain normative statements does not refer to a (conditional) duty, but to an institutional power. Consider for instance "in order to perform a real estate transaction, buyers and sellers must sign a written contract". In this sort of cases, 'must' is derived from practical necessity ("to be obliged to"), more than normative aspects ("to have the obligation to"): e.g. if buyer and seller *want* to perform a sale, they don't have any other way but signing a contract.

Their interaction is visualized in Fig. 1. The *regulation* is the effect of the normative positions currently holding. Note that all *-ive* elements (explicit, intentional) can be replaced by the wider *-ing* class (including implicit and non-intentional mechanisms).

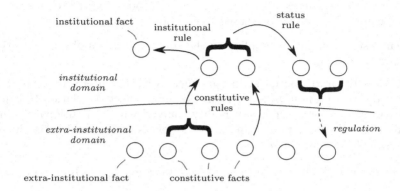

Fig. 1. Coupling between institutional and extra-institutional domains

Sources of Facts. The initial definitions of constitutive and regulative rules given by Searle (1, 2, 3) are centered around *acts*, but later authors soon extended them to *events*, to *states of affairs*, and then to *facts*. Unfortunately, 'facts' can be quite different things depending on the tradition upon which the author builds, consciously or not. From an ontological perspective, facts are arrangements of entities, objects, events/actions, or processes. From an epistemic perspective, facts are justified true beliefs about such arrangements or occurrences, and therefore transport propositional content. Which of these perspectives are we referring to when dealing with constitutive rules?

Considering an agentive perspective, the associated philosophical problem would be to settle whether these facts are *directly perceived* facts or *representationally mediated* facts. The distinction between *presentation* and *representation* is a traditional argument in phenomenology, e.g. [24, pp. 144–145], but it has recently returned in analytic philosophy with the discussion about the 'bad argument' [25]. Entering into the details of this debate is out of scope here; however, observing the reconstruction we have developed so far, illustrated in Fig. 1, we can argue that the *whole mechanism of constitution can be seen as a prototypical mechanism of re-presentation*. In effect, 'counts-as' can be interpreted also as 'stands-for'. Institutional facts are prototypical mediators and therefore represented facts. On the other hand, extra-institutional facts may be perceived (i.e. non-mediated) facts, or representations, if their meaning is built upon other institutions (the use of language nicely fits with the second case). We do not need to specify them further.

3.3   Separating Static and Dynamic Aspects

In general, systems can be divided into two categories (cf. [26]):

- *transformational systems*, characterized mostly by static, timeless, steady aspects, which can be easily represented in functional terms;
- *reactive systems*, characterized by dynamic, temporal, asynchronous aspects, which cannot be easily represented in functional terms;

A similar distinction can be applied to the sub-components of an institutional interpretative system.

Static, Conditional Aspects. In agreement with the literature, conditional classification or *subsumption* is plausibly the most effective relation to capture static extra-institutional aspects of reality charged with institutional meaning. For instance, "bikes counts as vehicles". The related rule would be in the form of a *classificatory constitutive rule*:

$$\text{In context C, an entity of type X counts as an entity of type Y.} \tag{4}$$

Within the institutional system, we can also consider rules that are not grounded on extra-institutional facts, but operate only at the institutional level. These may be definitional, for instance "a check in which the king cannot meet the attack counts as checkmate", or "a formal charge which addresses a public officer counts as an impeachment". In these specific cases, constitution is rather an *is-a* relation and the associated *definitional institutional rule* would be:

$$\text{An entity of type Y1 is an entity of type Y2.} \tag{5}$$

However, most of institutional rules are *status rules*, mapping institutional notions (Y) to normative aspects (Z), i.e. deontic and potestative characterizations. Related examples are "a promise counts as an obligation", "in case of emergency, a mayor has the competence to declare the state of emergency" (considering both promise and emergency as institutional facts, cf. Sect. 5):

$$\text{An entity of type Y implies the existence of an entity of type Z.} \tag{6}$$

In this case it is not a matter of definition: the two entities are different, a promise *is not* an obligation, and an emergency *is not* a competence. From a logical point of view, these rules function as remapping of the parametric content specifying one entity into the other, e.g. the promise of doing A implies the duty of doing A.

Dynamic, Procedural Aspects. Generally speaking, the term *act* refers both to a performance and to its outcome. However, from the outcome, we can always refer back to the action. For instance, "a promise counts as an obligation" can be rephrased as "positing a promise counts as undertaking an obligation", i.e. in terms of an initiating event. The result is an *institutional event rule*:

$$\text{An event of type Y1 implies the occurrence of an event of type Y2.} \tag{7}$$

To consider the relation at the production level (with the creation of the promise) rather than at the outcome level (the settled promise) is, in this example, only a matter of taste. If the promise is removed, so is the obligation. This example does not support the introduction of a new modeling dimension. Let us consider then another example: "raising a hand during an auction counts as making a bid". This is a *constitutive event rule*:

$$\text{In context C, an event of type X counts as an event of type Y.} \qquad (8)$$

In this case, there is a decoupling from the 'brute' result of the hand-raising action and its institutional counterpart: we may let the hand go down, but our bid would remain. These dynamic aspects of reality are not reducible at the level of outcome, and the procedural/event component of the constitution plays a crucial role. For those, the traditional logic notation is problematic, because logic conditionals require an adequate machinery to deal with incremental change.[9] Similar problems have been studied in *contrary-to-duty* (CTD) obligations [27].

4 Constitutive Dimensions of Institutional Power

Raising a hand to make a bid is an example of action conducted in the physical reality to obtain a result in the institutional domain. If we turn our attention from the action to the agent, we have already observed that what enables the social participant to produce the intended institutional outcome is being disposed, besides the practical ability, with the relevant *institutional power* (also *ability*, *capacity* or *competence*, depending on the tradition). Without this power, the agent would be not able to constitute the outcome. What, then, is the relation between institutional power and constitutive rules? Our proposal elaborates on this notion in terms of dispositions.

In general, a *disposition* is a precondition necessary to reach, at the occurrence of an adequate *stimulus*, a now only potential state. This transformation, and the resulting outcome, count as the *manifestation* of the disposition. Typical examples are being fragile or being soluble.[10] Dispositions are *requirements for change* (e.g. an element can be dissolved in a solution only if the element is soluble). On the other hand, they provide also behavioural *expectations* about the referent entities (a soluble element is expected to dissolve in a solution). Applying this notion to our domain, we can define *institutional power* as a *disposition whose manifestation is the creation, destruction or modification of institutional entities*. This definition is wider than the one usually encountered

---

[9] On the other hand, when a relation can be represented between the outcomes, the procedural model requires the introduction of adequate revision mechanism for operational closure, and therefore, it becomes less efficient from a representational perspective.

[10] Disposition is a long-debated notion in philosophy, especially in metaphysics. Lewis provides in [28] a famous critique to the classic account based on logic conditionals, and a reformulation in causation terms, which is compatible with the present proposal.

in legal scholarship. For instance, offering, or infringing the law, are actions usually not considered associated to *legal capabilities*. The first because, differently from accepting an offer, it does not create any obligation. The second because it is not a type of action promoted by the legal system. However, from a formal point of view, they do entail consequences at institutional level.[11]

Evidently, physical actions performed in a specific context become vectors to *constitute* institutional facts through constitutive event rules. This concerns the *performance* component of institutional power. Other orthogonal components used in specifying institutional power concern the minimal requirements for the *qualification* of the performer to the *role* he is enacting and the *delimitation* of the institutional *subject-matter* on which the power may be exercised. Considering these three dimensions, we organize in Table 1 the examples of legal specifications of power reported by Hart in [23, p. 28]. The case of judicial officer could be extended similarly to other public officers. In dispositional terms, with some approximation, qualification defines the *disposition*, performance defines the *stimulus* and delimitation provides ingredients to specify the *manifestation*. In terms of constitutive rules, the first component can be related to classificatory rules (4), the second to constitutive event rules (8), and the third defines or constrains the *codomain* of status rules (6).

Table 1. Specifications of institutional power defined by law, examples.

	Private persons	Judicial officers	Legislative authority
Qualification	Minimum requirements of personal qualification (*capacity*)	Manner of appointment, qualifications for and tenure of judicial officer	Qualifications of identity of the members of the legislative body
Performance	Manner and form in which the power is exercised (*execution, attestation*)	Procedure to be followed in the court	Manner and form of legislation, procedure to be followed
Subject-matter	Variety of rights and duties which may be created	Jurisdiction	Domain over which the power may be exercised

5 On the Ontological Status of Constitution

The previous sections clarify how constitution functions, but we haven't yet investigated what type of relation constitution is. One way to approach this topic is to start by addressing the domains of its terms.

Ontological Stratification of Institutions. Amongst the authors reviewed in Sect. 2, only Hindriks [19] and Boer [20] explicitly elaborate and argue for an *ontological distinction* between institutional and extra-institutional (including 'brute') realms. It is plausible that also the others share, implicitly or tacitly, a similar perspective. In contrast, Searle rejects in several points of his works

---

[11] In a similar spirit, Sartor extends in [29] *action-power* with *generic-power*, that can be associated to natural events as well (e.g. death, timeouts, etc.).

the idea that there are different levels in reality (e.g. [3, p. 1]). However, as connotation is contextual, the *same* extra-institutional facts may yield different institutional outcomes depending on the context, and, therefore, this argument is difficult to maintain: at least from a formal point of view, Searle seems to conflate constitution and identity relations.[12] Secondly, this argument overlooks the existence of a plurality of institutions, and of institutional interpretations, and thus the intrinsic possibility of conflicting institutional outcomes.

Informal and Formal. Interestingly, the ontological distinction between intra- and extra-institutional domains results in a framework affine with the *legal abstract model* proposed by Breuker [30], advancing the idea that institutional layers are built upon a *common-sense* knowledge layer. Consider the analysis of promise given by Conte for the X-type of rule: "a promise counts as the undertaking of an obligation". His interpretation insists on the fact that the meaning of promise lies already in linguistic practice as a fundamental *speech act*, and consequently, the proposed rule is merely descriptive. In Hindriks's terms, however, the rule can be interpreted as an import rule, which, in a legal context, would instantiate a legal obligation (thus protected by law). For this reason, it would be a different rule than the one followed in social practice. The nature of the 'promise' term is not settled, however. When there is not a definite constitutive rule that specifies the criteria for which a promise can be accepted as a *valid* promise, the institutional system can be seen as relying on the meaning constituted at extra-institutional level. The resulting mechanism can be modeled in two ways:

- by introducing an implicit constitutive rule that remaps the extra-institutional fact in a cloned institutional reference for institutional import;
- by considering connotation and import collapsing into the same link, directly associating the constitutive fact to the normative fact.

The second is evidently simpler, and avoids the introduction of unnecessary links. However, the first solution is interesting, as it prepares for consequent developments. In effect, it is reasonable to expect the enactment of an explicit constitutive rule in all cases in which the original extra-institutional term is acknowledged to introduce non-predictability in the functioning of institutional mechanisms. For instance, in certain contexts, promises are considered valid (the speech act of promising counts effectively as an institutional promise) only when they are in written form, plausibly because in oral form they turned out to be insufficiently reliable. Thus, we may conclude that *explicit constitutive machinery ultimately responds to the requirement of reducing the frictions caused by different interpretations of what moulds the institutional matter.*

Emergence and Supervenience. Strangely enough, the recognition of different *ontological strata*, i.e. a division of reality in domains to be treated for the

---

[12] The canonic form of constitutive rules (1) implies that when we are not in C, X may not count as Y. This shows that it is impossible that constitution corresponds to identity, as X would be equal to Y in certain cases, and not equal to Y in others.

most part separately, would be, in principle, compatible with Searle's attempt to provide a *naturalistic* account of language [3, p. 61]. In effect, natural sciences approach reality depending on various factors, such as the dimensional scale in focus (e.g. particle physics vs astrophysics). Theories and accounts associated to these approaches are often so incompatible, that they may be seen as targeting different realities. Maintaining this distinction furnishes a framework compatible with the analysis and treatment of *emergent properties* or *emergent phenomena*, i.e. those arising out of more fundamental ones, but not reducible to them.

In philosophy, several authors have attempted to capture the relation amongst different *ontological strata* working with the notion of *supervenience*. In the simplest form, "we have supervenience when there could be no difference of one sort without differences of another sort" [31, p. 14]. Considering for instance the physical reality, we may say that the macroscopic level *supervenes* the microscopic level because any difference observed at the macroscopic level necessarily implies a difference at the microscopic level. But the notion is applied in other domains as well, e.g. in support of the recognition of "the existence of mental phenomena, and their non-identity with physical phenomena, while maintaining an authentically physicalist world view" [32]. In other words, supervenience makes explicit an intrinsic ontological asymmetry: e.g. mental or institutional states cannot change without having a change occurring at the physical level.

What is Constitution? Why supervenience is relevant for constitutive rules? Even without referring to supervenience, Hindriks [19] expresses a similar intuition, citing Baker's analogy with aesthetic relations. A painting does not directly 'define' its own beauty (determination), nor 'cause' it (material production), but it '*constitutes*' it. The connection of a painting with its beauty is a classical example of the use of supervenience (although more debated than the macro-micro scenario).[13] The notion of supervenience is compatible with the idea of *constitution* advanced by this work: constitutive (classificatory or event) rules can be seen as reifying the interactions between extra-institutional and institutional domains, with the latter supervening the former.[14] Informally stated, many events (conditions) may occur (hold) in the world which are irrelevant from an institutional point of view. However, if in a certain moment the institutional domain was found to be different, this means that something necessarily changed in the extra-institutional (e.g. 'brute') domain as well: i.e. a part of the constitutive base must have triggered such a change at institutional level.

Towards the Operationalization of Alignment. The previous analysis suggests an alternative approach in testing whether two representations are aligned. In the literature, due to the prominent focus on their classificatory function, constitutive rules are usually specified via a *subsumption* relation. Subsumption

---

[13] If supervenience holds, it is impossible that there are two paintings that are the same from a physical point of view (e.g. for their distribution of colours), but they are different in respect of how beautiful they are (to respond to relativist critics, we should add for the same observer and in the same mental state).

[14] This idea was briefly presented in [33] as well, but it remains underspecified.

between two prototypical entities is verified when all the properties of one entity match a sub-set of the properties of the other. However, in the previous sections we showed that the classificatory view is not sufficient to capture all the types of constitution. In this context, *supervenience* offers a better frame than subsumption: we do not target the verification of an equal (sub-set of) properties, but of a fit alignment of differences after change. Intuitively, given two behavioural models, when the execution of the supposedly supervenient model exhibits a change, we should verify that some aligned change occurs in the supposedly base model. A preliminary operationalization following this idea has been presented in [34].

6   Conclusion and Further Developments

The paper revisits the notion of *constitutive rules*, attempting an integration and synthesis of previous contributions. The intuition to carefully distinguish declarative components from reactive components came after the examples of conflation in both cognitive and computational domains remarked by Kowalski and Sadri [35]. Our analysis confirms that the nature of constitutive rules is complex, and suggests that this complexity is due to the integration of the different types of interactions that may occur between 'brute' (or better, extra-institutional) and institutional domains.

The study is functional to a more general research objective: the alignment of representations of law (norms), of implementations of law (e.g. services), and of intentional characterizations of behaviour (cases) [36]. With respect to representation of law, we presented in [37] a revisitation of Hohfeld's framework in interactional terms; in [27] we investigated the *contrary-to-duty* (CTD) constructs studied in deontic logic. With respect to representation of behaviour, we introduced in [38] an agent architecture based on the notions of *commitment*, *affordance*, *expectation* and *susceptibility*, interpreted in analogy with Hohfeldian notions. This paper focuses on the theoretical aspects about the connection between extra-institutional and institutional components, but, as the other references show, our current efforts are also directed on establishing a unifying formal visual notation (based on Petri Nets), in support to our theoretical proposal.

Evidently, the constitution of institutional meaning follows the sense of constitutive rules (from behaviour to institutional domain) but it also implements a feedback on behaviour through regulation. Furthermore, social systems adapt to institutional mechanisms—a phenomenon observable through the emergence of "nomotropic" behaviours, i.e. of "acting in light of rules" (which is different from "in conformity with rules") [39]—to which social systems respond again by modifying their own institutional mechanisms. In the full picture, constitutive rules establish a *structural coupling* between the two domains. However, because adaptation mechanisms are much slower than operational mechanisms, on shorter temporal scales the coupling is asymmetrical. This assumption allows to associate constitution to the notion of *supervenience*, thus enabling the verification of alignment, but the analysis of the institutional dynamics accounting for the change of norms remains to be investigated.

References

1. Searle, J.R.: Speech Acts: An Essay in the Philosophy of Language. Cambridge University Press, Cambridge (1969)
2. Searle, J.R.: Intentionality: An Essay in the Philosophy of Mind. Cambridge University Press, Cambridge (1983)
3. Searle, J.R.: Making the Social World: The Structure of Human Civilization. Oxford University Press, Oxford (2010)
4. Roversi, C.: Acceptance is not enough, but texts alone achieve nothing. A critique of two conceptions in institutional ontology. Rechtstheorie 43(2), 177–206 (2012)
5. MacCormick, N.: Norms, institutions, and institutional facts. Law Philos. 17(3), 301–345 (1998)
6. Ruiter, D.W.P.: Structuring legal institutions. Law Philos. 17(3), 215–232 (1998)
7. Conte, A.G.: L'enjeu des règles. Droit et Société 17–18, 125–146 (1991)
8. Jones, A., Sergot, M.: A formal characterisation of institutionalised power. J. IGPL 4, 427–443 (1996)
9. Boella, G., van der Torre, L.: Constitutive norms in the design of normative multiagent systems. In: Toni, F., Torroni, P. (eds.) CLIMA 2005. LNCS (LNAI), vol. 3900, pp. 303–319. Springer, Heidelberg (2006). https://doi.org/10.1007/11750734_17
10. Dennett, D.C.: The Intentional Stance, 7th edn. MIT Press, Cambridge (1987)
11. von Wright, G.H.: Norm and Action: A Logical Enquiry. Routledge & K. Paul, London (1963)
12. Bulygin, E.: On norms of competence. Law Philos. 11(3), 201–216 (1992)
13. Peczenik, A.: On Law and Reason. Kluwer, Dordrecht (1989)
14. Jones, A.J., Sergot, M.: Deontic logic in the representation of law: towards a methodology. Artif. Intell. Law 1(1), 45–64 (1992)
15. Grossi, D.: Designing invisible handcuffs, formal investigations in institutions and organizations for multi-agent systems. Ph.D. thesis, University of Utrecht (2007)
16. Atkinson, K., Bench-Capon, T.J.M.: Levels of reasoning with legal cases. In: Proceedings of the ICAIL 2005 Workshop on Argumentation in AI and Law (2005)
17. Lindahl, L., Odelstad, J.: Intermediate concepts in normative systems. In: Goble, L., Meyer, J.-J.C. (eds.) DEON 2006. LNCS (LNAI), vol. 4048, pp. 187–200. Springer, Heidelberg (2006). https://doi.org/10.1007/11786849_16
18. Ransdell, J.: Constitutive rules and speech-act analysis. J. Philos. 68(13), 385–399 (1971)
19. Hindriks, F.: Constitutive rules, language, and ontology. Erkenntnis 71(2), 253–275 (2009)
20. Boer, A.: Legal theory, sources of law and the semantic web. Ph.D. thesis, University of Amsterdam (2009)
21. Hage, J.: Separating rules from normativity. In: Araszkiewicz, M., Banas, P., Gizbert-Studnicki, T., Pleszka, K. (eds.) Problems of Normativity, Rules and Rule-Following. LAPS, vol. 111, pp. 13–22. Springer, Cham (2015). https://doi.org/10.1007/978-3-319-09375-8_2
22. Beer, S.: Brain of the Firm. Wiley, New York (1995)
23. Hart, H.L.A.: The Concept of Law, 2nd edn. Clarendon Press, Oxford (1994)
24. Husserl, E.: The Shorter Logical Investigations. Taylor & Francis, Abingdon (2002)
25. Searle, J.R.: Perceptual intentionality. Organon F 19, 9–22 (2012)
26. Harel, D., Pnueli, A.: On the development of reactive systems. In: Apt, K.R. (ed.) Logics and Models of Concurrent Systems. NATO ASI Series (Series F: Computer and Systems Sciences), vol. 13, pp. 477–498. Springer, Heidelberg (1985). https://doi.org/10.1007/978-3-642-82453-1_17

27. Sileno, G., Boer, A., van Engers, T.: A Petri net-based notation for normative modeling: evaluation on deontic paradoxes. In: Proceedings of MIREL 2017: Workshop on MIning and REasoning with Legal texts, in conjunction with ICAIL 2017 (2017)
28. Lewis, D.: Finkish dispositions. Philos. Q. **47**, 143–158 (1997)
29. Sartor, G.: Fundamental legal concepts: a formal and teleological characterisation. Artif. Intell. Law **14**(1), 101–142 (2006)
30. Breuker, J., den Haan, N.: Separating world and regulation knowledge: where is the logic? In: Proceedings of ICAIL 1991: 3rd International Conference on Artificial Intelligence and Law, pp. 92–97 (1991)
31. Lewis, D.K.: On the Plurality of Worlds. B. Blackwell, Oxford (1986)
32. Brown, R., Ladyman, J.: Physicalism, supervenience and the fundamental level. Philos. Q. **59**(234), 20–38 (2009)
33. Hage, J., Verheij, B.: The law as a dynamic interconnected system of states of affairs: a legal top ontology. Int. J. Hum.-Comput. Stud. **51**(6), 1043–1077 (1999)
34. Sileno, G., Boer, A., van Engers, T.: Bridging representations of laws, of implementations and of behaviours. In: Proceedings of the 28th International Conference on Legal Knowledge and Information Systems (JURIX 2015). FAIA, vol. 279 (2015)
35. Kowalski, R., Sadri, F.: Integrating logic programming and production systems in abductive logic programming agents. In: Polleres, A., Swift, T. (eds.) RR 2009. LNCS, vol. 5837, pp. 1–23. Springer, Heidelberg (2009). https://doi.org/10.1007/978-3-642-05082-4_1
36. Sileno, G.: Aligning law and action. Ph.D. thesis, University of Amsterdam (2016)
37. Sileno, G., Boer, A., van Engers, T.: On the interactional meaning of fundamental legal concepts. In: Proceedings of the 27th International Conference on Legal Knowledge and Information Systems (JURIX 2014). FAIA, vol. 271, pp. 39–48 (2014)
38. Sileno, G., Boer, A., van Engers, T.: Commitments, expectations, affordances and susceptibilities: towards positional agent programming. In: Chen, Q., Torroni, P., Villata, S., Hsu, J., Omicini, A. (eds.) PRIMA 2015. LNCS (LNAI), vol. 9387, pp. 687–696. Springer, Cham (2015). https://doi.org/10.1007/978-3-319-25524-8_52
39. Conte, A.G.: Nomotropismo: agire in-funzione-di regole. Sociologia del diritto **27**(1), 1–27 (2000)

The Truth in Law and Its Explication

Hajime Yoshino$^{(\boxtimes)}$ (iD)

Meiji Gakuin University, Tokyo, Japan
hyoshino@ls.meijigakuin.ac.jp

Abstract. This paper discusses what types of truth play their role in law and in what way such types of truth can be explicated. For this purpose, this paper applies the logical viewpoint and method of predicate logic to clarify the logical structure of legal sentences and legal reasoning through their application. This paper presents its central argument that the concept of truth in law is to be classified into three types of truth, i.e., truth as fact, truth as validity and truth as justice, and provides their formal semantic foundation. This paper analyzes the way to explicate truth as validity and truth as justice in the ways of intensional and extensional explications on the one hand and in the way of the reasoning of justification and the reasoning of creation on the other hand.

Keywords: Truth · Validity · Justice · Rule · Fact · Logic
Predicate logic · Legal object sentence · Legal meta-sentence
Reasoning of justification · Reasoning of creation · Explication of truth

1 Introduction

The concept of truth has played a great role in law. This paper at first aims to clarify in what dimensions the concept of truth plays its role in law. In other words, it aims to clarify what types of truth play their role in law. Secondly, it aims to clarify in what way, to be precise, through what inference, such truths in law can be determined.

In order to realize these purposes, this paper applies the classical mathematical logic, i.e., predicate logic to discuss the topic of truth in law. Through the application of this method, this paper shortly clarifies the logical structure of legal sentences (Sect. 2) and legal reasoning (Sect. 3), both of which will be invoked to the discussion of the concepts of truth in law. This paper then presents its central argument that the concept of truth in law is to be classified into three types of truth, i.e., (1) truth as fact, (2) truth as validity, and (3) truth as justice (Sect. 4). It provides the formal semantic foundation of these three types of truth in law (Sect. 5). It discusses further the way to explicate the concepts of truth as validity and truth as justice in law. In doing so, it analyzes not the abstract concept of truth as validity or justice itself but the legal sentences which are conceived as valid or just. It also discusses the way of clarification in terms of the intension and extension of the concepts on the one hand and of the reasoning of legal justification and the reasoning of legal creation on the other hand (Sect. 6). This paper concludes by summarizing its achievements and listing further tasks which are still to be solved (Sect. 7).

© Springer Nature Switzerland AG 2018
U. Pagallo et al. (Eds.): AICOL VI-X 2015–2017, LNAI 10791, pp. 56–71, 2018.
https://doi.org/10.1007/978-3-030-00178-0_4

2 The Logical Structure of Legal Sentences and Its Representation

The concept of truth plays its role concerning sentences. In other words, sentences can be said that they are true or false. The concept of truth also plays its role in the reasoning, which operates with sentences. Therefore, to discuss the concept of truth in law in terms of logic, it is necessary, as a preparing exercise, to clarify the logical structure of legal sentences and its representation.

To clarify the logical structure of legal sentences, we apply the logical method to them. The method of logic, which is applied to this paper to analyze legal sentences and reasoning, is the method of classical mathematical logic, especially the first order predicate logic. One may ask: why is a special logic of norms like Deontic Logic[1] developed for norms not applied to legal sentences? The reason is this: the predicate logic is effectively applicable to legal sentences on the one hand and it is questionable whether real laws use the deontic conceptions of "obligation", "prohibition" and "permission" presented by Deontic Logic, and therefore, we do not need the calculation between them defined by such logic of norms on the other hand. Such logics that have been presented so far are so weak that they cannot adequately represent real legal sentences describing complex legal states of affairs. Also, sometimes, paradoxes have appeared in their application to legal arguments. Those paradoxes could not emerge if one applied first order predicate logic to legal arguments.[2]

To logically formalize law, we should analyze law into the minimal units of legal sentences and construct law as their logical connection. The author presents three fundamental types of legal sentences as the minimal units which have been found through the author's study on the construction of legal knowledge base systems [11, 16, 17].

These three fundamental types of legal sentences which are broken down into two further sub-types are:

(1) Legal rule sentences and fact sentences
(2) Legal element sentences and complex sentences
(3) Legal object sentences and meta-sentences

2.1 Legal Rule Sentences and Fact Sentences

Legal rule sentences are sentences that have the following syntactic structure:
$$\forall X\{a(X) \leftarrow b(X)\}.^3$$

---

[1] Georg Henrik von Wright has developed Deontic Logic [8].

[2] The author shows that Ross's paradox could not emerge if one applied the classical propositional logic correctly to normative arguments [9]. The author also demonstrates that the paradox of "Contrary-to-Duty Imperatives" presented by von R. M. Chisholm does not occur if one formalizes the imperatives by means of predicate logic [10].

[3] This is a predicate logical formula in which a string which begins with the upper cases is used for variables and a string with the lower cases for constants.

Legal fact sentences on the other hand have the following syntactic structure:

$$b(x1).$$

This structure of legal sentences, i.e., dividing them into rule sentences and fact sentences, enables jurists to apply legal rule sentences to fact sentences of the problems to deduce a decision as a conclusion of a logical inference based on the logical inference rule of Modus Ponens. If a legal rule sentence like $\forall X\{a(X) \leftarrow b(X)\}$ and a legal fact sentence like $b(x1)$ are set as premises, the conclusion $a(x1)$ is logically deduced based on Modus Tollens. The inference is represented as follows: $\forall X\{a(X) \leftarrow b(X)\}\&b(x1) \Rightarrow a(x1)$.[4] Here, the structure of "sentence" and the "inference" are closely connected.

2.2   Legal Element Sentences and Complex Sentences

Legal element sentences mark the smallest units of legal sentences. Legal complex sentences are the combination of legal element sentences. For example, a contract is a legal complex sentence and an article of the contract is a legal element sentence. The "United Nations Convention on Contracts for the International Sale of Goods" ("CISG") is a legal complex sentence, whereas CISG "Article 23 A contract is concluded at the moment when an acceptance of an offer becomes effective" is a legal element sentence. Each legal sentence has a unique name. Through the introduction of these conceptual devices, the author breaks law into its smallest elements while also reconstructing it logically from those elements on the way it exists in fact.[5]

2.3   Legal Object Sentences and Meta-sentences

A legal object sentence regulates an obligation for people to perform a certain action. Therefore, a legal object fact sentence is formalized in the following predicate logical formula:

is_obligatory(Person, Action).[6]

A concrete example of a legal object fact sentence and its predicate logical formula is:

ofs1: Bernard is obligated to pay the price $5000 to Anzai.

ofs1: obligated('Bernard',pay('Bernard', $5000, 'Anzai',T))

If this sentence is used or asserted in an inference, it is meant that "Bernard is obligated to pay the price $5000 to Anzai" is legally true. Jurists have represented this

---

[4] The author feels that the structure of law, in the form of rule and fact sentences, might be one of the great subconscious inventions by mankind and/or a miracle made by God.

[5] The advantage of the concept of the legal complex sentences is to be able to deal with the validity of legal element sentences which belong to a legal complex sentence all at once by determining the validity of the relevant complex sentence. This relationship is regulated by implicit fundamental legal rules which later will be logically formalized as mr01 and mr3aa1 in the Sect. 6.5.

[6] "*Person*" and "*Action*" are used for the valuables for persons and for actions.

kind of situation that a legal sentence which represents an obligatory state of affairs is legally true by means of legal meta-sentences using the predicate "valid".

A legal meta-sentence[7] regulates the validity of another legal sentence.[8] Therefore, they should have the predicate representing "valid,"[9] and the terms for legal sentences, whose validity is in question, and the terms for the scope of validity (in which scope of time, places, people and matters the sentence is valid). An example of a legal meta-fact sentence on the legal object fact sentence *ofs1* explained above (where the scope of the validity is restricted only to time) and its predicate logical formulae is:

mfs1: ofs1 is valid on February 23rd, 2016:

mfs1: is valid(ofs1,23_02_2016).

The author has introduced the sentences describing the "justness" of other legal sentences as a subclass of the concept of legal meta-sentences. Thus, the following sentences are also legal meta-sentences:

mfs2: Sentence ofs1 is just on October 15, 2016.

Its predicate logical representation is:

mfs2: just(ofs1, 2016_10_15).

In the examples above of *ofs1* and *mfs1*, when it is proven in the legal inference that the legal meta-sentence *mfs1* is true, it is conceived that the legal object sentence *ors1* is valid in fact and that the state of affairs of the obligation represented by the object sentence exists in the legal world. How these types of legal meta-sentences can be inferred will be discussed in the foregoing chapter (Sect. 6).

These conceptual devices of legal sentences can logically represent real legal sentences used in law as they exist and logically formalize the inference to decide the validity of legal sentences as they are done.

3   The Logical Structure of Legal Reasoning

Legal sentences are developed through legal reasoning. The author clarifies the structure of the legal reasoning in terms of the reasoning of legal justification and the reasoning of legal creation.

3.1   The Logical Structure of the Reasoning of Legal Justification

The reasoning of legal justification is the reasoning to justify legal sentences as the consequences of logical deductions from "valid" (legally true) legal rule sentences together with "true" (factually true) fact sentences. The logical deduction is based on the inference rule of "Modus Ponens":

---

[7] The terminology "meta" originates from Tarski's "meta-language" [7].

[8] The author got the idea of "legal meta sentence" from H.L.A. Hart's "secondary rules." Cf. Hart, H. L.A., The concept of law, Oxford 1961, p. 79; 2nd edition, Oxford University Press, NY 1994, p. 80.

[9] The predicate is not restricted to the noun "validity." Other predicate which represent the conception of the validity are available, e.g., "is valid," "become valid," "become null," "is terminated," and so on.

$$((A \Rightarrow B)\&A) \Rightarrow B$$

The rule of Modus Ponens is a fundamental inference scheme of the reasoning of justification in law, especially in the reasoning of the application of law to given cases.

3.2   The Logical Structure of the Reasoning of Legal Creation

The reasoning of legal creation (or discovery)[10] is the reasoning to newly create legal sentences which are necessary to constitute the reasoning of justification. The logical structure of reasoning of legal creation is clarified in terms of two related types of reasoning: (1) generating hypothetical legal sentences and (2) testing these hypothetical legal sentences.

(a) The Logical Structure of Reasoning for Generating Legal Sentences. The reasoning behind generating hypothetical legal sentences is not the deduction but the abduction or induction. The abduction takes place when a fact sentence is generated and the induction, on the contrary to that, takes place when a rule sentence is generated according to the author's definition.

An example of **abduction** is as follows:

(1) A goal sentence:	$q(a)$
(2) A rule sentence:	$q(X) \leftarrow p(X)$
(3) A fact sentence generated as a hypothesis:	$p(a)$

(1)   A goal $q(a)$ is to be proven as true.
(2)   There is a rule $q(X) \leftarrow p(X)$ which has the goal $q(X)$ as a head of the rule.
(3)   To prove goal $q(a)$ by the application of the rule, the necessary fact sentence is generated through the abduction.

The abduction is mainly performed to confirm the fact of the given event, which may fulfill the requirement of the relevant legal rule sentence that is applied to the case.

An example of an **induction** is as follows:

(1) A goal sentence:	$q(a)$
(2) A fact sentence:	$p(a)$
(3) A rule sentence generated as a hypothesis:	$q(X) \leftarrow p(X)$

---

[10] It may be common in traditional legal theories to use the terminology of "discovery", not of "creation," to indicate such non-deductive legal reasoning. However, the word "discovered" should be used for the case that one finds an object or a rule which already exists. Legal sentences which are necessary to constitute the reasoning of justification do not beforehand exist but are actually "created" by the applicators of law, which will be discussed later. Therefore, it is better not to use "discovery" but to use "creation".

The induction is mainly performed to create a new rule sentence which is necessary to solve the problem adequately in correspondence to the situation of society. [11]

(b) The logical structure of the reasoning for testing the generated legal rule sentences. In relation to Karl Popper's falsification theory [4], the author thinks that the logical structure of the reasoning for testing the generated hypothetical legal rule sentences is "Modus Tollens", which is represented in propositional logical formulas as follows:

$$(P \to Q) \& \neg Q \Rightarrow \neg P$$

This shows: If Q is followed from P, and Q is negatively evaluated, i.e., falsified, then the negative evaluation of P is followed, i.e., P is falsified.

4 The Concepts of Truth in Law – Truth as Fact, as Validity and as Justice

The author thinks that three types of truth are used in law: (1) truth as fact, (2) truth as validity and (3) truth as justice.

4.1 The Truth as Fact

"Truth as fact" concerns whether sentences describing the facts of cases are factually true or false. If sentences describing the state of affairs of the case are factually true, then the relevant state of affairs is regarded as existing in the factual world.

4.2 The Truth as Validity

"Truth as validity" concerns whether legal (rule) sentences are legally true or false. If it is proven that a legal meta-sentence describing the validity of another legal (rule) sentence is true, then the state of affairs described by the latter legal (rule) sentence is regarded as the case in the legal world. Therefore, it is applicable. The concept of truth as validity plays its role in the application of legal rules to solve problems.

It is remarkable that jurists have represented this concept of legal truth using the predicate "valid" or "validity" and produced the system of legal rule sentences according to which the (legal) truth of given legal sentences, i.e. whether they are (legally) true or false, is determined.

For example, if a legal meta-fact sentence which describes the validity of a legal object sentence representing an obligation of a person to do a certain action is proven as true, the obligation of the person to take the action is regarded as existing in the legal world.

---

[11] The reasoning of generating a more abstract general rule sentence from many individual concrete/specific rule sentences is also called "induction". This reasoning has basically the same inference structure as this.

If a legal meta-fact sentence which describes the validity of a legal rule sentence is proven as true, the meaning of the rule sentence regulating a certain matter is regarded as being the case. The legal rule sentence is applied for activating logical inferences using the inference rule of Modus Ponens, as explained above in Sects. 2.1 and 3.1.

Below, the author tries to make a visual expression about this relationship between the proof of the validity of a legal rule sentence and the activation of the logical inference, applying the relevant legal rule sentences, in Fig. 1.

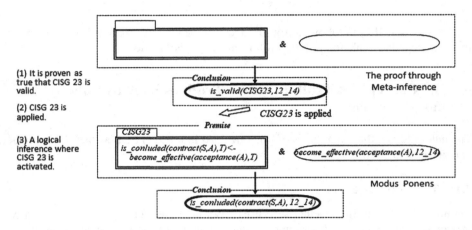

Fig. 1. The relationship between the inference to prove the validity of a legal rule sentence and the inference in which the relevant valid legal rule sentence is applied.

(1) It is proven as true that CISG[12] Article 23 is valid on December 14, 2016. The Article expresses: "A contract is concluded when an acceptance of an offer becomes effective". (2) CISG 23 is applied to solve the problem of a contract on the day. (3) As the legal rule sentence of Article 23 is proven as valid (legally true) in the legal world, a logical inference is activated through the application of the rule sentence of Article 23 based on the inference rule of Modus Ponens. As a result, it is proven that the contract is concluded on December 14, 2016.

4.3   The Truth as Justice

"Truth as justice" concerns whether legal (rule) sentences are just or unjust. If a meta-sentence describing that a legal (rule) sentence is just is proven as true, then the latter legal (rule) sentence is just and therefore the state of affairs described by this legal (rule) sentence is conceived as just in the legal world.

---

[12] CISG is the abbreviation of "United Nations Convention on Contracts for the International Sale of Goods".

How can the above interpretation "truth as fact", "truth as validity" and "truth as justice" be semantically founded? The author will provide their formal semantic foundation below by applying the scheme of the definition of truth in logic by Tarski.

5 The Formal Semantic Foundation of the Concepts of Truth in Law

The concept of truth in classical logic, especially in the predicate-calculus, is formally defined by Tarski [6, 7]. In the following paragraphs, the outline of Tarski's interpretation of the concept of truth will be presented in a concise manner. The following symbols will be used: Φ: a single term predicate; i: an interpretation-functor; $\alpha_1, \ldots, \alpha_n$: an individual constant or variable.

$$(A) : \Phi(\alpha_1, \ldots, \alpha_n) \text{ is } \textbf{\textit{true}} \text{ under } i \text{ if } <i(\alpha_1), \ldots, i(\alpha_n)> \ \in i(\Phi), \text{ and}$$

$$(B) : \Phi(\alpha_1, \ldots, \alpha_n) \text{ is } \textbf{\textit{false}} \text{ under } i \text{ if } <i(\alpha_1), \ldots, i(\alpha_n)> \ \notin i(\Phi)$$

(A) and *(B)* are equivalent to *(A)* with *"if and only if"* instead of *"if"*.

Accordingly, when a one-term predicate applies to an individual constant or variable being part of the set which is the extension of the interpreted predicate, then the respective statement-formula is true and, if not, then it is false. For a better understanding of this principle, an illustration will be given with a one-term predicate below in Fig. 2.

Field of Interpretation

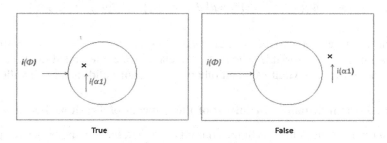

True   False

Fig. 2. The definition of the concept of formal truth in logic.

Based on the foregoing demonstrations, one should point out that the definition by Tarski of the concept of truth of logic is constructed purely formally. It does not matter by what criteria the fulfillment must be decided. According to the definition by Tarski, the logical calculus needs, as a presupposition, nothing but the purely formal principle of bivalence, namely, that a value of two possible values "true" ("1") or "false" ("0") is allocated uniformly to every sentence [10]. Legal sentences which law and legal reasoning consist of can be evaluated as valid or invalid and as just or unjust. Here, the bivalence principle is valid so that legal sentences can be evaluated as true or false in the sense of classical logic. There is no difficulty for the predicate logic to be applied to law.

5.1   The Formal Semantic Definition of the Concept of Truth as Fact

The Tarski-type of the definition of the concept of truth described above can be applied to define the concept of truth as fact:

$$(A_1) : \Phi(\alpha_1 \ldots, \alpha_n) \text{ is } \textbf{\textit{factually true}} \text{ if } <i(\alpha_1), \ldots, i(\alpha_n)) > \; \in i(\Phi)$$

$$(B_1) : \Phi(\alpha_1, \ldots, \alpha_n) \text{ is } \textbf{\textit{factually false}} \text{ if } <i(\alpha_1), \ldots, i(\alpha_n)) > \; \notin i(\Phi)$$

When an interpreted constant or variable falls under the class of the interpreted predicate, then the predicate formula is *factually true (A₁)* and otherwise it is *factually false (B₁)*.

5.2   The Formal Semantic Definition of the Concept of Truth as Validity

The Tarski-type of the definition of the truth concept described above can be applied to interpret the concept of truth as validity as follows:

$$(A_2) : \Phi(\alpha_1 \ldots, \alpha_n) \text{ is } \textbf{\textit{valid}} \text{ if } <i(\alpha_q), \ldots, i(\alpha_n)) > \; \in i(\Phi)$$

$$(B_2) : \Phi((\alpha_1 \ldots, \alpha_n) \text{ is } \textbf{\textit{invalid}} \text{ if } <i(\alpha_1), \ldots, i(\alpha_n)) > \; \notin i(\Phi)$$

When a constant or variable comes under a predicate, i.e., when an interpreted individual constant or –variable falls under the class of the interpreted predicate, then the predicate formula is **valid** *(A₂)* and otherwise it is **not valid**, namely **invalid** *(B₂)*.

5.3   The Formal Semantic Definition of the Concept of Truth as Justice

The Tarski-type of the definition of the concept of truth described above can be applied to interpret the concept of truth as the concept of justice:

$$(A_3) : \Phi(\alpha_1 \ldots, \alpha_n) \text{ is } \textbf{\textit{just}} \text{ if } <i(\alpha_1), \ldots, i(\alpha_n)) > \; \in i(\Phi)$$

$$(B_3) : \Phi((\alpha_1\dots,\alpha_n) \text{ is } \textbf{\textit{unjust}} \text{ if } <i(\alpha_1),\dots,i(\alpha_n)) > \notin i(\Phi)$$

When an individual constant or – variable comes under a predicate, i.e. when an interpreted individual constant or – variable falls under the class of the interpreted predicate, then the predicate formula is **just** *(A₃)* and otherwise it is **unjust** *(B₃)*.

These definitions show that the concepts of validity and justice can be treated as the concept of truth in logic. But they do not intend to provide any criterion on validity or on justice, namely any criterion to determine whether a given legal rule sentence is valid or just. However, as it is proven that validity and justice can be conceived as truth in logic, we can now proceed to discuss how the concept of truth as validity and the concept of truth as justice could be explicated when we conceive validity and justice as truth in logic.

6 The Ways to Explicate the Concepts of Truth in Law

How can we explicate the concepts of truth in law? The way to explicate the concept of existing objects is conceivable on the following two ways: the intensional explication and the extensional explication.

6.1 The Intensional Explication of an Object

The intensional explication is to describe the intension, i.e., the nature of the object. Let us have a look at the explication of "dog": A dog is "a highly variable domestic mammal (Canis familiaris) closely related to the gray wolf" (by Merriam-Webster).

6.2 The Extensional Explication of an Object

The extensional explication is to give examples of the objects which are included in the set represented by the term, for example, in the case of the extensional explication of "dog", to designate mammals which have the nature of a dog.

6.3 The Mutual Relationship Between the Intensional and the Extensional Explication

The intensional explication of the objects is related to the extensional explication, in the sense that the extension of the objects is decided when the intension of the objects is decided.

6.4 The Explication of the Concept of Truth Itself or the Explication of True Legal Sentences?

How can we intensionally or extensionally explicate the concept of truth in law? According to the author's opinion, the abstract concept of truth itself can neither be explicated well intensionally nor extensionally as an object like a dog.

However, sentences which are to be confirmed as true, i.e., **true sentences**, can be explicated intensionally and extensionally. It would be useful for the science of law and legal practices if the methods to decide legally true sentences were provided. In the following, the author will discuss the way to explicate the concepts of truth as validity and truth as justice in the way to determine valid legal sentences and just legal sentences. (The concept of truth as fact will be discussed in the authors future studies)

6.5   The Way to Determine Valid Legal Sentences

Valid legal sentences are decided through legal reasoning. In the reasoning, legal meta-rule sentences, which regulate the validity of legal sentences, are applied. Therefore, this reasoning can be called "legal meta-inference" [11].

The Way to Intensionally Explicate Valid Legal Sentences. Based on the relation between the intension and the extension of a concept, as explained above, the extension of a concept is determined when the intension of the concept is determined. The author thinks that the way to intensionally identify legally valid sentences is to identify legal meta-rule sentences which regulate the validity of legal sentences. To raise legal meta-rule sentences can be a kind of an intensional description of valid legal sentences criteria. To find and raise legal meta-rule sentences, which determine valid legal rule sentences under the given circumstance, is an extensional explication of the relevant legal meta-rule sentences themselves. However, it is an intensional explication of the valid legal rule sentences, because the extension of valid legal rule sentences under the given circumstance is determined through the application of the raised legal meta-rule sentences to the circumstance. The author will raise several legal meta-rule sentences below.

In real positive laws, there is a great amount of legal rule sentences which regulate the validity of legal sentences. There are also several implicit fundamental legal meta-rules as legal common sense. Those legal meta-rule sentences are united under the following most fundamental meta-rule sentence (MFMR):

$$(mr0) : \forall S \, \forall T \, \forall T1 \{is\_valid(S, T) \leftarrow$$
$$become\_valid(S, T1) \, \& \, before(T1, T) \, \&$$
$$not((become\_null(S, T2) \, \& \, before(T2, T)))\}.$$

Positive legal meta-rule sentences and implicit fundamental legal meta-rule sentences regulate the determination of the first part of the requirement or of the second part of the requirement of this rule sentence. To determine the first part of the requirement, the following fundamental legal meta-rule sentence must be implicitly valid (From here on, the Universal Quantifier "$\forall$" is eliminated.):

$$(mr01) : become\_valid(S, T) \leftarrow$$
$$element\_sentence(S, CS) \& complex\_sentence(CS) \& become\_valid(CS, T).$$

This rule regulates: an element sentence S becomes valid at time T if it is an element of the complex-sentence CS and the complex sentence becomes valid at time T.

To determine whether the complex sentence becomes valid at time T, the following fundamental legal meta-rule sentence must be implicitly valid:

$$(mr3aa1) : becomes\_valid(CS, T) \longleftrightarrow$$
$$complex\_sentence(CS)\&formed(CS, T1)\&before(T1, T)\&$$
$$not(invalid(CS, T))\&$$
$$(((starting\_point(T2, CS)\&has\_come(T, T2))v$$
$$(condition(Co, CS)\&fulfilled(Co, T)))v$$
$$T = T1).$$

This rule regulates: a complex sentence CS becomes valid a time T, if it is formed at time $T1$ being before T and it is not invalid, and while the complex sentence CS includes a starting time point of validity and the time point has come at T or while it includes the condition of the validity and the condition is fulfilled at time T or $T1$ is T.

As a contract is a complex sentence, CISG[13] Article 23 "A contract is concluded when an acceptance of an offer becomes effective." is applicable to determine the first part of the requirement of the legal fundamental meta-rule *mr3aa1*. In this way, further positive legal meta-rule sentences (CISG articles 14 - 24) are applicable to determine whether a contract is formed.

Positive legal sentences which describe "rights" are to be considered as legal meta-sentences [13]. They mainly regulate the fulfillment of the first part of the MFMR *(mr01)* in the way that the executions of rights make relevant sentences become valid. In addition, they partially regulate the second part, for example in the way that the execution of the right of cancelling a contract as a legal complex sentence makes the contract become null.

To raise legal meta-rule sentences in this way, is a way to intentionally explicate valid legal sentences.

The Way to Extensionally Explicate Valid Legal Sentences. To infer all legally valid sentences is the way to extensionally explicate legal valid sentences. Valid legal sentences can be determined and therefore raised through the legal meta-inference, where legal meta-rule sentences, which are an intensional description of legally valid sentences, are applied.

If one could install the necessary and sufficient amount of legal meta-rule sentences in a legal knowledge base, one could theoretically let computers infer the whole legal sentences which are valid at a certain time point, through the application of legal meta-rule sentences. In this way, the extension of valid legal sentences can theoretically be determined through a computer aided legal reasoning system.

---

[13] CISG is an abbreviation of "United Nations Convention on Contracts for the International Sale of Goods."

Whereby it is to be noted that the validity of legal sentences is relative with respect not only to "time" but also to "place", "person" and "matter" to which the relevant legal sentences are applied. In practicing legal reasoning, one should individually determine whether a candidate of a legal rule sentence being applied to solve a legal problem is legally valid at a certain time, at a certain place, for a certain person and regarding a certain matter.

6.6   The Way to Determine just or Unjust Legal Sentences

Justice of law is one of the central topics of law, especially for the philosophy of law. But it has been considered that it is difficult for a science to clarify the concept of justice. Here, the author does expect that this paper's approach to the concept of justice, which considers the justice of law as a kind of truth of law and does not deal with the abstract concept of justice itself but with "just or unjust legal sentences", makes a scientific approach to justice possible.

The way to determine just legal sentences. As justice in law is a type of truth as clarified above, the justness of a legal sentence is proven when it is logically deduced from other just legal sentences. However, the problem is how other just legal sentences can be confirmed. In positive laws, there are many legal meta-rule sentences that regulate the determination of valid legal sentences (Cf. [12, 13, 15]), whereas there is no positive legal rule sentence which regulates the determination of just legal sentences. This suggests that the reasoning of justification does not play a big role in determining just legal sentences, but mainly the reasoning of creation or discovery will play its role in determining just legal rule sentences.

The inference scheme of the reasoning of creation as a falsification represented as Modus Tollens, explained in Sect. 3.2 (b), can be analyzed more precisely as follows (by identifying the system of the already existing legal rule sentences (R) and the added hypothetical legal rule sentence $(r1)$ and by representing the event to which the relevant rule sentences are applied as (E) and the consequence resulting from the application of $r1$ together with R as (C)).

$$\{(R \cup r1)\&E \to C\}\&\neg C \Rightarrow \neg r1$$

This scheme can be read as follows: If legal rule sentences which are merged of the already existing legal rule sentences R with a hypothetical legal rule sentence $r1$ are applied to an event of the case E, then the consequence C will result from their application. However, the consequence is to be negatively evaluated as $\neg C$. Therefore, the hypothetical legal rule sentence is to be negatively evaluated as $\neg r1$ [14].

This type of falsification reasoning should be performed for a sufficient number of times to make clear that the relevant hypothetical legal sentence will bring no serious unjust result and that the legal sentence can, therefore, be confirmed as tenable or relatively just. The whole inference scheme of the falsification reasoning which leads to a just legal sentence, being confirmed as not falsified, is represented in Scheme 1:

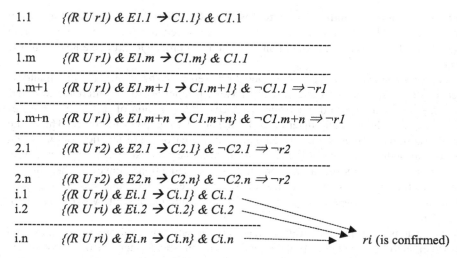

1.1 $\{(R \cup r1) \& E1.1 \rightarrow C1.1\} \& C1.1$

1.m $\{(R \cup r1) \& E1.m \rightarrow C1.m\} \& C1.1$

1.m+1 $\{(R \cup r1) \& E1.m+1 \rightarrow C1.m+1\} \& \neg C1.1 \Rightarrow \neg r1$

1.m+n $\{(R \cup r1) \& E1.m+n \rightarrow C1.m+n\} \& \neg C1.m+n \Rightarrow \neg r1$

2.1 $\{(R \cup r2) \& E2.1 \rightarrow C2.1\} \& \neg C2.1 \Rightarrow \neg r2$

2.n $\{(R \cup r2) \& E2.n \rightarrow C2.n\} \& \neg C2.n \Rightarrow \neg r2$

i.1 $\{(R \cup ri) \& Ei.1 \rightarrow Ci.1\} \& Ci.1$

i.2 $\{(R \cup ri) \& Ei.2 \rightarrow Ci.2\} \& Ci.2$

----

i.n $\{(R \cup ri) \& Ei.n \rightarrow Ci.n\} \& Ci.n$ ⟶ ri (is confirmed)

Scheme 1. Reasoning of falsification to test hypothetical legal rules

We should analyze past arguments over justice to find out in which way, intensionally or extensionally, they have tried to identify just or unjust legal sentences. We should analyze them further from the viewpoint of the reasoning of legal creation or discovery.

The Way to Intensionally Explicate Just or Unjust Legal Sentences. To the question of "What is justice?", Aristotle answered: "Justice is equality" [1]. This is an intensional explication of the concept of justice. Hereby, the next question arises immediately: How can "equality" play its role to decide whether a legal sentence is just?

Here, the author only tries to answer to the second question. Legal rule sentences are to be evaluated, in terms of justice, in possible results of the application of the relevant legal rule sentences to the problems which are to be solved. The results can be evaluated in terms of the criteria of "equality". If the application of the relevant legal rules causes such results which would be unequal, then the legal rules are to be evaluated as unjust. Here, the inference of the legal creation based on Modus Tollens (explained above) will play its role.

It is further necessary to discuss how the inequality of the results of the application of the relevant legal rule sentence is evaluated. The author cannot avoid leaving the discussion of this problem open until, in the future, the analysis of real legal arguments regarding "equality" will be done.

In this sense, the theories of justice that try to provide the nature of justice, like Aristotle, who did with "equality", stand on the way to intensionally explicate just legal sentences.

The Way to Extensionally Explicate Just Legal Sentences. Natural law theories in modern times like Pufendorf's seem to have provided a system of just legal rule sentences [5]. This is an example of an extensional approach to explicate just legal rule sentences.

How can the extension of such just legal rule sentences be acquired? This should be precisely analyzed from a logical point of view. In contrast to the inference to determine the extension of valid legal rule sentences, the extension of just legal sentences cannot even be theoretically determined by means of a computer inference. This is the case because the former is determined based on the reasoning of justification, in which the logical deduction plays its role, as far as necessary and sufficient legal meta-rule sentences are presupposed as the premise of the deduction. However, the latter is related to the legal reasoning of creation where, directly, only unjust legal rule sentences can be identified through the falsification inference as it was explained in Sect. 6.6.

The extension of just legal rule sentences in the sense of legal rule sentences which passed enough falsification tests and therefore are confirmed as tenable or relatively just can only be extended step by step at the moment. This still requires an evaluator's hardworking brain and debates between people because no practicable computer program has yet been developed for this reasoning. The algorithm for such a computer program should be researched intensively. The very computer simulation of these falsification tests – in which the prediction of the result of the application of hypothetical legal rule sentences plays an important role – is needed to be developed for a genuine science of law.

7   Conclusion

The author believes that this paper has provided an overview of the concepts of truth in law from the logical point of view.

The first achievement of this paper is to have presented three sorts of the concept of truth in law, i.e., (1) truth as fact, (2) truth as validity and (3) truth as justice. It has also formally and semantically founded such a classification of the concepts of truth in law.

The second achievement is that this paper has analyzed the inference to determine the concepts of truth as validity and truth as justice in terms of an intensional or extensional way on the one hand and in terms of the reasoning of justification and creation of legal sentences on the other hand.

One of the future tasks related to this paper is to discuss the inference, to determine truth as fact. It is necessary to clarify the inference which determines that legal fact sentences are factually true or false.

Another future task is to clarify the logical structure of the inference to determine "just" legal sentences more precisely. It is especially necessary to analyze real arguments in positive law theories and legal philosophies regarding just legal sentences.

Acknowledgements. This paper was written by the author during his studies as a visiting professor at the Christian-Albrechts-Universität zu Kiel (CAU), Faculty of Law, and during his studies as a visiting scholar at Northeastern University School of Law (NUSL). The author is grateful to both schools for having provided a good research environment. The author expresses his deep appreciation, especially to the host Prof. Robert Alexy together with his colleague Prof. Ino Augsberg, Prof. Rudolf Meyer-Pritzl, Prof. Joachim Jickeli, and Prof. Michael Stöber at CAU as well as the host Prof. Sonia Elise Rolland together with her colleague Dean Prof. Jeremy R. Paul, Prof. Karl E. Klare, and Prof. Patrick Cassidy at the NUSL. Finally, the author would also like to express his gratitude to his student assistants Sven Petersen, Regina Kardel, Dennis Hardtke, and Amanda Dennis for their devoted assistance.

References

1. Aristotle: Politics, 2nd edn. University of Chicago Press, Chicago (2013). Edited and Translated by Carnes Lord. 1282b 22
2. Chisholm, R.M.: Contrary-to duty imperatives and deontic logic. Analysis **24**, 33–36 (1963)
3. Jørgensen, J.: Imperative and logic. Erkenntnis **7**, 88–296 (1937, 1938)
4. Popper, K.: The Logic of Scientific Discovery, p. 30. Hutchinson, London/New York (1959)
5. Pufendorf, S.: De Jure Naturae et gentium libri octo. Amsterdam edition (1688), 143 ff. The translation by Oldfather, 208 ff
6. Tarski, A.: The semantic conception of truth and the foundation of semantics. J. Philos. Phenomenol. Res. **4**, 341–375 (1944)
7. Tarski, A.: The concept of truth in formalized language. In: Tarski, A. (ed.). Logic, Semantics, Metamathematics, pp. 152–278, 167–168. Oxford University Press (1933, 1936)
8. von Wright, G.H.: Deontic logic. Mind **LX**, 1 (1951)
9. Yoshino, H.: Zu Ansätzen der Juristischen Logik. In: Tammelo (ed.) Strukturierungen und Entscheidungen im Rechtsdenken, pp. 279–282. Wien, New York (1978)
10. Yoshino, H.: Über die Notwendigkeit einer besonderen Normenlogik als Methode der juristischen Logik. In: Klug, U., Ramm, T., Rittner, F., Schmiedel, B. (eds.) Gesetzgebungstheorie, Juristische Logik, Zivil- und Prozeßrecht, pp. 140–161. Springer, Heidelberg (1978). https://doi.org/10.1007/978-3-642-95317-0_13
11. Yoshino, H.: The systematization of legal meta-inference. In: Proceedings of the Fifth International Conference on Artificial Intelligence and Law, pp. 266–275 (1995)
12. Yoshino, H.: The systematization of law in terms of the validity. In: Proceedings of the Thirteenth International Conference on Artificial Intelligence and Law, Danvers MA, pp. 121–125 (2011)
13. Yoshino, H.: The logical analysis of the concept of a right in terms of legal meta-sentence. In: Proceedings of Internationales Rechtsinformatik Symposion (IRIS), pp. 305–312 (2012)
14. Yoshino, H.: Justice and Logic, Jusletter IT 11, September 2014
15. Yoshino, H.: The concept of truth in law as the validity. In: Yoshino, H., et al. (ed.) Truth and Objectivity in Law and Morals, Stuttgart, pp. 13–31 (2016)
16. Yoshino, H., et al.: Legal expert system — LES-2. In: Wada, E. (ed.) LP 1986. LNCS, vol. 264, pp. 34–45. Springer, Heidelberg (1987). https://doi.org/10.1007/3-540-18024-9_20
17. Yoshino, H.: Legal expert project. J. Adv. Comput. Intell. Tokyo **1**(2), 83–85 (1997)

From Words to Images Through Legal Visualization

Arianna Rossi[✉] and Monica Palmirani

Università di Bologna, CIRSFID, via Galliera 3, 40121 Bologna, Italy
{arianna.rossi15,monica.palmirani}@unibo.it

Abstract. One of the common characteristics of legal documents is the absolute preponderance of text and their specific domain language, whose complexity can result in impenetrability for those that have no legal expertise. In some experiments, visual communication has been introduced in legal documents to make their meaning clearer and more intelligible, whilst visualizations have also been automatically generated from semantically-enriched legal data. As part of an ongoing research that aims to create user-friendly privacy terms by integrating graphical elements and Semantic Web technologies, the process of creation and interpretation of visual legal concepts will be discussed. The analysis of current approaches to this subject represents the point of departure to propose an empirical methodology that is inspired by interaction and human-centered design practices.

Keywords: Privacy · Legal design · Visualization · Legal XML
Legal semantic web · Interpretation · Interaction design
Human-centered design

1 Introduction

It is a common experience that legal terms, licenses, consent requests and in general any legal notice overload web applications. At the same time, they are ignored by most users, especially by digital natives. This is a paradox: on the one hand, overregulation. On the other hand, individuals' disregard. For these reasons, interest towards the visualization of legal clauses is growing with the aim of capturing and retaining individuals' attention, while providing intelligible and effective communication. In this light, the current research aims to model a theory for the visual representation of legal documents, with a concrete application to privacy terms.

To create visualizations in our research, we intend to leverage the different layers through which legal documents can be represented in the Semantic Web: text, structure, legal metadata, legal ontology and legal rules [32]. After having offered a complete and correct representation of a privacy policy on all these levels, we plan to build an additional layer on top of them: the visualization. However, it can be argued that it is indispensable to address the topic of visual

© Springer Nature Switzerland AG 2018
U. Pagallo et al. (Eds.): AICOL VI-X 2015–2017, LNAI 10791, pp. 72–85, 2018.
https://doi.org/10.1007/978-3-030-00178-0_5

representation of legal knowledge and its interpretation, specifically by answering the following questions:

1. What are the benefits and the risks of visualized legal information?
2. How can legal visualizations be generated?
3. How can machine-readable legal data be leveraged to create visualizations and what are the advantages?
4. Is it possible to ensure a correct interpretation of legal visualizations?

In the present position paper, we intend to provide a preliminary answer to these questions. Firstly, after having outlined the research scenario, some successful cases of legal visualizations will be presented. Next, the possibility to build semi-automatic visualizations on semantically-enriched legal data will be discussed. Then, the connection among communication theories, interaction, design and legal hermeneutics will be briefly introduced, alongside the interpretative process carried out when legal information is transformed into a machine-readable format. Current approaches for the generation and interpretation of visualizations adopted by legal scholars and legal designers will also be examined. Finally, some empirical design-oriented suggestions to address this topic will be made. Our intention is to implement and test them in the ongoing research described below.

2   Research Scenario

During an ongoing research, we propose semi-automatic visualizations of privacy policies and consent agreements (see also [31]). The debate around data protection is extremely topical: concerns about the practices of collection and processing of personal data are spreading, while regulations to protect data subjects are enforced. In the European Union, the principle of transparency laid down in Article 12 of the General Data Protection Regulation [13] (hereafter, GDPR) mandates the provision of intelligible and easily accessible information on data practices. The aim is that of empowering individuals to be knowledgeable about how their data is used and, as a consequence, to make informed decisions [2], for instance when they choose a certain service over another or when they consent to certain processing operations.

However, privacy disclosures are typically not read or not understood [37]. The use of visual cues has been proposed as a possible solution [17,33], since it has been demonstrated that they can enhance the effectiveness of legal communication (see next Section). Furthermore, it is the GDPR itself that suggests the use of icons "to give in an easily visible, intelligible, and clearly legible manner a meaningful overview of the intended processing" [13, Article 12(7)]. For these reasons, a privacy icon set is under development [23]. But its creation has raised some questions about the possibility of misrepresenting the legal terms during their conversion into visual elements, as well as the possibility of misinterpreting the visualizations (as it has emerged from some studies, e.g. [19,30]).

3   Background

3.1   Legal Visualizations and Legal Design

The discussion on the comprehensibility of legal sources must be understood as a part of the emerging research area of Legal Design, which is "the application of human-centered design to the world of law, to make legal systems and services more human-centered, usable, and satisfying" [18]. Thanks to the online environment, the legal message has exited the exclusive realm of lawyers. This means that new methods of communication must be considered to allow any individual, even a layperson, to access and understand legal information. In some contexts, as pointed out earlier, this is mandated by the law. We have entered a new era where design, communication and information technology must produce novel, user-friendly interfaces to the law [10].

Although the total absence of graphics is typical of modern legal texts, with exceptions such as the highway code and patents [6], this tendency is changing. For instance, principles of information design and graphic design have been applied to contracts [26–28], in order to produce user-friendly legal documents that are able to elicit information effectively, easily and quickly. As for what concerns the privacy ecosystem, innovative ways of communication and presentation are arising, although these attempts are rare and scattered [16]. In these experiments, visualization is crucial. Indeed, the support of visual elements helps unburden the cognitive load that derives from reading, navigating and understanding cumbersome documents, such as legal texts. There exist several different visual representation techniques, depending on the type of information, on the addressee, on the context, on the goal etc. For instance, flowcharts (Fig. 1) can express complex conditional structures that are typical of legal texts better than prose, whereas swimlane tables (Fig. 2) can highlight vis-a-vis the roles, rights, and responsibilities of different stakeholders [27]. Graphical symbols, such as icons (Fig. 3), can also be used in legal texts to foster understanding, memorization, and quick information retrieval. The present research around the generation and interpretation of visual elements focuses on this latter type of visualizations.

3.2   Legal Visualizations and Legal Informatics

Legal visualizations can be integrated into legal informatics. In fact, both research areas are concerned with the management of the complexity of legal knowledge [15]. Moreover, both disciplines deal with the representation of legal information: one in a visual format, the other in a machine-readable format. Semantic Web technologies allow the automated processing of semantically-enriched, machine-interpretable information, that can even be rendered graphically. For instance, visualizations were generated from XML marked-up legislative data to display the complexity of legal order overtime[1] [22] and of the Italian legislative procedure[2].

---

[1] http://lodpiemonte.cirsfid.unibo.it.
[2] http://code4italy.cirsfid.unibo.it.

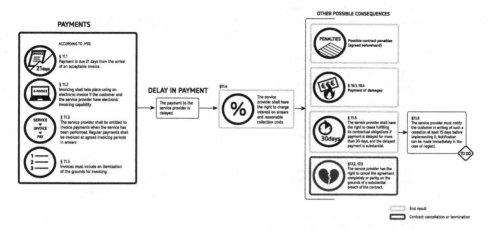

Fig. 1. Example of flowchart used to elicit payment procedures and consequences of delayed payments in the visual guide for the Finnish terms of public procurement [27]. ©2013 Aalto University & Kuntaliitto ry. Licensed under CC-BY-ND 3.0.

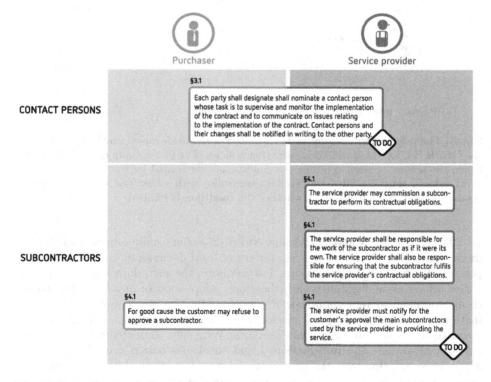

Fig. 2. Example of swimlane table used to illustrate the parties' rights and responsibilities in the visual guide for the correct with Finnish terms of public procurement [27]. ©2013 Aalto University & Kuntaliitto ry. Licensed under CC-BY-ND 3.0.

Annex 1 - Presentation of the particulars referred to in Article 13a (new)

1) Having regard to the proportions referred to in point 6, particulars shall be provided as follows:

ICON	ESSENTIAL INFORMATION	FULFILLED
	No personal data are **collected** beyond the minimum necessary for each specific purpose of the processing	
	No personal data are **retained** beyond the minimum necessary for each specific purpose of the processing	
	No personal data are **processed** for purposes other than the purposes for which they were collected	
	No personal data are **disseminated** to commercial third parties	
	No personal data are **sold or rented out**	
	No personal data are retained in **unencrypted** form	

COMPLIANCE WITH ROWS 1-3 IS REQUIRED BY EU LAW

(a) Privacy icons and their description in a table

(b) Graphical symbols to signal the fulfillment of the conditions laid down in the second column

Fig. 3. The tabular format proposed in Annex 1 of the draft report on the proposal for the GDPR [14] for standardised information policies. The first column contains privacy icons, the second column contains the conditions represented by the icons, while the third column must be filled by the data controller with either one of the graphical symbols of Fig. 3b, depending on whether the condition is fulfilled.

The legal XML standard Akoma Ntoso [25] offers unique opportunities to model the structural and semantic content of legal documents, so that it can be processed by software applications. Furthermore, the metadata layer of Akoma Ntoso allows great flexibility and, therefore, adaptation of any legal document to any ontological representation of concepts [4]. The machine-readable information that is captured by the mark-up enriches and is in turn enriched by the resources available on the (legal) Semantic Web [32], thus creating a complex network of sources and information. Legal ontologies enrich the Akoma Ntoso XML representation with the necessary semantic level that permits the connection between text and legal rules. Another legal XML language, LegalRuleML [3], can integrate Akoma Ntoso for what concerns the mark-up of the logical structure of legal rules. For instance, it can model deontic norms (obligations, permissions, prohibitions, rights) and can manage negations.

The structural, semantic, logical and ontological layers of a legal document can, thus, provide the information needed to propose a semi-automatic visualization of its content [31]. Furthermore, the encoding of legal content in a machine-readable format provides the opportunity to interact with it in order to customize its presentation for an intended audience and in a certain context. For instance, automated tools have been proposed to build interactive visualizations of contractual terms according to the input provided by users [29].

4 Legal Visualizations: From Representation to Interpretation

4.1 Communication, Design, Hermeneutics, and Visualizations

Visualization provides an alternative, supplementary manner of conveying legal content (concepts, norms, etc.) to the traditional text-based legal communication. The nature of communicative processes must be briefly introduced[3] in order to analyze the role of interpretation in legal visualizations. Communication is basically constituted by an encoder (the addresser) who sends a message to a decoder (the addressee) who receives and makes sense of that message (and reacts according to her sense-making) [20]. However, communication does not merely correspond to the exact match between the encoders' intended meaning of the message and the decoders' sense-making result: it is rather a continuous process of meaning negotiation between them. Design can be considered as a sort of communication: the designer gives a certain meaning to an artifact (e.g. a certain element of a graphical user interface) and the user interprets how, where, and when the artifact can be used [35]. However, no matter how carefully an artifact is designed, its meaning is not objective nor static: users unfold and decode the message (embedded by designers in signs like words, icons, command buttons, interface layouts etc.) while they interact with the system [36]. This is why, designers should provide users with all possible means (e.g. hints, explanations, etc.) to facilitate their sense-making of interface signs.

A comparable interactive meaning negotiation activity takes place in legal hermeneutics. Meaning does not derive solely from the intentions of the legislator nor from the activity of the legal interpreter: meaning is constantly produced within an interpretative dialogue among author, text and interpreter in specific contextual conditions. Thus, interpretation cannot be unique, it can only be coherent and correct according to shared criteria [38]. The theory of legal interpretation provides not only an explanation for one of the possible meanings, but also a methodology based on arguments, reasoning and values, that can justify one possible interpretation in the light of a certain social context and of a certain case [1]. On the other hand, common sense or preunderstanding can support legal experts to carry out their analysis to obtain a correct interpretation [9].

---

[3] A comprehensive approach to communication theories goes well beyond the scope of this paper.

Similarly, the visualization of legal content should be sufficiently evocative to produce in its addressees a visual perception comparable to the preunderstanding activity, in order to ensure a correct decoding of the visual legal message. In fact, the graphical representation has the goal of making legal terms more accessible and understandable. However, if wrongly interpreted, it would create obscurity in lieu of transparency. It is one thing to rely on a shared visual vocabulary (e.g. the Highway Code) and to depict concrete objects (e.g. patents or technical regulations). It is another thing to represent abstract or complex concepts with arbitrary symbols. For instance, user studies reveal that misinterpretation of privacy icons can occur [19,30] (the latter on the icons in Fig. 3). In these cases, the designer embedded a certain meaning in a symbol, which however did not meet other individuals' expectations and understanding, for instance due to different cultural backgrounds. Moreover, the visualization should also provide the necessary information to account for the methodology used to obtain a graphical representation of a certain legal concept.

In this scenario, two different issues must be addressed: firstly, define the criteria for the choice of a certain visual representation for a legal concept and, secondly, define a methodology for the induction of the correct legal concept in the decoder of a legal visualization.

4.2   Machine-Readable Representation and Interpretation

Even the analysis and consequent XML mark-up of legal documents cannot abstain from interpretation. Although the expertise of legal knowledge engineers who mark up the text guarantees the reliability of the annotation [25], in some cases multiple semantic annotations which represent different legal interpretations are unavoidable [3]. This is why the metadata section of the XML documents provides relevant information on the interpretation (for instance about the authoritativeness of the annotator) [24]. Furthermore, multiple metadata layers about different interpretations of the same document are possible [4]. Despite the possibility of multiple annotations, legal mark-up disambiguates uncertain concepts and clarifies meanings [25], thus it can represent a solid basis to build visualizations. Finally, the concepts of a certain domain, that are captured by the document mark-up, can be formalized and organized in an ontology, which lowers the personal bias in the selection, interpretation, and representation of legal knowledge. This shared formalization can also contain the graphical representation of its concepts, that will thus have a precise, stable, and machine-interpretable meaning [23].

4.3   Iconography, Legal Design and Interpretation

Nevertheless, although it is a common understanding that images are a universal language [7,12], visualized legal content allows greater freedom of interpretation than written text: indeed, "[i]mages are potentially more anarchic than words" [6, p. 89]. Because of the lack of a comprehensive theoretical framework for visual legal communication, methodological questions on the creation, analysis and evaluation of legal visualizations have been raised [8,11] and some (yet incomplete) answers have been suggested.

Iconographical and iconological methods developed by image disciplines have been compared to legal hermeneutics, on the grounds that these disciplines aim to uncover different layers of meaning and discover the deepest one [6]. Image disciplines and hermeneutics have developed similar interpretative approaches: the pre-iconographic description of the image elements resembles the preliminary analysis of individual words and sentences of the legal text; the iconographical analysis recalls the interpretation of the historical development, systematic analysis and context of the norm; finally, the iconological interpretation looks for the deeper meaning and purpose of the picture, similarly to the teleological interpretation of the law. Brunschwig's seminal work [7] originates from the same premises, but she also proposes a sound methodology for the creation of legal visualizations. The author applies methods of "visual rhetoric" derived from classical rhetoric (in particular from the *elocutio* process), to the Swiss Civil Code and transforms norms into drawings, especially through the application of "visual figures of speech" (i.e. visual association, visual synecdoche, visual symbolization, etc.). The transformation process of text into pictures is inherently arbitrary, but the correctness and understandability of the images depend on the following principles: 1. application of graphical elements drawn from traditional legal iconography; 2. their appropriateness to the time and place; 3. their appropriateness to the target audience (e.g. age, background, etc.); 4. compliance with Gestalt psychology principles (e.g. simplicity, clarity, organization, etc.); 5. aesthetics.

The same principles are usually respected by legal designers. They draw best practices from human-centered design and they usually cooperate with legal experts and other individuals with diverse backgrounds [5,10] to graphically elaborate concepts with the end-user of the legal document in mind. Although legal design does not explicitly tackle legal interpretation, this approach guarantees, on the one hand, the correctness of the visual representation of legal concepts thanks to the knowledge of legal experts [7] and, on the other hand, it considers the characteristics of the user that could influence the interpretation (i.e. age, education, culture) [33]. Indeed, the design process starts with empirical studies (e.g. surveys and interviews) and observations that reveal users' needs and characteristics, so that designers do not project on them their own beliefs and assumptions [5]. The process ends with user-testing, which is an empirical evaluation of the legal visualized document, e.g. in terms of comprehension of the legal meaning embedded in visualizations [26].

5   Suggestions for a Visual Legal Interpretation Framework

As illustrated above, there still lacks a comprehensive framework for legal text interpretation with the explicit aim of generating visualizations and for the interpretation of visualized legal content. However, the approaches illustrated above (cf. Subsect. 4.3) represent an essential point of departure to propose empirical solutions to the interpretation of legal visualizations, which is essential to our current research. Brunschwig [7] proposes clear, practical guidelines for the legal design process, but some aspects must be re-elaborated and integrated for our particular research topic. Firstly, this approach was proposed for paper documents, whereas privacy policies live in an online and interactive environment. Secondly, despite her sound methodology, the author does not offer a solution to the possibility of multiple interpretation of pictorial norms. Thirdly, the degree of comprehensibility and engagement of the legal drawings was not studied. By contrast, the effectiveness of legal design principles and practices has been proven [26–28], but a couple of aspects must be stressed to guarantee an appropriate representation and interpretation of data protection notions. In the first place, participatory design [34] must be the preferred framework so that ordinary users are consulted not only before and after the design process, but also during it. Should this not be the case, if a legal visual message is clear and unambiguous for its creators (e.g. legal and design experts), all the other users (the message decoders) will not necessarily assign the same meaning to it. In the second place, the graphical creation cannot only represent the view of one single group. Although less personal than the work of one person, it would not be representative of all the user-groups (e.g. designers, lawyers, computer scientists, laypeople, etc.) and, thus, its meaning could be ambiguous.

5.1 Moving Forward: Participation, Representativeness, Customization

We now propose an empirical methodology that is inspired by the aforementioned approaches and by current design practices to visualize the information expressed in privacy policies. The methodology is based on three pillars, that we believe should be integrated to propose an answer to the questions raised in the introduction: participation, representativeness and customization.

Participation. The knowledge of legal experts ensures the correct interpretation of the privacy concepts that must be rendered graphically, whereas the expertise of graphic designers together with existing good practices guarantee the quality of visualization. Since privacy and data protection notions are legal but also technical in nature, in this specific context even the knowledge of IT professionals is valuable. However, even ordinary users need to be involved in the creation stage to ensure that the graphical representation of the legal concepts mirrors their mental model. For instance, a technical expert and a layperson might represent the concept of "personal data" differently[4], because diversity

---

[4] Indeed, this tension became visible during a participatory workshop that we organized for the generation of privacy icons [21]. "Data" was initially represented as a cylinder, which is part of a shared visual vocabulary in computer science. It was, however, not understandable by those without technical background, thus it was transformed into the less specialist, but more widespread representation of a file folder.

in experiences and knowledge produces different mental images of it. "Participation stands in contrast with the cult of the specialist" [34, xi]: during the design process, users should cooperate with experts to reach a compromise that considers as many different points of view as possible. In this way, ordinary users become message encoders who will probably shape the visual message in a more comprehensible way for ordinary message decoders like themselves.

Representativeness. It is questionable whether the legal graphical representations will be interpreted in the same way as intended by the group of creators, even if this is multidisciplinary and takes into account expert as well as non-expert views. To reach the greatest level of agreement among message encoders and decoders, an open consultation or a crowdsourcing experiment about the correspondence between a certain graphical element and a certain legal concept could be launched. Then, an accuracy measurement of image-concept matching and of interpersonal agreement must be applied, in order to determine which visualizations can be considered the most representative of certain concepts for a significant number of individuals. Of course, it is necessary to determine what this means according to the specific context. In the case of the data protection icons, they aim to become a EU standard: they should, therefore, be sufficiently and consistently evocative for individuals with dozens of different nationalities, different ages, different backgrounds, etc., which is no easy task.

Customization. Although the outlined suggestions aim to find the highest degree of agreement to ensure correspondent interpretations, it is objectionable whether one single representation is ideal for every typology of user. Unlike contracts that are usually destined to a specific user-group (e.g. businesspeople, engineers, etc.), privacy policies address any type of person: from well-educated teenagers to technology-illiterate pensioners. This is why a unique interpretation is difficult to achieve, while customization could provide a viable solution. Privacy policies are not fossilized on paper, but can be rather conceived as online graphical, possibly dynamic, interfaces. Thus, a certain degree of customization that responds to the different needs and characteristics of different users can be envisaged. Culture, age, technical proficiency, linguistic proficiency and legal knowledge are some of the features that must guide the creation of the visualization and, consequently, its interpretation. At the same time, users themselves must have the possibility to initiate the customization. For instance, different users could choose between different degrees of visualization: from a maximum of textuality (e.g. for lawyers) to some degree of pictoriality (e.g. for teenagers).

Moreover, as seen above, interaction is a fundamental part of the interpretative process: the user assigns meanings to the elements of an interface while using it (in our case, the privacy policy) and can even adjust the meanings as the interaction proceeds. Users could be given the opportunity to opt for the kind of visualization they will better understand and remember, as exemplified by the online learning platform Memrise[5]. For instance, an old user and a young

---

[5] https://www.memrise.com.

user might need two different representations of the "justice" concept in order to interpret it correctly: one might prefer the long-established, traditional sign of a scale, whilst for the other the icon of Batman might be more meaningful. All the information gathered from the interaction of users could then be sent back to the source, confirming or rejecting the visualization proposed by the encoders. The results of this iterative process can be considered for subsequent re-elaborations (e.g. all children interpret the image of "Batman" as "justice").

5.2   A Methodology for Legal Visualizations

In the current research, different disciplines interlace to offer a methodological framework (see also [23]) for the generation and interpretation of visual elements that represent legal information of many kinds. The proposed framework is open to argument and does not intend to provide any final solution to the debate. However, in this specific context of research, it does provide an answer to some of the questions raised throughout the article.

First of all, the appropriateness of the visualization of a certain concept is supported, to a certain extent, by the legal XML mark-up of the privacy policy, the metadata that provides information on the mark-up process (e.g. annotations, exceptions, context, jurisdiction, etc.), and by the legal ontology that organizes and formalizes the meanings of a certain legal domain, e.g. the EU data protection laws. Semantic web technologies that tranform information into a machine-readable format can, thus, provide a first layer of interpretation of a certain legal domain knowledge in a specific context that can inform the generation of visual cues. Even the specific legal framework can provide direction for the visualization of legal notions: for instance, it is the GDPR to mandate which information must be provided to the final user and how they must be visualized (e.g. through icons, as opposed to other visual elements).

Moreover, interdisciplinary cooperation of (design, legal, technical) experts and non-experts in the stage of transforming concepts into visualizations also decreases the chances of personal bias [5]. The expertise of designers ensures that the proposed visual representation is coherent with the lessons drawn by previous experiments and good practices in legal design. Moreover, even the sense-making process of end-users (typical message decoders) is considered: in the first place, by involving them in the design phase; in the second place, by carrying out user testing to establish whether a certain image is as evocative as intended by those who created it; in the third place, by allowing customization that depends on the users' profile and on their interaction with the graphical interface.

Nevertheless, there exist cases where these measures could be insufficient to guarantee easy recognition. For instance, if the concepts are abstract, visualizations can be arbitrary and only their standardization and widespread adoption can guide a correct interpretation. The same holds when the symbol is comprehensible, but it is the notion to which it refers to be unfamiliar for the addressee (e.g. the notion of "pseudonymization"). In the best case, the image will be sufficiently evocative to suggest its meaning and create a preunderstanding in the user's mind. Should this not be the case, this can be solved only through education to privacy and data protection.

6 Conclusions and Future Work

In this position paper, the topic of interpretation of legal visualizations has been discussed. We have illustrated the shortcomings of traditional legal communication and, on the contrary, the many advantages that the visualization of the law grants. However, the pictorial representation of concepts opens up multiple interpretations and, in the legal domain, this ambiguity must be faced. This is why we have suggested an approach based on Semantic Web technologies and human-centered design that aims to guarantee representativeness of privacy pictorial representations to the highest possible degree, also through engagement and participation of multiple stakeholders in the design phase. Equally, some practical considerations on the role of interaction to realize customization and tailored visualizations have been proposed to address individual differences. In conclusion, the generation of one single "right" image is not desirable: there might be more than one easily intepretable picture, but it depends on the context, the type of representation, the background of the decoder, etc. The proposed methodology is being currently implemented and integrated with best practices already in use, in order to test whether it can represent a solution for the generation and interpretation of legal visualizations.

References

1. Alexy, R.: Interpretazione giuridica. In: Enciclopedia delle scienze sociali. Treccani (1996)
2. Article 29 Data Protection Working Party: Guidelines on transparency under regulation 2016/679, 17/EN WP260, December 2017
3. Athan, T., Governatori, G., Palmirani, M., Paschke, A., Wyner, A.: LegalRuleML: design principles and foundations. In: Faber, W., Paschke, A. (eds.) Reasoning Web 2015. LNCS, vol. 9203, pp. 151–188. Springer, Cham (2015). https://doi.org/10.1007/978-3-319-21768-0_6
4. Barabucci, G., Cervone, L., Palmirani, M., Peroni, S., Vitali, F.: Multi-layer markup and ontological structures in Akoma Ntoso. In: Casanovas, P., Pagallo, U., Sartor, G., Ajani, G. (eds.) AICOL -2009. LNCS (LNAI), vol. 6237, pp. 133–149. Springer, Heidelberg (2010). https://doi.org/10.1007/978-3-642-16524-5_9
5. Berger-Walliser, G., Barton, T.D., Haapio, H.: From visualization to legal design: a collaborative and creative process. Am. Bus. Law J. **54**(2), 347–392 (2017)
6. Boehme-Nessler, V.: Pictorial Law: Modern Law and the Power of Pictures. Springer, Berlin (2010). https://doi.org/10.1007/978-3-642-11889-0
7. Brunschwig, C.: Visualisierung von Rechtsnormen: legal design. Ph.D. thesis, University of Zürich (2001)
8. Brunschwig, C.R.: On visual law: visual legal communication practices and their scholarly exploration. In: Schweihofer, E., et al. (eds.) Zeichen und Zauber des Rechts: Festschrift für Friedrich Lachmayer, pp. 899–933. Editions Weblaw, Bern (2014)

9. Canale, D.: La precomprensione dell'interprete è arbitraria? Etica Politica **1**, 1–42 (2006)
10. Curtotti, M., Haapio, H., Passera, S.: Interdisciplinary cooperation in legal design and communication. In: Schweighofer, E., et al. (eds.) Co-operation. Proceedings of the 18th International Legal Informatics Symposium IRIS, pp. 455–462 (2015)
11. Curtotti, M., McCreath, E.: Enhancing the visualization of law. In: Law via the Internet Twentieth Anniversary Conference, Cornell University (2012)
12. Esayas, S., Mahler, T., McGillivray, K.: Is a picture worth a thousand terms? Visualising contract terms and data protection requirements for cloud computing users. In: Casteleyn, S., Dolog, P., Pautasso, C. (eds.) ICWE 2016. LNCS, vol. 9881, pp. 39–56. Springer, Cham (2016). https://doi.org/10.1007/978-3-319-46963-8_4
13. European Parliament, Council of European Union: Regulation (EU) 2016/679 of the European Parliament and of the Council of 27 April 2016 on the protection of natural persons with regard to the processing of personal data and on the free movement of such data, and repealing Directive 95/46/EC (General Data Protection Regulation). O.J. L 119, 4 May 2016, pp. 1–88 (2016)
14. European Parliament. Committee on Civil Liberties, Justice and Home Affairs: Draft report on the proposal for a regulation of the european parliament and of the council on the protection of individuals with regard to the processing of personal data and on the free movement of such data (general data protection regulation) [com(2012) 0011 - c7–0025/2012 - 2012/0011 (cod)], 21 November 2013
15. Geist, A., Brunschwig, C., Lachmayer, F., Schefbeck, G.: Multisensory law and legal informatics: a comparison of how these legal disciplines relate to visual law. In: Strukturierung der Juristischen Semantik - Structuring Legal Semantics. Editions Weblaw (2011)
16. Haapio, H., Hagan, M., Palmirani, M., Rossi, A.: Legal design patterns for privacy. In: Schweighofer, E. (ed.) Data Protection/LegalTech Proceedings of the 21st International Legal Informatics Symposium IRIS 2018, pp. 445–450. Editions Weblaw, Berlin (2018)
17. Hagan, M.: User-centered privacy communication design. In: Twelfth Symposium on Usable Privacy and Security (SOUPS 2016). USENIX Association (2016)
18. Hagan, M.: Law by design (2017). http://www.lawbydesign.co
19. Holtz, L.-E., Nocun, K., Hansen, M.: Towards displaying privacy information with icons. In: Fischer-Hübner, S., Duquenoy, P., Hansen, M., Leenes, R., Zhang, G. (eds.) Privacy and Identity 2010. IAICT, vol. 352, pp. 338–348. Springer, Heidelberg (2011). https://doi.org/10.1007/978-3-642-20769-3_27
20. Jakobson, R.: Closing statement: linguistics and poetics. In: Style in Language, pp. 350–377 (1960)
21. Legal Design Lab: Design workshop for eu general data protection regulation, July 2017. http://www.legaltechdesign.com/design-workshop-for-eu-general-data-protection-regulation/
22. Palmirani, M., Cervone, L.: Measuring the complexity of the legal order over time. In: Casanovas, P., Pagallo, U., Palmirani, M., Sartor, G. (eds.) AICOL -2013. LNCS (LNAI), vol. 8929, pp. 82–99. Springer, Heidelberg (2014). https://doi.org/10.1007/978-3-662-45960-7_7
23. Palmirani, M., Rossi, A., Martoni, M., Hagan, A.: A methodological framework to design a machine-readable privacy icon set. In: Schweighofer, E. (ed.) Data Protection/LegalTech Proceedings of the 21st International Legal Informatics Symposium IRIS 2018, pp. 451–454. Editions Weblaw, Wien (2018)

24. Palmirani, M., Vitali, F.: Akoma-ntoso for legal documents. In: Sartor, G., Palmirani, M., Francesconi, E., Biasiotti, M. (eds.) Legislative XML for the semantic Web. LGTS, vol. 4, pp. 75–100. Springer, Dordrecht (2011)
25. Palmirani, M., Vitali, F.: Legislative XML: principles and technical tools. Inter-American Development Bank (2012)
26. Passera, S.: Beyond the wall of text: how information design can make contracts user-friendly. In: Marcus, A. (ed.) DUXU 2015. LNCS, vol. 9187, pp. 341–352. Springer, Cham (2015). https://doi.org/10.1007/978-3-319-20898-5_33
27. Passera, S.: Flowcharts, swimlanes, and timelines. J. Bus. Tech. Commun. **32**, 229–272 (2017)
28. Passera, S., Haapio, H.: Transforming contracts from legal rules to user-centered communication tools: a human-information interaction challenge. Commun. Des. Q. Rev. **1**(3), 38–45 (2013)
29. Passera, S., Haapio, H., Curtotti, M.: Making the meaning of contracts visible-automating contract visualization. In: Proceedings of the 17th International Legal Informatics Symposium IRIS 2014 (2014)
30. Pettersson, J.S.: A brief evaluation of icons in the first reading of the european parliament on COM (2012) 0011. In: Camenisch, J., Fischer-Hübner, S., Hansen, M. (eds.) Privacy and Identity 2014. IAICT, vol. 457, pp. 125–135. Springer, Cham (2015). https://doi.org/10.1007/978-3-319-18621-4_9
31. Rossi, A., Palmirani, M.: A visualization approach for adaptive consent in the European data protection framework. In: Parycek, P., Edelmann, N. (eds.) CeDEM 2017: Proceedings of the 7th International Conference for E-Democracy and Open Government, pp. 159–170. Edition Donau-Universität Krems, Krems (2017)
32. Sartor, G., Palmirani, M., Francesconi, E., Biasiotti, M.A.: Legislative XML for the Semantic Web: Principles, Models, Standards for Document Management, vol. 4. Springer, Dordrecht (2011). https://doi.org/10.1007/978-94-007-1887-6
33. Schaub, F., Balebako, R., Durity, A.L., Cranor, L.F.: A design space for effective privacy notices. In: Eleventh Symposium On Usable Privacy and Security (SOUPS 2015), pp. 1–17 (2015)
34. Schuler, D., Namioka, A.: Participatory Design: Principles and Practices. CRC Press, Boca Raton (1993)
35. de Souza, C.S.: Semiotic engineering: bringing designers and users together at interaction time. Interact. Comput. **17**(3), 317–341 (2005)
36. de Souza, C.S.: Semiotics. In: Soegaard, M., Dam, R.F. (eds.) The Encyclopedia of Human-Computer Interaction, 2nd edn. The Interaction Design Foundation, Aarhus (2013)
37. TNS Opinion & Social: Special Eurobarometer 431 Data Protection. Technical report, European Commission, Directorate-General for Justice and Consumers, Directorate-General for Communication (2015)
38. Viola, F., Zaccaria, G.: Diritto e interpretazione: lineamenti di teoria ermeneutica del diritto, Laterza (2013)

Rules and Norms Analysis and Representation

A Petri Net-Based Notation
for Normative Modeling: Evaluation
on Deontic Paradoxes

Giovanni Sileno[1,2]($\boxtimes$), Alexander Boer[1], and Tom van Engers[1]

[1] Leibniz Center for Law, University of Amsterdam, Amsterdam, The Netherlands
g.sileno@uva.nl
[2] LTCI, Télécom ParisTech, Université Paris-Saclay, Paris, France

Abstract. Developing systems operating in alignment with norms is not a straightforward endeavour. Part of the problems derive from the suggestion that law concerns a system of norms, which, in abstract, in a fixed point in time, could be approached and expressed atemporally, but, when it is contextualized and applied, it deals with a continuous flow of events modifying the normative directives as well. The paper presents an alternative approach to some of these problems, exemplified by well-known deontic puzzles, by extending the Petri net notation, most common in process modeling, to Logic Programming Petri Nets. The resulting visual formalism represents in a integrated, yet distinct fashion, procedural and declarative aspects of the system under study, including normative ones.

Keywords: Contrary-to-duty · Deontic puzzles · Logic Programming
Petri nets · Normative modeling

1 Introduction

Puzzles and paradoxes are tools for bringing conceptualizations to their boundary conditions, and are therefore relevant for testing formal notations. The deontic logic community has devoted special attention to *paradoxes* constructed with *contrary-to-duty* (CTD) structures (see e.g. [3,4,9,11,17,22]). These are "paradoxes" because, although the normative statements look plausible in natural language, when each sentence is formalized in *standard deontic logic* (SDL)—the *paper tiger* of normative modeling—either the set of formulas is inconsistent, or one of the formulas is a logical consequence of another formula (e.g. [2]).

Definition 1 (Contrary to Duty). *A contrary-to-duty (CTD) structure is a situation in which a* primary obligation *exists, and with its violation, a secondary obligation* comes into existence.

The importance of CTDs lies in more than just their theoretical aspects: CTDs are fundamental to normative modeling, because they are at the base

© Springer Nature Switzerland AG 2018
U. Pagallo et al. (Eds.): AICOL VI-X 2015–2017, LNAI 10791, pp. 89–104, 2018.
https://doi.org/10.1007/978-3-030-00178-0_6

of *compensatory norms*, prototypical in e.g. contracts. The problem carries definite applicative concerns. This intuitively simple structure produces complex structures of obligations, prohibitions or permissions applying to sequences of violations or satisfactions relative to the conduct of agents in a regulated social system. Moreover, the secondary obligation may directly contradict the primary obligation. In this case, the conflict *has* to be solved to decide a course of action (i.e. "I am obliged, but I am forbidden, so what should I do?"). This consideration highlights the problem of specifying and treating preferences between idealities, or, in more agentive terms, priorities between commitments.

In this work, we focus on testing CTD structures on Logic Programming Petri Nets (LPPN).[1] This modeling notation has been introduced in [25] with the purpose of integrating and distinguishing in the same visual representation *declarative* aspects (concerning terminology, ontological constraints, normative directives, etc.) and *procedural* aspects (mechanisms, processes, courses of actions, etc.) of the reference system. The resulting common representational ground is proposed as a basis to support a continuous re-alignment in administrative organizations of representations of *law* (norms), of *implementations of law* (services as business processes), and of *action* (behavioural scripts, use cases, possibly intentionally characterized). The notation aims therefore to cover a wider class of models (business processes embedded with normative positions, scenarios issued from narratives, agent scripts, etc.) than what usually studied by deontic logic. Furthermore, beside its visual power (in principle increasing its accessibility), it enjoys computational properties as distributed computation, i.e. it does not require the reference to a global state.[2]

The connection of normative modeling with Petri nets is not new; see e.g. [18,19], and more recently [23]; however, these works mainly focus on events and factual conditions, overlooking normative characterizations. Other works, such as [24], have proposed using Petri nets to formalize contracts; with respect to these, the present proposal is more specific, as it focuses on minimal CTDs (through the lens of deontic puzzles), but also more general, as it considers the inclusion of declarative bindings in the model.

The paper is organized as follows. In Sect. 2, we will present *Logic Programming Petri Nets* (LPPN), delineating the notation and introducing informally a simplified version of its semantics. In Sect. 3, we will review a series of examples, all, save the first, copied from the literature. For each of them, we will propose models of the corresponding scenarios, and attempt to clarify part of the issues encountered in SDL. Discussion and further developments end the paper. A formalization of the propositional version of LPPN can be found in the appendix.

---

[1] Prototypes of LPPN interpreters are available on http://github.com/s1l3n0/pypneu and http://github.com/s1l3n0/lppneu.

[2] Cf. the recent extension to standard deontic logic by Gabbay and Straßer [6] integrating reactive constructs, an approach in many aspects dual to the present proposal.

2   Logic Programming Petri Nets

Petri nets are a simple, yet effective computational modeling representation featuring an intuitive visualization (see Fig. 1). They consist in directed, bipartite graphs with two types of nodes: *places* (visually represented with circles) and *transitions* (with boxes). A place can be connected only to transitions and vice-versa. One or more *tokens* (dots) can reside in each place. The execution of Petri nets is also named "token game": transitions *fire* by consuming tokens from their input places and producing tokens in their output places.[3]

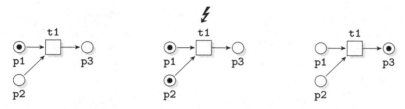

(a) not enabled transition, before firing   (b) enabled transition and firing   (c) the transition has fired

Fig. 1. Example of a Petri net and of its execution (but also of a LPPN *procedural component* when labels are propositions).

Despite their widespread use in computer science, electronics, business process modeling and biology, Petri nets are generally considered not to be enough expressive for reasoning purposes; in effect, they do not refer explicitly to any informational or representational concept. In their simplest form, tokens are indistinct, and do not transport any data. Nevertheless, usually modelers introduce labels to set up a correspondence between the *modeling* entities and the *modeled* entities. This practice enables them to read the results of a model execution in reference to the modeled system, and therefore it becomes *functional to the use* of the notation, although it is not a requirement for the execution in itself. Further interaction is possible if these labels are processed according an additional formalism, as for instance with the *Coloured Petri Net* (CPN) notation [13], which, for many aspects, is a descendant of *Predicate/Transition Nets* [7]. If its expressiveness and wide application provide reasons for its adoption, the CPN notation introduces many details which are unimportant in our setting (e.g. expressions on arcs); more importantly, it still misses the requirement of processing declarative bindings, necessary, for instance, to model terminological relationships. We opted therefore for an alternative notation.

Whereas Petri nets specify *procedural* mechanisms, LPPNs extend those (a) with Prolog-like *literals* as labels, attached on places and transitions; (b) with nodes specifying (logic) *declarative bindings* on places and on transitions.

---

[3] For an overview on the general properties of Petri nets see e.g. [21].

The notation builds upon the intuition that places and transitions mirror the common-sense distinction between *objects* and *events* (e.g. [1]), roughly reflecting the use of *noun/verb* categories in language [14]: the procedural components can be used to model *transient* aspects of the system in focus; the declarative components to model *steady state* aspects, i.e. those on which the transient is irrelevant or does not make sense (e.g. terminology, ontological constraints, etc.).

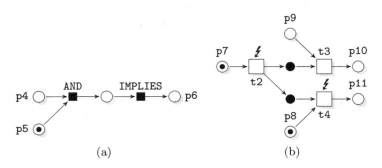

Fig. 2. Examples of LPPN *declarative components*: (a) defined on places, corresponding to the Prolog/ASP code: `p6 :- p4, p5. p5.` (b) defined on transitions, instantaneously propagating the firing where possible (the `IMPLIES` label on black circles is left implicit).

In this paper, for simplicity, we will consider only propositional labeling; with this assumption, the execution model of the LPPN procedural component is the same of *Condition/Event* nets, i.e. Petri nets whose places are not allowed to contain more than one token. For this reason, the Petri net in Fig. 1 can be interpreted as an example of LPPN specifying a procedural mechanism. However, the LPPN notation introduces also logic operator nodes (or *l-nodes*), which apply on places or on transitions. An example of a sub-net with l-nodes for places (small black squares) is given in Fig. 2a. These are used to create logic compositions of places (via operators as `NEG`, `AND`, `OR`, etc.), or to specify logic interdependencies (via the logic conditional `IMPLIES`). Similarly, transitions may be connected declaratively via l-nodes for transitions (black circles) as in Fig. 2b. These connections may be interpreted as channels enabling *instantaneous propagation* of firing. In this case, it is not relevant to introduce operators as `AND` because, for the interleaving semantics, only one source transition may fire per step. To simplify the visual burden, we might leave the `IMPLIES` label implicit, exploiting the sense of the arrow to specify the direction of the relation. Operationally, these declarative components are treated integrating the *stable model semantics* used in *answer set programming* (ASP) [15]. This was a natural choice because process execution exhibits a prototypical 'forward' nature, and ASP can be interpreted as providing forward chaining. A formalization of propositional LPPNs can be found in the Appendix.

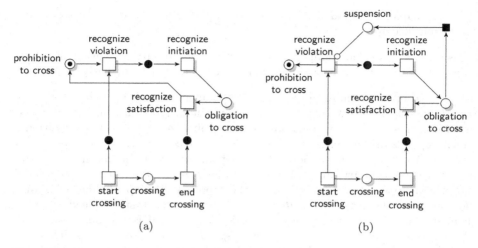

Fig. 3. A minimal, conflicting and event-based *contrary-to-duty* (CTD) structure: a secondary obligation is created after the violation of a primary obligation, and in conflict with it. The CTD may be interpreted: (a) as an *exception*; or (b) as *overriding* the primary obligation. The second is the most accepted option.

3 Deontic Exercises

3.1 Crossing or Not Crossing?

Let us start from this minimal, conflicting CTD structure:

> *You are forbidden to cross the road.*
> *If you are crossing the road, (you have to) cross the road!*

This rule of conduct is perfectly plausible: most parents say something similar to their children at some moment. However, its translation in basic deontic logic is not direct. The text suggests, in effect, an underlying model in terms of action: a state-based interpretation would miss the implicit initiation/termination events that make the action-wise prescription sound, and namely:

> *You are forbidden to cross the road.*
> *If you have started to cross the road, you are obliged to finish crossing.*

This *transitional* aspect can be easily mapped on a LPPN, separating the experiential world from the institutional world, with the second synchronized to the first via *constituting links* determining what *counts as* violation or satisfaction.[4]

---

[4] With respect to constitutive rules, the LPPN notation enables to easily distinguish *classificatory constitutive rules* (e.g. "a bike counts as a vehicle") from *constitutive event rules* (e.g. "raising a hand counts as making a bid"), as they are modeled respectively using black boxes or black circles. Most formalizations of constitutive rules consider only on the first aspect (e.g. [10]), cf. the overview in [27].

In principle, two modeling options are available in regard to the secondary obligation; it can interpreted:

- as an *exception*, thus temporarily retracting the primary obligation (Fig. 3a);
- as *overriding* the primary obligation, which persists concurrently (Fig. 3b).

The second option requires an additional treatment, because it brings two contrary/opposite positions to hold concurrently. Similarly to what suggested in the literature, this can be solved introducing an explicit *ordering* between positions, which depends on how close to *ideal* is the world/context they are referring to (see e.g. [16, 22]). In the proposed Petri net an aspect of this mechanism—the fact that the secondary obligation is put in force *in response to the violation* of the primary one—is already reified in the topology. To capture the remaining part, i.e. that the second is *contextually overriding* the first, we need to order them in the opposite sense: the last obligation created is the one with most priority and should be the only active, *suspending* the previous ones. This can be done introducing an *inhibiting arc* (visualized in Fig. 3b as an arrow with a circle-shaped head).[5] The resulting design can be seen as a model of *salience*.

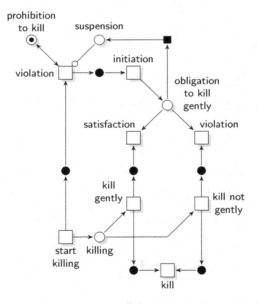

Fig. 4. *Gentle murderer* case.

---

[5] Inhibiting arcs goes from places to transitions. If the input place of an inhibiting arc is occupied, its output transition is disabled.

3.2   Gentle Murderer

The previous CTD model gives us the basic instruments to proceed. Let us start from the classic case of the "gentle murderer", given by Forrester [5]:

It is forbidden to kill,
but if one kills, one ought to kill gently.

This example is very similar to the previous one, except that the target of the secondary obligation is subsumed by the target of the first one. Because our notation explicitly accounts for a declarative dimension for events, we can directly map this relation (Fig. 4).

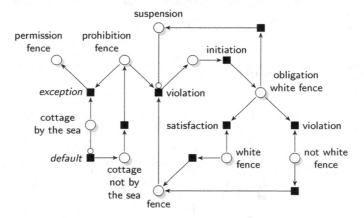

Fig. 5. *White fence* case.

3.3   White Fence

Now, we consider a static and extended variation proposed by Prakken and Sergot [22], the "white fence" case:

There must be no fence.
If there is a fence, it must be a white fence.
If the cottage is by the sea, there may be a fence.

This example shows the importance of distinguishing exceptions from overriding effects due to CTDs (and therefore supports the second interpretation of CTD given in Sect. 3.1). In principle, a rule specifies a CTD if its premise is the negation of the target of the obligation in the consequent of another rule. A rule specifies an exception if it has as consequent the negation of the consequent of another rule, *and* it has a lower *priority* than the first one (exceptions are by definition subordinate to some *normal* conditions). In effect, the two rules can be read as referring to a *priority-based representation* [26]. Considering part of the "white fence" case in propositional form, we have:

$$Forb(fence) \qquad sea \rightarrow Perm(fence)$$

which can be translated to the corresponding *constraint-based* representation:

$$\neg sea \rightarrow Forb(fence) \qquad sea \rightarrow Perm(fence)$$

This treatment gives a hint as to how to deal with *exceptions*—that is, it helps make explicit an enchaining of negations of the premises following the inverse ordering of salience. The fastest solution to avoiding conflicts in the case of belief revision is to not reify directly the *default* position (in this case, prohibition against having a fence), but to generate it through a *default rule* [26]:

$$not\ sea \rightarrow Forb(fence)$$

The resulting model is illustrated in Fig. 5.

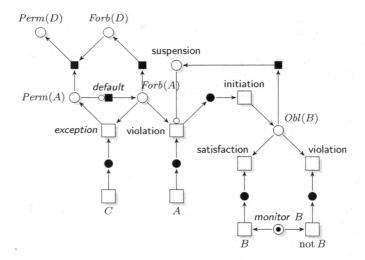

Fig. 6. *Privacy act* case.

3.4 Privacy Act

Recently, Governatori [8] has proposed the case of a Privacy Act (fictional, but based on actual Australian normative provisions):

i. *The collection of personal information is forbidden, unless acting on a court order authorising it.*

  ii. *The destruction of illegally collected personal information before accessing it is a defence against the illegal collection of the personal information.*
 iii. *The collection of medical information is forbidden, unless the entity collecting the medical information is permitted to collect personal information.*

The following deontic interpretation is proposed:

  i. Forbidden A. If C, then Permitted A.
 ii. If Forbidden A and A, then Obligatory B.
iii. Forbidden D. If Permitted A, then Permitted D.

A, B, C, and D in this specific case are actions; (ii) specifies a CTD, (i) and (iii) provide rules based on a priority-based representation. As before, we extract explicitly the defaults. The negation of permission of A in (iii) can be interpreted as the prohibition of A, thus converging to the default in (i). For completeness, we have reported in Fig. 6 the monitoring place from which the event B or not B is recognized.

3.5 Detachment Principles

In the deontic logic literature, two types of "detachment principles" are recognized as relevant. The first is called *factual detachment* (FD):

$$p \wedge Obl(q|p) \rightarrow Obl(q) \tag{1}$$

The second is known as *deontic detachment* (DD):

$$Obl(p) \wedge Obl(q|p) \rightarrow Obl(q) \tag{2}$$

In our framework, a conditional directive or commitment is seen as a *susceptibility* to a condition that *creates* or *implies* the directive depending upon whether the connective is a *causal* or *logical dependence*. The two principles can be then translated using the LPPN notation. Focusing on the logical dependence case, the result is seen in Fig. 7. The pictures show that the first principle is satisfied by the notation semantics; on the contrary, the second principle, which is based on an *anticipation* of the normal conditional, is not satisfied.

3.6 Derived Obligation

Consider these two sentences:

- *Bob's promise to meet you commits him to meeting you.*
- *It is obligatory that if Bob promises to meet you, he does so.*

Although in natural language their difference is arguable, in the literature they have been formalized using two distinct deontic formulations:

- $p \rightarrow Obl(m)$
- $Obl(p \rightarrow m)$

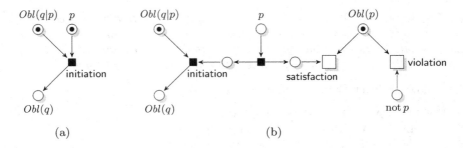

Fig. 7. Factual and deontic detachments.

What is the difference between the two formulations in our framework? The second formula can be translated with the consideration that the obligation of *something* consists of two recognition rules about satisfaction and violation, by default anchored respectively to *something* and to ¬*something*. As an object, the conditional within the obligation can be transformed using the *material implication*.[6] The result are reported in Fig. 8. As we see in the picture, both models are violated in the same situation (p and ¬m); however, the second includes the recognition of a satisfied situation not accounted for in the first (¬p). In other words, the first derived obligation precisely discriminates the elements producing the violation. The second takes an explicit position also on the satisfying elements.

3.7   Chisholm's Paradox

At this point, we can finally model the "paradox" proposed by Chisholm [4]:

> It ought to be that Jones goes (to the assistance of his neighbors).
> It ought to be that if Jones goes, then he tells them he is coming.
> If Jones doesn't go, then he ought not tell them he is coming.
> Jones doesn't go.

This was seen as a paradox, because if we model it as:

i. $Obl(go)$
ii. $Obl(go \rightarrow tell)$
iii. $\neg go \rightarrow Forb(tell)$
iv. $\neg go$

---

[6] The specific example from which we started is not based on a logic conditional, but on a causal connective, at least in the case of "if Bob promises to meet you, then he does so". In this case, the use of material implication is not a perfect fit, as the temporal shift between the promise and the meeting falsifies the derived constraint, at least on a transient basis. On a steady state analysis, however, this simplification may be applied.

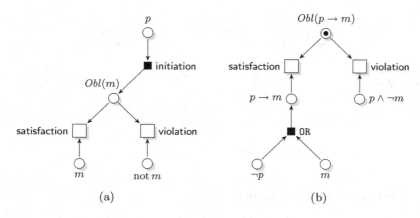

Fig. 8. Derived obligation modeled as $p \to Obl(m)$ or as $Obl(p \to m)$.

and we apply both deontic and factual detachments, we find an inconsistency. More precisely, from (i) and (ii), using of deontic detachment, we derive $Obl(tell)$, while from (iii) and (iv), using factual detachment, we derive $Obl(\neg tell)$. However, representing this model using our notation as in Fig. 9, we do not find any specific issue. The fact $\neg go$ satisfies $Obl(go \to tell)$, but violates $Obl(go)$, and for this reason, $Forb(tell)$ is instantiated. Depending on whether $tell$ becomes true, this may or may not be violated.

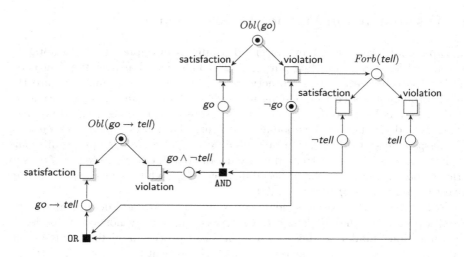

Fig. 9. *Chisholm's paradox* case.

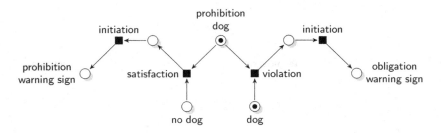

Fig. 10. *Residential neighbourhood* case.

3.8 Residential Neighbourhood

As we observed above, the difference in natural language between the two types of derived obligations is arguable. In order to show what would happen if we interpret the two as conditional obligations, we consider the non-agent version of the Chisholm's paradox proposed by Prakken and Sergot [22]:

> *There must be no dog.*
> *If there is no dog, there must be no warning sign.*
> *If there is a dog, there must be a warning sign.*
> *There is a dog.*

Written in this way, the modeling is straightforward (Fig. 10).

4 Discussion and Further Developments

At superficial level, the paper presented examples of application of a notation introduced for wider modeling purposes [25]. This served as an important exercise to (partially) evaluate its practical functionality, as one may capture the subtle problems related to modeling in a certain domain (in this case normative modeling) only by approaching the specific issues that have been raised by practitioners and scholars in that domain. The introduction of *defaults*, *exceptions*, and *suspensions* in the notation presented here is a preliminary proposal. Some of these aspects have been treated more in more detail elsewhere (e.g. *defaults* in priority-based rule-bases [26], proceeding along [12]), while others require further investigation (e.g. *suspension*, cf. [20]).

Nevertheless, the exercise yields concrete practical and theoretical results. From a practical point of view, it makes a case supporting normative modeling with notations similar to those used in business process modeling, thus potentially facilitating cross-fertilization between theoretical to operational settings. From a theoretical point of view, we observed for instance that our conceptual framework does not entail the *deontic detachment* principle, hinting at a more general *minimal commitment* taken by the notation. In other words, i.e. the notation does not provide any rule *a priori* to conclude whether $Obl(A) \wedge Obl(B)$ is the same as $Obl(A \wedge B)$. This neutral starting point can be used to evaluate the alternative impact of different axioms proposed in the literature, in affinity with approaches like *input/output logic* [17].

More importantly, while working on these exercises, we appreciated the crucial interplay between static and dynamic aspects (one of the issues underlying many deontic puzzles). The LPPN notation, requiring the explicitation of procedural and declarative aspects, highly facilitated this task, but our exercise suggests further research on the modeling methodology. For instance, in Chisholm's paradox, we considered *go* and *tell* as labels of places, but strictly speaking, they should be attached to transitions (as in the *privacy act* case). With this choice, we would require making explicit the *occurrence* of the events as places, in order to evaluate the material implication. Does this simplification hint at a more general pattern? We modeled the nodes concerning violation and satisfaction as l-nodes only when their transformational nature was certain. In general, however, they may be *transformational* (when they simply identify whether a violation or satisfaction holds at the moment) or *reactive* (when they reify the fact that a violation occurred in that moment, or when they cause any change on the inputs, e.g. removing the obligation)—note again the interplay between static and dynamic aspects. In the future, an investigation of boundary cases may help in formulating a more general theory on how to decide upon the level of abstraction, and about whether it is possible to identify or elaborate general patterns, that, depending on circumstances, are read in one form or in the other.

A   Formalization

Here we present a simplified version of the LPPN notation considering only a *propositional* labeling. We start from the definition of propositional literals derived from ASP [15], accounting for strong and default negation.

Definition 2 (Literal and Extended literals). *Given a set of propositional atoms A, the set of* literals $L = L^+ \cup L^-$ *consists of* positive literals *(atoms)* $L^+ = A$, negative literals *(negated atoms)* $L^- = \{-a \mid a \in A\}$, *where '$-$' stands for* strong negation.[7] *The set of* extended literals $L^* = L \cup L^{not}$ *consists of* literals *and* default negation literals $L^{not} = \{notl \mid l \in L\}$, *where 'not' stands for* default negation.[8]

We denote the basic topology of a Petri net as a procedural net.

Definition 3 (Procedural net). *A procedural net is a* bipartite directed graph *connecting two finite sets of nodes, called* places *and* transitions. *It can be written as* $N = \langle P, T, E \rangle$, *where* $P = \{p_1, \ldots, p_n\}$ *is the set of* place *nodes;* $T = \{t_1, \ldots, t_m\}$ *is the set of* transition *nodes;* $E = E^+ \cup E^-$ *is the set of* arcs *connecting them:* E^+ *from transitions to places,* E^- *from places to transitions.*

---

[7] Strong negation is used to reify an explicitly false situation (e.g. "It does not rain").

[8] Default negation is used to reify a situation in which something cannot be retrieved/inferred (e.g. 'It is unknown whether it rains or not').

LPPNs consists of three components: a procedural net specifying causal or temporal relationships, and two declarative nets specifying respectively logical dependencies at the level of objects or ongoing events (on places), and on impulse events (on transitions). Furthermore, *propositional* LPPNs build upon a boolean marking on places (like *condition/event* nets).

Definition 4 (Propositional Logic Programming Petri Net). *A proposi-tional Logic Programming Petri Net $LPPN_{prop}$ is a Petri Net whose places and transitions are labeled with literals, enriched with declarative nets of places and of transitions. It is defined by the following components:*

- $\langle P, T, PE \rangle$ *is a procedural net; PE stands for* procedural edges*;*
- $C_P : P \to L^*$ *and* $C_T : T \to L$ *are labeling functions, associating literals respectively to places and to transitions;*
- $OP = \{\neg, -, \wedge, \vee, \to, \leftrightarrow, \dots\}$ *is a set of logic operators.*
- *LP and LT are sets of* logic operator nodes *(in the following called* l-nodes*) respectively for places and for transitions.*
- $C_{LP} : LP \to OP$ *maps each l-node for places to a logic operator; similarly,* $C_{LT} : LT \to OP$ *does the same for l-nodes for transitions.*
- $DE_{LP} = DE^+_{LP} \cup DE^-_{LP}$ *is the set of arcs connecting l-nodes for places to places; similarly,* $DE_{LT} = DE^+_{LT} \cup DE^-_{LT}$ *for l-nodes for transitions and transitions.*[9]
- $M : P \to \{0, 1\}$ *returns the marking of a place, i.e. whether the place contains (1) or does not contain (0) a token.*

Note that if $LP \cup LT = \varnothing$, we have a *strictly procedural* $LPPN_{prop}$, i.e. a standard binary Petri net. If $T = \varnothing$, we have a *strictly declarative* $LPPN_{prop}$, that can be directly mapped to an ASP program.

With respect to the *operational semantics*, the execution cycle of a LPPN consists of four steps: (1) given a "source" marking M, the bindings of the declarative net of places entail a "ground" marking M^*; (2) an enabled transition is selected to *pre-fire*, so determining a "source" *transition-event* e; (3) the bindings of the declarative net of transitions entail all propagations of this event, obtaining a set of *transition-events*, also denoted as the "ground" *event-marking* E^*; (4) all transition-events are fired, producing and consuming the relative tokens. The steps (1) and (3) are processed by an ASP solver: the declarative net of places (respectively transitions) is translated as *rules*, tokens (transition-events) are reified as *facts*; the ASP solver takes as input the resulting program and, if satisfiable, it provides as output one or more ground marking (one or more sets transition-events to be fired). For the steps (2) and (4), the operational semantics distinguishes the *external* firings (started by the execution) from the *internal* firing, immediately propagated (triggered by the declarative net of transitions).

---

[9] Note that $DE^-_{LT} \subseteq (T \cup P) \times LT$, i.e. these edges go from transitions *and* places (modeling contextual conditions) to l-nodes for transitions.

Definition 5 (Enabled transition). *A transition t is* enabled *in a ground marking M^* if a token is available for each input places:*

$$Enabled(t) \equiv \forall p_i \in \bullet t, M^*(p) = 1$$

Similarly to what marking is for places, we consider an *event-marking* for transitions $E : T \rightarrow \{0, 1\}$. $E(t) = 1$ if the transition t produces a transition-event e. Each step s has a "source" event-marking E.

Definition 6 (Pre-firing). *An enabled transition t pre-fires at a step s if it selected to produce a* transition-event:

$$\forall t \in Enabled(T) : t \text{ pre-fires} \equiv E(t) = 1$$

As we apply an *interleaving semantics* for the pre-firing, the interpreter selects only one transition to pre-fire per step; for any other t', $E(t') = 0$.

Definition 7 (Firing). *An enabled transition t fires by propagation, consuming a token from each input place, and forging a token in each output place:*

$$\forall t \in Enabled(T) : t \text{ fires} \equiv$$
$$E^*(t) = 1 \leftrightarrow \forall p_i \in \bullet t : M'(p_i) = 0 \; \wedge \; \forall p_o \in t\bullet : M'(p_o) = 1$$

References

1. Breuker, J., Hoekstra, R.: Core concepts of law: taking common-sense seriously. In: Proceedings of Formal Ontologies in Information (2004)
2. Broersen, J., van der Torre, L.: Ten problems of deontic logic and normative reasoning in computer science. In: Bezhanishvili, N., Goranko, V. (eds.) ESSLLI 2010-2011. LNCS, vol. 7388, pp. 55–88. Springer, Heidelberg (2012). https://doi.org/10.1007/978-3-642-31485-8_2
3. Carmo, J., Jones, A.: Deontic logic and contrary-to-duties. In: Gabbay, D.M., Guenthner, F. (eds.) Handbook of Philosophical Logic, vol. 8, pp. 265–343. Springer, Dordrecht (2002). https://doi.org/10.1007/978-94-010-0387-2_4
4. Chisholm, R.M.: Contrary-to-duty imperatives and deontic logic. Analysis **24**(2), 33–36 (1963)
5. Forrester, J.W.: Gentle murder, or the adverbial Samaritan. J. Philos. **81**(4), 193–197 (1984)
6. Gabbay, D.M., Straßer, C.: Reactive standard deontic logic. J. Log. Comput. **25**(1), 117–157 (2015)
7. Genrich, H.J.: Predicate/transition nets. In: Brauer, W., Reisig, W., Rozenberg, G. (eds.) ACPN 1986. LNCS, vol. 254, pp. 207–247. Springer, Heidelberg (1987). https://doi.org/10.1007/978-3-540-47919-2_9
8. Governatori, G.: Thou shalt is not you will. Technical report, NICTA (2015)
9. Governatori, G., Rotolo, A.: Logic of violations: a gentzen system for reasoning with contrary-to-duty obligations. Australas. J. Log. **4**, 193–215 (2006)
10. Grossi, D., Meyer, J.J.C., Dignum, F.: Classificatory aspects of counts-as: an analysis in modal logic. J. Log. Comput. **16**(5), 613–643 (2006)

11. Hansen, J., Pigozzi, G., Van Der Torre, L.: Ten philosophical problems in deontic logic. Normative Multi-agent, pp. 1–26 (2007)
12. Horty, J.F.: Rules and reasons in the theory of precedent. Legal Theory **17**(1), 1–33 (2011)
13. Jensen, K.: Coloured Petri Nets: Basic Concepts, Analysis Methods and Practical Use. Springer, Heidelberg (1996). https://doi.org/10.1007/978-3-662-03241-1
14. Kemmerer, D., Eggleston, A.: Nouns and verbs in the brain: implications of linguistic typology for cognitive neuroscience. Lingua **120**(12), 2686–2690 (2010)
15. Lifschitz, V.: What is answer set programming? In: Proceedings of the 22th AAAI Conference on Artificial Intelligence (2008)
16. Makinson, D.: Five faces of minimality. Stud. Log. **52**, 339–379 (1993)
17. Makinson, D., Van Der Torre, L.: Input/output logics. J. Philos. Log. **29**, 383–408 (2000)
18. Meldman, J., Fox, S.: Concise petri nets and their use in modeling the social work (Scotland) Act 1968. Emory Law J. **30**, 583–630 (1981)
19. Meldman, J., Holt, A.: Petri nets and legal systems. Jurimetr. J. **12**(2), 65–75 (1971)
20. Meneguzzi, F., Telang, P., Singh, M.: A first-order formalization of commitments and goals for planning. In: Proceedings of the 27th AAAI Conference on Artificial Intelligence, pp. 697–703 (2013)
21. Murata, T.: Petri nets: properties, analysis and applications. Proc. IEEE **77**(4), 541–580 (1989)
22. Prakken, H., Sergot, M.: Contrary-to-duty obligations. Stud. Log. **57**(1), 91–115 (1996)
23. Purvis, M.A.: Dynamic modelling of legal processes with petri nets. Ph.D. thesis, University of Otago (1998)
24. Raskin, J.F., Tan, Y.H., van der Torre, L.: How to model normative behavior in Petri nets. In: Proceedings of the 2nd ModelAge: Workshop on Formal Models of Agents, pp. 223–241 (1996)
25. Sileno, G.: Aligning law and action. Ph.D. thesis, University of Amsterdam (2016)
26. Sileno, G., Boer, A., van Engers, T.: A constructivist approach to rule bases. In: Proceeding of the 7th International Conference on Agents and Artificial Intelligence (ICAART 2015) (2015)
27. Sileno, G., Boer, A., van Engers, T.: Revisiting constitutive rules. In: Proceedings of the 6th Workshop on Artificial Intelligence and the Complexity of Legal Systems (AICOL 2015) (2015)

Legal Patterns for Different Constitutive Rules

Marcello Ceci[⊠], Tom Butler, Leona O'Brien, and Firas Al Khalil

GRCTC, University College Cork, Cork, Ireland
{marcello.ceci,tbutler,leona.obrien,
firas.alkhalil}@ucc.ie

Abstract. The research for solutions for compliance is mainly focused on the representation of regulative rules, i.e. the imperatives that the industry is asked to comply to. Yet, a relevant part of the legal knowledge contained in regulation cannot be expressed in terms of deontic statements, and is instead represented as *constitutive rules*. This concept was first introduced by philosophers of language such as J.L. Austin and J.R. Searle and further developed in legal philosophy, where constitutive statements are classified in categories according to their legal effects. The present paper presents a heuristic approach for the representation of alethic statements as part of a methodology aimed at ensuring effective translation of the regulatory text into a machine-readable language. The approach is based on a classification of constitutive statements contained in the work of legal philosophers A.G. Conte and G. Carcaterra. The methodology includes an intermediate language, accompanied by an XML persistence model, and introduces a set of "legal concept patterns" to specifically represent the different constitutive statements. The paper identifies five patterns for the corresponding constitutive statements found in financial regulations: legal definitions, commencement rules, amendments, relative necessities, and party to the law statements.

Keywords: Constitutive rules · Legal patterns · Legal definitions
Meta-rules · SBVR

> *"Comprendere un diritto significa sapere che cosa esso è, sapere che cosa è significa possederne la definizione."*
> Understanding a right implies knowing what it is, and knowing what it is implies possessing its definition.
>
> Carcaterra [9, p. 25].

1 Introduction

Assessing compliance means checking the correspondence of an activity with a set of norms. Here, norm is intended as the interpretation of a rule contained in a regulation. To assess compliance, we need two pieces of information: one about the activity, and the other about the interpretation of the regulation. In order to speed up the process of compliance assessment, we thus need a machine-readable interpretation of the law.

© Springer Nature Switzerland AG 2018
U. Pagallo et al. (Eds.): AICOL VI-X 2015–2017, LNAI 10791, pp. 105–123, 2018.
https://doi.org/10.1007/978-3-030-00178-0_7

Great are the potentials of semantic web technologies to express semantics of legal texts, especially in terms of legal references (e.g. LegalDocML [24]) and legal scope (e.g. LKIF [8]). Several rule languages exist that manage legal rules, and rest on solid logical foundations (e.g. LegalRuleML, see survey [13]). Unfortunately, those layers of technology are difficult for lawyers to grasp, and the related solutions are still out of their reach.

The goal of the research presented in this paper is to represent regulations for GRC tasks in financial industry. To achieve this, we developed a Regulatory Interpretation Methodology (RIM) to guide a Subject Matter Expert (SME, e.g. the legal expert) and a Semantic Technology Engineer (STE) in a collaborative process of transformation of the regulatory text into machine-readable information [1].

To represent the semantics of regulatory requirements in a machine-readable format with a SME-friendly process we built an intermediate language based on SBVR (Semantics of Business Vocabulary and Business Rules [25]). SBVR is a powerful instrument for building a vocabulary representing business activities [34, p. 14], but unfortunately it isn't suitable – as is – for the representation of legal rules in a machine-readable format: besides SBVR being designed for human-to-human communication across a business and not for automatic reasoning, some of its components are falling short in capturing legal concepts, such as constitutive rules.

Philosophy of language [3, 32] identified two types of rules: regulative rules and constitutive rules. Previous work describes our approach to regulative rules [12]. The present paper discusses the representation of constitutive rules, which, despite not being requirements themselves, still play more than a marginal role in compliance assessment.

1.1   Scope

The present paper focuses on the issue of representing alethic statements (including legal definitions, meta-rules, statements of facts) in a machine-readable way. The proposed solution employs an intermediate language based on SBVR and follows the classification drawn in legal philosophy for constitutive statements. Because the research is focused on compliance, constitutive statements are seen as complementary, and represented only to the extent necessary to define and specify the effects of regulative statements. Legal philosophy identifies different categories of constitutive rules, and this paper follows these classifications in order to represent their semantics. The paper introduces the concept of **legal concept patterns**, that work as templates to represent constitutive norms with fixed effects, and presents five legal concept patterns for capturing five types of constitutive rules.

This paper is structured as follows: Sect. 2 introduces the concept of constitutive rules and the relevant doctrine on them. Section 3 introduces legal concept patterns, used to represent constitutive norms as explained in Sect. 4.

2   Constitutive Rules

In legal theory, constitutive norms[1] are the result of declarative acts [6]. These norms introduce new abstract classifications of existing facts and entities. Those classifications are called institutional facts (e.g. marriage, money, private property) and they emerge from an independent ontology of "brute" physical facts. Differently from regulative rules, constitutive norms have no deontic content: they do not introduce obligations, prohibitions or permissions. Instead, they typically take the following form:

$$(a) \text{ counts as } (b) \text{ in context } (c)$$

In order to capture these rules, it is thus necessary to identify three elements:

– a material (or previously identified) phenomenon (*token*);
– an abstract concept that is created by the constitutive rule itself (*type*);
– a limited area of application (*context*).

Two additional elements, the (alethic) modality and the legal source, are in common with regulative rules. Constitutive norms are also called "determinative rules" [18]. In LegalRuleML, that class is represented as *ConstitutiveStatement* node element. In Normative Multi-Agent systems, they are formalized as belief rule of normative agents: from a knowledge representation point of view, they behave as data abstraction in programming languages [7]. An investigation of the logic underlying "count-as" statements is performed by Grossi [20], including a wide survey of the existing attempts to provide a formalization for constitutive norms and count-as conditionals [21]. In it, the diversity of formal approaches is evident. Seven strands of research are identified [21, p. 429]: contextual aspects of counts-as; classificatory aspects of counts-as; counts-as and actions; counts-as and conventions; counts-as as grounded on dedicated agents; counts-as as related to regulative norms; counts-as as related to the definition of legal terms.

This multiplicity of approaches suggests that a unique formalization is not capable of representing all the possible aspects of constitutive norms. Furthermore, the distinction [19] of counts-as statements in classificatory counts-as, proper classificatory

---

[1] The concept of constitutivity, as distinguished from the regulative effects of norms, was first introduced by John Rawls [27], with the following distinction: "justifying a practice and justifying a particular action falling under it... [by meaning for] practice any form of activity specified by a system of rules which defines offices, roles, moves, penalties, defenses, and so on, and which gives the activity its structure". Austin [3] investigated the phenomenon of the *performative utterances*, defining them as: "Utterances [...] that [...] do not 'describe' or 'report' or constate anything at all, are not 'true or false,' and the uttering of [which] is, or is a part of, the doing of an action, which again would not normally be described as, or as 'just,' saying something" (pp. 5–6). The concept of performative utterances was later refined by Searle [32] into that of speech acts and constitutive rules, defined as follows: "[R]egulative rules regulate antecedently or independently existing forms of behaviour [...]. But constitutive norms do not merely regulate, they create or define new forms of behaviour. The rules of football or chess, for example [...] create the very possibility of playing such games" (p. 33).

counts-as, ascriptive counts-as and constitutive counts-as, is a proof of the hetero-geneity of such statements, not only in their form but also in their effects.

SBVR's restricted language does not explicitly include institutional facts or con-stitutive norms, although it has a rule category called structural (or definitional) rules that can be used for the purpose. These rules are represented in the language through alethic statements instead of deontic statements.

The rest of this section will present part of the research conducted in philosophy of law on the subject of constitutive rules with the aim of identifying a taxonomy of constitutive rules.

2.1   On the Constitutivity of Rules

Over the last decades the Italian school of legal philosophy introduced distinctions within constitutive statements [9, 14, 16, 22]. According to Carcaterra [9, p. 61], the constitutive statement "produces, at the very moment when it enters into force, the effect that is its scope and content". Carcaterra distinguishes two meanings of constitutivity in legal norms: according to the first meaning, constitutivity is a process downright creator of legal effects (or states of affairs). Rules carrying such constitutivity correspond to Searle's declarative speech acts [33, pp. 16–20]. In the second meaning, constitutivity is the process of creation of acts and facts with a specific legal meaning. Such meaning of constitutivity differs from that of declarative speech acts, rather resembling the creative attitude of Searle's "rules that are constitutive of speech acts".

According to this distinction, we can distinguish two types of constitutivity: thetic-constitutivity (from θέσις, "affirmation") directly creates its object (a legal effect or state of affairs), while eidetic-constitutivity (from εἶδος, shape) rather creates the abstract concept of its object, thus making such legal effect or state of affairs possible in the legal system. An example of thetic-constitutive rule (a declarative speech act) would be a marriage celebrated by a public officer (as it creates the legal bond between two individuals) or the divorce sentence of a judge (as it removes it), while examples of an eidetic-constitutive rule (a statement constitutive of speech acts) would be the laws that establish such procedures and effects (marriage and divorce).

Conte [14, pp. 82–83] classifies those rules as conditions for their regulated entity: then, an eidetic-constitutive rule is a necessary condition and a thetic-constitutive rule is a sufficient condition. These two types of constitutive rules are different, and this duality cannot be reduced or simplified, as argued by Roversi [29].

2.2   Relative Necessities as Constitutive Statements

According to Sartor [31], "in many cases, when a legal text uses the words must, ought, may, or can, it does not express obligations or permissions in the sense discussed above, but it conveys a completely different notion, which is parasitical on the idea of a normative conditional."

Consider those cases in which, for example, the law says that a petition or contract must or must not be done in a certain way, or that it can or cannot contain certain terms. In these cases, the law establishes what we may call a relative necessity: it establishes that certain requirements have (or don't have) to be satisfied for a certain legal result to be obtained in a certain way. Often, the specification of this result is left to further normative propositions. For instance, suppose that in a legal text, after stating that "whoever appropriates the property of others is going to be punished as a thief", it is stated that "the appropriator must have the intention of getting permanent possession of the stolen object". Clearly, there is no legal obligation to have such intention. The "must" signals a necessity, relative to the normative antecedent which determines subjection to punishment for theft. It indicates that the elements explicitly contained in the antecedent of the rule on theft are not really sufficient to produce the effect indicated in that rule: a further element, namely, the intention to appropriate, is also required to instantiate the precondition of the rule.

We may use the term anankastic – from the Greek word Ἀνάγκη, necessity – to characterise the (anankastic) propositions expressing this kind of necessity. As we may have normative propositions expressing anankastic connections, we may also have propositions denying (excluding) such connections. However, the basic and constant meaning of the anankastic must consist in what Sartor calls relative necessity, that corresponds to the combination of the following propositions (1) and (2):

(1) if A then B

(2) C must be realized for B to be determined according to (1)

Being considered equivalent to the following proposition (3):

(3) if A and C then B.

According to Conte [15, p. 362], *anankastic-constitutive* rules create a (necessary) condition for their regulated entity, rather than being themselves a condition.

2.3 A Taxonomy of Constitutive Statements

The considerations of the previous paragraphs allow us to identify three types of constitutive rules, namely:

- rules that directly constitute new entities and are sufficient conditions for the new entity to exist (*thetic-constitutive* rules);
- rules that merely create the possibility of new entities and are necessary conditions for the new entity to exist (*eidetic-constitutive* rules);
- rules that, without constituting new entities, introduce necessary conditions for them to exist (*anankastic-constitutive* rules).

Azzoni, scholar of Conte, completed this taxonomy adding *noetic-constitutive* rules (directly constituting new entities with necessary and sufficient conditions, e.g. the *Grundnorm* of a legal system), *metathetic-constitutive* rules (introducing a sufficient condition, e.g. the rule of the House of Lords Act 1999 that grants the right to membership to 90 hereditary peers) and *nomic-constitutive* rules (introducing a necessary and sufficient condition, e.g. the rule in Article 12 of the Constitution of Ireland saying that "The President is elected by direct vote of the people") [4, p. 161]. Azzoni's taxonomy is represented in Table 1. Introducing *noetic* and *nomic* constitutive rules, however, exalts some critical points in the taxonomy [30, pp. 1289 ff.], which is outside of the scope of the present paper.

Table 1. The six types of constitutive statements as identified by Azzoni [4].

	Declarative speech act	Constitutive of speech act
Necessary	Eidetic	Anankastic
Sufficient	Thetic	Metathetic
Nec + Suf	Noetic	Nomic

This taxonomy suggests that, when dealing with constitutive rules, we need to ask two questions:

- Is the posed condition necessary, sufficient, or both?
- Does it create its effect directly or indirectly?

Answering these questions helps in defining the effects of constitutive rules[2]. Specifically, answering the first question helps to determine its logical formulation. In our research, the second question helps in distinguishing rules that affect the legal source from rules that have only affect the single interpreted rules or entities.

In a more recent work [6], conceived for rationalization of legislative drafting for automation purposes, what we define so far as "constitutive statements" are classified alternatively as constitutive rules or metarules (see Table 2).

Table 2. Constitutive rules and metarules found in legal texts as identified by Biagioli [5].

Classes	Rules	Arguments
Constitutive rules		
Definition	Term	definiendum, definiens
	Procedure	addressee, counterpart, action, object
Creation	Institution	addressee
	Organization	addressee
Attribution	Power	addressee, counterpart, activity, object
	Liability	addressee, counterpart, activity, object
	Status	addressee, object
Metarules		
Application	Inclusion	partition
	Exclusion	partition
Modification	Repeal	partition, position, out, in
	Insertion	partition, position, out, in
	Substitution	partition, position, out, in

---

[2] It is however necessary to be careful in the classification of constitutive rules because it can change depending on the perspective taken [29]: there are views where all rules are constitutive, or none of them are.

2.4 Constitutive Rules for Compliance

In financial regulations, our research has so far identified five types of constitutive statements. We will now present these, describing how each of them specifies the generic form "(*a*) counts as (*b*) in context (*c*)" introduced at the beginning of this section.

– *Legal definitions*: these rules, often contained in the first article of regulations, specify the meaning (*a*) of specific terms (*b*) that are found throughout the regulative text or in a subpart of it (*c*). When terms specifically appear in *legal definitions*, the interpretation of their meaning cannot be arbitrary: every time they occur in the text, they must be understood as meaning the exact combination of words (or sentences) that appear in the definition (*a*). In this sense, legal definitions are creators of intermediate legal concepts, one of the ways to represent constitutivity [28]. Legal definitions are thus *eidetic constitutive rules* in the distinction made by Carcaterra [10]: they are in fact called "stipulated definition" by Guastini [22]. They are thus *constitutive of speech act*, not *speech act* themselves: to have the latter we need also the rules that tell us the legal valence of that concept [30, p. 1278]. When exhaustive (intensional definitions), legal definitions are actually *nomic* constitutive rules, as they do not only define what something *is* (the definiens), but also what something *isn't* (the negation of the definiens). This is true only for intensional definitions, while extensional definitions are, strictly speaking, not *eidetic* rules [30, p. 1278]. For our representation we treat all legal definitions as *declarative speech acts*, and therefore intensional definitions are *noetic* constitutive rules while extensional definitions are *thetic* constitutive rules.
– *Commencement rules*: these rules indicate a (directly or indirectly identified) time parameter (*a*) as the starting point for the validity (*b*) of the regulation (or part of it) (*c*). Commencement rules are *eidetic* constitutive rules in the distinction made by Carcaterra [10], and they are really descriptive, as they do not constitute alone the legal effect: to constitute it, in fact, we also need the rules that describe the legal valence of the concept of *validity*. For reasons of simplicity in our representation, however, in our work we treat commencement rules as *thetic* constitutive rules.
– *"Party-to-the-law" statements*: these rules extend the subjective or objective dimension (*b*) of the norm (*c*), by identifying new addressees (*a*) to it. Imposing a sufficient condition, and its effects being mediated (by the other conditions of the target rule) makes it a *metathetic* constitutive rule.
– *Relative necessities*: Rules restricting the subjective or objective dimension (*b*) of the norm (*c*), by identifying a limitation (*a*) to it. These rules, as explained in Sect. 2.2, pose new limit on the subjective or objective aspect of another rule. They are similar to legal definitions except they do not create a new intermediate concept. Because they impose a necessary condition and their effect is mediated (by the other conditions in the target rule) they are *anankastic* constitutive rules.
– *Amendments*: these rules modify the legal source (*c*), either by adding, removing, or modifying (*a*) the textual content (*b*). Some theorists don't classify these as constitutive rules but rather as meta-rules [5]. According to Carcaterra [9], repeal laws are definitely *thetic*, because their effect (the disappearance of the norm from the legal system) is immediate.

With help from the classification of Carcaterra et al. explained in Sect. 2.3, we can group together these constitutive statements depending on their category, and model their content and effects consequently. We see two groups here: one is composed by *commencement* and *amendment*, who are speech acts, immediately laying their effects either on a legal source or on single rule statements, and the second is composed by *legal definition*, *relative necessity* and *party to the law*, which are rules constitutive of speech acts (and in fact they lay their effects mainly in the vocabulary section and in single rule statements). While legal definitions pose necessary and sufficient conditions, and explicitly introduce an intermediate legal concept (which in turn translates to an autonomous vocabulary entry in SBVR), relative necessities and party-to-the-law statements introduce necessary and sufficient conditions respectively, and do not explicitly create intermediate legal concepts. In SBVR these two statements can be represented in the rulebook, by limiting or extending one or more factors of one or more conditions, or in the vocabulary, creating an intermediate concept or "convenience form" (see Sect. 4.2) that applies within the context.

In order to support the lawyer's work on regulations, it is necessary to capture – and represent in the formal model – the semantics of those five types of constitutive rules. This activity complements the work on regulative rules in producing a complete representation of the semantics of a regulation.

3   Legal Concept Patterns

The specific needs of the research presented in this paper suggested a rather heuristic approach in representing constitutive rules: the focus on regulatory compliance, and thus on regulative norms, means that the constitutive norms are ancillary norms, used to specify and extend the semantics of the requirements. For the same reason, the abstract model does not involve the representation of Hohfeldian powers and thus it is not possible to represent rules attributing powers.

The use of SBVR as a basis for the intermediate language, and the creation of the Regulatory Interpretation Methodology, creates the possibility of an ad-hoc solution where the templates for constitutive rules are specified in the methodology documentation (the "Protocol") in the style of a user manual, and their semantics can be specified within the vocabulary part, through general entries that constitute a template (i.e. $thing^1$ counts as $thing^2$ in *context*). The literature supports this approach for representing constitutive rules since, as explained in the previous section, it highlights the risks and limitations of a omni-comprehensive, generic approach to their representation.

The transformation of regulatory language into SBVR is aimed at providing the knowledge engineers with an unambiguous, understandable text while at the same time maintaining the implicit legal knowledge that is expressed by the original legal fragment. This, however, is not always possible: some legal concepts exist, that can be expressed only by a specific combination of words. Also, sometimes a certain combination of words has a specific legal meaning, corresponding to a precise legal figure. In these cases, the risk exists that aspects of the legal figure are lost in the passage from the legal text to the machine-readable information. In order to store the semantics of these legal figures in the knowledge base we need specific patterns which, in turn, take into account the limitations coming from the targeted formal language backing the knowledge base.

For example, saying that "law x applies to entity/activity y" doesn't necessarily mean that the law performs some particular action: if the statement following the "party to the law" pattern, then it means that for the entity or activity y new obligations apply, i.e., the entity or activity y must comply to the obligations of the law x. In the computable model, the rule should therefore be represented as "it is necessary that entity/activity y *counts as* addressee *in* law x", but can a computer scientist in charge with the formal model (an STE) independently do this when he reads the original "law x applies to entity/activity y"?

A second example is the sentence "in the present law, a handshake has the value of an agreement" which corresponds to the constitutive statement "handshake counts as agreement in Law X". Being an extensional *legal definition*, that statement introduces a sufficient condition ("it is necessary that handshake *counts as* agreement *in* **Law X**") but not also a necessary condition ("it is impossible that [something that is] not [a] handshake counts as agreement in **Law X**"), which would be the case in presence of an intensional definition such as "A meeting of minds with the understanding and acceptance of reciprocal legal rights and duties as to particular actions or obligations counts as agreement in Italian Law". Should the computer scientist (STE) know about legal definitions, their status of thetic-constitutive rules, and the distinction between extensional and intensional definitions, in order to correctly translate the structured English into the formal model? Or should instead be the legal expert (SME) the one in charge of this identification, and deliver to the STE not only the sentence in structured English, but also an indication in the Terminological Dictionary that the sentence follows a specific template with specific semantics?

To represent sentences and forms with specific legal meaning, we thus introduce *legal concept patterns*. Legal concept patterns are related to similar figures, known in the literature e.g. as "technical relations" [5, 17] or "logical relations" (e.g. Hohfeldian relations [23]).

Legal concept patterns are created in the form of a verb concept with generic verb concept roles (e.g. the Legal Definition pattern "definiens *counts as* definiendum *in* context"). When the SME meets a rule that follows one such pattern (e.g. "handshake *counts as* agreement *in* Italian Civil Law"), a verb concept entry is created and the applicable pattern is indicated as a specific attribute. The roles played by the verb concept roles in the pattern definition are important, as they determine the classification of the instances found in the single rules: e.g. the Legal Definition pattern "definiens *counts as* definiendum *in* context" tells the STE where to locate the information related to "definiens", "definiendum" and "context" in the rule "handshake *counts as* agreement *in* Italian Civil Law" (i.e. handshake is the definiens, agreement is the definiendum, and Italian Civil Law is the context)[3].

---

[3] It is also possible to extend the basic patterns into more complex forms by further specifying its verb concept roles, even introducing verb concepts as roles (e.g. adding the vocabulary entry "person1 *shakes hands with* person2" with the attribute "general concept: handshake" results in the more complex pattern "person1 *shakes hands with* person2 *counts as* agreement *in* **Law X**" – see Fig. 1).

Generally, legal concept patterns enhance the interaction between SME and STE during the iterative process of translation by allowing both users to refer to concepts that are defined both in their legal valence (for the SME) and in their formal model (for the STE). When a STE finds "handshake *counts as* agreement" and doesn't know how to model it in the machine-understandable knowledge base, the STE can ask the SME to point at a legal concept pattern to specify the intended legal meaning. The SME would refer e.g. to the *legal definition* pattern that indicates "definiens counts as definiendum in context", and this would at the same time specify the role of the terms handshake and agreement in the formal model, for the STE, and remind the SME that e.g. according to the Protocol (RIM – Regulatory Interpretation Methodology) the context of legal definitions must be explicitly stated.

Legal concept patterns thus assist SMEs in conveying legal content in a way that is understandable by the STE, without abandoning the legal language constructs that express a specific meaning[4].

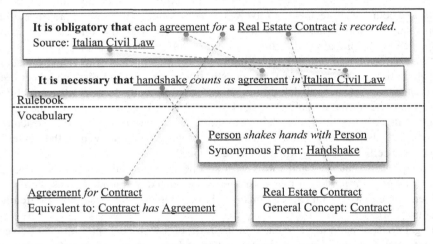

Fig. 1. Example of an implicit ontology built using SBVR. In the example, any occurrence of the verb concept "person shakes hands with person" that is referred to a Real Estate Contract is implicitly inferred as being subject to duty of recording. Additional vocabulary entries such as the noun concept "Real Estate Contract" and the verb concept "Agreement for Contract" enrich the implicit ontology further.

---

[4] By combining the SBVR attributes "general concept" and "synonymous (form)", the Legal Concept Patterns, and verb concept roles, the SMEs effectively build taxonomies – and even simple ontologies – covering portions of the knowledge base (see Fig. 1). Those ontologies are built independently, but can be linked together (e.g. through a common term or pattern). In this way, the burden of enriching the ontology is shared between the SME and the STE, with the first building modules of a legal ontology to express legal concepts, leaving to the latter only the task of merging and consistency checking.

In regulatory interpretation, legal concept patterns can be used for three purposes:

- When **defined in the protocol**, to help representing the most important legal figures. A number of legal concept patterns are introduced in the RIM documentation, that can be used to express common legal concepts. Their use however is not compulsory: the SME can decide to ignore them for their first iterations, relying on them only to disambiguate resulting vocabulary and rules when required by the STE (see the last point).
- When **defined by SMEs within their SBVR transformation**, to represent recurring (also non-legal) patterns easily (see business definitions and convenience forms in Sect. 4.2).
- When **used within SME-STE iterations**, to disambiguate concepts and keep track of the incremental process. Because legal concept patterns are documented both in their legal model (for the SME to understand) and in their machine-understandable formal model (for the STE to understand), they are the common ground that allows the feedback between the two and the progressive refinement of the knowledge base.

4   Legal Concept Patterns for Constitutive Rules

We model constitutive rules according to the doctrine explained in Sect. 2, not using formal logics as suggested in the state-of-the art [19, 20] – as this would be too abstract for an SME to use – but rather modelling single types of constitutive rules as predefined legal concept patterns. Table 3 shows the list of legal concept patterns currently available for constitutive rules:

4.1   General Properties of a Constitutive Rule

In this section we are going to present the common attributes of constitutive rules, and then introduce the five legal concept patterns that specify those attributes for the five types of constitutive rules identified in the table above, with an indication of the meaning of the variables and on the effect that these constitutive rules have on the regulative rules contained within the context of application of these constitutive rules. As illustrated in Fig. 2, all constitutive rules share five main attributes:

- Modality
- Source
- Token
- Type
- Context

Every constitutive statement has exactly one constitutive **modality** out of three possible values (possibility, impossibility, necessity). This attribute indicates the modality in which the original rule entry in the rulebook has been modelled by the SME: a necessity statement can in fact be transformed into an equivalent impossibility statement (and vice versa), but it still makes sense, for authoring purposes, to specify which

Table 3. The list of legal concept patterns currently available for constitutive rules. For each of them, we show the syntax that these patterns normally use in legal language, followed by the syntax used in our research to capture those statement in a uniform way.

Legal Concept	Pattern
Constitutive Rule (generic template)	it is necessary that <u>thing$_1$</u> *counts as* <u>thing$_2$</u> *in* <u>context</u>
Legal Definition	<u>definiendum</u> *means* <u>definiens</u> = it is necessary that <u>definiens</u> *counts as* <u>definiendum</u> *in* <u>context</u> it is impossible that not <u>definiendum</u> *counts as* <u>definiens</u> *in* <u>context</u>
Party-to-the-law	<u>law</u> *applies to* <u>Thing</u> Synonymous Form: it is obligatory that <u>thing</u> *complies with* <u>law</u> = it is necessary that <u>thing</u> *counts as* <u>addressee</u> *in* <u>context</u>
Relative Necessity	<u>addressee</u> *must be* <u>qualified</u> = it is impossible that not <u>qualified</u> *counts as* <u>addressee</u> *in* <u>context</u>
Commencement	<u>law</u> *comes into force on* <u>date</u> = it is necessary that <u>date</u> *counts as* <u>start date</u> *in* <u>rule</u> *or* <u>source</u>
Amendment	<u>old text</u> *is* <u>repealed</u> *in* <u>context</u> <u>new text</u> *is* <u>added</u> *in* <u>context</u> <u>old text</u> *is replaced by* <u>new text</u> *in* <u>context</u> = it is necessary that <u>new text</u> *counts as* <u>old text</u> *in* <u>context</u>

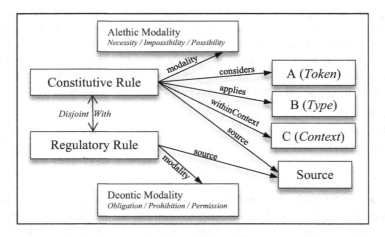

Fig. 2. Ontology of a constitutive rule.

modality was originally employed. The modality also identifies necessary and/or sufficient conditions: sufficient conditions are in fact represented as necessities, while necessary conditions are represented as impossibilities of the opposite. For example, the sufficient condition of a legal definition is "it is necessary that definiens counts as definiendum in context", while its necessary condition is "it is impossible that not definiendum counts as definiens in context".

Source is a general element in SBVR, and our application uses LegalDocML [24] for its representation in a machine-understandable format.

Token and **type** change depending on the legal concept pattern being used, as the present work does not define their semantics (and the semantics of "counts as") at a generic level [20]. This is when the classification proposed by the legal theory and presented in Sect. 2 turns out useful, as it can be used to guide the design choices. While the dichotomy thetic/ipothetic has not been given too much importance (the distinction itself being criticized also in the theory [30, p. 1291]), the distinction of the type of condition being posed (necessary or sufficient) played a major role in distinguishing and modelling those rules.

Finally, every constitutive statement has a **context**. In legal theory, the context of a constitutive rule is used to identify the limits within which the constitutive effects of the rule take place. In our approach, the concept of context is used in a slightly different way: it represents the domains where the rule is relevant. This difference becomes evident when dealing with commencement rules (see below): while in the legal theory the context of a commencement rule is the entire legal system (jurisdiction), in our approach it is used to indicate which legal fragments have their coming into force date affected by the commencement rule. Context can be specified in terms of themes, activities, rulebooks, or sources. For legal rules, the context must include a legal source. The context determines which regulative rules are affected by the constitutive rule.

4.2   The Legal Concept Pattern for Legal Definitions

Legal definitions are eidetic-constitutive rules because they create the *possibility* of a *speech act*. In legal theory they are called *constitutive definitions* and reduced to a thetic-constitutive rule and an agreed definition. Semantic Web frameworks treat them as *technical relations* [17]. In our model we treat extensional definitions as sufficient conditions and intensional definitions as necessary and sufficient conditions. In this latter case we need two rules to represent this condition: the first stating the necessity of it and the second stating the impossibility of the opposite (see Sect. 4.1).

Our approach captures legal definitions by using the rule that is attached to a vocabulary entry (the *definiendum*). Token and type are *definiens* and *definiendum* respectively, and *context* is the context of the definition, i.e. the act(s) where it applies. For regulative rules whose source is within such context, the *definiens* and *definiendum* are thus equivalent: the *definiens* can be replaced with the *definiendum*, and vice versa. Figure 3 shows the replacement of the word "relevant bank". Other examples:

- (*defining a noun concept*) It is necessary that trade *has value* more than 10k USD counts as Relevant Trade in Code of International Trade.

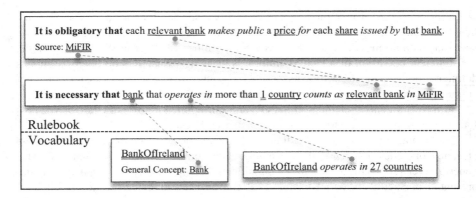

It is obligatory that each relevant bank *makes public* a price *for* each share *issued by* that bank.
Source: MiFIR

It is necessary that bank that *operates in* more than 1 country *counts as* relevant bank *in* MiFIR

Rulebook
Vocabulary

BankOfIreland
General Concept: Bank

BankOfIreland *operates in* 27 countries

Fig. 3. Example of the relationship between an operative rule and the legal definition of a noun concept. Please note that the two vocabulary entries do not result from an interpretation of the regulatory text but rather from internal company data.

- (*defining a verb concept*) It is necessary that person *helps* person that *commit* crime *counts as* person *participates in* crime *in* **Italian Criminal Code**.

Legal Definitions vs. Business Definitions and Convenience Forms

When modelling the representation of concept definitions, it is important to distinguish legal definitions (explicitly introduced by legal texts) from business definitions (created within the company or industry, or by the SMEs themselves).

In our approach, business definitions also cover what in SBVR is defined as "convenience form": in regulatory texts, it is common that parts of text are repeated several times. For example, locutions such as "Market operators and investment firms operating a trading venue" and "bonds, structured finance products, emission allowances and derivatives traded on a trading venue" are found several times in the MiFIR[5] regulatory text. To make the work less repetitive, and to increase human readability of the interpreted rules, the SME can use convenience forms for these locutions (e.g. "trading operator" for the first, and "traded instrument" for the second) in the rulebook, and then define them in the terminological dictionary. As a result, during the process of interpretation the SME divides the regulatory statement into one requirement (regulatory rule, a deontic statement in the rulebook) and one or more definitions (constitutive rule, a structural statement in the terminological dictionary). This process is also very valuable towards automatizing some phases of the translation: once defined, those forms can in fact be automatically detected by NLP tools, thus easing the process of writing SBVR rulebooks. Please note that, from a legal-philosophical point of view, legal definitions are themselves convenience forms [28, 29, p. 112], only with an authoritative value derived from the legal system they are part of.

---

[5] Regulation (EU) No. 600/2014 of the European Parliament and of the Council of 15 May 2014 on markets in financial instruments and amending Regulation (EU) No. 648/2012.

In our approach the distinction between legal definitions on one side, and business definitions and convenience forms on the other, is explicitly stated in the rulebook, as every rule is either a legal rule (legal definition) or a business rule (a business definition or a convenience form). Further distinction between the latter two is to be found in the context: while business rules are valid within a certain class of actions (e.g. pertaining to a specific business activity or industry, or to a specific company), convenience forms are valid within a certain rulebook (because they are subjective, ad-hoc solutions for the simplification of the interpretation job at hand).

4.3   The Legal Concept Pattern for Commencement Rules

Commencement rules are thetic-constitutive rules, as they directly modify the validity of the norms contained in the legal source indicated as context [26]. Token is a date, while type is either a start or an end date of validity. Context is the legal source whose efficacy times are affected. Regulative rules within the context have their applicability restricted by the start and/or end date, as shown in Fig. 4. Examples:

- (*start date*) MIFID II Comes into force on January 10th, 2014.
  It is necessary that January 10th, 2014 counts as efficacy start in MIFID II.
- (*end date*) MIFID I Stops being into force on January 10th 2014.
  It is necessary that January 10th, 2014 counts as efficacy end in MIFID I.
- (*start and end date*) Article 13 is in force from January 1st, 2014 to December 31st, 2014.
  It is necessary that January 1st, 2014 counts as efficacy start in Article 13.
  It is necessary that December 31st, 2014 counts as efficacy end in Article 13.
- (*end and start date*) Article 13 is suspended from June 1st 2014 to June 15th 2014.
  It is necessary that June 1st, 2014 counts as efficacy end in Article 13.
  It is necessary that June 14th, 2014 counts as efficacy start in Article 13.

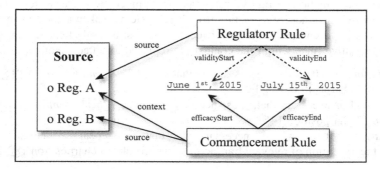

Fig. 4. Ontological model of the relationship between a regulatory rule and a commencement rule. The dashed properties of the regulatory rule are inferred.

4.4   The Legal Concept Pattern for Party-to-the-Law Statements

Party-to-the-law statements are metathetic-constitutive rules, as they create the possibility of "new speech acts" by specifying a new category of addressees for an existing speech act. Token is one (or more) person(s); type is "the addressee of a norm" or "the co-responsible of the breach" or other similar legal liability figures; context is the norm or legal text. Regulative rules within the context have now potentially new addressees. Examples:

- *(context as a legal source)* It is necessary that <u>Person</u> that *participates in* <u>crime counts as</u> <u>subject to the law</u> *in* <u>Article 13</u>
- *(context as an interpreted norm)* It is necessary that <u>Person</u> that *participates in* <u>crime</u> *counts as* <u>subject to the law</u> *in* <u>Obligation_L_143</u>.

4.5   The Legal Concept Pattern for Relative Necessities

Relative necessities (see Sect. 2.2) are the converse of party-to-the-law statements, as they identify necessary conditions for the regulative rule. On this aspect, they are anankastic-constitutive rules. Token is the new requirement; type is the target condition contained in the context; context is the target regulatory statement(s) or legal source. Regulatory statements within the context have their condition extended with the new requirements.

Because they are necessary conditions, they are better expressed as impossibility statements, stating the impossibility of negating the condition. Example:

- It is prohibited that <u>appropriator</u> *steals* <u>object</u>
- It is impossible that <u>person</u> that not *has* <u>intention</u> *to keep* <u>object</u> *counts as* <u>appropriator</u> *in* <u>Rule1</u>.

4.6   The Legal Concept Pattern for Amendments

Amendments are thetic-constitutive rules, as they immediately create new states of affairs (insert/remove/modify regulation from legal system). Token is the new text, type is the old text, and context is the target location as a structural element (e.g. article, clause). Regulative rules within the context are replaced/repealed. Examples:

- *(substitution)* It is necessary that <u>"10"</u> *counts as* <u>"15"</u> *in* <u>Article 13 charposition 134-135</u>.
- *(new text)* It is necessary that, <u>", as specified in Article *13bis*"</u> *counts as* <u>new text</u> *in* <u>Article 13 charposition 145</u>.
- *(repeal)* It is necessary that <u>repeal</u> counts as <u>"with the exception of relevant transactions"</u> in <u>Article 13 charposition 180-227</u>.

4.7   Possibility Statements

SBVR possibility statements can be used for representing exceptions [13]. They can also be used for representing *eidetic* (or, in some cases, *metathetic*) constitutive rules or rules that attribute Hohfeldian powers ("ESMA will publish technical standards on what constitutes a prevalent market condition"): because these rules introduce events that may or may not happen, the purpose is not to trigger automatic conclusions out of those statements, but only to record the eventuality of them to happen and the legal relevance attributed by the law to such administrative acts. Because the scope of our research is regulatory compliance, this information is only marginally relevant and thus needs to be recorded but not semantically enriched. From a theoretical point of view, such statements are constitutive to the extent to which they attribute a new power (as noted previously, Hohfeldian powers are not represented in our approach). In all other cases, e.g. when they foresee the publishing of some documentation, these statements have no constitutive power as they are statements *de jure condendo* and not *de jure condens* [11, p. 19, 30, p. 1273].

5   Conclusions

The paper presented results from applied research on compliance regarding the representation of alethic statements in an intermediate language that is human-readable and that can be mapped to a machine-understandable language. The solution applies notions from philosophy of language and philosophy of law to AI & Law, identifying different types of constitutive statements.

The paper claims that, in order to capture the different legal effects of these statements, we need to represent them through distinct models, with different semantics but a similar syntax, emanation of a general "constitutive rule" pattern.

Legal concept patterns are thus conceived to fill the gap between the SME and STE in the process of translating the regulatory text into machine-readable information, a process that is collaborative and iterative. This process, and this solution, are part of the Regulatory Interpretation Methodology (RIM), that governs the translation process.

Applications of legal concept patterns and the RIM include: building a knowledge base and exploring it; modelling the effects of alethic statements in the document metadata (for metarules) or in the rulebook/vocabulary (for constitutive rules); mapping the knowledge to external ontologies such as FIBO or FIRO (Financial Industry Regulatory Ontology [2]) for reasoning and queries; mapping to a (defeasible) rule language.

In FIRO, reasoning capabilities rely on axiomatization of rules through conditions and factors. The model for regulative rules is explained in previous work [2], while the model for constitutive rules is currently under construction.

The next step for the research is to find a logical formulation for the types of constitutive statement, similarly to what has been done [13] for regulative rules. This will allow the definition of the logical expressivity necessary to represent them in a rule language. Outside of constitutive rules, but towards the same goal of logical formalization, the attention will focus on the formalization of keywords (especially logical operators and quantifiers). The research is also investigating the application of NLP techniques to speed up the translation process, especially in the most repetitive tasks.

Acknowledgments. This work is mainly supported by Enterprise Ireland (EI) and the Irish Development Authority (IDA) under the Government of Ireland Technology Centre Programme.

References

1. Abi-Lahoud, E., O'Brien, L., Butler, T.: On the road to regulatory ontologies. In: Casanovas, P., Pagallo, U., Palmirani, M., Sartor, G. (eds.) AICOL -2013. LNCS (LNAI), vol. 8929, pp. 188–201. Springer, Heidelberg (2014). https://doi.org/10.1007/978-3-662-45960-7_14
2. Al Khalil, F., Ceci, M., Yapa, K., O'Brien, L.: SBVR to OWL 2 mapping in the domain of legal rules. In: Alferes, J.J.J., Bertossi, L., Governatori, G., Fodor, P., Roman, D. (eds.) RuleML 2016. LNCS, vol. 9718, pp. 258–266. Springer, Cham (2016). https://doi.org/10.1007/978-3-319-42019-6_17
3. Austin, J.L.: How to Do Things with Words, 2nd edn. Oxford University Press, Oxford (1962)
4. Azzoni, G.: Condizioni costitutive. Rivista Internazionale di Filosofia del Diritto **63**, 160–191 (1986)
5. Biagioli, C.: Modelli Funzionali delle Leggi: Verso Testi Legislativi Autoesplicativi. European Press Academic Publishing, Firenze (2009)
6. Biagioli, C., Sartor, G.: Regole e atti linguistici nel discorso normativo: studi per un modello informatico-giuridico. Nuovi Modelli Formali del Diritto. Il Ragionamento Giuridico nell'Informatica e nell'Intelligenza Artificiale, CLUESP (1993)
7. Boella, G., van der Torre, L.: Regulative and constitutive norms in normative multiagent systems. In: KR 4, pp. 255–265 (2004)
8. Boer, Alexander, Winkels, Radboud, Vitali, Fabio: MetaLex XML and the legal knowledge interchange format. In: Casanovas, Pompeu, Sartor, Giovanni, Casellas, Núria, Rubino, Rossella (eds.) Computable Models of the Law. LNCS (LNAI), vol. 4884, pp. 21–41. Springer, Heidelberg (2008). https://doi.org/10.1007/978-3-540-85569-9_2
9. Carcaterra, G.: Le Norme Costitutive. Giuffrè, Milan (1974)
10. Carcaterra, G.: La Forza Costitutiva delle Norme. Bulzoni, Rome (1979)
11. Carcaterra, G.: Le regole del Circolo Pickwick. Nuova Civiltà delle Macchine **3**, 16–23 (1985)
12. Ceci, M., Al Khalil, F., O'Brien, L.: Making sense of regulations with SBVR. In: RuleML 2016 Challenge, Doctoral Consortium and Industry Track hosted by the 10th International Web Rule Symposium (2016)
13. Ceci, M., Al Khalil, F., O'Brien, L., Butler, T.: Requirements for an intermediate language bridging legal text and rules. In: MIREL 2016 Workshop, held within JURIX 2016, Nice, France, 13 December 2016 (2016)
14. Conte, A.G.: Konstitutive regeln und deontik. In: Morscher, E.S. (ed.) Ethik. Akten des Fünften Internationalen Wittgenstein-Symposiums (Kirchberg am Wechsel, 1980), pp. 82–86. Hölder-Pichler-Tempsky, Wien (1981)
15. Conte, A.G.: Materiali per una tipologia delle regole. Materiali per una Storia della Cultura Giuridica **15**, 345–368 (1985)
16. Conte, A.G.: Regola costitutiva in Wittgenstein. In: Conte, A.G. (ed) Filosofia del Linguaggio Normativo. I, pp. 237–54. Torino (1° ed. 1981) (1995)
17. Francesconi, E.: A description logics framework for advanced accessing and reasoning over normative provisions. Artif. Intell. Law **22**, 291–311 (2014)
18. Gordon, T.F., Governatori, G., Rotolo, A.: Rules and norms: requirements for rule interchange languages in the legal domain. In: Paschke, A., Governatori, G., Hall, J. (eds.) Rule Interchange and Applications, pp. 282–296. Springer, Berlin (2009)
19. Grossi, D., Meyer, J.J.C., Dignum, F: Modal logic investigations in the semantics of counts-as. In: Proceedings of the Tenth International Conference on Artificial Intelligence and Law (ICAIL 2005), pp. 1–9. ACM, June (2005)

20. Grossi, D., Meyer, J.J.C., Dignum, F.: Classificatory aspects of counts-as: an analysis in modal logic. J. Logic Comput. **16**(5), 613–643 (2006)
21. Grossi, D., Jones, A.J.I.: Constitutive norms and counts-as conditionals. In: Gabbay, D., Horty, J., Parent, X., van der Meyden, R., van der Torre, L. (eds.) Handbook of Deontic Logic and Normative Systems. College Publications, Milton Keynes (2013)
22. Guastini, R.: Six concepts of "constitutive rule". In: Eckhoff, T., Friedman, L.M., Uusitalo, J. (eds.), Vernunft und Erfahrung im Rechtsdenken der Gegenwart (Reason and Experience in Contemporary Legal Thought: Proceedings of the 11th World Congress of IVR, Helsinki 1983), pp. 261–269. Rechtstheorie Beiheft 10 (1986)
23. Hohfeld, W.N.: Some fundamental legal conceptions as applied in judicial reasoning. Yale Law J. **23**, 16–59 (1913)
24. OASIS: Akoma Ntoso Version 1.0 Part 1: XML Vocabulary. Committee Specification Draft 01/Public Review Draft 01, Standards Track Work Product, 14 January 2015
25. Object Management Group: Semantics of Business Vocabulary and Rules. May 2015. http://www.omb.org/spec/SBVR/1.3/
26. Palmirani, M., Ceci, M., Radicioni, D., Mazzei, A.: FrameNet model of the suspension of norms. In: Proceedings of the 13th International Conference on Artificial Intelligence and Law, pp. 189–193. ACM (2011)
27. Rawls, J.: Two concepts of rules. Philos. Rev. **64**, 3–32 (1955). https://doi.org/10.2307/2182230
28. Ross, A.: Tû-tû. Harv. Law Rev. **70**(5), 812–825 (1957). https://doi.org/10.2307/1337744
29. Roversi, C.: Costituire: Uno Studio di Ontologia Giuridica. Giappichelli, Turin (2012)
30. Roversi, C.: Sulla duplicità del costitutivo. RIFD, Quaderni della Rivista Internazionale di Filosofia del Diritto **8**, 1251–1295 (2012)
31. Sartor, G.: Fundamental legal concepts: a formal and teleological characterisation. Artif. Intell. Law **21**, 101–142 (2006)
32. Searle, J.R.: Speech Acts: An Essay in the Philosophy of Language. Cambridge University Press, Cambridge (1969)
33. Searle, J.R.: A taxonomy of illocutionary acts. In: Gunderson, K. (ed.) Language, Mind and Knowledge, pp. 344–369. University of Minnesota, Minneapolis (1975)
34. Van Haarst, R.: SBVR Made Easy. Conceptual Heaven, Amsterdam (2013)

An Architecture for Establishing Legal Semantic Workflows in the Context of Integrated Law Enforcement

Markus Stumptner[1](✉) [iD], Wolfgang Mayer[1] [iD], Georg Grossmann[1],
Jixue Liu[1], Wenhao Li[1], Pompeu Casanovas[2,3], Louis De Koker[2] [iD],
Danuta Mendelson[4] [iD], David Watts[2], and Bridget Bainbridge[2]

[1] University of South Australia, Adelaide, Australia
Markus.Stumptner@unisa.edu.au
[2] La Trobe Law School, La Trobe University, Melbourne, Australia
[3] Autonomous University of Barcelona, Barcelona, Spain
[4] Deakin Law School, Deakin University, Melbourne, Australia

Abstract. Traditionally the integration of data from multiple sources is done on an ad-hoc basis for each analysis scenario and application. This is a solution that is *inflexible*, incurs *high costs*, leads to "silos" that prevent sharing data across different agencies or tasks, and is unable to cope with the modern environment, where workflows, tasks, and priorities frequently change. Operating within the Data to Decision Cooperative Research Centre (D2D CRC), the authors are currently involved in the Integrated Law Enforcement Project, which has the goal of developing a federated data platform that will enable the execution of integrated analytics on data accessed from different external and internal sources, thereby providing effective support to an investigator or analyst working to evaluate evidence and manage lines of inquiries in the investigation. Technical solutions should also operate ethically, in compliance with the law and subject to good governance principles.

Keywords: Natural language processing of legal texts
Law enforcement investigation management

1 Introduction

This paper presents ongoing research of the Australian government-funded Data to Decisions Cooperative Research Centre (D2D CRC).[1] Australia's national security and law enforcement agencies are faced with a deluge of intelligence and other data. Data from sources as varied as financial transactions, immigration movements, vehicle

---

A previous version of this paper was presented at the Third Workshop on Legal Knowledge and the Semantic Web (LK&SW-2016), EKAW-2016, November 19th, Bologna, Italy.

[1] http://www.d2dcrc.com.au/.

© Springer Nature Switzerland AG 2018
U. Pagallo et al. (Eds.): AICOL VI-X 2015–2017, LNAI 10791, pp. 124–139, 2018.
https://doi.org/10.1007/978-3-030-00178-0_8

registrations, call charge records, criminal histories, airline data, social media services, etc. results in a flood of information in disparate formats and with widely varying content. In Australia, such data is often held by individual federal, state or territory agencies and inter-agency access to and sharing of data is generally subject to multiple laws and complicated rules and agreements [20, 21]. Accessing relevant data as well as linking and integrating them in a correct and consistent way remains a pressing challenge, particularly when underlying data structures and access methods change over time. In addition to this challenge, a large volume of data needs to be handled. Usually only a fraction of current volumes can be analyzed. The Big Data challenge is to extract maximum value from this flood of data through the use of smart analytics and machine enablement.

Traditionally the integration of data from multiple sources is done on an ad-hoc basis for each analytical scenario and application. This is a solution that is *inflexible*, *costly*, entrenches "silos" that prevent sharing of results across different agencies or tasks, and is unable to cope with the modern environment, where workflows, tasks, and priorities frequently change. Working within the D2D CRC, one group of authors of this article are currently involved in the Integrated Law Enforcement Project, which has the goal of developing a federated data platform to enable the execution of integrated analytics on data accessed from different external and internal sources, in order to provide effective support to an investigator or analyst working to evaluate evidence and manage lines of inquiry in the investigation. This will be achieved by applying *foundational semantic technologies* based on the *meta-modelling* of data models and software systems that permit alignment and translation by use of *model-driven transformations* between the different APIs, services, process models and meta-data representation schemes that are relied upon by the various stakeholders. It will also provide easily adapted interfaces to third party data sources currently outside of the stakeholders' reach, such as financial transactions. The other group of authors are involved in the D2D CRC's Law and Policy Program, which aims to identify and respond to the legal and policy issues that arise in relation to the use of Big Data solutions by Australian law enforcement and national security agencies.

A 2015 systematic ACM review and mapping [1] of papers on online data mining technology intended for use by law enforcement agencies identified eight main problems being addressed in the literature: (i) financial crime, (ii) cybercrime, (iii) criminal threats or harassment, (iv) police intelligence, (v) crimes against children, (vi) criminal or otherwise links to extremism and terrorism, (vii) identification of online individuals in criminal contexts, and (viii) identification of individuals. The survey also included an array of technologies capable of application to Open Source Intelligence (OSINT), i.e. data collected from publicly available sources in the fight against organized crime and terrorism: Artificial Intelligence, Data Fusion, Data Mining, Information Fusion, Natural Language Processing, Machine Learning, Social Network Analysis, and Text Mining.

Data integration in this context raises serious legal compliance and governance challenges. While the *Onlife* Manifesto considers the use of self-enforcing technologies as the exception, or a last resort option, for coping with the impact of the information revolution [2], nothing prevents the regulation of OSINT in accordance with existing legislation and case law, international customary law, policies, technical protocols, and best practices [3]. Indeed, compliance with existing laws and principles is a precondition for the whole process of integration, as information acquisition, sharing and analysis must occur within the framework of the rule of law.

We have taken this complex set of issues into account in our paper on architecture and information workflows. In order to foster trust between citizens and national security and law enforcement agencies, a commitment to transparency and respect for privacy must be preserved. However, addressing these issues in practice is difficult; in order to achieve a good outcome a more nuanced approach may be required. For example, an insistence upon 'full transparency' may not be desirable for citizens and law enforcement agencies alike if it undermines operational secrecy. Rather, the goal is to identify an outcome that maintains public accountability, understanding that to do so requires effort. The identification of relevant legal, regulatory and policy requirements is the starting point of this process.

2   Architectural Challenges

2.1   Data Integration and Matching

Many prototypes for data matching exist [4]. Matching systems rely either on hand-crafted rules or use simple lexical similarity and concept tree based similarity measures. Complex data structures and entire Service API interface specifications are not covered. Besides extensions for complex structures, simplification of human input and incremental match maintenance are open issues for further research.

Mapping of relational data sources to semantic models is still a predominantly manual activity. Standards, such as XML-DB and RDB2RDF can represent only syntactic mappings. Academic tools (e.g., Karma) allow mapping of relational sources to rich semantic models based on past mappings. Incremental match maintenance (if the model on either side evolves) and support for query APIs and meta-data attributes are not supported in the current tools.

Linked data uses standards such as RDF and OWL for linking knowledge sources in the Web. Although links can be established manually or with the help of various application- and source-specific algorithms, dealing with the semantic interpretation of links spanning multiple sources, the integration of data models, meta-data, and the possible unintended consequences of linking entities is often left to application programmers.

NIEM[2] has emerged as a standard for information exchange between government agencies in the U.S.A. The standard specifies data models for specific message exchanges (in XML format) between two endpoints, and covers core data elements that are commonly understood and defined across domains (e.g. 'person', 'location') as well as community specific elements that align with individual domains (e.g. immigration, emergency management, screening). However, the standard is weak in relation to meta-data and provenance information, and security considerations are orthogonal. Moreover, the architecture is designed for enterprise application integration, not Big Data

---

[2] National Information Standard Model, https://www.niem.gov/.

analytic interfaces. There is no equivalent standard in Europe yet although the EU General Data Protection Regulation (GDPR) (2016/679), which comes into force in May 2018, is motivating its development [5].

Current research focuses on schema mapping where a relationship between data specifications is established [4, 6] in a semi-automated way and requires a domain ontology. Current challenges include dealing with the evolution of schema- and data structure, for example, how to re-establish links across data sources that have been changed, integrating data on the record level – not only on the schema level, and integration of data streams which is particularly important for integration of events.

2.2 Meta-Data

Meta-data management is addressed in various proprietary ways in most commercial databases, intelligence tools, and Big Data platforms. A federated meta-data mechanism is required that spans multiple vendor tools and can capture and manage meta-data such as provenance, data quality, and linkage information at the right granularity (attribute/fact level) for a policing and intelligence context.

Linking data and data access processes to related legal policies and workflows is required but often not provided explicitly. Although there are a growing number of databases that use licenses (CC), most of them do not contain any reference to licenses [7]. Yet, there are some research attempts to compose them [8] or to facilitate their use within a copyright term bank [10], or through a general framework [9].

Meta-data approaches for linked data platforms, such as Resource Description Framework (RDF) annotations, are not standardized and possess no widely agreed-upon semantics. The W3C is currently working on security standards for linked data.[3] However, this standard will be generic and may not meet the specific needs of intelligence and policing applications (e.g. it will lack the capacity to establish and preserve the provenance of the meta-data, which is critical when dealing with data that is sourced across governmental or organisational boundaries). Temporal aspects and the degree of confidence in meta-data are also not considered.

Information governance is as important in Big Data initiatives as in traditional information management projects. Gartner has identified information governance as one of the top three challenges of Big Data analytics initiatives.[4] SAS is also singling out information governance and data quality as major challenges to the success of analytics projects.[5]

In traditional information management initiatives, the focus has been on absolute control of the data attributes such as accuracy, consistency, completeness and other data quality dimensions. Initiatives such as meta-data management and master data management have assisted in creating 'single versions of the truth' for sharing information assets [33].

---

[3] https://www.w3.org/Metadata/.

[4] Gartner Data & Analytics Summit 2017. 20–21 February/Hilton Sydney.

[5] SAS Institute (Suite of Analytics Software), esp. Best Practices in Enterprise Data Governance, https://www.sas.com.

Big Data initiatives involving the placement of disparate data sets into 'data lakes' for analysis have significant information governance issues as they have the potential to force knowledge of contextual awareness and semantic understanding. Once analytical models have been created their operationalization will be restricted without data curation and lineage metadata.

2.3 Workflow Orchestration

Commercial tools predominantly rely on proprietary implementations of analytic tool chains and workflows. Although there is some support for exchange of analytical processes (e.g., through an UIMA specification) in commercial tools (Leidos TeraText) tools are confined to a federation comprising a single vendor's analytic tool chain in many cases. Some platforms, e.g. SAS IM, can access Hadoop file systems and generate analytic scripts for such Map-Reduce architectures. Big Data frameworks (Hadoop, YARN, RabbitMQ) support efficient and flexible data pipelines but require configuration and custom code for integration with vendor tools for each individual application.

Scientific workflow tools (Kepler, Taverna) provide process design and limited execution monitoring and (coarse-grained) provenance mechanisms. However, extensions and novel meta-data models are required to suit the specific tools for policing/analytics and fine-grained provenance.

If more than a few selected data sources are accessed in a data pipeline, data access itself can become an issue since end-user analysts cannot be expected to know all of the underlying technical data models and languages used by the individual systems (e.g., (Geo)SPARQL, (Geo)JSON, XML, etc.). Effective end-user analytic processes therefore must abstract from source-specific query languages at the user level. There is ample academic work on query translation, but mostly for relational databases [11].

Existing analytic tools/products assume that all data is available locally, and require (at least partial) ETL/ingest and indexing of data to facilitate linking, matching, search, deduplication, and quality checking. If federated cross-platform analytic processes are to be supported, systematic mechanisms are required for managing cached and replicated data across vendor tool chains, and local updates made in an intelligence tool should be fed back into the federation.

Multiple workflows and policies may apply to analysis tasks (in particular to identity resolution), individual cases and agencies, and workflows may differ based on availability of data, timeline, and security credentials. As such, in addition to executing a given analytic process it is also desirable to suggest and configure suitable analytic processes specific to the analyst's situation.

3 Architectural Overview

The overall architecture for an Integrated Law Enforcement System is described in Fig. 1. The architecture comprises 8 broad categories of services depicted as blue rectangles.

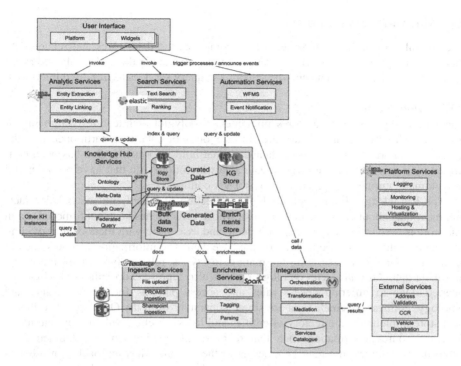

Fig. 1. Architecture overview

The chosen approach is consistent with the TOGAF Architecture Development Method [28], in that requirements management within the project is ongoing and changing stakeholder requirements, changes in partnerships, and technological innovation result in updates to the specifics. With regard to managing strategies according to the approaches listed in [27], the setting of the project can be categorised as a bottom up approach (due to the independence of different agencies), open specifications, and a focus on technical integration and a reference architecture approach. Centralisation efforts that may lead to a more top-down approach are underway but at this point not clear in terms of their impact.

The project has defined an open architecture for data/meta-data management and analytic processes. As such it will translate the best practices from Enterprise Application Integration to the "Big Data" analytic pipelines. The work addresses aspects related to data and metadata modelling and storage, modelling and execution of analytic processes across multiple analytic tools and data sources. Central to this architecture is a framework for effective semi-interactive entity linking and querying of linked data. The project has been working on a comprehensive data management framework that relies on a well-defined shared data and meta-data model supported by vendor-agnostic interfaces for data access and execution of processes comprising analytic services offered by different tools. In the following sections we discuss the main elements of the architecture.

3.1   Knowledge Hub Services

The central *Knowledge Hub Services* area comprises the data stores and related data management services. It governs the repository of data held in the node of the federated architecture and exposes data and the schema via query services to front-end interfaces.

3.1.1   Data Stores

The Knowledge Hub's data stores implement a polyglot architecture comprising of multiple technologies tailored to different categories of data. It is partitioned into the Curated Data area which includes databases that hold information that has been confirmed by a user, and the Generated Data area which hold data that have been derived by automatic enrichment processes but not yet confirmed.

The Knowledge Graph store holds the collection of linked entities. It holds facts and meta-data about entities and their links whose veracity has been confirmed. Data in this store is predominantly structured, linked, and associated with meta-data, providing a semantic entry point for operating on the base data. The information is represented in terms of an Ontology describing the main entity types, relation types, their attributes, and meta-data attributes. The ontology itself is also represented explicitly and can be queried. Due to differing access rules and access patterns for data/meta-data and ontology, entities/links/meta-data are stored separately from the Ontology. The linked data store implements a directory of entities and links enriched with appropriate meta-data and source information such that detailed information can be obtained from authoritative sources that may be external to the system. This approach is needed as data in the law enforcement domain is dispersed among a number of systems owned and operated by different agencies. As such no centrally controlled database can feasibly be put in place in the foreseeable future.

The Bulk Data store holds documents and binary objects (e.g., videos), and the enrichments store holds derived information that may facilitate analysis and can be promoted into the curated data area. As curated and generated data exhibit different lifecycles, volume, and access patterns, these are held in separate data stores.

3.1.2   Ontology and Meta-Data

The contents of the data stores are governed by an Ontology that describes the domain-specific taxonomy of entity types, their properties, and relationships. Akin to a schema definition in a relational database, the ontology acts as a reference for knowledge organization and aids in the integration of information stemming from external sources, where it acts as a reference for linking and translating information into a form suitable for the knowledge hub. The adoption of a linked data approach supported by an ontology provides the flexibility needed to evolve data and schema over time and supports semantic interpretation of the linked elements.

The ontology has been designed specifically for the law enforcement domain and includes a broad spectrum of data types, including structured entities such as persons, organizations, vehicles, communication events, and their relationships; and unstructured data including text documents, video and audio recordings. The ILE ontology is too large to reproduce it in full in this paper; it comprises 19 high-level domain concepts which are further refined into a total of ~ 140 concepts and a taxonomy of ~400 specialized relationship types. The full ontology has been documented in [23]. These domain concepts are closely aligned with the draft National Police Information Model (NPIM), complemented with relevant aspects drawn from the NIEM standard[6] and concepts related to case management. The provenance model is an extension of PROV-O [24].

The ontology is complemented by a meta-data ontology that defines the meta-data attributes that are associated with each entry in the knowledge hub. Meta-data information includes information about provenance, links to entries in external systems and document store, temporal qualification, security and access control descriptors, and information about acquisition process and modification events. Meta-data is one of the cornerstones of information management in the knowledge hub, as the process and timing of information acquisition must be documented meticulously in order to satisfy the legal requirements related to evidence collection. Meta-data elements can be attached to each element (entity, property, link). This relatively fine-grained approach has been selected to be able to support entity linking and merging of information stemming from multiple external sources. The resulting data and meta-data model serve as the foundation for information use, governance, data quality protocols, analytic pipelines, exploration and justification of the results.

3.1.3   Query Services

The services exposed by the Knowledge Hub component relate to querying, keyword search, and meta-data access. At the time of writing, the implementation of the architecture supports structured and keyword search queries about related entities. Graph matching and graph analytics are not currently implemented directly in the hub and must be performed in external tools.

The architecture embraces location- and representation transparency principles that enable front-end applications to access data irrespective of *where* the data is stored and rely on a uniform representation defined by an ontology irrespective of *how* the data is stored in a source system. If a knowledge hub node cannot satisfy a query based on the information it holds, queries to external system can be spawned to acquire the requested information. For this purpose, each knowledge hub maintains a registry of sources that can be queried for information. Adapters for each source type abstract from the specific technologies and message formats used to access the sources. The results obtained from other systems are then expressed in the common representation and merged into a consolidated list of results using entity linking and ranking algorithms.

3.2   Ingestion and Integration Services

Ingestion services provide functions for importing (bulk) data from external systems, such as legacy case management systems and document repositories. The ingestion process follows a pipeline architectural style where data is processed and enriched in stages: data is acquired from the source system, the content is indexed, entities are extracted, annotated with meta-data and provenance information, and linked to relevant

---

[6] https://www.niem.gov/.

existing information in the knowledge hub. The results are represented in terms of the ontology and added to the knowledge hub.

The heterogeneity in representation and data format among different sources presents challenges related to information interpretation and transformation into the ontology used within the data platform. Declarative data transformation methods are employed to convert the different external representations into a common data model and link the resulting structure to the ontology governing the knowledge hub. Ontology matching techniques [11] are used in a semi-interactive process to match and convert user supplied data, and graph mining and matching techniques have been developed to improve the mapping of implicit relationships discovered between extracted entities. The mapping from proprietary data representations to the representation used in the knowledge hub is performed via declarative transformation specified in the Epsilon Transformation Language framework [25]. This approach enables flexible configuration of the transformation rules as sources are added. Moreover, the explicit representation of the transformation facilitates analysis of impact of changes as the internal ontology evolves.

Interoperability with existing data sources and systems can be achieved by constructing executable mappings from the (meta-)data model to the individual system's data models and APIs. Our work goes beyond existing Extract-Transform-Load (ETL) and data access approaches in that the mapping will facilitate bi-directional communication to allow for propagating updates to/from the federated knowledge hub, and model-driven mapping technologies will facilitate maintenance of schema transformations in case source systems undergo extensions or data format changes. We intend to rely on proven meta-modelling techniques for early detection and semi-automated resolution of mapping problems at the interfaces to legacy systems. This approach will help avoid problems related to failing ETL processes and subtle issues arising from changing data sources. Currently, these issues are predominantly left for manual resolution by software engineers.

The pursued approach is well-established in Enterprise Application integration but has only recently been considered in the form of "Big Service" integrated pipelines [12], where a shared architecture comprising of an integrated shared data model and implementation-agnostic service APIs is described. This project aims to translate this idea to the policing and intelligence domain where Big Data requirements are prevalent. Given that the number of sources relevant to policing and intelligence has been increasing, unless systematic data management and access mechanisms are implemented, data quality, provenance and maintenance issues are likely to worsen if the current siloed approach is continued.

3.3 Analytic Services

Analytic services related to the data platform include entity extraction from unstructured text [26], entity linking, similarity calculation and ranking. Entity linking and ranking methods that are effective for sparse data are being developed. Moreover, the inclusion of meta-data attributes in the resolution and ranking calculations is a distinguishing feature of this work. Services provided by commercial tools, such as network analysis and entity linking/resolution solutions, can be integrated in the modular architecture.

The project will provide an efficient, open orchestration platform for Big Data applications that can incorporate capabilities from multiple tools made available through services. Integration of multiple COTS tools will furthermore enable analysts to use familiar languages and tools for exploring information and semi-interactive linking/resolution while relying on capabilities beyond their single tool to perform search, linking, analysis tasks. For static information models, specific-purpose tool chains could be coded by software engineers; however, for end-user specified analytic pipelines and evolving linked data models (e.g. case-specific taxonomies) a comprehensive data and processing architecture is needed.

For efficiency of certain analytic tasks, data may need to be replicated and indexed in multiple locations, subject to security and data access considerations. Keeping these cached copies consistent is a non-trivial problem that we will address through leveraging incremental data propagation and eventual consistency mechanisms. This capability will benefit end users who can rely on automation of complex data management processes, avoid batch ETL jobs and error-prone manual coding of data/metadata transformation pipelines, and improve data consistency and meta-data capture.

3.4 Automation Services

Automation services provide workflow and process orchestration functions. Workflow services will facilitate the enactment of work processes such as acquiring authorization and warrants. Supported by a set of user-facing "widgets" and a library of tasks and processes, common standard processes can be planned and automatically triggered and executed. Process standardization for common tasks may improve efficiency and compliance with policies and legal requirements. In the domain of law enforcement, some processes vary depending on the context of the investigation. A task ontology for investigation planning could capture the semantics of key process steps as well as machine-interpretable descriptions of the roles of various actors and data objects, e.g. evidence, in the investigation process. Automatic configuration of workflows and tracking of their execution may reduce the potential for errors. Moreover, appropriate provenance and chain of evidence can be established by linking the information obtained in the course of an investigation with the process activity and timeline that led to its acquisition. At the time of writing, the automation services component is not yet implemented in software.

3.5 Security

Information security is one of the main concerns in a system designed for law enforcement. Trust in the sharing platform is paramount as an absence of trust and security protocols will prevent sharing of most data. Any data sharing platform in this domain needs to be capable of operating in a multi-agency environment where each agency may have its own security and information sharing policies and protocols. It is difficult to envision a single system and access control policy that would simultaneously satisfy all stakeholders' requirements.

The approach taken in the architecture presented here rests on two principles: (i) a fine-grained security model where access privileges can be associated with each individual fact that in the knowledge hub (akin to the Accumulo database management systems), and (ii) a federated network of linked knowledge hubs that collaborate to provide access to information. The granular access privilege model enables precise control of what information can be disclosed (e.g. some attributes and relationships associated with selected entities may be classified or restricted whereas others may be accessible to all authorized users). The federated architecture aims to build trust in the sharing platform by maintaining control of data access within each individual source organization. Queries are dispatched to multiple nodes and executed under the local node's access policy. The results are then transmitted and collated at the originating node where a query was posed. At the time of writing, the precise access control model and full implementation of the access federation remain the subject of future work.

3.6   Legal Workflow Processing

Another key concern is the incorporation of constraints into the workflow execution to ensure compliance with laws, policies and procedures, including agency legislation and applicable privacy requirements. Natural Language parsing can be used to elicit event specifications that could then be translated into business rules in an executable formal language and issued to an event processor in the knowledge hub [19]. These rules would be used to check and guarantee conformance of analytic processes/workflows and data usage.

At present, there exists a substantive body of works on law and semantic languages —LegalXML, LegalRuleML, RDF and legal ontologies in OWL modelling interoperability and reasoning [13]. However, in the field of policing, law enforcement and security, research and experience have shown that this relationship is by no means simple. Law and policies are subject to contextual and dynamic interpretation across different jurisdictions, legal systems and policy environments [22]. Legal requirements cannot be comprehensively itemized/programmed, nor can the rule of law, privacy and data protection be hard-coded, in particular, where judgement or an exercise of discretion is required [14, 15]. Thus, indirect strategies [16] and design tactics [17], including privacy engineering and risk management, will need to be employed to ensure both compliance with the Australian legal system, and beyond that, the proactive adoption of privacy and data protection safeguards and ethical principles. [18].

3.7   Example

The system has not been tested with end-users users, but the following provides an example illustrating its application and the legal challenges faced by the designers. In the context of police investigations, work processes can be supported by partially automated workflows that help investigators carry out activities efficiently while, at the same time, ensuring that each activity is linked to appropriate supporting information. For example, the planning underpinning an application for a search warrant of premises by an officer of the Australian Federal Police in terms of the *Crimes Act 1914* (Cth) could be partly automated.

The common law imposed significant restrictions on the use of search and seizure powers by government officials and constables based on the inviolability of property interests:

> Against that background, the enactment of conditions, which must be fulfilled before a search warrant can be lawfully issued and executed, is to be seen as a reflection of the legislature's concern to give a measure of protection to those interests. To insist on strict compliance with the statutory conditions governing the issue of a search warrant is simply to give effect to the purpose of the legislation.[7]

The law therefore provides a range of control measures to protect the rights of individuals affected or potentially affected by a search warrant. Apart from the procedures prescribed by the *Crimes Act 1914*, outlined in this example, other Acts may also be relevant, for example the *Australian Federal Police Act 1979* (Cth) and the *Privacy Act 1988* (Cth). There would also be internal agency procedures to be followed, including the Commonwealth Director of Public Prosecution's *Search Warrant Manual* for obtaining and executing warrants under Commonwealth law. A range of legal questions may therefore arise and these may differ from case to case.

Section 3E of the *Crimes Act 2014* sets out a number of requirements that must be met before a valid search warrant can be issued. In broad terms, a successful search warrant application involves two steps. The first is to assemble the necessary material necessary to enable the applicant to present sufficiently persuasive material, on oath or affirmation, to enable an 'issuing officer' to be satisfied 'that there are reasonable grounds for suspecting that there is, or there will be within the next 72 h, any evidential material at the premises.'[8] The second is for the issuing officer, once so satisfied, to address the requirements set out in Section 3E(5) in the warrant itself. These include a description of the offence to which the warrant relates,[9] a description of the premises to which the warrant relates[10] and the kinds of evidential material to be searched for.[11]

The background processes that are needed to support compliance with requirements such as these could be automated using a federated data architecture. Investigation planning could be supported by an ontology describing goals and activities that may be conducted in the course of an investigation. Each goal would be associated with supporting sub-goals and activities as well as information requirements. If an element is added to the investigation plan, subordinate elements could be automatically added and, where possible, executed automatically. This would require a careful preparatory work, as each line of investigation may rise separated legal issues.

For example, if an investigator adds a line of inquiry (e.g. representing the criminal history, if any, of the owner of the premises) to the investigation plan in the case management system, the integrated information architecture as described in this paper would automatically enable a search of its knowledge hub for relevant information, including the criminal history of the subject, whether the person owns a registered

---

[7] *George v Rockett* (1990) 170 CLR 104 at pp. 110–111.

[8] S 3E(1) of the *Crimes Act 1914*.

[9] S 3E(5)(a) of the *Crimes Act 1914*.

[10] S 3E(5)(b) of the *Crimes Act 1914*.

[11] S 3E(5)(c) of the *Crimes Act 1914*.

firearm and, where relevant, whether previous applications were made for warrants relating to the same person or premises, and their outcomes. The system would then populate an application for an arrest warrant, which, after being sworn or affirmed by the applicant, could be presented, potentially automatically, to the issuing officer and the applicant would be informed of the outcome. If the outcome is positive, execution of the warrant must be planned. To facilitate risk mitigation, the system could further determine whether there is information indicating that other persons reside at the same address, whether they pose a potential threat, or whether there are any potential threats linked to surrounding premises and their occupants that should be considered. Such information may be obtained from data sources within law enforcement, such as a case management system containing structured person records, documents and notes; and from sources external to the agency, such as council rate bills, electoral roll information, and information extracted from social media posts by the subject. Linking this information to the corresponding elements in the investigation plan facilitates a more comprehensive and efficient consideration of available information and automation facilitates appropriate execution of mandated investigation practices.

Many legal questions arise in relation to the design of an effective automated system, for example: What are the different types of information that an investigator would wish to access? Where relevant information is highly sensitive to another investigation conducted by a different team, is the investigator entitled to access that information? Once collected for purposes of the warrant, can personal information of the occupants and residents in the area be used and stored for future investigations? Where answers to these legal questions may be clear, they may differ across Australian states and territories [29, 30], and the architecture should be flexible enough to accommodate all legal requirements. In this project we are therefore addressing two separate but linked sets of problems: (i) the coexistence of both artificial and human decision-making and information processes; and (ii) the modelling of specific legal requirements arising from different legal and government sources [31, 32]. We are considering a blended "RegTech" perspective[12] to be applied to law enforcement and security with the due legal protections in place.

4   Intention and Future Work

This paper outlined the data management architecture for supporting law enforcement agencies under development at the D2D CRC. Although some of it is confidential at a granular level, the architectural overview, meta-data driven integration, and legal workflow processing can be disclosed for academic and scientific discussion. We have shown that extensible domain ontologies and semantic meta-data are an essential pillar of long-term data management in a domain where the variety of data and complex analytical processes are dominant. In the law enforcement domain, work processes, mandated procedures-, approval- and data acquisition processes are just as important as the collected information. Moreover, in the age of advanced data analytics, discoveries

---

[12] http://www.investopedia.com/terms/r/regtech.asp.

are increasingly based on automated collection and analysis of data. As a result, questions related to the way in which these processes are conducted and under what circumstances their results may be used are increasingly important and must be considered simultaneously with the design of the business processes and supporting information systems. We contend that policy models for law enforcement and national security purposes should and can be based on an appropriate understanding and implementation of all relevant legal requirements. We intend to further explore the specific requirements pertaining to policing and the wider law enforcement context in Australia and devise appropriate models and implementations that can support and govern the information sharing activities conducted within and across organizational boundaries.

References

1. Edwards, M., Rashid, A., Rayson, P.: A systematic survey of online data mining technology intended for law enforcement. ACM Comput. Surv. (CSUR) **48**(1), 15 (2015)
2. Pagallo, U.: Good onlife governance: on law, spontaneous orders, and design. In: Floridi, L. (ed.) The Onlife Manifesto. Being Human in a Hyperconnected Era, pp. 161–177. Springer, Cham (2015). https://doi.org/10.1007/978-3-319-04093-6_18
3. Casanovas, P.: Cyber warfare and organised crime. A regulatory model and meta-model for open source intelligence (OSINT). In: Taddeo, M., Glorioso, L. (eds.) Ethics and Policies for Cyber Operations. PSS, vol. 124, pp. 139–167. Springer, Cham (2017). https://doi.org/10.1007/978-3-319-45300-2_9
4. Alexe, B., ten Cate, B., Kolaitis, P.G., Tan, W.C.: Designing and refining schema mappings via data examples. In: Proceedings ACM SIGMOD International Conference on Management of Data, pp. 133–144 (2011)
5. Rodríguez-Doncel, V., Santos, C., Casanovas, P., et al.: Legal aspects of linked data – The European framework. Comput. Law Secur. Rev. (2016). https://doi.org/10.1016/j.clsr.2016.07.005
6. Bellahsene, Z., Bonifati, A., Rahm, E.: Schema Matching and Mapping. Data-Centric Systems and Applications. Springer, Heidelberg (2011). https://doi.org/10.1007/978-3-642-16518-4. ISBN 978-3-642-16517-7
7. Rodriguez-Doncel, V., Gómez-Pérez, A., Mihindukulasooriya, N.: Rights declaration in linked data. In: Hartig, O., et al. (eds.) COLD. CEUR, vol. 1034 (2013). http://ceur-ws.org/Vol-1034/RodriguezDoncelEtAl_COLD2013.pdf
8. Governatori, G., Rotolo, A., Villata, S., Gandon, F.: One license to compose them all. In: Alani, H., et al. (eds.) ISWC 2013. LNCS, vol. 8218, pp. 151–166. Springer, Heidelberg (2013). https://doi.org/10.1007/978-3-642-41335-3_10
9. Cardellino, C., et al.: Licentia: a tool for supporting users in data licensing on the web of data. In: Proceedings of the 2014 International Conference on Posters & Demonstrations Track, vol. 1272. CEUR-WS.org (2014)
10. Rodríguez-Doncel, V., Santos, C., Casanovas, P., et al.: A linked term bank of copyright-related terms. In: Rotolo, A. (ed.) Legal Knowledge and Information Systems, pp. 91–99. IOS Press, Amsterdam (2015)
11. Knoblock, C.A., Szekely, P.A.: Exploiting semantics for big data integration. AI Mag. **36**(1), 25–38 (2015)

12. Xiaofei, X., Sheng, Q.Z., Zhang, L.-J., Fan, Y., Dustdar, S.: From big data to big service. IEEE Comput. **48**(7), 80–83 (2015)
13. Casanovas, P., Palmirani, M., Peroni, S., van Engers, T., Vitali, F.: Special issue on the semantic web for the legal domain, guest editors editorial: the next step. Semant. Web J. **7** (2), 1–13 (2016)
14. Boella, G., Humphreys, L., Muthuri, R., van der Torre, L., Rossi, P.: A critical analysis of legal requirements engineering from the perspective of legal practice. In: Seventh IEEE Workshop on Requirements Engineering and Law, pp. 14–21. IEEE RELAW (2014)
15. Koops, B.J., Leenes, R.: Privacy regulation cannot be hardcoded. A critical comment on the 'privacy by design' provision in data-protection law. Int. Rev. Law Comput. Technol. **28**(2), 159–171 (2014)
16. Casanovas, P., Arraiza, J., Melero, F., González-Conejero, J., Molcho, G., Cuadros, M.: Fighting organized crime through open source intelligence: regulatory strategies of the CAPER Project. In: Proceedings of the 27th Annual Conference on Legal Knowledge and Information Systems, JURIX-2014, pp. 189–199. IOS Press, Amsterdam (2014)
17. Colesky, M., Hoepman, J.H., Hillen, C.: A critical analysis of privacy design strategies. In: IEEE Symposium on Security and Privacy Workshops, pp. 33–40 (2016). https://doi.org/10. 1109/spw.2016.23
18. Maurushat, A., Bennet-Moses, L., Vaile, D.: Using 'big' metadata for criminal intelligence: understanding limitations and appropriate safeguards. In: Proceedings of the 15th International Conference on Artificial Intelligence and Law, pp. 196–200. ACM (2015)
19. Selway, M., Grossmann, G., Mayer, W., Stumptner, M.: Formalising natural language specifications using a cognitive linguistic/configuration based approach. Inf. Syst. **54**, 191–208 (2015)
20. Bennet Moses, L., Chan, J., De Koker, L., et al.: Big Data Technology and National Security - Comparative International Perspectives on Strategy, Policy and Law Australia. Data to Decisions CRC (2016)
21. Parliamentary Joint Committee on Law Enforcement. In: Inquiry into the Gathering and Use of Criminal Intelligence (2013). http://www.aph.gov.au/~/media/wopapub/senate/ committee/le_ctte/completed_inquiries/2010-13/criminal_intelligence/report/report.ashx
22. Pagallo, U.: Online security and the protection of civil rights: a legal overview. Philos. Technol. **26**, 381–395 (2013)
23. Grossmann, G., et al.: Integrated Law Enforcement Platform Federated Data Model. Technical report, Data to Decisions CRC (2017)
24. Lebo, T., et al.: Prov-o: The PROV Ontology. W3C Recommendation (2013)
25. Kolovos, D.S., Paige, R.F., Polack, F.A.C.: The epsilon transformation language. In: Vallecillo, A., Gray, J., Pierantonio, A. (eds.) ICMT 2008. LNCS, vol. 5063, pp. 46–60. Springer, Heidelberg (2008). https://doi.org/10.1007/978-3-540-69927-9_4
26. Del Corro, L., Gemulla, R.: Clausie: clause-based open information extraction. In: Proceedings of the 22nd International Conference on World Wide Web. ACM (2013)
27. Mondorf, A., Wimmer, M.A.: Requirements for an architecture framework for pan-european e-government services. In: Scholl, H.J., et al. (eds.) EGOVIS 2016. LNCS, vol. 9820, pp. 135–150. Springer, Cham (2016). https://doi.org/10.1007/978-3-319-44421-5_11
28. Open Group Standard TOGAF Version 9.1 Document Number: G116. ISBN 9789087536794
29. Watts, D., Bainbridge, B., de Koker, L., Casanovas, P., Smythe, S.: Project B.3. In: A Governance Framework for the National Criminal Intelligence System (NCIS), Data to Decisions Cooperative Research Centre, La Trobe University, 30 June 2017

30. Bennet-Moses, L., de Koker, L.: Open secrets: balancing operational secrecy and transparency in the collection and use of data for national security and law enforcement agencies. Melb. Univ. Law Rev. **41**(2) (2017)
31. Bainbridge, B., de Koker, L., Watts, D., Mendelson, D., Casanovas, P.: Identity Assurance, 'Pattern of Life' and Big Data Analytics Report. Project B.1: Identity Assurance, Law and Policy Program. Data to Decisions Cooperative Research Centre, La Trobe University, May 2017
32. Mayer, W., Stumpfner, M., Casanovas, P., de Koker, L.: Towards a linked information architecture for integrated law enforcement. In: Poblet, M., Plaza, E., Casanovas, P. (eds.), Linked Democracy: Artificial Intelligence for Democratic Innovation, IJCAI-2017 Workshop, August, Melbourne, CEUR, pp. 15–37 (2017). http://ceur-ws.org/Vol-1897/
33. Berson, A., Dubov, L.: Master Data Management and Data Governance, 2nd edn. McGraw-Hill Education, New York (2010)

Contributions to Modeling Patent Claims When Representing Patent Knowledge

Simone R. N. Reis[1]([⊠]) [iD], Andre Reis[2] [iD], Jordi Carrabina[3] [iD],
and Pompeu Casanovas[1,4] [iD]

[1] Institute of Law and Technology, Faculty of Law,
Universitat Autònoma de Barcelona (UAB), Bellaterra, Spain
simonerosa.nunes@e-campus.uab.cat,
pompeu.casanovas@uab.cat
[2] Institute of Informatics, UFRGS, Porto Alegre, Brazil
andre.reis@inf.ufrgs.br
[3] Cephis, Universitat Autònoma de Barcelona, Bellaterra, Spain
jordi.carrabina@uab.cat
[4] CRC D2D, La Trobe Law School, Bundoora, Melbourne, Australia
p.casanovasromeu@latrobe.edu.au

Abstract. This paper discusses the modeling of patent claims in ontology based representation of patent information. Our contributions relate to the internal structure of the claims and the use of the all-element rule for patent coverage. Starting from the general template for the structure of the claim, we present contributions to (1) visualization of claims, (2) storing claim information in a web semantics framework, and (3) evaluating claim coverage using Description Logic.

Keywords: Patent · Ontology · Claim structure · All-element rule
Web semantics · Description logics

1 Introduction

Patents are a form of intellectual property aimed to protect human inventions. Basically, the inventor discloses her invention through a patent document and in exchange he or she receives temporary exclusivity rights to practice (manufacture, sell, etc.) the invention. The patent document has several sections, namely: abstract, description, claims and drawings. The section that legally determines what is protected by a patent is the claim section [1, 2]. In this sense, the exact wording of the claims is very important and should receive a closer attention [3, 4]. The wording of the claims is firstly written by the inventor (or his/her patent attorney or agent), but this is not necessarily the final writing. During the application process, claim wording will probably suffer modifications in the final text, as requested by an examiner associated with the government office that issues the patent rights if they are granted. The modifications of the text are often necessary so that the claims represent an original invention for which the inventor receives exclusivity rights.

© Springer Nature Switzerland AG 2018
U. Pagallo et al. (Eds.): AICOL VI-X 2015–2017, LNAI 10791, pp. 140–156, 2018.
https://doi.org/10.1007/978-3-030-00178-0_9

Several works have been proposed in claim interpretation, i.e. legally determine the invention that is protected by the claims of a patent. The PhD thesis of Fabris [5] includes an analysis of claim interpretation in Europe and Brazil. The book edited by Manzo [6] covers claim interpretation in several countries, containing chapters written by local specialists. However, neither Fabris [5] nor Manzo [6] cite the all-element rule widely used in patent interpretation. The so-called all-element rule states that a product is covered by a patent when the product contains all the elements recited in at least one of the claims of the patent.

Notice that modeling patent knowledge is different from modeling patent law knowledge. Ramakrishna and Paschke [14] use first a semi-formal representation format for representing legal (procedural) norms, enriched by an annotated semantic representation later on. However, they do not address the modeling of patent claims, they only address the representation of legal texts. They propose the use of the so-called "Elementary Pragmatics" (EP) approach to modelling patent laws and associated pragmatics, i.e. jurisprudence texts complementing the text of the law.

Wang [7] describes how to legally avoid patent infringement, based on claim interpretation and explicitly describes the all-element rule. The all-element rule is also explicitly described in the work of Schechter and Thomas [8]. Considering the all-element rule, we have identified that there is a lack of works that make an effort to (1) visually analyze claim interpretation, (2) store claim information in a web semantics framework, and (3) evaluating claim coverage using different types of logic such as Description Logic and Deontic Logic. Our work intends to present contributions to these three aspects, as described in the next paragraphs.

It is worth to notice that visualization and visual analytics constitute a recent trend in legal analysis [16]. "Visual law" trends have been already introduced to represent content in legal semiotics [32], human rights law [33], contracts [34, 35], user-centered privacy design [36], risks and security [37], crisis mapping [15], and co-regulatory mobile applications [38]. A better "visualized" interface has been proposed for e-government executable modelling [39], patent statistics representation for quality management [40], and adaptive consent in the European data protection framework [43].

We will concentrate on the logical representation concerning patent coverage visualization content. We choose intuitive tools to face it for practical reasons, as we had in mind usable and shareable interfaces with end-users. Visual analysis of claims using Venn diagrams [9] is advanced by Brainard [10], but only the relationship among claims is discussed, pointing out that dependent or derived claims are more restrictive. Brainard´s work lacks a more precise discussion of infringement by comparing the elements of an object to the elements of a claim. In this work, we propose the representation of elements of a claim as sets visually represented as Venn diagrams. This is different of the representation proposed by Brainard, where only complete claims were represented as sets. We argue that by representing individual elements of a claim as sets, the all-element rule can be better visualized, and the inventors can better understand what is protected and what is not protected by a specific claim.

Considering web semantics frameworks for patent information modeling, many approaches have been proposed. The work of Ramakrishna and Paschke [14] is more devoted to the representation of knowledge of patent law than to represent the knowledge of patent documents. Other works [11, 17–31] that are devoted to model patent documents knowledge do not address the internal structure of the claims. Among these works, a comprehensive approach to model patent document knowledge presented by Giereth et al. [11] stands out. The second contribution of this paper is to extend the ontology proposed by Giereth et al. to include information about the internal structure of the claims, which is absent from the work of Giereth et al.

Concerning the processing of patent concepts an algorithm to compute concept difference was proposed by Karam and Paschke [12]. The third contribution of this paper is to describe how the all-element rule can be considered when processing patent document information represented as Description Logic. We also discuss Deontic Logic in this context.

This paper is organized as follows. Section 2 describes the structure of a patent, including the internal structure of claims. Claim structure is discussed in Sect. 3. A similar presentation for the relationship among claims is made in Sect. 4. Our contributions to represent ontological information of claims are described in Sect. 5. The second contribution of the paper, representing patent claim information with web semantics, is discussed in Sect. 5.1. Processing claim information using Description Logic, is described in Sect. 5.2. Conclusions are presented in Sect. 6.

2   The Structure of a Patent

In this section we discuss the structure of a patent. In order to illustrate this discussion, we refer to Fig. 1, which presents the major patent upper level concepts and relations for patent structure as proposed by Giereth et al. [11]. Notice that the structure of a patent, according to Giereth et al. is composed of some non-textual content (i.e. figures) and some textual content consisting of title, abstract, description and claim (sic).

The modelling proposed by Giereth et al. lacks a more detailed description of patent claims. Both from an internal structure of a claim point of view, as well as from a standpoint from the relationship among the different claims in the patent. In fact a patent may have several claims, which can make references to previous claims, forming a complex layered claiming structure, as it will be discussed later. It is very rare for a patent to have just a single claim, a typical patent has more than one claim. When a patent has a single claim (instead of having multiple claims), this is a sign that the patent has been poorly written.

2.1   The Structure of a Patent Claim

The internal phrasal structure of a patent claim must follow a well-defined pattern, according to the World Intellectual Property Organization (WIPO). This structure is discussed in the WIPO Patent Drafting Manual [13]. The general structure is shown in Fig. 2a, while an example is shown in Fig. 2b. The general structure of a patent claim consists of (i) a preamble, (ii) a transitional phrase (or transition) (iii) and the body of the claim, which recites one or more elements.

The preamble defines the nature of the invention being claimed. For instance, it might be common to have almost identical claims in a single patent where the only distinction is the preamble. It would be possible for a patent to claim very similar

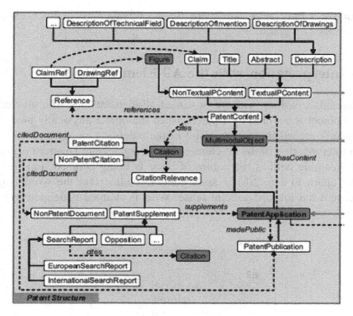

Fig. 1. Major patent upper level concepts and relations for patent structure as proposed by Giereth et al. [11] (the figure presented here is a verbatim partial reproduction of Fig. 2 from [11])

Preamble, transition:	An apparatus, comprising:
Element (#e1);	a plurality of printed pages;
Element (#e2); and	a binding configured to hold the printed pages together; and
Element (#e3).	a cover attached to the binding.
(a) general structure	*(b) one example*

Fig. 2. The structure of a patent claim, according to WIPO [13].

inventions in the form of a method, an algorithm or a computer program, just by having claims with different preambles. From a patent drafting point of view, most patent offices worldwide require the preamble to be separated from the transition by a comma, as shown in Fig. 2.

The transitional phrase determines the relationship among the nature (defined by the preamble) and the elements of the body. In the example of Fig. 2(b), the transition is the verb *comprising*. Notice that from a punctuation point of view, the transition is separated from the preamble by a comma and separated from the body by a colon.

The body of the claim consists of one of more elements and the relationship among them. In the example of Fig. 2, the body of the claim consists of three distinct elements: e1 (a plurality of printed pages); e2 (a binding configured to hold the printed pages together); and e3 (a cover attached to the binding). The elements may be separated by a semicolon or by a line break, but there is no obligation to indicate explicitly the different elements of a claim.

3   Claim Interpretation with the All-Element Rule

Claim interpretation is done with the so-called all-element rule. The all-element rule states that an object is covered by a patent when the object physically presents all the elements verbally recited in a single claim of the patent.

A visual interpretation of the all-element rule using a Venn Diagram is presented in Fig. 3. The preamble defines the nature of what is being claimed. For instance, the nature of the claim in Fig. 2(b) is an apparatus. Notice that the word apparatus is chosen because it has a broad general sense. What is claimed is defined by the nature

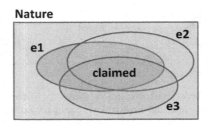

Fig. 3.   Visual Interpretation of the all-element rule.

(preamble) of the claim, restricted by the elements recited in the claim. In the case of the claim in Fig. 2(b), it has three elements (e1, e2 and e3). These three elements restrict the nature of the claim, and the claimed invention is given by the intersection among the three elements. This is illustrated in Fig. 3.

1.   Is the object an *apparatus*?
2.   Does the object comprise *a plurality of printed pages*?
3.   Does the object comprise *a binding configured to hold the printed pages together*?
4.   Does the object comprise and *a cover attached to the binding*?

Fig. 4.   Questions to detect coverage of claim in Fig. 2b using the all-element rule.

The interpretation of a patent with the all-element rule can be done through a set of questions about the nature and the presence of the elements in the object. In order to decide if an object is covered by the claim in Fig. 2(b), the questions in Fig. 4 should be asked.

A given object is covered by the claim in Fig. 2(b) when the answer for each of the questions in Fig. 4 is yes. When the answer for any of these questions is no, the object is not covered by the claim in Fig. 2(b).

4   Relationship Among the Claims of a Patent

A patent typically contains more than one claim. The reasoning for this, from a patent strategy is that patent claims can possibly be invalidated during patent litigation. This way, having more than one claim makes the patent more robust during litigation. Typically, a well written patent has more than one claim.

The claims of a patent can be of two different types: independent and dependent claims. An independent claim does not make reference to any other claim in the patent. A dependent claim makes reference to at least one of the previous claims of the patent. For example, we illustrate an independent claim and a derived claim in Fig. 5. The claim presented in Fig. 5(a) is an independent claim comprising two elements. The derived (or dependent) claim presented recited in Fig. 5(b) adds a third element to the two elements inherited through the reference to the first claim. In this sense, the claim in Fig. 5(b) has three elements: one recited in the claim and two inherited by reference. Notice that the claim in Fig. 5(b) could be rewritten in independent format by textually reciting all the three elements in the body of the claim. The claim in Fig. 2(b) could be a possible rewriting of the claim in Fig. 5(b) in independent form. In this sense, the claims from Figs. 2(b) and 5(b) have the same legal coverage, as they have the same nature and the same elements.

1) An apparatus, comprising:
   a plurality of printed pages; and
   a binding configured to hold the printed pages together.

(a) an independent claim

2) An apparatus, according to claim 1, further comprising:
   a cover attached to the binding.

(b) a derived claim

Fig. 5.   An independent claim and a derived claim.

The coverage of the claims in Fig. 5 can be discussed by using the all-element rule. This coverage is illustrated in Fig. 6(a) for the claim in Fig. 5(a). As shown in the figure, the claim in Fig. 5(b) adds a third element to the two already existing in Fig. 5 (a). The added element acts as a restriction or limitation, further limiting the coverage of the claim from Fig. 5(b), with respect to the claim from Fig. 5(a).

As a consequence of the all-element rule, as illustrated in Fig. 6, a derived claim tends to be narrower than the claim it refers to. This is always true when the reference is made to add new elements to an existing claim.

The interpretation of a patent with the all-element rule can be done through a set of questions about the nature and the presence of the elements in the object. In order to decide if an object is covered by the claim in Fig. 5(a), the questions in Fig. 7 should be asked.

A given object is covered by the claim in Fig. 5(a) when the answer for all the three questions in Fig. 7 is yes. When the answer for any of these questions is no, the object is not covered by the claim in Fig. 5(a). Concerning the claim in Fig. 5(b), it is equivalent to the claim in Fig. 2(b). This way, the set of questions to detect coverage of the claim in Fig. 5(b) is the same set of questions as shown in Fig. 4 for the equivalent claim in Fig. 2(b).

Apparatus

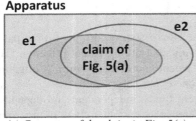

(a) Coverage of the claim in Fig. 5(a)

Apparatus

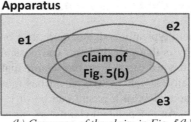

(b) Coverage of the claim in Fig. 5(b)

Fig. 6. Coverage of the claims from Fig. 5. Element e1 is "*a plurality of printed pages*"; element e2 is "*a binding configured to hold the printed pages together*"; and element e3 is "*a cover attached to the binding*".

1. Is the object an *apparatus*?
2. Does the object comprise *a plurality of printed pages*?
3. Does the object comprise *a binding configured to hold the printed pages together*?

Fig. 7. Questions to detect coverage of claim in Fig. 5a using the all-element rule.

5   Patent Ontologies and Claims

Several approaches have been proposed for ontological modeling in the patent domain [11, 12, 17–31]. However, none of these approaches discusses the structure of the claims in detail. Additionally, the relationship among a set of claims is not discussed in these previous publications either.

In the following we discuss some extensions of our view to the two most relevant approaches we found for ontological patent information representation. Giereth et al. [11] carried out a broad ontological approach for patent knowledge based on web semantics (OWL). Karam and Paschke [12] set a description logic approach to model patents claims and performing differences. Both can benefit from our analysis of patent claim structure and the all-element rule.

5.1   Representing Patent Claim Information with WEB Semantics

Giereth et al. [11] is based on web semantics (OWL) including (i) patent metadata, (ii) patent classification (according classifications proposed by patent offices), (iii) patent internal structure, and (iv) patent drawings.

As previously discussed, Fig. 1 reproduces the model for patent internal structure proposed by Giereth et al. [11]. Notice that their proposed model for internal structure only makes reference to a single *Claim* as part of its textual content (TextualIPContent, in Fig. 1). We propose to have a more detailed model that includes a list of independent claims. Each dependent claim would be linked to the claim it refers to (i.e., the parent claim), possibly through a dependence tree. For each claim, the structure composed of preamble (nature), transitional phrase (or transition), and the body of the claim would

Table 1. Proposed xml markers for patent claim content storage.

xml marker	Role in claim description
<claims> </claims>	Claim section
<claim> </claim>	Individual claim
<parent> </parent>	Parent claim
<preamble> </preamble>	Preamble
<transition> </transition>	Transition
<elements> </elements>	Element section
<element> </element>	Individual element

be stored. The claim would contain a list of all of its elements. The suggested xml markers are shown in Table 1.

5.2 Processing Claim Information with Description Logic

Karam and Paschke [12] proposed a description logic approach to model patents claims and performing differences. According the authors, *"their work was motivated by an application in the context of patent applications valuation. In this context one needs to compare the claims of the patent with previous patents solving a similar problem"*. This affirmation is true, but it can be more precisely described when the all-element rule is taken into account. The result section of Karam and Paschke [12] is composed of two examples, which we will discuss in the following sub-sections considering patent claim structure and the all-element rule.

5.2.1 Discussion About Example 1 from Karam and Paschke [12]

The example 1 from Karam and Paschke [12] discusses a comparison of a patent application against a previous patent. The patent application *"is for a chair with only one leg having a seat made only of a light material"*, which indicates that this description is being claimed, i.e. it can be found in a claim of the application, even if the provided text in the example is not in the form of a claim. This claim is represented in Description Logic by the formula in Eq. (1). The previous patent *"describes a chair with three legs and having one seat made of light wood"*, which is represented in Description Logic by the formula in Eq. (2).

$$= 1hasLeg \sqcap \exists hasSeat.(\forall hasMaterial.Light) \tag{1}$$

$$= 3hasLeg \sqcap \exists hasSeat.(\forall hasMaterial.(Wood \sqcap Light)) \tag{2}$$

Karam and Paschke [12] proposed an algorithm to compute the difference between concepts expressed in Description Logic. Their algorithm returns as answer the formula in Eq. (3), which reads *"at most one leg"* for the difference between Eqs. (1) and (2). We agree that the differences between the two concepts reside mainly in the number of legs presented by the chairs in the application and in the previous patent. However, we do not agree that the difference can be expressed as *"at most one leg"*, in a way that is meaningful for patent interpretation. In fact, the expected difference would be two legs, which does not correspond to Eq. (3). Unfortunately, Karam and Paschke [12] do not verbalize the meaning of Eq. (3), which makes difficult to check for possible typos in the equation.

$$\leq 1 hasLeg \tag{3}$$

The comparison between the individual elements of the patent application and the previous patent in example 1 are shown in Table 2. From an all-element rule standpoint, the question is whether the claimed elements in the application were already present in the previous patent. From Table 2, it is clear that element e2 is present in both the application and the previous patent. It is also easy to see that the previous patent has the element e3 of the application, even if it uses wood as the light material. The difference resides in element e1, concerning the number of legs, but the difference is not "*at most one leg*". From a patent law point of view, the following concerns can be raised. First, the examiner would probably not allow the word only in a claim as *only one leg* means *not having more than one leg*, and the form *not having* is not a valid form of claiming. The patent agent should use the wording *exactly one leg*, which is admissible. Second, any patent agent would try to use the broader formulation *at least one leg* while claiming, but then the previous patent would be valid prior art, as a chair with three legs has *at least one leg*.

Table 2. The comparison of the elements in the patent application and in the previous patent in example 1 from Karam and Paschke [12].

Element	Element in the application	Element in the previous patent
e1	Only one leg	Three legs
e2	One seat	One seat
e3	Seat of light material	Seat of light wood

5.2.2 Discussion About Example2 from Karam and Paschke [12]

The example 2 from Karam and Paschke [12] discusses a comparison between a patent application for a watch and an existing physical watch. The application is for "*a watch with at least two displays that are bright*", which is expressed in Description logic by the formula in Eq. (4). The existing physical watch has one display that is analogical and has one display that is not analogical, which is written in Description Logic through the formula in Eq. (5). According to Karam and Paschke [12], their algorithm to compute differences between formulas returns the formula in Eq. (6), as answer for the difference between Eqs. (4) and (5). The formula in Eq. (6) reads "*all displays are bright*". We agree with the difference provided as answer in this example by Karam and Paschke [12].

$$> \; = 2hasDisplay \sqcap \forall hasDisplay.Bright \tag{4}$$

$$\exists hasDisplay.Analogical \sqcap \exists hasDisplay.\neg Analogical \tag{5}$$

$$\forall hasDisplay.Bright \tag{6}$$

The comparison between the individual elements of the patent application and the existing physical watch in example 2 are shown in Table 3. From an all-element rule standpoint, the question is once again if the claimed elements in the application were already present in the existing watch. From Table 3, it is clear that element e1 is present in the existing watch. However, element e2 is not present in the existing watch, so it is not a valid prior art for the patent, meaning that the patent could potentially be granted due to the novelty provided by element e2.

Table 3. The comparison of the elements in the patent application and in the existing watch in example 2 from Karam and Paschke [12].

Element	Element in the application	Element in the existing watch
e1	Has two or more displays	Has two displays
e2	All displays are bright	Not present

Notice that Karam and Paschke [12] introduce an algorithm to compute the difference between two concepts expressed through Description Logic to be used in patent valuation. They also propose to use the difference algorithm to compute the difference between two concepts. However, they do not discuss whether the difference algorithm can be applied altogether with the all-element rule. In fact, Karam and Paschke [12] conclude their work stating that "*a direction for future work would be to investigate the decision making process based on the results returned by the difference and empirical rules derived from experts decisions*". We believe that the discussion provided herein helps to work into this direction by clarifying the role of the all-element rule in experts' decision-making.

6 Representing the All-Element Rule with Descriptive Logic and Deontic Logic

In this section, we express the all-element rule in terms of Descriptive Logic [12] and in terms of Deontic Logic [41]. This is done in the next two subsections. The importance of representing claims in Descriptive Logic and in Deontic logic is justified by the existence of frameworks for automatically computing logic difference between concepts, such as the one presented in [12].

6.1 All-Element Rule in Description Logic

The all-element rule takes the general form of Eq. (7) when written in Description Logic. There will be one of these formulas for each claim in the patent, taking into account all the elements in the claim. Equation (7) is read in such a way that an object covered by the claim has to have all elements recited in the claim; meaning that an object that "*has element e1 and has element e2 and has element en*" is covered by the claim. In order for a physical object not to be covered by the claim represented by Eq. (7) it must follow the conditions given by Eq. (8). Equation (8) is read in such a way that an object not covered by the claim should not have all of the elements recited in the claim; meaning that an object that "*either has not element e1 or has not element e2 or has not element en*" is not covered by the claim. The same applies for a previous patent not describing prior art.

$$= hasElement.e1 \sqcap hasElement.e2 \sqcap \ldots \sqcap hasElement.en \tag{7}$$

$$= \neg hasElement.e1 \sqcup \neg hasElement.e2 \sqcup \ldots \sqcup \neg hasElement.en \tag{8}$$

6.2   All-Element Rule in Standard Deontic Logic

Considering Deontic Logic [41], we have a similar modeling as well. There are early developments by Nitta [44] and Roberts (as quoted in [45]). From our perspective, the all-element rule takes the general form of Eq. (9) when written in Standard Deontic Logic. There will be one of these formulas for each claim in the patent, taking into account all the elements in the claim. Equation (9) is read in such a way that an object covered by the claim has an obligation O to have all elements recited in the claim; meaning that an object that "element e1 is obligatory and element e2 is obligatory and element en is obligatory" for an object covered by the claim. In order for a physical object to be permitted, i.e. not covered, by the claim represented by Eq. (9) it must follow the conditions given by Eq. (10). Equation (10) is read in such a way that an object is permitted P (i.e., the object is not covered by the claim) when the object does not have all the elements recited in the claim; meaning that the object is permitted if "*either it has not element e1 or it has not element e2 or it has not element en*". The same applies for a previous patent not describing prior art.

$$Oe1 \wedge Oe2 \wedge \ldots \wedge Oen \tag{9}$$

$$P(\neg e1 \vee \neg e2 \vee \ldots \vee \neg en) \tag{10}$$

7   A Practical Example

As a practical example we examine the claims in the United States Patent 5960411, also known as the one-click patent by Amazon [42]. The first five claims of the patent are reproduced in Table 4. The nature of all claims is a method. The first claim is an independent claim; the four other claims are derived directly from claim 1 by adding an extra element. The way the claims are derived results in the Venn diagram presented in Fig. 8.

Notice that the first claim can be considered as composed of eight distinct elements. Figure 9 highlights these eight elements by using the proposed xml markers listed in Table 1. Figure 9 also provides the markup for all the tags presented in Table 1,

Table 4. The first five claims in United States Patent 5960411 [42].

1.	A method of placing an order for an item comprising: under control of a client system, displaying information identifying the item; and in response to only a single action being performed, sending a request to order the item along with an identifier of a purchaser of the item to a server system; under control of a single-action ordering component of the server system, receiving the request; retrieving additional information previously stored for the purchaser identified by the identifier in the received request; and generating an order to purchase the requested item for the purchaser identified by the identifier in the received request using the retrieved additional information; and fulfilling the generated order to complete purchase of the item whereby the item is ordered without using a shopping cart ordering model
2.	The method of claim 1 wherein the displaying of information includes displaying information indicating the single action
3.	The method of claim 1 wherein the single action is clicking a button
4.	The method of claim 1 wherein the single action is speaking of a sound
5.	The method of claim 1 wherein a user of the client system does not need to explicitly identify themselves when placing an order

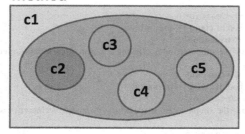

Fig. 8. Relationship among the first five claims in United States Patent 5960411 [42] represented as a Venn diagram.

highlighting the hierarchy of the information. The fact that all the elements are explicitly indicated allows for a more easy application of the all-element rule, including visualization of claim hierarchy, as presented in Fig. 8.

8 General Discussion

This paper presented several different aspects of modeling knowledge about patent documents. The discussion was focused on modeling patent claims, especially in the light of the all-element rule. In this regard, we have demonstrated that organizing the claims by having a clear view of the elements, parent claims and the process of

```
<claims>
  <claim #1>
    <preamble>A method of placing an order for an item </preamble>
    <transition> comprising: </transition>
      <elements>
        <element>under control of a client system,</element>
        <element>displaying information identifying the item; and </element>
        <element>in response to only a single action being performed, sending a request to
          order the item along with an identifier of a purchaser of the item to a
          server system; </element>
        <element>under control of a single-action ordering component
          of the server system, receiving the request; </element>
        <element>retrieving    additional    information    previously    stored    for    the    purchaser
          identified by the identifier in the received request; and</element>
        <element>generating an order to purchase the requested item for the purchaser identified
          by    the    identifier    in    the    received    request    using    the    retrieved    additional
          information; and</element>
        <element>fulfilling the generated order to complete purchase of the item</element>
        <element>whereby    the    item    is    ordered    without    using    a    shopping    cart    ordering
          model. </element>
      </elements>
  </claim>
  <claim #2> <parent> #1 </parent>
    <preamble>The method of claim 1 </preamble>
    <transition>wherein </transition>
    <elements>
        <element> the    displaying    of    information    includes    displaying    information    indicating
          the single action. </element>
    </elements>
  </claim>
  <claim #3> <parent> #1 </parent>
    <preamble>The method of claim 1</preamble>
    <transition>wherein </transition>
    <elements> <element>the single action is clicking a button. </element></elements>
  </claim>
  <claim #4> <parent> #1 </parent>
    <preamble>The method of claim 1</preamble>
    <transition>wherein </transition>
    <elements> <element> the single action is speaking of a sound. </element> </elements>
  </claim>
  <claim #5> <parent> #1 </parent>
    <preamble>The method of claim 1 </preamble>
    <transition>wherein</transition>
    <elements>
      <element>a    user    of    the    client    system    does    not    need    to    explicitly    identify    themselves
        when placing an order. </element> </elements>
  </claim>
</claims>
```

Fig. 9. Proposed xml markers for patent claim content storage.

derivation from parent claims allow for a better visualization of claim hierarchy through Venn diagrams. The clear view of the elements also allows creating claim descriptions for frameworks that process claims expressed as Description Logic or Deontic Logic. An example of such frameworks is the one proposed in [12]. We acknowledge that our observations rely on the validity of the all-element rule. In the next section we discuss the prevalence of the all-element rule for several countries.

8.1   Prevalence of the All-Element Rule

One could argue that the observations made herein rely on the all-element rule, and therefore are only valid in countries where such rule applies. We agree, and still our work is useful in several countries where it applies, notably the United States of America. We also highlight that WIPO (World Intellectual Property Organization) makes extensive use of this rule, including in *Wipo Patent Drafting Manual* [13]. We also know by the experience of some co-authors of this paper, that WIPO uses questions based on the all-element to test student knowledge on patent infringement and prior art. Also, the Spanish patent law was recently modified and the new law includes a mention to claim elements that can be understood as an adoption of the all-element rule. For all these reasons, we believe that the all-element rule will be increasingly followed by European countries in the future. This way, we believe the all-element rule will be used in a larger number of national patent offices in the future, making the work presented here more relevant.

9   Conclusion

This paper aims at extending ontologies and ontological frameworks to represent patent documentation. We highlight the need to store and process information about patent claims. Claims are the section of a patent with the function of defining what is covered by the patent. Our first contribution shows how its representation can benefit from using the all-element rule, visualizing them through Venn diagrams. The second contribution extends the ontology proposed by Giereth et al. to include information about the internal structure of the claims. Our third contribution describes how the all-element rule can be considered when processing patent document information represented as Description Logic and Standard Deontic Logic. Considering that the claim section represents the core of patent document knowledge, we believe these three contributions will be essential for an effective knowledge modeling of patent documents. In the next future, we plan to extend these arguments further, and explore other possibilities for modeling patents (e.g. in non-Standard Logic). Another open area for future work is the possibility of using natural language processing methods for the automatic identification and extraction of the proposed claim models from patents described in natural language.

Acknowledgements. This research was partially funded by Meta-Rule of Law (DER2016-78108-P, Spain). André Reis was supported by Brazilian funding agencies CAPES (Grant BEX 0466/15-8) and CNPq (Grant 312086/2016-4).

References

1. Corcoran, P.: It is all in the claims! [IP Corner]. IEEE Consum. Electron. Mag. **4**(3), 83–89 (2015)
2. Rackman, M.I.: Inventors: protect thyself: careful attention to the claims section will go far toward establishing patent validity and extending the scope of protection. IEEE Spect. **15**(2), 54–60 (1978)
3. Emma, P.: Writing the claims for a patent. IEEE Micro **25**(6), 79–81 (2005)
4. Osenga, K.: Linguistics and patent claim construction. Rutgers Law J. **38**, 61–108 (2006)
5. Guerra Fabris, R.: La determination de l'objet du Brevet en Droit Bresilien et Europeen. Université de Strassbourg. Ph.D. thesis, 22 June 2012
6. Manzo, E.: Patent Claim Interpretation - Global Edition, 2014–2015 edn. LegalWorks, 24 October 2014
7. Wang, S.-J.: Designing around patents: a guideline. Nat. Biotechnol. **26**(5), 519–522 (2008)
8. Schechter, R., Thomas, J.: Principles of Patent Law (Concise Hornbook Series). West Academic Publishing, St. Paul (2007)
9. Parks, H., Musser, G., Burton, R., Siebler, W.: Mathematics in Life, Society, and the World. Prentice Hall, Upper Saddle River (2000)
10. Brainard, T.D.: Patent claim construction: a graphic look. J. Pat. Trademark Off. Soc. **82**, 670 (2000)
11. Giereth, M., et al.: A modular framework for ontology-based representation of patent information. In: Proceedings of the 2007 Conference on Legal Knowledge and Information Systems: JURIX 2007, The Twentieth Annual Conference, pp. 49–58. IOS Press (2007)
12. Karam, N., Paschke, A.: Patent valuation using difference in ALEN. In: 25th International Workshop on Description Logics, p. 454 (2012)
13. Wipo Patent Drafting Manual. Available from WIPO at the following page address. http://www.wipo.int/edocs/pubdocs/en/patents/867/wipo_pub_867.pdf
14. Ramakrishna, S., Paschke, A.: A process for knowledge transformation and knowledge representation of patent law. In: Bikakis, A., Fodor, P., Roman, D. (eds.) RuleML 2014. LNCS, vol. 8620, pp. 311–328. Springer, Cham (2014). https://doi.org/10.1007/978-3-319-09870-8_23
15. Poblet, M.: Visualizing the law: crisis mapping as an open tool for legal practice. J. Open Access Law **1**, 1 (2013)
16. Casanovas, P., Palmirani, M., Peroni, S., van Engers, T., Vitali, F.: Special issue on the semantic web for the legal domain guest editors' editorial: the next step. Semant. Web J. **7**(2), 1–13 (2016)
17. Soo, V.-W., Lin, S.-Y., Yang, S.-Y., Lin, S.-N., Cheng, S.-L.: A cooperative multi-agent platform for invention based on patent document analysis and ontology. Expert Syst. Appl. **31**(4), 766–775 (2006)
18. Bermudez-Edo, M., Noguera, M., Hurtado-Torres, N., Hurtado, M.V., Garrido, J.L.: Analyzing a firm's international portfolio of technological knowledge: a declarative ontology-based OWL approach for patent documents. Adv. Eng. Inform. **27**(3), 358–365 (2013)
19. Trappey, C.V., Trappey, A.J., Peng, H.Y., Lin, L.D., Wang, T.M.: A knowledge centric methodology for dental implant technology assessment using ontology based patent analysis and clinical meta-analysis. Adv. Eng. Inform. **8**(2), 153–165 (2014)
20. Lim, S.-S., Jung, S.-W., Kwon, H.-C.: Improving patent retrieval system using ontology. In: 30th Annual Conference of IEEE, 2004, IECON 2004, vol. 3, pp. 2646–2649. Industrial Electronics Society (2004)

21. Ghoula, N., Khelif, K., Dieng-Kuntz, R.: Supporting patent mining by using ontology-based semantic annotations. In: Proceedings of the IEEE/WIC/ACM International Conference on Web Intelligence (WI 2007). IEEE Computer Society, Washington, DC, USA, pp. 435–438 (2007)

22. Zhi, L., Wang, H.: A construction method of ontology in patent domain based on UML and OWL. In: 2009 International Conference on Information Management, Innovation Management and Industrial Engineering, Xi'an, pp. 224–227 (2009)

23. Law, K.H., Taduri, S., Law, G.T., Kesan, J.P.: An ontology-based approach for retrieving information from disparate sectors in government: the patent system as an exemplar. In: 2015 48th Hawaii International Conference on, System Sciences (HICSS), Kauai, HI, pp. 2096–2105 (2015)

24. Trappey, Amy J.C., Trappey, C.V., Chiang, T.-A., Huang, Y.-H.: Ontology-based neural network for patent knowledge management in design collaboration. Int. J. Prod. Res. **51**(7), 1992–2005 (2013)

25. Hsu, A.P.T., Trappey, C.V., Trappey, A.J.C.: Using ontology-based patent informatics to describe the intellectual property portfolio of an e-commerce order fulfillment process. In: ISPE CE 2015, pp. 62–70 (2015)

26. Nédellec, C., Golik, W., Aubin, S., Bossy, R.: Building large lexicalized ontologies from text: a use case in automatic indexing of biotechnology patents. In: Cimiano, P., Pinto, H.S. (eds.) EKAW 2010. LNCS (LNAI), vol. 6317. Springer, Heidelberg (2010). https://doi.org/10.1007/978-3-642-16438-5

27. Li, M., Zheng, H.T., Jiang, Y., Xia, S.T.: PatentRank: an ontology-based approach to patent search. In: Lu, B.-L., Zhang, L., Kwok, J. (eds.) ICONIP 2011. LNCS, vol. 7062. Springer, Heidelberg (2011). https://doi.org/10.1007/978-3-642-24955-6

28. Wang, F., Lin, L.F., Yang, Z.: An ontology-based automatic semantic annotation approach for patent document retrieval in product innovation design. In: Rui, H. (ed.) Applied Mechanics and Materials, vol. 446, pp. 1581–1590. Trans Tech Publications, Zurich (2014)

29. Calvert, J., Joly, P.B.: How did the gene become a chemical compound? The ontology of the gene and the patenting of DNA. Soc. Sci. Inf. **50**(2), 157–177 (2011)

30. Li, Z., Tate, D.: Interpreting design structure in patents using an ontology library. In: ASME 2013 International Design Engineering Technical Conferences and Computers and Information in Engineering Conference, IDETC/CIE (2013)

31. Zhai, D., Liu, C.: Research on patent warning index-system ontology modeling and its application. In: Proceedings of the 4th International Conference on Innovation and Management, vols. I and II, pp. 2051–2055 (2007)

32. Cyras, V., Lachmayer, F., Schweighofer, E.: Visualization as a tertium comparationis within multilingual communities. Baltic J. Mod. Comput. **4**(3), 524 (2016)

33. Hagan, M.: The human rights repertoire: its strategic logic, expectations and tactics. Int. J. Hum. Rights **14**(4), 559–583 (2010). https://doi.org/10.1080/13642980802704312

34. Haapio, H.: Contract clarity and usability through visualization. In: Marchese, F.T., Banissi, E. (eds.) Knowledge Visualization Currents, pp. 63–84. Springer, London/Heidelberg (2013). https://doi.org/10.1007/978-1-4471-4303-1_4

35. Haapio, H., Hagan, M.D.: Design patterns for contracts. In: Networks. Proceedings of the 19th International Legal Informatics Symposium IRIS, pp. 381–388 (2016)

36. Hagan, M.: User-centered privacy communication design. In: Twelfth Symposium on Usable Privacy and Security (SOUPS 2016), Denver, Colorado, June 22th–24th (2016). https://www.usenix.org/conference/soups2016/workshop-program/wfpn/presentation/hagan

37. Hall, P., Heath, C., Coles-kemp, L.: Critical visualization: a case for rethinking how we visualize risk and security. J. Cybersecur. **1**(1), 93–108 (2015)

38. Poblet, M., Teodoro, E., Gonzalez-Conejero, J., Varela, R., Casanovas, P.: A co-regulatory approach to stay safe online: reporting inappropriate content with the MediaKids mobile app. J. Fam. Stud. (2016). https://doi.org/10.1080/13229400.2015.1106337
39. Olbrich, S., Simon, C.: Process modelling towards e-government – visualisation and semantic modelling of legal regulations as executable process sets. Electron. J. E-gov. **6**(1), 43–54 (2008). www.ejeg.com
40. Laub, C.: On legal validity—using the work of patent courts for quality management: the statistical reutilization of patent court appeal decisions. J. World Intellect. Prop. **16.3–4** (2013), 168–188 (2013)
41. Hilpinen, R., McNamara, P.: Deontic logic: a historical survey and introduction. In: Gabbay, D., Horty, J., Parent, X., van der Meyden, R., van der Torre, L. (eds.) Handbook of Deontic Logic and Normative Systems, p. 80. College Publications, London (2013)
42. Hartman, P., Bezos, J.P., Kaphan, S., Spiegel, J.: Method and system for placing a purchase order via a communications network. United States Patent 5960411
43. Rossi, A., Palmirani, M.: A visualization approach for adaptive consent in the European data protection framework. In: Parycek, P., Edelmann, N. (eds.) Proceedings of the 7th International Conference for E-Democracy and Open Government, CeDEM 2017, pp. 159–170. Donau-UniversitŠt Krems, Krems (2017)
44. Nitta, K., Nagao, J., Mizutori, T.: A knowledge representation and inference system for procedural law. New Gener. Comput. **5**(4), 319–359 (1988)
45. Jones, A.J., Sergot, M.: Deontic logic in the representation of law: towards a methodology. Artif. Intell. Law **1**(1), 45–64 (1992)

Modeling, Execution and Analysis of Formalized Legal Norms in Model Based Decision Structures

Bernhard Waltl[(✉)], Thomas Reschenhofer, and Florian Matthes

Software Engineering for Business Information Systems, Department of Informatics,
Technische Universität München, Boltzmannstr. 3,
85748 Garching bei München, Germany
b.waltl@tum.de, {reschenh,matthes}@in.tum.de

Abstract. This paper describes a decision support system to represent the semantics of legal norms. The focus is on designing and software-technical implementing of a comprehensive system to support model based reasoning on legal norms and enabling end-users to create, maintain, and analyze semantic models, i.e. ontologies, representing structure and semantics of norms.

A model based expression language (MxL) has been developed to coherently support the formalization of logical and arithmetical operations. MxL is intended to define complex, nested, strongly-typed, and functional operations. The paper summarizes research on the design and implementation of a legal expert system built upon model based decision structures. Thereby, three different components, namely a model store, a model execution component, and an interaction component have been developed. The formalization, execution, and analysis is shown on German child benefit regulations.

Keywords: Legal expert system · Deductive reasoning
Rule-based system · End-user centered · Domain specific language

1 Introduction

The formalization of normative texts, regarding to various aspects, e.g., propositional, deontological, temporal, defeasible, etc., is well studied [1–3] and led to valuable principles allowing complex formal reasoning on given laws or contracts. The execution of algorithmically processable formalizations requires the translation of the textual representation, which is a complex and manual task [4]. Advances in natural language processing have at most led to tools or algorithms supporting end-users during analysis, interpretation, and application of legal rules [5]. The user perspective during the formalization process of legal rules has earned rather less attention within the last decades [6]. Higher attention has user-enabled formalization of arguments drawn [7].

© Springer Nature Switzerland AG 2018
U. Pagallo et al. (Eds.): AICOL VI-X 2015–2017, LNAI 10791, pp. 157–171, 2018.
https://doi.org/10.1007/978-3-030-00178-0_10

The paper presents selected related approaches and ontologies for legal reasoning in Sect. 2. In Sect. 3 the model based formalization is introduced and illustrated on a concrete example from the German tax law. The design and implementation with a strong focus on end-user perspective of the resulting decision support system is summarized in Sect. 4. The automated analysis of decision structures and their representation are presented in Sect. 5. Finally critical and concluding remarks are discussed in Sect. 6.

2   Related Work

Within the last decades many attempts have been made to formalize legal systems, respectively legal rules. Thereby, the contributions made by the AI and law community have significantly improved the understanding of the possibilities and limitations of formalization [1].

2.1   A Quick Glance at Legal Expert Systems

Legal expert systems (LES) are well-studied throughout the domain of artificial intelligence and law [1]. Highly tailored to the legal domain the usage of those systems was left up to experts with knowledge in both legal sciences and computer science.

The reasoning within legal expert systems, can be differentiated into several categories, such as rule-based systems (e.g., [7]), case-based reasoning (e.g., [8]), neural nets (e.g., [9]), fuzzy logic (e.g., [10]), Bayesian networks (e.g., [11]), etc. An additional step towards more comprehensive LES was reasoning on (legal) ontologies [12–14]. Expressing logical constraints and relationships between those knowledge objects can be done with description logics, e.g., web ontology language (OWL). Thereby, OWL allows the definition of constraints and axioms in ontologies. Many prior attempts used the W3C standard for modeling ontologies based on RDF and OWL. OWL suffers of the possibility to formalize arithmetical or complex logic operations. Since OWL is an description logic, it was not designed to be used for arithmetical expressions or as first-order (or higher order) predicate language.

Latest approaches on the formalization of legal norms using LegalRuleML have investigated structured processes to move from a natural language to a controlled natural language focusing on the pragmatics of legal reasoning [15]. In the model proposed by Ramakrishna they need two roles, namely legal practitioner and a knowledge engineer, to formalize the semantics in an independent rule representation format, namely LegalRuleML. Another very interesting approach was implemented by [16]. The authors focused on the implementation of a rule management architecture integrating a defeasible inference engine.

2.2   End-User Oriented Decision and Reasoning Systems

Enabling end-users to understand, analyze, and model use cases, which are relevant to them, e.g., user stories, has become an important paradigm in the domains of software engineering. Thereby, the focus is on providing modeling languages, i.e. notations, that are expressive enough to capture all relevant issues of a particular domain while remaining simple enough to be used by end-users. Well-known examples of those end-user oriented modeling languages are UML (Unified Modeling Language [17]), BPMN (Business Process Modeling Notation [18]), CMMN (Case Management Modeling Notation [19]), or DMN (Decision Model and Notation [20]).

BPMN focuses on business modeling and specification [18]. Many attempts have already been made to adapt the BPMN to enable automated compliance checks regarding pre-defined executable rules [21]. The most recent standards provided by the OMG (Object Management Group) have a more specific focus on supporting modeling decision structures in work flows, e.g. business processes or adaptive cases. Both, the CMMN and the DMN, provide end-users with functionality to specify complex decision structures, such as decision tables [20, Clause 8].

This brief sketch of the development shows how important the end-users orientation and empowerment has been for the success of modeling notations. It also shows, that the provision of executable semantics has always been an important part of the standardizations efforts. Within the last years more and more effort has been spent on formalizing work flows and decision structures. This heavily increases the transparency of business processes and adaptive cases and allows optimizations and leveraging of efficiency and effectiveness.

3   Model Based Formalization of Normative Regulations

3.1   The German Child Benefit Regulation

The German child benefit regulation is part of the tax law and can be formalized using an ontological, i.e., model-based approach. The relevant articles from the law are German tax income act §32, and §§62–78. §32 legally defines the term "child" and what attributes are necessary for human beings to be considered as children regarding the German tax law. We expressed the semantics of the types, attributes and the relations in a UML class diagram (see Fig. 1).

The class diagram represents the user-defined semantic model. The result of this model is still the result of a manual interpretation process, which can be supported by analytics from the NLP framework, e.g., [22], to automatically classify legal norms, such as obligations and permissions.

The semantic model consists of four different types, namely *Taxpayer*, *Residence*, *Child*, and *Employment*. Each type has atomic attributes, indicated by '-', and derived attributes, indicated by '/'. For the purpose of this model, calculation of child benefit, it is sufficient for the *Taxpayer* to have only one atomic attribute *name* of type string. In addition, the *Taxpayer* has two derived attributes *isQualified* and *sumChildbenefit*. Both are defined through a MxL expression, which is a strongly typed domain specific model based expression language (see Sects. 3.2 and 4.1).

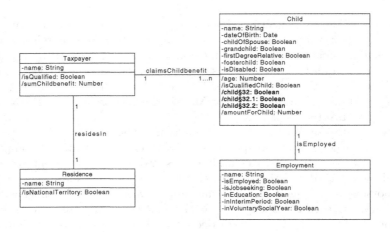

Fig. 1. A semantic model for the German child benefit claim.

3.2 Model Based Formalization

We show the appropriateness of our approach by a concrete example from the German tax law, namely the determination if a taxpayer is eligible for retrieving child benefit and the calculation of child benefit. Different conditions have to be fulfilled, which are stated in German tax law.

Type Definitions. For the determination of the child benefit the German tax law requires several different types, namely taxpayer, child, residence, and employment.

$$t \in taxpayer \tag{1}$$

$$c_j \in child, \ j \in \mathbb{N} \tag{2}$$

$$r \in residence \tag{3}$$

$$e \in employment \tag{4}$$

Relations. The types have relations among each other, which have to be formalized. Thereby, we can restrict our model to three different relations (see Fig. 1). The relation between a taxpayer and its child (5), between a taxpayer and its residence (6), and finally between a child and its employment (7).

$$claimsChildBenefit \subseteq taxpayer \times child :$$
$$(t, c_j) \in claimsChildBenefit \implies k_j \ is \ t's \ j^{th} \ child \tag{5}$$

$$residesIn \subseteq taxpayer \times residence :$$
$$(s, w) \in residesIn \implies taxpayer \ t \ lives \ in \ r \tag{6}$$

$$isEmployed \subseteq child \times employment :$$
$$(c_j, e) \in isEmployed \implies child \ c_j \ is \ employed \tag{7}$$

Derived Attributes and Rules. Finally, the different types have attributes, such as name, birth date, etc., that are required during the reasoning process. Those attributes can either be atomic attributes or derived attributes. The first kind of attributes describe those that inherently belong to a concrete type (e.g., name is of type string). The latter ones are those attributes that can be inferred from other attributes. Consequently, derived attributes consist of the definition, i.e. expression, containing the required information on how the attributes is determined.

The following equations describe how the different attributes, which are required during the determination of child benefit, are defined. The notation for accessing an attribute of a type is the '.' (dot). E.g., $c_j.dateOfBirth$ means the dateOfBirth attribute from the jth child.

$$c_j.age := \lfloor NOW - c_j.dateOfBirth \rfloor \tag{8}$$

$$
\begin{aligned}
c_j.isQualifiedChild := c_j.child\S32 \wedge \\
(c_j.childOfSpouse \\
\vee\, c_j.grandchild \\
\vee\, c_j.firstDegreeRelative \\
\vee\, c_j.fosterchild)
\end{aligned} \tag{9}
$$

$$
\begin{aligned}
c_j.child\S32 := c_j.age < 18 \\
\vee\, c_j.isDisabled \\
\vee\, c_j.\S32.4.1 \\
\vee\, c_j.\S32.4.2
\end{aligned} \tag{10}
$$

$$
\begin{aligned}
c_j.\S32.4.1 := (c_j.age > 18 \wedge c_j.age < 21) \\
\wedge\, \neg e.isEmployed \\
\wedge\, \neg e.isJobseeking
\end{aligned} \tag{11}
$$

$$
\begin{aligned}
c_j.\S32.4.2 := (c_j.age > 18 \wedge c_j.age < 25) \\
\wedge\, (e.inEducation \\
\vee\, e.inInterimPeriod \\
\vee\, e.inVoluntarySocialYear)
\end{aligned} \tag{12}
$$

The Eqs. (9)–(12) specify the different conditions that are defined by law qualifying a child to be considered during the calculation for child benefit. The claim can arise from different articles from the tax law. For example §32 states that a child, which is younger than 18 or disabled is eligible. Beside, it is also considered as child if the conditions in §32.4.1 or §32.4.2 are met.

$$
\begin{aligned}
C^t := \{c_j \in child | (t, c_j) \in claimsChildbenefit \\
\wedge\, c_j.isQualifiedChild\} \; for \; t \in taxpayer
\end{aligned} \tag{13}
$$

$$t.isQualified := r.isNationalTerritory, \; (t, r) \in livesIn \tag{14}$$

The Eqs. (13) and (14) ensure that a child is related to a taxpayer and that the taxpayer lives within the national territory.

$$t.sumChildbenefit :=$$
$$\begin{cases} \sum_{c_j \in C^t} c_j.amountForChild & if\ t.isQualified \\ 0 & if\ \neg t.isQualified \end{cases} \tag{15}$$

$$c_j.amountForChild := \begin{cases} 190 & if\ 1 \le j \le 2 \\ 196 & if\ 3 \le j \le 4 \\ 221 & if\ 5 \le j \end{cases} \tag{16}$$

The remaining two Eqs. (15) and (16) determine the amount for the child benefit based on the number of eligible children.

MxL - a Model Based Expression Language. The model based expression language (MxL) as a type-safe domain specific language was developed in our research group (see [23]) to support reasoning within a generic meta-model based information system.

The meta model based information system incorporates the MxL for defining executable semantics based on a semantic model. MxL users to apply simple (e.g., arithmetic) and higher-order functions (e.g., query operations), and to compose them to complex and nested expressions. In addition it allows the access to methods and operations implemented in Java and can easily be extended by additional operators and functions.

An important property of MxL is its type-safety: It ensures that expressions are valid regarding their static semantics and thus supports users in defining consistent expressions with respect to the user-defined semantic model. Furthermore, MxL's type-safety enables the system to resolve dependencies between expressions, which in turn enables an automated adoption of expressions if referenced elements of the semantic model change.

In order to enhance the usability of MxL, we implemented helpful UI features, e.g., syntax highlighting for better readability, auto-completion including elements of the semantic model, and error localization in case of syntactic and semantic errors.

4   The Model Based Legal Expert System

4.1   Executable Semantics of Legal Norms

To represent the content of legal norms in model based decision structures two aspects need to be differentiated to fully capture the executable semantics: Firstly, the structural semantics of legal norms (see Sect. 4.1). Secondly, the behavioral semantics of legal norms (see Sect. 4.1).

Modeling Structural Semantics of Legal Norms. Modeling structural properties of the norms' content is necessary to capture mandatory legal concepts with their attributes and relations. The meta model based information system [23] empowers end-users to iteratively and collaboratively define semantic models. End-users create and manage domain-specific types as well as corresponding attributes and relations, e.g., a type *Taxpayer* with a relation *residesIn*, or another type *Child* with the attribute *dateOfBirth* and the derived attribute *age*. Since the semantic model is stored in a collaborative environment, i.e. service oriented architecture for the model store, it can be revised by other users. They can refine the model by adding additional types, attributes or relations. They could also remove or add different kinds of constraints, e.g., cardinality constraints (the number of minimal and/or maximal values an attribute has to have), or type- and structure-related constraints, e.g., data types of attributes. As illustrated in Fig. 1, the cardinality of the *Taxpayer*'s relation *Child* is defined to be *1...n*, which allows a taxpayer to claim child benefit for different children.

Modeling Behavioral Semantics of Legal Norms. Besides the semantic structure of legal concepts the behavioral aspects focus is on the interconnection and the reasoning dependencies within structural components, namely types, attributes, and relationships.

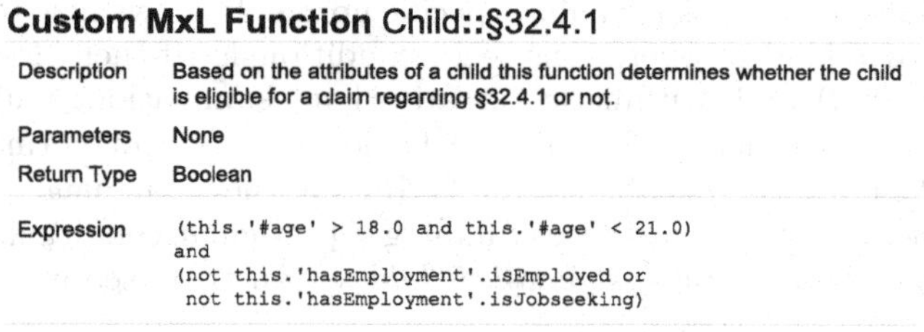

Custom MxL Function Child::§32.4.1

Description	Based on the attributes of a child this function determines whether the child is eligible for a claim regarding §32.4.1 or not.
Parameters	None
Return Type	Boolean

Expression	`(this.'#age' > 18.0 and this.'#age' < 21.0)`
	`and`
	`(not this.'hasEmployment'.isEmployed or`
	`  not this.'hasEmployment'.isJobseeking)`

Fig. 2. Definition of the function *§32.4.1*. A short description, the input parameters, the return type, and the MxL expression are provided.

The listing below shows the formalization of the normative structure deciding on whether a child is eligible for child benefit or not. Thereby, the function uses logical and arithmetical operations to combine numeric (e.g., *greater-than*) and boolean attributes (e.g., *or, and, not*) of the child. It corresponds to the derived attribute definition of Eq. 11 in Sect. 3 (Fig. 2).

(this.'#age' > 18.0 and this.'#age' < 21.0)
  and
(not this.'hasEmployment'.isEmployed or
  not this.'hasEmployment'.isJobseeking)

The decision structure belongs to a child instance, which can be accessed using the *this* keyword. The semantics of the keyword is the same as in object oriented programming languages, namely accessing the attributes or methods from the same instance. Consequently, if the value of the derived attribute $c_j.\S32.4.1$, $c_j \in child$, $j \in \mathbb{N}$ is read, the decision structure above is evaluated and the result calculated.

We can combine and nest the functions to define a function *sumChildbenefit* (see below) determining how much a given taxpayer t receives. The function reflects the Eqs. 13 (line 7), 15 (line 1 and 7), and 16 (line 4–6) of Sect. 3.

```
1  if not this.'isQualified' then 0
2  else
3    let betrag = (children: Sequence) =>
4      if children.count() <= 2 then children.count() * 190
5      else if children.count() = 3 then 2 * 190 + 1 * 196
6      else 2 * 190 + 1 * 196 + (children.count() − 3) * 221
7    in betrag(find(Child).where(c => c.'isQualifiedChild'))
```

If a given taxpayer *tp* is not eligible, the function returns 0. Otherwise, the function determines the number of children for which the taxpayer can claim the benefit. Based on this result, the function calculates the amount that a taxpayer will receive based on a formal calculation prescription derived from the law. This small example demonstrates how partial expressions can be defined as separate custom functions in order to formalize specific norms. It shows how to apply and combine different kind of operations, e.g., conditionals (if-then-else) or logical (and, or, not, etc.) and arithmetic (greater-than, summation, multiplication, etc.) operations, in order to formalize behavioral aspects of normative texts. In addition it shows the capabilities of MxL as a query language, that allows complex queries to retrieve instances fulfilling a particular condition, such as all children having the attribute *isQualifiedChild* set on true (see line 7 in listing above).

4.2 Software Components of the Model Based Legal Expert System

Jandach [24] analyzed different notions of legal expert systems in 1993 with a particular focus the concepts and characteristics that address LES for civil law systems, more specifically the legal system in Germany. Several attempts have been made to implement decision structures, arising from German legal texts, into rule-based systems. However, hardly any attempt has been made to formalize German laws using a model based, i.e., ontological approach, with a reasoning engine that enables users to define expressions and infer knowledge using propositional logic, first-order predicate logic, and arithmetical logic alike.

Based on Jandachs classification of the different components of legal expert systems, namely knowledge base, inference engine, explanation component, knowledge caption component, and dialog component, we designed a software system, which's components are shown in Fig. 3.

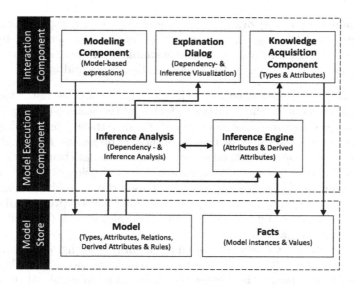

Fig. 3. System architecture consisting of a model storage, model execution components, and interaction components.

The system's components can be classified into three different groups, namely a model store, a model execution component, and an interaction component. Each group is implemented by multiple different software components.

Model Store. The model storage component contains the definition of the model, i.e., ontological description, and the facts provided by the end-user.

Model. A model is described by its types with their attributes, i.e., scheme, and the relations between types. Our implementation differentiates between two types of attributes: atomic attributes and so call derived attributes. Atomic attributes consist of concrete values and have a basic data type, such as number, date, text, enumeration, boolean, and sequence. In contrary, derived attributes are expressed as rules, formalized in a model based expression language (MxL), which is a strongly-typed and functional domain specific language (DSL).

Facts. The instantiation of a model is done through the provision of facts. Those facts are stored as explicit records in the model store. Each model instance has a unique identifier and name which is used for unambiguous identification. An instance does not need to assign a value to each attribute. The attributes are optional and null-value (empty attributes) are allowed.

For our implementation we used a meta-model based information system to implement the model storage component. This meta-model based information system holds all the information about the scheme of the ontology, i.e., model, as well as the instances (facts) of a concrete model. The system allows the formalization of different models, that are logically separated into disjoint workspaces (data rooms).

Model Execution Component. The model execution components are built on top of the model storage and accesses the database of facts, i.e., instantiation of types with concrete values for the available attributes, and the database containing the information about the schema, i.e., types and attributes.

Inference Engine. The reasoning on the given facts considering the formalized rules requires access to the database of facts and the storage holding the information about the expressions required to determine the derived attributes. The input parameters and the return values of those expressions are strongly typed. The inference engine is developed in Java and retrieves data from the meta model based information system. The MxL was designed using "Beaver - a LALR Parser Generator"[1]. The inference engine offers end-users to define semantics of derived attributes in functional expressions, and allows expression of first and second order logic as well as the definition of complex queries (projection, selection, and transformation).

Inference Analysis. Closely connected to the inference engine is the inference analysis component. This component allows the inspection of complex expressions. On the one hand it is possible to get the information about the abstract syntax tree (AST) of an expression. It allows overviews on the provided and derived facts in an object diagram like visualization (see Sect. 5.1). On the other hand the component offers functionality to view complex data flows based on the input parameters to inspect the resulting derived attribute (see Sect. 5.2).

Interaction Component. The improvements of modern software systems with regard to user experience can be considered as one of the main successes of software engineering in the last decade. End-user development and human-centered design thinking have become an established methodology in designing and implementing software systems. Beside the provision of bare functionality, such as logical reasoning, LES need to provide user interfaces that do not overexert users. Instead it will be the challenge for the legal informatics domain to enable end-users to use LES and leverage the full potential that they offer.

In our system the modeling component is separated from the knowledge acquisition component and the explanation dialog:

Modeling Component. Users, e.g., legal data scientists or legal knowledge engineers, are supported during the creation of the model with its attributes and relations by an appropriate modeling component. The modeling component offers functionality to add new types to a model and easily add attribute definitions and derived attribute definitions (MxL). Thereby, the users are supported with a graphical user interface that runs completely as web application.

---

[1] http://beaver.sourceforge.net/, last access on 03/01/17.

Knowledge Acquisition Component. The insertion of facts is done in a separate component, which has been exclusively designed for this purpose. Thereby, types and attributes, describing a case, can be added by the users. Since the model attributes are typed a first type checking is performed within the interface. It is not possible to insert not compatible types, such as text if number is required. The knowledge acquisition components show the inferred values of the derived attributes.

Explanation Dialog. To reconstruct the conclusion that was made by the system, users need functionality providing them with information about the reasoning procedures. This explanation dialog visualizes the information from the inference analysis component. Thereby, given a particular derived attribute the user gets information about the underlying MxL expression and the abstract syntax tree showing the different data values and operators that contribute to the overall result.

4.3   Execution and Computation of Models in a Collaborative Environment

The three interaction components of our system, namely modeling component, explanation dialog and the knowledge acquisition component (see Fig. 3), are developed as collaborative web application components. Each of them can be used through a web browser. They access a shared model store containing the model and the instances via a REST API. This enables users to create new models, i.e., types, attributes, and relations, and share them with other users. Additionally, it is possible to maintain and refine existing models that a user has created prior or that another user created.

The creation of decision structures through the system components is separated from the components handling the instantiation of models and their execution. The knowledge acquisition component, shown in Fig. 4, is structured in to three views: the model view on the left, the form view in the middle, and the document view on the right:

Model view. The model view is an interactive JavaScript component providing an overview of the semantic model. It enables users to select and unselect types, such as the 'Taxpayer' (see Fig. 4), which is highlighted and to which details are shown in the form view and document view. This view shows the relations between types and the cardinalities of those relations. Note, that multiple relations can exist between two types although this is not shown in Fig. 4.

Form view. The area in the middle of the screen is the form view which is vertically divided into 4 regions, namely the title of the selected type, a list of attributes, a list of relations, and a list of derived attributes. This view offers the user the functionality to graphically add new model instances and provide them with proper facts (attributes and relations). The attributes form the atomic properties that belong to a particular type and the references indicate the relations to instances of another type, e.g., 'Residence' or 'Child'.

The derived attributes list shows the evaluated MxL expressions. In addition it offers the functionality to access the explanation dialog by clicking on the question mark beside the input box of a derived attribute (see Sect. 5.1). Since all attributes are strongly typed, the user interface prevents the input of wrongly typed facts, e.g., number instead of boolean.

Document view. The document view allows access to information from a textual resource that was used during the creation of the model. This is considered be valuable since it provides additional information to the form view based on the legislative or jurisdictional texts. Figure 4 shows article 1 entitled "Steuerpflicht" (engl. tax liability) from the the German tax law.

The knowledge acquisition component is a central view of the system and allows the creation of new model instances and the inspection of existing ones. The modeling component is strictly separated from this view. It is not possible to modify the model in the knowledge acquisition phase.

Fig. 4. The front-end of the knowledge acquisition component consisting of three areas: (a) model overview (left), (b) a form-based input dialog distinguishing between attributes, relations and derived attributes (middle), and (c) a set of textual documents to provide additional information about the decision structure (right).

It is necessary to carefully distinguish between the interpretation and application, e.g., subsumption, of a legal norm. Transferring the idea of interpretation of norms to the model based reasoning approach, the interpretation can be considered as the modeling phase. During the modeling phase a legal expert or a group of legal experts formalize the decision structures and specify the required types, attributes, and relations. During a subsequent subsumption phase, legal experts provide the system with facts that constituent themselves in instances of types with concrete attributes and relations. Given this instantiation as input, the model execution component deductively derives new information. It is not necessary that every attribute of an instance is provided the execution component can reason on partially filled types and attributes as well. It is designed to determine as much new information as possible based on the given input.

Once the information of the reasoning structures are modeled and the instances with their attributes and relations are provided, the system is capable of automatically inspecting the reasoning structures regarding data flows and dependencies, which is going to be discussed in the next chapter.

5 Analysis of Decision Structures for End-Users

5.1 Attribute-Based Dependency Trees

Derived attributes, which semantics are specified using the model-based expression language, can potentially consist of complex and nested functional expressions. Those expressions are evaluated before the attribute is accessed in the model store. This read event triggers the evaluation and the execution of the expressions.

A dependency tree for a given derived attribute can automatically be generated by the inference analysis component and forwarded to the dialog component which renders the resulting tree. Thereby, the leaves of the given tree denote either constants, atomic variables, such as 'isEmployed' or 'isJobseeking' (both boolean), or other derived attributes, such as '#age'. The nodes within the tree constitute the various logical and arithmetical operations, such as 'GreaterThan' or 'And', that evaluated during the execution.

The dependency tree view is widely used in semantic program analysis. It enables end-users to understand and reconstruct how the different input parameters contribute to the final result. Consequently, this view fosters the comprehensibility and traceability of a complex decisions structures.

5.2 Interactive Data Flow Graphs

In addition to means for collaborative modeling, model based reasoning, and inspection of attribute-based dependency trees the system offers a holistic perspective to view and explore the data flow throughout a semantic model. This data flows can again be represented as directed graphs, where the nodes represent attributes or types and the edges represent the usage or contribution within a subsequent type or derived attribute. Thereby, the inference analysis component inspects the data flow during the execution of expressions and passes this information to the dialog component, which renders and visualizes the interactive graphs.

For instance, the data flow graph allows the analysis of contributing variables to the derived attribute 'isQualifiedChild' of a child (Eqs. 9–12 in Sect. 3.2). Thereby, it can be seen which attributes influence each other and how it is determined whether a child is eligible for retrieving a benefit or not. It also allows the inspection, which facts are given by a particular instance and how a change in the facts would influence the different attributes resulting into claims that someone has or has not.

6   Conclusion

This paper is a contribution enabling end-users to create executable models representing the semantics of statutory texts, i.e. laws. Based on the theory and prior approaches in the domain of artificial intelligence, in particular legal expert systems and ontologies, we designed an implemented a model based expert system focusing on the end-users perspective. We divided the system into three different components: a model store, a model execution component, and an interaction component.

The model store is a meta-model based information systems persisting the model, i.e. schema, consisting of types, attributes, derived attributes, relations and the facts, i.e. instances of the model. The model execution component is a deductive reasoning engine providing a domain specific language enabling end-users to create executable rules defining the derived attributes. The interaction component is a web based application fostering collaborative access to the model store to create and maintain models and to provide facts. In addition the system has components to analyze the dependency tree of derived attributes and the data flow within a model.

References

1. Bench-Capon, T., et al.: A history of AI and Law in 50 papers: 25 years of the international conference on AI and Law. Artif. Intell. Law **20**, 215–319 (2012)
2. Sartor, G.: Legal Reasoning: A Cognitive Approach to the Law, Ser. A Treatise of Legal Philosophy and General Jurisprudence. Springer, Dordrecht (2005)
3. Rissland, E.L., Ashley, K.D., Loui, R.P.: AI and law: a fruitful synergy. Artif. Intell. **150**(1–2), 1–15 (2003)
4. van Engers, T.M., van Doesburg, R.: First steps towards a formal analysis of law. In: Proceedings of eKNOW (2015)
5. Francesconi, E. (ed.): Semantic Processing of Legal Texts: Where the Language of Law Meets the Law of Language. Springer, Heidelberg (2010)
6. Liao, S.-H.: Expert system methodologies and applications–a decade review from 1995 to 2004. Expert Syst. Appl. **28**(1), 93–103 (2005)
7. Prakken, H., Sartor, G.: Law and logic: a review from an argumentation perspective. Artif. Intell. **227**, 214–245 (2015)
8. Ashley, K.D., Rissland, E.L.: A case-based approach to modeling legal expertise. IEEE Expert **3**(3), 70–77 (1988)
9. Aikenhead, M.: Uses and abuses of neural networks in law. Santa Clara Comput. High Tech. LJ **12**, 31 (1996)
10. Gerathewohl, P.: Erschließung unbestimmter Rechtsbegriffe mit Hilfe des Computers: Ein Versuch am Beispiel der angemessenen Wartezeit bei §142 StGB. Dissertation, Eberhard-Karls-Universität, Tübingen (1987)
11. Timmer, S.T., Meyer, J.-J.C., Prakken, H., Renooij, S., Verheij, B.: A structure-guided approach to capturing Bayesian reasoning about legal evidence in argumentation. In: Proceedings of the 15th International Conference on Artificial Intelligence and Law, pp. 109–118 (2015)
12. Francesconi, E. (ed.): Proceedings of LOAIT 2010 -: IV Workshop on Legal Ontologies and Artificial Intelligence Techniques

13. Wyner, A.: An ontology in OWL for legal case-based reasoning. Artif. Intell. Law **16**(4), 361–387 (2008)
14. Casanovas, P., Biasiotti, M. A., Francesconi, E., Sagri, M.T. (eds.): Proceedings of LOAIT 2007: II Workshop on Legal Ontologies and Artificial Intelligence Techniques (2007)
15. Ramakrishna, S., Paschke, A.: A process for knowledge transformation and knowledge representation of patent law. In: Bikakis, A., Fodor, P., Roman, D. (eds.) RuleML 2014. LNCS, vol. 8620, pp. 311–328. Springer, Cham (2014). https://doi.org/10.1007/978-3-319-09870-8_23
16. Islam, M.B., Governatori, G.: Ruleoms: a rule-based online management system. In: Proceedings of the 15th International Conference on Artificial Intelligence and Law. ACM, pp. 187–191 (2015)
17. Object Management Group: Unified Modeling Language (UML) 2.4.1 Infrastructure. http://www.omg.org/spec/UML/2.4.1/
18. Object Management Group: Business Process Model and Notation (BPMN), Version 2.0
19. Object Management Group: Case Management Model And Notation Version 1.0
20. Object Management Group: Decision Model and Notation Version 1.0
21. Governatori, G. (ed.): Law, logic and business processes. In: 2010 Third International Workshop on Requirements Engineering and Law (RELAW) (2010)
22. Waltl, B., Matthes, F., Waltl, T., Grass, T.: LEXIA: a data science environment for Semantic analysis of German legal texts. Jusletter IT (2016)
23. Reschenhofer, T., Monahov, I., Matthes, F.: Type-safety in EA model analysis. In: IEEE EDOCW (2014)
24. Jandach, T.: Juristische Expertensysteme: Methodische Grundlagen ihrer Entwicklung. Springer, Heidelberg (1993). https://doi.org/10.1007/978-3-642-84978-7

Causal Models of Legal Cases

Ruta Liepina[1](✉)(iD), Giovanni Sartor[1,2], and Adam Wyner[3]

[1] Law Department, European University Institute, Florence, Italy
Ruta.Liepina@EUI.eu
[2] CIRSFID, University of Bologna, Bologna, Italy
[3] School of Law and Department of Computer Science, Swansea University,
Swansea, UK

Abstract. Legal causation is a complex aspect of legal reasoning. Due to its significant role in the attribution of legal responsibility, it is important that there is a clear understanding of the requirements for establishing and reasoning with causal links. This paper presents preliminary results of modelling causal arguments based on the legal decisions with particular focus on physical causation. We introduce a semi-formal framework for reasoning with causation that uses strict and defeasible rules for modelling factual causation arguments in legal cases. We further discuss the complex relation between formal, common sense, norm and policy based considerations of causation in legal decision making with particular focus on their role in comparing alternative causal explanations.

Keywords: Causation · Law · Evidence · Legal reasoning

1 Introduction

This study is inspired by the theoretical challenges of establishing causation.[1] We focus on cases addressed by the US Vaccine Injury Court [17] and in particular the *Althen's* decision [1]. In vaccine cases a Special Master has the task of 'determining the types of proceedings necessary for presenting the relevant evidence and ultimately weighing the evidence in rendering a final, enforceable decision' [2]. While the Special Master has the training and experience in addressing causation in vaccine cases, uncertainties remain, concerning not only specific decisions on causality, but also the criteria to be used in such decisions. In fact, in the *Althen's* decision, the Special Master affirmed that the criteria for establishing a satisfactory causal connection is 'an unresolved legal issue'; and moreover, he emphasised that 'without articulate standards providing guidance [on causation], the experts bring their own beliefs and biases into the courtroom'.

---

[1] The current article is version of our semi-formal causal argumentation framework, which was presented at AICOL Workshop, JURIX 2017, Luxembourg, Luxembourg. Another version was presented at the Evidence and Decision Making Workshop in ICAIL 2017, London, United Kingdom; that work is being reworked for publication.

© Springer Nature Switzerland AG 2018
U. Pagallo et al. (Eds.): AICOL VI-X 2015–2017, LNAI 10791, pp. 172–186, 2018.
https://doi.org/10.1007/978-3-030-00178-0_11

With causation being an active area of research and having practical implications, this paper discusses the connection between the cause-in-fact and legal causation as observed in the case law. Our study aims to provide analysis of the arguments establishing the cause-in-fact. This paper contributes to the current state of art by providing a logic-based approach designed for causal argument analysis in the law. While our study is at its early stages, it has already shown that it is possible to capture important aspects of causal reasoning in the law. Despite many more challenges that have to be addressed before causal issues can be fully understood in the law, this is a step towards argument modelling and assessment with the potential to support practical analysis of civil law cases (especially those relying on expert testimonies).

We present our analysis in three main sections. In Sect. 2, we begin by introducing the relevant theories of causation and the facts of the case study. We focus on the legal and formal approaches of causation. These use various logic and common sense reasoning tools and have the potential to be applied in law. In Sect. 3, we introduce a semi-formal framework for modelling causal arguments in legal cases with notions of causal and evidential links as well as strict and defeasible rules. We present an application of our framework through a case analysis of *Althen's* vaccine injury case. We model two conflicting causal arguments as presented by the medical experts in the case. We comment on the use of causal language and logical structures present in the expert testimonies. In Sect. 4, we further discuss the complex relationship between formal, common sense, norm and policy based considerations of causation in legal decision making, with particular focus on their role in comparing alternative causal explanations. In Sect. 5, we conclude with discussion of future developments of our framework, including norm based extensions.

2   Background

Our interdisciplinary study aims to bridge the formal theories of causation and the needs of the practical field of law. As many other areas that concern themselves with causal issues, law has adapted various domain specific measures to deal with causality [12]. In this section, we introduce two current views on causation: Hart and Honoré's NESS [9, 19], which represents the legal perspective, and Halpern and Pearl's [8] formal theory of 'actual causation'. We also introduce the facts and legal norms of the working case example.

2.1   Theories of Causation

Causation is a theoretically rich field [3], but not all discussions are relevant in legal analysis. Here, we discuss two groups of approaches of causal analysis, starting with Hart and Honoré's [9] theory of necessary and sufficient conditions in common sense analysis in law. We then present a formal theory of causation, Halpern and Pearl's [8] actual causation.

Legal Causation: Hart and Honoré's Approach. With 'Causation in the Law', Hart and Honoré [9] shaped the discussions of causation in the field of legal theory in at least two major ways: (1) through the distinction between the cause-in-fact and legal causation in legal responsibility attribution; and (2) through defining a more restricted version of the existing counterfactual approaches in the law[2] based on the conditionality of necessary and sufficient conditions [9,12,19]. Cause-in-fact in law is established based on the factual information available in the case. However, only some of the causal links are sufficient for attributing legal responsibility in the case. These legal causes are governed by the rules and policy considerations. Following the definition of legal responsibility attribution in [12], it can be satisfied on the following three grounds: '(a) the conduct of the person; (b) the causal connection between the conduct of the person and the given harm; and (c) the fault legally implied by the conduct of the person'. While (a) and (c) are given, it is the task of the judge and the jury to reason about the causal connection defined in (b). A number of things, such as multiple causes or absence of action under the duty of care can increase the complexity of establishing a causal link and consequently complicate the task of legal responsibility attribution. An example of over-determination in the medical domain can occur when there is more than one contributor to the patient's injuries. Moreover, there can be issues with foreseeing the effects of how certain types of substances react with medical preconditions. While it might be possible to determine the physical causes in such cases with some level of accuracy, for policy reasons the judge in the case might wish to lower the standards of the proof to allow for the victim to be compensated based on non-causal considerations, such as fairness, or suffering of the patient. It is important to distinguish between the different types of causation in order to design a framework that supports legal reasoning. The second contribution by Hart and Honoré is their discussions about the necessary and sufficient conditions for the outcomes. The supporters [19] of this view argue that in 'a specific situation a causally relevant condition is a necessary element of a set of conditions jointly sufficient for the harmful outcome', or the so-called NESS test, where the cause is a necessary element of a sufficient set of conditions. The NESS approach allows one to pick out the cause with more precision compared to the *sine qua non* approach. In order to compare alternative causal models, the NESS approach appeals to the idea of generalisations about causal relations [10], where causal models would be based on instantiations of such generalisations to compare alternative models.

Causation in AI and Law: Halpern and Pearl's Approach. Causation has been described as one of the essential bonds of the universe as perceived and understood by humans [3]. Indeed, it seems inconceivable that everyday or specialised reasoning could be coherent without the causal elements. In the sub-field of artificial intelligence and law, causation holds a central role in understanding and modelling legal reasoning and legal responsibility attribution [12]. This mat-

---

[2] The most common approach in law being *sine qua non*: 'but for the action, the result would not have happened'.

ter has been approached from various perspectives, including logic [11,13,16], statistics [5], argumentation [17,18], and new task specific approaches [6,14]. These approaches are not exclusive, and we argue that a combination of these and legal approaches introduced above provide a more comprehensive solution for causal analysis in the law. Our framework was inspired by several of the current state of art approaches, but especially by the considerations of Halpern and Pearl's 'actual causation'.

Halpern and Pearl's [7,8] 'actual causation' is a formal approach to causal analysis that allows for comparison of alternative explanations based on normality, typicality and default notions. What distinguishes this approach from others is the method of modelling causal relations through interventions. Halpern and Pearl try to avoid the ambiguity in determining the cause and effect by modelling causal events through structural equations. Actual causation can model more complex causal relations and is a good competitor with the NESS test. Furthermore, Halpern and Hitchock have developed an extension of the theory that allows for alternative causal explanations to be compared [8], based on the notions of normality, defaults and typicality. The idea behind this extension is to compare the alternative causal explanations based on the closeness to what has been defined as the normal state of the relevant events. For instance, when multiple agents could have prevented a harmful event, causal responsibility could be attributed to the omission of the agent who had the obligation to prevent it. The authors claim that it can be based on various criteria, including statistical data, moral norms, and prescribed norms. The latter are especially relevant to considerations in law.

Towards a Semi-formal Approach. The approaches we have just presented show the complexity of causal attribution. Any adequate model of causality has to take into account the issues addressed by such authors. In particular the model by Halpern and Pearl appears to be the most promising, and we aim to expand our approach so that it includes the ideas developed by these authors.

However, we think that for modelling many legal cases, a simpler approach is sufficient. Even if the model will not yet capture some causal issues (overdetermination, pre-emption, etc.), it may help us to understand cases that do not involve such subtleties. We need a sufficient representation that works with the presentations of information in the cases. This is the purpose of the model that will be presented in the next sections.

Below, we introduce the working example of the *Althen's* case. We then provide our framework for capturing the causal reasoning, which is later applied to the *Althen's* case. Finally, we contrast the various approaches to causal models in Sect. 4, showing how the formalism can aid legal discussion and *vice versa*.

2.2 The Althen's Case

The *Althen's* Special Master's decision [1] is our source for evidentiary and legal issues in relation to causation. We focus on how the cause-in-fact is established based on the conflicting testimonies from the expert witnesses explaining the symptoms observed on Mrs. Althen, and how the special master reasons about these causal arguments to attribute legal responsibility in the case.

Facts of the Case: The case concerns Mrs. Althen (petitioner) and her worsening health conditions after receiving a tetanus toxoid (TTV) vaccine. Prior to the vaccines, petitioner was reasonably healthy. After roughly two weeks from the vaccination date, petitioner started reporting various symptoms ranging from blurred vision, to steady headache and temporal loss of vision. The complaints and hospital visits continued for the following three years. Petitioner underwent various types of treatments and extensive medical testing (MRI, EEG, blood tests) that showed inconclusive results for acute-disseminated encephalomyelitis (ADEM), multiple sclerosis, and vasculitis. Petitioner subsequently applied to the Vaccine Court for compensation, which requires that petitioner establishes a causal link between the TTV and ADEM.

Legal Criteria: For a causal link to be successfully proven in the US Vaccine Court, the vaccine either has to be listed on the approved 'Vaccine Injury Table' or the petitioner has to satisfy the causation-in-fact conditions set out by the court (off-table vaccine injury). This case involves an off-table vaccine injury. This case involves an off-table vaccine injury. The claimant's burden (also known as the Stevens test) can be summarised as follows: "the claimant has to show by preponderant evidence that the vaccination brought about her injury by providing a medical theory causally connecting the vaccination and the injury, a logical sequence of cause and effect showing that the vaccination was the reason for the injury, and a showing of a proximate temporal relationship between vaccination and injury; if the claimant satisfies this burden, she is entitled to recover unless the government shows, also by a preponderance of evidence, that the injury was in fact caused by factors unrelated to the vaccine".

In this paper, we mostly focus on the criterion that requires a 'logical sequence of cause and effect'. We claim that our semi-formal model is able to support expert witness testimonies in meeting this criterion.

Expert Witness Testimonies: There were three expert witnesses assigned to this case, of which we discuss two competing testimonies. Dr. Smith for petitioner arguing for the positive causal link between TTV and ADEM, and Dr. Safran for respondent rejecting the causal link.

The experts agreed that it is theoretically possible that the TTV can cause ADEM. However, the main disagreement was whether in this particular scenario the TTV which instigated the reaction, where healthy cells were attacked and demyelinated. Dr. Smith supported his opinion by referring to the medical theory of cell degeneracy, which shows cell modification through evolution and can explain T cell reaction after a vaccine. The theory of cell degeneracy is based on the premise that TTV can attack and destroy both bad (antigen) and good (myelin) cells, as the antigen and myelin are *sufficiently similar*. Dr. Safran, while accepting the general causal theory of degeneracy, denies the link in this particular case on two grounds. Firstly, he argues that antigen and myelin cells are not proven to be sufficiently similar. Secondly, the symptoms observed on the patient can be better explained by multiple sclerosis. Based on this information that has been abstracted from the case, we will model the causal explanations given by the experts. We decided to focus on the expert testimonies due to their core value in decision making in the vaccine courts. Furthermore, these testimonies provide detailed information on the causal claims made in the case, and the special master carefully examines them and weights them for the legal responsibility attribution.

3   Semi-formal Framework and Case Analysis

In this section, we present a semi-formal framework for assessing causal links. Then we use this framework to capture the views expressed by Dr. Smith and Dr. Safran on the causal relation between TTV and ADEM. Our analysis is meant to accommodate the causal relations that are presented as the core disagreements between the parties and shed some light on the structure of the arguments provided by the expert witnesses. Other matters are out of scope at this moment, in particular, the dynamics of dialogue, belief change, and time. Rather, it is a static model that lays out all the information available. It makes explicit some of the otherwise implicit assumptions that are highlighted in the course of the presentation of the expert testimony and by way of attack.

3.1   Semi-formal Framework

Our semi-formal framework is a propositional language to represent and reason with basic facts/events and causal relations between them. Our model has basic knowledge structures and rule schemes using the structures.

Basic Knowledge Structures. There are several basic knowledge structures: factual propositions; predicates for similarity and evidentiality; causal links; and inference rules.

Factual Propositions. A factual proposition has the form

$$\pm H(X)$$

where X is a positive or negative literal. $H(X)$ states that the literal X *holds* and $\neg H(X)$ that this was not the case. For instance $H(TTV)$ and $H(\neg TTV)$ are such literals, affirming respectively, that it holds that tetanus toxoid vaccination was performed, and that it holds that this was not the case. We assume that $H(X)$ and $H(\neg X)$ are incompatible, and that $H(\neg X)$ is indeed equivalent to (it strictly implies and is implied by) $\neg H(X)$. For instance $H(\neg TTV)$ is equivalent to $\neg H(TTV)$.

Similarity and Evidentiality. The case scenario also includes reasoning with similarity and evidentiality, which we introduce as a relation and a predicate, respectively. For similarity, we have

$$Sim(X, W)$$

which is understood as the propositional content of X is similar to the propositional content of W (and vice versa). For evidentiality, we have

$$EV(X)$$

which is understood to represent the existence of evidence for the propositional content of X.

Causal Links. Causal links are represented as

$$C(L, X, Y)$$

where L takes values 1 or 2, and X and Y are factual propositions. $L = 1$ indicates that cause X always (necessarily) produces effect Y, and $L = 2$ indicates that cause X usually (normally) produces effect Y. The causal links and levels of causal links loosely correspond to the language used by the reasoners.[3] For instance, $C(1, TTV, TCellAct)$ is an expression that TTV and $TCellActivation$ have the *always causal* relation, as the witnesses present it.

Inference Rules. We use strict and defeasible inference rules represented as

$$X_1 \ldots X_n \to Y$$

for strict rules, and

$$X_1 \ldots X_n \Rightarrow Y$$

for defeasible rules, where $X_1, \ldots X_n, Y$ are factual propositions.

We assume that strict rules allow for contrapositive reasoning. For our purposes it is sufficient the contrapositive inference where, given all antecedents of a defeasible rule except X, and the negation of the rule's consequent, we can infer X's negation. Thus we assume that a strict rule stands for the set of all of its contrapositions. A contrapositive of a strict rule

$$X_1 \ldots X_n \to Y$$

is a rule

$$X_1 \ldots X_{i-1}, \neg Y, X_{i+1}, \ldots X_n \to \neg X_i$$

---

[3] At the initial stages of the study, we annotated the decision identifying causal and accompanying hedging expressions. After identifying the main causal links in the case, we ranked the various expressions in two levels of strength. For instance, *'a probable causal relation between tetanus toxoid and two injuries'*, *'it is more probably than not the case that tetanus toxoid can cause the injuries suffered here'* are examples of level 2 (usually causal) support.

For instance, if a knowledge base contains the rule

$$H(X) \wedge C(1, X, Y) \rightarrow H(Y)$$

it also contains a rule

$$\neg H(Y) \wedge C(1, X, Y) \rightarrow \neg H(X)$$

Accordingly, if Y does not hold and X strongly causes Y, we can infer that X does not hold, for otherwise Y should hold.

To capture the reasoning of the experts in our cases, we need to supplement the general framework above with some schemes for rules.

General Rule Schemes. There are general rule schemes for causal rules, similarity, and evidence (including abduction).

Causal Rules. Rule schemes R1 and R2 capture the inferential relevance of causal relations

$$[R1.] \ H(X) \wedge C(1, X, Y) \rightarrow H(Y)$$

captures the inferential meaning of necessary causal links. If the precondition holds and the causal link is level 1, we strictly conclude that the effect holds.

$$[R2.] \ H(X) \wedge C(2, X, Y) \Rightarrow H(Y)$$

captures the inferential meaning of defeasible causal links. If the precondition holds and the causal link is level 2, we defeasibly conclude that the effect holds, but can have exceptions.

Similarity. The case scenario also includes reasoning with similarity, in particular, it is assumed that similar facts cause the same effect. This is captured by the following scheme for defeasible conditionals:

$$[R3.] \ Sim(X, W) \wedge C(L, X, Y) \Rightarrow C(L, W, Y)$$

Evidence. Finally, our experts reason with evidence. First, it is assumed that having evidence for a proposition defeasibly implies that this proposition holds:

$$[R4.] \ EV(X) \Rightarrow H(X)$$

Evidence plays two roles in our domain. First, it may *establish facts that contradict the conclusion of a causal inference*. This will defeat the causal argument leading to the conclusion contradicted by the evidence. If that argument culminates with the effect of a level 1 causal relation, defeat may extend to the precondition of that causal relation via contraposition.

Second, evidence may provide *abductive support for establishing the antecedent of a level 1 causal relation*. In fact, it seems that our experts assume that given a necessary causal relation and its effect, we can abductively infer the precondition. We capture this aspect of their reasoning through the following pattern defeasible conditionals:

$$[R5.] \; H(Y) \wedge C(1, X, Y) \Rightarrow H(X)$$

meaning, that we can defeasibly infer the precondition X when we have established its effect. For instance, given evidence of certain symptoms, we can defeasibly infer that these symptoms hold by R4; moreover, if such symptoms are strictly caused by an illness, we can defeasibly infer that the illness holds by R5.

3.2 Models in the Language

In this section we apply the semi-formal framework to represent the relations as described in the case by the expert witnesses.

We shall use the following atoms, representing the circumstances that are relevant to our case:

Factual Atoms

TTV - tetanus toxoid vaccination being injected in the patient
$ADEM$ - acute-disseminated encephalomyelitis illness
MS - multiple sclerosis
$TCellAct$ - the chemical process of tetanus toxoid vaccination activating T cells
$AntigDestr$ - antigen cells destroyed (T cells should target this, wanted effect)
$MlnDest$ - myelin cells destroyed (T cells should not target this, unwanted effect)
$Symp(Mono)$ - monophasic symptoms occur. This means that the symptoms that occurred just once. $-Symp(Mono)$ means here that the symptoms occurred on multiple occasions.

We use the following causal links to represent the causal claims of the expert witnesses:

C1. Tetanus toxoid vaccination always causes T-cell activation: $C(1, TTV, TCellAct)$
C2. T-cell activation always causes antigen destruction: $C(1, TCellAct, AntigDestr)$
C3. T-cell activation usually causes myelin destruction: $C(2, TCellAct, MlnDestr)$
C4. Myelin destruction usually causes ADEM: $C(2, MlnDestr, ADEM)$
C5. ADEM usually causes monophasic symptoms: $C(2, ADEM, Symp(Mono))$
C6. Multiple sclerosis usually causes recurrent symptoms: $C(2, MS, -Symp(Mono))$

3.3 The Arguments of the Expert Witnesses in *Althen's*

We now model the arguments of Dr. Smith and Dr. Safran in *Althen's*.

Dr. Smith. Given the language and rules above, we model the reasoning by Dr. Smith. He argues for a causal link between the TT vaccine and ADEM.

The argument starts from the explicit assumption of TTV (given as a fact) and uses the strict and defeasible rules to model the reasoning process and justification of linking the vaccination, symptoms and illness. In particular, Dr. Smith's argument is based on the explicit assumption $Sim(AntigDestr, MlnDestr)$ and implicit assumption $C(2, ADEM, Symp(Mono))$ (an assumption exposed by another witness' counter-argument). We take these assumptions as assertions in Dr. Smith's model. We give the assumptions, rules, and inferences in sequence, labelling the reasoning steps by agent.

Dr. Smith's Model: The rules for Dr. Smith's argument, based on the rules proposed above:

1. $H(TTV)$
2. C(1, TTV, TCellAct)
3. $H(TTV) \land C(1, TTV, TCellAct) \to H(TCellAct)$
4. $H(TCellAct)$ (from 1, 2, and 3)
5. $C(1, TCellAct, AntigDestr)$
6. $Sim(AntigDest, MlnDest)$ (similarity assumption by Smith)
7. $Sim(AntigDest, MlnDest) \land C(1, TCellAct, AntigDestr) \Rightarrow C(2, TCellAct, MlnDestr)$ (an instance of the rule scheme that similar effects are caused by the same cause)
8. $C(2, TCellAct, MlnDestr)$ (from 5, 6, 7)
9. $H(MlnDestr)$
10. $C(2, MlnDestr, ADEM)$
11. $H(MlnDestr) \land C(2, MlnDestr, ADEM) \Rightarrow H(ADEM)$
12. $H(ADEM)$
13. C(1, ADEM, Symp(Mono))
14. $H(ADEM) \land C(1, ADEM, Symp(Mono)) \to H(Symp(Mono))$
15. $H(Symp(Mono))$

Smith can also build an additional argument for ADEM, this time based on the evidence of the symptoms.

1. $EV(Symp(Mono))$
2. $EV(Symp(Mono)) \Rightarrow H(Symp(Mono))$
3. $H(Symp(Mono))$
4. $C(1, ADEM, Symp(Mono))$
5. $H(Symp(Mono)) \land C(1, ADEM, Symp(Mono)) \Rightarrow H(ADEM)$ (instance of the abduction rule)
6. $H(ADEM)$

Dr. Safran. Dr. Safran's objections against the causal link between the TTV and ADEM can be summarised into two main arguments. Firstly, he argues against Dr. Smith's claim that myelin and antigen cell destruction are sufficiently similar for the vaccine to make an error in distinguishing between these processes.

This argument consists in the single claim

1. $\neg Sim(AntigDest, MlnDest)$

Secondly, Dr. Safran argues against the conclusions based on the monophasic symptoms, he claims that the evidence shows that the symptoms observed on the patient are clearly reoccurring. Therefore, its condition cannot be $ADEM$, since $ADEM$ is described as a monophasic disease in the medical literature.

His argument against $ADEM$ is is the following:

1. $EV(C(1, ADEM, Symp(Mono)))$
2. $EV(C(1, ADEM, Symp(Mono))) \Rightarrow C(1, ADEM, Symp(Mono))$
3. $C(1, ADEM, Symp(Mono))$
4. $\neg H(Symp(Mono))$
5. $\neg H(Symp(Mono)) \wedge C(1, ADEM, Symp(Mono)) \rightarrow \neg H(ADEM)$ (by transposition of the rule $H(ADEM) \wedge C(1, ADM, Symp(Mono)) \rightarrow H(Symp(Mono))$
6. $\neg H(ADEM)$

Furthermore, Dr. Safran provides an alternative explanation for the illness stating that recurrent symptoms can be linked with multiple sclerosis, and therefore, he defeasibly concludes for multiple sclerosis.

1. $C(2, MS, \neg Symp(Mono))$
2. $H(\neg Symp(Mono))$
3. $H(MS) \wedge C(2, MS, \neg Symp(Mono)) \Rightarrow H(\neg Symp(Mono))$
4. $H(MS)$

Multiple sclerosis indeed provides an explanation of the evidence, as he sees it, i.e., as including non-monophasic (recurrent) symptoms $H(\neg Symp(Mono))$.

3.4   Preliminary Assessment

Preliminary results show that our semi-formal framework is able to capture the core points of witness arguments in the causal analysis in the *Althen's* case. In addition to modelling the causal relations and their relative strengths, we also intend to integrate a level of evidential reasoning from the evidence to a supported conclusion. This is especially helpful in legal reasoning where the parties are expected to justify their arguments by showing how the evidence links to their claims. We also observed that there is a mix of everyday and legal causal expressions with causal language often being accompanied by hedging expressions. We observed that witnesses used the language of uncertainty, which required our framework to integrate degrees of belief to portray the nature of discussions in the court. This suggests a possible development using statistical approaches to further improve the causal models to reflect causal reasoning present in the courtrooms.

Legally relevant causal arguments are often at the heart of legal disputes, therefore, investigating and modelling these links from various perspectives enables more thorough analysis of the reasoning involved. Our aim was to capture how causal links are established in the Vaccine Court assessing expert witness testimonies. The advantage of our approach is shown by the fact that the arguments modelled for causal analysis have been scrutinised, and an additional layer of justification based on defeasible rules has been added. At the moment, there is a lack of consistency in assessing causal links in courts according to the guidelines. We believe that with better understanding of the causal links and their justifications, these guidelines could be improved for greater consistency and predictability in the courts. What we have observed in this particular case is the continuous reference to the normative guidelines without fully explaining what is meant by 'medical causation', 'logical sequence', etc. Our semi-formal analysis is intended to explicitly represent causal and evidential reasoning for these concepts.

While we agree that law is a practical field and does not necessarily have to engage in a philosophical debate on causation, it is important that such an essential component of decision making as causation is not left undefined. It is of especial importance when relying on expert witness testimony where personal bias can play a role [18].

4   Causation and Burden of Proof

Thus far, we have mainly focused on establishing and modelling the cause-in-fact. However, the mere link of physical events and effects constitutes only a component of the task of attributing legal responsibility and, more generally, legal reasoning. The work of a decision maker involves assessing the causal explanations presented by the parties and experts, then deciding which of the explanations is the most appropriate according to a complex set of criteria, including the rules set out by the legislators and previous courts. In this section, we examine how formal theories can support the choice between alternative causal models, and we propose extensions that are needed to accommodate their use in legal reasoning.

Two approaches of interest here are the generalisation theory by Hart and Honoré [9], and normality theory by Halpern and Pearl [8]. According to the generalisation theory, one can establish 'particular causal links as instances of generalisations' of the cause and effect [10]. This theory heavily relies on common sense understanding of causation. It has the advantage of simplifying the discussion about causation in cases where the choice of the alternative explanations is based on subjective assessment and provides limited rationality, as it is commonly observed in everyday reasoning. It is also useful in cases where there is an agreement as to what the generalisation of the causal link is. For instance, taking a billiard ball, it can be agreed that we can generalise about the movement and impact of the billiard ball on the table and the effects it might cause in a particular context. While this approach is on many levels intuitive and reflects many instances of human reasoning, it has two serious flaws. Firstly, it emphasises human reasoning about causation as 'arbitrary and irrational', which is not necessarily the case and is not a satisfactory justification in the legal discourse [19]. And secondly, there is a very limited set of generalisations people can agree on, where most of them do not help resolving disagreements. On the other side of the spectrum, there are approaches that emphasise the rational and quantitative nature of causal decisions by employing statistical methods of reasoning with causation [5]. These provide the advantage of showing rational means of choosing particular causal explanation over another, but as observed in the *Althen's* case, experts and decision makers often lack the tools and information to make such quantitative claims.

To some extent, our approach is similar to the generalisation theory, since we say nothing about *how* the relation is established, which is the crux of much philosophical discussion. Yet, our approach is significantly less arbitrary and irrational in that we provide plausible and useful causal reasoning rules; moreover, in a scientific setting, there are meaningful generalisations that are agreed upon (or at least disagreed on, which may lead to further empirical testing). While establishing the causal relation is a significant matter, this is beyond what we address here, which is to represent and clarify the causal arguments as they are provided in a legal case.

Based on our observations in the case study and the work of Walker and his team in the Vaccine Injury Project [2], it can be said that there is a combination of common sense and formal reasoning based on a diverse pool of evidence. One of the challenges in the cases, where the Special Masters rely heavily on expert input to determine cases, is to balance the standards of proof between what is accepted in various domains involved [17], i.e., medical proof and legal burden of proof [4, 15]. Legal proof in the vaccine cases does not amount to the proof as considered in science. There are also other considerations that the judges have to take into account that might not always fit into strictly rational frameworks. To better reflect legal reasoning about causation, we believe that there is a need for a norm-based analysis.

Halpern and Pearl [8] have proposed the use of normality, typicality and default measures in comparing causal explanations. Each of the terms is vaguely defined to reflect the notions of strength in the ways these can be supported by evidence. To give a flavour of these, some aspects of normality can be covered by social norms (descriptive) and legal norms (prescriptive), while typicality can be supported by statistical evidence or various templates of causal observations in life. These provide a formal way of comparing the alternative explanations based on how close such scenarios are to the 'normal world'. This approach has the advantage of reflecting how human reasoners build counterfactual scenarios. The shortcoming, as with the generalisation theory, is the loose definitions of the terms and criteria of setting norms.

Our idea is to apply these theories of generalisation and normality to a set of cases to establish a pattern of norms used to prove a causal link for legal responsibility attribution. Our hypothesis is that by surveying a set of class action vaccine cases, we would be able to identify the causal arguments and reasoning patters that establish the 'normal world'. Based on such patterns, the reasoning and justification behind causal links are uncovered, and new arguments can be built allowing that case outcomes might be predicted in the same restricted domain. Furthermore, we intend to utilise the semi-formal framework in modelling cause-in-fact arguments in other legal cases.

5 Conclusions and Future Work

The overall aim of this line of research is to develop an approach that identifies, formally models, and supports reasoning with causation in a manner that is relevant to the legal domain. In this paper, we have introduced a semi-formal approach for modelling causal arguments in law based on strict, defeasible and causal relations. As it can be seen from our preliminary results, we have mainly focused on simple causal relations that are expressed through complex arguments in the court. The proposed rules can be reused to model similar cases in the vaccine court and have the potential to model a large variety of causal issues.

As part of the future work, we intend to use the methods and insights developed here to tackle more challenging causal issues. Furthermore, we plan to integrate preference relations and argument assessment in our framework to accommodate some of the decision making tasks based on causal relations. Such an endeavour would employ both qualitative and quantitative analytical tools in determining liability attribution based causal expressions used by the reasoners. There is a lot more that needs to be done to understand and automate the arguments and reasoning based on causal models, but we agree with the other specialists in the field [12], that it is work worth pursuing to add some of the missing pieces in the puzzle of legal reasoning and argumentation.

References

1. Althen v Secretary of HHS, The Court of Federal Claims, Golkiewicz, Chief Special Master, 2003 WL 21439669 (2003)
2. Research Laboratory for Law, Logic & Technology, Vaccine Injury Project. http://www.lltlab.org/projects/data-projects/vaccineinjury-project/. Accessed 10 Nov 2017
3. Beebee, H., Hitchcock, C., Menzies, P.: The Oxford Handbook of Causation. Oxford University Press, Oxford (2009)
4. Bex, F., Walton, D.: Burdens and standards of proof for inference to the best explanation: three case studies. Law Probab. Risk 11(2–3), 113–133 (2012)
5. Chockler, H., Fenton, N., Keppens, K., Lagnado, D.: Causal analysis for attributing responsibility in legal cases. In: Proceedings of the 15th International Conference on Artificial Intelligence and Law, pp. 33–42. ACM (2015)
6. Giunchiglia, E., Lee, J., Lifschitz, V., McCain, N., Turner, H.: Nonmonotonic causal theories. Artif. Intell. 153(1–2), 49–104 (2004)
7. Halpern, J.Y.: Actual Causality. MIT Press, Cambridge (2016)

8. Halpern, J.Y., Hitchcock, C.: Actual causation and the art of modeling. In: Dechter, R., Geffner, H., Halpern, J. (eds.) Heuristics, Probability, and Causality: A Tribute to Judea Pearl, pp. 383–406. College Publications, London (2010)

9. Hart, H.L.A., Honoré, T.: Causation in the Law. Oxford University Press, Oxford (1985)

10. Honoré, T.: Causation in the law. In: Zalta, E.N. (ed.) The Stanford Encyclopedia of Philosophy. Winter 2010 Edition (2010)

11. Kowalski, R., Sergot, M.: A logic-based calculus of events. In: Schmidt, J.W., Thanos, C. (eds.) Foundations of Knowledge Base Management, pp. 23–55. Springer, Heidelberg (1989). https://doi.org/10.1007/978-3-642-83397-7_2

12. Lehmann, J., Breuker, J., Brouwer, B.: Causation in AI and law. Artif. Intell. Law **12**(4), 279–315 (2004)

13. Lehmann, J., Gangemi, A.: An ontology of physical causation as a basis for assessing causation in fact and attributing legal responsibility. Artif. Intell. Law **15**(3), 301 (2007)

14. Mueller, E.: Commonsense Reasoning: An Event Calculus Based Approach. Morgan Kaufmann, Burlington (2014)

15. Prakken, H., Sartor, G.: A logical analysis of burdens of proof. In: Kaptein, H., Prakken, H., Verheij, B. (eds.) Legal Evidence and Proof: Statistics, Stories, Logic. Ashgate, Aldershot (2009)

16. Turner, H.: A logic of universal causation. Artif. Intell. **113**(1–2), 87–123 (1999)

17. Walker, V., Vazirova, K., Sanford, C.: Annotating patterns of reasoning about medical theories of causation in vaccine cases: toward a type system for arguments. In: ArgMining@ ACL, pp. 1–10 (2014)

18. Walton, D.: Argumentation Methods for Artificial Intelligence in Law. Springer, Heidelberg (2005). https://doi.org/10.1007/3-540-27881-8

19. Wright, R.W.: The NESS account of natural causation: a response to criticisms (2011)

Developing Rule-Based Expert System for People with Disabilities – The Case of Succession Law

Michał Araszkiewicz[1]([⊠]) and Maciej Kłodawski[2]

[1] Department of Legal Theory, Faculty of Law and Administration,
Jagiellonian University, Kraków, Poland
michal.araszkiewicz@uj.edu.pl
[2] Department of Legal Theory, Faculty of Law and Administration,
University of Zielona Góra, Zielona Góra, Poland
m.klodawski@wpa.uz.zgora.pl

Abstract. This paper presents the features of a moderately simple legal expert system devoted to solving the most frequent legal problems of disabled persons in Poland. The authors focused on the structure of legal expert system and methodology used for the sake of its development. The succession law of Poland has been selected in the paper as the illustrative domain, because the modelling of the succession procedures delivers sufficient material to reveal the most important issues concerning project of the legal expert system.

Keywords: Legal expert system · Legal problems of disabled persons
Rule-based reasoning · Succession law

1 Introduction

This paper presents a selection of results of the project "New applications in the judiciary against the exclusion of people with disabilities"[1]. The authors of this paper were members of an interdisciplinary team encompassing 7 people, among them lawyers, a doctor of arts, an expert on integration of people with disabilities and a computer scientist. The aim of the project was to develop a set of documents (interactive court forms, contract templates, instructions) as well as informative infographics and finally a modest legal expert system that would enhance access to justice for people with disabilities. The project encompasses not only the domains of law that are specifically interesting for people with disabilities, but also the most common domains such as succession law or accommodation law. It was assumed that people with disabilities are particularly vulnerable to potential problems related to those basic fields. The project assumed the use of simplified plain language (rather than formalistic legal language) as well as attractive graphical form. Its results should be assessed as

---

[1] Financed from the EEA Funds in the frame of the program and realized in years 2015–2016 by INPRIS – Institute for Law and Society, a NGO concerned, *inter alia*, with legal policy, new technologies and access to justice (the website of the organization is accessible at http://www.inpris.pl/en/home/).

U. Pagallo et al. (Eds.): AICOL VI-X 2015–2017, LNAI 10791, pp. 187–201, 2018.
https://doi.org/10.1007/978-3-030-00178-0_12

interesting from the point of view of usage of simple information technology tools in legal aid systems. It is worth noting that in Poland the system of legal aid is on the early stage of development.

The present contribution is therefore focused on representation of actual reasoning of lawyers (in particular, asking proper questions to the clients/users and adequately reacting to the information provided by them) rather than on application of a more advanced technology for the sake of generation of valuable output in a procedure that does not resemble actual legal reasoning. Therefore, this paper is closer to the field of computational legal theory rather to the domain of applied legal AI [13]. Apart from its practical value, the expert system provides insights concerning the structure of norms of the modeled domains, the optimal procedure of information gathering with regard to the issue in question, as well as to the content of the investigated domain itself. Due to the technological limitations present in the project from its initial steps to the very end, and therefore lesser relevance of such issues such as combinatorial explosion or handling inconsistencies (all potential inconsistencies were eliminated manually), the analysis of computational features is not included here.

The authors of the present paper, as experts in law, were responsible for preparation of the legal content of the interactive documents, the infographics and for the content and the logical structure of legal expert system which was then implemented by the programmer - Michał Szota - in the Angular framework in JavaScript. This paper focuses on the structure of legal expert system and methodology used in its development. The order of investigations is as follows. In Sect. 2 we discuss the characteristics of the developed legal expert system on the background of the state of art. Section 3 discusses the illustrative domain chosen for the aims of the present paper: the succession law of Poland. Although the expert system encompasses also other selected topics (such as eviction and social benefits procedures), during our works we found the modelling of the succession procedures the most challenging task. Section 4 shows an example of adoption of the chosen methodology. Section 5 presents the application in action. Section 6 presents a discussion and directions of further research.

2   The Basic Assumptions of the Legal Expert System

The works on the legal expert system in the project were based on the following assumptions.

- The developed system is purely a rule-based one. No Case-Based Reasoning, probabilistic or argumentative components were planned to be included in the system – therefore it was a challenging task to select domains and problem fields that may be adequately represented without resort to richer knowledge representation tools.
- The system is designed to deal with recent fact situations; the content of legal system was fixed for the date of March the 1st, 2016. The system models concrete versions of normative acts and does not deal with any intertemporal problems, as opposed to the system developed for instance by Yoshino [8].

- The functioning of the system is typical for classical legal expert systems: first defining the issue to be decided and then determining an answer to the issue by providing answers by the user to the questions asked by the system.
- The questions asked by the system should be either "yes or no" questions (where an answer is dictated by application of a well-defined concept), or a question about quantities of certain objects.
- The system assumes negation as failure: if it is not known to the user that a state of affairs S holds, it is concluded that S does not hold.
- The terms used in "yes or no" questions should be extensionally unequivocal, i.e. it should be obvious even for a lay person whether the state of affairs designated by the term holds in the world or not. In case of any interpretative problem the user of the system is referred to consult a lawyer.

Although it is clear that adoption of the abovementioned assumptions has to lead to development of a product of rather limited application, they enabled us to focus exclusively on modelling of legal information representable by rules. As Bench-Capon rightly notes [3], rule-based legal expert systems give the user the information what questions should be asked in order to solve a legal problem, rather than an actual solution to such concrete problem. It is trivial to note that much of the work in the field of AI and Law has been developed since the 80s precisely to enable the legal reasoning models to deal with issues of vagueness, open texture and context-sensitivity, to mention classifying legal problem into simple and hard cases [4], the use of CBR structures in argumentation [1, 2], joining rules with CBR in hybrid systems [6] and recently the use of argumentation schemes theory to legal interpretation [7]. As the present expert system was assumed not to make use of any of these components, our theoretical aim was to re-explore the expressiveness of rule-based expert systems and methods to efficiently develop them from the raw legal text. Taking into account the results of the famous modelling of British Nationality Act [5] we were also interested in identification of potential gaps in the system of law. Importantly, due to the temporal and financial limitations, it was not foreseen in the project to develop a domain-independent shell of the system or its (onto)logical architecture. Therefore, the developed and implemented application is able only to represent the knowledge contained therein, is not able to learn and each extension of its knowledge base requires manual work. However, on the other hand, the application correctly resolves the legal problems which may be posed by the users.

3   Description of the Domain

Although the legal expert system consists of 6 components (applications), here, due to limitations of space, we choose the domain of succession law as illustrative material, therefore limiting our examples to the functioning of two applications: one modelling statutory succession and another one dealing with testamentary succession, both under Polish law.

In Polish law statutory provisions related to succession law are gathered mostly in the Civil Code[2] (hereinafter "PCC"), enacted in 1964. The legislator constantly keeps classic division into testamentary succession and statutory succession, derived from Roman law. In the structure of the PCC these characteristic for European private law's types of succession are separated only partially, what means that they are connected not only by many general inheritance provisions and rules common both for testamentary and statutory succession (e.g. unworthiness regulated in Art. 928 of the PCC, which means that an heir may be adjudged unworthy by a court of law if, for instance, he has intentionally committed a serious crime against the decedent), but also by tangled, at least prima facie, rules (e.g. rule regulated in Art. 967 § 1 of the PCC, which states that if a person entitled to be the testamentary heir does not want to or may not be an heir, a statutory heir who the share allocated to this person fell to shall be obliged to perform ordinary legacies, instructions and other dispositions of the decedent which encumber this person, unless the decedent decides otherwise). Other rules, specific strictly for given type of succession (e.g. related to testamentary succession accrual, regulated in Art. 965 of the PCC, which is explained extensively in further part of present paper), refer to some provisions in "go there and back" way, creating sometimes necessity of iteration in algorithm.

The rule common for both types of succession in Polish law is that, as stated in Art. 924 of the PCC, the inheritance shall be opened upon the death of the decedent. In statutory succession that means no statements are needed to make someone an heir. Almost everyone (exception concerns unworthy persons), who simply is alive and belongs to group of relatives entitled by law to inherit, may acquire the estate.

The crucial difference between statutory and testamentary succession under Polish law is dependence on action, at least one, of the decedent. Testamentary succession requires the declaration of intent of the decedent. Although testamentary succession may seem more complex than statutory succession in Polish law, this finding is illusory. Statutory succession becomes intricate for instance when family of the decedent contains numerous relatives of the decedent. Then amount of calculations, fixed shares in the estate and relations of rules determining the shares of heirs in the estate – some of which may be ascendants, descendants or siblings – arise. Also factors from beyond the law, for example fact, that some of descendants are not alive, must be taken into account.

4 Methodology

The development of any of the components of the legal expert system consisted of the following steps.

1. Definition of the legal issue to be decided by the system and its sub-issues.
2. Identification of statutory provisions relevant for the modelling.

---

[2] Journal of Laws from 2016, item 380, with further amendments (http://dziennikustaw.gov.pl/DU/2016/380/1).

3. Initial transformation of the statutory provisions into rules expressed in any language rich enough to express natural numbers, separately for each of the sub-issues.
4. Determination of a list of sufficient conditions for the negative answer to the legal issue in question.
5. Determination of a list of the remaining legal issues to be taken into account to provide a final answer to the legal issue in question.
6. Development of an exhaustive list of "yes or no" or quantitative questions such that:
   (a) Providing answers to all questions from the list yields an unequivocal and legally adequate answer to the legal issue in question;
   (b) It is determined first whether any of the sufficient conditions for the negative answer hold;
   (c) The sequence of questions is the shortest one possible;
   (d) One question asks for one piece of information (here understood as a simple proposition with no connectives), unless it is possible to ask a complex question without significant risk of its misinterpretation by the user.
7. Development of a list of rules dictating the system what it should do in reaction to a given answer to a particular question, where the options are as follows:
   (a) Present an information "please use the algorithm X" if according to the initial information given by the user he should not use the present application, but another one;
   (b) Present an information "explanation" if the question concerns legal term or complex factual issue and it is assumed that the user will handle the question after acquiring and understanding the explanation;
   (c) Present an information "please consult a lawyer" if the question uses an open-textured term or if the degree of complexity of legal issue initially described by the user is too high;
   (d) Present a screen "you do not inherit estate after the deceased person" if any of the sufficient conditions for such conclusion is satisfied;
   (e) Go to the next question in the sequence;
   (f) Provide a final answer to a legal issue in question, for instance calculate a share of a person by application of a certain formula, or simply give the answer, if no calculations are necessary.

Let us show how this methodology was employed with regard to the legal issue of statutory succession.

The legal issue is defined as follows: (1) is the user of the system a statutory successor of the deceased person and (2) if an answer to the question (1) is positive, what is the share of the user in the estate? Let us note that due to the fact of existence of different groups of precedence among the set of statutory successors under Polish law, this legal issue is divided into sub-issues concerning inheritance of persons belonging to different groups. In the system, we have distinguished the following categories of potential users of the "Statutory Succession" application: Spouse, Child, Grandchild or Grand-grandchild (for practical reasons, this category has not been extended further), Sibling, Siblings' children or grandchildren, Parent, Grandparent, Children of the deceased spouse.

The set of statutory provisions for the modelling was chosen on the basis of internal systematization of the PCC, where provisions ranging from Art. 931 to the Art. 940 together from a Title II entitled "Statutory Succession".

In the third step, statutory provisions expressed in natural language were transformed into rules expressed in a simplified first-order language. Let us consider the following provision of the PCC (the translations to English are taken from the Legalis system published by C.H. Beck, 2017 and Lex system published by Wolters Kluwer, 2017):

Art. 931 of the PCC
§ 1. The children of the deceased and his spouse shall, by virtue of statutory law, be appointed to inherit first; they shall inherit in equal parts. However, the part of the spouse cannot be lesser than one fourth of the entire estate.
§ 2. If a child of the deceased did not survive opening the inheritance, that share of the estate which would have been his shall pass to his children in equal parts. This provision shall apply respectively to more distant descendants.

Taking into account the existence of groups of precedence in the Polish law of statutory succession, one may easily note that the quoted provision comprises two types of information: (1) it defines the first group of precedence and (2) it provides a formula for calculation of the share of the successor. It was noted earlier that such reconstructions are done separately for each sub-issue. For instance, if we are concerned in developing a set of questions and rules for the calculation of a share of a spouse, the following rules are reconstructed from the quoted provision.

Sub-issue: SPOUSE
Formula 1. IF [the number n of the inheriting children shares $\leq$ 2] THEN [spouse's share = $1/n$]
Formula 2. IF [the number n of the inheriting children shares > 2] THEN [spouse's share = 1/4]
[inheriting child] = [a child of the deceased person alive during the time of death of the deceased person] and [not excluded from succession]
[inheriting children share] = [a share of an inheriting child] or [a share of inheriting children of an inheriting child]

Let us note that the latter definition allows for recursive nesting of further inheriting children shares in the previously considered inheriting children shares, but it does not have an effect on calculation of the spouse's share.

The determination of sufficient conditions for negative answer to the legal sub-issue in question is relatively simple; apart from the general conditions for exclusion from succession which are applicable to any successor, there are two specific conditions excluding the spouse from succession:

• Being in the state of separation with the deceased person during the death of the latter,
• The deceased person, before the time of death, filed a lawsuit for divorce or separation against the spouse, based on the fault of the spouse, and this lawsuit was justified.

A circumstance modifying the formulas for calculation of the spouse's share is the absence of inheriting children shares. In such situation, the spouse inherits in concurrence with parents of the deceased. We will provide the formulas for calculation of the spouse's share below together with the set of questions.

The sequence of questions, with rules determining the reactions of the system to the answers given by the user, is as follows. It should be noted that the following presentation is not the code of the application (which was developed in Java) but the representation of the sequence of questions which encompasses both substantial rules (on the merit of law) and procedural steps (such as "go to" instructions). The procedural steps are introduced to give the Reader the sense of sequence of questions. The sequence is important because the sufficient conditions of negative answer to the legal question are investigated. The procedural steps are marked by capital letters. Let us stress that this exposition serves as faithful representation of actual steps that are taken by a competent lawyer dealing with this domain (where in reality of course procedural steps are made implicitly) and it does not represent the actual code of the Java program.

1. Is it the case that in the time of death of the deceased person you were in separation with that person? Y/N
   a. IF Y, THEN END.
   b. IF N, THEN GO TO 2.
2. Is it the case that before death, the deceased person filed a lawsuit against you for divorce or separation based on your fault? Y/N
   a. IF Y, THEN END; PLEASE CONSULT A LAWYER (reason: the said lawsuit must be justified, which is a context-sensitive term).
   b. IF N, THEN GO TO 3.
3. Did the deceased person have children who were alive during the time of death of the deceased person, or who had children who were alive during the time of death of the deceased person?
   a. IF Y, THEN PROVIDE A NUMBER. APPLY Formula 1 or Formula 2.
   b. IF N, THEN GO TO 4.
4. Is it the case that both parents of the deceased person were alive during the deceased person's death? Y/N
   a. IF Y, THEN spouse's share = ½.
   b. IF N, THEN GO TO 5.
5. Is it the case that one of the parents of the deceased person was alive during the deceased person's death? Y/N
   a. IF Y, THEN spouse's share = ½.
   b. IF N, THEN spouse's share = 1.

Let us note that in the sub-issue described above, only one legal problem was classified as requiring a consultation with a lawyer.

Let us now present adoption of the methodology with regard to an issue of testamentary succession: accrual. On the contrary to the legal issue of statutory succession, the legal issue of testamentary succession is defined as follows:

(1) Is the testament valid?
(2) Has the testament been revoked?
(3) Are there any other persons specified in the testament, except for the user of the system?

(4) Is the user of the system a person appointed as a heir in the testament?
(5) If an answer to the question (4) is positive, what is the share of the user in the estate?

It must be noted that enlarged, in comparison to statutory succession, group of issues is a consequence of fact that the user is entitled to inherit not directly by law, but by the will of the decedent expressed in the testament. Therefore an examination which concerns both legal (validity) and factual (revocation) state of the testament must be a part of algorithmic way to solution.

Moreover, the will might concern different issues, for instance (I) a role of each person specified in the testament by the decedent, (II) amount of persons specified in the testament, (III) a part of the estate being object of the testament. The issue (I) is most complex as it comprises 5 different types of the decedent's will among the distinguished in testamentary succession under Polish law:

(i)   to make specified person a heir, namely to appoint to the estate – Art. 959 of the PCC and the following in Section II of Title III in Book IV of the PCC,

(ii) to make a specified person a legatee (ordinary legacy), namely to oblige a statutory or testamentary heir to render specific property-related performance for the benefit of the specified person – Art. 968 § 1 of the PCC,

(iii) to make a specified person a sublegatee (sublegacy), namely to encumber a legatee with the ordinary legacy – Art. 968 § 2 of the PCC,

(iv) to make a specified person a bequeathed (specific bequest), namely to decide in a testament drawn up in the form of a notarial deed that a specified person shall acquire the object of the bequest upon the opening of the inheritance – Art. 981[1] § 1 of the PCC,

(v)   to encumber specified person with the instruction (instruction), namely to impose on an heir or a legatee the obligation of specific acting or refraining from acting without making anyone a creditor – Art. 982 of the PCC.

Due to assumed limitations of the user we decided to project algorithm as part of the expert system which can solve only situation of heirs (i). In remaining cases the user of the system is referred to consult a lawyer, because thorough interpretation of the testament and distinguishing of types of the decedent's will are required. We also decided to exclude the (III) question from algorithm, as the assumed aim of algorithm of testamentary succession, similarly to algorithm of statutory succession, is calculate the share of the user in the estate and the answer to the (III) does not have an impact on this answer in any manner. Furthermore it must be mentioned that questions (3) and (4) are followed in algorithm by series of questions related to specific testamentary succession institutions like substitution or accrual.

The set of statutory provisions for the modelling was chosen on the basis of internal systematization of the PCC, where provisions ranging from Art. 941 to the Art. 967 together from Section I ("Testament") and Section II ("Appointment of Heir"), both being a part of Title III entitled "Disposition in Case of Death".

As regards the third step, the user, after selecting "Testamentary Succession", always follows – on the contrary to statutory succession – one path which obviously may lead him to different solutions.

Let us present the sequence of questions, with rules determining the reactions of the system to the answers given by the user, in testamentary succession. It must be noted that algorithm starts with questions about unworthiness, subsequently is followed by questions (1) and (2) described above and only successful result of those steps leads to the questions presented below. Also essential are two hereunder provisions:

Art. 960 of the PCC
If the decedent appointed several heirs to the estate or to a specified part of the estate without determining their shares in the estate, they shall inherit in equal parts

Art. 965 of the PCC

If the decedent has appointed several testamentary heirs and one of them does not want to or may not be an heir, the share allocated to him shall fall to the remaining testamentary heirs in proportion to the shares falling to them (accrual), unless the decedent decides otherwise.

The sequence of questions, with rules determining the reactions of the system to the answers given by the user, is as follows. It should be noted again that the following presentation is not the code of the application, but a representation of a set of questions, encompassing both substantial rules and procedural steps.

1. Are there any other persons specified in the testament, except for the user of the system? Y/N
   a. IF Y, THEN GO TO 1A;
   b. IF N, THEN GO TO 1B.
   (explanation: step 1B. and the following B. steps are not related with the accrual, so they are omitted)
1A. Are all of persons specified in the testament heirs? Y/N
   a. IF Y, THEN GO TO 2A;
   b. IF N, THEN END; PLEASE CONSULT A LAWYER
   (reason: ordinary legacy, sublegacy, specific bequest and instruction, are difficult institutions of testamentary succession, so thorough legal interpretation of the testament is required)
2A. Input a total amount of heirs in the testament (including the user) NUMBER(H)
   (explanation: number must be > 1, which is logical consequence of decision made in step 1.)
   a. IF NUMBER(H) = 1, THEN WAIT FOR NUMBER > 1;
   b. IF NUMBER(H) > 1, THEN GO TO 3A.
3A. Did the decedent specify in the testament the user's share in the estate? Y/N
   a. IF Y, THEN INPUT USER'S SHARE [S(1)] AND GO TO 4A;
   b. IF N, THEN LEAVE UNKNOWN [U(1)] AND GO TO 4A.
   (explanation: algorithm memorises [S(1)] and [U(1)] values)
4A. Did the decedent specify in the testament the other heir's share in the estate? Y/N
   (explanation: the question 4A. iterates H − 1 times and algorithms retains to memory each obtained value)
   a. IF Y, THEN INPUT HEIR'S SHARE [S(2)] AND GO TO 5A.
   b. IF N, THEN LEAVE UNKNOWN [U(2)] AND GO TO 5A.
   (explanation: algorithm memorises [S(2)] and [U(2)] values)

5A. Does the other heir specified by the decedent want to or may become an heir? Y/N
   (information: the user obtains a visually assisted explanation presented on the additional screen)
   a. IF Y, THEN
      i. IF Y IN 3A. AND IF Y OR N IN 4A., THEN user's share = [S(1)]
      ii. IF N IN 3A. AND IF Y IN 4A., THEN user's share = 1 − [S(2)]
      iii. IF N IN 3A. AND IF N IN 4A., THEN user's share = 1/H *(in presented example: ½)*
         (explanation: according to Art. 960 of the PCC; steps i., ii. and iii. are not related with the accrual institution, so we present them only as a sample calculation)
   b. IF N, THEN GO TO 6A.
6A. Did the decedent specify whom fall share in the estate allocated to the heir, who does not want to or may not be an heir? Y/N
   a. IF Y, THEN GO TO 1C.
      (explanation: step 1C. and the following C. steps. are not related with the accrual, so they are omitted)
   b. IF N, THEN GO TO 7A.
7A. Has the decedent excluded accrual towards the heir who does not want to or may not be an heir?
   (information: the user obtains a visually assisted explanation presented on the additional screen)
   a. IF Y, THEN
      i. IF Y IN 3A. AND IF Y OR N IN 4A., user's share = [S(1)]
      ii. IF N IN 3A. AND N IN 4A., THEN user's share = 1/H of the estate *(in presented example: ½)*
         (explanation: according to Art. 960 of the PCC)
      iii. IF N IN 3A. AND Y IN 4A., THEN user's share = 1 − [S(2)]
   b. IF N, THEN
      i. IF Y IN 3A. AND Y IN 4A., THEN user's share = [S(1)] + [S(1)] * [S(2)]
      ii. IF Y IN 3A. AND N IN 4A., THEN user's share = [S(1)] + [S(1)] * {1 − [U(2)]}
      iii. IF N IN 3A. AND Y IN 4A., THEN user's share = {1 − [U(1)]} + {1 − [U(1)]} * [S(2)]
      iv. IF N IN 3A. AND N IN 4A., THEN user's share = 1 − [U(1)]} + {1 − [U(1)]} * {1 − [U(2)]}

It must be noted that when [S(1)] + [S(...)] + [S(H)] > 1, algorithm informs the user, that sum of all shares (expressed as fractions) must be no greater than 1 (as 1 represents the maximum possible value to be divided in the testament), and if the user is certain about [S(1)] + [S(...)] + [S(H)] > 1, he is advised by algorithm to consult a lawyer. The similar situation occurs in opposite case, i.e. [S(1)] + [S(...)] + [S(H)] < 1 − (1) the decedent probably made a mistake in determining the shares of the various heirs or (2) the decedent intentionally described the shares, which do not cover the entire estate. In both cases exists a discrepancy between the amount of shares and the size of the entire estate and the user is advised by algorithm to consult a lawyer.

5   Expert System in Action

In this section we present selected screens captured from the Javascript interactive application available at http://www.inpris.pl/infografika/2016/index.php. The entire application is accessible only in Polish language version, so we shortly summarize content of each screen below each Figs. 1, 2, 3, 4, 5, 6 and 7. All graphics being part of

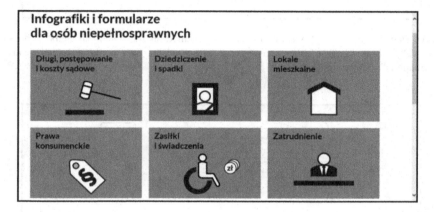

Fig. 1. Initial screen of the interactive application (from the left, upper row "debts, litigation and its costs", "inheritance and estates", "accommodation"; from the left, lower row "consumer rights", "social benefits", "employment").

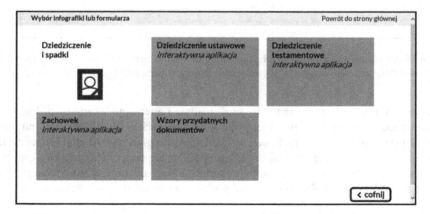

Fig. 2. Sub-menu "inheritance and estates". "Statutory succession" (upper centre) and "testamentary succession" (upper right) algorithms are separated. Also present (lower row) are "legitim" algorithm (on the left) and "models documents in the polish succession law".

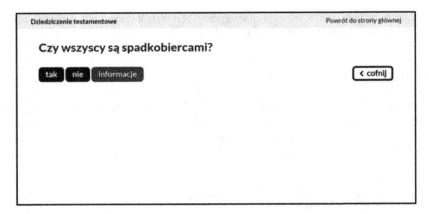

Fig. 3. Step 1A (question "Are all of persons specified in the testament heirs?", possible answers "yes" or "no") of the accrual case presented in Sect. 4. blue button leads to "informations". (Color figure online)

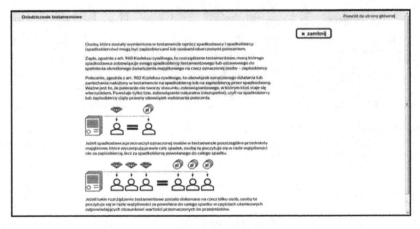

Fig. 4. Explanation available after clicking on blue button presented in Fig. 3. This screen explains differences between heirs, legatees and instructed persons. (Color figure online)

the application have been designed by prof. Justyna Lauer from Academy of Fine Arts in Katowice (Akademia Sztuk Pięknych w Katowicach). We asked for and were granted permission from prof. Lauer, as well from programmer Michał Szota, to the presentation of screen captures of the application in this paper. The graphics combine text and pictures and aim to enhance the understanding of the presented content. The language used in the application is a simplified version of statutory language.

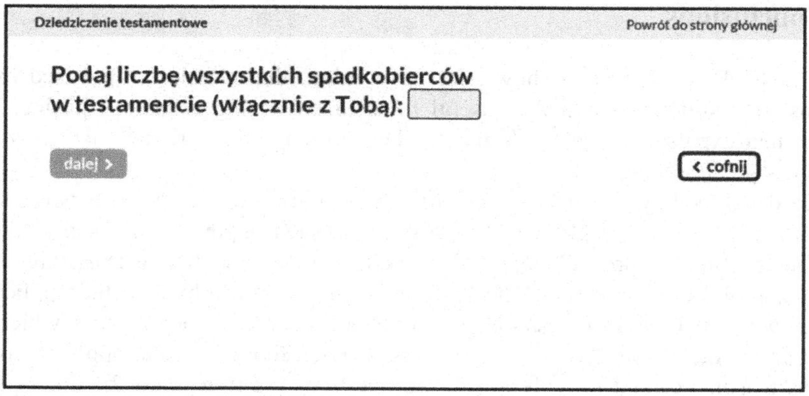

Fig. 5. Step 2A of the accrual case presented in Sect. 4. The user must input amount of all heirs, including the user.

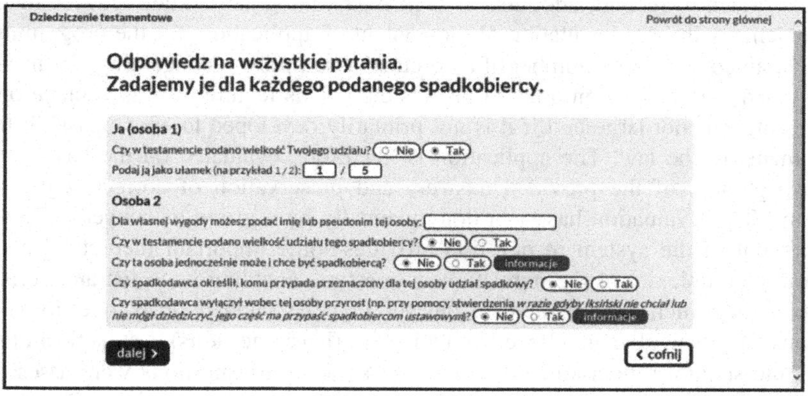

Fig. 6. Steps 3A–7A of the accrual case (questions aforementioned in Sect. 4).

Fig. 7. Solution of the case presented in Sect. 4 (a sample consistent with variant 7A. b. ii.).

6 Conclusions

The project described above shows, in our opinion, that classical rule-based expert systems may still be assessed as useful tools in enhancing access to justice, even though their expressive power is limited and even though they are not backed by a set of (onto)logical assumptions.

The developed system enables us to rise questions concerning the benefits stemming from similar simple projects. In our opinion, such implementations are valuable even though their theoretical import is limited. We may identify at least three main advantages of similar projects. The first advantage is quite obvious: the application enables a broader circle of people to access the content of legal rules which are important for they in their day-to-day activities. Even though similar applications, for obvious reasons, cannot provide for all the questions the user might be interested to ask, they still provide answers to many questions and they rise the user's awareness of problems which require an advice from a professional lawyer. Therefore, similar systems, development of which is not very expensive, may play an important role in legal aid systems. Second, adoption of such methodological attitude reduces many of the problems with implementation of the content of application, for the programmer is not constrained by a large number of theoretical assumptions (concerning, for instance, the assumed ontology, definitions of objects etc.). This feature is an advantage only if an application is not large and if it is not primarily developed to encompass all future amendments to the law. The application is, therefore, evaluated on the basis of substantial rightness of the provided answers and preservation of correct sequence of questions. This evaluation has been done manually by a group of lawyers. Third, the development of the system in question provides some important theoretical insights concerning complexity of the regulation in question, enabling us to list and count the questions for which an unequivocal answer may be yielded (easy questions), and questions which involve an advice from a lawyer (hard questions). Let us recall that in case of the statutory inheritance of a spouse, 4 (out of 5) questions were assessed as easy ones. Similar result has been obtained for the determination of a user's share in case of accrual, however, this involved putting more information into the set of procedural rules.

The presented examples of modules of the system show that the modest set of tools is sufficient to model quite complex issues, provided that they involve well-defined concepts or numbers. In the future we are intending to develop the system further, to include a CBR component and intertemporal issues as well as a module related to the problem of legal interpretation, including doctrinal interpretation of the concepts contained in the application. We are particularly concerned with the latter issue, for enhancement of rule-based systems with a base of cases has been a known approach from the early days [6]. The introduction of an argumentative knowledge concerning legal interpretation may lead to a more fine-grained elaboration of hard questions. A rule-based implementation of the argumentative schemes used for statutory interpretation [7, 9–12] should enhance the system's usefulness not only for its primary users, but for professional lawyers, too. This component of the system would prepare the user for a meeting with a lawyer by providing an information what kind of information (for instance, on conflicting interpretations) should be expected with respect to a given question.

The scope of the project did not encompass systematized evaluation of the application by potential users. The functionalities of the system were assessed and validated by professional lawyers. It is intended that such evaluation is performed in the later stages of the project.

References

1. Aleven, V.: Teaching case-based argumentation through a model and examples. Ph.D. Dissertation, University of Pittsburgh, Graduate Program in Intelligent Systems (1997)
2. Ashley, K.: Modeling Legal Argument: Reasoning with Cases and Hypotheticals. MIT Press, Cambridge (1990)
3. Bench-Capon, T.: What makes a system a legal expert? In: Schäfer, B. (ed.) Twenty-Fifth Annual Conference Legal Knowledge and Information Systems, JURIX 2012, pp. 11–20. IOS Press, Amsterdam (2012)
4. Gardner, A.L.: An Artificial Intelligence Approach to Legal Reasoning. MIT Press, Cambridge (1987)
5. Sergot, M., Sadri, F., Kowalski, R., Kriwaczek, F., Hammond, P., Cory, H.T.: The British nationality act as a logic program. Commun. ACM **29**, 370–386 (1986)
6. Skalak, D., Rissland, E.: Arguments and cases: an inevitable intertwining. Artif. Intell. Law **1**, 3–44 (1992)
7. Walton, D., Sartor, G., Macagno, F.: Contested cases of statutory interpretation. Artif. Intell. Law **24**, 51–91 (2016)
8. Yoshino, H., et al.: Legal expert system—LES-2. In: Wada, E. (ed.) LP 1986. LNCS, vol. 264, pp. 34–45. Springer, Heidelberg (1987). https://doi.org/10.1007/3-540-18024-9_20
9. Żurek, T., Araszkiewicz, M.: Modelling teleological interpretation. In: Verheij, B., Francesconi, E., Gardner, A.L. (eds.) Proceedings of the Fourteenth Conference on Artificial Intelligence and Law, ICAIL 2013, pp. 160–168. ACM, New York (2013)
10. Sartor, G., Walton, D., Macagno, F., Rotolo, A.: Argumentation schemes for statutory interpretation: a logical analysis. In: Hoekstra, R. (ed.) Twenty-Seventh Annual Conference Legal Knowledge and Information Systems, JURIX 2014, pp. 11–20. IOS Press, Amsterdam (2014)
11. Macagno, F., Sartor, G., Walton, D.: Argumentation schemes for statutory interpretation. In: Araszkiewicz, M., Myška, M., Smejkalová, T., Šavelka, J., Škop, M. (eds.) International Conference on Alternative Methods of Argumentation in Law, ARGUMENTATION 2012, pp. 31–44. Masaryk University, Brno (2012)
12. Araszkiewicz, M.: Towards systematic research on statutory interpretation in AI and law. In: Ashley, K. (ed.) Twenty-Sixth Annual Conference Legal Knowledge and Information Systems, JURIX 2013, pp. 15–24. IOS Press, Amsterdam (2013)
13. Schäfer, B.: Formal models of statutory interpretation in multilingual legal systems. Statut. Law Rev. **38**(3), 310–328 (2017)

Legal Vocabularies and Natural
Language Processing

EuroVoc-Based Summarization
of European Case Law

Florian Schmedding[1]([✉]), Peter Klügl[1], David Baehrens[1], Christian Simon[2],
Kai Simon[3], and Katrin Tomanek[4]

[1] Averbis GmbH, Tennenbacher Str. 11, 79106 Freiburg, Germany
{florian.schmedding,peter.kluegl,david.baehrens}@averbis.com
[2] INTER CHALET Ferienhaus-Gesellschaft mbH,
Heinrich-von-Stephan-Str. 25, 79100 Freiburg, Germany
c.simon@interchalet.com
[3] European Patent Office, Rijswijk, The Netherlands
[4] VigLink Inc., 333 Bush Street, San Francisco, CA 94110, USA
katrin.tomanek@gmx.de

Abstract. This work reports on the ongoing development of a multi-lingual pipeline for the summarization of European case law. We apply the TextRank algorithm on concepts of the EuroVoc thesaurus in order to extract summarizing keywords and sentences. In a first case study, we demonstrate the feasibility and usefulness of the presented approach for five different languages and 18 document sources.

1 Introduction

The ongoing harmonization of the various legal systems across the European Union constantly increases the importance of the pan-European legal system. For example, national case law decisions from the higher courts become immediately effective in the legal system of each member state. Consequently, legal professionals must consider more and more all member state's national legislation and jurisdiction when researching the context of their causes.

However, such researches are difficult due to the intrinsic diversity of the European Union. Legal information is spread over several national and European repositories and is, of course, published in different languages. Additionally, the format and the structure of legal documents depend heavily on their origin and often there are no standardized cross-references to the related documents. Accordingly, there is a growing need for information systems that enhance the access to the pan-European legislation and jurisdiction. A thorough overview on the corresponding backgrounds is elaborated by Boella et al. [3], a more technical view on the characteristics of the legal domain is presented by the authors of the Eunomos system [2]. Beside text classification and document clustering (see

C. Simon, K. Simon and K. Tomanek—The contributions were developed while this author was working at Averbis GmbH.

U. Pagallo et al. (Eds.): AICOL VI–X 2015–2017, LNAI 10791, pp. 205–219, 2018.
https://doi.org/10.1007/978-3-030-00178-0_13

Boella et al. [4] and Schweighofer et al. [31], for example), text summarization is an important feature of these systems.

Being confronted with large bodies of documents that must be scrutinized with great precision, legal professionals greatly benefit from document summaries [24]. In turn, with respect to the size of the legal repositories, automated document summarization greatly simplifies the operation of legal information systems. Regarding the diverse origins of the legal documents, the system must process different formats and languages uniformly.

In this work, we report on our experiences and ongoing work on both aspects. We approach the first by generating two kinds of summaries, controlled keyword and sentence summaries. The keywords are based on the EuroVoc terminology and hence not only descriptive but do also relate documents across languages. For both summaries we pursue the language-independent graph-based TextRank algorithm [23]. However, it benefits from a language-specific preprocessing. Regarding the second, we are currently dealing with five important European languages: Bulgarian, English, French, German, and Italian. Our natural language processing is based on UIMA [13], a framework for the orchestration of individual text analysis engines, facilitating the clear separation between language-dependent and language-independent parts of the pipeline. Thus, the extension to another language is fairly easy—only the language-specific components have to be added.

We evaluated our results with questionnaires send to legal experts asking them to rate the automatically selected keywords and sentences. Their answers show the feasibility of our approach. Additionally, we invited them to select the keywords and sentences that summarize the document in their opinion. Together with the previous answers we hope to gain insights and clues for the improvement of our system and its further adjustment to the legal domain.

The rest of the paper is structured as follows: Sect. 2 gives a short overview of the related work on text summarization of legal documents and on approaches based on the UIMA framework. The multilingual pipeline is introduced in Sect. 3 and the text summarization of European case law is described in Sect. 4. Section 5 presents the results of the case study and Sect. 6 concludes with a summary.

2   Related Work

Text summarization is an active and thriving field of research due to the fact that its importance grows with the increasing amount of available textual information. An overview of this research area, its historical development and categorization of approaches is given in various survey articles (cf. Gupta and Lehal [17], Nenkova and McKeown [25], Dalal and Malik [7], and Elfayoumy and Thoppil [9]). Especially Alemany et al. [1] provide a comprehensive overview of earlier systems. Another recent summary focused on multilingual approaches for summarization can be found in Sarkar [30]. Most publications classify approaches for text summarization into diverse categories, for example, extractive and abstractive, single document and multi document, language dependent and language independent, and other categories based on the purpose or target users (cf. Sarkar [30]). Following this, the approach pursued in this work can be classified as extractive, single document and language independent.

The legal domain is predestined for text summarization and attracts a considerable amount of interest. In the following, we present a selection of recent and representative approaches for text summarization in the legal domain (in chronological order). An extended overview of previous work can be found in Moens [24].

The LetSum system [12] extracts summarizing sentences dependent on the thematic structure of juridical decision. After preprocessing for tokenization, sentence splitting and part-of-speech tagging is applied, the separate segments concerning decision data, introduction, context, juridical analysis and conclusion are identified. Their content is filtered by removing passages like citations and large paragraphs. Then, separate heuristics optimized for a specific segment type are applied in order to extract best candidates, which are proportionally joined for the final summary.

The work of Saravanan et al. [29] and Hachey and Grover [18] follows up on the idea of improving legal text summarization using segmentation in rhetorical roles. Saravanan and Ravindran [29] apply Conditional Random Fields with adapted feature sets to identify segments of seven rhetorical roles. In these segments, key sentences are extracted using term distribution models. Hachey and Grover [18] define the identification of roles as well as the extraction of summarizing sentences as a classification task and compare different machine learning models like Naive Bayes, Support Vector Machines and Maximum Entropy. Yousfi-Monod et al. [34] also learn supervised Naive Bayes models for summarization of legal documents. They evaluated different combinations of surface, emphasis and content features for English and French documents concerning immigration, tax and intellectual property. In Chieze et al. [6], an automatic summarization system for English and French legal documents is described.

Kim et al. [19] developed an extractive summarization algorithm based on directed and disconnected graphs with asymmetric edge weights. Furthermore, they do not need to specify the compression rate and are able to provide summarizing sentences with a high cohesion. Galgani et al. [14] argue that approaches for summarization that are based on a single technique are not able to provide sufficient results in divergent domains. They propose to build summarizers customized for specific domains by a rule-based combination of different elements like frequencies, centrality, citations and linguistic information. The increased engineering effort for this approach is faced with an incremental knowledge acquisition framework. While most publications automatically evaluate their approaches using Rouge [22], they additionally presented results using human evaluators. In another approach, Galgani et al. [15] emphasized the usefulness of citation graphs in legal documents for text summarization. They combined elements of cited and citing documents and validated that best performing combinations depend on the domain.

In contrast to this previous work on text summarization in the legal domain, we do not target the development of novel techniques. This work utilizes an established technique for language independent summarization and investigates architectural requirements, feasibility and results for multilingual case law. The experimental results are reported using human evaluators only. From this architectural perspective, an additional branch of related work concerning UIMA can be identified. DKPro Keyphrases [10] is a UIMA-based framework for keyphrase extraction experiments and thus facilitates the evaluation as well as the development of new approaches. The ATLAS platform [26] provides a framework based on UIMA for multilingual natural language processing supporting several European languages. The authors report that the planned summarization component will be based on LexRank [11] and Open Text Summarizer[1]. A demonstrator of the platform covers legal documents of the European Union that are categorized using the EuroVoc thesaurus. Multilingual natural language processing is in general a well understood and supported use case in UIMA, which can be ascertained by diverse publications [20,21,28,32].

3   Multi-lingual Document Processing

Clearly, a legal information system in a pan-European setting is confronted with different languages (and distinct scripts—Latin and Cyrillic). Therefore, when it comes to natural language processing, this should be done in a flexible and robust way, i.e., the language coverage should be easily extensible. However, there must be a common ground such that new components can be included free of interference.

The UIMA framework [13] has proven to provide the necessary means to these requirements paying special attention to the interoperability of components. Individual components—the analysis engines—are orchestrated in the processing pipeline and communicate with each other through adding or modifying meta information stored in the Common Analysis Structure (CAS) which contains the currently processed document. This information is represented by typed feature structures based on a common type system and thus suited for robust applications with predictable behavior and results.

Additionally, the UIMA framework comes with a powerful built-in support for horizontal scaling achieved by distributing the requests via an ActiveMQ[2] message broker to available processing endpoints. This is not only handy when facing vast amounts of data but also helpful if some pipeline components are not thread-safe. In this case, the workload can be easily parallelized by registering multiple instances of the same pipeline at the broker which then takes care of spreading the requests to a free instance, completely transparent to the user.

Our pipeline is depicted in Fig. 1. The reminder of this section introduces its language-dependent components and the EuroVoc concept mapper.

---

[1] http://libots.sourceforge.net/.
[2] http://activemq.apache.org/.

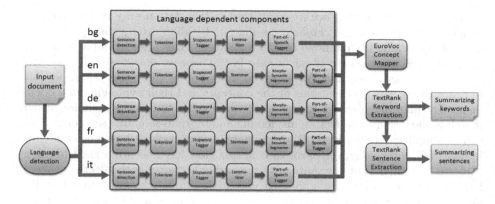

Fig. 1. Overview of the multilingual pipeline for text summarization.

3.1 NLP Components

Sentence detection segments the documents into sentences, which is an important task for extractive text summarization. While this is a well-understood problem, it can provide challenges if the sentence splitter also needs to handle headlines and listings correctly. We adapted and evaluated rule-based approaches and probabilistic models based on Maximum Entropy for case laws in different languages with the result that the rule-based components prevailed. The tokenizer creates meaningful elements of text (tokens) for further processing and the stopword tagger identifies tokens that carry no semantics for this given domain, most often tokens of closed word classes like determiners. The stemmer, lemmatizer and morpho-semantic segmenter [8] are applied to reduce words to their stem, basic form or morphologically meaningful units, respectively. Finally, the part-of-speech tagger identifies the word class of a token.

The actual configuration of components for a specific language depends on the availability of the components for that language. Partly, we rely on third-party components, which influences the selection of previous components. A specific part-of-speech tagger, for example, may require a certain type of tokenzier. The language-specific part-of-speech tags are reduced to a universal part-of-speech tagset [27] for further usage by the language-independent components.

3.2 EuroVoc

EuroVoc[3] is a multilingual, multidisciplinary thesaurus created and managed by the Publications Office of the European Union. It is utilized by European Parliament and national governments amongst other for indexing. The thesaurus consists of 21 area fields and 127 microthesauri with translations for over 20 languages. It provides almost 7000 concepts with varying amount of synonyms per language.

---

[3] http://eurovoc.europa.eu/.

In the context of this work, we utilize the translation only of the five languages Bulgarian, English, French, German and Italian. Many concepts are too general concerning the intended task. The concept "Law", for example, is hardly useful for describing the content of case law. Thus, we blacklisted 37 concepts mostly of the legal domain. We apply an extension of the ConceptMapper [33] in order to identify the mentions of the concepts and their synonyms in a document. The matching process supports different lookup techniques including exact matches, part-of-speech tags, stems, lemma and morpho-semantic segments. Possible ambiguities are resolved through removing concepts that have been matched by an auxiliary synonym in favor of concepts that have been matched by their preferred synonym. For any ambiguity remaining hereafter each affected concept is also removed. While this approach may look simple compared to other disambiguation components of our pipeline (for example, statistics and dictionary based) it has shown sufficiently good performance for plenty of use cases. So we achieve a precise, robust and reliable extraction of EuroVoc concepts.

4   Summarization of Case Law

The pipeline introduced in the last section contains two components that are responsible for generating the essential elements for the text summaries of European case law. While the first one identifies valuable keywords, the second one extracts sentences which makeup the final summary. Both components are based on the TextRank algorithm [23]. In this section, we first repeat the basic ideas of this algorithm and then describe how it is applied to identify summarizing keywords and sentences.

4.1   TextRank

The TextRank algorithm conceived by Mihalcea and Tarau [23] is an approach to rank elements of text documents, for example, in order to extract keywords that outline their topic. Unlike supervised systems, it relies exclusively on information drawn from the text itself and is principally independent of the document content and language. However, as Mihalcea and Tarau show, its results are generally better if natural language processing is applied to the text before.

The basic idea of the algorithm is the transformation of the text into a graph containing the elements in question as nodes. Edges between the nodes are introduced according to the relationship between the respective elements and thus the PageRank algorithm [5] is applicable for assigning a ranking score to each element.

PageRank is adequate for undirected and directed edges. For cases where weighted edges are more appropriate for modeling the relationship between the text elements Mihalcea and Tarau propose an adjusted version of the original scoring formula. For instance, they use it to compute the most important sentences of a document where the edges between two nodes describe the similarity among two sentences.

While TextRank scores single elements only, a post-processing may be used to refine the results. For instance, Mihalcea and Tarau join a selected token with its adjacent ones in order to generate more meaningful keywords.

4.2 EuroVoc Keyword Extraction

In contrast to the pure TextRank algorithm that generates free keywords, we want to choose the keywords from distinguished candidates contained in a controlled vocabulary. This has two advantages: First, each candidate includes a list of synonyms that enable the normalization of different tokens onto a precise keyword. Second, the normalization reveals similarities among documents containing the same concepts but different synonyms or being written in another language.

Despite using controlled keywords we do not need to specifically adjust the TextRank algorithm to it. The recognition of concepts from the vocabulary is performed independently before the keyword extraction takes place. As proposed by Mihalcea and Tarau, we restrict the domain of the nodes to nouns and adjectives that are identified by the natural language preprocessing. Additionally, we reject tokens that are shorter than three characters or that contain no letters or numbers.

According to Mihalcea and Tarau, the TextRank results improve when the nodes refer to normalized word forms. We use therefore segments (based on morphological analysis) for English and German, lemmas for Italian and Bulgarian, and stems for French. Each form is the preferred normalization for the corresponding language in our natural language processing pipeline. For creating the edges we relate each normalized form with the neighboring ones inside a window size of three. The mapping between nodes and previously determined concepts occurs in the post-processing step. It is achieved as follows:

1. The score of a concept is computed as the average score of the nodes representing it, compensating the number of words within the corresponding synonym.
2. As each concept may appear at several positions inside the text, equal concepts are grouped into clusters.
3. Each cluster is represented by the concept occurrence having the highest score among those contained in the cluster.

After sorting the obtained clusters according to the representative score in descending order, the best concepts appear at the beginning of the resulting list. Finally, the preferred synonyms pertaining to selected concepts are used to generate a set of legible keywords.

4.3 Sentence Extraction

Like above for the keyword extraction, we apply the EuroVoc vocabulary for detecting summary sentences. Distinct from the summarization method used

Very useful Useful Not useful Misleading Human (5) Summary Sentence

Very useful	Useful	Not useful	Misleading	Human (5)	Summary Sentence
●	●	●	●	☐	For nearly half a century, legal aid provided out of public funds was the main source of funding for those of modest means who sought to make or (less frequently) defend claims in the civil courts and who needed professional help to do so.
				☐	By this means access to the courts was made available to many who would otherwise, for want of means, have been denied it.
				☐	But as time passed the defects of the legal aid regime established under the Legal Aid and Advice Act 1949 and later statutes became more and more apparent.
●	●	●	●	☐	While the scheme served the poorest well, it left many with means above a low ceiling in an unsatisfactory position, too well off to qualify for legal aid but too badly off to contemplate incurring the costs of contested litigation.
				☐	There was no access to the courts for them.

Fig. 2. Excerpt of an exemplary questionnaire for rating the text summarization.

by Mihalcea and Tarau, where sentences are the immediate result of the graph processing (cf. Subsect. 4.1), we identify them based on the keyword extraction.

Having computed the sorted list of clusters, we start with the first and look at the text position of its representing concept. The enclosing sentence gets selected for the summary. In order to avoid duplicates, concepts that are already contained in a previously chosen sentence are skipped. The procedure repeats with the next cluster until the desired number of sentences is collected or no more keywords or sentences are available.

5   Case Study

While the pipeline for text summarization is still subject to further improvement, we prepared an initial case study that provides some insights in the general feasibility and applicability of the presented approach. Furthermore, we hope to gain clues about possible starting points to improve the running system. Figure 2 shows an excerpt of an exemplary questionnaire for rating the results. As an initial test data set, we prepared a collection of 100 documents—20 documents from different courts for each of the languages English, French, Italian, German, and Bulgarian. The exact amount of documents and their sources are summarized in Table 1.

To assess the quality of the automatically generated text summaries and keywords, we conducted a survey of the selection and utility of the document descriptions. Therefore, we asked the available human experts from the legal domain (native speakers or business fluent) to evaluate summaries and keywords on the test corpus of documents using predefined questionnaires. They were encouraged to rate the utility of the automatic descriptions in the categories of "Very useful", "Useful", "Not useful" to "Misleading". Additionally, they are allowed to select the five most important summary sentences and keywords from the documents themselves. This supplementary information is utilized to calculate precision and recall for the summaries and keywords. These auxiliary scores provide, however, only limited expressiveness[4] since multiple equivalent summaries may exist and despite a suggested one is rated as useful a different may be chosen by the expert.

---

[4] Therefore, precision and recall are always marked with asterisks.

Additionally, the pipeline suggests up to twelve keywords and eight sentences, and the experts did not always select five keywords or sentences, even if some of the proposed elements were rated as useful. These circumstances greatly decrease the evaluation scores but nevertheless they provide helpful insights for further development.

Table 1. Amount, language and source of the documents utilized in the case study.

Language	Source	Documents	Total
English	EUR-Lex	8	
	Judiciary.gov.uk	4	20
	Supreme Court (UK)	4	
	House of Lords Judgments	2	
French	EUR-Lex	10	20
	Legifrance	10	
Italian	Guistizia Amministrativa	10	20
	Corte Costituzionale	10	
Bulgarian	EUR-Lex	8	
	Varhoven Kasatsionen Sad	4	20
	Varhoven Administrativen Sad	4	
	Portal "Sadebni aktove" - Vish Sadeben Savet	4	
German	EUR-Lex	4	
	Rechtsinformationssystem (at)	2	
	Bundesverfassungsgericht	2	
	Bundesgerichtshof	2	
	Bundesverwaltungsgericht	2	20
	Bundesfinanzhof	2	
	Bundesarbeitsgericht	2	
	Bundessozialgericht	2	
	Bundespatentgericht	2	

5.1   Results

From a total of 100 questionnaires (20 judgments for each of the languages English, French, German, and Italian, and Bulgarian) we got expert utility ratings for 660 automatically generated summary sentences and 1070 keywords. This is a response rate of 95.5% and 96.4%, respectively. The participants also selected 468 sentences and 366 keywords for content description. Thus, whereas for the sentences almost five were selected per document, less than four were selected in the keyword case.

Table 2 shows the rated utility by language for the automatic keywords. The majority of the English and German keywords are judged helpful (>60% useful or very useful). On the other hand, the keywords in French, Italian, and Bulgarian failed to describe the contents in roughly 75% of the cases. Additionally, Table 2 contains the aggregated utility rating of the automatic summaries broken down by document language. For the languages of English, French, and German more than 75% have been found useful or even very useful. For Italian, half of the summaries were rated not useful while for Bulgarian 60% were helpful. The approximated precision and recall scores range in the anticipated low regions as explained above. Concerning the keywords, a negative amplitude can be observed for Bulgarian, and concerning summaries, for Bulgarian and English.

Table 2. Keywords and sentences by language

	Keywords					Sentences				
	de	en	fr	it	bg	de	en	fr	it	bg
Very useful	0.07	0.43	0.02	0.03	0.03	0.10	0.38	0.00	0.14	0.05
Useful	0.53	0.20	0.22	0.18	0.27	0.75	0.40	0.78	0.26	0.55
Not useful	0.33	0.30	0.76	0.72	0.62	0.12	0.13	0.22	0.47	0.33
Misleading	0.06	0.00	0.00	0.04	0.01	0.03	0.04	0.00	0.02	0.02
Not rated	0.00	0.07	0.00	0.04	0.08	0.00	0.05	0.00	0.10	0.06
Precision*	0.24	0.23	0.19	0.24	0.16	0.24	0.11	0.25	0.26	0.17
Recall*	0.64	0.63	0.68	0.64	0.55	0.31	0.18	0.27	0.40	0.25

Tables 3 and 4 display the ratings for keywords and sentences broken down to the different sources. The keywords in only half of the sources are rated helpful or very helpful at the majority. However, the summaries received more positive feedback. Only three sources are rated negative at the majority.

5.2   Discussion

The results of the questionnaires indicate that the EuroVoc terminology might not be useful for extracting summarizing keywords in European case law. Only the keywords in German and English documents have been rated positive. The identified keywords can, however, be utilized to create useful summaries, which can be observed for the positive utility ratings of German and English documents, but also for French and Bulgarian documents. The extracted sentences for the two latter languages are rated useful or very useful for the majority, while their keywords received overall negative feedback. Only Italian documents could not keep pace.

No dependencies can be observed between the ratings and the precision and recall scores. The evaluation scores for summarizing keywords are distributed in the same region regardless of their utility. The summarizing sentences of English received the most positive feedback by the legal experts, who stated that the sentences seem to be manually selected. Interestingly, these English documents obtained the lowest precision and recall scores. This leads to another point of

Table 3. Keywords by source

	Bundesar- beitsgericht	Bundesfi- nanzhof	Bundesge- richtshof	Bundespa- tentgericht	Bundesso- zialgericht	Bundesver- fassungsge- richt	Bundesver- waltungsge- richt	Corte Co- stituzionale	EUR-Lex
Very useful	0.21	0.25	0.00	0.05	0.08	0.04	0.05	0.06	0.23
Useful	0.67	0.46	0.62	0.25	0.63	0.58	0.79	0.15	0.19
Not useful	0.13	0.21	0.24	0.60	0.29	0.29	0.00	0.73	0.52
Misleading	0.00	0.08	0.14	0.10	0.00	0.08	0.16	0.01	0.01
Not rated	0.00	0.00	0.00	0.00	0.00	0.00	0.00	0.05	0.05
Precision*	0.13	0.29	0.10	0.15	0.33	0.38	0.42	0.25	0.20
Recall*	0.30	0.70	0.40	0.60	0.80	0.90	0.80	0.61	0.61

	Guistizia Ammini- strativa	House of Lords	Judiciary	Legifrance	Rechtsinfor- mationssys- tem	Sadebni aktove	Supreme Court	Varhoven Administra- tiven Sad	Varhoven Kasatsio- nen Sad
Very useful	0.00	0.23	0.40	0.03	0.00	0.00	0.31	0.00	0.00
Useful	0.21	0.27	0.21	0.31	0.29	0.25	0.35	0.25	0.35
Not useful	0.70	0.23	0.31	0.66	0.63	0.75	0.33	0.75	0.65
Misleading	0.08	0.00	0.02	0.00	0.04	0.00	0.00	0.00	0.00
Not rated	0.02	0.27	0.06	0.00	0.04	0.00	0.00	0.00	0.00
Precision*	0.22	0.17	0.15	0.27	0.17	0.15	0.25	0.19	0.19
Recall*	0.69	0.53	0.47	0.77	0.80	0.50	0.60	0.64	0.56

reference that the utility is a more important rating than the evaluation scores for assessing the summarization. The reason behind may be the aforementioned existence of several useful summaries. The average number of candidate keywords and sentences shown in Table 5 supports this presumption. English documents are generally longer than those of other languages. Consequently, more appropriate keywords can be extracted and more summarizing sentences exist.

A closer look at the results dependent on the source reveals some interesting insights. The EUR-Lex documents were processed in all languages but Italian. Here, 84% of the summarizing sentences haven been rated useful or very useful. This is a clear indication that the presented approach is capable to extract useful summaries in the different languages. Most of the summarizing document of German sources are rated positive, up to 94% and 100% useful or very useful for "Bundessozialgericht" and "Bundesverfassungsgericht" respectively. Documents from the Austrian source "Rechtsinformationssystem" received more negative than positive ratings. More work needs to be invested in order to investigate the reasons, e.g., the increased amount of not useful keywords. The discrepancy between the evaluation scores and the utility rating can also be observed for the sources. The two sources "Bundessozialgericht" and "Bundesverfassungsgericht" obtained the best feedback, but also completely differing evaluation scores. While the first one counts to be worst sources with a precision and recall of 0.08 and 0.09, the second one achieved the best precision and recall scores with 0.50 and 0.60 respectively. This is also an indication of a possibly low interrater agreement.

Table 4. Sentences by source

	Bundesarbeitsgericht	Bundesfinanzhof	Bundesgerichtshof	Bundespatentgericht	Bundessozialgericht	Bundesverfassungsgericht	Bundesverwaltungsgericht	Corte Costituzionale	EUR-Lex
Very useful	0.06	0.19	0.15	0.00	0.00	0.17	0.17	0.28	0.30
Useful	0.81	0.75	0.69	0.71	0.94	0.83	0.67	0.24	0.52
Not useful	0.06	0.00	0.15	0.29	0.06	0.00	0.17	0.41	0.12
Misleading	0.06	0.06	0.00	0.00	0.00	0.00	0.00	0.04	0.03
Not rated	0.00	0.00	0.00	0.00	0.00	0.00	0.00	0.04	0.03
Precision*	0.13	0.19	0.08	0.14	0.06	0.50	0.42	0.28	0.18
Recall*	0.20	0.30	0.10	0.10	0.09	0.60	0.45	0.43	0.25

	Giustizia Amministrativa	House of Lords	Judiciary	Legifrance	Rechtsinformationssystem	Sadebni aktove	Supreme Court	Varhoven Administrativen Sad	Varhoven Kasatsionen Sad
Very useful	0.00	0.06	0.31	0.00	0.00	0.00	0.22	0.00	0.00
Useful	0.29	0.59	0.47	0.78	0.45	0.41	0.41	0.75	0.69
Not useful	0.53	0.06	0.22	0.22	0.55	0.56	0.25	0.25	0.28
Misleading	0.00	0.03	0.00	0.00	0.00	0.00	0.13	0.00	0.00
Not rated	0.17	0.25	0.00	0.00	0.00	0.03	0.00	0.00	0.03
Precision*	0.24	0.03	0.13	0.35	0.27	0.16	0.13	0.22	0.13
Recall*	0.36	0.06	0.20	0.35	0.30	0.25	0.19	0.33	0.19

Table 5. Average number of candidate keywords and sentences per language

	de	en	fr	it	bg			de	en	fr	it	bg
Keywords	44.8	119.8	30.0	30.2	23.3		Sentences	97.2	431.8	60.2	51.6	87.6

Overall, the initial results of the questionnaires are very promising and supplied us with useful insights for further development. Text summarization in Italian documents needs to be improved in general. Furthermore, the reduced recall for some sources can indicate a low coverage of the terminology for a subdomain.

6   Conclusions

In this work, we presented an approach to automatically extract controlled keywords and sentence summaries for legal documents from diverse origins and in different languages. We also evaluated the utility of the generated keywords through user ratings and alternative keyword selections by legal experts.

We found, that there are major differences in the utility of keywords in the different languages. While the majority of English and German summary sentences and keywords were found useful, the results are mixed for French, Italian, and Bulgarian. By comparison of the utility ratings between keywords and summary sentences in these languages, we have shown for French and Bulgarian that our approach is capable to generate useful summary sentences although the extracted keyword terms from the EuroVoc terminology do not provide useful keywords by themselves. Moreover, from the expert selections of keywords, we have seen that the EuroVoc terminology is suitable for some of them only. We provided evidence that for Italian other vocabularies are likely to cover the legal domain more appropriately.

The example of case law from the EUR-Lex source displayed indications that our approach is able to automatically extract summary sentences in the different European languages. Here, 84% of the keywords were rated as helpful by the human experts.

Many interesting possibilities for future work remain. The summarization pipeline is still ongoing work, but its results are already useful and prove the feasibility of the architecture and approach. This enables us to further improve any adjusting screw ranging from specialization of the sentence splitter to more sophisticated algorithms for text summarization. An important step will be a more standardized and automatized evaluation of the pipeline with established evaluation metrics like ROUGE [22] and datasets like the HOLJ corpus [16] or the Legal Case Reports Data Set[5]. A promising option is the integration of citation information as in [15].

Regarding the processing of documents in different languages, we have established a reliable and extensible pipeline. Our approach has proven capable of running several distinct components within a uniform framework and we have shown how to cleanly separate language-specific from language-independent processing steps. By the help of the broker middleware we were able to increase the pipeline throughput although some of the components did not have native support for parallelization.

Acknowledgments. Parts of this work have been supported by the European Commission under the 7th Framework Programme through the project *EUCases*–EUropean and National CASE Law and Legislation Linked in Open Data Stack (grant agreement no. 611760). We do also gratefully acknowledge the effort spent by all legal experts for finishing the questionnaires.

References

1. Alemany, L.A., Castellón, I., Climent, S., Fort, M.F., Padró, L., Rodríguez, H.: Approaches to text summarization: questions and answers. Inteligencia Artif. Rev. Iberoamericana de Inteligencia Artif. 8(22), 79–102 (2004)
2. Boella, G., Caro, L.D., Humphreys, L., Robaldo, L., Rossi, P., Torre, L.: Eunomos, a legal document and knowledge management system for the web to provide relevant, reliable and up-to-date information on the law. Artif. Intell. Law **24**(3), 245–283 (2016)
3. Boella, G., et al.: Linking legal open data: breaking the accessibility and language barrier in European legislation and case law. In: Proceedings of the 15th International Conference on Artificial Intelligence and Law, ICAIL 2015, pp. 171–175. ACM, New York (2015)

---

[5] http://archive.ics.uci.edu/ml/datasets/Legal+Case+Reports.

4. Boella, G., Di Caro, L., Rispoli, D., Robaldo, L.: A system for classifying multi-label text into EuroVoc. In: Proceedings of the Fourteenth International Conference on Artificial Intelligence and Law, ICAIL 2013, pp. 239–240. ACM, New York (2013)

5. Brin, S., Page, L.: The anatomy of a large-scale hypertextual web search engine. Comput. Netw. ISDN Syst. **30**(1–7), 107–117 (1998)

6. Chieze, E., Farzindar, A., Lapalme, G.: An automatic system for summarization and information extraction of legal information. In: Francesconi, E., Montemagni, S., Peters, W., Tiscornia, D. (eds.) Semantic Processing of Legal Texts: Where the Language of Law Meets the Law of Language. LNCS (LNAI), vol. 6036, pp. 216–234. Springer, Heidelberg (2010). https://doi.org/10.1007/978-3-642-12837-0_12

7. Dalal, V., Malik, L.: A survey of extractive and abstractive text summarization techniques. In: 6th International Conference on Emerging Trends in Engineering and Technology (ICETET), pp. 109–110. IEEE (2013)

8. Daumke, P., Schulz, S., Markó, K.: Subword approach for acquiring and cross-linking multilingual specialized lexicons. In: Workshop on Acquiring and Representing Multilingual, Specialized Lexicons at LREC 2006 (2006)

9. Elfayoumy, S., Thoppil, J.: A survey of unstructured text summarization techniques. Int. J. Adv. Comput. Sci. Appl. **5**(4), 149–154 (2014)

10. Erbs, N., Santos, P.B., Gurevych, I., Zesch, T.: DKPro keyphrases: flexible and reusable keyphrase extraction experiments. In: Proceedings of the 52nd Annual Meeting of the Association for Computational Linguistics: System Demonstrations, pp. 31–36. ACL (2014)

11. Erkan, G., Radev, D.R.: LexRank: graph-based lexical centrality as salience in text summarization. CoRR abs/1109.2128 (2011)

12. Farzindar, A., Lapalme, G.: LetSum, an automatic legal text summarizing system. In: Legal Knowledge and Information Systems, pp. 11–18 (2004)

13. Ferrucci, D., Lally, A.D.A.M.: UIMA: an architectural approach to unstructured information processing in the corporate research environment. Nat. Lang. Eng. **10**(3–4), 327–348 (2004)

14. Galgani, F., Compton, P., Hoffmann, A.: HAUSS: incrementally building a summarizer combining multiple techniques. Int. J. Hum.-Comput. Stud. **72**(7), 584–605 (2014)

15. Galgani, F., Compton, P., Hoffmann, A.G.: Summarization based on bi-directional citation analysis. Inf. Process. Manag. **51**(1), 1–24 (2015)

16. Grover, C., Hachey, B., Hughson, I., et al.: The HOLJ corpus: supporting summarisation of legal texts. In: Proceedings of the 5th International Workshop on Linguistically Interpreted Corpora (LINC) at Coling 2004 (2004)

17. Gupta, V., Lehal, G.S.: A survey of text summarization extractive techniques. J. Emerg. Technol. Web Intell. **2**(3), 258–268 (2010)

18. Hachey, B., Grover, C.: Extractive summarisation of legal texts. Artif. Intell. Law **14**(4), 305–345 (2006)

19. Kim, M.-Y., Xu, Y., Goebel, R.: Summarization of legal texts with high cohesion and automatic compression rate. In: Motomura, Y., Butler, A., Bekki, D. (eds.) JSAI-isAI 2012. LNCS (LNAI), vol. 7856, pp. 190–204. Springer, Heidelberg (2013). https://doi.org/10.1007/978-3-642-39931-2_14

20. Kontonasios, G., Korkontzelos, I., Ananiadou, S.: Developing multilingual text mining workflows in UIMA and U-compare. In: Bouma, G., Ittoo, A., Métais, E., Wortmann, H. (eds.) NLDB 2012. LNCS, vol. 7337, pp. 82–93. Springer, Heidelberg (2012). https://doi.org/10.1007/978-3-642-31178-9_8

21. Kontonatsios, G., Thompson, P., Batista-Navarro, R.T., Mihaila, C., Korkontzelos, I., Ananiadou, S.: Extending an interoperable platform to facilitate the creation of multilingual and multimodal NLP applications. In: Proceedings of the 51st Annual Meeting of the Association for Computational Linguistics: System Demonstrations, pp. 43–48 (2013)
22. Lin, C.Y.: ROUGE: a package for automatic evaluation of summaries. In: Marie-Francine Moens, S.S. (ed.) Text Summarization Branches Out: Proceedings of the ACL 2004 Workshop, pp. 74–81. Association for Computational Linguistics, Barcelona (2004)
23. Mihalcea, R., Tarau, P.: TextRank: bringing order into texts. In: Proceedings of Empirical Methods for Natural Language Processing, pp. 404–411 (2004)
24. Moens, M.F.: Summarizing court decisions. Inf. Process. Manag. **43**(6), 1748–1764 (2007)
25. Nenkova, A., McKeown, K.: A survey of text summarization techniques. In: Aggarwal, C.C., Zhai, C. (eds.) Mining Text Data, pp. 43–76. Springer, Boston (2012). https://doi.org/10.1007/978-1-4614-3223-4_3
26. Ogrodniczuk, M., Karagiozov, D.: ATLAS multilingual language processing platform. Procesamiento del Leng. Nat. **47**, 241–248 (2011)
27. Petrov, S., Das, D., McDonald, R.T.: A universal part-of-speech tagset. In: Calzolari, N., et al., (eds.) Proceedings of the 8th International Conference on Language Resources and Evaluation (LREC 2012). European Language Resources Association (ELRA), Istanbul, May 2012
28. Rocheteau, J., Daille, B.: TTC TermSuite: a UIMA application for multilingual terminology extraction from comparable corpora. In: Proceedings of the 5th International Joint Conference on Natural Language Processing (IJCNLP), Chiang Mai, Thailand, pp. 9–12 (2011)
29. Saravanan, M., Ravindran, B., Raman, S.: Improving legal document summarization using graphical models. Front. Artif. Intell. Appl. **152**, 51–60 (2006)
30. Sarkar, K.: Multilingual summarization approaches. In: Computational Linguistics: Concepts, Methodologies, Tools, and Applications, pp. 158–177 (2014)
31. Schweighofer, E., Rauber, A., Dittenbach, M.: Automatic text representation, classification and labeling in European law. In: Proceedings of the 8th International Conference on Artificial Intelligence and Law, ICAIL 2001, pp. 78–87. ACM, New York (2001)
32. Strötgen, J., Gertz, M.: Multilingual and cross-domain temporal tagging. Lang. Resour. Eval. **47**(2), 269–298 (2013)
33. Tanenblatt, M., Coden, A., Sominsky, I.: The ConceptMapper approach to named entity recognition. In: Calzolari, N., et al., (eds.) Proceedings of the Seventh conference on International Language Resources and Evaluation (LREC 2010). European Language Resources Association (ELRA), Valletta, May 2010
34. Yousfi-Monod, M., Farzindar, A., Lapalme, G.: Supervised machine learning for summarizing legal documents. In: Farzindar, A., Kešelj, V. (eds.) AI 2010. LNCS (LNAI), vol. 6085, pp. 51–62. Springer, Heidelberg (2010). https://doi.org/10.1007/978-3-642-13059-5_8

Towards Aligning *legivoc* Legal Vocabularies by Crowdsourcing

Hughes-Jehan Vibert[1], Benoit Pin[2], and Pierre Jouvelot[2(✉)]

[1] Ministère de la Justice, Paris, France
hughes-jehan.vibert@justice.gouv.fr
[2] MINES ParisTech, PSL University, Paris, France
{benoit.pin,pierre.jouvelot}@mines-paristech.fr

Abstract. *legivoc* is the first Internet-based platform dedicated to the diffusion, edition and alignment of legal vocabularies across countries. Funded in part by the European Commission and administered by the French Ministry of Justice, *legivoc* offers a seamless path for governments to disseminate their legal foundations and specify semantic bridges between them. In this system description paper, we outline the general principles behind the *legivoc* framework and provide some ideas about its implementation, with a particular focus on the state-of-the-art tools it includes to help crowdsource the alignment of legal corpora together.

Keywords: Legivoc · Classification · Legal foundations

1 Introduction

Easy and seamless access to law is of key import to states, institutions, businesses and citizens. Such a challenge is compounded when dealing with states that admit multiple languages, such as Belgium or Switzerland, or supranational institutions that embed states with different, even if sometimes similar, legal systems such as the European Union (EU) or the United Nations. Providing tools that help handling such diversity is of paramount importance in a connected world where open e-government and access to knowledge anytime anywhere are taken for granted.

Yet, when dealing with legal systems from different countries and/or languages, "in order to build a bilingual tool [and hence a multilingual one] granting access to legal terminology databases, translation will not be the only issue. Equivalence relationships between languages are not sufficient to convey the modalities of judicial systems connecting to one another. They shall be kept as such under the right circumstances, but one must search for the depth of the degree of relationship intrinsically binding two legal systems: that degree is called *functional equivalence*" [15]. Aligning functionally equivalent concepts in a seamless and consistent manner is one of *legivoc* main goals.

legivoc (all in lower case) is an Internet-based database platform dedicated to the management of multiple legal information terminologies, with a particular focus on vocabularies and their alignments [4]. The *legivoc* system is designed to be used both interactively and also as an automated Web service, interoperable with other document management tools or international legislation or translation systems, via a dedicated

U. Pagallo et al. (Eds.): AICOL VI-X 2015–2017, LNAI 10791, pp. 220–232, 2018.
https://doi.org/10.1007/978-3-030-00178-0_14

Application Programing Interface (API). The *legivoc* web site[1] is open and running, although in an "alpha" version for the time being.

The main goals of *legivoc* are: (1) to provide access, within a unique framework and using a general formalism, to (ultimately) all the legal vocabularies of the Member States of the EU; (2) to foster the use of best practices regarding the encoding of these vocabularies using Internet standards such as the Simple Knowledge Organization System (SKOS) and Uniform Resource Identifier (URI); (3) to encourage the creation of alignment information between these vocabularies, helping provide bridges between judicial systems based on different laws and languages.

The French Ministry of Justice spearheads the project, partly funded by the European Commission and the Ministries of Justice of the Czech Republic, Spain, Finland, France, Italy and Luxembourg. ARMINES and MINES ParisTech are the lead scientific advisors and implementation specialists for the *legivoc* project.

legivoc is intended to be used directly by law and judicial experts, for instance when dealing with cross-border legal issues or planning new legislative regulations. For such a purpose, knowing how a legal notion in a given vocabulary relates to similar ones in other countries, a so-called alignment is a key asset. We show how *legivoc* can be extended so that entering such information is a very intuitive operation, with the idea of relying on crowdsourcing efforts (where dedicated individuals perform useful tasks for the community, as in Wikipedia) to enrich its vocabularies.

The rest of this system description paper is structured as follows. In Sect. 2, we survey the current and planned systems that provide services somewhat related to the ones we focus on with *legivoc*. Section 3 introduces briefly the structure of *legivoc* and typical use cases. Section 4 focuses on the alignment process, which intends to build upon international crowdsourcing efforts to enrich the *legivoc* database. Section 5 outlines the communication capabilities embedded within *legivoc*, for use by the systems that want to take advantage of it. We introduce short- and long-term future work in Sect. 6, while concluding in Sect. 7.

2 Related Work

For years, computer-based tools have been a staple of legal departments that provide juridical help to both legal experts and citizens. We review here some of such systems, focusing on the ones that support multilingual functionalities, and put them in perspective with *legivoc* goals.

EuroVoc [16] is a multilingual (27 languages), multidisciplinary thesaurus that classifies all EU activities into about 6,800 labeled categories; organized into a 8-level hierarchy, it is used to loosely group related descriptors. EuroVoc users include the European Parliament, the Publications Office of the EU (which manages the thesaurus), national and regional parliaments in Europe as well as national governments. It was developed to (manually) categorize all relevant documents in order to perform multi-lingual and cross-lingual search and retrieval in potentially very large document

---

[1] www.legivoc.org.

collections. *legivoc* differs from Eurovoc by its focus on legal terminologies and their alignment, while Eurovoc only seeks to define labels that can be used to summarize all kind of subject matters addressed in EU documents.

CELLAR [5] is multilingual, semantic-based service provided by the Publications Office of the EU. It is based on a bibliographical ontology specifically designed to encompass all the material issued by the Office, together with its associated metadata. *legivoc* uses the same format as CELLAR, namely SKOS, to encode its taxonomies, but plans to address law systems both inside and outside of the EU, while using automated tools to enrich its database from a variety of sources. Moreover, *legivoc* intends to ultimately bootstrap its content-building effort via crowdsourcing and gamification.

EUR-Lex [6] is another effort from the EU which, when completed, will provide free access to the European law material (treatises, directives, jurisprudential data...) in 24 languages. It uses European Legislation Identifiers (ELI [7, 8]), which uniquely identify documents. The intent behind *legivoc* is to provide the same wealth of multilingual coverage but on a more limited data set, namely legal vocabularies, together with alignment information between concepts, which will be of use to both legal experts and translators, and even possibly the public-at-large. *legivoc* concepts are identified by specific SKOS concepts, although linking them with ELI-identified documents could be a valuable addition to the alignment goal targeted by *legivoc*.

The Inter-Active Terminology for Europe (IATE [9]) is a 10-year old, EU-funded web-based system that focuses on EU-specific terminology. Its almost 8.5 million entries target issues well beyond the world of law, up to agriculture or information technology, targeted by *legivoc*. Moreover, alignment information between similar concepts is not present in IATE.

The World Law Dictionary Project [10] (supported by TransLegal and nine law faculties) intends to provide alignment information from an online database in English to their equivalent in other languages. The use of a pivot language, here English, is a key distinguishing feature from *legivoc*, which in particular for political reasons, must remain language-agnostic.

3 *legivoc* 1.0

legivoc materializes as a Web site providing a state-of-the-art multilingual system for the creation, edition and alignment of international legal vocabularies (see Fig. 1. *legivoc* home page).

3.1 User Interface and Capabilities

In its current (6/2015) state, *legivoc* enables registered users to access the legal vocabularies of 13 Member States plus Switzerland, in addition to a global one managed by Eurovoc[2]. These vocabularies exist in multiple languages; these translated

---

[2] www.eurovoc.europa.eu.

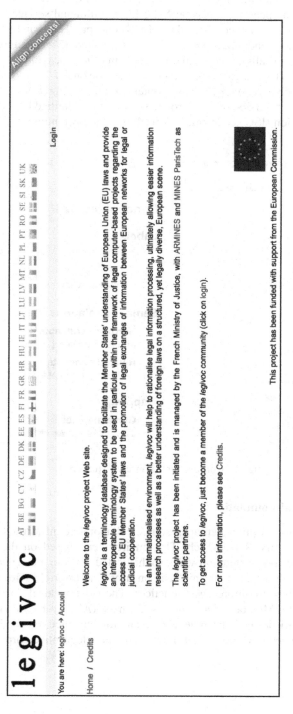

Fig. 1. *legivoc* home page

versions have been either provided by the Member States themselves or automatically translated via the European Commission MT@EC multilingual service [3].

Words in vocabularies are considered as SKOS concepts. They can be (1) visualized in various forms (text, dendogram, SKOS source), (2) edited, (3) related to more or less abstract concepts or (4) aligned to similar concepts in other vocabularies (see Sect. 4). We illustrate part of a typical display of a concept, here the one of "civil law" (see Fig. 2. Concept for "droit civil" (excerpt)). It was obtained, after a search for "droit civil" in *legivoc*, via the French version of the Eurovoc vocabulary, identified by its International Standard Organization (ISO) code eu, followed by its *legivoc* number, 523.

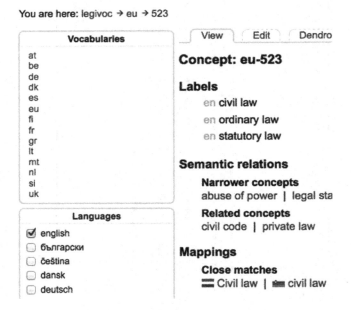

Fig. 2. Concept for "droit civil" (excerpt)

3.2   Technological Foundations

legivoc is built on top of plinn[3], an open-source collaborative infrastructure developed at ARMINES and MINES ParisTech. This environment, based on the Zope multi-purpose Web framework system, provides sophisticated ways to manage documents in various formats, with a particular emphasis on users' access rights, for security purposes, and workflows, to enforce best practices. The existing legal vocabularies provided by the State Members use various formats (ASCII, Excel, Word, XML, SKOS...); thus heuristics have been developed and implemented to encode them into a common *legivoc*-specific SKOS format. Introducing new legislative corpora, e.g., from

---

[3] www.plinn.org.

countries wishing to join *legivoc*, requires the design and implementation of new approximate algorithms, unless the data is already encoded into the *legivoc* SKOS format, which is strongly advised.

As an example, the SKOS encoding used by *legivoc* for the "droit civil" concept (see Fig. 2. Concept for "droit civil" (excerpt)) is provided below (see Table 1). After a constant list of definitions specifying the chosen encoding formats, each concept is given a unique number (here 523 in the Eurovoc vocabulary). Alignment information (see Sect. 4) is then followed by a list of alternate and preferred labels. The list of exact strings corresponding to each label completes the whole specification.

Table 1. SKOS encoding of the "droit civil" concept (excerpt)

```
@prefix dct: <http://purl.org/dc/terms/> .
@prefix legivoc: <http://legivoc.org/namespaces/2014/legivoc#> .
@prefix rdf: <http://www.w3.org/1999/02/22-rdf-syntax-ns#> .
@prefix rdfs: <http://www.w3.org/2000/01/rdf-schema#> .
@prefix skos: <http://www.w3.org/2004/02/skos/core#> .
@prefix skosxl: <http://www.w3.org/2008/05/skos-xl#> .
@prefix xml: <http://www.w3.org/XML/1998/namespace> .
@prefix xsd: <http://www.w3.org/2001/XMLSchema#> .

<http://eurovoc.europa.eu/523> a skos:Concept ;
  skos:closeMatch <http://legivoc.org/be/932>,
    <http://legivoc.org/fi/1619>,
    <http://legivoc.org/fi/2270>,
    <http://legivoc.org/nl/3792>, ...
  skos:narrower <http://eurovoc.europa.eu/164>,
    <http://eurovoc.europa.eu/186>,
    <http://eurovoc.europa.eu/3497> ...
  skos:related <http://eurovoc.europa.eu/5496>
    <http://eurovoc.europa.eu/576> ;
  skosxl:altLabel <http://eurovoc.europa.eu/523/label/11>,
    <http://eurovoc.europa.eu/523/label/13>,
    <http://eurovoc.europa.eu/523/label/15>, ...
  skosxl:prefLabel <http://eurovoc.europa.eu/523/label/0>,
    <http://eurovoc.europa.eu/523/label/1>,
    <http://eurovoc.europa.eu/523/label/10>, ...
<http://eurovoc.europa.eu/523/label/0> a skosxl:Label ;
  skosxl:literalForm "гражданско право"@bg .
<http://eurovoc.europa.eu/523/label/1> a skosxl:Label ;
  skosxl:literalForm "Derecho civil"@es .
...
```

Even though the presence of such diverse formats and possibly incompatible semantics is a clear challenge and the existence of a general, widely adopted vocabulary format would be a desirable feature, we take, with *legivoc*, a "can-do" approach, and try to leverage existing corpora instead of waiting for an eventual standard. In fact, our own *legivoc* SKOS format can be seen as a first proposal in this direction.

legivoc strongly adheres to W3C standards, such as (1) the Resource Description Framework (RDF), which uses 3-tuples (subject, predicate, object), also called triples, to represent data, (2) the URI naming convention, to denote such resources, (3) SKOS, an RDF-based representation format for vocabularies, and (4) the SPARQL Protocol and RDF Query Language (SPARQL), to search and access triples in an effective and expressive manner.

IT specialists can write and execute (possibly from a remote site, see Sect. 5) *legivoc* SPARQL commands to answer specific requests emanating from law or judicial experts (see Fig. 3. Querying the Greek vocabulary).

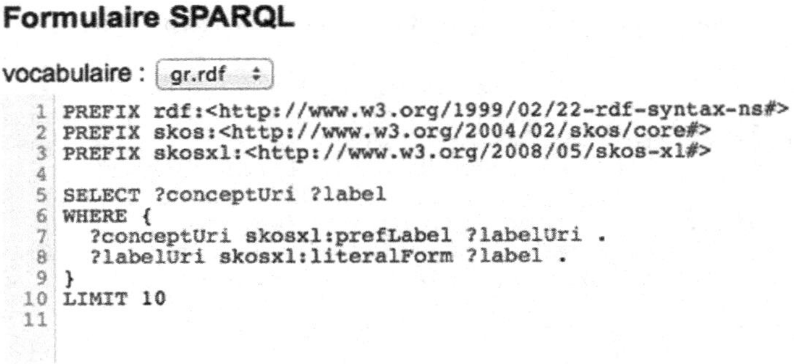

Formulaire SPARQL

vocabulaire : [gr.rdf ‡]

```
1  PREFIX rdf:<http://www.w3.org/1999/02/22-rdf-syntax-ns#>
2  PREFIX skos:<http://www.w3.org/2004/02/skos/core#>
3  PREFIX skosxl:<http://www.w3.org/2008/05/skos-xl#>
4
5  SELECT ?conceptUri ?label
6  WHERE {
7      ?conceptUri skosxl:prefLabel ?labelUri .
8      ?labelUri skosxl:literalForm ?label .
9  }
10 LIMIT 10
11
```

Fig. 3. Querying the Greek vocabulary

In this particular example, one asks for the list of all concepts, given by their URI, and their preferred labels, as strings, present in the Greek vocabulary. An excerpt of the output is given below (see Fig. 4. Greek concepts and labels (excerpt)).

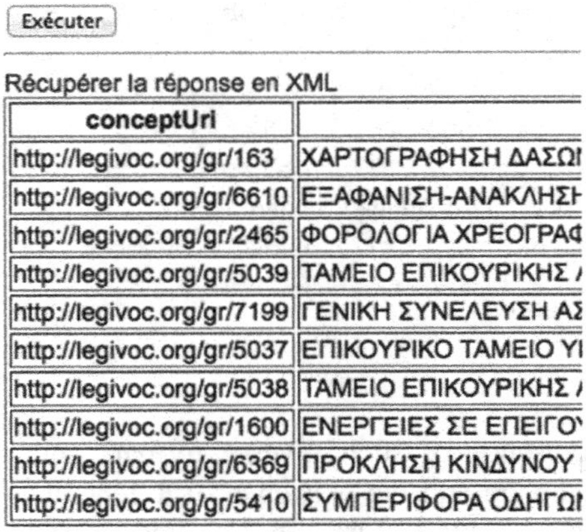

[Exécuter]

Récupérer la réponse en XML

conceptUri	
http://legivoc.org/gr/163	ΧΑΡΤΟΓΡΑΦΗΣΗ ΔΑΣΩΙ
http://legivoc.org/gr/6610	ΕΞΑΦΑΝΙΣΗ-ΑΝΑΚΛΗΣΗ
http://legivoc.org/gr/2465	ΦΟΡΟΛΟΓΙΑ ΧΡΕΟΓΡΑΦ
http://legivoc.org/gr/5039	ΤΑΜΕΙΟ ΕΠΙΚΟΥΡΙΚΗΣ /
http://legivoc.org/gr/7199	ΓΕΝΙΚΗ ΣΥΝΕΛΕΥΣΗ ΑΣ
http://legivoc.org/gr/5037	ΕΠΙΚΟΥΡΙΚΟ ΤΑΜΕΙΟ ΥΙ
http://legivoc.org/gr/5038	ΤΑΜΕΙΟ ΕΠΙΚΟΥΡΙΚΗΣ /
http://legivoc.org/gr/1600	ΕΝΕΡΓΕΙΕΣ ΣΕ ΕΠΕΙΓΟΥ
http://legivoc.org/gr/6369	ΠΡΟΚΛΗΣΗ ΚΙΝΔΥΝΟΥ
http://legivoc.org/gr/5410	ΣΥΜΠΕΡΙΦΟΡΑ ΟΔΗΓΩΙ

Fig. 4. Greek concepts and labels (excerpt)

4 Alignment Management

Alignment is a feature supported by SKOS, via the predefined `closeMatch`, `exactMatch`, `broadMatch`, `narrowMatch` and `relatedMatch` mapping properties that can relate two concepts in a somewhat hierarchical manner. Table 1 provides an example of alignment information; there, for instance, the concept of "droit civil" is mentioned as a close match to Concept 932 in the Belgian corpus (also called "Burgerlijk Recht", in Flemish – recall that Belgium admits two official languages). We believe the new approach to alignment management, described below, is one of the key features of *legivoc*.

4.1 Collecting Alignments

Introducing alignment information between vocabularies greatly enriches the semantic knowledge already embedded in *legivoc*. Yet, the size of the *legivoc* database, with its (up-to-now) 13 vocabularies sporting each an average number of concepts in excess of 7,000, would make this an expensive undertaking if one were to only use the text-based concept (and alignment) editor provided by *legivoc*.

One possible approach to handle data in such high volumes is to rely on automatic semantic analysis tools and techniques, e.g., machine learning, to suggest possible alignments to the user, an approach akin to the one advocated, for instance, for the EUCases project [14]. Given the more homogeneous nature of our data (only vocabularies), we decided to try another route.

We designed a streamlined and intuitive alignment environment within *legivoc* so that any benevolent user can help improve, in a friendly and even possibly "fun" way, the budding ontology induced by alignments. We indeed expect *legivoc* alignment content to be built from the ground up via crowdsourcing, building upon ideas stemming from human computation [1]. Providing a natural affordance for the introduction of alignments, using a simple but dynamic graphical user interface (see below), is a first step towards motivating the law community.

Another tool to increase participation we have had in mind from the very start of the project is gamification [2, 11], which has been shown to significantly improve intrinsic motivation in a wide variety of situations [12] and, interestingly enough, even when dealing with alignment in natural languages [18]. We view the entirely graphical and playful interface we designed, in opposition to mostly menu- and text-based interfaces seen in more traditional ontology-building tools such as Tematres [13] for instance, as a first step in this direction.

With its unique alignment extension environment, *legivoc* is now open (in read mode) to any user interested in participating in this ontology-building effort by providing new alignment information. To register as a legivoc user, the only user data required is a valid email address and an optional Twitter account. Indeed, all alignments are reported on Twitter, enabling following users to discover in real time when new alignments are being added and by whom, thus creating a sense of community and challenge. New alignments are currently checked a posteriori by law experts, to prevent as much as possible the input of possibly incorrect or conflicting information in the *legivoc* database; if need be, malevolent users could be blocked in short order and their actions reverted by a SPARQL command. In the future, this group of experts could be supported by selected digital volunteers (see for instance [17] for examples of such programs).

4.2 Using Alignments in *legivoc*

There are currently in *legivoc* three new modalities for introducing, in an intuitive manner, new concept alignments involving two different vocabularies. They vary according to how the relevant concepts are found:

- *list*, where concepts are displayed in alphabetic order;
- *search*, where the user inputs keywords to *legivoc*, which returns a list of concepts matching those words;
- *pick*, where the system chooses at random a given concept, and challenges the user to find a related concept in the other vocabulary.

The user then only has to mouse-select one concept in a given vocabulary and drag it on top of the other concept, in the second vocabulary. This process is made even easier and more informed via the use of dendograms, which display in an intuitive manner the hierarchical structure of law concepts (see Fig. 5. Aligning the UK and English-translated Spanish vocabularies, for a particularly rich example).

A typical illustration of the alignment environment is provided above (same figure). The top half of the screen is dedicated to the UK vocabulary, in list mode (by clicking twice on a concept name, here "communication", its partly elided dendogram has appeared), while the second half is in search mode on the Spanish vocabulary. Note that we use the English version of the Spanish law, obtained via MT@EC. The user has already dragged the blue bullet along the word "Media and the press" on top of "Public communication", thus creating an alignment, reported in the left window.

As described above, we are currently experimenting on the motivational aspects of our approach. As already mentioned and as graphically indicated by the ticked box dedicated to alignment tweeting, all alignments are tweeted on the @legivoc account, in the hope of motivating users. We also intend to use in the future this medium to keep users informed of *legivoc* developments and upgrades. Ultimately, users could also contribute their own tweets on this account, on a limited basis.

5 Using *legivoc* as a Web Service

We already alluded to the possibility of accessing *legivoc* remotely. This can currently be done in two ways: structured or not.

- The first one is via SPARQL commands (see Sect. 3) sent to a dedicated *legivoc* URL: legivoc.org/sparql_form. The first argument, query, is a string corresponding to the command to run, while the second one, db, is the ISO country code of the vocabulary on which the command is to be run. The output uses the XML format required by the SPARQL specifications. This service allows arbitrary,

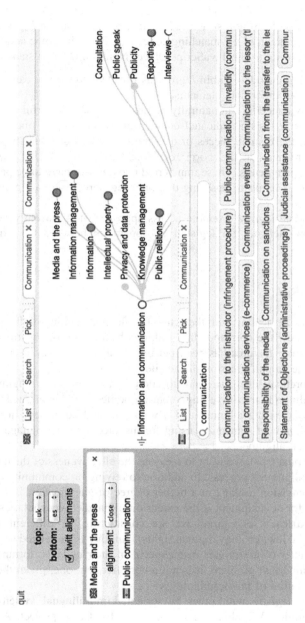

Fig. 5. Aligning the UK and English-translated Spanish vocabularies

non-modifying requests to be run on the *legivoc* database, thus providing a powerful and generic API for remote users and servers.

- The second access method is via the `legivoc.org/search_concepts` URL. It can be used to perform non-structured, textual searches on the *legivoc* database. The output, which includes the matching concepts URIs, with some additional data, is formatted according to the JavaScript Object Notation (JSON) standard.

Alignments, being encoded within *legivoc* as full-fledged triples, can be retrieved remotely as well as all other data elements.

Obvious security concerns can naturally be raised by such powerful remote access mechanisms. *legivoc* relies on dedicated cookies to ensure proper, fine-grained user rights management; these small pieces of data are transferred and locally stored after performing POST requests at the `legivoc.org/logged_in` URL, with proper name and password parameters. These transferred cookies will have to be passed along subsequent data access requests, ensuring that only registered users are granted access to the system.

In order to validate *legivoc*'s remote access approach, it is currently being tested within the legicoop[4] network for legislative cooperation between the Ministries of Justice of the EU.

6 Future Work

Future work will first be dealing with the actual full-fledged opening of the *legivoc* web site, and assessing how the corresponding traffic is handled by our platform. Unitary testing of all of *legivoc* features has been performed, and a few key users have been granted access to the "alpha" version of the site.

At a more theoretical level, we want to address reasoning over alignment information, e.g., regarding (1) transitive alignment properties ("if a is aligned with b and b is aligned with c, then the alignment of a with c should be present in the *legivoc* database") or (2) alignment semantics, using for instance natural language processing tools to infer implicit alignments.

On the motivational front, we want to measure the effectiveness of the tools used in *legivoc* to fuel the alignment process. In addition to relying on community effects, one could, if need be, envision looking at a higher degree of gamification.

Another venue for development is the extension of handled vocabularies, for either more countries (Africa is one target we are considering) or different application domains (commercial law, ecology, human rights). Another issue related to vocabulary extension is the matter of the proper management of their updates; fortunately, even though this is an important problem, it is not a very frequent one, given the generally relatively slow evolution of law terminology.

Finally, linking *legivoc* with other law-oriented multilingual systems presents interesting opportunities. We already mentioned the EU-Cases project. Another fascinating prospect could be Eunomos [19], currently dedicated to customer law and

---

[4] www.legicoop.eu.

where *legivoc* data could be used to extend its current analysis procedures and application domain [20].

7 Conclusion

We presented a new approach to the alignment input process for the international legal vocabularies stored within the *legivoc* infrastructure. Heavily based on existing W3C standards, it offers both an intuitive and even possibly "fun" interactive interface and a remote API. We rely on motivational techniques based on social networks tools such as Twitter to (hopefully) increase the amount of alignment information required to make *legivoc* a success.

The goal pursued by the *legivoc* project, and the joined forces of computer systems, AI and advanced HCI techniques, is to provide a key tool for economic, legal and political intelligence. Ultimately, we will be looking at ways of offering our enhanced data in Open access mode, while enforcing some country-specific copyright restrictions.

Acknowledgments. We thank Claire Medrala for her help with the implementation of the *legivoc* Twitter interface. We also thank the anonymous reviewers of the 2015 LST4LD and AICOL workshops for helping us improve our paper.

References

1. Michelucci, P. (ed.): Handbook of Human Computation. Springer, New York (2013). https://doi.org/10.1007/978-1-4614-8806-4
2. Deterding, S., Sicart, M., Nacke, L., O'Hara, K., Dixon, D.: Gamification using game-design elements in non-gaming contexts. In: CHI 2011 Extended Abstracts on Human Factors in Computing Systems (CHI EA 2011). ACM (2011)
3. Pilos, S.: European Commission Machine Translation and Public Administrations. Legivoc conference, Brussels, Belgium (2014). www.youtube.com/watch?v=B_rDUisXaB8. Accessed 7 Dec 2015
4. Vibert, H.-J., Jouvelot, P., Pin, B.: Legivoc - connecting law in a changing world. J. Open Access Law **1**(1), 1–19 (2013)
5. www.joinup.ec.europa.eu/sites/default/files/da/c3/de/CESAR-community_CELLAR.pdf. Accessed 7 Dec 2015
6. www.eur-lex.europa.eu/homepage.html. Accessed 7 Dec 2015
7. www.eur-lex.europa.eu/eli/reg/2013/216. Accessed 7 Dec 2015
8. www.eli.fr/en. Accessed 7 Dec 2015
9. www.iate.europa.eu/about_IATE.html. Accessed 7 Dec 2015
10. www.translegal.com/legal-english-dictionary. Accessed 7 Dec 2015
11. Walz, S., Deterding, S. (eds.): The Gameful World. The MIT Press, Cambridge (2014)
12. Rigby, C.S.: Gamification and motivation. In: [11] (2014)
13. www.vocabularyserver.com. Accessed 8 Dec 2015
14. www.eucases.eu. Accessed 7 Dec 2015
15. Mazet, G.: Jurilinguistique et informatique juridique. IRETIJ, Université de Montpellier (2001)

16. www.eurovoc.europa.eu. Accessed 17 Mar 2016
17. www.onlinevolunteering.org. Accessed 12 May 2017
18. Poesio, M., Chamberlain, J., Kruschwitz, U., Robaldo, L., Ducceschi, L.: Phrase detectives: utilizing collective intelligence for internet-scale language resource creation. In: Proceedings of the 24th International Joint Conference on Artificial Intelligence (IJCAI 2015). AAAI Press (2015)
19. Boella, G., Di Caro, L., Humphreys, L., Robaldo, L., Rossi, P., van der Torre, L.: Eunomos, a legal document and knowledge management system for the web to provide relevant, reliable and up-to-date information on the law. Artif. Intell. Law **24**, 245–283 (2016)
20. Boella, G., Di Caro, L., Robaldo, L.: Semantic relation extraction from legislative text using generalized syntactic dependencies and support vector machines. In: Morgenstern, L., Stefaneas, P., Lévy, F., Wyner, A., Paschke, A. (eds.) RuleML 2013. LNCS, vol. 8035, pp. 218–225. Springer, Heidelberg (2013). https://doi.org/10.1007/978-3-642-39617-5_20

Data Protection in Elderly Health Care Platforms

Angelo Costa[1], Aliaksandra Yelshyna[2], Teresa C. Moreira[2],
Francisco C. P. Andrade[2], Vicente Julian[3], and Paulo Novais[1(✉)]

[1] Centro ALGORITMI, University of Minho, Braga, Portugal
{acosta,pjon}@di.uminho.pt
[2] School of Law, University of Minho, Braga, Portugal
yelshyna@gmail.com, {tmoreira,fandrade}@direito.uminho.pt
[3] Departamento de Sistemas Informáticos y Computación,
Universitat Politècnica de València, Valencia, Spain
vinglada@dsic.upv.es

Abstract. Ambient Assisted Living provides solutions to the increasing cognitive problems that affect the elderly population. To provide all features possible, Ambient Assisted Living projects require access to personal and private information of their users. Currently, the legal issues arisen in Ambient Assisted Living are a hot topic in the European Union, especially aspects regarding unsupervised data processing and cross-sharing of personal information. In this paper it is presented the iGenda project, which is a Cognitive Assistant inserted in the Ambient Assisted Living area which aims to build safe environments that adapt themselves to one's individual needs. However, one of the issues is the protection of the data flowing within the system and the protection of user's fundamental rights. It is also presented the principles and legal guarantees of data protection and transmission, and legal aspects are explained, embracing appropriate solutions to technological features that may be a threat.

Keywords: Healthcare platform · Ambient Assisted Living
Data protection · Privacy · IGenda

1 Introduction

The dramatic increase in average life expectancy during the 20th century was achieved due to social and economic stability and medical improvements [18]. According to the UN report, in the year 2050 the elderly population is expected to be over 2 billion [18]. This growth of human longevity and birth rate decrease is threatening the sustainability of health systems and forces to rethink health care planning and provision [19].

Furthermore an important issue is the great medical care that the elderly population needs. Currently there are efforts to provide technological solutions, based on the Ambient Intelligence (AmI) and Ambient Assisted Living (AAL)

© Springer Nature Switzerland AG 2018
U. Pagallo et al. (Eds.): AICOL VI-X 2015–2017, LNAI 10791, pp. 233–244, 2018.
https://doi.org/10.1007/978-3-030-00178-0_15

concepts, which allow their users to stay at home, providing medical assistance through the use of devices and services that connect them with their physicians and medical staff [7,11,12,16,20].

The AAL is focused in people with some form of disabilities; the frameworks developed usually target the elderly population. The two main reasons why the elderly are chosen are: the considerable size of population they represent and the challenge that they pose as most possess more than one disability.

In recent years, some projects developed became a reference to the AAL area, because their goals, architecture or innovation. These projects are: AAL4ALL [15], Care4Balance [1], RelaxedCare [13]. The AAL4ALL has presented new ways of communicating with heterogeneous devices and services using the IEEE 11073 and the HL7 as base standards, which are commonly used in the medical area. The Care4Balance presented a new perspective in terms of gathering information of the caregiver and care-receiver. The RelaxedCare aims to create a novel social network that connects its platform users with their relatives. There are more projects but these are what seem more relevant in the area. The AAL area differs from the medical area because the information it has and the environment where the platforms are deployed.

Medical devices are tested and certified to achieve a high level of protection for human health and safety and a good functioning without any harm or malpractice to its users (Directives 90/385/EEC, 93/42/EEC and 98/79/EC). Therefore, they are very restricted in terms of features and the type of information the possess or generate. AAL projects usually require complete information about the users because most of the features rely on Artificial Intelligence processes, which consume big amounts of data.

The use of the AmI and AAL systems may present some difficult issues from a legal point of view due to the monitoring procedures and the cross-sharing of sensible information intend a serious risk of privacy loss. The AAL4AAL made several efforts to create a standard that encompasses the exigencies that AAL projects require, this would allow them to be equivalent to medical devices in terms of legal frameworks. Until now there are no advances in this field. Therefore, AAL projects have been barred the access to the medical environment, although that did not stop the development of medical features hoping that the regulations change.

Field tests performed on these projects, and others, reveal that there is a generalized acceptance by the elderly population and by the medical staff. The successful results show that these type of projects are needed and there is a market for them. The issue relies on the privacy and data protection. Something that the RelaxedCare project is working on, because there is nothing more prone to invade privacy than a social network. Enforcing encryption and social tools, as social spheres can be a way of keeping private data secure. One approach of attempted encryption is introduced by Doukas et al. [6], which proposes the introduction of Public Key Infrastructure (PKI) encryption [17] on sensor gateways, disabling middle-man attacks and packet sniffing. This security level is appropriate to secure remote data transmission, where data has to pass several internet nodes but it has a high computational cost. This is unfeasible to be implemented in internal data exchanges. The number of connections established in just one second rely on fast response, thus the overhead required is impractical. Furthermore, the complexity of AAL systems communications exceed the peer-to-peer type, which would require multiple keys to each user, increasing substantially the complexity of the encryption/decryption process.

This paper presents a discussion of the dichotomy between the current legal framework and ALL technology using the iGenda as an example, focusing on the privacy and data protection concerns. The aim is to find solutions to harmonize the technological advances and data protection requirements for current and future laws.

In the following section it is going to be presented an AAL platform, iGenda, showing the data transferred and user access to it. In Sect. 2 it is presented the current data protection framework and the legal warranties related to the AAL action area. Section 3 explains legal aspects of data storage and access law procedures. And finally, Sect. 4 presents the conclusions of the paper.

2   The iGenda Example

The AAL and AmI aim to build safe environments that adapt themselves to one's individual needs. Typically used in home environments (that can be adapted to nursing homes and others alike) AAL platforms are built with cost in mind, thus resorting to commercially available devices and software to implement their features. The goal is to deliver medical assistance to one's home, therefore decreasing hospital stays and visits sustaining the familiar feeling that a home provides.

The use of AAL systems require a large amount of personal information about the users of those systems, such as personal health record, data about social contacts, domestic activities, and physical location.

To better demonstrate the AAL concept we present the iGenda project [4, 5,10] that is an AAL platform that uses mobile devices and sensor systems to collect and process vital data, displaying them via mobile devices or the iGenda administration web-page. These procedures aim to improve the well-being of the users (the care-receivers) by creating a compendium of health data that can help to identify health problems or critical events.

In terms of features, the iGenda primary feature is to be a communication platform with an calendar manager that intelligently schedules regular events, plans social events and, directed to the medical staff, schedules medical appointments with the care-receivers, facilitating the creation of shared events.

There are three major actors in iGenda: the care-receivers (elderly or mentally impaired people), the caregivers (physicians or family/relatives), and the relatives (family and friends). They have access to specific information tailored to them, according to their needs. For instance, the care-receivers have no need to receive extensive medical information as it would only confuse them.

Apart from these three actors there is also the technician who is a trained professional responsible for the iGenda system and who is bound by a contract.

iGenda relies on data, in fact, without a large amount of data about its users it will not operate correctly. The platform uses a profiling method based on likes and dislikes of the users so it can suggest activities that please them. Thereon, the platform can schedule shared events of leisure activities that please all the participants and that also comply with the active-aging objective.

To find activities that are pleasant to all of the users, the system searches their activities database for similar events. The events have their own ontology, which relies on well-defined tags to each activity. Therefore, all activities are described the same way and their introduction is done by a iGenda technician. The similar activities are ranked by a weighted algorithm that analyses each activity classification (according to each user) and produces a new classification. The higher classified activity is then scheduled in a timeframe common to all participants (that anyone has no activities). For instance, if 4 users (that know eachother) like playing cards and have the Monday afternoon free the iGenda is able to schedule a card game on that time period.

Furthermore, the caregivers have the responsibility to care for the care-receivers that are assigned to them (they can be formal or informal, such as relatives or friends) and receive extended health or personal information about each care-receiver, effectively entering the private sphere of each user.

One of the great privacy protection issue is that in iGenda (and in most of the AAL projects) the information is shared and viewed by several users, some are bound by confidentiality obligations and others are not. Furthermore, the information will be present in iGenda as long as possible, e.g., at least as a specific user is registered in the system but in may be present for a longer period. These choices were taken so the platform is able to relate all information and social connections, thus being able to provide accurate event suggestions and health reports that are grounded to the common medical history.

3   The Data Protection Framework for AAL Systems

European Union legislation on personal data protection is presented by the Directive 95/46/EC (Personal Data Protection Directive) that was adapted in Portugal by the Law 67/98, 26 October on Data Protection (Portuguese Data Protection Act) and Directive 2002/58/EC (Directive on Privacy and Electronic Communications). The currently applicable Directive 95/46/EC is being revised and in the near future will be replaced by the General Data Protection Regulation (GDPR) which establishes rules adapted to the digital era and aims to harmonize data protection rules in the EU, introducing some new principles of data protection: data protection by default and data protection by design, which will then guarantee that data protection safeguards are being incorporated in all planning phases of development of the AAL solutions.

iGenda (and AAL platforms in general) collect and process personal and health data which is particularly sensitive and therefore requires special protection in accordance with the Directive 95/46/CE and Convention for the Protection of Individuals with regard to Automatic Processing of Personal Data

(Convention N.° 108). In Portugal, article 35 of the Portuguese Constitution stipulates a general prohibition of processing personal data, forbidding the use of informatics for the treatment of data concerning the private life of the citizens [9]. On the other hand, both the Portuguese Law 67/98 and the Directive 95/46/CE have specified that, within the prohibition of processing sensitive data, in addition to all data concerning the private life of the citizens, health, sexual and genetic data must be also included. However, there is an obvious exception to this general prohibition: the case when the data subject expressly consents, through free informed will, without any kind of coercion, being totally aware of all the effects arising out of his/her manifestation of will [2]. This requirement of a free and express consent is obviously related with the legal principles of personal data protection. First of all, the principle of transparency, meaning that the person responsible for the data collection and processing must be clearly identified and the data subject must be informed on its purpose and also on the delays for keeping the data, as well as the possibility and conditions of its communication to third parties.

One of the this principles that constitutes the truly fundamental and main principle of data protection is the limitation principle or purpose principle (partially embodied in article 6°, n. 1, paragraph (b) of the Directive and in article 5°, n. 1, paragraph (b) of the Portuguese Law 67/98). The referred principle prohibits further processing that is incompatible with the original purpose(s) of the collection. Personal and health data collected via AAL should only be processed for the purpose of providing AAL services and should not be used for any way incompatible with those purposes.

Article 6° of the Directive and article 5°, n. 1, paragraph (c) of the Portuguese Law 67/98 incorporate this principle of proportionality by stating that personal data must be adequate, relevant, and not excessive in relation to the intended and legitimate purposes for which personal data are collected and/or processed. Also, the processing of personal data must be strictly limited to the minimum required to achieve the AAL objectives, according to the minimization principle. In addition, each consultation of personal data that is available through the AAL should be justified by a real necessity of providing care, treatment or medicine prescription.

The proportionality principle is associated to the quality of the personal data which imposes personal data to be pertinent, kept up-to-date and not excessive in relation to the purpose for which they are collected. The treatment of personal data can only take place when it is indispensable for the initial purpose and irrelevant data should not be collected (article 6°, n. 1, paragraph (c) of the Directive).

According to the retention principle the collected data should not be retained in these systems for longer than necessary (see article 6°, n. 1, paragraph (e) of the Directive 95/46/CE and article 5°, n. 1, paragraph (e) of the Portuguese Law 67/98). This is an ambiguous principle as the maximum time is not defined and can be abused. This principle is established to prevent abuses and enforce legal protection if abuses are done. In the case of AAL projects, and in iGenda, some features require the collected data to be permanent, and that constitutes an abuse of privacy. Therefore, this issue is more relatable to ethical concerns, as while it is not illegal to keep the information a large period of time it may be considered unethical because users may not be aware of such time period. It is hard to fathom the concept of "forever" and what it means, thus most people cannot make an informed decision about the data their are surrendering.

In AAL platforms the care-receiver has the right to access and verify, without any need of substantiation, if the data concerning himself/herself are (or not) correct and updated. The provision of this information is necessary to satisfy the requirement of fair and lawful processing under the Data Protection Directive and also ensures informational self-determination [2,14].

4 Legal Aspects for Data Storage

The main issue of AAL platform consists on using sensors and profiling techniques that create a large amount of personal information (including health data) flowing the system. However, the health data is considered by European and Portuguese law as "sensitive data", thus requiring reinforced protection. Nevertheless, monitoring and profiling must be done in order to accomplish the minimal requirements for the platform operation, which does not mean that legal aspects are breached. It's important to guarantee the protection of the personal data in the iGenda project, in a way allowing the care-receiver to benefit from the available services and, at the same time, having all warranties of fundamental rights being respected.

4.1 Health Data

All AAL platforms must collect health data about their users and store it for historical operations, personal health records and future medical actions based on previous conditions. Therefore, iGenda is confronted with the difficult decision of which categories of personal data, particularly health data, should be collected and stored.

Health data is sensitive data according to Portuguese and European law and its processing may not be authorized in all situations, unless there is an explicit consent of the data subject and additional data security measures are available (article 8° of the Directive and article 15 nr. 3 of the Portuguese Law 67/98). An exception to the requirement of free and informed consent occurs when the care-receiver is temporarily unable to express consent (for instance, because he/she is in coma or totally unconscious) and, yet, the data collection or processing is absolutely essential in order to protect a vital interest of the care-receivers (usually life or death situations) and in this case, the fundamental right to life will always prevail [3]. Another important exception is the treatment of medical data for purposes of preventive medical actions, medical diagnosis, care or management of healthcare services that are carried out by health professional obligated to professional secrecy [2].

The delicate issue of AAL systems and iGenda platform is centered in the establishment of limits to this huge flow of collection, storing and transmission of health data, and these are related with the application of the data protection principles. Since it is crucial to observe fundamental rights of the individual (especially regarding the right to be left alone or the right to be forgotten) so, the data must only be stored while it is absolutely indispensable, assuring a balance between the collected data and the purposes of its collection and processing [2]. The care-receiver must always be informed about the presence of sensors and cameras and what type of personal data is being processed and for what purposes the data is planned to be used, according to article 11° of the Data Protection Directive. Additionally, to guarantee that only personal data that is necessary for each specific purpose is processed, we recommend that AAL platforms should be created with a mechanism of privacy by design and also a privacy impact assessment before it is used.

The Data Protection Directive directly and indirectly affects the process of keeping information about the medical history of the people that are supervised by AAL platforms. In fact, data protection principles represent an important limit to the processing and conservation of personal data under any form, mainly imposing restrictions in the elaboration of automatic profiles based on the personal data treated. To provide a secure and reliable medical diagnosis, it is imperative to have knowledge about previous medical problems. Therefore, by shortening the lifespan of the information, the Directive restricts the provision of any type of diagnosis and just responds to immediate problems.

4.2   Profiling

The essential feature in the iGenda that requires a large amount of personal data is the profiling technique. It automatically creates a database that mirrors the user's personality to better emulate the user's choices in non-critical decisions. In this database, each user is clearly identified and each one has its own profile type, such as care-receiver, the caregiver, and other users.

In accordance with the general rules of Data Protection Directive, when the construction of user's profiles take place, the iGenda (seen in this context as an entity) always informs the care-receiver with the following information: the precise purpose of the collection and processing of his/her personal data (e.g., for diagnosis, prevention), identity and contact details of data consumer, the precise categories of personal data the platform will collect and process, the recipients of the data entitled with the right of access and rectification, ensuring the transparency of all of the process of collection and treatment of personal data and the revelation of information to third parties [8].

These profiles contains various categories of personal data that require different degrees of confidentiality, therefore, each user has different access conditions to the database that includes explicit consent and special technical barriers for data protection.

4.3   Data Access Feature

iGenda features social interaction in highly heterogeneous group of people, connecting several of its users and sharing non-vital information among them. The issue that arises is that there is the possibility of building true knowledge from the crossing of non-vital information. Thus, by propagating previous rules, each individual may require being exempt from this feature and the removal of all information related to him/her. This right is associated to the right to be forgotten and the right to be let alone [2]. The care-receiver should be able to ask about the access of each party and be allowed the possibility of rectification, deletion or blocking of any parties or entities involved in the exchange of information within iGenda. Furthermore, the possibility of sharing personal data is also kept under control of the care-receiver: him/her can deny the collection and processing of his/her personal data and refuse access to optional information using privacy-friendly default options [2], with the downside of losing some or all iGenda features and services.

In the data protection domain, the integrity of the system and the control by the individual on data of his own can be achieved by the use of privacy-enhancing technologies and transparency-enhancing technologies as instruments capable of helping in the fulfilment of the requirements of informational self-determination [8]. The iGenda platform includes regular internal checks and controls of database access, which serve as a protection against intrusions. Therefore, the module of the Agenda Manager keeps a record of every connection made through a logging registry, which registers every communication tunnel established.

Nevertheless, iGenda intensely uses personal data. That is why data security must be implemented directly in the architecture of AAL (privacy by design), from the early design stages. The privacy by design approach has been addressed by the European Commission in their proposal for a General Data Protection Regulation and it can be a solution to some of the legal problems raised by the cross exchange of health data in iGenda, while preserving a high level of data protection. Currently, the iGenda provides some features that followed the privacy by design concept, e.g., encryption of data, login requirements for sensitive data, communication obfuscation, etc. These are not enough and more is needed to keep the information secure. Moreover, privacy by design has to be carefully considered, as it is relatable to technology and social factors. In terms of iGenda, the privacy by design is considered only applied to the technological features, implementing encryption here possible, assuring digital signatures and enforcing secure database access and communication tunnelling.

5   Technological Implementations

As explained before, iGenda has already some security features implemented. One is the secure access defined by user/password pair. Dealing with mobile devices, there is the possibility of others operating the device unlawfully. The visual interfaces are designed to be simple, and some information is directly displayed but, sensible and private information is protected with identification and passwords. The digital signature assures that the sender of events is the real person. The issue with the iGenda is that currently it does not enforce encryption on the message per se, but the content is stamped with the digital signature. The multi-agent system that sustains the iGenda provides ontologies and encryption to the underlying message system, which for internal messages of the platform is secure enough but not to exchange them over the internet.

Technologically speaking, security measures have their positives and negatives. While the positive are easy to see, the negatives are usually increased complexity and time and resources consumption. While common users may consider that spending a few seconds more in sending a message is acceptable, in a large scale system that time is not trivial nor unnoticeable. For instance, PKI encryption is a proven secure method, but it takes an considerable amount of time to be encoded or decoded (up to a few seconds) that shows an impact when implemented in low computing power systems like sensor platforms [6]. We have considered different approaches, like each user possessing a computer system at home that could decentralize the information but, that would only increase the number of security measures that would have to be implemented. So, the only solution to this issue is to wait for more advanced sensor systems that will have embedded encryption protocols. Until then, we will in the near future implement encryption in the messaging service of the smartphones, reinforcing the strength of the digital signature, but accept non-encrypted messages from other systems.

In terms of database security, the implementation relies on the database provider tools that encrypts in real-time its contents. The issue is the access to the information, and that is considered a social issue. The automatized services do not rely on people to operate and serves the information to the ones who require them. This situation shifts the burden of responsibility to the users. iGenda technicians will be scrutinized and under a non-disclosure confidential contract, which enforces these agents to be private about the information that they edit. Thus, the main issue related to the databases is the time that information is kept.

The profiling methods (and the medical information) require that the information about the users are kept at least during the time he/she is registered in the platform, and in some cases even more. For instance, if a specific user influenced or shared activities with others its information has to stay on the platform even if the user quits the service. It is our belief that other users must not have reduced services due to others actions, meaning that to keep the actions' history of each user intact, all the participants must be correctly identified. This is a difficult issue to resolve as it goes against two directives, the right to be forgotten and the retention principle. While the retention principle is somewhat easy to be met (as explained before), the right to be forgotten is only partially possible. There are two approaches to achieve it, delete all data related to the user who wishes to opt-out and void the assumption that users should not be impaired by other users actions; or to delete only part of the data and go against the legal ruling. Currently the iGenda is able to partially deleting the information of the users that which to opt-out, eliminating all private information but keeping social information (e.g. name and friends information) and to delete all information available. Although the latter option is not recommended by us.

As it happens in real life, one cannot be simply deleted from others lives and the interactions performed do not suddenly become vacant of that person. As interaction occurs there will always be some type of information trail. Therefore, until the Data Protection Directive encompasses new rules about social networks and information sharing it will be impossible to have iGenda features fully compliant.

6 Conclusions

The present study of the iGenda project has focused mainly on analysis in what measure its technical features stay in accordance with the legal requirements, in terms of privacy and data protection and what must be enforced to keep data transmission and processing within the legal boundaries. Along the previous sections, we have shown that the procedures of the AAL platforms, besides the potential risks of privacy loss and unauthorized access to personal data, can be used in accordance with the current data protection framework.

However, in order to benefit from the iGenda services and, at the same time, to guarantee all fundamental rights, the care-receiver needs to be allowed to make use of his legal right on informational self-determination by taking control on his own data flowing within the system. The acceptability of AAL projects also depend on an adequately high level of data protection and privacy that is why security-relevant issues must be identified in the preliminary stages of development. The environments here AAL projects operate are sensitive and most require that the frameworks are secure and without information breaches. We may consider that by the current standards the iGenda is able to be implemented in home environments, but to nursing homes, where the complexity increases exponentially, there legal considerations (and ethical) become a very important subject. Considering that the main players are the nursing homes, the acceptability by them to embrace the iGenda can be questioned and refuted.

The main concern is definitely the protection of the care-receiver and of the data flowing within the system, in a way allowing him/her to benefit from the available services and, at the same time, having all his/her fundamental rights being guaranteed. It was possible to observe that AAL projects are able to follow current laws but not without losing important features in terms of functionality that would be essential to improve ones' health condition.

Acknowledgements. This work has been supported by COMPETE: POCI-01-0145-FEDER-007043 and FCT-Fundação para a Ciência e Tecnologia within the Project Scope UID/ CEC/00319/2013. A. Costa thanks the Fundação para a Ciência e a Tecnologia (FCT) the Post-Doc scholarship with the Ref. SFRH/BPD/102696/2014. This work is also partially supported by the MINECO/FEDER TIN2015-65515-C4-1-R.

References

1. Care4Balance (2015). http://www.aal-care4balance.eu/
2. e Castro, C.S.: Direito da Informática - Privacidade e Dados Pessoais. Almedina (2005)
3. Correia, L.B.: Direito da Comunicação Social. Direito da comunicação social, vol. 1. Almedina (2005)
4. Costa, Â., Castillo, J.C., Novais, P., Fernández-Caballero, A., Simoes, R.: Sensor-driven agenda for intelligent home care of the elderly. Expert. Syst. Appl. **39**(15), 12192–12204 (2012). https://doi.org/10.1016/j.eswa.2012.04.058
5. Costa, Â., Novais, P., Corchado, J.M., Neves, J.: Increased performance and better patient attendance in an hospital with the use of smart agendas. Log. J. IGPL **20**(4), 689–698 (2011). https://doi.org/10.1093/jigpal/jzr021
6. Doukas, C., Maglogiannis, I., Koufi, V., Malamateniou, F., Vassilacopoulos, G.: Enabling data protection through PKI encryption in IoT m-Health devices. In: 2012 IEEE 12th International Conference on Bioinformatics & Bioengineering (BIBE), pp. 25–29. IEEE, November 2012
7. Grauel, J., Spellerberg, A.: Attitudes and requirements of elderly people towards assisted living solutions. In: Mühlhäuser, M., Ferscha, A., Aitenbichler, E. (eds.) AmI 2007. CCIS, vol. 11, pp. 197–206. Springer, Heidelberg (2008). https://doi.org/10.1007/978-3-540-85379-4_25
8. Hert, P., Gutwirth, S., Moscibroda, A., Wright, D., González Fuster, G.: Legal safeguards for privacy and data protection in ambient intelligence. Pers. Ubiquitous Comput. **13**(6), 435–444 (2008)
9. Marques, G., Martins, L.: Direito da Informática. Almedina (2006)
10. Novais, P., Costa, R., Carneiro, D., Neves, J.: Inter-organization cooperation for ambient assisted living. J. Ambient. Intell. Smart Environ. **2**(2), 179–195 (2010). https://doi.org/10.3233/AIS-2010-0059
11. O'Grady, M.J., Muldoon, C., Dragone, M., Tynan, R., O'Hare, G.M.P.: Towards evolutionary ambient assisted living systems. J. Ambient. Intell. Humanized Comput. **1**(1), 15–29 (2009)
12. Rashidi, P., Mihailidis, A.: A survey on ambient-assisted living tools for older adults. IEEE J. Biomed. Health Inform. **17**(3), 579–590 (2013)
13. RelaxedCare (2015). http://www.relaxedcare.eu/en/
14. Rouvroy, A., Poullet, Y.: The right to informational self-determination and the value of self-development: reassessing the importance of privacy for democracy. In: Gutwirth, S., Poullet, Y., Hert, P., Terwangne, C., Nouwt, S. (eds.) Reinventing Data Protection? pp. 45–76. Springer, Netherlands (2009). https://doi.org/10.1007/978-1-4020-9498-9_2
15. Sousa, F., et al.: An ecosystem of products and systems for ambient intelligence - the AAL4ALL users perspective. Stud. Health Technol. Inform. **177**, 263–71 (2012)

16. Sun, H., Florio, V.D., Gui, N., Blondia, C.: Promises and challenges of ambient assisted living systems. In: 2009 Sixth International Conference on Information Technology: New Generations, pp. 1201–1207. IEEE (2009)
17. Tepandi, J., Tšahhirov, I., Vassiljev, S.: Wireless PKI security and mobile voting. Computer **43**(6), 54–60 (2010)
18. United Nations: World Population Ageing, vol. 7 (2009)
19. United Nations: Population estimates and projections section. Technical report (2012)
20. Villacorta, J.J., del Val, L., Jimenez, M.I., Izquierdo, A.: Security system technologies applied to ambient assisted living. In: Lytras, M.D., Ordonez De Pablos, P., Ziderman, A., Roulstone, A., Maurer, H., Imber, J.B. (eds.) WSKS 2010. CCIS, vol. 111, pp. 389–394. Springer, Heidelberg (2010). https://doi.org/10.1007/978-3-642-16318-0_46

Assigning Creative Commons Licenses to Research Metadata: Issues and Cases

Marta Poblet[1(✉)], Amir Aryani[2], Paolo Manghi[3], Kathryn Unsworth[2],
Jingbo Wang[4], Brigitte Hausstein[5], Sunje Dallmeier-Tiessen[6],
Claus-Peter Klas[5], Pompeu Casanovas[7,8],
and Victor Rodriguez-Doncel[9]

[1] RMIT University, Melbourne, Australia
marta.pobletbalcell@rmit.edu.au
[2] Australian National Data Service (ANDS), Caulfield East, Australia
[3] ISTI, Italian Research Council, Pisa, Italy
[4] Australian National University, Canberra, Australia
[5] GESIS – Leibniz Institute for the Social Sciences, Mannheim, Germany
[6] CERN, Geneva, Switzerland
[7] IDT, Autonomous University of Barcelona, Barcelona, Spain
[8] La Trobe University, Bundoora, Australia
[9] Universidad Politécnica de Madrid, Madrid, Spain

Abstract. This paper discusses the problem of lack of clear licensing and transparency of usage terms and conditions for research metadata. Making research data connected, discoverable and reusable are the key enablers of the new data revolution in research. We discuss how the lack of transparency hinders discovery of research data and make it disconnected from the publication and other trusted research outcomes. In addition, we discuss the application of Creative Commons licenses for research metadata, and provide some examples of the applicability of this approach to internationally known data infrastructures.

Keywords: Semantic web · Research metadata · Licensing · Discoverability
Data infrastructure · Creative commons · Open data

1 Introduction

The emerging paradigm of open science relies on increased discovery, access, and sharing of trusted and open research data. New data infrastructures, policies, principles, and standards already provide the bases for data-driven research. For example, the FAIR Guiding Principles for scientific data management and stewardship [21] describe the four principles—findability, accessibility, interoperability, and reusability—that should inform how research data are produced, curated, shared, and stored. The same principles are applicable to metadata records, since they describe datasets and related research information (e.g. publications, grants, and contributors) that are essential for data discovery and management. Research metadata are an essential component of the open science ecosystem and, as stated in [17], "for a molecule of research metadata to

© Springer Nature Switzerland AG 2018
U. Pagallo et al. (Eds.): AICOL VI-X 2015–2017, LNAI 10791, pp. 245–256, 2018.
https://doi.org/10.1007/978-3-030-00178-0_16

move effectively between systems, the contextual information around it - the things that are linked to, must also be openly and persistently available".

Yet, finding relevant, trusted, and reusable datasets remains a challenge for many researchers and their organisations. New discovery services address this issue by drawing on open public information, but the lack of transparency about legal licenses and terms of use for metadata records compromises their reuse. If licenses and terms of use are absent or ambiguous, discovery services lack basic information on how metadata records can be used, to what extent they can be transformed or augmented, or whether they can be utilised as part of commercial applications. Ultimately, legal uncertainty hinders investment and innovation in this domain.

The rest of this paper is organised as follows: Sect. 1 presents the most widely adopted research metadata protocols and practices; Sect. 2 provides some global figures about the types of licenses used for research metadata; Sect. 3 identifies the main stakeholders; Sect. 4 reviews the most common choices for metadata licenses and discusses both advantages and disadvantages of such choices; Sect. 5 offers six compact case studies from different research data services. Finally, the conclusion raises some questions to guide future work.

2   Research Metadata Protocols and Practices

A number of instruments covering the management of research metadata are currently available. For example, the Open Archives Initiative (OAI) developed the Protocol for Metadata Harvesting OAI-PMH to facilitate interoperability between repositories and metadata service providers [14]. OAI-PMH enables harvesting the metadata of open access repositories such as PubMed, Arxiv, HAL, the Wikipedia [4], or the World Bank's Open Knowledge Repository (OKR).

The Dublin Core Metadata Initiative (DCMI) promotes interoperability and reusability in metadata design and best practices by developing semantic standards and recommendations, model-based specifications, and syntax guidelines, such as the Singapore Framework for Dublin Core Application Profiles or the DCMI Abstract Model.[1]

The RIOXX Metadata Guidelines,[2] implemented by more than 50 institutional repositories in the UK [20], have adopted NISO's "Recommended Practice on Metadata Indicators for Accessibility and Licensing of E-Content"[3] to add a tag (<license_ref>) with a reference to a URI carrying the license terms [13]. The main goal is to provide a mechanism of compliance with the RCUK policy on open access.

While the adoption of these instruments paves the way for technical standardisation, the discussion subsists with regard to the licensing options available and the implications of such choices. The issues arise out of the complexity of contractual obligations that the different types of licenses create, the extent of copyright laws in

---

[1] http://dublincore.org/specifications/.

[2] http://rioxx.net/.

[3] http://www.niso.org/apps/group_public/project/details.php?project_id=118.

different jurisdictions, or the difficulties of attribution when metadata are combined or remixed. Since a distinctive feature of high-quality metadata is that "it is created once and then reused as needed" [2], transparency and predictability are essential. The available options come with different requirements, conditions, and scope.

3 Current Use of Creative Commons (CC) Licenses in Research Metadata

Although many scientific data repositories live behind firewalls in proprietary environments, the Web houses thousands of scientific data repositories whose study is now possible. Marcial et al. [12] manually chose 100 diverse scientific data repositories and analysed 50 of their characteristics. While copyright issues were out of their scope, two of the observations referred to the input and output metadata's rights–distinguishing between the terms a contributor has to accept before uploading a new record and the license under which the entire metadata collection is offered. The text excerpts included in the 100 data repositories referring to these matters showed a huge variety of custom-made licenses and only two mentions to CC licenses were reported. The earliest data for this study were collected in 2007 and there is some evidence that the use of standardized licenses has dramatically increased since then. Yet, an updated study is still needed.

The Registry of Research Data Repositories by re3data.org (a service of DataCite) makes its data available for research under an API.[4] The Registry, now "the largest and most comprehensive registry of data repositories available on the web" [15] publishes an overview of existing international repositories for research data from all academic disciplines and as of September 2016, listed 1692 data repositories. An analysis of these repositories reveals that 269 (16%) of repositories made an explicit mention to CC licenses with a valid URI, while only 17 to Open Data Commons or 9 to GNU licenses. While these data require some caution (for example, the World Bank's Open Knowledge repository applies CC-BY 3.0 in most cases but it does not provide the corresponding URI) they offer a good snapshot of the current adoption of CC licenses in the research metadata ecosystem.

4 Main Stakeholders

The following stakeholders can benefit from assigning Creative Commons (CC) licenses to the research public metadata:

- Research Management Software Vendors: Assigning CC licenses to research public metadata will encourage software vendors to incorporate this data into their systems, leading to better automation in data entry and discovery capabilities of research management platforms.

---

[4] https://www.re3data.org/.

- Research Institutions: Better research management systems can reduce the cost of data entry for universities, and enable discovery of research collaboration opportunities. In addition, universities will be able to demonstrate their collaboration networks on the public domain using derivative analytics from CC licensed research metadata.
- Research Infrastructures (including data repositories): research metadata are the key enablers in creating interoperability between research infrastructures; particularly for research data repositories, public metadata enables connecting datasets across multiple systems and enables better discovery and reuse of the research output.
- Researchers: At present, finding related and relevant research, research data and other scholarly works is not a trivial task for most researchers. Better discovery tools augmented with public metadata would enable researchers to find related research and research collaborators, hence finding new research opportunities.
- Publishers: A clear indication on the applicable CC licenses would help to eliminate the uncertainties about possible consequences of reusing/republishing metadata.
- Funders: The collective effort by universities, publishers, infrastructure providers and software vendors can enable funders to have a better understanding of the impact of their funding; moreover, better research collaboration discovery can improve the return on investment.

5 Applying Creative Commons Licenses to Research Metadata

We address the issue of assigning clear licenses and terms of use for public research information by reviewing two frequently used Creative Commons (CC) licenses for public metadata records: CC0 and CC-BY. Creative Commons discourages the use of its NonCommercial (NC) or NoDerivatives (ND) licenses on databases intended for scholarly or scientific use, and they are not open licenses according to the definition of 'open" by the Open Knowledge Foundation.[5] It is important to note that CC0 and CC-BY are not the only open licenses available, as Open Data Commons, to refer to another popular option, offers three legal tools – the Public Domain Dedication and License (PDDL), the Attribution License (ODL-By) and the Open Database License (ODBL)—which covers the European sui generis database right (although now this is also the case of CC 4.0 licenses). The choices will depend on the objects to be licensed (creative contents, data, databases, etc.), the clauses and terminology that come with each choice, the derived contractual obligations, and the mechanisms of enforcement available to the licensor.

The most accessible form of CC instrument is CC0—"No Rights Reserved" (also known as Public Domain Dedication).[6] This is the choice of research data services such as Dryad or Figshare for their generated metadata. Increasingly, a number of cultural

---

[5] http://opendefinition.org.
[6] https://creativecommons.org/about/cc0.

institutions such as the Tate Gallery, the Museum of Modern Art (MoMA), the Walters Art Museum, or the Thyssen Foundation are also releasing their metadata with the CC0 document.

Nevertheless, there are some doubts about the force of the CC0 waiver in some jurisdictions (e.g. under Australian law), especially with regard to moral rights. As AusGOAL alerts, "the disclaimer that accompanies CC0, at present, may be ineffective in protecting the user from liability for claims of negligence."[7] The main issue with assigning a CC0 document to research metadata is the responsibility to collect the original records with the CC0 waiver. According to the Creative Commons definition (CC0 2016) "You should only apply CC0 to your own work, unless you have the necessary rights to apply CC0 to another person's work."[8] Hence, unless adequate provisions are taken, metadata aggregators or repositories would not be able to assign the CC0 license to records created by other sources. This is why, for instance, Europeana releases all its metadata with the CC0 document and requires its data providers to waive all IP rights to the metadata provided. Likewise the Digital Public Library of America (DPLA) requires all data and metadata donors to attach a CC0 document to any donation [6].

Another popular CC tool for open access works is the CC-BY license that enables third parties to distribute the work with attribution to the original author. CC 4.0 now makes this requirement more flexible as it can be done 'in any reasonable manner based on the medium, means, and context in which you share the licensed material".[9] A potential issue when assigning CC-BY licenses to aggregated metadata is that the sources of metadata records are not always clear. Who owns metadata records? The researcher who described the work? The research institution who owns the IP? Moreover, the CC-BY license requires to "indicate if changes were made" which adds to the complexity of enriching metadata by aggregators (CC-BY 2016). Given these options, assuming Copyright in metadata seems to be the safest approach. As Aus-GOAL advises, "recent developments in Australia have led to the situation where it is unclear which data is subject to copyright. In this situation, Australian researchers have to take a pragmatic approach and it would seem desirable to assume copyright as subsisting in all data created in the course of research, and ensure that it is licensed accordingly. No harm can come from this approach." [3]. ANDS adds to this, "It will still serve as a useful way to make known how you would like to be attributed, in addition to applying a limitation of liability and warranty clause to the data" [1]. In cases where it is clear that copyright does not subsist in the aggregated metadata, applying a CC Public Domain mark would suffice, provided the rights to do so have been established, including consideration that copyright for the material may subsist in other jurisdictions.

---

[7] https://www.ands.org.au/working-with-data/publishing-and-reusing-data/licensing-for-reuse/faq-for-research-data-licensing-and-copyright.

[8] https://creativecommons.org/share-your-work/public-domain/cc0/.

[9] https://creativecommons.org/licenses/by-nc-sa/4.0/legalcode.

6   Case Studies

6.1   CERN

The European Organization for Nuclear Research[10] is a hub for the High-Energy Physics community. The laboratory is used to handling complex and large-scale datasets. Among many other things, CERN operates a range of platforms and services related to scholarly information that serve specific community needs. For the purpose of this case study, two of them should be highlighted here. Both are openly accessible to the public and aim at fostering (re)use of the disseminated materials. One is INSPIREHEP, the main scholarly information platform in high-energy physics, aggregates information from all relevant community resources. Historically this mainly concerns preprints, but recently has also been extended to include research data. On top of the content and its metadata, the service provides 'author pages' (with ORCID integration) compiling information about researchers from the scholarly records available on INSPIRE [8]. The metadata on this platform are shared with a CC0 waiver, with the expectation that third parties or researchers themselves will use the available information to compile new services, such as citation statistics. The second example concerns CERN Open Data which is a dedicated portal to publish data, software and accompanying research materials such as documentation, trigger files, and tutorials to enable reuse by any interested audience. Objects are shared with Open Science licences, data and metadata with the CC0 waiver, and software with the GNU General Public License (GPL). CC0 was determined to be the best option for promoting the widest possible exploitation of the curated datasets. In addition, users are asked to cite the datasets whenever they publish a result based on the shared datasets. Each dataset is provided with a DOI to facilitate that process (according to Force 11 Data Citation Recommendations). So far the feedback on the choices made has been positive and highlighted the appreciation of clear, international and liberal license conditions for such materials.

6.2   da|ra

da|ra is a registration agency for social science and economics data in Germany.[11] It is run by the GESIS Leibniz Institute for the Social Sciences and ZBW Leibniz Information Center for Economics, in cooperation with DataCite (the international consortium promoting research data as independent citable scientific objects). This infrastructure lays the foundation for long-term, persistent identification, storage, localization and reliable citation of research data via allocation of DOI names. Each DOI name is linked to a set of metadata and presents the properties of resources, their structure and contextual relations. The da|ra Metadata Schema [9] provides a number of mandatory elements – six core properties –that have to be submitted by the data centres at the time of data registration. Although da|ra complies with the official

---

[10] https://home.cern/.

[11] http://www.da-ra.de/.

DataCite Metadata Schema, it has broadened the DataCite metadata by adding some specific properties related to the social sciences and economics. Therefore data centres may also choose other optional properties to identify their data. da|ra reserves the right to share provided metadata of the registered research data with information indexes and other entities. Under German law most of the formal metadata are not subject to copyright because the threshold of originality is not sufficient enough. [10]. As da|ra supports the open metadata principles the metadata of the registered research data are available under CC0 1.0 to encourage all metadata providers (data centres, data repositories, libraries, etc.) to make their metadata available under the same terms. Since 2016 da|ra has been offering access to the metadata using the Open Archives Initiative Protocol for Metadata Harvesting [14]. The da|ra OAI-PMH Data Provider is able to disseminate records in various formats such as DDI-Lifecycle 3.1 and OAI DC.

6.3   NCI

The National Computational Infrastructure (NCI)[12] at the Australian National University (ANU) has evolved to become Australia's peak computing centre for national computational and Data-intensive Earth system science. More recently NCI collocated 10 Petabytes of 60+ major national and international environmental, climate, earth system, geophysics and astronomy data collections to create the National Environmental Research Interoperability Data Platform (NERDIP). Data Collection management has become an essential activity at NCI. NCI's partners (CSIRO, Bureau of Meteorology, Australian National University, and Geoscience Australia), supported by the Australian Government and Research Data Storage Infrastructure (RDSI) and Research Data Services (RDS), have established a national data resource that is co-located with high-performance computing. NCI uses license conditions, national/international regulations as guidance for data governance. The license file is required as the very first step of our data publishing process, this requirement has greatly pushed the progress of the license investigation within the data provider's agency. The license files are published jointly with data through NCI's OpenDAP server[13]. More than half of NCI's data collection projects have license files published with the metadata records. The access and use constraints of the rest collections are still being investigated. Most of the data are quality assured for being 'published' and made accessible as services under Creative Commons Attribution (CC-BY) 4.0 as they are sourced from commonwealth government agencies [9]. However, some geophysical surveys were conducted through Australian state government, where the state license is applied while discussion about moving state license to CC-BY4.0 is happening. Other type of licenses exist for our international data collections, such as Earth System Grid Federation (ESGF[14]) require every single user to register an OpenID as the way to agree with the ESGF license, Copernicus Sentinel Data and Service Information regulated by

[12] http://nci.org.au.
[13] http://dapds00.nci.org.au/thredds/catalog/licenses/catalog.html.
[14] https://esgf.llnl.gov/.

EU law[15], European Centre for Medium-Range Weather Forecasts[16] data has more strict license[17] for data access and usage so that it is only available to NCI users who agree with the license and can only access data through Raijin supercomputer. Different license often means different project code on the file system as we need to grant different type of access to each individual project. Therefore, the license condition has become one of the important indicators for our data management practice. The metadata associated with data collection are available under CC-BY4.0. They are publicly available for users to query the metadata catalogue entries. Our collection level metadata has also been harvested by national and international aggregators such as Research Data Australia (RDA) and International Directory Network of Committee on Earth Observation Satellites (CEOS).

6.4 OpenAIRE

The OpenAIRE[18] infrastructure is the point of reference for Open Access and Open Science in Europe (and beyond) [11]. Its mission is twofold: enabling the Open Science cultural shift of the current scientific communication infrastructure by linking, engaging, and aligning people, ideas, resources, and services at the global level; monitoring of Open Access trends and measuring research impact in terms of publications and datasets to serve research communities and funders. To this aim, OpenAIRE offers services [19] that collect, harmonize, de-duplicate, and enrich by inference (text mining) or end-user feedback, metadata relative to publications, datasets, organizations, persons, projects and several funders from all over the world.

As for any repository aggregation system, access and usage rights of the 25 million records collected by the OpenAIRE system plays a rather important role in the lifecycle of the overall infrastructure. However, from an analysis run in January 2017, out of 2500 publication repository services (supporting the OAI-PMH protocol standard) registered in the OpenDOAR directory[19], only 9 expose metadata license information: 3 with CC-0, 2 with CC-BY, and 4 which require a permission for commercial use, 3 with CC-0 and 1 with CC-BY. Repository managers, as well as their institutions, seem to convene that metadata records are generally free of access and reuse, and underestimate the importance of licensing. In order to cope with this "legal gap", starting from the end of 2017, OpenAIRE services will request data source managers to accept Terms of Agreement where they are informed of the intention of OpenAIRE to collect the records, transform/enrich them, and make the accessible to third-parties with provenance information. The aggregated OpenAIRE graph is exported via standard protocols (e.g. HTTP-REST search, LOD, OAI-PMH) and formats, and the metadata records are available under CC-0, with no restriction of embargo or re-use. This ToA based approach seemed the only reasonable solution in order to offer properly usable

---

[15] http://dapds00.nci.org.au/thredds/fileServer/licenses/fj7_licence.pdf.

[16] https://www.ecmwf.int/.

[17] http://dapds00.nci.org.au/thredds/fileServer/licenses/ub4_licence.pdf.

[18] https://www.openaire.eu/.

[19] http://www.opendoar.org/.

metadata obtained from a large set of unlicensed data sources: the aggregating system can safely carry on its function, as metadata records are collected on request of the repository managers.

6.5 ResearchGraph

Research Graph[20] is an example of value added to data infrastructures by third-party services. Research Graph is a collaborative project by a number of international partners that links research information (datasets, grants, publications and researchers) across multiple platforms (Fig. 1). This initiative uses the research metadata to construct a graph of scholarly works, and this graph connects data and publications with multiple degrees of separation. The outcome enables a researcher to search the graph for a particular publication or research project and discovers a collaboration network of researchers who are connected to this work (or topic). The main consideration for such a service is the ability to read, connect and transform metadata, and without clear licensing or terms of use, this platform would not be able to include a data infrastructure in the graph. In addition, given the mixture of licences provided by different

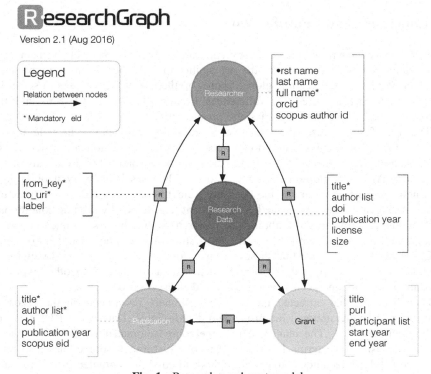

Fig. 1. Research graph metamodel

---

[20] http://researchgraph.org/.

contributors the constructed graph is not publically available as a single dataset. Instead, it had to be split into separate clusters where the license for each cluster can be defined from the individual sources. For example, Research Graph holds a cluster of nodes about Australian Research Grants and Australian Research Data without any explicit license provided by the metadata source. As such the given cluster, cannot be integrated into systems that require CC0 license. On the contrary, Research Graph composed of clusters from da-ra and CERN metadata records that all contain well-described license leading to a much more usable network of scholarly communication that can be used by commercial and open access systems with clear terms of use. For systems with heterogeneous data sources, it is often difficult to find a minimum technical requirement for all connected components, as such a hybrid technical approach can be adopted to enable interoperability between systems. However, in the case of Research Graph, this is very difficult to achieve due to lack of legal interoperability between information systems.

Figure 1 shows the Research Graph metamodel. The metamodel contains three four main Research Graph node types: Researcher, Research Data, Publication and Grant. The metadata of all these nodes require well defined terms of use to enable consuming and processing by research management systems and other information systems.

7   Conclusions and Future Work

In this paper we have raised the need for a transparent regime of metadata licensing and have briefly reviewed the state-of-the art application of open licenses to research metadata. We have offered some global figures on the use of CC licenses in scientific research metadata, explored the differences between CC0 and CC-BY, and the approach taken by five data registries and/or repositories.

The use of standardized licenses fosters reusability and science in general, and choosing CC or alternative well-known licenses favours the automatic discovery of usable datasets (e.g. *search by license*), which can be accomplished by means of the re3data.org API. An additional advantage of CC licenses is their availability in a machine-readable form, namely, the license document contains a RDFa which enable further intelligent processing of the license content (e.g. search by specific conditions).

The examples reviewed did not include research funding bodies, an integral part of the meta-research ecosystem [16] and the integration of researcher identifiers (such as ORCID); hence, we believe that these are areas for future investigation. Likewise, it could be further investigated if research metadata, as compared to other types of metadata, have enough specificity to require a dedicated set of licenses.

Data licensing has attracted the attention of many researchers in the fields of Semantic Web, computational linguistics and deontic logic. Datasets of RDF licenses do exist already [18]. The challenge of developing automated frameworks able to generate licensing data terms from heterogeneous distributed sources has also been addressed [7]. NLP techniques to extract rights and conditions granted by licenses and return them into RDF have been applied [5]. We believe that these technical solutions offer a number of advantages and deserve to be monitored, reused, and tested in real scenarios.

However, the context-dependent problems and ambiguities highlighted in this paper still survive, such as the discussion of how to share the metadata generated in scientific research, whether it should accrue the public domain or, rather, whether scientists and research organisations should retain a legal expression of attribution, including the implications of such choices. For example, if assigning CC licenses to remixed metadata requires modifying the records at the source (or get consent from all creators involved), the process can be difficult to escalate.

This is a domain that requires some *previous* positioning before making decisions about the appropriate heuristics for end-users interfaces. The underlying philosophy and assumptions about building semi-automated ecosystems for data science face practical legal, commercial, and political issues that require attention.

References

1. ANDS: Australian National Data Service guide on Metadata stores solutions (2016). http://www.ands.org.au/guides/metadata-stores-solutions. Accessed 5 May 2016
2. ANDS: Guides 2016, Copyright, data and licensing guide (2016). http://ands.org.au/guides/copyright-data-and-licensing
3. AusGoal: Research data FAQs (2016). http://www.ausgoal.gov.au/research-data-faqs. Accessed 9 May 2016
4. Bianchini, L.: Metadata in scientific publication (2012). https://www.mysciencework.com/omniscience/metadata-in-scientific-publication. Accessed 9 May 2016
5. Cabrio, E., Palmero Aprosio, A., Villata, S.: These are your rights. In: Presutti, V., d'Amato, C., Gandon, F., d'Aquin, M., Staab, S., Tordai, A. (eds.) ESWC 2014. LNCS, vol. 8465, pp. 255–269. Springer, Cham (2014). https://doi.org/10.1007/978-3-319-07443-6_18
6. Cohen, D.: CC0 (+BY) (2013). http://www.dancohen.org/2013/11/26/cc0-by/. Accessed 5 May 2016
7. Governatori, G., Rotolo, A., Villata, S., Gandon, F.: One license to compose them all. In: Alani, H., et al. (eds.) ISWC 2013. LNCS, vol. 8218, pp. 151–166. Springer, Heidelberg (2013). https://doi.org/10.1007/978-3-642-41335-3_10
8. Hecker, B.L.: Four decades of open science. Nat. Phys. **13**(6), 523–525 (2017)
9. Helbig, K., Hausstein, B., Koch, U., Meichsner, J., Kempf, A.O.: da|ra Metadata Schema. Version: 3.1. GESIS - Technical reports 2014/17 (2014). http://doi.org/10.4232/10.mdsdoc.3.1. Accessed 24 July 2017
10. Klimpel, P.: Eigentum an Metadaten? Urheberrechtliche Aspekte von Bestandsinformationen und ihre Freigabe. In: Handbuch Kulturportale, Online-Angebote aus Kultur und Wissenschaft. Eds. Ellen Euler, Monika Hagedorn-Saupe, Gerald Maier, Werner Schweienz and Jörn Siegelschmidt, Berlin/Boston, pp. 57–64 (2015). https://irights.info/artikel/eigentum-an-metadaten-urheberrechtliche-aspekte-von-bestandsinformationen-und-ihre-freigabe-2/26829. Accessed 24 July 2017
11. Manghi, P., Bolikowski, L., Manola, N., Shirrwagen, J., Smith, T.: Openaireplus: the European scholarly communication data infrastructure. D-Lib Mag. **18**, 9–10 (2012)
12. Marcial, L.H., Hemminger, B.M.: Scientific data repositories on the Web: an initial survey. J. Am. Soc. Inf. Sci. **61**, 2029–2048 (2010). https://doi.org/10.1002/asi.21339
13. NISO RP-22-2015: Access License and Indicators, January 2015. http://www.niso.org/apps/group_public/download.php/14226/rp-22-2015_ALI.pdf. Accessed 6 Sept 2016

14. OAI: The open archives initiative protocol for metadata harvesting (2015). https://www.openarchives.org/OAI/openarchivesprotocol.html. Accessed 5 May 2016
15. Pampel, H., Vierkant, P., Scholze, F., Bertelmann, R., Kindling, M., Klump, J., et al.: Making research data repositories visible: The re3data.org Registry. PLoS ONE 8(11), e78080 (2013)
16. Poblet, M., Aryani, A., Caldecott, K., Sellis, T., Casanovas, P.: Open-Access grant data: towards meta-research innovation. In 27th International Conference on Legal Knowledge and Information Systems: Jurix 2014, pp. 125–130 (2014)
17. Porter, S.: A new research data mechanics. Digital Science White Paper (2016). https://s3-eu-west-1.amazonaws.com/pfigshare-u.../ANewResearchDataMechanics.pdf
18. Rodríguez Doncel, V., Gómez-Pérez, A., Villata, S.: A dataset of RDF licenses. In: Hoekstra, R. (ed.) Legal Knowledge and Information Systems. The Twenty-Seventh Annual Conference, JURIX-2014, pp. 187–189. IOS Press, Amsterdam (2014)
19. Schirrwagen, J., Manghi, P., Manola, N., Bolikowski, L., Rettberg, N., Schmidt, B.: Data curation in the OpenAire scholarly communication infrastructure. Inf. Stand. Q. 25(3), 13–19 (2013)
20. Walk, P.: RIOXX adoption reaches a half-century (2016). http://www.rioxx.net/2016/04/12/rioxx-adoption-reaches-a-half-century/. Accessed 7 Sept 2016
21. Wilkinson, M., Dumontier, D., Mons, M.: The FAIR guiding principles for scientific data management and stewardship. Sci. Data 3, 160018 (2016). https://doi.org/10.1038/sdata.2016.18%5b21%5d

Dataset Alignment and Lexicalization to Support Multilingual Analysis of Legal Documents

Armando Stellato[1(⊠)], Manuel Fiorelli[1], Andrea Turbati[1],
Tiziano Lorenzetti[1], Peter Schmitz[2], Enrico Francesconi[2,3(⊠)],
Najeh Hajlaoui[2], and Brahim Batouche[2]

[1] ART Group, Department of Enterprise Engineering, University of Rome Tor
Vergata, Via del Politecnico 1, 00133 Rome, Italy
stellato@uniroma2.it,
{fiorelli, turbati}@info.uniroma2.it,
tiziano.lorenzetti@gmail.com
[2] Publications Office of the European Union, Luxembourg City, Luxembourg
{Peter.SCHMITZ,
Enrico.Francesconi}@publications.europa.eu,
{Najeh.HAJLAOUI,
Brahim.BATOUCHE}@ext.publications.europa.eu
[3] Institute of Legal Information Theory and Techniques (ITTIG),
Consiglio Nazionale delle Ricerche (CNR),
Via dei Barucci 20, 50127 Florence, Italy

Abstract. The result of the EU is a complex, multilingual, multicultural and yet united environment, requiring solid integration policies and actions targeted at simplifying cross-language and cross-cultural knowledge access. The legal domain is a typical case in which both the linguistic and the conceptual aspects mutually interweave into a knowledge barrier that is hard to break. In the context of the ISA[2] funded project "Public Multilingual Knowledge Infrastructure" (PMKI) we are addressing Semantic Interoperability at both the conceptual and lexical level, by developing a set of coordinated instruments for advanced lexicalization of RDF resources (be them ontologies, thesauri and datasets in general) and for alignment of their content. In this paper, we describe the objectives of the project and the concrete actions, specifically in the legal domain, that will create a platform for multilingual cross-jurisdiction accessibility to legal content in the EU.

1 Introduction

The construction of the European Union is one of the most relevant political success stories of the last decades, able to guarantee a space of freedom, justice and democracy for millions of European citizens, based on the free exchange of people, information, goods and services.

However, complex, multilingual and multicultural as Europe is, it cannot rely on political success and good intentions alone: the objectives of its unification must be

© Springer Nature Switzerland AG 2018
U. Pagallo et al. (Eds.): AICOL VI–X 2015–2017, LNAI 10791, pp. 257–271, 2018.
https://doi.org/10.1007/978-3-030-00178-0_17

underpinned by solid integration policies and targeted actions, considering and dealing with the heterogeneities that lay at the basis of the foundation of EU itself.

The legal domain is an emblematic example of this heterogeneity: while united under common goals and ethics, each of the Member States retains its own laws and regulations. These need to be aligned to the common directions and indications provided by the EU Parliament, while keeping their independence and bindings to the constitutions characterizing each nation. The differences are not technically limited to the regulations per se, being the whole fabric of knowledge bond to the cultural and societal heritage of a nation. For instance, the French concept "tribunaux administratifs" cannot be translated in English as "administrative tribunals". The English word for "tribunaux" in fact is "courts" while the "administrative tribunals" are administrative commissions which are comparable, mutatis mutandis, to the French "autorités administratives indépendantes" [1]. There is however, as this example shows, a linguistic problem as well, as it is important that the reached semantic consensus on recognized similarities and affinities be available and accessible in different languages.

In such a scenario, the European digital eco-system should be made ready to support seamless and cross-lingual access to Member States' legislations, accounting for their differentia as well as their relatedness under the common umbrella of the EU.

With this objective to pursue, and in a broader context including, but not limited to, the domain of jurisprudence and law, in 2010 the EU defined the so-called European Interoperability Framework, namely a set of recommendations and guidelines to support the pan-European delivery of electronic government services. This framework aims at facilitating public administrations, enterprises and citizens to interact across borders, in a pan-European context. Such guidelines cover different aspects of social, commercial and administrative relations among different European actors, like multilingualism, accessibility, security, data protection, administrative simplification, transparency, reusability of the solutions.

One of the main objectives of such guidelines is to establish semantic interoperability between digital services, having the potential to overcome the barriers hampering their effective cross-border exploitation, which means making information exchange not only understandable by humans but also understandable and processable by machines, as well as establishing correspondences between concepts in different domains and languages, or represented in different digital tools (like controlled vocabularies, classification schemas, thesauri).

In the context of the Public Multilingual Knowledge Infrastructure (PMKI), a project funded by the ISA² programme[1] with the aim to overcome language barriers within the EU by means of multilingual tools and services, we are addressing Semantic Interoperability at both the conceptual and lexical level, by developing a set of coordinated instruments for advanced lexicalization of RDF resources (be them ontologies, thesauri and datasets in general) and for alignment of their content.

In this paper, we will show how the realization of such an objective will enable seamless, multilingual, cross-legislative retrieval and analysis of legal content, and will show how the PMKI project will contribute to such a vision by detailing it objectives

---

[1] https://ec.europa.eu/isa2/

and milestones. The rest of the paper is organized as follows: Sect. 2 provides more motivations for our effort and describes use case scenarios. In Sect. 3 a brief overview on the evolution of models for representing lexical resources is given. Section 4 introduces the PMKI project, while Sect. 5 details the actions of the project and their outcomes in the legal domain. Section 6 concludes the paper.

2   Use-Case Scenarios

There are several scenarios in the management and access to legal content that would benefit from a thorough approach to conceptual and lexical integration.

2.1   Semantic Integration

As shown in [2], a typical use case for the adoption of legal ontologies is their application to specialist domains (e.g. industry standards), which in turn opens up different interaction possibilities between the legal knowledge (e.g. norms and regulations) and the one pertaining to the specialized domain (e.g. a domain ontology related to the aforementioned industry standards). Alignments between legal ontologies and specialized domain ontologies should be considered as precious resources per se, as well as the systems and frameworks that support the creation of such artifacts.

Semantic integration between analogous legal knowledge resources developed in different countries is also important, in order to facilitate the understanding of alien concepts through those closer to one's own culture or, at least, through general shared conceptualizations. For instance, the Italian thesaurus TESEO[2] (TEsauro SEnato per l'Organizzazione dei documenti parlamentari: Senate Thesaurus for the organization of parliamentary documents) is a classification system, originally developed by the Italian Senate and now used in the most relevant databases of the Senate, Chamber of Deputies and of some regions of Italy. Even in the multilingual environment characterizing the EU, the monolingual TESEO (its concepts are expressed in Italian only) keeps its relevance due to its tight connection to the Italian law regulation system and culture (TESEO includes a mix of specific legal concepts and more general topics). It is thus an irreplaceable resource for semantically indexing information from the abovementioned Italian data and document bases. At the same time, aligning TESEO to other resources, such as the EU's multilingual thesaurus EuroVoc[3], the multilingual thesaurus of the EU, allows for cross-cultural and cross-lingual (EuroVoc is available in 26 languages, chosen from those spoken by EU Member States and candidate countries) mediated access to any content indexed through it. While EuroVoc obviously lacks the specificities that TESEO can offer to the Italian interested user, it still provides a best-mediated access modality, universally accepted and officially adopted within the EU.

---

[2] https://www.senato.it/3235?testo_generico=745

[3] http://eurovoc.europa.eu/

2.2   Natural Language Understanding

Another very important scenario (which, in turn, includes a plethora of use cases) concerns the identification and extraction of relevant information. The identified information can be exploited in a variety of tasks, such as:

Annotation of Document Corpora. In the legal domain law references, articulated in proper structures (e.g. law, article, paragraph), are important indexing elements for documents. Being able to search corpora by including explicit constraints on mentioned regulations is a powerful feature for legal search engines. For instance, a lawyer could access to the full list of trials registered for a given court, and extract all judgements that include a mention of a given law (or a set of laws), eventually specifying portions of them. However, discovering references is not trivial, as it implies both being able to parse the structure of a law mention (a mix of natural language processing capabilities and of background knowledge about the existing laws is required) and being able to recognize the so called "popular expressions" for referring to these laws. For instance, in Italy the expression "Bossi-Fini" is a specific term referring to the law n° 189 of 30th July 2002, establishing policies about immigration and employment of migrants. This popular expression is originated by the names of the first signatories, Gianfranco Fini and Umberto Bossi, at that time vice-president of the cabinet and minister for institutional reforms and devolution respectively, and is often adopted even in specialized literature. A proper lexicalization even – and actually, most importantly – in the same language of the country adopting that law is thus important in order to recognize the variety of expressions that refer to the same precise legal entity.

Knowledge Building. While the previous scenario deals with the identification of mentions of entities already defined and structured in specific areas of knowledge, it is also important to be able to build new knowledge by analyzing language content. The development of specialized domain ontologies can be partially automated by applying terminology extraction techniques to document corpora [3] in order to identify the entities that will be later elaborated into ontology classes and properties. The analysis of relations [4] in the text can help both the development of new knowledge as well as – when legal content is available – the production of alignments between legal and domain ontologies.

Cross-lingual Recognition. The availability of terms in multiple languages allows for efficient retrieval of the same conceptual information in various languages. However, the analysis of language content (for any of the two tasks above) requires more fine-grained lexical background knowledge than just mere terminology. Being able to describe, in different languages, the single components forming compound terms, the several forms in which these can be declined/conjugated, their lexical variations etc. is a necessary step which has to be carried on even for those languages different from the one spoken in the country where that knowledge originated.

It appears evident how all the tasks above would benefit from proper lexicalization of the knowledge resources involved, performed by adopting well established standards for the representation of lexical information and of the lexical-semantic interface with ontologies. Reuse of existing resources modeled according to these standards should be also encouraged, to minimize the effort for lexicalizing knowledge resources. In the next section, we will provide an excursus over models for lexical resources that have been proposed in the last 20 years of research on (computational) linguistics.

3   State of the Art on Linguistic Resources and Language Representation

"The term linguistic resources refers to (usually large) sets of language data and descriptions in machine readable form, to be used in building, improving, or evaluating natural language (NL) and speech algorithms or systems" [5].

Multiple efforts have been spent in the past towards the achievement of consensus among different theoretical perspectives and systems design approaches. The Text Encoding Initiative (www.tei-c.org) and the LRE-EAGLES (Expert Advisory Group on Linguistic Engineering Standards) project [6] are just a few, bearing the objective of making possible the reuse of existing (partial) linguistic resources, promoting the development of new linguistic resources for those languages and domains where they are still not available, and creating a cooperative infrastructure to collect, maintain, and disseminate linguistic resources on behalf of the research and development community.

A popular resource which got a broad diffusion characterized by exploitation in both applications and scientific studies is WordNet [7, 8]. Being a structured lexical database, presents a neat distinction between words, senses and glosses, and is characterized by diverse semantic relations like hypernymy/hyponymy, antonymy etc.... Though not being originally realized for computational uses, and being built upon a model for the mental lexicon, WordNet has become a valuable resource in the human language technology and artificial intelligence. Due to its vast coverage of English words, WordNet provides general lexico-semantic information on which open-domain text processing is based. Furthermore, the development of WordNets in several other languages [9–11] extends this capability to trans-lingual applications, enabling text mining across languages.

A more recent effort towards achieving a thorough model for the representation of lexical resources is given by the Lexical Markup Framework [12]. LMF, which has obtained ISO standardization (LMF; ISO 24613:2008), can represent monolingual, bilingual or multilingual lexical resources. The same specifications are to be used for both small and large lexicons, for both simple and complex lexicons, for both written and spoken lexical representations. The descriptions range from morphology, syntax, computational semantics to computer-assisted translation. The covered languages are not restricted to European languages but cover all natural languages. The range of targeted NLP applications is not restricted. LMF is able to represent most lexicons, including the above mentioned WordNet.

With the advent of the Semantic Web and Linked Open Data, a number of models have been proposed to enrich ontologies with information about how vocabulary elements have to be expressed in different natural languages. These include the Linguistic Watermark framework [13, 14], LexOnto [15], LingInfo [16], LIR [17],

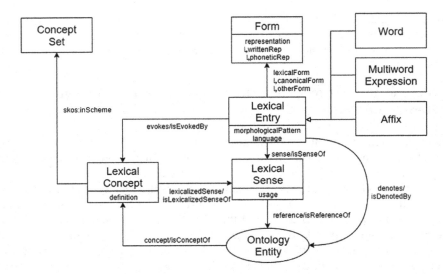

Fig. 1. The OntoLex-lemon model

LexInfo [18] and, more recently, *lemon* [19]. The *lemon* model envisions an open ecosystem in which ontologies[4] and lexica for them co-exist, both of which are published as data on the Web. It is in line with a many-to-many relation between: (i) ontologies and ontological vocabularies, (ii) lexicalization datasets and (iii) lexical resources. Lexicalizations in our sense are reifications of the relationship between an ontology reference and the lexical entries by which these can be expressed within natural language. *lemon* foresees an ecosystem in which many independently published lexicalizations and lexica for a given ontology co-exist.

In 2012, an important community effort has been made to provide a common model for Ontology-Lexicon interfaces: the OntoLex W3C Community Group[5] was started with the goal of providing an agreed-upon standard by building on the aforementioned models, the designers of which are all involved in the community group.

The OntoLex-*lemon* [20] model (see Fig. 1) developed by the OntoLex Community Group is based on the original *lemon* model, which by now has been adopted by a number of lexica [21–24], and as such was taken by the group as the basis for developing an agreed-upon and widely accepted model. The *lemon* model is based onto the idea of a separation between the lexical and the ontological layer following Buitelaar [25] and Cimiano et al. [26], where the ontology describes the semantics of the domain and the lexicon describes the morphology, syntax and pragmatics of the words used to express the domain in a language. The model thus organizes the lexicon

---

[4] It would be more appropriate to adopt the term "reference dataset" (including thus also SKOS thesauri and datasets in general), to express data containing the logical symbols for describing a certain domain. In line with the traditional name OntoLex (and thus the ontology-lexicon dualism), we will however often refer to them with the term ontology.

[5] http://www.w3.org/community/ontolex/

primarily by means of *lexical entries*, which are a word, affix or multiword expression with a single syntactic class (part-of-speech) to which a number of *forms* are attached, such as for example the plural, and each form has a number of *representations* (*string forms*), e.g. written or phonetic representation. Entries in a lexicon can be said to *denote* an entity in an ontology, however normally the link between the lexical entry and the ontology entity is realized by a *lexical sense* object where pragmatic information such as domain or register of the connection may be recorded.

In addition to describing the meaning of a word by reference to the ontology, a lexical entry may be associated with a *lexical concept*. Lexical concepts represent the semantic pole of linguistic units, mentally instantiated abstractions which language users derive from conceptions [27]. Lexical concepts are intended primarily to represent such abstractions when present in existing lexical resources, e.g. synsets for wordnets.

Finally, linguists have acknowledged [28] the benefits that the adoption of the Semantic Web technologies could bring to the publication and integration of language resources, thus denoting a convergence of interests and results rarely occurring before. A concrete outcome of this convergence is given by the Open Linguistics Working Group[6] of the Open Knowledge Foundation, which is contributing to the development of a LOD (Linked Open Data) (sub)cloud of linguistic resources, known as LLOD[7] (Linguistic Linked Open Data).

4   The PMKI Project

Public Multilingual Knowledge Infrastructure (PMKI) is launched as an ISA2 action to answer claims from the European Language Technology Community such as the multilingual extension of the Digital Single Market, the increase of the EU cross-border online service. It aims to provide support for the EU economy in particular to SMEs to overcome language barriers and to help to unlock the e-Commerce potential within the EU implementing the necessary multilingual tools and features and helping to build the Connecting Europe Facility Automated Translation (CEF.AT) Platform - a common building block implemented through the CEF programme.

The project aims to create a set of tools and facilities, based on Semantic Web technologies, aimed to support the language technology industry as well as public administrations, with multilingual tools in order to improve cross border accessibility of public administration services and e-commerce solutions. In practical terms, overcoming language barriers on the Web means creating multilingual vocabularies and language resources, establishing links between them as well as using them to support accessibility to services and goods offered through the Internet.

The objective of PMKI is to implement a proof-of-concept infrastructure to expose and to harmonize internal (European Union institutional) and external multilingual resources aligning them in order to facilitate interoperability. It could support the

---

[6] http://linguistics.okfn.org/

[7] http://linguistic-lod.org/llod-cloud

knowledge layer of the multilingual infrastructure for Europe. Additionally, the project aims to create a governance structure to extend systematically the infrastructure by the integration of supplementary public multilingual taxonomies/terminologies.

PMKI is a pilot project to check the feasibility of the proposed solutions and to prepare the roadmap to convert such proof-of-concept into a public service.

5 Specific Actions with Reusable Outcomes in the Legal Domain

The proposed PMKI action meets the recommendations included in the European Interoperability Strategy (EIS)[8]. The adherence to specific standards for describing language resources, and the creation of an interoperability platform to manage them, comply with the main approaches and "clusters" of the EIS (reusability of the solutions, interoperability service architecture in the EU multilingual context, implication of ICT on new EU legislation, as well as promotion of the awareness on the maturity level and of the shareability of the public administration services).

Similarly, the proposal meets the recommendations and principles of the European Interoperability Framework (EIF)[9], regarding multilingualism, accessibility, administrative simplification, transparency, and reusability of the solutions. The creation of a public multilingual knowledge infrastructure will allow EU public administrations to create services that can be accessible and shareable independently from the language actually used, as well as the SMEs to sell goods and service cross-border in a Digital Single Market.

As we have shown in Sect. 2, the outcomes of such initiatives are prodrome for supporting document analysis, indexing and retrieval as well as cross-legislation access to legal content. In the next sections we will present the main actions foreseen in our contribution to the PMKI project and their potential in supporting the above objectives.

5.1 Comparative Study and Selection of Semantic Web Standards for Describing Multilingual Resources

A study has been conducted, embracing available web standards for multilingual resources at large, thus including multilingualism in ontologies, terminologies and specifically in lexical resources.

Due to the nature of the resources in PMKI, within the project different recommendations or even popular vocabularies will be adopted:

SKOS [29]: the W3C recommendation for formalizing thesauri, terminologies, controlled vocabularies and other knowledge resources characterized by shallow semantics. It is worth noticing that the terminological level solely supports the identification of concepts by giving them names (and alternative lexical references) but cannot be considered to be a lexicon nor any sort of advanced lexical resource, as any sort of

---

[8] http://ec.europa.eu/isa/documents/isa_annex_i_eis_en.pdf
[9] http://ec.europa.eu/isa/documents/isa_annex_ii_eif_en.pdf

lexical description taking into account phenomena such as morphology, lexical relations etc. are considered, by definition, to be out of the scope of a thesaurus.

SKOS-XL [30]: As for the general definition of thesauri, SKOS does not address complex lexical descriptions of its elements. However, SKOS is extended by the SKOS-XL vocabulary which provides reified labels by means of the class skosxl:Label. SKOS terminological properties have their equivalents (identified by homonymous local names) in the new namespace, that is: skosxl:prefLabel, skosxl:hiddenLabel, skosxl:altLabel in order to relate concepts with these reified labels.

OntoLex-Lemon. We already described this model in Sect. 3. As the model is relatively recent, there is still not much support for developing resources according to its vocabulary. As explained in the next section, we will develop a system, integrated into an already mature ontology/thesauri development environment, for the development of lexicons and for interfacing lexical knowledge with ontological one.

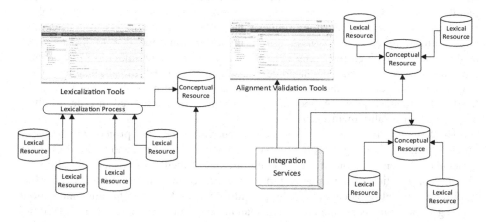

Fig. 2. PMKI integration framework, general architecture

Other Models and Schemes. The above vocabularies represent the core of the selected models for development and alignment of resources in PMKI. The support for OntoLex will however not be limited to the enrichment of SKOS thesauri, and OWL ontologies or generic RDF datasets can be lexically enriched with OntoLex lexical descriptions with no loss of generality. Similarly, the above choices do not obviously prevent the adoption of specific metadata vocabularies, domain/application ontologies etc....

5.2   Systems for Semantic and Lexical Integration of Multilingual Resources

Support for integration will be implemented two-fold: by realizing a framework for alignment of semantic resources (thesauri, ontologies etc.) and by the development of a system for the development of lexicons according to the OntoLex vocabulary and for the lexical enrichment of semantic resources with lexical information.

Even though a pilot project in nature, PMKI is not a research project, it in fact aims at building up on well-established research results and existing technologies and at converging towards a concrete proposal for an integration framework.

The general concept behind the framework is depicted in Fig. 2, focused on the interaction of systems aimed at supporting the two tasks previously defined.

Semantic Integration Framework. The architecture foresees the presence of semantic integration services accessed by RDF management systems. The separation between the two is dictated by the different requirements in terms of interaction modalities, performance and results. RDF Management Services, whether single-user desktop applications or centralized collaborative platform, require high interaction with the user, averagely-low response times and, in the case of collaborative systems, the capacity to serve in real time several users accessing diverse projects. These platforms may offer manual or semi-automatic alignment functionalities, which though have to be performed with a low impact on system resource, and possibly replicated across several parallel requests. Conversely, Semantic Integration systems may instead act as token-based service providers, receiving requests to load and align datasets of considerable size, performing their function in non-trivial execution time due to the intensive analysis of the involved resources and dedicating considerable amount of resources to these tasks. After each alignment process has been completed, the alignment services may release the token to the requesting peer and start the next alignment task at the head of the request queue. A pool of processors may be considered in order to allow parallelization of alignment tasks.

The Semantic Integration System developed within the pilot project will be based on GENOMA [31], a, highly configurable alignment architecture, and on MAPLE [32], a metadata-driven component for the configuration of mediators, which will allow for seamless application of the same alignment techniques on datasets modeled according to different modeling vocabularies, by providing vocabulary-specific implementations of the general analysis engine tasks. The manual/semi-automatic alignment capabilities will be provided by VocBench [33], a collaborative RDF management system for the development and maintenance of RDF ontologies thesauri and datasets, based on a service-oriented RDF management platform [34], recently updated to its third version [35] through another funded action of the ISA^2 program. As part of a coordinated action with the PMKI project, VocBench will also feature interaction modalities with the Semantic Integration system developed within PMKI.

Lexicon Development and Lexical Enrichment of Knowledge Resources. The OntoLex model is relatively young and, as such, it is still not widely supported by most mature technologies for data management. In a recent paper [36] describing the expressive power of VocBench 3 custom forms, the authors show how the custom form mechanism could be used to define complex lemon-patterns. As VocBench 3 provides a general-purpose editing environment with specific facilities for the editing of SKOS and SKOSXL thesauri and OWL ontologies, extending the system with dedicated support for OntoLex-Lemon seems thus a natural way to cover this need.

In PMKI, VocBench will thus be improved to support the OntoLex-Lemon model in two different scenarios: developing Lexicons based on the OntoLex vocabularies and enriching semantic resources with lexical content. The two scenarios may be interwoven, as it will be possible to develop lexical entries specifically for semantic resources as well as reuse lexical content from existing lexicons in order to enrich the semantic resource with it. In most real applications, the two possibilities will not be alternative to each other: while a lexicon can usually provide domain-independent lexical entries, the description of specific concepts in a domain/application ontology often requires the definition of new complex terms, thus requiring in turn to state how the proper combination (at the lexical level) of single lexical entries would generate the accurate description of the conceptual elements. This implies the creation of further lexical entries describing the multiword, syntagmatic structure of the lexical representation of the complex concept. The inspiring work for such evolution of VocBench comes from past works concerning semi-automatic enrichment of ontologies by reuse of lexical resources [37] and exploitation of language metadata [13, 38], which can now benefit from the standardization of this metadata for the Linked Open Data [39, 40].

Fig. 3. Aligning concepts between EU EuroVoc and Italian Senate's TESEO thesauri

5.3 Realization of Concrete Semantic Alignments and Lexical Enrichments and Assessing

In the pilot project, a certain amount of alignments and lexicalizations will be produced. The objective is not only to produce the resources per-se, but to provide golden-standards that can be used in the later stage to evaluate the alignment systems.

Developing a gold standard mapping dataset is however not an easy task, due to the difficulty, even for humans, to lose potential matches in datasets of even modest size. Not incidentally, the Ontology Alignment Evaluation Initiative (OAEI), an initiative, implemented as a contest, which aims at evaluating the state of the art of ontology alignment tools, [41] mostly offers test beds of relatively small size and rarely updates the list of these mappings. Furthermore, evaluation of mappings sent by the participants, in the cases involving large datasets does not rely entirely on the standard and involves instead manual scrutiny, in order to take into account potentially correct mappings missing from the oracle.

We thus decided to divide the kind of contributions for dataset alignment in two steps: a vertical exploration of a humanly-computable subdomain of the two thesauri, and a larger attempt at mapping complete resources. The first result guarantees the creation of a reliably sound and complete set of mappings, while a larger alignment on the whole resources will be produced later on in the project, by means of semi-automatic processes, reusing the same systems that we will validate through the first result. An alignment that will be considered for production is the one – already mentioned in the example in Sect. 2.1 – between EuroVoc and TESEO (see Fig. 3).

Concerning lexicalizations, EuroVoc, as a central hub in the EU scenario, has, also in this case, been selected as the target conceptual resource. Candidate lexical resources for the results to be produced within the pilot are WordNet, being probably the most popular lexical resource and, for analogous reasons and more specifically in the EU scenario, IATE[10], the InterActive Terminology for Europe. However, both these resources do not provide the rich lexical and morphological descriptions representing the added value brought by the OntoLex model. For this reason, other resources such as BabelNet, or other lexicons still not modeled in OntoLex, will be taken into consideration. In the latter case the process will be two-fold: porting resources to OntoLex, which is a result per se, and then using them to lexicalize (part of) EuroVoc.

6 Conclusions

In this paper, we have presented the objectives and roadmap of the PMKI project and how its outcomes will directly and positively affect access to legal content and foster its exploitation in various scenarios. The multicultural, multi-jurisdictional and multilinguistic nature of the European Union has always been considered an asset rather than an obstacle, as it is through their differences that the Member States can learn from each other, benefiting from distinct experiences and approaches. Making these experiences truly and effectively comparable by lowering the language barriers and by harmonizing/connecting different though overlapping concepts and regulations is the objective of initiatives such as PMKI. Even though a pilot project, PMKI will aim to pave the way for analogous efforts while still contributing the community with tangible results in terms of systems and frameworks for alignment and lexicalization of heterogeneous resources.

References

1. Francesconi, E., Peruginelli, G.: Opening the legal literature portal to multi-lingual access. In: Proceedings of the Dublin Core Conference, pp. 37–44 (2004)
2. Antonini, A., Boella, G., Hulstijn, J., Humphreys, L.: Requirements of legal knowledge management systems to aid normative reasoning in specialist domains. In: Nakano, Y., Satoh, K., Bekki, D. (eds.) JSAI-isAI 2013. LNCS (LNAI), vol. 8417, pp. 167–182. Springer, Cham (2014). https://doi.org/10.1007/978-3-319-10061-6_12

---

[10] http://termcoord.eu/iate/

3. Velardi, P., Navigli, R., Cucchiarelli, A., Neri, F.: Evaluation of ontolearn, a methodology for automatic population of domain ontologies. In: Ontology Learning from Text: Methods, Applications and Evaluation. IOS Press, Amsterdam (2005)

4. Pennacchiotti, M., Pantel, P.: Automatically harvesting and ontologizing semantic relations. In: Buitelaar, P., Cimiano, P. (eds.) Ontology learning and population: bridging the gap between text and knowledge. Frontiers in Artificial Intelligence. IOS Press, Amsterdam (2008)

5. Cole, R.A., Mariani, J., Uszkoreit, H., Zaenen, A., Zue, V. (eds.): Survey of the State of the Art in Human Language Technology. Cambridge University Press, Cambridge (1997)

6. Calzolari, N., McNaught, J., Zampolli, A.: EAGLES Final Report: EAGLES Editors Introduction. Pisa, Italy (1996)

7. Miller, G.A., Beckwith, R., Fellbaum, C., Gross, D., Miller, K.: Introduction to WordNet: An On-line Lexical Database (1993)

8. Fellbaum, C.: WordNet: An Electronic Lexical Database. WordNet Pointers. MIT Press, Cambridge, MA (1998)

9. Vossen, P.: EuroWordNet: A Multilingual Database with Lexical Semantic Networks. Kluwer Academic Publishers, Dordrecht (1998)

10. Roventini, A., et al.: ItalWordNet: a large semantic database for the automatic treatment of the Italian language. In: First International WordNet Conference, Mysore, India, January 2002

11. Stamou, S., et al.: BALKANET: a multilingual semantic network for the Balkan languages. In: First International Wordnet Conference, Mysore, India, pp. 12–14 (2002)

12. Francopoulo, G., et al.: Lexical markup framework (LMF). In: LREC2006, Genoa, Italy (2006)

13. Pazienza, M.T., Stellato, A., Turbati, A.: Linguistic Watermark 3.0: an RDF framework and a software library for bridging language and ontologies in the semantic web. In: 5th Workshop on Semantic Web Applications and Perspectives (SWAP2008), Rome, Italy, 15–17 December 2008, CEUR Workshop Proceedings, FAO-UN, Rome, Italy, vol. 426, p. 11 (2008)

14. Oltramari, A., Stellato, A.: Enriching ontologies with linguistic content: an evaluation framework. In: The Role of Ontolex Resources in Building the Infrastructure of Web 3.0: Vision and Practice (OntoLex 2008), 31 May, Marrakech, Morocco, pp. 1–8 (2008)

15. Cimiano, P., Haase, P., Herold, M., Mantel, M., Buitelaar, P.: LexOnto: a model for ontology lexicons for ontology-based NLP. In: Proceedings of the OntoLex07 Workshop (held in conjunction with ISWC 2007) (2007)

16. Buitelaar, P., et al.: LingInfo: design and applications of a model for the integration of linguistic information in ontologies. In: OntoLex 2006, Genoa, Italy, pp. 28–34 (2006)

17. Montiel-Ponsoda, E., Aguado de Cea, G., Gómez-Pérez, A., Peters, W.: Enriching ontologies with multilingual information. Nat. Lang. Eng. **17**, 283–309 (2011)

18. Cimiano, P., Buitelaar, P., McCrae, J., Sintek, M.: LexInfo: a declarative model for the lexicon-ontology interface. Web Semant. Sci. Serv. Agents World Wide Web **9**(1), 29–51 (2011)

19. McCrae, J., et al.: Interchanging lexical resources on the Semantic Web. Lang. Resour. Eval. **46**(4), 701–719 (2012)

20. Cimiano, P., McCrae, J.P., Buitelaar, P.: Lexicon Model for Ontologies: Community Report, 10 May 2016. Community Report, W3C (2016). https://www.w3.org/2016/05/ontolex/

21. Borin, L., Dannélls, D., Forsberg, M., McCrae, J.P.: Representing Swedish lexical resources in RDF with lemon. In: Proceedings of the ISWC 2014 Posters & Demonstrations Track a Track Within the 13th International Semantic Web Conference (ISWC 2014), Riva del Garda, Italy, pp. 329–332 (2014)

22. Ehrmann, M., Cecconi, F., Vannella, D., McCrae, J.P., Cimiano, P., Navigli, R.: Representing multilingual data as linked data: the case of BabelNet 2.0. In: Proceedings of the Ninth International Conference on Language Resources and Evaluation (LREC-2014), Reykjavik, Iceland, 26–31 May 2014, pp. 401–408 (2014)

23. Eckle-Kohler, J., McCrae, J.P., Chiarcos, C.: lemonUby—a large, interlinked syntactically-rich lexical resources for ontologies. Semant. Web J. (2015 accepted)

24. Sérasset, G.: Dbnary: wiktionary as a LMF based multilingual RDF network. In: Proceedings of the Eighth International Conference on Language Resources and Evaluation (LREC-2012), Istanbul, Turkey, 23–25 May 2012, pp. 2466–2472 (2012)

25. Buitelaar, P.: Ontology-based Semantic Lexicons: Mapping between Terms and Object Descriptions. In: Huang, C.-R., Calzolari, N., Gangemi, A., Lenci, A., Oltramari, A., Prevot, L. (eds.) Ontology and the Lexicon: A Natural Language Processing Perspective. Cambridge University Press, Cambridge (2010)

26. Cimiano, P., McCrae, J., Buitelaar, P., Montiel-Ponsoda, E.: On the role of senses in the ontology-Lexicon. In: Oltramari, A., Vossen, P., Qin, L., Hovy, E. (eds.) New Trends of Research in Ontologies and Lexical Resources, pp. 43–62. Springer, Berlin (2013). https://doi.org/10.1007/978-3-642-31782-8_4

27. Evans, V.: Lexical concepts, cognitive models and meaning-construction. Cognit. Linguist. **17**(4), 491–534 (2006)

28. Chiarcos, C., McCrae, J., Cimiano, P., Fellbaum, C.: Towards open data for linguistics: linguistic linked data. In: Oltramari, A., Vossen, P., Qin, L., Hovy, E. (eds.) New Trends of Research in Ontologies and Lexical Resources, pp. 7–25. Springer, Berlin (2013). https://doi.org/10.1007/978-3-642-31782-8_2

29. World Wide Web Consortium (W3C): SKOS Simple knowledge organization system reference. In: World Wide Web Consortium (W3C) (2009). http://www.w3.org/TR/skos-reference/. Accessed 18 Aug 2009

30. World Wide Web Consortium (W3C): SKOS simple knowledge organization system eXtension for labels (SKOS-XL). In: World Wide Web Consortium (W3C). http://www.w3.org/TR/skos-reference/skos-xl.html. Accessed 18 Aug 2009

31. Enea, R., Pazienza, M.T., Turbati, A.: GENOMA: GENeric Ontology Matching Architecture. In: Gavanelli, M., Lamma, E., Riguzzi, F. (eds.) AI*IA 2015. LNCS (LNAI), vol. 9336, pp. 303–315. Springer, Cham (2015). https://doi.org/10.1007/978-3-319-24309-2_23

32. Fiorelli, M., Pazienza, M.T., Stellato, A.: A meta-data driven platform for semi-automatic configuration of ontology mediators. In: Chair, N.C., et al. (eds.) Proceedings of the Ninth International Conference on Language Resources and Evaluation (LREC'14), May 2014. European Language Resources Association (ELRA), Reykjavik, Iceland, pp. 4178–4183 (2014)

33. Stellato, A., Rajbhandari, S., Turbati, A., Fiorelli, M., Caracciolo, C., Lorenzetti, T., Keizer, J., Pazienza, M.T.: VocBench: a web application for collaborative development of multilingual thesauri. In: Gandon, F., Sabou, M., Sack, H., d'Amato, C., Cudré-Mauroux, P., Zimmermann, A. (eds.) ESWC 2015. LNCS, vol. 9088, pp. 38–53. Springer, Cham (2015). https://doi.org/10.1007/978-3-319-18818-8_3

34. Pazienza, M.T., Scarpato, N., Stellato, A., Turbati, A.: Semantic Turkey: a browser-integrated environment for knowledge acquisition and management. Semant. Web J. **3**(3), 279–292 (2012)

35. Stellato, A., et al.: Towards VocBench 3: pushing collaborative development of thesauri and ontologies further beyond. In: 17th European Networked Knowledge Organization Systems (NKOS) Workshop, 21st September 2017, Thessaloniki, Greece (2017)

36. Fiorelli, M., Lorenzetti, T., Pazienza, M.T., Stellato, A.: Assessing VocBench custom forms in supporting editing of lemon datasets. In: Gracia, J., Bond, F., McCrae, John P., Buitelaar, P., Chiarcos, C., Hellmann, S. (eds.) LDK 2017. LNCS (LNAI), vol. 10318, pp. 237–252. Springer, Cham (2017). https://doi.org/10.1007/978-3-319-59888-8_21
37. Pazienza, M.T., Stellato, A.: An environment for semi-automatic annotation of ontological knowledge with linguistic content. In: Sure, Y., Domingue, J. (eds.) ESWC 2006. LNCS, vol. 4011, pp. 442–456. Springer, Heidelberg (2006). https://doi.org/10.1007/11762256_33
38. Pazienza, M.T., Sguera, S., Stellato, A.: Let's talk about our "being": a linguistic-based ontology framework for coordinating agents. Appl. Ontol. Spec. Issue Form. Ontol. Commun. Agents 2(3–4), 305–332 (2007)
39. Fiorelli, M., Stellato, A., McCrae, J.P., Cimiano, P., Pazienza, M.T.: LIME: the metadata module for OntoLex. In: Gandon, F., Sabou, M., Sack, H., d'Amato, C., Cudré-Mauroux, P., Zimmermann, A. (eds.) ESWC 2015. LNCS, vol. 9088, pp. 321–336. Springer, Cham (2015). https://doi.org/10.1007/978-3-319-18818-8_20
40. Fiorelli, M., Pazienza, M.T., Stellato, A.: An API for OntoLex LIME datasets. In: OntoLex-2017 1st Workshop on the OntoLex Model (co-located with LDK-2017), Galway (2017)
41. Shvaiko, P., Euzenat, J.: Ontology matching: state of the art and future challenges. IEEE Trans. Knowl. Data Eng. 25(1), 158–176 (2013)

A Multilingual Access Module to Legal Texts

Kiril Simov[1]([✉]), Petya Osenova[1], Iliana Simova[1],
Hristo Konstantinov[2]([✉]), and Tenyo Tyankov[2]

[1] Linguistic Modelling Department, IICT-BAS, Sofia, Bulgaria
{kivs,petya,iliana}@bultreebank.org
[2] APIS, Sofia, Bulgaria
{ico,tencho}@apis.bg

Abstract. The paper introduces a Multilingual Access Module. This module translates the user's legislation query from its source language into the target language, and retrieves the detected texts that match the query. The service is demonstrated in its potential for two languages – English and Bulgarian, in both directions (English-to-Bulgarian and Bulgarian-to-English). The module consists of two submodules: Ontology-based and Statistical Machine Translation. Since both proposed submodules have some drawbacks, they are used in an integrated architecture, thus profiting from each other.

Keywords: Multilingual access · Query translation · Query expansion

1 Introduction

Processing of legal data has been in the focus of NLP community for the recent years. A lot of resources have been compiled and made available to the community. This holds especially for the legal documentation of EU (EuroParl[1], JRC Acquis[2], EAC-ECDC[3], etc.). Rich thesauri and ontologies have been produced (such as, Eurovoc[4], lkif-core[5]). At the same time, processing modules have been developed for the aims of information retrieval. There are also a number of projects dedicated to the smart access to legal data. These are OpenLaws[6], EUCases[7], e-CODEX[8], etc.; focused conferences, such as JURIX[9], among others. Our paper presents a multilingual module for accessing legal texts. It uses two approaches for the translation of users' queries – ontology-based and statistical. The experiments showed that the results are better when both components are used in combination. Although the multilingual nature of the module is demonstrated for two languages – English and Bulgarian, it is scalable also to other languages.

---

[1] http://www.statmt.org/europarl/.
[2] http://optima.jrc.it/Acquis/index_2.2.html.
[3] https://ec.europa.eu/jrc/en/language-technologies/ecdc-translation-memory.
[4] http://open-data.europa.eu/data/dataset/eurovoc.
[5] https://github.com/RinkeHoekstra/lkif-core.
[6] http://www.openlaws.eu/?page_id=1004.
[7] http://www.eucases.eu/start/.
[8] http://www.e-codex.eu/about-the-project.html.
[9] http://jurix2015.di.uminho.pt/.

© Springer Nature Switzerland AG 2018
U. Pagallo et al. (Eds.): AICOL VI-X 2015–2017, LNAI 10791, pp. 272–286, 2018.
https://doi.org/10.1007/978-3-030-00178-0_18

The structure of the paper is as follows: in Sect. 2 the main background issues are outlined. Section 3 focuses on the Ontology-based Translation module. Section 4 discusses Statistical Machine Translation Module. Section 5 presents the parameters of the integration between the two modules and describes the evaluation. Section 6 concludes the paper.

2 Background

In this paper we report on the design and development of Multilingual Access Module (MLAM) for full text search within legal documents in English and Bulgarian. The MLAM translates user queries in both directions: from Bulgarian to English and from English to Bulgarian. A typical user query is a list of key words and phrases. The user query is evaluated over a set of documents loaded in a full text search engine which performs searches for relevant documents. Thus, our goal is to deliver an adequate translation service for the user queries.

In the module two complementary technologies are exploited. The first technology is based on Ontology-to-Text relation. In this case, the system relies on a common ontology with augmented lexicons. The lexicons are mapped in such a way that the conceptual information within the ontology corresponds to the meaning of the lexical items. Having lexicons for different languages aligned to the same ontology is a prerequisite for the accurate translation of the corresponding lexical items. In addition to the lexicons, special chunk grammars are needed to recognize the lexical items in the text. Such grammars are important especially for languages with rich morphology and/or free word order.

The exploitation of ontologies in translation provides some additional functionality of performing query expansion on the basis of inference within the ontology. In our module we implemented two query expansion procedures: (1) expansion via subclasses and (2) expansion via related classes. Both of them are presented in our ontologies: Syllabus ontology and Eurovoc multilingual taxonomy. After performing the query expansion, the new set of classes is translated to the target language using the appropriate lexicons.

We expect that the user queries will be mainly related to the above mentioned domain ontologies which are also employed for document indexing. They reflect the specific content of the documents in the EUCases database. Nevertheless, the users should not be restricted to specify their queries only through the lexical items from the available lexicons. Thus, MLAM needs to provide translation also for words and phrases that are not in the lexicons. In order to solve this problem, we exploited a statistical machine translation module trained on domain specific parallel corpora. This module in combination with the ontology-based module provides alternative translations to the lexicon items and thus covers the missing translations for out-of-vocabulary words and phrases.

3   The Ontology-Based Translation Module

The design and implementation of the Ontology-based translation module of MLAM exploits the ontology-to-text relation approach [7, 8]. We started with classification of ontologies with respect to their precision provided by Nicola Guarino[10]:

Lexicon: machine readable dictionaries; vocabulary with natural language definitions.
Simple Taxonomy: classifications.
Thesaurus: WordNet; taxonomy plus related terms.
Relational Model: Light-weight ontologies; unconstrained use of arbitrary relations.
Fully Axiomatized Theory: Heavy-weight ontologies.

The two ontologies to be used in the project – Syllabus ontology and Eurovoc multilingual taxonomy – are at the middle of this classification. The first one is a relational model by its creation, and the second one is a thesaurus. Thus, they provide a limited inference which we exploit for query expansion. Both of them are considered domain ontologies, but are not aligned to an upper ontology.

3.1   Ontology-to-Text Relation

Here we represent briefly the two main components that define the ontology-to-text relation necessary to support the tasks within our project. These components are: (terminological) lexicon and a concept annotation grammar.

The lexicon plays a twofold role in our architecture. First, it interrelates the concepts in the ontology to the lexical knowledge used by the grammar for recognizing the role of the concepts in the text. Second, lexicon represents the main interface between the user and the ontology. This interface allows for the ontology to be navigated or represented in a natural for the user way. For example, the concepts and relations might be named with terms used by the users in their everyday activities and in their own natural language. This might be considered as a first step to a contextualized usage of the ontology in a sense that the ontology might be viewed through different terms depending on the context.

Thus, the lexical items contain the following information: a term, information determining the context of the term usage, and grammatical features providing the syntactic realization within the text. In the current implementation of the lexicons the contextual information is simplified to a list of a few types of users (lawyers, judges, etc.). With respect to the relations between the terms in the lexicon and the concepts in the ontology, there are two main problems: (1) there is no lexicalized term for some of the concepts in the ontology, and (2) there are lexical terms in the domain language which lack corresponding concepts in the ontology.

---

[10] Invited Mini-course on Ontological Analysis and Ontology Design. First Workshop on Ontologies and lexical Knowledge Bases - OntoLex 2000. Sozopol, Bulgaria.

The first problem is solved by adding also non-lexicalized (fully compositional) phrases to the lexicon. These varieties of phrases or terms for a given concept are used as a basis for construction of the annotation grammar. Having them, we would capture different wordings of the same meaning in the text. The picture below shows the mapping varieties. It depicts the realization of the concepts (similarly for relations and instances) in the language. The concepts are language independent and they might be represented within a natural language as form(s) of a lexicalized term, or as a free phrase. In general, a concept might have a few terms connected to it and a (potentially) unlimited number of free phrases expressing this concept in the language. Some of the free phrases receive their meaning compositionally regardless their usage in the text, other free phrases denote the corresponding concept only in a particular context. In our lexicons we decided to register as many free phrases as possible in order to have better recall on the semantic annotation task. In case of a concept that is not-lexicalized in a given language we require at least one free phrase to be provided for this concept. See Fig. 1.

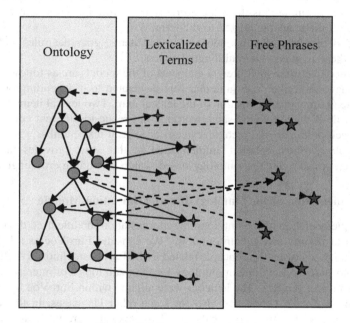

Fig. 1. Ontology-to-text relation

We could summarize the connection between the ontology and the lexicons in the following way: the ontology represents the semantic knowledge in form of concepts and relations with appropriate axioms; and the lexicons represent the ways in which these concepts can be realized in texts in the corresponding languages. Of course, the ways in which a concept could be represented in the text are potentially infinite in number. For that reason we aimed at representing in our lexicons only the most frequent and important terms and phrases.

The second component of the ontology-to-text relation, the concept annotation grammar, is ideally considered as an extension of a general language deep grammar which is adopted to the concept annotation task. Minimally, the concept annotation grammar consists of a chunk grammar for concept annotation and (sense) disambiguation rules. The chunk grammar for each term in the lexicon contains at least one grammar rule for recognition of the term. As a preprocessing step we consider annotation with grammatical features and lemmatization of the text. The disambiguation rules exploit the local context in terms of grammatical features, semantic annotation and syntactic structure, and also the global context, such as the topic of the text, discourse segmentation, etc.

For the implementation of the annotation grammar we rely on the grammar facilities of the CLaRK System (Simov et al. 2001).

The creation of the actual annotation grammars started with the terms in the lexicons for the corresponding languages. Each term was lemmatized and the lemmatized form of the term was converted into a regular expression of grammar rules. Each concept related to the term is stored in the return markup of the corresponding rule. Thus, if a term is ambiguous, then the corresponding rule in the grammar contains a reference to all the concepts related to the term.

Figure 2 depicts the relations between lexical items, grammar rules and the text. We exploit these relations for multilingual access.

The relations between the different elements of the models are as follows. A lexical item could have more than one grammar rule associated to it depending on the word order and the grammatical realization of the lexical item. Two lexical items might share a grammar rule if they have the same wording, but relate to different concepts in the ontology. Each grammar rule recognizes zero or several text chunks.

The ontology-to-text relation, implemented in this way, provides facilities for solving different tasks, such as ontology-based search (including crosslingual search).

3.2   Implementation of the Ontology-Based Translation Module

Our first implementation of the ontology-based translation module used the EuroVoc[11] multilingual taxonomy as its main ontology. We consider EuroVoc as a light-weight ontology. EuroVoc covers the concepts related to the European Union activities. In this respect we consider it as a domain ontology for the main topics of interest to the users of EUCases project services. The lexicons were aligned within EuroVoc for the official languages of European Union and also for some other languages. In this respect, it provides the necessary inventory for the two languages that are important to us: Bulgarian and English. It can be extended further for the other represented languages. The actual concepts are mapped via numerical identifiers. The concepts are arranged in domains and microthesauri. Each domain is divided into a number of microthesauri. A microthesaurus is considered as a concept scheme with a subset of the concepts that are part of the complete EuroVoc thesaurus. The main relations encoded in EuroVoc

---

[11] http://eurovoc.europa.eu/.

that we exploit are: "skos:broader"[12], "skos:related" and "xl:pre-fLabel", defined in http://www.w3.org/2009/08/skos-reference/skos.html and http://www.w3.org/TR/skos-reference/skos-xl.html documents. Table 1 contains a few examples of the interrelations of concepts in EuroVoc. With the help these relations we define different query expansion approaches.

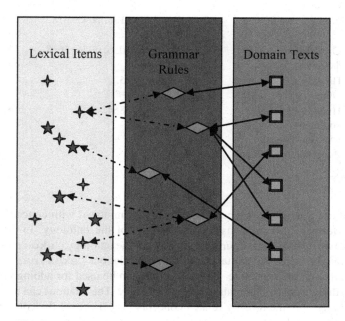

Fig. 2. Relations between lexical items, grammar rules and text

As it was mentioned above, on the basis of all terms related to a given concept identifier, a regular expression is created. Each rule annotated the recognized text with the corresponding identifier. In the cases of ambiguous terms, the text was annotated with several identifiers. The annotation grammars were applied over the user query string and each recognized term was presented by the corresponding concept identifiers. After the complete analysis of the input query, the text was converted into a list of identifiers. In some cases, a specific substring of the user query might not be recognized as a term in the lexicon. In this case, the substring remained unanalyzed. For example, for the concept 1460[13] the grammar rule in the CLaRK system would look like: <"EU">, <"financial">, <"instrument"> → <concept v = "1460"/>, where the first part of the rule would recognize the term in the text and this text would be annotated with the XML fragment from the right part of the rule.

---

[12] Also its reverse relation "skos:narrower".

[13] See the first row in Table 1.

Table 1. In the table the relations between concepts in EuroVoc thesaurus are presented. The relations show the complexity of the graph in the thesaurus.

Concept ID	Bulgarian term	English term	skos:narrower	skos:related
1460	Финансов инструмент на Общността	EU financial instrument	**1052**, 2054, 2609	*862*, 1851, 2511, 4370, 5472
1052	Фондове на ЕС	EC funds	**5138**, 5643, 978	973, 4055, 8549, 862
5138	Структурни фондове	Structural funds	1056, 4056, 5668	5472, *5499*, 5580, 5847
862	Помощ на Общността	EU aid	852	–
5499	Икономическо и социално взаимодействие	Economic and social cohesion	5864	*5643*
5643	Фонд за сближаване	Cohesion Fund	–	–

After the user query was executed, the text was annotated with concept identifiers. Then we performed query expansion on the basis of the ontology. In this case, we exploited the two relations that define the structure of the ontology: "skos:narrower" and "skos:related". As the table shows, both relations "skos:narrower" and "skos:related" are transitive. These relations can be used for adding new concept identifiers to those from the annotation of the user query. The relations can be used in two ways: (1) getting only the directly related concepts, or (2) getting the concepts that are related via transitive closure of the relations.

In the first implementation, we performed a transitive closure for the relation skos:broader and only direct related concepts for the relation skos:related. Here we present the processing steps of the user query: EU financial instrument:

Step 1: Text annotation
Step 2: Query expansion applying transitive closure of skos:narrower
Step 3: Query expansion applying skos:related
Step 4: Deleting the repeated concepts
Step 5: Translation to the other language

In this step each concept identifier is substituted with the corresponding terms in the other language. The result for our example includes phrases in Bulgarian:

финансов инструмент на ЕС помощ на ЕС поддържащ механизъм земеделска валутна политика европейска парична система рамка за подкрепа на общността фондове (ЕС) европейски фонд за валутно сътрудничество европейски фонд за развитие европейски фонд за приспособяване към глобализацията структурни фондове икономическо и социално взаимодействие структурен разход подходящ район за развитие европейски фонд за регионално развитие регионална помощ регионално планиране регионална политика на ЕС структурно приспособяване европейски социален фонд фиор европейски фонд за ориентиране и гарантиране на земеделието секция „ориентиране" фонд за сближаване ФЕОГА европейски фонд за ориентиране и гарантиране на земеделието – секция „гарантиране" нов инструмент на общността европейска инвестиционна банка заем от общността заем на европейска инвестиционна банка инициатива за европейски растеж заем на европейско обединение за въглища и стомана помощ на европейско обединение за въглища и стомана заем на ЕВРАТОМ ЕВРАТОМ заем, получен от ЕС международен заем

This translation of the expanded query is used for retrieval of the appropriate documents from the full text search system.

The approach for query expansion is based on the intuition that when someone searches for a concept they are interested in all subconcepts of the given one as well as related concepts with step one from the initial concept because the related concepts that are far from the initial concept could introduce too much unrelated content. In order to provide more flexible control over the query expansion we have implemented the following combinations:

NQE: No query expansion
QNA: Query expansion using transitive closure of the relation `skos:narrower`
QRE: Query expansion using the relation `skos:related`
QNR: Query expansion using both relations

The implementation provides a possibility for the user to select the translation direction: Bulgarian-to-English, English-to-Bulgarian as well as the query expansion approach: one of the above. As one can see, there are many ways for query expansion. The best one would depend on the domain, the task and so on. After the evaluation of this module we will improve it to achieve a better performance.

4   Statistical Machine Translation Module

As it was mentioned above, our task is to handle the out-of-vocabulary items for the lexicons aligned to the ontologies, and also to provide a module for translation of user queries based on statistical machine translation. User queries are mainly lists of key words and phrases which we expect to be domain dependent. Thus the parallel corpora on which Statistical Machine Translation system (SMT) are trained become very important. As a system for statistical machine translation we selected Moses[14]. Moses is a data-driven and state-of-the-art machine translation system. It provides three types of translation model implementations: phrase-based models, where n-grams ("phrases") are the basic units of translation, hierarchical or syntax-based models, where information about the structure of the parallel data can be incorporated, and factored translation models, where additional linguistic information (e.g., lemma, part-of-speech tag) can be integrated into the translation process.

Moses has two main components – a training pipeline and a decoder. The training pipeline includes various tools for data pre-processing (e.g., for tokenisation, lower-casing, removing very long sentences on the source or target side of the training data,

---

[14] http://www.statmt.org/moses/.

etc.), for accessing external tools for data alignment (GIZA++), language model building (SRILM, KenLM, IRSTLM, RandLM), and implementations of popular tuning algorithms. The Moses decoder tries to find the highest scoring sentence during translation, or outputs a ranked list of translation candidates with additional information. Standard tools for the evaluation of translations (e.g., BLEU scorer) are also available. In addition to parallel data in the form of plain text, Moses can be used to decode data represented as confusion networks or word lattices. In this way, ambiguous input data, such as the output of an automatic speech recognizer, or a morphological analyzer, can be processed to reduce erroneous hypothesis.

Two machine translation systems were created for the language pairs English-Bulgarian and Bulgarian-English by the Moses open source toolkit (see [4]). Parallel data from several sources was used to train factored translation models [3], which can be viewed as an extension to standard phrase-based models, where more linguistic information can be utilized in the translation process in addition to word forms.

4.1 Used Corpora

Parallel Corpora
We used several parallel corpora:
SETimes[15] (154K sentences)
A parallel corpus of news articles in the Balkan languages, originally extracted from http://www.setimes.com. Here we use the Bulgarian-English part which was cleaned within the European EuroMatrixPlus project[16]. We manually checked the alignment for more than 25000 sentences. The rest was automatically cleaned from sentence pairs that were suspicious with respect to their translation.
Europarl[17] (380K sentences)
The parallel texts were extracted from the Proceedings of the European Parliament.
Bulgarian-English BTB lexicon (9K word translations)
This is a lexicon created by professional lexicographers especially for machine translation purposes.
JRC Acquis[18] (364K sentences)
Parallel texts were extracted from the European Union legislation.
EAC-ECDC[19] (7K sentences)
These sentences were extracted from translation memories published on the above web page. The sentences were extracted manually because of the many alignment discrepancies.
APIS Legal Corpus (3844 sentences)

---

[15] http://opus.lingfil.uu.se/SETIMES.php.

[16] http://www.bultreebank.org/EMP/.

[17] http://www.statmt.org/europarl/.

[18] http://optima.jrc.it/Acquis/index_2.2.html.

[19] https://ec.europa.eu/jrc/en/language-technologies/ecdc-translation-memory.

These sentences were extracted from parallel texts covering parts of Bulgarian legislation.

The parallel data was cleaned semi-automatically. Non-translated sentences in the Bulgarian data were detected and removed together with their equivalents in the English data. Empty sentences or sentences longer than 80 words were removed with the Moses script clean-corpus-n.perl. The parallel data was lowercased for training. In the parallel data corpora we used mainly domain related corpora, but we also included an out-of-domain corpus in order to cover more general language usage.

Monolingual Corpora

Additionally, the following data sets were used for the creation of suitable language models: **Bulgarian**: National Reference Corpus (1.4M sentences) and the Bulgarian data from the parallel corpora. **English**: Europarl (2M sentences) and the English data (without Europarl) from the parallel corpora.

4.2   Data Analysis

The basic units of translation in Factored translation models are vectors of factors, where a factor is usually a linguistic property attached to word forms, such as the lemma, part-of-speech tag, or morphological properties associated with the word. In the current settings, we make use of the linguistic analyses produced by the Bulgarian pipeline btb-pipe (implemented partially within the EU-Cases project) and the English system ixa-pipes (see [1]). In the preprocessing step, we perform sentence splitting, tokenization, part-of-speech tagging, and lemmatization of the Bulgarian and English parallel corpora.

The Bulgarian data was processed with the pipeline btb-pipe, which includes rule-based, hybrid, and statistical components. It performs tokenization and sentence splitting jointly. The tagging module assigns tags from a rich tagset [6], which encodes detailed information about the morphosyntactic properties of words. In the experiment, simplified POS tags were used as factors for translation to avoid data sparseness issues. Lemmatization is based on rules, generated with the help of a morphological lexicon.

For the processing of the English part of the data we created a wrapper for the modules of the ixa-pipes system [1] ixa-pipe-tok (version 1.7.0), and ixa-pipe-pos (version 1.3.3). The wrapper includes an additional module which generates factored output, suitable for use with the Moses factored system. The first module, ixa-pipe-tok, takes plain text input, and carries out rule-based tokenization and sentence segmentation. The next step in the pipeline, ixa-pipe-pos, includes POS tagging and lemmatization. For tagging we selected one of the provided POS models for English – Perceptron [2]. The wrapper provides the option to preserve the number of lines in the input and output English file. This option should be used in the processing of parallel corpora to ensure that the resulting factored output can be aligned to its corresponding Bulgarian file in case when the English file contains more than one sentence on certain lines.

4.3   Translation Models

During training, a mapping between the source and target language linguistic factors, produced in the previous step, is established. The following lines describe the alternatives which were chosen for the two translation directions.

The SRI Language Modeling Toolkit (SRILM) [4] was used to build 5-gram language models for the two translation systems. Two types of language models were used by both systems – word-form-based and part-of-speech-tags-based ones. For the word-based language models we used Kneser-Ney smoothing, while part-of-speech-tag-based models were smoothed with the Witten-Bell method.

Both systems were tuned with minimum error rate training (MERT) (see [5]) implementation provided as part of the Moses toolkit. The English-to-Bulgarian translation system uses two types of factors – wordform and POS tag. The wordform of the source language is mapped to the wordform and POS tag factors on the target language side. Additionally, the proposed wordform and POS tag sequences are evaluated with the corresponding language models.

The Bulgarian-to-English system uses three types of factors – word-form, lemma, and part-of-speech tag. In this translation scenario a source word form is again mapped to the target word form and tag, but if no translation is found for the word, its lemma is used instead. This greatly helps with data sparseness issues caused by the rich morphology of Bulgarian. Once again two language models were employed, one for tags and one for wordforms. The translation process can be divided into the following steps:

1. The input is processed with the corresponding pipeline, and factors are generated.
2. The factored data is lower-cased (Moses script lower-case.perl).
3. The factored data is translated with the corresponding model.
4. The translation output is de-tokenized (Moses script de-tokenizer.perl).

The translation output is re-cased (a Moses re-caser model was trained for each translation direction). The evaluation of the statistical model showed the following BLEU scores, presented in Table 2.

Table 2. The BLUE scores for the statistical machine translation modules

	BG-EN	EN-BG
BLEU	23.39	23.70

These results show that only statistical models are not sufficient for the real applications.

5   Integration and Evaluation of Both Models

Both translation modules have some drawbacks. The ontology-based translation module is not able to disambiguate ambiguous terms because of the lack of annotated corpora from where a statistical model to be learnt. It also cannot translate out-of-vocabulary text. Such out-of-vocabulary text might have new paraphrases of existing concepts in the ontology or complete unrelated keywords or phrases. The statistical machine translation module also might not be able to use enough contexts in the user search query to translate some keywords or phrases in the right way. Also, the SMT module is not able to translate words that are not mentioned in the training corpus. For that reason sometimes the translation contains words in the source language. In order to handle these drawbacks of both modules and to gain from their complementary performance, we ingrate them in the following way.

First, we translate the user query Q by each of the modules. The results are Qot and Qsmt. Each of them could contain substrings from the source language. We delete them from the two translated queries. Then we concatenate the two strings. The result is Qtrans. This result is used for the full text search in a document database in the target language.

For the actual tests we have selected three queries from the list of queries provided by APIS[20]. The goal of the selected queries is to test the translation service on different levels of specificity of the queries. Because the translation service is based on the EuroVoc thesaurus, two of the queries are selected to correspond to terms in EuroVoc and one is not corresponding to a term in EuroVoc. The queries were originally in Bulgarian. First they were translated to English by a professional translator working with legal texts. We consider these translations as original queries in English. Then the queries were translated in both directions by people that know English, but are not professional translators. In this way, we simulate the case in which the users of the service will translate their queries by themselves. When we have the original queries and their human translations, we perform translation of each query by the service in three modes: simple translation, translation with query expansion using the relation skos:narrower (Query Expansion 1), and translation with query expansion using the relation skos:narrower and skos:related (Query Expansion 2). The following table summarises the variants of the three queries:

Q1 English Original (EO1): "consumer protection"
Q1 English Human Translation (EH1): "consumer protection"
Q1 English Simple Translation (ES1): "consumer protection"
Q1 English Query Expansion 1 (E11): "consumer protection" "consumer information" "european consumer centres network" "product quality" "product life" "product designation" "consumer movement" "product safety" "defective product"
Q1 English Query Expansion 2 (E21): "consumer protection" "housing law" "advertising" "advertising malpractice" "food safety" "producer's liability" "public health" "restriction on competition" "consumer information" "labelling" "social labelling" "european consumer centres network" "product quality" "competitiveness" "designation of origin" "industrial manufacturing" "quality control of agricultural products" "quality standard" "quality control circle" "product life" "product designation" "consumer movement" "product safety" "safety standard" "defective product"
Q1 Bulgarian Original (BO1): "защита на потребителите"

Q1 Bulgarian Human Translation (BH1): "защита на потребителите"

Q1 Bulgarian Simple Translation (BS1): "защита на потребителите"

Q1 Bulgarian Query Expansion 1 (B11): "защита на потребителя" "потребителска информация" "мрежата от европейски потребителски центрове" "качество на продукта" "живот на продукта" "наименование на продукт" "движение на потребители" "безопасност на продукта" "дефектен продукт"

Q1 Bulgarian Query Expansion 2 (B21): "защита на потребителя" "жилищно право" "реклама" "незаконни рекламни практики/недобросъвестна реклама" "хранителна безопасност" "отговорност на производителя" "обществено здраве" "ограничение на конкуренцията" "потребителска информация" "етикетиране" "социално класиране" "мрежата от европейски потребителски центрове" "качество на продукта" "конкурентност" "обозначение за произход" "промишлено производство" "качествен контрол на земеделска продукция" "стандарт за качество" "кръг за контрол на качество" "живот на продукта" "наименование на продукт" "движение на потребители" "безопасност на продукта" "стандарт за безопасност" "дефектен продукт"

Q2 English Original (EO2): "green area"

Q2 Bulgarian Original (BO2): "зелени площи"…[21]

Q3 English Original (EO3): "child support"

Q3 Bulgarian Original (BO3): "издръжка на дете"…[22]

The evaluation of the queries is with the operator AND for the words within the quotes and operator OR between different quotes. Each query was evaluated with respect to the search system provided by APIS and each returned document was evaluated by an independent subject knowing only the original query (and never having seen the translations). Each document was evaluated by assigning one of the following three categories: *exact match*, *non-exact match* and *no match*.[23] The non-exact match is necessary because in many cases the document is relevant to the original query, but the content of the query itself is not mentioned in the document. The documents returned by the queries in group of queries for each original query were put together and each of the documents was evaluated with respect to the three categories. Because the returned documents for some of the queries overlap, the actual number of the evaluated documents is smaller than the expected 400 documents. The following table represents the number of all documents in the group. See Table 3.

On the basis of these results we can draw some conclusions. For general queries from a thesaurus (Query 1 in Table 3) the performance slightly decreases in the cases of query expansion (B11, B21, E11, E21 in Table 4). For specific queries from a

---

[21] Some of the queries were skipped due to the space limits.

[22] The English and the Bulgarian queries are very similar to each other.

[23] The traditional evaluation in terms of precision and recall as well as in terms of their combinations is not possible in our setup, because we do not have a large set of documents and appropriate set of queries. Creation of such a test set is a time-consuming task which is outside of the work, reported here.

Table 3. The number of documents per query type.

Query group	Number of documents	Exact	NonExact	No
Q1 Bulgarian	272	182	56	34
Q1 English	244	194	18	32
Q2 Bulgarian	181	42	8	131
Q2 English	196	14	8	174
Q3 Bulgarian	264	146	8	110
Q3 English	164	78	12	74

thesaurus or for queries translated automatically without the usage of a thesaurus the performance improves in all cases except one case – B23. In case of general queries the number of non-exact match documents drastically increase in comparison to exact matches. To sum up, in cases when the users are not sure in their own translation of the query they are interested in, it is better to use the automatic translation service. If the users look also for similar documents that contain no exact match, then they might prefer to use the query expansion module.

The evaluation is given in the following Table 4.

Table 4. The manual evaluation of the documents per query.

Query	Exact	NonExact	No	Query	Exact	NonExact	No
(BO1)	90	6	4	(EO1)	92	0	8
(BH1)	90	6	4	(EH1)	92	0	8
(BS1)	90	6	4	(ES1)	92	0	8
(B11)	60	22	18	(E11)	78	9	13
(B21)	50	28	22	(E21)	59	23	18
(BO2)	36	6	76	(EO2)	12	6	84
(BH2)	19	6	57	(EH2)	8	8	82
(BS2)	36	6	76	(ES2)	12	6	84
(B12)	36	6	76	(E12)	12	6	84
(B22)	36	6	76	(E22)	12	6	84
(BO3)	90	6	4	(EO3)	40	4	56
(BH3)	47	1	52	(EH3)	40	4	56
(BS3)	58	4	38	(ES3)	62	10	28
(B13)	58	4	38	(E13)	62	10	28
(B23)	44	4	52	(E23)	65	6	29

6 Conclusions

The paper reports on a multilingual access module to legal data, which combines two approaches to translation of users' queries – ontology-based and statistical.

The experiments showed that the applicability of the module is better when both modules are combined to work together. Both modules require the availability of appropriate data – lexical resources and ontologies for the ontology-based one as well as big high-quality corpora for the statistical one.

Our future work includes the following streamlines: testing the presented ideas on other languages; evaluation on the combined module setting; qualitative evaluation of the results with real users; query expansion with Linked Open Data reasoning.

References

1. Agerri, R., Bermudez, J., Rigau, G.: IXA pipeline: efficient and ready to use multilingual NLP tools. In: Proceedings of the Ninth International Conference on Language Resources and Evaluation (LREC 2014) (2014)
2. Collins, M.: Discriminative training methods for hidden Markov models. In: Proceedings of the ACL-02 Conference on Empirical Methods in Natural Language Processing, vol. 10, pp. 1–8 (2002)
3. Koehn, P., Hoang, H.: Factored translation models. In: Proceedings of the 2007 Joint Conference on Empirical Methods in Natural Language Processing and Computational Natural Language Learning, pp. 868–876 (2007)
4. Koehn, P., et al.: Moses: open source toolkit for statistical machine translation. In: Proceedings of the 45th Annual Meeting of the ACL on Interactive Poster and Demonstration Sessions, pp 177–180 (2007)
5. Och, F.J.: Minimum error rate training in statistical machine translation. In: Proceedings of the 41st Annual Meeting on Association for Computational Linguistics, vol. 1, pp. 160–167 (2003)
6. Simov, K., Osenova, P., Slavcheva, M.: BTB-TR03: BulTreeBank morphosyntactic tagset BTB-TS version 2.0 (2004)
7. Simov, K., Osenova, P.: Applying ontology-based lexicons to the semantic annotation of learning objects. In: Proceedings from the Workshop on NLP and Knowledge Representation for eLearning Environments, RANLP-2007, pp. 49–55 (2007)
8. Simov, K., Osenova, P.: Language resources and tools for ontology-based semantic annotation. In: Oltramari, A., Prévot, L., Huang, C.-R., Buitelaar, P., Vossen, P. (eds.) OntoLex 2008 Workshop at LREC 2008, pp. 9–13. Published by the European Language Resource Association ELRA (2008)
9. Simov, K., Peev, Z., Kouylekov, M., Simov, A., Dimitrov, M., Kiryakov, A.: CLaRK - an XML-based System for Corpora Development. In: Proceedings of the Corpus Linguistics 2001 Conference, 553–560 (2001)

Combining Natural Language Processing Approaches for Rule Extraction from Legal Documents

Mauro Dragoni[1]([✉]), Serena Villata[2], Williams Rizzi[3], and Guido Governatori[4]

[1] Fondazione Bruno Kessler, Trento, Italy
dragoni@fbk.eu
[2] CNRS, I3S Laboratory, Paris, France
villata@i3s.unice.fr
[3] Universitá degli Studi di Trento, Trento, Italy
wrizzi@fbk.eu
[4] NICTA Queensland, Brisbane, Australia
guido@governatori.net

Abstract. Legal texts express conditions in natural language describing what is permitted, forbidden or mandatory in the context they regulate. Despite the numerous approaches tackling the problem of moving from a natural language legal text to the respective set of machine-readable conditions, results are still unsatisfiable and it remains a major open challenge. In this paper, we propose a preliminary approach which combines different Natural Language Processing techniques towards the extraction of rules from legal documents. More precisely, we combine the linguistic information provided by WordNet together with a syntax-based extraction of rules from legal texts, and a logic-based extraction of dependencies between chunks of such texts. Such a combined approach leads to a powerful solution towards the extraction of machine-readable rules from legal documents. We evaluate the proposed approach over the Australian "Telecommunications consumer protections code".

1 Introduction

Applying deontic reasoning techniques to real world scenarios has to face the challenge of processing natural language texts. On the one side, all codes and legal documents of public institutions and companies are expressed in natural language, and it is very unlikely to have a structured (possibly machine-processable) representation of the deontic conditions contained in such documents. On the other side, automated reasoning techniques need to process formal conditions to infer further information, or to check whether the observed behavior is compliant with such conditions, or whether a violation occurred. In this kind of frameworks, the basic representation of a legal rule is as follows: $sup\_received\_complaint \Rightarrow [Obl]inform\_consumer\_process$ meaning that a supplier has to inform the consumer of the complaint procedure upon reception of a complaint. Note that this kind of rules are not always clearly identifiable in legal texts, and this task is difficult even for humans, becoming challenging for an automated system. Defining systems able to tackle this task in an automated way is a main challenge that received a lot of attention in the past years from the legal information systems community, and heterogeneous approaches have been proposed, e.g., [1,2]. This interest is due, not only to the difficulty for humans to address such a task, but also to the fact that the task is extremely time consuming for humans, and (even partially) automating it to reduce the amount of work demanded to humans would become a valuable support.

Despite the huge number of proposed approaches, the problem of extracting rules or conditions from legal texts is still open. In this paper, we start from the observation that, given the difficulty of the task, the adoption of a single Natural Language Processing (NLP) approach to solve it would not lead to satisfiable results, as witnessed by very limited adoption of the current frameworks. The research question we answer in this paper is: *How to combine different NLP approaches to extract in an automated way a set of rules from natural language legal texts?* This question breaks down into the following subquestions: *(1)* How to deal with the variability of natural language texts for the identification of the deontic components of each rule?, and *(2)* How to combine a syntax-based approach and a semantic-based one to identify the terms composing each rule, and correctly assign them as being the antecedent/consequent of the rule?

To answer these questions, we adopt and combine a set of NLP techniques. More precisely, our framework for automated rules generation exploits the Stanford Parser to obtain the grammatical representation of the sentences, and WordNet[1] to deal with the variability of the language in expressing the deontic components in natural language legal texts. We combine this syntactic-based rules extraction approach, relying on the well known Stanford Parser, together with a logic-based approach, exploiting the Boxer framework [3] for the extraction of logical dependencies between chunks of text. The results of the evaluation of our combined framework on a section of the Australian "Telecommunications consumer protections code" show the feasibility of the proposed approach, and foster further research in this direction. The advantage of our approach is that there is no need to learn how to extract the rules building a huge annotated data set of legal documents as for machine learning approaches.

The remainder of this paper is as follows: Sect. 2 discusses the related literature and compares it to the proposed approach. Section 3 presents the overall framework for automated rules extraction, and Sect. 4 describes the evaluation setting.

2   Related Work

The automated processing of legal texts to extract some kind of information is a challenge that received a lot of attention in the literature. [4] address an automated processing of legal texts exploiting NLP techniques: they aim at classifying

---

[1] https://wordnet.princeton.edu/.

law paragraphs according to their regulatory content and extracting text fragments corresponding to specific semantic roles relevant for the regulatory content, while our goal is to extract rules with deontic modalities from legal texts. [5], instead, propose an automated framework for the semantic annotation of provisions to ease the retrieval process of norms, [6] present a knowledge extraction framework from legal texts, and [7] present a tool for extracting requirements from regulations where texts are annotated to identify fragments describing normative concepts, and then a semantic model is constructed from these annotations and transformed into a set of requirements. Also in these cases, the goal of the automated processing of legal texts is different. [1] present an automated concept and norm extraction framework that adopts linguistic techniques. The goal of this paper is the same as ours: an automated norm/rules extraction system will help in saving knowledge analysts a lot of time, and it also contributes to a more uniform knowledge representation of such formal norms/rules. However, the adopted methodology is different: they exploit Juridical (Natural) Language Constructs (JLC) that formalize legal knowledge using NLP by introducing a set of predefined natural language constructs to define a subset of all possible legal sentences. This kind of "patterns" is identified in the text thanks to the identification of noun and verb phrases, and then they are translated into formal rules. Similarly to them, we define "patterns" for detecting the deontic rules, but we combine two approaches to lead to better results: we rely on the structured representation of the sentence returned from the parser and its logical one returned from Boxer. Finally, [1] do not consider the identification of deontic modalities in rules, and no evaluation of their automated norms extraction framework is provided thus results cannot be compared. [8] use machine learning for Dutch regulations, [9,10] do the same for Italian ones. These approaches classify documents or sentences, differently from our methodology where rules are extracted from the structural representation of legal texts. Finally, [2] present a linguistic-based approach to extract deontic rules from regulations. As underlined by the authors, Stanford parser has not been evaluated against legal sources, that is the what we do in our own framework and they do as well. However, we do not exploit the General Architecture for Text Engineering, and our approach does not require to annotate the legal texts. To obtain satisfiable results, we combine the result of the parser together with the logical dependencies between chunks of text extracted from the document through Boxer. An experimental comparison with the performances reported in these works is difficult as the data sets used to evaluate them are not available. [11] present a framework to automatically extract semantic knowledge from legislative texts. A similarity with our work is that, instead of using pattern matching methods relying on lexico-syntactic patterns, they propose to adopt syntactic dependencies between terms extracted with a syntactic parser. The idea, on which the present paper is grounded as well, is that syntactic information are more robust than pattern matching approaches when facing length and complexity of the sentences. The difference consists in the kind of information extracted, legal rules in our case, and three semantic labels, namely active role, passive role, and involved object in their work.

3   The Framework

The combined NLP approach implemented in this paper adopts several components to automatically generate rules from natural language legal texts. In particular, it exploits the following elements described in more details later on in this section: (i) a lightweight ontology describing the deontic linguistic elements allowing for the identification of the obligations, permissions, and prohibitions in legal texts; (ii) a lightweight ontology describing how the natural language text is structured, and how punctuation can be interpreted for helping the extraction of rules[2]; (iii) a NLP library, namely, the Stanford Parser library[3], used for parsing natural language sentences to retrieve their grammatical representation. We decided to adopt Stanford Parser as it is the reference parser for parsing natural language sentences in English; (iv) a Combinatory Categorial Grammar (CCG) parser tool including the Boxer framework [3], used for extracting logical dependencies between chunks of text from the document.

The resulting combined framework is an extension of the approach presented in [12]. In particular, the following drawbacks have been addressed with respect to [12]: (i) the deontic ontology has been extended by extracting from Word-Net [13] all synsets related to the meaning of the Obligation, Permission, and Prohibition concepts (as described in Subsect. 3.1). In this way, we are able to improve the precision of the term annotation activities with the deontic labels; (ii) the set of the patterns used for detecting deontic rules has been enriched; (iii) a parallel branch integrating the functionalities of the CCG parser has been integrated to analyze the text from a different perspective. The analysis results obtained by the CCG parser are then merged with the output of the NLP-only branch for extracting the final set of rules. Figure 1 shows the pipeline of the proposed framework.

After the preliminary steps consisting in the extraction of the text from source documents, and the composition of the separated sentences generated by the extractor, the structured representation of the text follows two parallel branches implementing two different analysis techniques. In the lower branch, the modules of the Stanford NLP library are applied for tagging sentence content, and building the related tree for extracting the terms contained in each sentence. Then, the deontic ontology is applied to annotate each term with the appropriate label, i.e., obligation, permission, prohibition. Finally, the system looks for patterns within the terms set of each sentence in order to compose the rules.

---

[2] Note that these ontologies are explicitly called *lightweight* ontologies as they are not expected to be used to normalize the concepts of legal text by mapping the legal terms into concepts in ontology, and obtain the meaning of the text by using the ontology structure. They uniquely provide a support for detecting the deontic components in legal texts and the structure of such texts, respectively.

[3] http://nlp.stanford.edu/software/lex-parser.shtml.

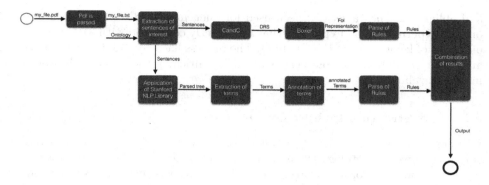

Fig. 1. The pipeline of the proposed framework.

In the upper branch, instead, the CCG parser is applied to the full sentence to extract logic relationships between terms. Then, the output of the CCG parser is used for confirming the rules extracted through the lower branch, and for discovering new relationships between terms that have not been detected by applying the patterns adopted by the NLP parser. Each component of the pipeline is now detailed.

3.1 Deontic Lightweight Ontology

The deontic lightweight ontology, called `normonto`, has been designed to support the system in the automated identification of the normative component of the rules. More precisely, this ontology is exploited to identify whether a term expresses a prohibition, a permission, or an obligation. Even if several ontologies have been proposed in the latest years to represent such a kind of knowledge in different contexts, the aim of the `normonto` ontology is not to represent and model legal concepts but to specify the lexicon used to express permissions, prohibitions and obligations in natural language legal texts. For this reason, we specify the three main concepts called `Obligation`, `Permission`, and `Prohibition`. The lexicon used to express the normative component in legal texts is represented in the ontology as individuals of such subclasses. For instance, the individual `must` identifies an obligation, thus it belongs to the class `LexicalTermObl`, and the individual `not_be_allowed` identifies a prohibition, thus belonging to the class `LexicalTermPro`. Note that this ontology is intended to be general purpose and extensible, and differently from the text structure ontology we present in the next section, it can be exploited by the system to extract the deontic component of the rules from heterogeneous legal texts. Finally, the ontology is intended to model the legal lexicon in English. Further extensions to cover multilingual rules extraction are considered for future research. The selection of the keywords modeled as individuals in the ontology has been performed by starting from a basic set of keywords related to the concepts of prohibition, permission, and obligation. Such a set has been used for querying WordNet to extract synonyms, hypernyms, and hyponyms that are directly connected with each element of the set of keywords mentioned above. The process has been run for three times and, after each step, the content extracted for enriching the ontology has been manually validated.

3.2   Text Structure Lightweight Ontology

In order to support the NLP algorithm in the analysis of different textual structures, a lightweight ontology, defining the main elements of the text organization, has been modeled in order to effectively address our particular use case. Depending on the text structure that has to be analyzed, it might be necessary to model different lightweight ontologies dedicated to those particular purposes.

Concerning the concepts definition, we modeled three main concepts: (i) `Document`, defining the conceptualization of the entire text to analyze; (ii) `TextChunk`, defining a single piece of text containing valuable information (i.e. antecedent or consequent of the rule that has to be extracted); and (iii) `Punctuation`, defining the meaning that specific punctuation signs may have in the text from the computational point of view (for instance, the ";" sign may be used for splitting sentences).

Concerning individuals, we modeled each block of the text as a new individual instantiating the `TextChunk` object. This way, we are able to represent each sentence of the text, or part of it, as a new element of the ontology in order to allow the definition of their semantic relations used by the system for the extraction of the rules.

Besides concepts and individuals, we define two object properties (`hasGeneralChunk` and `hasPart`, the second one modeled as `inverseOf` of the first one) and one data property (`hasText`). The two object properties are used for modeling the hierarchical relationships between different `TextChunk`-objects; while, the `hasText` data property allows to associate the natural language text with the correspondent individual.

3.3   Extraction of Sentences

The analysis of the text starts with the extraction of sentences of interest that are subsequently used for the text analysis. The extraction of such sentences is done by exploiting the structured nature of the text that generally characterizes legal documents where a bullet-based representation is used for describing normative conditions. As first step, we map single text chunks contained in the bullet representation of the document to the lightweight ontology. In this way, we are able to manipulate a linked structure of the text easing the extraction of the full sentences. By considering the structured representation of the text as a tree, we reconstruct the set of full sentences to analyze by starting from the root of the tree and by concatenating, for each .possible path, the text chunks found until the leaves are reached. Let us consider an excerpt of the document used as test case (Sect. 4) showing the structured representation of one of the norms contained in the document:

```
(1) - Acknowledging a Complaint:
(2) --- immediately where the Complaint is made in
        person or by telephone;
(3) --- within 2 Working Days of receipt where the
        Complaint is made by:
(4) ----- email;
(5) ----- being logged via the Supplier's website
        or another website endorsed
        by the Supplier for that purpose;
(6) ----- post; and
(7) ----- telephone and a message is recorded
        without direct contact with a
        staff member of the Supplier.
```

By performing the mapping between the text and the lightweight ontology, the resulting assignments are the "Level 1" to the first chunk, "Level 2" to the second and third ones, and "Level 3" to the others. By navigating through the tree representation, the sentences extracted from the text are the concatenations of the following text chunks (based on the ids written at left of each chunk): "1-2", "1-3-4", "1-3-5", "1-3-6", "1-3-7". As in Sect. 3.2, the punctuation elements are used as regulators for deciding where to split sentences in case of complex structures. Sentences extracted at this step are then used for the extraction of the single terms.

3.4 The Use of the Stanford NLP Library

The extraction of rules from natural language legal texts requires the use of tools able to provide a grammatical structure of the text that may be exploited for inferring the different components of a logical rule. The facilities available for having an effective representation of sentences are very limited. By analyzing the state of the art, one of the most prominent library is the one provided by Stanford. Such a library includes a Tree Parser able to produce a tree-based representation of each sentence and to tag them with grammatical prefixes. Moreover, the parser includes also a facility able to produce a set of grammatical relations explained which dependency elapses between two terms. The role of the parser is to work out the grammatical structure of sentences, for instance, which groups of words go together and which words are the "subject" or the "object" of a verb. The Stanford Tree Parser is a probabilistic parser using knowledge of language gained from hand-parsed sentences to try to produce the most likely analysis of new sentences. Even if statistical parsers still make some mistakes in exceptional cases, they commonly work very well and, currently, they are the most suitable solution for a preliminary text analysis. In the proposed approach, we decided to use the Stanford NLP library for parsing the extracted sentences, and to use the produced output as starting point for terms extraction. Let us consider the following sentence: "Suppliers must demonstrate, fairness and courtesy, objectivity, and efficiency by Acknowledging a Complaint within 2 Working Days of receipt where the Complaint is made by email." By parsing this sentence, we obtain the grammatical tree of the sentence shown below[4]:

```
(ROOT
  (S
    (NP (NNS Suppliers))
    (VP (MD must)
      (VP (VB demonstrate) (, ,) (VB fairness)
      (CC and)
      (NP
        (NP (NN courtesy) (, ,) (NN objectivity) (, ,)
          (CC and)
          (NN efficiency))
        (PP (IN by)
          (S
            (VP (VBG Acknowledging)
              (NP (DT a) (NN Complaint))
              (PP (IN within)
                (NP
                  (NP (CD 2) (JJ Working) (NNS Days))
                  (PP (IN of)
                    (NP (NN receipt)))))
              (SBAR
                (WHADVP (WRB where))
                (S
                  (NP (DT the) (NNP Complaint))
                  (VP (VBZ is)
                    (VP (VBN made)
                      (PP (IN by)
                        (NP (NN email)))))))))))))
    (. .)))
```

3.5   Extraction of Terms

Given the parsed version of each sentence, the next step consists to extract relevant terms from them. With "term" we do not mean a single word (or compound names) having a meaning in a vocabulary, but we mean a complex textual expression representing an entire concept. The extraction of the terms follows the identification of the subordinate sentences identified by the parser. In general, we interpret the beginning of a new sentence (or a subordinate one) as the beginning of a new term with some exceptions based on the content of the generated tree. Some examples are (i) if an extracted term starts with the expression "to VERB", the term is automatically concatenated with the previous one, and (ii) if an extracted term contains only one token, such a token is directly concatenated to the succeeding one. This mainly happens when tokens like "where", "what", etc. are parsed. Let us consider again the sample sentence of Sect. 3.4 where the analysis of the parsed representation leads to the identification of the following terms:

```
-: Suppliers must demonstrate fairness, and courtesy,
   objectivity and efficiency, by
a: Aknowledging a Complaint within 2 Working Days
   of receipt
b: where the Complaint is made by email
```

---

[4] For more details about the meaning of each tag and dependency clauses used by the parser, please refer to the official Stanford documentation: http://nlp.stanford.edu/software/dependencies_manual.pdf.

The first row is not marked as actual term but as "implicit" term. Indeed, as it will be explained in Sect. 4 concerning the document used as test case, some text chunks occur in many sentences. Such terms, independently by their eventual deontic meaning, are marked only once; while, for the other sentences, they are considered as "implicit" terms and they are not marked. The role of the "implicit" terms is to appear as antecedent of rules when, in a sentence, no terms are detected as antecedent, but consequent are identified. Two terms are identified here.

3.6   Annotation of Terms with Deontic Tags

After the extraction of terms, they have to be annotated with the deontic tags of Obligation, Permission, and Prohibition defined in the deontic lightweight vocabulary. We assign the deontic tags by applying a text processing approach. For each extracted term, we first verify if one of the lemmatized version of the labels of the vocabulary is present in the sentence; if yes, the term is annotated with the corresponding tag. A further check is performed to verify if, for example in case of verb, the label and the "not" auxiliary have been split during the term extraction in two consecutive terms. Indeed, if this happens, the identified deontic tag has to be changed. For instance, for the labels "must" and "must not" the deontic tags used are, respectively, the "Obligation" and the "Prohibition" ones. In the example, the only term in which a deontic element is identified is the implicit one that is annotated with the "Obligation" tag due to the label "must":

```
-: Suppliers must demonstrate fairness, and courtesy,
   objectivity and efficiency, by [O]
a: Aknowledging a Complaint within 2 Working Days of
   receipt
b: where the Complaint is made by email
```

3.7   Combination of Terms for Rule Definition

The last step consists in the definition of the rules obtained by combining the extracted and annotated terms. For creating the rules, we apply a set of patterns to the terms in order to detect what is the antecedent and the consequent of each rule. Due to space reasons, we are not able to report all patterns defined in the system, but only some of them:

```
[O] Term1
WHERE Term2        Rule: Term2 => [O] Term1

IF Term1
[O] THEN Term2     Rule: Term1 => [O] Term2

[O] Term1
UNLESS Term2       Rule: Term2 => [P] NOT Term1

[O] Term1
WHEN Term2
AFTER Term3        Rule: Term2 AND Term3 => [O] Term1
```

It is important to highlight that, in case a deontic tag is used for anno-tating an implicit term, such a tag is inherited by the first term following the implicit one. This happens because implicit terms are not taken into account for generating the rules.

Finally, by considering the annotated terms shown in Sect. 3.6 and by apply-ing the first pattern due to the presence of the "where" label, the generated rule is: b => [O] a.

3.8   The Use of the CCG Parser

The CCG parser has been integrated for performing a logic analysis of each sentence in order to find relationships between the contained words. Indeed, semantic representations produced by the CCG parser, known as Discourse Rep-resentation Structures (DRSs), can be considered as ordinary first-order logic formulas and can be exploited to find semantic connections between each word extracted from the sentences. The aim of the integration of such a component is to support the NLP pipeline described above in detecting the relationships between the sentences from which the Stanford parser is not able to extract any information through the application of the pattern-based mechanism (Sect. 3.7). The exploitation of such logical relationships allows to improve the general effec-tiveness of the rules extraction system.

Consider the following example of the output generated by the CCG parser (Fig. 2) and of the linguistic graph that we build starting from the relationships between words found by the parser (Fig. 3).

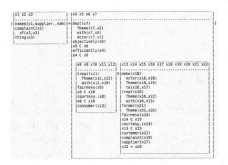

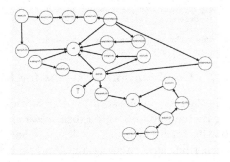

Fig. 2. Example of output generated by the CCG parser.

Fig. 3. Example of the linguistic graph built by starting from the relationships between words found by the parser.

Graph's connections are exploited for two purposes. First, for sentences where deontic rules have been extracted by the NLP-only pipeline, we verify if the CCG parser finds relationships between the terms involved in the rule (the effectiveness of the pipeline by considering the different scores between these rules will be discussed in Sect. 4). Second, for sentences where deontic rules are not detected by the NLP-only pipeline, in particular by the pattern-based mechanism, if the CCG parser identifies logical relationships between the terms contained in the sentence, a new deontic rule is created and stored in the rules set.

4   Evaluation

The evaluation is based on the novel Australian Telecommunications Consumer Protections Code, TC628-2012 (TCPC) effective from September 1st, 2012, in particular Sections 8.2.1(a)–8.2.1(c) pertaining Compliant Management. The section describes the obligations a telecommunication service provider has to comply with when they receive a complaint from customer or consumer (for the purpose of TCPC, Section 2 Terms and Definitions customer or consumer are treated as synonymous).

The text under analysis contains a single top level clause (8.2.1) which is then divided in 3 subclauses. Furthermore, it contains 19 clauses at level 3, 16 clauses at level 4, and 4 level 5 clauses/conditions. The structure of the document (i.e., the organization of the clauses and their subclauses) indicates that the section contains 35 prima facie clauses.

For example, Section 8.2.1.a.(vii) states that:

advising the Consumer or former Customer of the proposed Resolution of their Complaint within 15 Working Days from the date the Complaint is received in accordance with clause 8.2.1 (a);

is mapped to the following prescriptive rule:

```
complaint => [O] inform_proposed_resolution_15_days
```

For the evaluation, we manually compared the rule-set manually generated by an analyst, and the set of rules automatically extracted using the methodology described in Sect. 3. Note that we cannot compare to a baseline as either none of the related work provides the evaluation results or the task they addressed is a different one thus results are not comparable.

For measuring the effectiveness of the system, we evaluated the following outputs and we compared them to the outputs contained in the manual created gold standard: *(i)* the number of correct sentences extracted from the text, *(ii)* the number of correct terms identified in the extracted sentences, *(iii)* the number of correct deontic components annotations performed on the identified terms, *(iv)* the number of correct rules generated from the extracted terms annotated with the deontic component, and *(v)* the impact of the CCG parser in supporting the detection of new patterns for generating rules.

By referring to the architecture described in Sect. 3, single blocks have been evaluated separately enabling a more fine-grained analysis of potential pitfalls in the effectiveness of system components. The evaluation of the lower branch of the pipeline consisted in the computation of the following values: *(i)* the number of sentences extracted correctly, *(ii)* the number of terms detected, *(iii)* the number of terms correctly annotated with the deontic tags, and *(iv)* the number of rules that have been generated correctly. While, the evaluation of the upper branch, consisted in measuring: *(i)* the agreement between the rules extracted from the CCG output and the ones generated by the lower branch, and *(ii)* the number of rules correctly extracted from the CCG output regarding sentences for which the lower branch generated anything.

Lower Branch Evaluation. The extraction of the sentences is the first performed task, the number of extracted sentences was 28 out of the same number of sentences contained in the gold standard. Therefore, concerning the first output the precision and recall of the system are 100%.

The second task is the identification of the terms within sentences. The gold standard contains 65 terms extracted by the analysts; our system is able to extract 59 terms whose 49 are correct. Therefore, the obtained recall is 90.78% and the precision is 83.05%, with a F-Measure of 86.74%. Concerning the assignment of the deontic annotation, 47 out of the 49 correctly identified terms have been annotated with the proper deontic component, leading to a precision of 95.92%.

The last step consists in determining which of the 36 rules contained in the gold standard have a counterpart in the automatically generated rule set composed by 41 rules. A rule r in the automatically generated set has a counterpart if there is a rule s in the manually generated set such that the proposition in the right hand side (or consequent) of s is mapped to the consequent of r. The number of rules satisfying this condition is 33 out of 36 with a Precision of 80.49% and a Recall of 91.67%.

Finally, the last operation is to determine which extracted rules have a full correspondence with the manually generated rules: 24 of the automatically extracted rules have a corresponding rule in the manually generated rule set. This means that, as final assessment, we obtain a recall of Precision of 66.67%.

Upper Branch Evaluation. The first evaluation performed on the upper branch of the pipeline was the measure of the agreement between the rules generated by the lower branch and the ones inferred from the output of the CCG parser. By starting from the output of the CCG parser, we firstly verify if words belonging to different terms are directly related by one of the logical modifiers used by the CCG parser for representing relationships between words. After the verification of the all generated relationships, we computed how many of them exist also in the set of the rules generated by the NLP parser used in the lower branch.

The set of relationships between terms extracted by the CCG parser contains 51 relationships and, by transforming them in rules, 35 of them have a counterpart (as defined in the previous paragraph) in the gold standard. With respect to the lower branch, the CCG parser was able to find 2 new rules having a counterpart in the gold standard. This means that the recall increased to 97.22% (35 rules detected out of 36), but the precision decreased to 68.63% due to the high number of relationships extracted by the CCG parser. Indeed, the CCG parser works at a more fine-grained logical-linguistic level with respect to the NLP-only parser; therefore, the detection of relationships between terms that are not actually a rule it is more easy.

Another interesting result is the number of deontic annotations that have been found by the CCG parser. The number of such annotations increased from 47 to 49 out of the 49 annotations contained in the gold standard by reaching a precision of 100.00%.

Finally, 29 out of the 35 rules found by the CCG parser have a full correspondence with the manually generated rules. This means that the synergistic use of the NLP-only and CCG parser led to an improvement of 5 rules by increasing the precision of the system from 66.67% to 80.56%.

Discussion of the Results. As we mentioned above, the text we analyzed contains 35 prima facie clauses, and some of these rules require to be decomposed in two sub-rules to fully capture the nuances of the conditions under which the obligations hold. For example, as we have seen in Sect. 3, Section 8.2.1.a.(xiii) splits in two clauses each requiring two rules. Furthermore, we would like to point out that the number of rules required to capture a norm could depend on the logical formalism used to reason with the rule. For example, if a condition of activation of an obligation is disjunctive, it is represented by two rules in the manually generated rule set. However, the disjunction could be represented by a single proposition encoding both of them. Thus, the number of rules required to model a normative clause depends on the underlying logic. This means that we can take as reference for the computation of the recall not the actual number of rules in the reference rule set, but the number of prima-facie clauses. In this case, the extracted rules cover 31 out of the 35 prima facie clauses. Finally, note that the examples used in this section (Section 8.2.1.a(vii) and 8.2.1a(xiii) are correctly identified by our system. Concerning error analysis, in most cases incorrect rules depend on the incorrect identification of the propositions in the first step, or on the fact that the rules contain implicit terms in the left-hand side to be derived from the right hand side. The correct treatment of these cases is left as future research.

5   Concluding Remarks

In this paper, we have presented a combined framework for the automated extraction of rules from legal texts. The framework exploits both syntax-based patterns extracted using the Stanford Parser, and logic-based ones extracted through the Boxer framework. Several steps need to be addressed as future research to improve the performance and the applicability of the system. First of all, we need to construct a gold standard of legal rules extracted from different kinds of legal texts in order to validate the proposed approach on a larger dataset, taking into account the variability of the legal documents. Second, we need to capture the co-reference links that are present in legal texts. For instance, consider a section of the code that starts with `Suppliers must provide Consumers with a Complaint handling process that [...]`. Then, in another part of the section, we have the following text A Supplier must take the following actions to enable this outcome. How to recognize what is "this outcome"? We need to establish that a co-reference occurred such that the outcome is to provide consumers with a compliant handling that satisfies the certain requirements. Third, we need to align the terms used in the legal text with the terms we want to use in the rules. As shown in our evaluation, the difference between the hand-written rules and the automated extracted ones is that different terms are used to constitute the same rules.

References

1. van Engers, T., van Gog, R., Sayah, K.: A case study on automated norm extraction. In: Proceedings of JURIX, pp. 49–58 (2004)
2. Wyner, A., Peters, W.: On rule extraction from regulations. In: JURIX 2011, pp. 113–122 (2011)
3. Curran, J.R., Clark, S., Bos, J.: Linguistically motivated large-scale NLP with c&c and boxer. In: Carroll, J.A., van den Bosch, A., Zaenen, A. (eds.) ACL 2007, Proceedings of the 45th Annual Meeting of the Association for Computational Linguistics, 23–30 June 2007, Prague, Czech Republic. The Association for Computational Linguistics (2007)
4. Soria, C., Bartolini, R., Lenci, A., Montemagni, S., Pirrelli, V.: Automatic extraction of semantics in law documents. European Press Academic Publishing (2005)
5. Biagioli, C., Francesconi, E., Passerini, A., Montemagni, S., Soria, C.: Automatic semantics extraction in law documents. In: ICAIL 2015, pp. 133–140 (2005)
6. de Araujo, D.A., Rigo, S., Muller, C., de Oliveira Chishman, R.L.: Automatic information extraction from texts with inference and linguistic knowledge acquisition rules. In: Web Intelligence/IAT Workshops, pp. 151–154 (2013)
7. Kiyavitskaya, N., et al.: Automating the extraction of rights and obligations for regulatory compliance. In: Li, Q., Spaccapietra, S., Yu, E., Olivé, A. (eds.) ER 2008. LNCS, vol. 5231, pp. 154–168. Springer, Heidelberg (2008). https://doi.org/10.1007/978-3-540-87877-3_13
8. de Maat, E., Winkels, R.: Suggesting model fragments for sentences in Dutch laws. In: Proceedings of LOAIT, pp. 19–28 (2010)
9. Brighi, R., Palmirani, M.: Legal text analysis of the modification provisions: a pattern oriented approach. In: ICAIL 2009, pp. 238–239 (2009)
10. Francesconi, E.: Legal rules learning based on a semantic model for legislation. In: Proceedings of SPLeT Workshop (2010)
11. Boella, G., Di Caro, L., Robaldo, L.: Semantic relation extraction from legislative text using generalized syntactic dependencies and support vector machines. In: Morgenstern, L., Stefaneas, P., Lévy, F., Wyner, A., Paschke, A. (eds.) RuleML 2013. LNCS, vol. 8035, pp. 218–225. Springer, Heidelberg (2013). https://doi.org/10.1007/978-3-642-39617-5_20
12. Dragoni, M., Governatori, G., Villata, S.: Automated rules generation from natural language legal texts. In: ICAIL 2015 Workshop on Automated Detection, Extraction and Analysis of Semantic Information in Legal Texts (2015)
13. Fellbaum, C.: WordNet: An Electronic Lexical Database. MIT Press, Cambridge (1998)

Analysis of Legal References in an Emergency Legislative Setting

Monica Palmirani[(✉)], Ilaria Bianchi[(✉)], Luca Cervone[(✉)],
and Francesco Draicchio

CIRSFID, University of Bologna, Bologna, Italy
{monica.palmirani,ilaria.bianchi,luca.cervone,
francesco.draicchio}@unibo.it

Keywords: NLP · URI · Legal XML · Modifications · Visualization
Network analysis

1 Introduction

Each legal system is a complex network of norms and the normative citations in the texts are the legal method for referring to other parts of the same legal system diachronically (dynamically over time) or synchronically (statically) (Palmirani and Brighi 2006). Normative citations are the textual part of a legal document that refers to another legal source in the same legal system (e.g., Sect. 3 of the Human Rights Act 1998 in the UK legal system) or also to other legal systems (e.g., European directives). One of the most relevant legislative techniques[1] uses citations to summarize the verbosity of norms, create semantic relationships between different normative resources, or amend the original text. We can classify citations using this taxonomy: (i) *internal* and *external* to the same document; (ii) *dynamic* or *static* at a given time (e.g., London Regional Transport Act 1984 and later London Regional Transport Act 1996); (iii) citations that express semantic *normative specification* (extension or restriction; see also interpretation); (iv) citations for referring to an already expressed piece of text already without duplicating it (*shortcut*); (v) citations that semantically connect different documents under the same topic (*clustering*). In all these cases citations set up an interesting apparatus for analyzing a country's legislative approach. In particular, it is possible to understand the legal drafting techniques adopted, as well as to detect anomalies in order to increase the effectiveness of normative action.

On the basis of these arguments, this paper investigates the references of a legal corpus of the ordinances issued by the Regional Commissioner for Emergency and Reconstruction over the first 18 months after the 2012 earthquake in Emilia-Romagna, Italy. The goal is to analyze the critical issues in the regulative strategy in emergency situations in order to help the lawmaker act better in future disasters, extract information concerning the number and the types of modifications produced, and support the debate on a national law on emergency in the wake of natural disasters.

---

[1] https://www.law.cornell.edu/citation/; http://filj.lawreviewnetwork.com/files/2011/10/EU_Citation_ Manual_2010-2011_for_Website.pdf; http://eur-lex.europa.eu/content/techleg/KB0213228ENN.pdf.

© Springer Nature Switzerland AG 2018
U. Pagallo et al. (Eds.): AICOL VI-X 2015–2017, LNAI 10791, pp. 301–313, 2018.
https://doi.org/10.1007/978-3-030-00178-0_20

The outcomes here presented are developed as part of the Energie Sisma Emilia research project, conducted by a consortium of universities in the Emilia-Romagna Region.[2,3] All the graphs are presented in dynamic visualization in web portal.[4] This makes it possible to cross-check groupings based on lexical-textual analysis and groupings based on structural elements.

2 Methodology

The earthquake struck in Emilia-Romagna Region[5] on 20 and 29 May 2012 and on 3 June 2012. The disaster area[6] includes 33 municipalities and stretches over 3,173 square meters across the region. The Commissioner for Emergencies issued 350 ordinances deliberated over a three-year period (2012–2015), so as to support the rebuilding, aid for the population, organization of the territory. The main research goal is to investigate the corpus of legislative ordinances so as to make more effective the legislative actions in emergency settings. Analyzing the legal citations and the correspondent references we can discover some dysfunctional behaviour in the lawmaking system, the concentration of some urgent topics, to detect weaknesses in normative area, to orient a more coordinated legislative action at the national level. In the Italian Senate there are several bills being debated on emergency situations. This analysis could provide useful input to that legislative debate.

The research at the University of Bologna was concentrated over the first 18 months, considering that we have a total of 252 ordinances were emitted between June 2012 to the end of 2013. We have concentrated our attention only on the pick of the emergency to depict urgent needs in the immediate disaster and to observe how legal drafting techniques could support them. We are not interested to investigate the post-emergency period (after 18 months) because other legal drafting mechanisms could be adopted closer to the normal rule of procedure. The work was divided into four main steps.

1. One group from the University of Modena was focused on building a clustering of the documents by thematic area. The clustering was produced with automatic text analysis — developed by Pavone[7] et al. — on the corpus of those ordinances, and has provided a list of main categories and subtopics. Four main topics have been singled out: (i) grant criteria and contributions; (ii) management of allocation of resources; (iii) urgent works for municipalities, school and church buildings; (iv) and interventions in support of the population.

---

[2] http://www.capp.unimo.it/pubbl/cappapers/Capp_p120.pdf.

[3] http://www.energie.unimore.it/.

[4] http://137.204.21.115/sisma-2012.

[5] http://www.regione.emilia-romagna.it/terremoto/gli-atti-per-la-ricostruzione.

[6] http://www.regione.emilia-romagna.it/terremoto/sei-mesi-dal-sisma/approfondimenti/il-documento-completo-della-regione-emilia-romagna.

[7] http://www.energie.unimore.it/analisi-lessico-testuale-delle-ordinanze-commissariali-un-contributo-alla-legge-nazionale-su-emergenza-e-ricostruzione/.

2. Using this list of topics, automatically extracted by the first research group, a second group of legal experts at the University of Bologna manually built a lifecycle map of the modifications that took place in the ordinance corpus. In meantime, the experts also classified the material and the partitions that had been modified. The goal was to investigate the lawmaker's behavior in taking legislative actions.
3. A third group at the University of Bologna extracted the references using a parser (see Sect. 1) for legislative documents (Palmirani and Brighi 2009; Palmirani and Cervone 2009).
4. A fourth group performed legal analysis of the results and defined the visualization using network-analysis graphs showing the correlation among the data extracted.

This methodology made it possible to evaluate the results of automatic extraction through the expertise of legal scholars. From a pure methodological perspective, this second method makes it possible to validate (a) the robustness of the cluster analysis produced through automatic text analysis and (b) the network analysis produced with Infomap (Pavone et al. 2016).

On 26 November 2015 the results of this analysis were presented to policymakers in Emilia-Romagna Region and to representatives of the Italian Parliament in order to provide inputs on which basis to enhance the legislative framework for emergency situations now making its way through Parliament.

3   From Citations to Neutral References

The normative citations in the digital-legislative-document collections are modelled using a regular grammar and identifier naming convention (e.g., URN:LEX,[8] ELI,[9] ECLI,[10] Opijnen 2017 AKN,[11] etc.) for transforming the narrative text into normalized references: persistent, machine-readable, univocal, meaningful, language-independent and human-understandable.[12] The goal in this work is to produce a canonical citation form independent of the different morphological variants used for the same conceptual citation (e.g., in Italy, Act 20/2012, Act no. 20 of 2012, or Legge 20 del 2012). This makes it possible to manage different versions the same citation over time. We adopt the Akoma Ntoso (Palmirani 2011; Palmirani and Vitali 2011) naming convention for translating textual citations into canonical form.

The transformation of the citations into neutral references is done using specific NLP parsers for Italian legislation already used with success in several research projects (Palmirani and Brighi 2009), and in particular in a project for the High Court of Cassation of Italy (about 50,000 documents of primary and secondary law). Different

---

[8] https://tools.ietf.org/pdf/draft-spinosa-urn-lex-09.pdf.

[9] http://eur-lex.europa.eu/legal-content/EN/TXT/?uri=CELEX:52012XG1026%2801%29.

[10] http://eur-lex.europa.eu/legal-content/EN/TXT/?uri=URISERV:jl0056.

[11] Akoma Ntoso Naming Convention verion 1.0, https://lists.oasis-open.org/archives/legaldocml/201407/msg00014/Akoma_Ntoso_Naming_Convention_Version-2014-07-30-wd12.doc.

[12] https://wiki.oasis-open.org/legalcitem/FundamentalRequirements3rd.

approaches for reaching with this goal are possible in the state of the art, such as (Bartolini et al. 2004; Palmirani et al. 2004; Biagioli et al. 2005; de Maat et al. 2006; Francesconi and Passerini 2007; Lesmo et al. 2013; Winkels and Boer 2014; Waltl and Florian 2014; Koniaris and Vassiliou 2014). However, the parser used by the authors is based on a hybrid approach that first generates the XML document's hierarchical structure so as to then refine the normative references with precision. After detecting the main parts (preface, preamble, body, conclusion), the parsers use about 6,000 patterns acquired from the High Court of Cassation XML corpus marked up by legal experts using the Norma-Editor system (Palmirani and Benigni 2007). The patterns of references are properly coded into regular expressions and then are used to find references to other documents. By exploiting the document's given XML structure, we can also contextualize. For instance, if a date is detected in the conclusion of the document, it is unlikely to be part of a reference, but if a date is detected in the preamble of the document, the date is likely to be a part of a reference that, because it is in the preamble, should be a static link. The same goes with the numbers of the articles. If the parser finds them within an article contained in a quoted structure, then the parser treats them as a part of the hierarchy of the cited document. The parser also uses vocabularies of frequent citations in legislative acts and ordinances so as to build the canonical form of the most frequent abbreviation (e.g., Constitutional Law, Civil Code, etc.) (Palmirani and Cervone 2013).

3.1 Parser Outcome

We detected 252 ordinances and 12,727 references. The references are sorted into three groups:

- modifications in the ordinance set extracted through the manual analysis of the legal experts;
- semantic citations between the ordinances elaborated using the parser and filtered with the modifications;
- semantic citations between national law and regional ordinances.

4 Modificatory Relationship Analysis

The modifications introduce complexity within a normative corpus, thus affecting the certainty of law, the clarity of the text being updated, and the simplicity with which norms can be applied. However, especially in a new emergency domain, modifications are necessary to introduce details, specify the norms' range of application, correct clerical and substantive errors, and extend procedural deadlines. An analysis of modifications makes it possible to evaluate the effectiveness of normative actions in the emergency situations and to provide instructions for the lawmaker so as to make norms more effective.

The modifications in the first 18 months were 814, made to 88 ordinances (from 22 June 2012 to 17 October 2013); 80% in 2012 (7 months after the event); 52% substitutions; 32% insertions; 5% clerical errors; 8% repeals; and 3% prorogations (Fig. 1). This work was conducted manually by legal experts, building the lifecycle of the normative documents. We adopt the modification taxonomy developed as part of the NormeInRete and Akoma Ntoso projects (Palmirani and Cervone 2014).

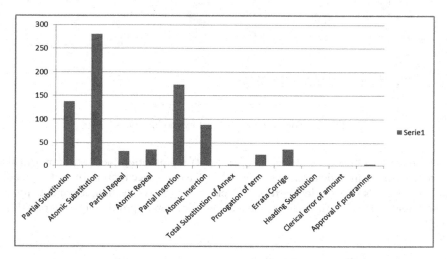

Fig. 1. Most frequent modifications using the Akoma Ntoso and NoremInRete taxonomy

The analysis highlights (a) the temporal period in which the modifications were concentrated (August 2012, October 2012, December 2012) and (b) the domain in which they acted (textual modifications in 2012 and prorogation of terms in 2013), and (c) which ordinances were mostly affected by the changes.

The most affected ordinances by modifications are nos. 51/2012, 29/2012, 57/2012, and 86/2012 (Fig. 2). Using the clustering analysis done by the University of Modena and Reggio Emilia, we have manually checked the classifications of each ordinance, finding that the most ammended ordinances belong to category 2 (Management of Resources) and category 4 (Assistance to the population) (Fig. 3).

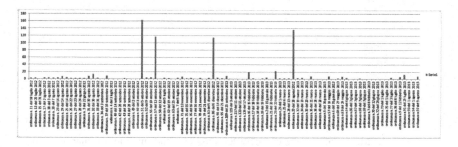

Fig. 2. Ordinances most affected by modifications

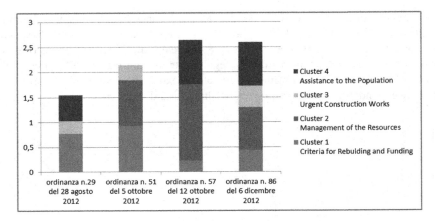

Fig. 3. Topics most amended by modifications.

We have also created a matrix graph (Fig. 4) representing the distribution of the different types of modifications over time. We have a concentration of textual modifications, due also to clerical errors, a lack of legislative technique, and template methodology. In the second year we have a concentration of prorogation of terms (blue dots).

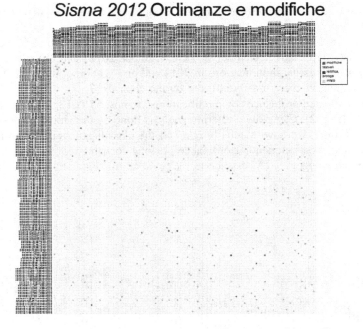

Fig. 4. Matrix of correlations between modified and modifier ordinances

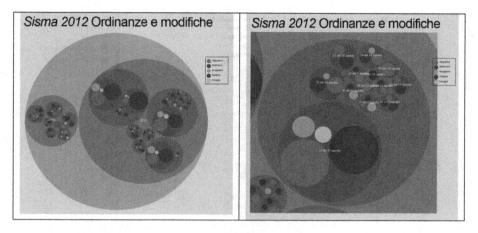

Fig. 5. Graphs showing the impact of modifications on the ordinance corpus

The same information were also described by using a navigable bubble graph (Fig. 5) on the Web that can be used to better analyse the data from a legal point of view. The data are sorted by year and month. Each bubble in the ordinance is intended to show the number of modifications within each type.

Another analysis was conducted for examining the evolution over time of modifications of the most modified ordinance n. 57/2012. The Fig. 6 presents the articles after 262, 305 and 535 days after the earthquake. The parallel lines pattern means that the same articles were subject of recursive modifications. This is a critical indicator that provides important information: those articles needed to be amended regularly due to the inadeguacy of the normative effectiveness. The colour expresses the topic of the modifcation.

5 Semantic References

The second goal was to analyse the semantic interconnection among ordinances in order assess whether there were critical normative topics that need complex policy by the decision-maker. Semantic web in legal domain is now quite developed (Casanovas et al. 2016). Other works in the state of the art other inspired our research (Winkels 2012, 2013, 2014; Bommarito and Katz 2010, 2017; Boulet et al. 2010).

The following dataset was built using the result of the parser analysis and filtering the normative references excluding the amendment link. The results (Fig. 7) stressed the presence of four islands that are grouped around major topics: green means "Assistance of the Population" norms; red means "Management of the Resources"; blu means "Criteria for Rebuiliding and Funding"; purpule means "Urgent construction works".

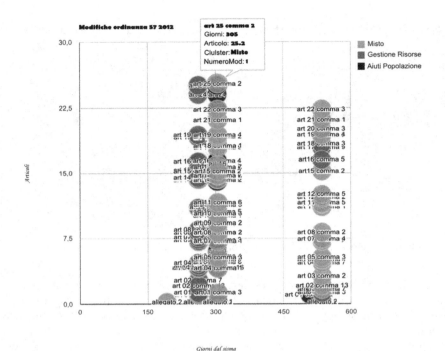

Fig. 6. Evolution of the modifications over time

The most cited ordinances are nos. 17/2012 (138), 57/2012(102), 82/2012 (72), and 19/2012 (69) (Fig. 8) and the topics that are most cited are "Assistance of the Population" and "Management of the Resources", the two main actions in the political agenda of the regional government (Fig. 9).

Another interesting visualization is the following matrix graph (Fig. 10), making it possible to see a regularity in the citation pattern. We can see parallel lines that indicate the frequency of citations from one active act (X axis) and the cited act (Y axis). The parallel lines mean that there is a template of citations (e.g., in the preamble) that all refer to the same legislative basis. The avarage of the citations from an ordinance to other ordinances is 6 references.

Another important analysis was intended to investigate the relationships among regional ordinances and national laws (Fig. 11). This contributes to a better understanding of which legislative actions could be useful at the national level to improve the regional legislative activities in emergency settings. In the Fig. 11 we could notice that the decree n. 74/2012 is the most cited. It is the decree of the emergency declaration in the geographic area. Other important primary law cited are: Act 122/2012, Act 340/2012, At 225/1992. The average number of citations from an ordinance to the national law is 31 references.

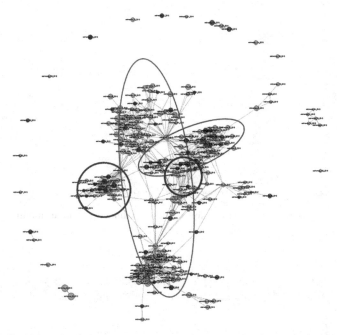

Fig. 7. Network of citations among ordinances filtered by amendment links

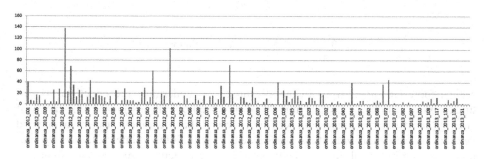

Fig. 8. Frequency of citations (passive citations) without modifications

6   Future Work

Our next work going forward will be focused on two goals: (i) to compare and cross-check results with the other team at the University of Modena and Reggio Emilia, which used a different approach (fuzzy linguistic and lexicon analysis of the text); and (ii) to find a more effective visualization for stressing the relationship between topics and modifications; (iii) to make dynamic the visualization in the web portal using real-time information in Akoma Ntoso. We aim to show the areas where the legislator was forced to amend frequently. This suggests that we need to pay more attention to these

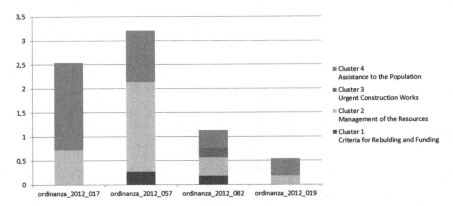

Fig. 9. Topics of most cited (passive citation) ordinances without modifications

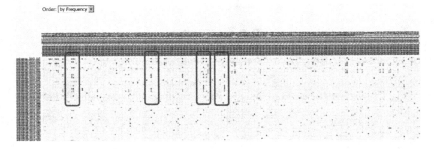

Fig. 10. Regularity in the active citations model.

critical topics in order to avoid modifications that undermine the effectiveness and timeliness of actions. A greater amount of modifications means greater dispersion of energy, effort, and resources, as well as problems having timely access to updated versions of each regulation; it also means dealing with different interpretations by end-users, making it difficult to give the process a single effective direction; and, finally, it means a lack of simplification for the citizens affected by the emergency situation, as well as corruption and mafia infiltration. We want also to improve the visualization of the frequency of the citations among ordinances using coloured nodes according to the prevalent topic (clusters) of the provisions. The more citations we have between ordinances, the greater the likelihood of finding a topic that needs attention by policymakers.

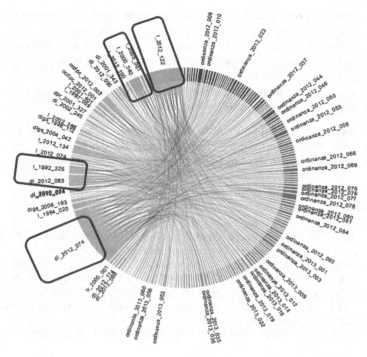

Fig. 11. Relationship between regional ordinances and national law

7 Conclusion

This research investigated the relationships between ordinances in the emergency setting, with the aim of detecting potential dysfunctional situations, thus providing helpful input for the regional and national lawmakers. Our analysis stressed the following points:

1. The ordinances do not follow a regular template, and this does not make it possible to avoid textual mistakes, clerical errors, or a deluge of modifications. The legal expert analysis stressed that the language is redundant and repetitive and can therefore create distortions in the automatic classification.
2. The consolidation of modifications is not an easy task, considering that the template of the ordinance is very flexible, unstructured, and variable, and the citations are not accurate in their fragmentation of partitions.
3. Citations among ordinances reveal a concentration of effort on two topics: (a) management of the rebuilding phase and (b) aid to the population. A national law regulating these aspects could speed up the reconstruction and improve quality of the life for the affected population.
4. Some topics are neglected in the first year: these include waste management and transportation for workers and employees. There is no energy plan in the first year; for example, no plan for managing toxic or radioactive waste coming from industry.

5. The annexes are too technical and verbose. They are substituted at least three times a year.
6. It is clear from Fig. 3 that there is no structural intervention plan and some actions (e.g., school) are recursively represented without any clear plan.
7. It is difficult to classify ordinances manually by their title.
8. The policy did not adequately address the issue of transparency so as to avoid corrupt behaviour and infiltration by the mafia.

A Web portal has been set up to illustrate the analysis of this work and to provide a new methodology for monitoring the effectiveness of legislative actions, especially in emergency situations where the timeliness is a key issue for decision-makers.

References

Bartolini, R., Lenci, A., Montemagni, S., Pirrelli, V., Soria, C.: Semantic mark-up of italian legal texts through nlp-based techniques. Proceedings of LREC **2004**, 795–798 (2004)

Biagioli, C., Francesconi, E., Passerini, A., Montemagni, S., Soria, C.: Automatic semantics extraction in law documents. In: ICAIL 2005 Proceedings of the 10th International Conference on Artificial Intelligence and Law, pp. 133–140. ACM, New York (2005)

Bommarito II, M.J., Katz, D.M.: A mathematical approach to the study of the united states code. Phys. A Stat. Mech. Appl. **389**(19), 4195–4200 (2010)

Bommarito II, M.J., Katz, D.M.: Measuring and Modeling the U.S. Regulatory Ecosystem. J. Stat. Phys. **168**, 1125–1135 (2017)

Boulet, R., Mazzega, P., Bourcier, D.: Network analysis of the French environmental code. In: Casanovas, P., Pagallo, U., Sartor, G., Ajani, G. (eds.) AICOL -2009. LNCS (LNAI), vol. 6237, pp. 39–53. Springer, Heidelberg (2010). https://doi.org/10.1007/978-3-642-16524-5_4

Casanovas, P., Palmirani, M., Peroni, S., van Engers, T., Vitali, F.: Semantic web for the legal domain: the next step. Semant. Web **7**(3), 213–227 (2016)

Francesconi, E., Passerini, A.: Automatic classification of provisions in legislative texts. Artif. Intell. Law **15**(1), 1–17 (2007)

Koniaris, M., Vassiliou, I.A.Y.: Legislation as a complex network: modelling and analysis of European Union legal sources. In: Hoekstra, R. (ed.) Legal Knowledge and Information Systems. JURIX 2014: The Twenty-Seven International Conference. Frontiers in Artificial Intelligence and Applications, vol. 260, pp. 143–152. IOS Press, Amsterdam (2014)

Lesmo, L., Mazzei, A., Palmirani, M., Radicioni, D.: TULSI: an NLP system for extracting legal modificatory provisions. Artif. Intell. Law J. **2013**(21), 139–172 (2013)

de Maat, E., Winkels, R., van Engers, T.: Automated detection of reference structures in law. In: van Engers, T.M. (ed.) Legal Knowledge and Information Systems. Jurix 2006: The Nineteenth Annual Conference, vol. 152, pp. 41–50. IOS Press, Amsterdam (2006)

van Opijnen, M., Palmirani M., Vitali, F., Agnoloni T.: Towards ECLI 2.0. In: 2017 International Conference for E-Democracy and Open Government, P6082, pp. 1–9. IEEE, Los Alamitos (2017). (atti di: 2017 International Conference for E-Democracy and Open Government, Krems, Austria, 17–19 May 2017)

Palmirani, M., Benigni, F.: Norma-system: a legal information system for managing time. In: Proceedings of the V Legislative XML Workshop, European Press Academic Publishing, FIRENZE, pp. 205–224 (2007). (atti di: V Legislative XML Workshop, Fiesole, Firenze, Italia, 14–16 Giugno 2007)

Palmirani, M., Brighi, R., Massini, M.: Processing normative references on the basis of natural language questions. In: DEXA 2004 Proceedings of the Database and Expert Systems Applications, 15th International Workshop, pp. 9–12. IEEE Computer Society (2004)

Palmirani M., Brighi R.: Legal text analysis of the modification provisions: a pattern oriented approach. In: Proceedings of the International Conference on Artificial Intelligence and Law (ICAIL) (2009)

Palmirani, M., Brighi, R.: Model regularity of legal language in active modifications. In: Casanovas, P., Pagallo, U., Sartor, G., Ajani, G. (eds.) AICOL -2009. LNCS (LNAI), vol. 6237, pp. 54–73. Springer, Heidelberg (2010). https://doi.org/10.1007/978-3-642-16524-5_5

Palmirani, M., Brighi, R.: Time model for managing the dynamic of normative system. In: Wimmer, M.A., Scholl, H.J., Grönlund, Å., Andersen, K.V. (eds.) EGOV 2006. LNCS, vol. 4084, pp. 207–218. Springer, Heidelberg (2006). https://doi.org/10.1007/11823100_19

Palmirani, M., Cervone, L.: Legal change management with a native XML repository. In: Governatori, G. (ed.) Legal Knowledge and Information Systems. JURIX 2009. The Twenty-Second Annual Conference, Rotterdam. 16th–18th December 2009, pp. 146–156. ISO Press, Amsterdam (2009)

Palmirani, M., Cervone, L.: A multi-layer digital library for mediaeval legal manuscripts digital libraries and archives. In: Communications in Computer and Information ScienceDigital Libraries and Archives, Communications in Computer and Information Science 2013, vol. 354, pp. 81–92. Springer, Heidelberg, 9–10 February 2012. (atti di: IRCDL 2012, Bari)

Palmirani, M., Cervone, L.: Measuring the complexity of the legal order over time. In: AI Approaches to the Complexity of Legal Systems, pp. 82–99. Springer, Heidelberg (2014)

Palmirani, M., Vitali, F.: Akoma-Ntoso for legal documents. In: Sartor, G., Palmirani, M., Francesconi, E., Biasiotti, M. (eds.) Legislative XML for the Semantic Web. Law, Governance and Technology Series, vol. 4, pp. 75–100. Springer, Dordrecht (2011). https://doi.org/10.1007/978-94-007-1887-6_6

Palmirani, M.: Legislative change management with Akoma-Ntoso. In: Sartor, G., Palmirani, M., Francesconi, E., Biasiotti, M. (eds.) Legislative XML for the Semantic Web. Law, Governance and Technology Series, vol. 4, pp. 101–130. Springer, Dordrecht (2011). https://doi.org/10.1007/978-94-007-1887-6_7

Pavone, P., Righi, R., Righi, S., Russo, M.: Text mining and network analysis to support improvements in legislative action. In: The Case of the Earthquake in Emilia-Romagna, Proceedings JADT2016, 7–10 giugno 2016, Nizza, Francia, pp. 237–247 (2016). ISBN 978-2-7466-9067-7

Waltl, B., Florian, M.: Towards measures of complexity: applying structural and linguistic metrics to german laws. In: Hoekstra, R. (ed.) Legal Knowledge and Information Systems. JURIX 2014: The Twenty-Seven International Conference. Frontiers in Artificial Intelligence and Applications, vol. 260, pp. 153–162. IOS Press, Amsterdam (2014)

Winkels R, Boer A.: Finding and visualizing dutch legislative context networks. In: Network Analysis in Law. Diritto Scienza Tecnologia, pp. 157–182 (2014)

Winkels, R., Boer, A., Plantevin, I.: Creating context networks in Dutch legislation. In: Ashley, K. (ed.) Legal Knowledge and Information Systems. JURIX 2013: The Twenty-Sixth International Conference. Frontiers in Artificial Intelligence and Applications, vol. 259, pp. 155–164. IOS Press, Amsterdam (2013)

Winkels, R., de Ruyter, J.: Survival of the fittest: network analysis of Dutch Supreme Court Cases. In: Palmirani, M., Pagallo, U., Casanovas, P., Sartor, G. (eds.) AICOL 2011. LNCS (LNAI), vol. 7639, pp. 106–115. Springer, Heidelberg (2012). https://doi.org/10.1007/978-3-642-35731-2_7

Legal Ontologies and Semantic Annotation

Using Legal Ontologies with Rules
for Legal Textual Entailment

Biralatei Fawei, Adam Wyner$^{(\boxtimes)}$, Jeff Z. Pan, and Martin Kollingbaum

Department of Computing Science, University of Aberdeen, Aberdeen, UK
azwyner@abdn.ac.uk

Abstract. Law is an explicit system of rules to govern the behaviour of people. Legal practitioners must learn to apply legal knowledge to the facts at hand. The United States Multistate Bar Exam (MBE) is a professional test of legal knowledge, where passing indicates that the examinee understands how to apply the law. This paper describes an initial attempt to model and implement the automatic application of legal knowledge using a rule-based approach. An NLP tool extracts information (e.g. named entities and syntactic triples) to instantiate an ontology relative to concepts and relations; ontological elements are associated with legal rules written in SWRL to draw inferences to an exam question. The preliminary results on a small sample are promising. However, the main development is the methodology and identification of key issues for future analysis.

1 Introduction

Law is an explicit system of rules to govern the behaviour of people. Legal practitioners must learn to apply legal knowledge to the facts at hand. The United States Multistate Bar Exam (MBE) is a professional test of legal knowledge, where passing indicates that the examinee understands how to apply the law. As such, the MBE provides a baseline for measuring the performance of a legal question answering system. We are primarily interested in modeling legal reasoning, wherein we reason from rules and facts to conclusions as well as provide explanations of reasoning. Such explicit modeling of legal reasoning is essential to legal practice, e.g. for appeals or development of the law. This paper proposes an automated question-answering mechanism (expert system) to answer legal questions of the United States Multistate Bar Exam (MBE).

The questions we used in our work are actual MBE questions published through the National Conference of Bar Examiners (NCBE). NCBE publishes these questions, multiple choice answers, and the correct "Gold Standard" answers. The example below shows question 7 from the July 1998 MBE, where answer "b." is correct.

The original MBE questions, which have four possible answers, were reorganized so that the main body of the text represents all the "background" knowledge from which we try to infer the answer[1]. From original given answer, the

---

[1] This is an abbreviated discussion. See [10] for what was done and why.

U. Pagallo et al. (Eds.): AICOL VI-X 2015–2017, LNAI 10791, pp. 317–324, 2018.
https://doi.org/10.1007/978-3-030-00178-0_21

part representing the *rationale* for either 'acquittal' or 'conviction' appears in the background knowledge (see sentence in bold below); otherwise, the background portions are the same. So, for example, from the background information in (a.), we should not infer "Mel should be acquitted.", while we should for (b.) we should.

a. *After being fired from his job, Mel drank almost a quart of vodka and decided to ride the bus home. While on the bus, he saw a briefcase he mistakenly thought was his own, and began struggling with the passenger carrying the briefcase. Mel knocked the passenger to the floor, took the briefcase, and fled. Mel was arrested and charged with robbery.* **He used no threats and was intoxicated**.

   Mel should be acquitted.

b. *After being fired from his job, Mel drank almost a quart of vodka and decided to ride the bus home. While on the bus, he saw a briefcase he mistakenly thought was his own, and began struggling with the passenger carrying the briefcase. Mel knocked the passenger to the floor, took the briefcase, and fled. Mel was arrested and charged with robbery.* **His mistake negated the required specific intent**.

   Mel should be acquitted.

The issue that we address is to extract information from the background and answer textual passages, associate the information with our knowledge base, and trigger rules to reason to the correct answer. Informally, we must understand and apply: the commonsense implications of violent acts, body-part relations, and possession; in addition, such facts must be tied to legal rules bearing on forced transfer of possession as well as consent. While providing solutions to such examples is difficult, we work with actual MBE questions to construct constrained models, which can be incrementally developed.

The novelty of the paper, which is preliminary work, is the integration of three main modules for modeling legal information: legal text annotation, legal ontology instantiation, and the application of legal rules. Related work is briefly reviewed in Sect. 2, followed by an outline of our approach (Sect. 3), results (Sect. 4), and closes with some discussion (Sect. 5).

2   Related Work

Existing legal question answering tools retrieve articles, extract chunks of information, and compare the retrieved information to the question in order to determine entailment [5]. A two layered approach for textual entailment was implemented [2], which works with Japanese Bar Exam data. However, the questions do not require legal reasoning and the approach is limited to handling issues arising from complex constraints in statute conditions. Kim et al. [1] seek relevant background information to facilitate inference in the questions by applying TF-IDF and a SVM to retrieve texts t1 relevant to a query t2, then measuring the similarity between t1 and t2 using paraphrase features and word embedding. However, the structure of the data used in these experiments is quite different from the bar exam considered in this research. Do et al. [9] applied a combination of SVM ranking and Convolution Neural Network techniques for information retrieval and legal question answering respectively.

There has been intensive research on textual entailment. Yet, these approaches do not address legal question answering. A pairwise syntactic similarity measure has been implemented in [8]. A dependency based paraphrasing was adopted in [7] for textual entailment. Arya et al. [6] implemented a knowledge base approach with different lexical resources to provide semantic and structural information for determining entailment. IBM DeepQA applies algorithms to identify answers for questions from both structured and unstructured sources of information [4].

Attention mechanism systems are based on sentence encoding [14,15] in which the decoder determines the part of sentence to focus on. They apply the Long Short-Term Memory (LSTM) networks to embed the premises and hypothesis into same vector space. Though, this approach provides more interplay between the embedded sentences, it involves deep sentence modeling, which require excessive training parameters and input of very long sequences [12]. These approaches lack the sort of legal knowledge and reasoning required for answering the MBE. Deciding entailment in this case requires the application of some legal rules residing in a knowledge base and some contextual information from the problem domain in answering such questions.

3   Approach

Broadly, in our approach, convergent tacks are taken to justify conclusions. For the first tack, the tool first extracts semantic triples from the source text, which are used to instantiate an OWL ontology [13] (see Subsect. 3.1). Such instantiations are used to ground predicates in the SWRL rules. Where a rule has all premises grounded with respect to the ontology, we can forward-chain to draw intermediate or final conclusions. For the second tack, keywords are used to identify relevant rules, which are those where the keyword matches the predicate of the rules conclusion (see Subsect. 3.2). Where a relevant rule is identified, backwards-chaining can be triggered, leading to searches for information to ground the premises. The two tacks can be interleaved until a justified conclusion is attained (a prediction of an answer); performance is evaluated with respect to the number of true positives versus false positives. Figure 1 shows the workflow used for the instantiation of the ontology and application of rules. In the following, we outline each of the subcomponents.

3.1   Text Processing, Keywords, Triples, and Ontology Instantiation

We apply standard NLP tools [3] of tokenisation, lemmatisation, and gazetteer lookup to both the Bg and Q texts. The gazetteer is a list of relevant legal

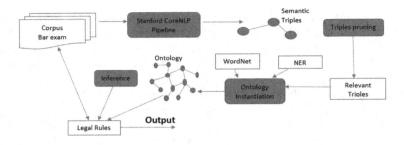

Fig. 1. Instantiating ontology from text

terminology. If a token in the text matches against the gazetteer, then it is extracted as a legal keyword. In our initial MBE example, Q contains two legal keywords *commit* and *robbery*. These keywords are used to filter triples as below.

In addition, we do part-of-speech annotation and parsing, followed by triple extraction, which are used to instantiate the OWL ontology, which consists of about 90 classes and 130 properties, represented in the $ALCHO$ description logic. Triples are a collection of three entities that represent a statement derived from the textual information and which are expressed as s-p-o (Subject-Predicate-Object). Semantic triples are important because they associate with the concepts and object-properties in the ontology, where the Subject and Object of the triples associate with concepts, and the predicate associates with an object-property. Triple extraction is done using the Stanford CoreNLP API package [3]. For example, from the sentence "Mel knocked the passenger to the floor", we can extract a triple with s = Mel, p = knock, and o = passenger.

However, the tool over-generates triples, that is, triples are created which are not relevant for the purpose of legal decision making. For example, other triples that are extracted are: [s = Mel, p = be, o = fire], [s = Mel, p = knock, o = passenger], [s = Mel, p = take, o = briefcase], [s = Mel; p = drink, o = quart], [s = mistake, p = negate, o = intent] etc. The first triple [s = Mel, p = be, o = fire] is not relevant. Hence, we remove irrelevant triples by comparing them to the keywords as well as the to the classes and object/data properties of the ontology. Where a match to a keyword or an instance or associated string is found, the relation is identified as a relevant triple for populating the ontology. For example, [s = Mel, p = take, o = briefcase] is a relevant triple because it matches the ontological relation [class = Person, objectproperty = take_property, class = Material], where "Mel" is an instance of Person, "briefcase" is an instance of Material, and "take" matches the string attribute of the object property take_property.

Furthermore, as extracted terminology may vary with respect to the ontology, we apply WordNet and NER, searching for relevant terminology that is lexically related; e.g., "knock" appears in the text and the ontological term is "forced", then we search in WordNet whether there is a relevant path (measured by similarity in the graph) connecting the terms. The threshold of similarity measure used is between 0.7 and 1.0 on a scale between 0 and 1, using the

Wu-Palmer path similarity (Wu and Palmer, 1994). Terminology that is similar may be used to match against the ontology.

3.2 Semantic Web Rule Language, Legal Rule Acquisition, Identification, and Execution

In this section, we briefly describe the Semantic Web Rule Language (SWRL) that is used in conjunction with the ontology and give an overview of how the rules are acquired, along with examples. We then explain how keywords are used to identify potentially relevant rules to execute followed by description of the execution of rules.

SWRL rules have a high-level abstract syntax to express Horn-like rules with an antecedent and a consequent. The rules are expressed in terms of OWL classes, properties, and individuals.

The legal SWRL rules that are developed in the approach are manually captured from criminal law and procedure rules found in bar examination preparatory material and in consultation with domain experts. Starting from a statement such as

> Robbery is when *property is taken from the person or presence of the owner and the taking is accomplished by using force or putting the owner in fear.* [11, p. 192].

we derive a rule, where the variables such as *?x* become grounded:

$own\_property(?x, ?y) \wedge forced\_person(?z, ?x) \wedge take\_property(?z, ?y) \wedge$
$differentFrom(?x, ?z) \rightarrow has\_committedRobbery(?z)$

The legal rules were manually created at this initial stage of development and, currently, we have about 20 criminal law rules.

Rules are activated either by ontological terminology that has been instantiated or by keywords. The search starts with legal keywords from the question statement. If the search is not successful, then keywords from the background information are combined with keywords in the question statement to search for the rule. For example, from "Mel should be acquitted", we extract the legal keyword *acquitted,* which can be used to trigger a more general rule, where *should_be_acquitted* is associated with the string *acquitted.*

$has\_committedRobbery(?x) \rightarrow has\_committed(?x, robbery) \wedge Robbery(robbery)$
$has\_committed(?x, ?y) \wedge did\_not\_intend(?x, ?y) \wedge Crime(?y)$
$\rightarrow should\_be\_acquitted\_of(?x, ?y)$

Forward chaining takes place if the expression representing the antecedent of a rule unifies with the terminological content of our legal ontology. Backward chaining takes place if the conclusion part of the rule unifies with the legal ontology. In that case, the antecedents are checked: if all antecedents also unify with the ontology, then the conclusion is accepted. If, however, some of the antecedents need to be checked, the tool returns to the source text to identify possible further useful information – the tool incrementally and "interactively" searches for an answer using as resources the MBE text itself, as well as the ontology, and the extracted legal rules.

With this implementation, the system searches in the legal knowledge base for criminal law rules that match legal keywords. Given instantiated object properties, a candidate legal rule can be:

$$own\_property(passenger, briefcase), \ forced\_person(Mel, passenger),$$
$$take\_property(Mel, briefcase) \text{ and } did\_not\_intend(Mel, robbery)$$

and since *Mel* and *passenger* are distinct, the system infers that *Mel has committed robbery*, which is a crime, as we have $Robbery \sqsubseteq Crime$ in the ontology. When this new knowledge of *Mel has committed robbery* is applied to the second rule, the system infers that *Mel* should be acquitted because the action was not an intended action. The axiom did_not_intend(?x, ?y) captured the information (s = mistake, p = negate, o = intent) at the rule level.

4 Results

Given 15 MBE questions, each with four possible answers, we have 60 question–answer pairs. Of these pairs, we found 15 true positives, 28 true negatives, and 17 false positives, giving a precision of 0.46, recall of 1, accuracy of 0.71, and an F1 measure of 0.63.

Examining the false positives, error analysis highlighted several problems: (1) polysemy, e.g. words such as *own, hold, possess*, are problematic; (2) We found examples where named entities are not recognised. For example, a *prosecutor* is a person. This problem could be solved using a legal named–entity recognizer; (3) Complex Compound Nouns are syntactically complex elements which are not recognised, e.g. *wrist watch*. Such compounds were made into sinlge lexical items and saved in the gazetteer.

5 Discussion

This paper describes an initial implementation of a rule-based legal question answering system to identify the correct answer to classic MBE exam questions. We used a rule-based approach and developed a question-answering legal expert system consisting of three modules implementing the functionality for legal text annotation, legal ontology instantiation, and the application of legal rules. In the future, we plan to introduce more legal knowledge, augment an NER tool adapted to the legal domain, and incorporate a large-scale common-sense knowledge base such as, for example, *YAGO*. Our system is still in an early development stage and our development approach is incremental. Nonetheless, we can identify patterns of legal reasoning, which we believe can be abstracted to facilitate further question-answering.

References

1. Kim, M.Y., Xu, Y., Lu, Y., Goebel, R.: Legal question answering using paraphrasing and entailment analysis. In: Tenth International Workshop on Juris-Informatics (JURISIN) (2016)
2. Kim, M., Goebel, R.: Two-step cascaded textual entailment for legal bar exam question answering. In: Proceedings of the International Conference on Artificial Intelligence and Law (2017)
3. Manning, C.D., Surdeanu, M., Bauer, J., Finkel, J.R., Bethard, S., McClosky, D.: The Stanford CoreNLP natural language processing toolkit. In: ACL (System Demonstrations), pp 55–60 (2014)
4. Ferrucci, D., Levas, A., Bagchi, S., Gondek, D., Mueller, E.T.: Watson: beyond jeopardy!. Artif. Intell. **199–200**, 93–105 (2013)
5. Monroy, A., Calvo, H., Gelbukh, A.: NLP for shallow question answering of legal documents using graphs. In: Gelbukh, A. (ed.) CICLing 2009. LNCS, vol. 5449, pp. 498–508. Springer, Heidelberg (2009). https://doi.org/10.1007/978-3-642-00382-0_40
6. Arya, A., Yaligar, V., Prabhu, R.D., Reddy, R., Acharaya, R.: A knowledge based approach for recognizing textual entailment for natural language inference using data mining. Int. J. Comput. Sci. Eng. **2**(06), 2133–2140 (2010)
7. Marsi, E., Krahmer, E., Bosma, W.: Dependency-based paraphrasing for recognizing textual entailment. In: Proceedings of the ACL-PASCAL WS on Textual Entailment and Paraphrasing, pp. 83–88 (2007)
8. Zanzotto, F.M., Moschitti, A., Pennacchiotti, M., Pazienza, M.T.: Learning textual entailment from examples. In: Proceedings of the Second PASCAL Challenges Workshop on Recognising Textual Entailment, vol. 6, no. 09, pp. 50–55 (2006)
9. Do, P.K., Nguyen, H.T., Tran, C.X., Nguyen, M.T., Nguyen, M.L.: Legal question answering using ranking SVM and deep convolutional neural network. In: Tenth International Workshop on Juris-Informatics (JURISIN) (2017)
10. Fawei, B., Wyner, A.Z., Pan, J.Z.: Passing a USA national bar exam: a first corpus for experimentation. In: Tenth International Conference on Language Resources and Evaluation, LREC 2016 (2016)
11. Emmanuel, S.L.: Strategies and Tactics for the MBE (Multistate Bar Exam). Wolters Kluwer, New York (2011)
12. Liu, P., Qiu, X., Huang, X.: Modelling interaction of sentence pair with coupled-LSTMs. arXiv preprint arXiv:1605.09090 (2016)
13. Pan, J.Z.: A flexible ontology reasoning architecture for the semantic web. IEEE Trans. Knowl. Data Eng. **19**(2), 246–260 (2007)
14. Chen, Q., Zhu, X., Ling, Z.H., Wei, S., Jiang, H., Inkpen, D.: Enhanced LSTM for natural language inference. In: Proceedings of the Second Workshop on Evaluating Vector Space Representations for NLP (RepEval 2017) (2017)

15. Kolawole John, A., Di Caro, L., Robaldo, L., Boella, G.: Textual inference with tree-structured LSTM. In: Bosse, T., Bredeweg, B. (eds.) BNAIC 2016. CCIS, vol. 765, pp. 17–31. Springer, Cham (2017). https://doi.org/10.1007/978-3-319-67468-1_2

16. Wu, Z., Palmer, M.: Verbs semantics and lexical selection. In: Proceedings of the 32nd annual meeting on Association for Computational Linguistics, pp. 133–138 (1994)

KR4IPLaw Judgment Miner - Case-Law Mining for Legal Norm Annotation

Shashishekar Ramakrishna[1]([✉]), Łukasz Górski[2], and Adrian Paschke[1]

[1] Freie Universität Berlin, Berlin, Germany
shashi792@gmail.com, paschke@inf.fu-berlin.de
[2] Nicolaus Copernicus University, Toruń, Poland
lgorski@mat.umk.pl

Abstract. The use of pragmatics in applying the law is hard to deal with for a legal knowledge engineer who needs to model it in a precise KR for (semi-)automated legal reasoning systems. The negative aspects of pragmatics is due to the difficulty involved in separating their concerns. When representing a legal norm for (semi-)automated reasoning, an important step/aspect is the annotation of legal sections under consideration. Annotation in the context of this paper refers to identification, segregation and thereafter representation of the content and its associated context. In this paper we present an approach and provide a proof-of-concept implementation for automatizing the process of identifying the most relevant judgment pertaining to a legal section and further transforming them into a formal representation format. The annotated legal section and its related judgments can then be mapped into a decision model for further down the line processing.

Keywords: LegalDocML · Case-law mining · Legal norms · Topic modeling

1 Introduction

In the domain of legal informatics there exists a necessity to '*simplify*' the induced vagueness in legal language. An approach to minimize the vagueness, or in other words to simplify the language, is by annotating of a legal section with its associated contextual background knowledge. Aggregation of such associated background knowledge removes many uncertainties during legal norm reasoning.

Annotation in the context of this paper refers to identification, segregation and thereafter representation of the legal content and its associated context.

In this paper, we present an approach and provide a proof-of-concept implementation for automatizing the identification of most relevant judgment pertaining to a particular legal section (in the domain of intellectual property) and further transforming them into a formal representation format. Thereby, the annotated legal section and the related judgments can be mapped into a decision model for further processing.

The paper is structured as follows: Sect. 2 provides a brief overview on research works related to our proposed approach. Section 3 discusses the notion of pragmatics and presents the important aspects of legal norm annotation. Sections 4 and 5 introduce to the overall system and specifically the new proof-of-concept implementation module

U. Pagallo et al. (Eds.): AICOL VI-X 2015–2017, LNAI 10791, pp. 325–336, 2018.
https://doi.org/10.1007/978-3-030-00178-0_22

for mining judgments. Sections 6 and 7 provide a detailed discussion on building a decision model and its further use. Section 8 evaluates the module based on well know information retrieval evaluation approach based on gold standards. Final Sect. 9 presents the conclusion and future works.

2 Related Work

A number of legal document annotation methods exist, including LegalRuleML [1, 2], LKIF [3] and LegalDocML [4], which stems from earlier Akoma Ntoso project [5]. LegalRuleML is an extension of RuleML [6] standard, aimed at enabling the exchange of legal semantic information (defined in laws, contracts, judgments) between legal documents, business rules and software applications. LKIF (Legal Knowledge Interchange Format) was designed to support the requirements of Semantic Web and Knowledge Representation domains. It supports a layered architecture, with distinct modules for terminological knowledge description (implemented with the use of Web Ontology Language - OWL) and rules (the extension of SWRL with negation of defeasible reasoning). The LegalDocML project describes a metadata format for documentation of parliamentary activities, such as debates, briefs, journals, as well as courts' decisions (opinions, judgments). It provides with a common data and metadata model that supports the temporal evolution of legal documents.

The research into text retrieval techniques (that match a set of documents against a user query) is vital for processing the increasing amount of electronic information [7]. There are, generally, two approaches to information retrieval in legal domain: manual knowledge engineering and those based on automated text analysis (natural language processing, NLP) [8]. Both techniques were used in the History Assistant project, aimed at finding interconnected judicial opinions [9]. Text mining was employed, for example, for legal argument extraction [10, 11]. Techniques similar to ours were used to build a law report recommendation system in the case of Sri Lankan judiciary [12]. The SMILE project is another project concerned with NLP, as it allowed to classify legal texts based on a set of classification concepts [13].

3 Legal Norm Annotation

3.1 Introduction- Pragmatics

3.1.1 What Is the Relationship Between Case-Law and Statute Law?

Even though the '*clarity*' of a legal provision is an idealistic aim that legislators are bound to achieve [14], it cannot be denied that the professional members of particular legal community - through their training and practical experience - tend to share a greater deal of particular contextual knowledge than ordinary layman [15]. Judgments provide a body of contextual knowledge that enhances the understanding of legal section under consideration. Therefore, when viewed in the lens of the theory of pragmatics, they enhance the meaning of legal norms. The inclusion of pragmatics, either directly from a legal section or from its interpretations provided via judgments therefore plays a very important role in capturing the interpretation concerning legal norms.

Despite the fact that both the courts and non-judiciary legal professionals share and adhere to the same legal interpretation guidelines (and could have been expected to easily arrive at the same result when interpreting legal provisions), the study of court opinions is a vital part of professional legal training, both in common law and civil law countries. The importance of contextual knowledge formalization has also been acknowledged in the area of legal informatics, with the development of the Ontology of Professional Judicial Knowledge (OPJK), a FAQ system for young judges [16]. Some legal theorists have as well viewed the process of applying the law (e.g. inventions/patent applications) as a non-verbal conversation between the legislature and members of judicature and executive (e.g. patent officer/examiner), and further - between a citizen and executive (e.g. the inventor and the patent office/examiner). Such conversation is guided by a set of conversational maxims, which - while obeyed or deliberately flouted - allow to decode the meaning of the utterance. The philosophical aspects of application of the theory of pragmatics in the domain of law are out of the scope of this paper. A philosophical framework addressing this concern was developed in other works [15, 17]. In the case of a semi-formal legal norm representation, the pragmatic aspect is also accounted for, at least in some of representation systems, e.g. the SBVR (cf. Sect. 7). This linguistic-based standard acknowledges the separation of *expression* and *meaning*: the semantic expression is enriched by relevant context, thus producing meaning (cf. [18]).

In this paper, we acknowledge that the semi-automatic annotation of legal sections facilitates the knowledge transfer even to people who are not as skilled in the domain of law (e.g. knowledge modelers).

3.2 Norm Annotation

Akoma Ntoso or Legal Document Markup Language (LegalDocML), a standard under OASIS for managing legal documents, provides a systematic mechanism for referencing documents based on URIs through sound ontological approach by designing metadata and relationships between documents and different versions of documents. Its provides a possibility to define a common format for most parliamentary activities. Of the possible document type handled by LegalDocML, few document types which are of our interest in domain of IP Laws are, **<legislativeDocs>**, comprising of '*acts*' *and* '*bills*', **<amendmentDocs>** related to amendments to any acts/bills/sections etc., and **<judgementDocs>**, pertaining to judgments, amicus briefs and other documents pertaining to any parliamentary activities concerning a law.

In addition to capturing (by annotation) the legal information from legal sections/paragraphs, we also annotate the landmark decisions pertaining to this legal section. Those supplementary annotations capture the pragmatic context in which such a legal section has to be applied. I.o.w, it defines new pragmatics, in terms of understanding and commitment, encompassing the legal section.

For the purpose of this paper, we focus only on the elements **<act>** and **<judgment>**. Further hierarchical subdivision of these elements into several classes is shown in Fig. 1. The **<meta>** element is used to capture all the meta-information concerning a

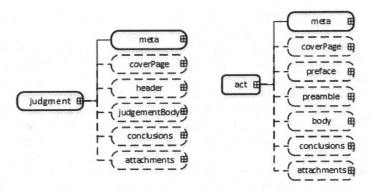

Fig. 1. 'Judgement' and 'Act' element hierarchical structure in LegalDocML

'*act*' or '*judgment*', the **<preface>**, defines document type (<docType>), document title (<docTitle>), document number (<docNumber>), date of assent (<docDate>), table of contents (<toc>). The **<preamble>** element defines '*citations*' i.e. list of other legislation resources that empower the current document and *recitals*, that provide the justification and motivation. Finally the **<Conclusions>** element describes the '*Signature*', '*date of signature*', '*place of signature*' etc. The **<judgment>** element, comprises of self descriptive sub-elements such as meta-information (**<meta>**), content of the judgment (**<judgementBody>**), verdict (**<conclusions>**), attachments pertaining to the judgment (**<attachments>**) etc. Identification and further annotation of such judgments while being of utmost importance, is a very time consuming process and requires digging through a sizable corpora of judgments. In pursue of automating the process we provide a proof-of-concept implementation, which mines for the most relevant judgments pertaining to the legal sections and further renders the selected judgments in a required formal representation format (in here, as LegalDocML).

4 KR4IPLaw System

Knowledge Representation for Intellectual Property Law (KR4IPLaw),[1] is an system (ecosystem) with modules built to bridging the gap between legal practitioners and knowledge modelers. The system is built on the KR4IPLaw framework, which in-turn loosely coupled with the OMGs Model Driven Architecture [19]. The current systems includes modules for representing legal knowledge at different level of granularity (Computational Independent, Platform Independent and Platform Specific). The system includes an inference engine Prova [20] to support reasoning on top of such represented legal knowledge. Further sections of this paper describes the functionalities of a newly added sub-module, the KR4IPLaw Judgment Miner. It is a tool to aimed at capturing the *a priori* information needed to build the decision model thereafter.

---

[1] http://kr4iplaw.wordpress.com.

5   KR4IPLaw Judgement Miner

The proof of concept system, as a simple I/O system, considers formally represented legal sections as input and produces the most relevant judgment or a set of judgments pertaining to the legal section. Whilst the current system is tailored to work with LegalDocML files, it can be very easily extended to other formal representations.

The inner stack of the module comprises of few translators, a search engine, a topic modeler, and query constructors. Translators help in extracting the required information from a LegalDocML file and thereby translating it to a format necessary for further processing and vice-versa. We integrate Apache Solr as a search engine - a high performance, scalable search server built based on Apache Lucene. The advanced caching and replication, the distributed search and easy integration of other modules makes it a better choice than existing search servers such as Minion [21] or Sphinx[2].

Case-law indexing is one of the important steps. CourtListner,[3] provides as a bulk download, the information pertaining to 361 jurisdictions of the United States courts. The data on CourtListener is a combination of many partial sources such as court websites, Public.Resource.Org and a donation from Law- box LLC, thus making it one of the most covered dataset available. The bulk data from the CourtListner is indexed by Solr.

For Solr scoring model, we use the Best Matching (BM25) algorithm [22] - a probabilistic Information Retrieval (IR) model against the well known TF-IDF - a vector space model for increased precision.

Solr provides the ability to create different user defined queries through its API. Solr query support different search patterns such as term, field, wildcard, fuzzy, proximity or range searches. Table 1 provides the list of search patterns available within this module.

To increase the accuracy of the search results, an obvious step would be to construct complex queries, which combine multiple patterns. One such pattern is the query boosting parameter which utilizes certain keywords to boost the search query and thereby altering its default ranking.

While such process of identifying keywords could be a manual operation, our module uses the topic model approach to automate the process of extracting and transforming the keywords, to be used as boosting terms. We integrate Mallets'[4] statistical natural language processing (NLP) and topic modeling modules. Within the NLP module, we integrate the Snowball stemmer [23] and provide legal dictionaries (e.g. USPTO- glossary[5]) as an exclusion list. As to the Topic Modeler module, we use the Parallel Topic Modeler [24], which realizes the Latent Dirichlet Allocation (LDA) model to compute the topics. The input to the topic modeler is the content part (i.e. legal paragraphs) of the LegalDocML file and we assume that the each document is composed of only a few dominant topics and each topic is composed of only a few

---

[2] http://sphinxsearch.com/.

[3] http://www.courtlistener.com/.

[4] http://mallet.cs.umass.edu/.

[5] http://www.uspto.gov/main/glossary/.

Table 1. KR4IPLaw search query patterns

Type	Pattern	Example
Term	"text"	"Supreme Court"
Field	text:"text"	court:"Supreme Court"
Boolean	AND, OR, NOT	"Supreme Court" OR "CAFC"
Wildcard	? or *	Supre?me or Supreme*
Fuzzy	~	Supreme ~
Range	TO	filed date: [20150601 TO 200150801]
Boosting	^	"Supreme Court"^10

dominant words. We set the hyper-parameters, α and β values to 0.01. The output from the topic modeller is used to build the complex query described hereinbefore. Additionally, the most frequently occurring terms from particular domains of law (i.e. *patent* in the case of patent law) were explicitly excluded from boosting parameters list, as they are routinely used in judgments and therefore are of little use for ranking purposes. The purpose built-in translator thereafter translates the obtained judgments from its XML-based native CourtListener format to a required formal judgment representation format (e.g. LegalDocML; in this case the conversion is realised with XSLT). With the annotation of legal sections and its relevant judgments completed, the next step is to integrate them into a decision model, so that further disaggregation and formal representation and reasoning can be performed.

6 Decision Model

The LegalDocML files representing the substantive laws and its relevant judgments are treated as a starting point for the decision model creation. The legal section is disaggregated from its vague substantive law semantics into a concrete procedural (norm) semantics, to extract the elementary concerns from the compound concerns of the statutory law.

Such procedural norms are usually provided in the forms of memos, instructions or guidelines and contain supplementary material pertaining to the interpretation of substantive laws and outline the procedure that is used for substantive law implementation. For example, in our earlier works, we have used the US patent law, as illustrative material in this respect, as the United States Patent and Trademark Office (USPTO), through its Manual for Patent Examination Procedure (MPEP), provides its examiners with such information. We transform such procedures into legal decision models, wherein, each decision point is a single procedure or a set of procedures to be carried out. The system provides a decision model representation module that utilizes UML activity diagram formalisms. Landmark decisions provide an additional means of interpretation, further supplementing the aforementioned guidelines. Hence their incorporation into decision model is of great importance.

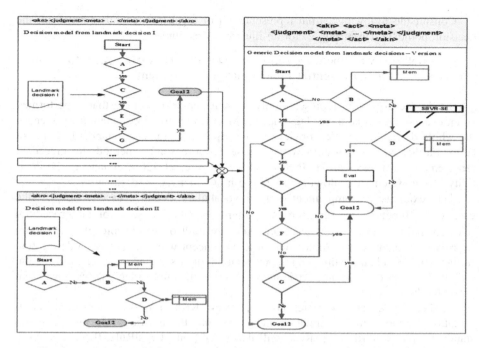

Fig. 2. Decision model for a legal section under consideration (adapted from [25]).

Figure 2[6], serves as an illustrative example of the above described approach of representing the procedural norms and their interpretations provided via judgments as decision models.

7   Representation and Reasoning

Further, we use the easy to understand decision models as basis for writing the legal norms and their elementary concerns in terms of constitutive vocabulary definitions and prescriptive behavioral legal rules in SBVRs Structured English. We can classify the mapping relationships as 1:1- wherein each decision is mapped into a single SBVR rule, 1:M- where, a single decision is mapped into many SBVR rules or an M:M relationship. Legal domain experts and trained formal knowledge engineers can work together in this formalization process using Structured English as common computational independent knowledge representation language.

---

[6] The textual content inside the decision model is left out on purpose to handle the space restrictions.

Consult the following partial representation of legal (procedural) norm from the decision point 'D' (from Fig. 2) for an illustratory example:

– It is obligatory thattheoffice action *includes* **Paragraph 7_33 01**,ifclaim *is_rejected_under* essential subject matter requirement.

Single decision point represents only a small part of reasoning that is performed when evaluating and applying legal norms. More complete representation is given by the whole decision tree. Yet, obviously, it is applicable rather in standard, non-hard cases. Further work might employ using case-based reasoning methods for precedent representation (in line with HYPO/CATO line of research [26]), enhancing the flexibility of the system and allowing for its use in a wider range of situations.

This example is complemented by a vocabulary defining used concepts, like essential_subject_matter requirement noun concept. The semi-formal procedural rules are built on legal facts, and **legal facts** are built on **legal concepts**[7] which are expressed by **legal terms**. Annotation of legal concept with the meta-data description further enables identification and representation of associated context information. A more in-depth discussions pertaining to SBVR and its use in legal domain has been presented by us in [27, 28].

Further, for formal rule representation, we use KR4IPLaw - a patent norm representation format, which seamlessly integrates into the existing rule representation standards like RuleML [29], ReactionRuleML [30] and LegalRuleML [1]. Figure 3 depicts the general structure of KR4IPLaw.

The module <rulePragmatics> holds all the pragmatic information which includes meta-information such as; <Sources> to identify the collection of legal resources relevant to the Legal document, <References> to provide an isomorphic relationship

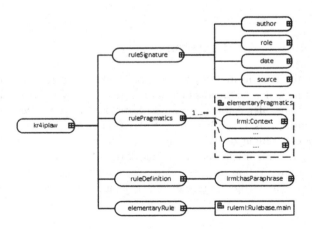

Fig. 3. KR4IPLaw: rule representation format.

---

[7] Represented using green color.

between the formal rule and the legally binding statements to the rule, <Authority>, <Jurisdictions>, <Associations>, <TimeInstants> etc. While the general structure provided here depicts the intended semantics to the formal representation formats, the authors would like to refer to a series of publications for a detailed discussion on it [31–33].

Further, for reasoning, the formal rule is transformed into a Platform Specific Model (PSM) rule representation format, Prova [20] - a semantic web rule language and a high expressive distributed rule engine- where the pragmatic information from the PIM layer, associated to a norm are handled with by *guards*.

8 Evaluation

8.1 Gold Standard

The proposed approach is evaluated on the well known precise-recall metric of information retrieval. An ordered set of judgments based on its relevance (i.e. on case-law citations[8]) to a legal section under consideration was created (a gold-standard or *ground truth judgment of relevance*)[9]. To evaluate the system for its cross domain performance, the gold standard included a minimum of 5 legal sections, each from different Intellectual Property (IP) Laws of the Code of Laws of the United States of America (U.S.C). As shown in Table 2, the legal sections from US Patent Law, Copyright law and Trademark law were considered. 20 most relevant, based on their number of citations pertaining to each legal section were identified. Relevance based on a citation count approach providing an easy-to-compute, context-free, and relatively accessible metric, may, in fact, be better for finding high-quality documents than sophisticated human or pattern recognition queries and models [34]. In total, the gold standard comprised of 300 judgments from courts of 361 jurisdictions within the US.

8.2 Precision and Recall

F-measure metric (i.e. the harmonic mean of the precision and recal) l is used for the results depiction. The F-measure for the judgments retrieved from the judgment-miner module is as shown below in Fig. 4. The F-measure is plotted for legal sections from different domains of the intellectual property law.

While vocabularies from US patent, trademark and copyright laws were introduced as an exception list for stemming, an observation made during this study was the necessity to perform a proximity search while indexing. This has been due to the fact that judges responsible for writing decisions use a slightly non-aligned nomenclature such as 35 USC 112 (a), 35 USC 112 First Paragraph or 35 USC sec 112 while referencing legal sections within a judgment.

---

[8] While the authors understand that an ideal approach is to use a expert driven gold standard construction, a common consensus on thus generated standards for relevance is debatable in the context of case-laws.

[9] http://github.com/shashi792/KR4IPLaw-Act2Judgement/KR4IPLaw_Gold_Standard.xlsx.

Table 2. Legal sections considered for the gold standard

Sec 35 U.S.C (patent law)	17 U.S.C (copyright law)	15 U.S.C (trademark law)
I 101 (inventions patentable)	107 (fair use)	1052 (registrable trademarks)
II 102 (novelty)	117 (computer programs)	1060 (assignment)
III 103 (non-obviousness)	201 (ownership)	1063 (opposition)
IV 112 (specification)	501 (infringement)	1070 (appeals)
V 271 (infringement)	1101 (unauthorized fixation)	1091 (supplemental register)

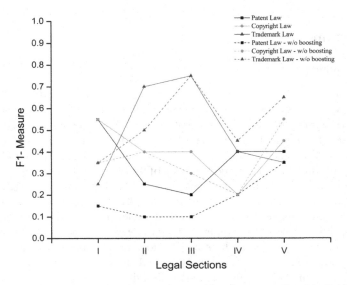

Fig. 4. F-measure (legal sections under consideration are as listed in Table 2)

While the use of boosting keywords resulted in significant result improvement in the domain of patent law, the outcome for copyright and trademark law remains satisfactory. Further improvement of results could be achieved by fine-tuning the proximity search method in case of those two domains.

9   Conclusion

The paper presented an approach and a proof of concept implementation for automatizing the process of identifying the most relevant judgment pertaining to a legal section and further transforming them into a formal representation format. To fine tune the retrieved judgments sorting order, we proposed an approach wherein topic modeling using LDA was used. Further these judgments were transformed into a formal representation format using a purpose built translator. In effect, any legal decision support system can facilitate the provided a priori information for its use in scenarios such as in-court argumentation.

References

1. Palmirani, M., Governatori, G., Rotolo, A., Tabet, S., Boley, H., Paschke, A.: LegalRuleML: XML-based rules and norms. In: Olken, F., Palmirani, M., Sottara, D. (eds.) RuleML 2011. LNCS, vol. 7018, pp. 298–312. Springer, Heidelberg (2011). https://doi.org/10.1007/978-3-642-24908-2_30
2. Athan, T., Boley, H., Governatori, G., Palmirani, M., Paschke, A., Wyner, A.: OASIS LegalRuleML. In: Proceedings of the Fourteenth International Conference on Artificial Intelligence and Law, pp. 3–12. ACM (2013)
3. Hoekstra, R., et al.: The LKIF core ontology of basic legal concepts. LOAIT **321**, 43–63 (2007)
4. Palmirani, M., Vitali, F.: Akoma Ntoso an open document standard for parliaments (2014)
5. Vitali, F., Zeni, F.: Towards a country-independent data format: the Akoma Ntoso experience. In: Proceedings of the V legislative XML Workshop, Florence, Italy, pp. 67–86. European Press Academic Publishing (2007)
6. Boley, H., et al.: Design rationale for RuleML: a markup language for semantic web rules. In: SWWS, vol. 1, pp. 381–401 (2001)
7. Lee, D.L., Chuang, H., Seamons, K.: Document ranking and the vector-space model. IEEE Softw. **14**(2), 67–75 (1997)
8. Maxwell, K.T., Schafer, B.: Concept and context in legal information retrieval. In: JURIX, pp. 63–72 (2008)
9. Jackson, P., Al-Kofahi, K., Tyrrell, A., Vachher, A.: Information extraction from case law and retrieval of prior cases. Artif. Intell. **150**(1), 239–290 (2003)
10. Wyner, A., Mochales-Palau, R., Moens, M.-F., Milward, D.: Approaches to text mining arguments from legal cases. In: Francesconi, E., Montemagni, S., Peters, W., Tiscornia, D. (eds.) Semantic Processing of Legal Texts. LNCS (LNAI), vol. 6036, pp. 60–79. Springer, Heidelberg (2010). https://doi.org/10.1007/978-3-642-12837-0_4
11. Ashley, K.D., Walker, V.R.: From information retrieval (IR) to argument retrieval (AR) for legal cases: report on a baseline study. In: Legal Knowledge and Information Systems. IOS Press (2013)
12. Firdhous, M.: Automating legal research through data mining. arXiv preprint arXiv:1211.1861 (2012)
13. Ashley, K., Brninghaus, S.: Automatically classifying case texts and predicting outcomes. Artif. Intell. Law **17**(2), 125–165 (2009)
14. Fuller, L.L.: The Morality of Law, vol. 152. Yale University Press, New Haven (1977)
15. Marmor, A.: The pragmatics of legal language. Ratio Juris **21**(4), 423–452 (2008)
16. Benjamins, V.R., Contreras, J., Casanovas, P., Ayuso, M., Becue, M., Lemus, L., Urios, C.: Ontologies of professional legal knowledge as the basis for intelligent it support for judges. Artif. Intell. Law **12**(4), 359–378 (2004)
17. Ramakrishna, S., Gorski, L., Paschke, A.: The role of pragmatics in legal norm representation. CoRR abs/1507.02086 (2015)
18. OMG: Semantics of Business Vocabulary and Business Rules (SBVR) v. 1.3 (2015)
19. Bézivin, J., Gerbé, O.: Towards a precise definition of the OMG/MDA framework. In: Proceedings of 16th Annual International Conference on Automated Software Engineering, 2001 (ASE 2001), pp. 273–280. IEEE (2001)
20. Kozlenkov, A., Paschke, A.: Prova rule language version 3.0 user's guide. http://prova.ws/index.html (2010)
21. Jeff, A., Stephen, G.: The minion search engine: indexing, search, text similarity and tag gardening. Technical report, Sun Microsystems, New York (2008)

22. Robertson, S., Zaragoza, H.: The Probabilistic Relevance Framework: BM25 and Beyond. Now Publishers Inc., Breda (2009)
23. Porter, M.F.: Snowball: a language for stemming algorithms (2001)
24. Newman, D., Asuncion, A., Smyth, P., Welling, M.: Distributed algorithms for topic models. J. Mach. Learn. Res. **10**, 1801–1828 (2009)
25. Ramakrishna, S.: First approaches on knowledge representation of elementary (patent) pragmatics. In: Joint Proceedings of the 7th International Rule Challenge, the Special Track on Human Language Technology and the 3rd RuleML Doctoral Consortium (2013)
26. Rissland, E.L., Ashley, K.D., Branting, L.K.: Case-based reasoning and law. Knowl. Eng. Rev. **20**(03), 293–298 (2005)
27. Ramakrishna, S., Paschke, A.: Bridging the gap between legal practitioners and knowledge engineers using semi-formal KR. In: The 8th International Workshop on Value Modeling and Business Ontology, VMBO, Berlin (2014)
28. Ramakrishna, S., Paschke, A.: Semi-automated vocabulary building for structured legal english. In: Bikakis, A., Fodor, P., Roman, D. (eds.) RuleML 2014. LNCS, vol. 8620, pp. 201–215. Springer, Cham (2014). https://doi.org/10.1007/978-3-319-09870-8_15
29. Boley, H., Paschke, A., Shafiq, O.: RuleML 1.0: the overarching specification of web rules. In: Dean, M., Hall, J., Rotolo, A., Tabet, S. (eds.) RuleML 2010. LNCS, vol. 6403, pp. 162–178. Springer, Heidelberg (2010). https://doi.org/10.1007/978-3-642-16289-3_15
30. Paschke, A.: Reaction RuleML 1.0 for rules, events and actions in semantic complex event processing. In: Bikakis, A., Fodor, P., Roman, D. (eds.) RuleML 2014. LNCS, vol. 8620, pp. 1–21. Springer, Cham (2014). https://doi.org/10.1007/978-3-319-09870-8_1
31. Ramakrishna, S., Paschke, A.: A process for knowledge transformation and knowledge representation of patent law. In: Bikakis, A., Fodor, P., Roman, D. (eds.) RuleML 2014. LNCS, vol. 8620, pp. 311–328. Springer, Cham (2014). https://doi.org/10.1007/978-3-319-09870-8_23
32. Paschke, A., Ramakrishna, S.: Legal RuleML Tutorial Use Case - LegalRuleML for Legal Reasoning in Patent Law (2013)
33. Ramakrishna, S., Gorski, Ł., Paschke, A.: A dialogue between a lawyer and computer scientist: the evaluation of knowledge transformation from legal text to computer-readable format. Appl. Artif. Intell. **30**(3), 216–232 (2016)
34. Bernstam, E.V., Herskovic, J.R., Aphinyanaphongs, Y., Aliferis, C.F., Sriram, M.G., Hersh, W.R.: Using citation data to improve retrieval from MEDLINE. J. Am. Med. Inform. Assoc. **13**(1), 96–105 (2006)

Towards Annotation of Legal Documents with Ontology Concepts

Kolawole John Adebayo$^{(\boxtimes)}$, Luigi Di Caro, and Guido Boella

Dipartimento di Informatica, Universita Di Torino,
Corso Svizzera 185, 10149 Turin, Italy
kolawolejohn.adebayo@unibo.it, {dicaro,guido.boella}@di.unito.it

Abstract. This paper describes a task of semantic labeling of document segments. The idea exploits ontology in providing a fine-grained conceptual document annotation. We describe a way of dividing a document into its constituent semantically-coherent blocks. These blocks are then used to perform conceptual tagging for efficient passage information retrieval. The proposed task interfaces other application areas such as intra-mapping of ontologies, text summarization and information extraction. The system has been evaluated on a task of conceptual tagging of documents and achieved a promising result.

Keywords: Conceptual tagging · Semantic annotation
Information retrieval · Passage retrieval · Text segmentation

1 Introduction

The deluge of electronically stored information (ESI), coupled with the data explosion on the Internet has practically necessitated developing frameworks for intelligent document processing. This is important since ESI is mostly unstructured. The Legal domain has also witnessed an unprecedented growth in the amount of ESI produced e.g., in the law courts, government assemblies etc., necessitating for repositories like Eurlex[1] etc. This comes with the responsibility of developing scalable retrieval techniques that provide legal practitioner an easy interface for retrieving information in a timely and efficient manner.

In this paper, we propose a passage retrieval system which works by segmenting a document into different semantically coherent parts based on the meaning of its content. In addition, the proposed system introduces a topic-like structure to an unstructured text since each of the segments relates to different concept/topic. The highlight of the proposed approach is how it automatically associates each segment of an input document to its respective concept from an ontology. We formalize this process as a Semantic Annotation task [5]. The rationale behind the proposed system is to provide practitioners and other end

---

[1] https://eur-lex.europa.eu/homepage.html.

© Springer Nature Switzerland AG 2018
U. Pagallo et al. (Eds.): AICOL VI-X 2015–2017, LNAI 10791, pp. 337–349, 2018.
https://doi.org/10.1007/978-3-030-00178-0_23

users with a fine-grained passage retrieval with a simple Natural Language Processing (NLP) tool that allows users to specify query using a controlled list of concept and the system retrieves not just the document related to the concept but specific part(s) of the document that is semantically related to the concept.

There are motivations for the proposed system. First, users are freed from the rigours associated with query formulation. This is important because many people understand their information need but the problem is how to effectively represent and present such information need to a retrieval algorithm. By providing a controlled list of descriptors, such problems are adequately taken care of. Secondly, by providing a fine-grained retrieval, the problem of *information overload* is solved. Information overload occurs when a system retrieves more information than its actually needed by a user, often requiring the user to manually inspect the retrieved item in order to locate the specific information of interest. This improves not just the *precision* but also the *recall* which is especially important in the legal domain. Moreover, concept mapping can support semantic query processing across disparate sources by expanding or rewriting the query using the corresponding information in multiple ontologies. More importantly, an Ontology can capture a domain knowledge in a machine understandable way, thereby providing a solution for solving semantic heterogeneity problem[2].

The method that we present in this paper is different from existing work in the way that we represent the meaning of a concept in an unsupervised way. Moreover, it does not directly rely on any Machine Learning (ML) methods. Instead, it is based on the expansion and enrichment of linguistic terms using some natural language processing techniques. The remaining parts of the paper are structured as follows. In Sect. 2, we review some related work. Section 3 contains a description of our algorithm and methods. Finally, we describe our experiment, the evaluation, and the result obtained in Sect. 4.

2   Related Work

Semantic Annotation (SA) formalizes and structure a document with well-defined semantics specifically linked to a defined ontology [23]. SA can be formalized as a 4-tuple (**a, b, c, d**), where a is the subject of the annotation, b is the object of the annotation, c is the predicate which defines the type of relationship between a and b, while d signifies the context in which the annotation is made. An ontology is a formal conceptualization of the world, capturing consensual knowledge [15]. It contains the concepts along with their properties and the relationship that exists between them. This study uses the Eurovoc[3] thesaurus as the ontology.

Generally, annotation can aid structured organization of documents for optimized search. For instance, users may search information by well-defined general concepts that describe the domain of information need rather than use keywords.

---

[2] E.g homonyms and synonyms.

[3] http://eurovoc.europa.eu/.

There are existing works which share similarity to the method proposed here. GATE [9] is a semi-automatic annotation system based on NLP. GoNTogle [5] uses weighted k-Nearest Neighbor (kNN) classifier for document annotation and retrieval. The authors in [24] developed a tool for ontology learning and population in the Semantic Web. Their approach utilizes Discourse Representation Theory and frame semantics for performing knowledge extraction. KIM [23] assigns semantic descriptions to Named Entities (NEs) in a text. The system is able to create hyperlinks to NEs in a text such that indexing and document retrieval is performed with the NEs. Regular Expressions (RE) have also been used to identify semantic elements in a text [16,17]. It works by mapping part of a text related to semantic context and matching the subsequent sequence of characters to create an instance of the concept. Another NE-based annotation tool is GERBIL [27] which provides rapid but extensive evaluation scheme for NE recognition tools for the semantic web. Application of these systems includes document retrieval especially in the semantic web domain [10,12].

The authors in [21] performed semantic annotation on legal documents for document categorization. Using *Eurovoc* concept descriptors on *EurLex*[4], a ML classifier was trained for multi-label classification. The authors' work is a supervised concept-to-document mapping, i.e., a document categorization where the concept(s) for a document is predicted by the ML classifier. In our work, we learn the concept representation in a completely unsupervised way, furthermore, instead of associating the concept to a whole document, our algorithm associate the specific segment(s) of document(s) to a concept once the algorithm determines that they have the same semantics.

Associating a concept to a document segment is only possible after finding the points in a text where there is a semantic drift. In our work, we identify these points by observing the distribution of topics in a text and how the topics change from one part of the document to another. Researchers working on Discourse structure have shown that a document is usually a mixture of topics and sub-topics [11]. Each topic discusses a theme of the document. Furthermore, topics sharing the same theme usually cohere, thus forming a form of *segment* or semantically align units. We incorporate this idea of topical segmentation of document such that concept(s) can be easily linked to any topical segment.

This part of our work follows the TextTiling algorithm [14] and a topic-modeling based improvement [25] which uses the Latent Dirichlet Allocation (LDA) [6]. These systems divide text into a contiguous, non-overlapping discourse units that correspond to the pattern of subtopics in a text. Some Semantic Textual similarity [19] ideas have also been incorporated for improved accuracy. The intuition here is that sentences that falls belonging to the same segment must be semantically similar.

We take a segment as an information unit in a document, defined by different levels of granularity, i.e., sentence, paragraph or section holding many paragraphs. The goal is to find a semantic correspondence between a concept

---

[4] An online database of EU government documents.

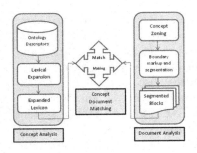

Fig. 1. The system architecture

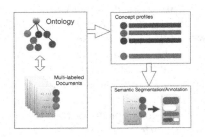

Fig. 2. A schematic representation of the concept-document mapping

descriptor and each topical segment. A high level structure of the proposed task is shown in Fig. 1.

The proposed system has diverse applications. As an example, legal documents usually contain many pages of information. A practitioner looking for specific information of interest from such documents would have to read through the pages before identifying the needed part even though the information that is being searched is contained within just a few paragraphs. With the proposed system, a user only has to specify a concept which represents the information need, and the system identifies and retrieves the particular segment(s) which is semantically related to the concept.

3   System Description

We use the *Eurovoc* thesaurus as the ontology and a collection from the *EurLex* website as documents to be processed. *EurLex* documents are already labeled with corresponding *Eurovoc* concept descriptors.

Consider a text in a collection of documents, where each document is associated to a set of concepts taken from a thesaurus σ (i.e., a multi-labeled text collection). In our work, instead of assuming a *Universe of Concept* (UoC) from the ontology, we use sets of concept already classified with that EurLex document.

We divide the task into 3 steps, i.e., *document analysis, concept analysis* and *concept-segment mapping*. The document analysis part performs topical document segmentation needed for the concept-segment mapping. The concept analysis step creates a profile for each concept, each profile is a unique symbolic signature capturing possible semantics of a concept. Concept profile can be viewed as a form of virtual document containing all possible descriptive information for that concept. The concept-Segment mapping part compare each profile and topical segment for similarity. Based on some heuristics, the system assigns the profile to the respective related segments. Figure 2 shows a pictorial representation of the details.

We now proceed to fully describe each step.

3.1 Document Representation

Given a text t_i and its sequence of sentences $Seq_i = <s_1, s_2, ..., s_k>$. The document analysis part aggregates all the sentences or paragraphs of the text that semantically align into a group. This semantically aligned group is called a segment, each of which can be directly mapped to the concept profile from an ontology. Basically, a topic segmentation algorithm tries to discover topic boundaries which symbolizes a semantic drift in the flow of topics within a document. These boundaries are then used to separate the sentences that is about individual topics, the group of aligned sentences must be coherent, hence a separate segment or topical unit.

In our work, topical segmentation is done based on an improved topic-modeling based Text Segmentation [25]. Our text segmentation implementation not only rely on topics but further incorporates a Semantic Nets[5] based similarity in order to improve segmentation accuracy. The approach follows the general template of the TextTiling [7,13] system. Generally, TextTiling algorithm uses the amount of word overlaps among contiguous sentences. It relies on the observations that the structure of a text is a function of its constituents terms. Using basic cues, it groups coherent sentences based on *word repetition* and *term co-occurrences* within a small axis and the extent of *word similarity*. A text is broken into pseudo-blocs, with each bloc comprising of k (3–5) adjacent sentences. A measure of relatedness is then obtained with cosine similarity of their vectors.

$$\cos(b_1, b_2) = \frac{\sum_{t=1}^{n} w_{t,b1} w_{t,b2}}{\sqrt{\sum_{t=1}^{n} w_{t,b1}^2 \sum_{t=1}^{n} w_{t,b2}^2}} \tag{1}$$

Where *b1* and *b2* are the two sentences compared. Highly similar blocs tend to form peaks and in contrast dissimilar blocs forms valleys, hence a boundary. Unlike TextTiling which uses only word repetition as evidence of coherence, we also compute semantic similarity using a WordNet-based Sentence similarity algorithm, this typically overcomes the problem of ambiguity in word usage [6]. Following the works of [25], we compute similarity between the LDA [6] generated topic vectors for each sentence in a candidate segment, this approach results in an improved performance. The reader is referred to [2] for detailed description of the text segmentation approach and algorithm.

3.2 Concept Representation

Once the topical segments of a document are identified, the next step is to retrieve the concepts that a document is manually labelled with on EurLex and then create a profile for each concept. A concept profile is essentially a signature which by design incorporates all the descriptive information of and/or about the

---

[5] We used WordNet concept distance to compute semantic similarity between adjacent sentences of a candidate segment according to a chosen window.
[6] E.g., synonymy and polysemy.

concept. Concept descriptors could range from unigram, bigrams to n-grams. Similarly to *query expansion*, if a concept descriptor has more than one word, we check if it is included in the WordNet as a word, e.g., the word *Jet-lag* has two joint terms (*jet* and *lag*). However, it is an entry in the WordNet as a single term. On the other hand, the word *public health* is not included in WordNet as a single term. In the second case, e.g., *public health*, we break the n-gram term into its constituent words, e.g., *public* and *health*. We then enrich the constituent term(s) in a process called *lexical expansion*.

The goal of lexical expansion is to retrieve semantically similar words such as synonyms from WordNet etc. We also obtain a top-k[7] related terms from a word embedding model obtained when the Word2vec [18] algorithm was trained on the Wikipedia dump[8]. The Word2Vec[9] is an algorithm capable of inducing semantic relatedness and similarity of words from a large corpus based on their Distributional features [26]. Given a word, it learns to predict the word that appears next to the given word, using past contextual information about that word obtained from the corpus.

The Gensim[10] implementation of the *Word2vec* algorithm uses *Skip-Gram* with *Hierarchical Softmax* which is widely preferred over the *Continous-Bag-of-Word* (CBOW) in terms of performance. The model obtained when the algorithm is trained over a corpus can be used to obtain semantically related words to a term. As an example, the model is able to understand that *Paris* is to *France* as *London* is to *England* thus capturing country-capital relationships based on knowledge extracted from the corpus when employed in a word analogy task.

The use of the word embedding model is important since some knowledge cannot not be derived from the WordNet. Recall that a concept does not have to appear in a text explicitly for humans to understand what the text is talking about, e.g., say a concept *soccer*, a document that contains terms like player, striker, goal, or even names like *Manchester United, Ronaldo, Messi* etc., is an indicator that the document is about soccer even without the word 'soccer' appearing in the document. Entries like *Manchester United* or *Ronaldo* which cannot be found in WordNet are easily captured by a word embedding model assuming that the related documents are included in the training set. Owing to its characteristics, Researchers have found that it is particularly useful for Information retrieval task [3,4,8,22].

To further enrich the profile, the ontology is traversed to obtain the neighours, e.g., ancestors, siblings and the children of a concept. The idea is that siblings of a concept are also semantically similar and the children could be more specific and less general than the parent node. Most importantly, using this information automatically disambiguates a concept. The profile of the neighours are also extracted and included in the profile of the concept. We call this *ontology*

---

[7] Where k is a chosen number and set as 3.

[8] English wikipedia dump was downloaded on July 30, 2015.

[9] https://code.google.com/p/word2vec/.

[10] https://github.com/RaRe-Technologies/gensim. Training Parameters: Context Window: 5, Neural Network layer size: 200, Minimum word count: 5.

enrichment. We say that the combination of the synonym sets from the Word-Net, the terms obtained from the ontology enrichment, and the related words obtained with the word embedding model constitute the profile for a concept. The profile $profile_{con}$, of a concept is defined as:

$$\overrightarrow{profile_{con}(a)} = \{Syn_{wn}(a)\} + \{Rterm_{we}(a)\} + \{Onto_{surround}(a)\} \quad (2)$$

Where Syn_{wn} is the set of synsets obtained from WordNet, $Rterm_{we}$ is the set of semantically related terms obtained from the word embedding model and $Onto_{surround}$ are the surrounding or neighours of a concept in the ontology.

The concept profile can be unnecessarily large due to duplicity of terms e.g. a synset obtained from WordNet may be returned by the word embedding model as well. It is therefore necessary to remove this redundancy. A concept profile is trimmed by removing any repeating term and those terms that are less semantically similar to the other terms in the profile. First, some randomly selected *baseline terms* whose similarity exceeds a threshold are selected. The threshold is heuristically determined and it ensures that those terms are highly semantically similar. The baseline terms are then used as a reference in measuring the similarity of every other terms in the profile. Similarity of other terms in the profile is calculated and a weight is assigned to each term based on the similarity score [1]. The weights of all the terms are then ranked and the top n ranked terms are selected while others are discarded. The result is that the concept profile contains a dense but highly semantic signature of the original concept. This reduces over-fitting of the profile with less useful terms. The trimmed profile $profile_{trimmed}$ is defined by:

$$\overrightarrow{profile_{trimmed}(a)} = \{t \quad | \quad SIM(baseline, t) > k\} \quad (3)$$

Where *baseline* is the set of chosen terms used to compare other terms, the *SIM* function returns a weight after computing similarity between a term in the profile and each of the baseline terms, k is a threshold for ranking, terms with weight less than k are discarded. For example, say a profile contain terms like {airport, transport, flight, shuttle, metro, wind}, we may safely assume that the word *wind* constitute mere noise to the profile as it is the least related to the others. Next, the terms in the trimmed profile are merged; in order to generate a sentential representation for the concept which is used for the concept-document mapping process.

3.3 Concept-Document Mapping

Concept-Document mapping can be viewed as finding a semantic correspondence between the semantic representation of a concept and the topical segment of a document. Recall that the concept profile for a particular document is built from the Eurovoc descriptors that the Eurlex document is already classified with. We can formalize the maping task as 4-tuple (Sen$_{form}$, Top$_{seg}$, Rel, Sim) where Sen_{form} is the sentential representation of a concept, Top_{seg} is the topical segment of a document, *Rel* is the semantic relationship between Sen_{form}, and

Top_{seg} which is represented by similarity metric Sim. Sim can be any vector distance metric like the Euclidean or Cosine similarity.

Matching a given concept to a text segment in a text is reduced to a simple semantic relatedness task between the sentential representation of each concept and the sentences in each segment. Thus, we can view it as a form of semantic similarity task. In order to compute similarity, we use two approaches. The first uses a cosine similarity metric. The issue with this approach is that Sen_{form} may not have many words in common with Top_{seg}, such that even if the two share words that are similar in meaning but with different lexicographic form, the cosine similarity will be low. The similarity obtained here is called $Sim1$.

Secondly, we compare each word in Sen_{form} with the words in Top_{seg}. However, some words in Top_{seg} may not be useful, e.g., stop words. We perform part-of-speech tagging using the Stanford POS tagger [20] in order to retain only the verbs, adjectives and nouns. We call the resulting set of words the Top_{seg} profile. Next, word-word similarity is done between the terms in Top_{seg} and those in Sen_{form}.

The word-word similarity computation is accomplished using a WordNet based similarity implementation. To derive similarity from WordNet, we used both the path length between each word as well as the depth function. Usually, longer path length between two concepts signifies lower similarity. The author in [19] introduced the depth function with the intuition that the words at the upper layer of a Semantic Net contains general semantics and less similarity while those at the lower layers are more similar. Therefore, a similarity assessment should be a function of both the depth as well as the path length distances between concepts. If f1(h) is a function of the depth and f2(l) is a function of the length, then the similarity between two word is given by:

$$S(w_1, w_2) = f1(h).f2(l) \qquad (4)$$

The length function is a monotonically decreasing function with respect to the path length l between two concepts. This is captured by introducing a constant alpha.

$$f2(l) = e^{-\alpha l} \qquad (5)$$

Likewise, the depth function is monotonically increasing with respect to the depth h of concept in the hierarchy.

$$f1(h) = \frac{e^{\beta h} - e^{-\beta h}}{e^{\beta h} + e^{-\beta h}} \qquad (6)$$

The similarity between two WordNet concepts is then calculated by:

$$S(w_1, w_2) = e^{-\alpha l} . \frac{e^{\beta h} - e^{-\beta h}}{e^{\beta h} + e^{-\beta h}} \qquad (7)$$

The author [19] empirically discovered that for optimal performance in Word-Net, α should be set to 0.2 and β set to 0.45. Since this approach considers only the similarity between two words, it is important to find a way to combine all the similarity scores that exceed a particular threshold. The aggregation function below is used:

$$\text{Sim} = \frac{\sum_{i,j}^{m,n} |S(w_i, w_j > x)|}{tCount} \tag{8}$$

Where $S(w_i, w_j)$ is the similarity score for two words, $tCount$ is the total number of the set of similarity scores that exceeds the threshold and Sim is the aggregating function combining all pairwise similarities. Past studies have shown that by encoding query and document terms with vectors from a word embedding model, combining the terms using for example a simple vector addition operator and then performing vector averaging, a retrieval system that is robust to language variability issues like synonymy and polysemy can be obtained [3,8]. We encode the terms in Top_{seg} and those in Sen_{form} with vectors from our trained word embedding model. Next, we obtain the representation for the concept and segment by performing vector addition and averaging of the terms in order to yield a single vector. The similarity between the concept vector and a segment vector is then computed with the Cosine similarity formula.

We call the WordNet based similarity score $Sim2$ and the similarity score from the word embedding is $Sim3$. The final similarity is obtained by the mean of the 3 similarities earlier calculated. This is given by the formula:

$$\text{cSim} = \frac{Sim1 + Sim2 + Sim3}{n} \tag{9}$$

Where n is the number of values combined, e.g., n = 3. Comparing each Sen_{form} to each Top_{seg} *profile* yields a vector of similarity scores for each Sen_{form}, e.g. assuming that a document has 3 topical segments, then a profile $Sen_{form}(con)$ of a concept *con* having vector $[0.8, 0.4, 0.2]$ means that its similarity score with the first topical segment is 0.8, second is 0.4 and third is 0.2 etc. A concept profile is said to be similar to the topical segment it has the highest similarity score with if it is Z[11] times higher than all other values else, the highest and the next highest sentences are both taken to be semantically close to the concept profile. The Z parameter is computed with the formula:

$$\text{Z} = \frac{a - b}{b} \times 100 \tag{10}$$

Where a and b are the highest and next highest values in the similarity scores vector of concept profile. In the example scores vector above, a = 0.8 and b = 0.40. Calculating z gives 1.00 which is greater than the threshold value for z. Thus the segment with score 0.8 is the only one tagged with that concept.

4   Evaluation

We selected 100 documents from EurLex website, 25 documents each from four different categories. EurLex is an open and regularly updated online database

---

[11] Ensures the highest similarity is at least z percent higher than the next highest value. By default, z = 0.3.

of over 3 million European Union documents covering EU treaties, regulations, legislative proposals, case-law, international agreements, EFTA documents etc. Documents are already classified using Eurovoc descriptors. We used the Eurovoc thesaurus as the ontology. EurLex and Eurovoc are both multilingual. Currently, it is available in 26 European languages. The documents downloaded are English versions from *Consolidated Acts* section of the website. Specifically, we selected documents under Transport Policy category. The sub-categories include {Transport Infrastructure, Inland Transport, Shipping, Air Transport}. We evaluated the system on a task of *conceptual tagging*.

Conceptual Tagging measures the performance of the system in correctly labeling a text segment with a concept. We measure the performance of the system against annotations from human judgment. To achieve this, all the documents were first automatically segmented into topical sections with our text segmentation algorithm. Two volunteers were asked to read each document and assign Eurovoc descriptors to the segments in the document as appropriate. The descriptors chosen for each document are those the document were classified with on EurLex website.

A segment may not be labeled with a concept descriptor if the volunteer annotators believed that there is no semantic relationship between it and any of the concept. Also, a segment can have more than one concept related to it. A third volunteer compares annotations from the first two volunteers, and where annotations do not correlate, decides the final annotation per document. The agreements were rated based on individuals judgment in labeling a text segment with a concept.

The same topical segments for each document were fed into the developed system. The goal of the system is to quantify the meaning of these segments and for each, select the concept that is most semantically related. Using the manual annotation as *Gold Standard*, we compared the performance of the system with that of manual annotation using the popular information retrieval metrics: Precision and Recall. The precision is the number of accurate tagging by the system in comparison to that of human annotators. The recall, on the other hand is the number of accurate tagging made by the system. Table 1 shows the results obtained under different categories of documents. We can see that we obtained the best precision and recall scores from 'Transport Infrastructure' documents while the worst results comes from 'Air Transport' category. Manual exploration

Table 1. Precision and recall across document genre

Domain of documents	No of documents	Precision (%)	Recall (%)
Transport infrastructure	25	0.74	0.77
Inland transport	25	0.71	0.73
Shipping	55	0.72	0.74
Air transport	25	0.68	0.71
Average score	100	0.71	0.73

of the documents reveal that the documents under this category with the best result are quite short (average of 3 pages) compared to those under Air Transport where the average number of pages was double that of the former. Overall, we obtained an average precision score of 71%, recall value of 73%, and an overall F_1 score of 72%.

5 Conclusion

The paper describes an approach to semantically link concepts to the parts of the document that the concept is semantically related to. The proposed concept-document mapping can aid conceptual information retrieval task such that users have a more fine-grained results, e.g., specific document part that satisfies the user query instead of the whole document. The Eurovoc thesaurus was used as the ontology of choice since EurLex documents are pre-labeled with descriptors. The task has useful applications in Information retrieval and extraction as well as text segmentation. For instance, a user who is more interested in a particular information in a document can easily specify such information need through a concept that describes such need. The system is then able to extract the specific portion containing the requested information need. Experimental result shows that the idea is feasible with a promising result. Future work will include an extended set of experiments by getting more volunteers to help with manual annotations require for thorough evaluation.

Acknowledgments. Kolawole J. Adebayo has received funding from the Erasmus Mundus Joint International Doctoral (Ph.D.) programme in Law, Science and Technology. Luigi Di Caro and Guido Boella have received funding from the European Union's H2020 research and innovation programme under the grant agreement No 690974 for the project "MIREL: MIning and REasoning with Legal texts".

References

1. Adebayo, K., Di Caro, L., Boella, G.: NORMAS at SemEval-2016 task 1: SEMSIM: a multi-feature approach to semantic text similarity. In: Proceedings of the 10th International Workshop on Semantic Evaluation, SemEval@NAACL-HLT 2016, San Diego, CA, USA, 16–17 June 2016, pp. 718–725 (2016)
2. Adebayo, K.J., Di Caro, L., Boella, G.: Text segmentation with topic modeling and entity coherence. In: Abraham, A., Haqiq, A., Alimi, A.M., Mezzour, G., Rokbani, N., Muda, A.K. (eds.) HIS 2016. AISC, vol. 552, pp. 175–185. Springer, Cham (2017). https://doi.org/10.1007/978-3-319-52941-7_18
3. Adebayo, K.J., Di Caro, L., Boella, G., Bartolini, C.: An approach to information retrieval and question answering in the legal domain, pp. 15–25 (2016)
4. Ai, Q., Yang, L., Guo, J., Croft, W.B.: Improving language estimation with the paragraph vector model for ad-hoc retrieval. In: Proceedings of the 39th International ACM SIGIR Conference on Research and Development in Information Retrieval, pp. 869–872. ACM (2016)

5. Bikakis, N., Giannopoulos, G., Dalamagas, T., Sellis, T.: Integrating keywords and semantics on document annotation and search. In: Meersman, R., Dillon, T., Herrero, P. (eds.) OTM 2010. LNCS, vol. 6427, pp. 921–938. Springer, Heidelberg (2010). https://doi.org/10.1007/978-3-642-16949-6_19
6. Blei, D.M., Lafferty, J.D.: Dynamic topic models. In: Proceedings of the 23rd International Conference on Machine Learning, pp. 113–120. ACM (2006)
7. Choi, F.Y.Y.: Advances in domain independent linear text segmentation. In: Proceedings of the 1st North American Chapter of the Association for Computational Linguistics Conference, pp. 26–33. Association for Computational Linguistics (2000)
8. Clinchant, S., Perronnin, F.: Aggregating continuous word embeddings for information retrieval. In: Proceedings of the Workshop on Continuous Vector Space Models and their Compositionality, pp. 100–109 (2013)
9. Cunningham, H., Maynard, D., Bontcheva, K., Tablan, V.: A framework and graphical development environment for robust NLP tools and applications. In: ACL, pp. 168–175 (2002)
10. Dill, S., et al.: A case for automated large-scale semantic annotation. Web Semant.: Sci. Serv. Agents World Wide Web 1(1), 115–132 (2003)
11. Halliday, M.A.K., Hasan, R.: Cohesion in English (1976)
12. Handschuh, S., Staab, S.: Authoring and annotation of web pages in cream. In: Proceedings of the 11th International Conference on World Wide Web, pp. 462–473. ACM (2002)
13. Hearst, M.A.: TextTiling: a quantitative approach to discourse segmentation. Technical report, Citeseer (1993)
14. Hearst, M.A.: TextTiling: segmenting text into multi-paragraph subtopic passages. Computational linguistics 23(1), 33–64 (1997)
15. Kiyavitskaya, N., Zeni, N., Mich, L., Cordy, J.R., Mylopoulos, J.: Text mining through semi automatic semantic annotation. In: Reimer, U., Karagiannis, D. (eds.) PAKM 2006. LNCS (LNAI), vol. 4333, pp. 143–154. Springer, Heidelberg (2006). https://doi.org/10.1007/11944935_13
16. Laclavík, M., Ciglan, M., Seleng, M., Krajei, S.: Ontea: semi-automatic pattern based text annotation empowered with information retrieval methods. In: Tools for Acquisition, Organisation and Presenting of Information and Knowledge: Proceedings in Informatics and Information Technologies, Kosice, Vydavatelstvo STU, Bratislava, part, vol. 2, pp. 119–129 (2007)
17. Laclavik, M., Seleng, M., Gatial, E., Balogh, Z., Hluchy, L.: Ontology based text annotation-OnTeA, pp. 280–284 (2006)
18. Le, Q.V., Mikolov, T.: Distributed representations of sentences and documents. arXiv preprint arXiv:1405.4053 (2014)
19. Li, Y., McLean, D., Bandar, Z.A., O'shea, J.D., Crockett, K.: Sentence similarity based on semantic nets and corpus statistics. IEEE Trans. Knowl. Data Eng. 18(8), 1138–1150 (2006)
20. Manning, C.D., Surdeanu, M., Bauer, J., Finkel, J.R., Bethard, S., McClosky, D.: The Stanford CoreNLP natural language processing toolkit. In: ACL (System Demonstrations), pp. 55–60 (2014)
21. Loza Mencía, E., Fürnkranz, J.: Efficient multilabel classification algorithms for large-scale problems in the legal domain. In: Francesconi, E., Montemagni, S., Peters, W., Tiscornia, D. (eds.) Semantic Processing of Legal Texts. LNCS (LNAI), vol. 6036, pp. 192–215. Springer, Heidelberg (2010). https://doi.org/10.1007/978-3-642-12837-0_11

22. Mitra, B., Diaz, F., Craswell, N.: Learning to match using local and distributed representations of text for web search. In: Proceedings of the 26th International Conference on World Wide Web, pp. 1291–1299. International World Wide Web Conferences Steering Committee (2017)

23. Popov, B., Kiryakov, A., Kirilov, A., Manov, D., Ognyanoff, D., Goranov, M.: KIM – semantic annotation platform. In: Fensel, D., Sycara, K., Mylopoulos, J. (eds.) ISWC 2003. LNCS, vol. 2870, pp. 834–849. Springer, Heidelberg (2003). https://doi.org/10.1007/978-3-540-39718-2_53

24. Presutti, V., Draicchio, F., Gangemi, A.: Knowledge extraction based on discourse representation theory and linguistic frames. In: ten Teije, A., et al. (eds.) EKAW 2012. LNCS (LNAI), vol. 7603, pp. 114–129. Springer, Heidelberg (2012). https://doi.org/10.1007/978-3-642-33876-2_12

25. Riedl, M., Biemann, C.: Text segmentation with topic models. J. Lang. Technol. Comput. Linguist. $27(1)$, 47–69 (2012)

26. Turney, P.D., Pantel, P., et al.: From frequency to meaning: vector space models of semantics. J. Artif. Intell. Res. $37(1)$, 141–188 (2010)

27. Usbeck, R., et al.: GERBIL: general entity annotator benchmarking framework. In: Proceedings of the 24th International Conference on World Wide Web, pp. 1133–1143. ACM (2015)

Reuse and Reengineering of Non-ontological Resources in the Legal Domain

Cristiana Santos[1(✉)], Pompeu Casanovas[1,4],
Víctor Rodríguez-Doncel[2], and Leendert van der Torre[3]

[1] Institute of Law and Technology (IDT-UAB), Barcelona, Spain
`cristiana.teixeirasantos@gmail.com`,
`pompeu.casanovas@uab.cat`
[2] Ontology Engineering Group,
Universidad Politécnica de Madrid, Madrid, Spain
`vrodriguez@fi.upm.es`
[3] University of Luxembourg, Luxembourg City, Luxembourg
`leon.vandertorre@uni.lu`
[4] Data to Decisions Cooperative Research Centre,
La Trobe Law School, Melbourne, Australia
`P.CasanovasRomeu@latrobe.edu.au`

Abstract. Instead of custom-building a new ontology from scratch, knowledge resources can be elicited, reused and engineered to develop legal ontologies with the goal of promoting the application of good practices and speeding up the ontology development process. This paper focuses on the *specificities* of non-ontological resources in the legal domain, and provides some guidelines of how these can be reused and engineered to enable heterogeneous resources integration within a legal ontology. The paper presents some examples of these processes using a case-study in the consumer law domain.

Keywords: Ontology engineering · Non-ontological resources
Legal ontology · MeLOn methodology · NeOn methodology

1 Introduction

Instead of custom-building a new legal ontology from scratch, knowledge resources are elicited from the legal domain, reused and engineered to develop legal ontologies[1], promoting the application of good practices.

Knowledge resources have been classified as ontological resources (ORs) or non-ontological resources (henceforth named NORs) [1]. This division regards the level of formalization. We will focus on the latter type. There is much literature for reusing and reengineering ORs [2, 3] and also ontology design patterns, but little about extracting knowledge from NORs in the legal domain, probably due to its *specificities,* delved in

---

[1] Ontologies are the chosen artifact to support the integration of data from multiple, heterogeneous legal sources, making information explicit and enabling the sharing of a common understanding of a domain.

© Springer Nature Switzerland AG 2018
U. Pagallo et al. (Eds.): AICOL VI-X 2015–2017, LNAI 10791, pp. 350–364, 2018.
https://doi.org/10.1007/978-3-030-00178-0_24

this paper. This subject is relevant as it has consequences at different levels, from knowledge acquisition, to ontology engineering.

There is a large amount of NORs that embody knowledge in the legal domain, that represent some degree of consensus for the legal community and possess *related semantics* that allows interpreting the knowledge contained therein. In fact, within this domain, NORs may correspond to some legal sources which consist on legislation, but also other relevant sources of e.g., case law, doctrinal interpretations, social rules; it is essential to connect this existing legal material to the ontology, even if its majority is not formalised, and hence not necessarily interoperable. NORs from this realm can be embedded in different and scattered sources of hard and soft law, such as classification schemes, thesauri, lexicons[2], textual corpora, among others, in a "patchwork" of "lego" pieces. The heterogeneity of the legal sources is observed at multiples levels: structural, semantic, and syntactic. To integrate information from multiple and heterogeneous knowledge sources, it is important to cope with the problem of legal knowledge representation, that consists in the balance between consensus and authoritativeness[3] [4] or, from the socio-legal perspective, dialogue and bindingness [5].

On the one hand, domain legal experts lack competencies in data modeling, and they often adopt technical tools (e.g., Protégé) without the necessary awareness of the technical consequences [6]. On the other hand, ontology developers, besides the data modeling perspective, should consider likewise compliance with the *specificities* of the juristic nature of legal NORs and of expert knowledge. A balanced combination would yield reliable actionable knowledge in a real world context, for a thorough understanding of the considered legal field is necessary to bring out explicit conceptualizations, to shape the design of the ontology and its population. Legal information *specificities* [7] and ontology interplay, in both its theoretical and engineering dimensions, are intrinsically connected. The interaction between legal concepts that affect the utilization of information is significative [6]. Hence, an interdisciplinary approach is essential towards representing machine-readable concepts and relationships from NORs in the legal domain, through the due processes of reusing and reengineering thereof. Hence, the research question of this paper is how to reuse non-ontological resources in the legal domain and their reengineering into ontologies. For such purpose we follow two complementary methodological approaches: (i) "Building Ontology Networks by Reusing and Reengineering Non Ontological Resources", Scenario 2 from *NeOn*[4] *methodology framework* (henceforward called *NeOn*) that explains how to build ontologies by reusing and reengineering non-ontological resources [1, 8–10]; and (ii) the Methodology for building Legal Ontology (henceforth called *MeLOn*) [6], developed by Monica Palmirani.

---

[2] A lexicon is the vocabulary of an individual person, an occupational group or a professional field, Glossary of Terms for the Standardization of Geographical Names, United Nations Group of Experts on Geographic Names, United Nations, New York, 2002.

[3] Regarding authoritativeness and bindingness, knowledge representation in the legal domain entails some peculiar features, because it is supposed that authority is somewhat embedded into the text.

[4] http://www.neon-project.org.

The observations held in this paper are built upon the construction of two legal ontologies named Relevant legal information for consumer disputes (RIC) and RIC-ATPI, referring to the relevant information in the domain of air transport passenger incidents [11].

The remainder of the paper is structured as follows. Section 1 describes the specificities of NORs in the legal domain. Section 2 refers to the main methodologies to build ontologies with NORS; Sect. 3 explains the NORs reuse and reengineering processes. Section 4 concludes the paper emphasizing the challenges and lessons learned while reusing and reengineering NORs from the legal domain.

2   Specificities of NORs in the Legal Domain

In this section we define NOR, providing some examples and we discuss the specificities of possible inputs (knowledge resources available for reuse) for building possible outputs (ontologies).

2.1   Non-ontological Resources

Non-ontological resources consist in:

(i)   knowledge resources that embody knowledge in the legal domain;
(ii) they represent some degree of consensus;
(iii) whose semantics have not been formalized by an ontology yet, but they possess related semantics which allow interpreting the knowledge they hold. Sometimes this semantics is explicitly specified in natural language on the document, thus fostering its reuse; however, in other cases, the semantics is implicit and this lack of formalization prevents us from using them as ontologies.

Using consensuated NORs portrays *benefits*: it favors interoperability of the used vocabulary, makes faster the ontology development process, lessens the knowledge acquisition bottleneck problems, reuse, browsing/searching, and follows good practices. NORs in the legal domain can be glossaries, classification schemes, dictionaries, taxonomies, thesauri and text. Table 1 exemplifies possible NOR for the legal domain.

2.2   Specificities of NORs in the Legal Domain

Yet, even cognizant of these benefits and amount of NORs in the legal domain, there are *specificities* to look upon: they present a complex multi-layered informational structure that should be considered when building a legal ontology. Some of these features are recursively evoked within any legal knowledge engineering process.

i.   *Validity of a legal source*, bounded both in time and jurisdiction;
ii. *Level of formalization*, in terms of being expressed in a logic formal system, as illustrated in Fig. 1, for they can possess weak or strong semantics, in the line of McGuinness [20]. Given the primacy of OWL ontologies, a description logics-centric discourse is justified.

Table 1. Examples of NORs in the legal domain.

Types of NOR	Definition	Examples
Glossary	*Terminological dictionary that contains designations and definitions from one or more specific subject fields. The vocabulary may be monolingual, bilingual or multilingual.* (ISO 1087:2000)	Customer complaint glossary[a], the Integrated Public Sector Vocabulary[b] (IPSV), Open Legal Terminology Dataset: IATE termbase,[c] ECRIS[d] as a shared terminology for the criminal domain
Classification scheme	*Descriptive information for an arrangement or division of objects into groups based on characteristics the objects have in common* (ISO 2004)	The classification of consumer complaints from the EU Commission (COM(2009) 346 final)
Dictionary	*A dictionary is a structured collection of lexical units with linguistic information about each of them* (ISO 1087-1:2000)	European Legal Taxonomy Syllabus [12]
Taxonomy	A taxonomy is the simplest variant of controlled vocabularies as it contains only terms that are organized into a hierarchical structure	The List of Extraordinary Circumstances by the NEBS is a taxonomic example[e]
Text corpora	Texts are among the strongest data available to acquire knowledge	Dataset of complaints, legislation
Thesauri	Thesauri are controlled vocabularies of terms in a particular domain with hierarchical, associative, and equivalence relations between terms (ISO 25964-1:2011)	Eurovoc[f]

[a]http://www.jarrar.info/CContology/
[b]http://doc.esd.org.uk/IPSV
[c]InterActive Terminology for Europe, now also available in TermBase eXchange (TBX) format.
[d]https://joinup.ec.europa.eu/sites/default/files/ckeditor_files/files/CR01(1).pdf
[e]https://www.ombudsman.europa.eu
[f]EuroVoc is a multilingual, multidisciplinary thesaurus covering the activities of the EU. Also available in XML and SKOS/RDF.

iii. *Hierarchy of the legal authority contained in legal sources*[5]. The legal domain itself defines a hierarchy of authority. Whilst legislation constitutes a primary source of law and it is binding, therefore, its authority is explicit, known soft law

---

[5] Legal knowledge structures are constructed in a different way than scientific knowledge structures. Whilst the natural sciences only deal with persuasive authority, meaning that the truth of a proposition does not depend on who states it, but only if empirical data supports it and/or is internally consistent, the law deals with binding authority, that is, statements from a particular source whose truth depends on that source, and other formal aspects, such as the law having been promulgated or statement being part of a verdict *ratio decidendi*.

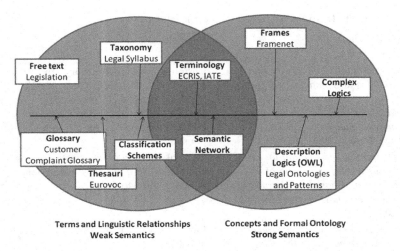

Fig. 1. Examples of knowledge resources distributed according to its level of formalization. On the left bubble, they are non-formal (i.e. not expressed in terms of a logic formal system). On the right bubble, they are formal. The lines shows that the more to the right, the more complex the formal system behind is.

sources comprising binding norms with a soft dimension may not be so explicit. A possible agreed-upon typology of legal sources relies on the legal hierarchy authority, shown in an informal way in Table 2 (for comprehension reasons and not for a discrete selection of the valid sources). Figure 2 exemplifies a hierarchy of knowledge sources. As illustrated, legislation, contractual terms and case law occupy the base of the pyramid. EU Commission Interpretative Communications and Recommendations are policy documents serving the purpose of providing legal certainty, for they facilitate a more homogenous application of the EU

Table 2. Classification of the primary and secondary sources of law

Primary sources of law

- Refer to legislation: rules of law created by a governmental body, e.g. constitutions, statutes and codes; regulations (from administrative agencies)
- Case-law
- Contracts
- These sources of primary law are binding

Secondary sources of law

- Legal doctrine (art. 38 (c) ICJ), which concerns legal scholarly writings and materials by legal scholars that explain, interpret or comment primary sources of law, such as: articles, legal commentaries, treatises, textbooks; legal encyclopedias, legal dictionaries, monographs
- Contain persuasive authority, which means that the court is not required to follow the analysis (non-binding)
- Soft law instruments, which are interpretative sources generally making open textured concepts operational (generally non-binding)

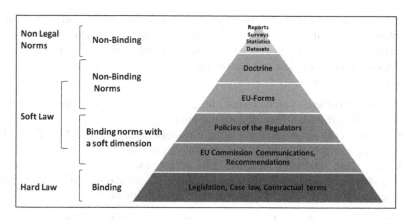

Fig. 2. Example of a hierarchy of knowledge resources.

Regulations and Directives, but lack on bindingness; these guidelines are intended to tackle the issues most frequently raised by national regulators and industry representatives. Reports and expert studies commissioned by the EU Commission, Eurobarometer, etc. help the preparation of texts and in decision-making, representing sources of knowledge but are non-binding.

iv. *Open textured concepts.* Inside the sources, vague concepts are subject to interpretation, e.g. reasonable measures, extraordinary circumstances, etc.

v. *Deontic legal operators.* Deontic legal terms, such as right, obligation, prohibition, permission, and sanction a.s.o. occur within legal and other normative documents dispersedly located.

vi. *Conjoint heterogeneity and fragmentation of the legal sources.* In the legal domain, NORs cannot be found in a single place, not even within one legislative text, but in a "patchwork" of "lego" pieces. *Patchwork* is the expression currently used to point at conjoint heterogeneity, e.g. privacy and data protection previous EU directive and from the intellectual property perspective, respectively [13, 14]. NORs "bricks" can be embedded in different and separate resources of hard and soft law, further articulated in case law and legal scholarship, scattered in a complex way in large textual corpuses, and reused in many different ways, depending on the area of law considered. They can be found in the sources indicated in Table 1;

vii. *Citations within and among sources*;

viii. *Closed, shared or open status of the resources.* As a result of the Open Data movement, legally backed by the PSI-Directive[6], fundamental legal sources of democratic societies, as legislation, court decisions and Parliamentary datasets, are freely available for reuse, and most of them have Uniform Resource Identifiers (URIs), being converted in linked data. Also the Eurovoc thesaurus, the

---

[6] Directive 2013/37/EU, CELEX:32013L0037.

IATE database, EU authority tables;[7] semantic interfacing between disparate national terminology repositories;[8] Identifiers such as the European Case Law Identifier (ECLI);[9] the European Legislation Identifier (ELI)[10] are open building blocks. Figure 3 depicts this status, from internal access to anyone.

ix. *Heterogeneity* on its:

- *type*: glossaries, dictionaries, lexicons, classification schemes and taxonomies, thesauri, textual corpora, etc.;
- *format*: only some possess machine-readable format, e.g. XML, PDF, HML, RDF, and the majority is free text, which is hard to process;
- *structure*: *unstructured* way, e.g. narratives; *semi-structured*, e.g. folksonomies[11]; and *structured*, e.g. databases, standards, catalogues, classifications, thesauri, lexicons, legal text, among others;

x. *Semantics of NORs*. NORS may possess explicit and implicit semantics:

- *explicit*: there are hierarchies, part-of relations and other structures explicitly expressed in natural language on the content documents, e.g. exceptions contained in legal text; and
- *implicit*: interpreting the knowledge they contain, e.g. recitals of legislation; terminologies emanated from relevant institutions with explicit definitions.

These peculiarities should be taken into account while building a legal ontology, transferring the legal material into a computational context.

3 Methodological Reuse-Based Approaches on NORs

Research on a reuse-based approach in ontology engineering methodologies presents a wide set of methods and tools for the ontologization of NORs, but mainly specific to a particular resource type, or to a particular resource implementation, developing ad-hoc solutions to transforming available resources into ontologies.

NeOn methodology provides guidelines for building ontologies by reengineering knowledge resources widely used within a particular community. Therefore we have used this methodology in our work, inheriting the activities of "search, assessing and

---

[7] The EU Metadata Registry: The Metadata Registry registers and maintains definition data (metadata elements, named authority lists, schemas, etc.) used by the different European Institutions involved in the legal decision making process gathered in the Interinstitutional Metadata Maintenance Committee (IMMC) and by the Publications Office of the EU in its production and dissemination process.

[8] The Legivoc project, http://legivoc.org/.

[9] Council conclusions inviting the introduction of the European Case Law Identifier (ECLI) and a minimum set of uniform metadata for case law, CELEX:52011XG0429(01).

[10] Council conclusions inviting the introduction of the European Legislation Identifier (ELI), CELEX:52012XG1026(01).

[11] A folksonomy is the result of personal free tagging of information and objects (anything with an URI) for one's own retrieval, T. Vander Wal. *Folksonomy coinage and definition*. 2007. http://www.vanderwal.net/folksonomy.html.

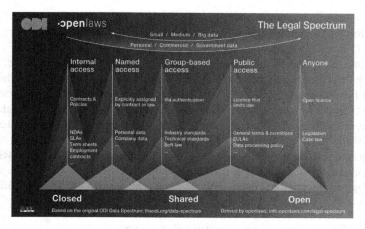

Fig. 3. Closed, shared and open knowledge resources, from Openlaws (https://openlaws.com/).

selecting" in the reuse process; and "reverse engineering, transformation and forward engineering" in the reengineering process, explained in Sects. 3.1 and 3.2 respectively. Nevertheless, *NeOn* does not refer to the domain specificities of legal knowledge encountered in Sect. 1.

There is relevant precedent work on ontology design within the legal domain, in particular, the *MeLOn* methodology, already implemented by a few scholars and used flexibly in ontology development projects within a diversity of use-cases in the legal domain [6, 15, 16]. This methodology was created for building legal ontologies in order to help legal experts modeling legal concepts using the principles of data modelisation. It comprises ten prescriptive methodological guidelines for building legal ontologies, from specification of requirements to implementatin and placing special emphasis to a thorough conceptual analysis and ontology evaluation[12] processes.

MeLOn regards NORs in its step 4 which entails the formation of a list of all the relevant terminology and subsequent production of a glossary of its main legal concepts. Accordingly, legislation, case law and other sets of legal norms should be consulted for determining the specific legal terminology. A glossary of terminology should have the form of a table with these column headings: term, definition by legal source (citing legal source, license, document, case law or legal theory, or common custom of the legal domain), link to normative/legal source, normalised definition (definition of term, made by the author of the new ontology, simplified or extended from a normative/legal source to fulfill the expectations of possible methodology users). The normalised definition should be a natural language description of the legal text using subject, predicate, object, with the aim to reuse the terms of the glossary as

---

[12] Evaluation parameters consist in: (i) completeness of the legal concepts definition; (ii) correctness of the explicit relationships between legal concepts; (iii) coherence of the legal concepts modelisation; (iv) applicability to concrete use-case; (v) effectiveness for the goals; (vi) intuitiveness for the non-legal experts; (vii) computational soundness of the logic and reasoning; (viii) reusability of the ontology and mapping with other similar ontologies.

much as possible and avoid duplicative or ambiguous terminology. In this way a legal expert is forced to create triples that can be aggregated later on into more abstract assertions (TBox or ABox).

Notwithstanding the significance of the pioneering work discussed above, it leaves space for enhancement regarding the NORs reuse process, as it provides high-level guidelines for ontology construction, but could provide an account of methodological steps, details and techniques employed. Three activities from *NeOn* could be added to this comprehensive methodology: criteria to search NORs, assess the set of candidates and the selection of the most appropriate NORs in the legal domain. We envisage that these granularity (provided with definitions of the resources, tables, examples of NORs) targets ontology practitioners with different backgrounds, encompassing domain experts, but also ontology engineers, final users, linguists, etc. which are lay to legal specificities.

4   NORs Reuse and Engineering Processes

In this section we present the NOR reuse and the NOR reengineering processes.

4.1   NORs Reuse Process

The NOR reuse process refers to the process of choosing the most suitable available NORs for the development of ontologies that, to some extent, cover the domain of the ontology being built and that normally reflect some degree of community consensus. The reuse process entails three activities: search, assessment ad selection of NORs explained below.

   (i)   *Searching for NORs.* This activity entails searching highly reliable websites, domain-related sites, and resources within organizations for NORs, using the terms included in the Ontology Requirement Specification Document, hence, according to the requirements and use-cases of the ontology;

  (ii) *Assessing the set of candidate NOR,* using three criteria: relevance, coverage and consensus, pursuant to the specificities delved in Sect. 1: primary and secondary sources of law, level of formalization, status of the resources, semantics and heterogeneity;

 (iii) *Selecting* the most appropriate NOR to be used to build the ontology;

    The purposive criteria to select and assess NOR can rely on relevance dimensions and consensus and coverage, provided below. For each of the resource and whenever possible, both the purpose and the components stemmed thereof should be made explicit.

- *Domain Relevance* (also denominated as *"domain relevance or legal authority, legal importance"*) [7, 16, 17] is two-folded, requesting the most important, or authoritative domain documents, within the specific legal domain, which the legal community considers relevant[13];

---

[13] Cfr. Point (iii) in Sect. 1.2 of the paper.

- *Cognitive Relevance*: the resources convening the users' cognitive and informational needs. Examples are conveyed in dataset of consumer's complaints, studies on user's search behaviour, studies on information-seeking behaviour of the considered users, etc.;
- *Situational Relevance*: the resources unfolding the user's problems or legal cases, which are mostly reported in case-law, in dataset of consumer com-plaints, and in domain reports;
- *Consensus and Coverage*: consensus among agreed-upon knowledge is a subjective and not quantifiable criterion. However, the reused resources should contain terminology already consensuated by the legal community, therefore the effort and time spent in finding out precise labels for the ontology terms decreased. Besides Eur-lex (where legislation and case-law can be retrieved), the EU Commission website on the topical domain might configure the relevant sources.

It is often the case that legal NORs in different languages have to be reused. Besides the challenges posed by multi-jurisdictional environments, the language issues become a problem by themselves - matching elements is hardened. These problems can be mitigated if linguistic models are used to mediate between resources. These linguistic models, like Ontolex[14] represent language information differentiating between lexical entries, senses and concepts, easing the task of integration of cross-language resources.

4.2 Non-ontological Resource Reengineering Process

Reuse of NORs process implies their reengineering into computational ontologies, exploiting the expressiveness and reusability of the RDF/OWL semantic web standards for knowledge representation. This process comprises two activities [9]. The definition of such activities and some examples are shown below. However, it is important to consider that not all NORs should be reengineered, like legislation, as its self-contained authoritativeness and authenticity needs to be guaranteed in its textual grounding, with a clear reference to the texts.

(i) *NOR reverse engineering*, whose goal is to identify NORs' underlying components and then create representations of the resources at different levels of abstraction (design, requirements and conceptual model). As an example, provision-types and their instances can be manually harvested from the selected sources, in order to develop a representation of the resource, a conceptual structure (e.g. a taxonomy) or instance data for the ontology.

(ii) *NOR transformation*, whose goal is to generate a conceptual model from each selected NOR. NOR transformation may include the following:

(ii.i) *TBox transformation*: transforms the content of the resource into an ontology schema (generating classes, relations, instances, as depicted in Fig. 4). Forms are usually useful to extract information due to its inherent classification scheme. As an example, the Air Passenger EU Complaint Form depicts domain incidents and their definitions (Fig. 5) used as classes in the RIC-ATPI domain ontology. Moreover, legal

---

[14] https://www.w3.org/community/ontolex/wiki/Final_Model_Specification.

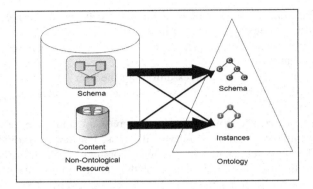

Fig. 4. NORs transformation activity. From the schema embedded in the resource, a conceptual model can be built.

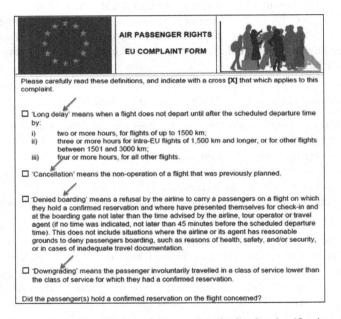

Fig. 5. Air passenger EU complaint form as an example of a classification scheme.

theory expresses the basic concepts (also called provision-types or systemic categories) common to (almost) all legal systems [22], e.g., obligation, permission, right, liability, sanction, legal act, cause, entitlement, etc. Legislative documents present (most of) these concepts and their stipulative definitions. The excerpt of the EC Regulation 261/2004 shown in Fig. 6 illustrates the extraction of anchoring provisions-types (requisite, right, exception, etc., that constitute classes of RIC ontology) that enable its transformation into the T-Box. The LegalRuleML metamodel [22] provides primitives

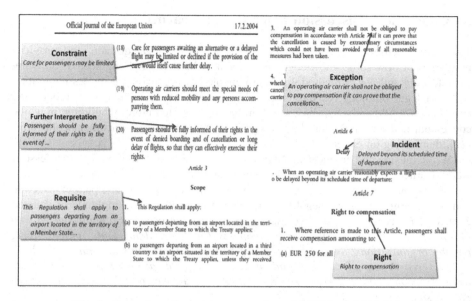

Fig. 6. Extraction of provisions-types from the EU Reg. 261/2004.

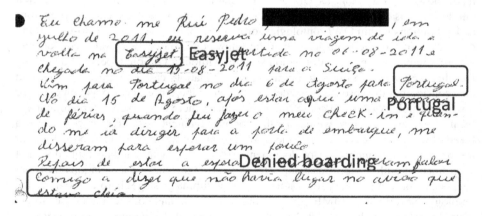

Fig. 7. Air transport passenger consumer complaint in Portuguese containing actual entities.

and their definitions, such as Permission, Obligation, Prohibition that can give a tax-onomic skeleton of a legal ontology.

(ii.ii) *ABox transformation*: converts the resource schema into an ontology schema, and resource content into ontology instances (generates classes, relations, instances and attributes);

(ii.iii) *Population*: transforms the content of the resource into instances of an existing ontology, as depicted in Fig. 7, where actual entities in this document ("Easyjet", "Portugal", "a denied boarding on 2011") will be class-instances of an ontology (as in RIC-ATPI ontology);

5 Conclusion: Discussion and Lessons Learned

This paper focuses on the *specificities* of NORs in the legal domain, and provides
guidelines of how some knowledge resources may be reuse and engineered following
both *MeLOn* and *NeOn* methodologies, to enable heterogeneous resources integration
within a legal ontology, as they are highly heterogeneous in their data model and
contents. We followed a text-based bottom-up approach to ontology building, in which
conceptual and terminological knowledge is contained in legal document collections
[22], demanding an expert-based analysis.

While reusing and engineering NORs, some problems occurred whilst other lessons
were learned and are hereby described and discussed. We argue that this
reuse/reengineering process should not only rely on a legal positivistic path of selecting
and interpreting norms, for legal knowledge can be used for an amplitude of situated
contexts and cases; thus, *"the representation of meaning becomes a multi-faceted web
of interactions between different components (methods, data, tools, places, time,
people, organizations, users, and so forth) and importantly, this meaning is in flux"*.
Hence, *"reordering of subjects and objects, or to truncate concepts to be simply
attributes can render current representations of knowledge in triple form rather
cumbersome to use"* [21].

Verification by domain experts was complex; mainly a presentation of drafts was
made possible. But tools as Grafoo[15] are claimed to be more intuitive for a non
ontologist; it is an open source tool that can be used to present the classes, properties
and restrictions within OWL ontologies, or sub-sections thereof, as easy-to-understand
diagrams. No specific management of the knowledge sources was followed, for they
were not integrated into an information system (without a version, type, etc.) due to the
fact that they were too many to be managed (legislation, case law, doctrine, etc.) and
also considering the absence of guidelines. Much as there is criteria to add an entity or
not to an ontology (through competency questions), there is no fixed criteria to manage
legal resources. Therefore we denote that the management of the resources requires a
breed of tools to store and manage them. We posit there was a limited reproducibility of
the processes: the annotation of documents (PDFs etc.) with standard tools does not
keep track of authorship, timestamp, etc. We are cognizant that annotations tools are
necessary for commenting on NORs as a preliminary stage before building the
ontology. Nevertheless, LIME editor[16] aims to annotate and connect the classes to the
texts. In order to make explicit the hidden semantics of the resource constituents, we
noticed the need of a domain expert. Furthermore, we used ad-hoc object properties of
the resource components extracted directly from the text. We acknowledge the
guidelines from *MeLOn* methodology to make explicit the hidden semantics in the
relations of the NOR terminology, which depend mostly on domain experts and
interpretation. We observed the need of clear criteria to select or disregard NOR
resources from the legal domain. By adapting *NeOn* methodology, we have decided for
three criteria: consensus, coverage and relevance dimensions (domain, situational,

---

[15] S. Peroni, "Grafoo," http://www.essepuntato.it/graffoo/.

[16] LIME editor, http://sinatra.cirsfid.unibo.it/demo-akn/.

cognitive), but others could be accustomed. Reengineering transformation approaches for legal text are required regarding TBox transformation, ABox transformation, Population, forward engineering, and reverse engineering.

We plan deepening on the epistemic grounding of this position paper in the immediate future, taking into account cooperative expert sharing in knowledge-acquisition and a user based evaluation on using the methods for reusing and reengineering NORs into ontologies to gain evidence on whether the usage of such granular guidelines leads to users being able to design ontologies faster and/or better quality standards [18, 19]. It is noteworthy that *"resources do not explicitly carry knowledge with them of how they were made, nor of how they should be understood, or used. Yet such knowledge is often vital to would-be consumers"* [21], hence, we envision a way to describe some of them in a machine-readable so that users can make informed decisions about the suitability of resources for their tasks and locate them. We aim to use Akoma Ntoso standard [23] to provide semantic information on top of selected legal text.

References

1. Suárez-Figueroa, M.C., Gómez-Pérez, A., Motta, E., Gangemi, A. (eds.): Ontology Engineering in a Networked World. Springer, Dordrecht (2012). https://doi.org/10.1007/978-3-642-24794-1

2. Breuker, J., Valente, A., Winkels, R.: Use and reuse of legal ontologies in knowledge engineering and information management. In: Benjamins, V.R., Casanovas, P., Breuker, J., Gangemi, A. (eds.) Law and the Semantic Web. LNCS (LNAI), vol. 3369, pp. 36–64. Springer, Heidelberg (2005). https://doi.org/10.1007/978-3-540-32253-5_4

3. Gangemi, A., Sagri, M.-T., Tiscornia, D.: A constructive framework for legal ontologies. In: Benjamins, V.R., Casanovas, P., Breuker, J., Gangemi, A. (eds.) Law and the Semantic Web. LNCS (LNAI), vol. 3369, pp. 97–124. Springer, Heidelberg (2005). https://doi.org/10.1007/978-3-540-32253-5_7

4. Francesconi, E.: Semantic model for legal resources: Annotation and reasoning over normative provisions. Semant. Web Leg. Domain Semant. Web 7(3), 255–265 (2016)

5. Casanovas, P.: Semantic web regulatory models. Philos. Technol. 28(1), 33–55 (2015)

6. Mockus, M., Palmirani, M.: Legal ontology for open government data mashups, pp. 113–124 (2017). https://doi.org/10.1109/CeDEM.2017.25

7. van Opijnen, M., Santos, C.: On the concept of relevance in legal information retrieval. Artif. Intell. Law 2017(25), 65–87 (2017)

8. Villazón-Terrazas, B., Suárez-Figueroa, M.C., Gómez-Pérez, A.: A pattern-based method for re-engineering nonontological resources into ontologies. Int. J. Semant. Web Inf. Syst. 6(4), 27–63 (2010)

9. Villazon-Terrazas, B.M.: Method for reusing and re-engineering non-ontological resources for building ontologies. Ph.D. thesis, UPC (2012)

10. Suárez-Figueroa, M.-C., Gómez-Pérez, A., Fernández-López, M.: The NeOn methodology framework: a scenario-based methodology for ontology development. Appl. Ontol. 10, 107–145 (2015)

11.
Santos, C., Rodriguez-Doncel, V., Casanovas, P., van der Torre, L.: Modeling relevant legal information for consumer disputes. In: Kő, A., Francesconi, E. (eds.) EGOVIS 2016. LNCS, vol. 9831, pp. 150–165. Springer, Cham (2016). https://doi.org/10.1007/978-3-319-44159-7_11

12. Gianmaria, A., Boella, G., et al.: European legal taxonomy syllabus: a multi-lingual, multi-level ontology framework to untangle the web of European legal terminology. Appl. Ontol. **11**(4), 325–375 (2017)

13. De Hert, P., Papakonstantinou, V.: The proposed data protection regulation replacing directive 95/46/EC: a sound system for the protection of individuals. Comput. Law Secur. Rev. **28**(2), 130–142 (2012)

14. Hunter, D., Thomas, J.: Lego and the system of intellectual property, 1955–2015, 7 March 2016. SSRN: http://ssrn.com/abstract=2743140

15. Rahman, M.: Legal ontology for nexus: water, energy and food in EU regulations. Dissertation thesis, Alma Mater Studiorum Università di Bologna. Dottorato di ricerca in Law, science and technology, 28 Ciclo (2016)

16. Santos, C.: Ontologies for legal relevance and consumer complaints. A case study in the air transport passenger domain. Dissertation thesis, Alma Mater Studiorum Università di Bologna. Dottorato di ricerca in Law, science and technology, 29 Ciclo (2017)

17. van Opijnen, M.: A model for automated rating of case law. In: 2013 ICAIL, NY, pp. 140–149 (2013)

18. Ramakrishna, S., Górski, Ł., Paschke, A.: A dialogue between a lawyer and computer scientist: the evaluation of knowledge transformation from legal text to computer-readable format. Appl. Artif. Intell. **30**(3), 216–232 (2016)

19. Casanovas, P., Casellas, N., Tempich, C., Vrandečić, D., Benjamins, R.: OPJK and DILIGENT: ontology modeling in a distributed environment. Artif. Intell. Law **15**(2), 171–186 (2007)

20. McGuinness, D.: Ontologies come of age. In: Fensel, D., Hendler, J., Lieberman, H., Wahlster, W. (eds.) Spinning the Semantic Web: Bringing the World Wide Web to Its Full Potential. MIT Press, Cambridge (2003)

21. Gahegan, M., Luo, J., et al.: Comput. Geosci. **35**, 836–854 (2009)

22. Francesconi, E., Montemagni, S., Peters, W., Tiscornia, D.: Integrating a bottom–up and top–down methodology for building semantic resources for the multilingual legal domain. In: Francesconi, E., Montemagni, S., Peters, W., Tiscornia, D. (eds.) Semantic Processing of Legal Texts. LNCS (LNAI), vol. 6036, pp. 95–121. Springer, Heidelberg (2010). https://doi.org/10.1007/978-3-642-12837-0_6

23. Athan, T., et al.: OASIS LegalRuleML. In: Proceedings of the Fourteenth International Conference on Artificial Intelligence and Law. ACM (2013)

24. Barabucci, G., Cervone, L., Di Iorio, A., Palmirani, M., Peroni, S., Vitali, F.: Managing semantics in XML vocabularies: an experience in the legal and legislative domain. In: 2009 Proceedings of Balisage (2010)

Ontology Modeling for Criminal Law

Chiseung Soh📧, Seungtak Lim, Kihyun Hong,
and Young-Yik Rhim(📧)

Intellicon Meta Lab., Seoul 06136, Korea
{soh, stlim, kihyun.hong, ceo}@intellicon.co.kr

Abstract. In the continental law system, more attention is paid to judicial interpretation to judge legal facts or actions than judicial precedents. Therefore, in the continental legal system, it is appropriate to express the law itself with knowledge such as legal ontologies or logical rules. To construct legal ontologies and rule-based methods, legal analysis by collaboration between legal experts and knowledge engineers should be preceded. This paper proposes a general model for designing criminal law ontologies and rules. First, we introduce the super-domain ontology that contains the common characteristics of criminal law. Then, we explain the rule design method of criminal law and present the application of the anti-graft act in Korea as an example.

Keywords: Criminal law ontology · Legal ontology model · SWRL rules
Legal reasoning · Super domain ontology

1 Introduction

Artificial intelligence (AI) has been increasingly applied to researches and services in specialized areas such as law and medicine. Most recent AI applications utilizes data-driven machine learning methods. However, these approaches are not transparent AI methods and are therefore not suitable for legal applications. AI applications in the legal field are generally required to be logically explainable implementations. In other words, the legal AI systems need to provide clear logics about their inferences and conclusions for solving legal problems. Therefore, machine and human readable legal knowledge representation and logical structure-based approaches are preferable to implement legal AI applications. There were several approaches to build such AI systems: Generalization of legal information [1], semantic web technology [2], legal ontology and rule designs [3, 17].

This paper presents ontology-based legal knowledge representation and logic based legal rule design. Especially, this paper focuses on the construction of criminal law ontology. It introduces the super-domain ontology as a general-purpose criminal law ontology with commonality of criminal law. It also explains how to construct judgment rules using the features of general criminal law. In addition, the proposed ontology model is applied to the Korean anti-graft act, which is one of criminal law.

Section 2 introduces related works on legal ontology. Section 3 describes the background of this paper. This section deals with the legal system, characteristics of criminal law, and Korean anti-graft act. The Korean anti-graft act is described as an

© Springer Nature Switzerland AG 2018
U. Pagallo et al. (Eds.): AICOL VI-X 2015–2017, LNAI 10791, pp. 365–379, 2018.
https://doi.org/10.1007/978-3-030-00178-0_25

example of criminal law. Section 4 introduces a criminal law ontology design. This section firstly reviews existing researches on legal and criminal ontologies, and on recent developments for legal analysis systems and legal ontology learning. Then, it presents the main idea of this paper, which is the design of an ontology for criminal law. Section 5 describes the application process of the proposed design for the Korean anti-graft act. Finally, this paper concludes with a discussion of the proposed design concept in Sect. 6.

2 Related Works

Various studies have been conducted on the design and construction of crime ontologies [3–5]. As part of the e-Court European project[1], Breuker [3] introduced ontology construction and reusability for the Leibniz Research Institute for law (LRI) ontology and the domain ontology of the Dutch Criminal Act (OCL.NL). The LRI-Core ontology consists of two parts, which are a concept and legal key element ontologies. The concept ontology describes physical, mental and abstract concepts, and the legal key element ontology describes the legal case, legal action, legal person, etc. Bezzazi [4] developed an ontology to identify what article of criminal law is applied to a cybercrime. Each legal article is defined as description logic and crime cases are classified by the logic. Bak and Jedrzejek [5] suggested an ontology model of financial fraud. They constructed the concept-wise ontology with a modular ontology and invented an inference method with Web Ontology Language[2] (OWL) and Semantic Web Rule Language[3] (SWRL).

Many studies on rule-based legal argumentation have been conducted [6–8]. Gordon [6] showed the syntax of the Legal Knowledge Interchange Format (LKIF) rule language and argumentation-theoretic semantics which are developed in the European ESTRELLA project[4]. The rules for those legal arguments were roughly composed of the provisions of the German family law. Contissa [7] introduced the legal rule-based system based on the Italian Copyright law. This is a support system creating and deploying rule-based knowledge models Ontologies are suitable for modeling legal knowledge because these represent resource relationships with inferable expressions. Governatori [8] applied a rule-based approach to the business process field.

The legal ontology is made up of ontology design based on the accurate legal analysis. Especially, legal analysis needs to be reviewed by legal experts because it requires interpretation based on the meaning of the legal texts and the purpose of the law. Knowledge engineers have actively worked with legal experts to conduct researches on legal analysis, information extraction and ontology generation. Many researches are conducted to automatically analyze legal sentences and construct legal knowledge bases, which are tagging semantic annotation for legal sentences with NLP

---

[1] http://cordis.europa.eu/project/rcn/56906_en.html.

[2] https://www.w3.org/TR/2012/REC-owl2-primer-20121211/.

[3] https://www.w3.org/Submission/SWRL/.

[4] http://www.estrellaproject.org/.

tools [9, 10], extracting rules from legal sentences with text structure lightweight ontologies or NLP parser [11, 12], and generating ontology from legal documents using NLP and ontology learning tools [13–16].

3 Legal System and Criminal Law in Korea

3.1 The Differences Between Continental Law and Common Law

Legal systems around the world generally fall into one of two main categories: continental law (civil law) and common law systems. The main difference between the two systems is that the continental law systems are codified, whereas the common law is normally uncodified. The continental law system is based on the statutory law and the Pandekten-system[5], and the deficiency of the law is supplemented by the precedents. The common law system is based on the customary law and the common law, and the precedents play a pivotal role. However, in the modern age, even common law countries adopt the statutory law form as a new legal system. In addition, the precedents are becoming more important in the continental law system, and the difference between the legal systems is getting smaller.

The Korean legal system follows the German legal system, which is based on the Roman law; the system has a hierarchical structure of the Constitution, law, enforcement ordinance and enforcement rules. The inside of each law follows the Pandekten-system.

3.2 Characteristics of Criminal Law

Law Types. Law is categorized into several law types, i.e., civil law, criminal law, etc., according to its characteristics. Figure 1 shows law types and their subordinate statutes (acts). Criminal law is a law that regulates crime and punishment. It specifies which punishments are imposed. In contrast, civil law is a general law of private law that regulates the rights and obligations arising from the relations between private law actors such as private persons and private juristic persons. Administrative law determines acts on the institutions, organizations, authorities and mutual relations of administrative entities (national and public organizations, etc.). It is also the upper laws of those regulating the legal relationships between the public entity and persons.

Nondeterministic Structure. As shown in Fig. 2, criminal law is described as having a nondeterministic structure as abstractly covering various real facts. On the contrary, civil law follows a deterministic structure because its provisions are concrete and univocal. For example, an assault offense is defined as "A person who uses violence against another shall be punished by imprisonment for not more than two years, a fine not exceeding five million won, detention, or a minor fine". It is difficult to determine the constituent requirements (corpus-delicti) of "assault" in a unique sense. All forms

---

[5] Pandekten-system begins with the general principles, followed by separate provisions governing particular areas of law.

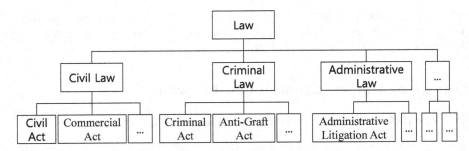

Fig. 1. Hierarchy of law and law types

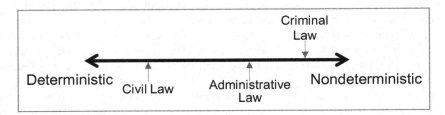

Fig. 2. Characteristics of law: deterministic vs nondeterministic

of tactics, such as sprinkling water, throwing objects, or wielding a bat, are considered "assault". Also, since the effect varies according to the type of "assault", "assault" acts as a categorical variable. In the case of bribery, it takes a continuous variable type constituent requirement (corpus-delicti), which varies depending on the amount of money received. Criminal law is similar to the abstracted legal requirement (corpus-delicti) and the triggered effect structure, but the premise of criminal ontology optimization is to analyze the nondeterministic structure and express it well by rules.

3.3   Korean Anti-graft Act

There are the Improper Solicitation and Graft Act[6] as an anti-corruption law in Korea, which is a part of criminal law. Traditionally, the sanctions for the prevention of corruption are governed mainly by bribery in criminal law. However, the effectiveness has been limited. Therefore, the Improper Solicitation and Graft Act was enacted in accordance with OECD Anti-Bribery Convention[7] and the precedents of anti-corruption legislation in some countries shown in Table 1.

The Improper Solicitation and Graft Act is divided into the action of improper solicitation and the action of graft. The sanctions against improper solicitation were

---

[6] http://elaw.klri.re.kr/kor_service/lawView.do?hseq=39287&lang=ENG.

[7] http://www.oecd.org/corruption/oecdantibriberyconvention.htm.

Table 1. An anti-graft act of other countries

Country or organization	Act title
OECD	Anti-Bribery Convention
USA	Foreign Corrupt Practices Act[a]
USA	Bribery, Graft, and Conflict of Interest Act[b]
UK	Bribery Act[c]
Singapore	Prevention of Corrupt Act[d]
Singapore	Corruption Confiscation of Benefits Act[e]

[a]https://www.justice.gov/criminal-fraud/foreign-corrupt-practices-act.
[b]http://law.justia.com/codes/us/2011/title-18/part-i/chapter-11.
[c]http://www.legislation.gov.uk/ukpga/2010/23/contents.
[d]search "Prevention of Corrupt Act" at http://statutes.agc.gov.sg/.
[e]search "CONFISCATION OF BENEFITS" at http://statutes.agc.gov.sg/.

intended to eradicate corrupt practices and to prohibit public officials from improper solicitation by enabling criminal sanctions beyond a simple code of ethics.

The penalty for graft was introduced to allow criminal punishment if a public official receives a certain amount of money or entertainment even unintentionally. A public official receives more than 1,000,000 KRW[8] in money or entertainment from a person who is not directly related to duties of the public official, he or she can be punished even though there is no intention for an immediate favor. If the person is directly related to duties of the public official, penalties are imposed even if the price is less than 1,000,000 KRW regardless of whether it is intending the return.

4 Approach of Criminal Law Ontology

4.1 Criminal Law Ontology Construction

The basic methodology of ontology design is to distinguish between a common part and a specific part of target design object. The common part is the set of the concepts shared by a domain or a sub-domain. Therefore, modularization and reuse of this part is an effective way to design an ontology. On the other hand, specific parts refer to domain-specific concepts. The LRI-core [3] and LKIF [17] ontologies are implemented in accordance with the basic design methodology. This paper proposes an ontology design that extends the LRI and LKIF ontology design by defining the common part of criminal law as a super domain. As shown in Fig. 3, the proposed design has the common and specific parts. Briefly, upper ontology, legal core ontology, and criminal ontology as super domains are common parts and legal domain ontologies are specific parts.

The upper ontology is independent of the legal domain and refers to the most basic concept. This includes abstract, physical, and mental concepts. Legal core ontology

---

[8] KRW is the Korean currency.

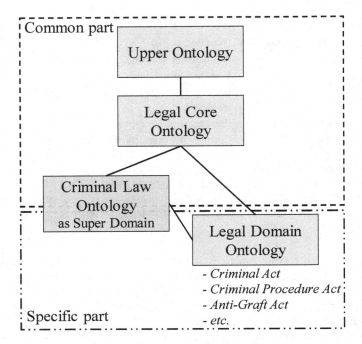

Fig. 3. A structure of legal ontology

consists of the basic elements of the law and contains the common concept of all laws. For example, legal act, legal situation, etc. Criminal law ontology is composed of common elements of all sub-laws (acts) of criminal law, which is called the super-domain. This includes basic elements of criminal law such as crime, punishment, and so on. This legal domain ontology, which reuses the elements of criminal law ontology, is built on laws belonging to criminal law. Criminal act, criminal procedure act, and the anti-graft act are implemented.

The design of a legal ontology is a representation of a relationship among the elements (such as a legal object, legal actions, legal effects, etc.) required for legal argument, the hierarchical structure between concepts, and concept description. Furthermore, the ontologies distinguish between common and specific parts to facilitate reuse and expansion of the knowledge base.

4.2   Judgment Rules of Criminal Law

This section describes the design process of judgment rules created by legal experts and ontologists. Because criminal law follows nondeterministic structure, it is easier to design judgment rules than other laws.

Tables 2 and 3 show the legal codes for private document counterfeit in some countries. The underlined passages in the articles indicate corpus-delicti and effects. The counterfeiting laws in each country are similar.

Figure 4 shows a diagram for corpus-delicti (constituent requirements) of the Article 231 of Korean Criminal Act[9] on counterfeiting. The Greek alphabets in Fig. 4 indicate the related terms of the articles in Table 2 and 3, and the numbers *1, 2, 3* are for the additional elements of 'counterfeiting', which are derived from legal theories and precedents.

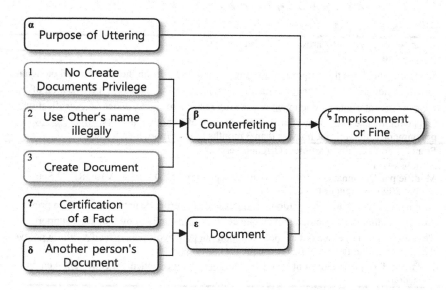

Fig. 4. A Diagram of constituent requirements and effects of counterfeiting in Korea

Table 2. Article on counterfeiting in Korea

Original version
제 231 조 (사 문서 등의 위조·변조) ^α 행사할 목적으로 권리·의무 또는 ^γ 사실 증명에 관한 ^δ 타인의 ^ε 문서 또는 도화를 ^β 위조 또는 변조한 자는 ^ζ 5 년 이하의 징역 또는 1 천만원 이하의 벌금에 처한다.

English version
Article 231 (Counterfeit or Alteration of Private Document, etc.) A person who, ^α for the purpose of uttering, ^β counterfeits or alters ^δ another person's ^ε document or drawing which pertains to right, duty, or a ^γ certification of a fact by assuming the capacity of another person, shall be punished by ^ζ imprisonment for not more than five years, or a fine not exceeding ten million won.

---

[9] http://elaw.klri.re.kr/kor_service/lawView.do?hseq=38891&lang=ENG.

Table 3. Articles on counterfeiting in some countries

Japanese' counterfeiting article – Original version

第百五十九条 $^\alpha$ 行使の目的で、$^\delta$ 他人の印章若しくは署名を使用して権利、 義務若しくは $^\gamma$ 事実証明に関する $^\varepsilon$ 文書若しくは図画を $^\beta$ 偽造し、又は偽造した他人の印章若しくは署名を使用して権利、義務若しくは事実証明に関 する文書若しくは図画を偽造した者は、$^\zeta$ 三月以上五年以下の懲役に処する。

Japanese' counterfeiting article – English version

Article 159

A person who, $^\alpha$ for the purpose of uttering, $^\beta$ counterfeits, with the use of a seal or signature of $^\delta$ another, a $^\varepsilon$ document or drawing relating to rights, duties or $^\gamma$ certification of facts or $^\beta$ counterfeits a $^\varepsilon$ document or drawing relating to rights, duties or $^\gamma$ certification of facts with the use of a counterfeit seal or signature of $^\delta$ another, shall be $^\zeta$ punished by imprisonment with work for not less than 3 months but not more than 5 years.

French's counterfeiting article – Original version

Article 441-1

Modifié par Ordonnance n°2000-916 du 19 septembre 2000 - art. 3 (V) JORF 22 Septembre 2000 en vigueur le 1er janvier 2002

$^\beta$ Constitue un faux toute altération frauduleuse de la vérité, de nature à causer un préjudice et accomplie par quelque moyen que ce soit, $^\varepsilon$ dans un écrit ou tout autre support d'expression de la pensée qui a $^\alpha$ pour objet ou qui peut avoir pour effet d'établir la preuve d'un droit ou d'un fait ayant des conséquences juridiques.

Le faux et l'usage de faux sont $^\zeta$ punis de trois ans d'emprisonnement et de 45000 euros d'amende.

French's counterfeiting article – English version

ARTICLE 441-1

(Ordinance no. 2000-916 of 19 September 2000 Article 3 Official Journal of 22 September 2000 in force 1 January 2002)

Forgery consists of $^\beta$ any fraudulent alteration of the truth liable to cause harm and made by any means in a $^\varepsilon$ document or other medium of expression of which the object is, or $^\alpha$ effect may be, to provide evidence of a right or of a situation carrying legal consequences.

Forgery and the use of forgeries is punished by $^\zeta$ three years' imprisonment and a fine of €45,000.

German counterfeiting article – Original version

§ 267 Urkundenfälschung

(1) Wer zur $^\alpha$ Täuschung im Rechtsverkehr $^{\beta,\,\varepsilon}$ eine unechte Urkunde herstellt, eine echte Urkunde verfälscht oder eine unechte oder verfälschte Urkunde gebraucht, wird mit $^\zeta$ Freiheitsstrafe bis zu fünf Jahren oder mit Geldstrafe bestraft.
etc.

German counterfeiting article – English version

Section 267 Forgery

(1) Whosoever $^\alpha$ for the purpose of deception in legal commerce $^{\beta,\,\varepsilon}$ produces a counterfeit document, falsifies a genuine document or uses a counterfeit or a falsified document, shall be liable to $^\zeta$ imprisonment not exceeding five years or a fine.
etc.

The counterfeiting action in Fig. 4 can be described using SWRL expression as follows:

$$hasSubject(?action, ?x) \wedge Person(?x) \wedge hasprivilege(?x, false)$$
$$\wedge isIllegalUseOtherName(?x, true)$$
$$\wedge createDocument(?x, true) \rightarrow Counterfeiting(?action)$$

The subject of the document forgery, that is, the person who forged the document becomes a principal offender of this crime. The SWRL of the logic is expressed as follows:

$$Counterfeiting(?action) \wedge Person(?x) \wedge hasSubject(?action, ?x)$$
$$\wedge hasObject(?action, ?document)$$
$$\wedge hasPurpose(?action, ?purpose)$$
$$\rightarrow isprincipalOffender(?action, ?x)$$

For example, in the case that nurse B wrote a false diagnosis in the name of doctor C for friend A, nurse B did not qualify to write the diagnosis and he or she made a false diagnosis by stealing the doctor's name. Nurse B becomes a principal offender of this crime. As shown in the case of document counterfeiting, legal arguments consist of corpus-delicti. These forms of argument are identical in all laws, especially criminal law.

5   Application to Anti-graft Act

This chapter presents an application of the proposed criminal law ontology to anti-graft act, which is one of criminal law. It also introduces the rules designed by analyzing the conditional articles of this Act.

5.1   Legal Domain Ontology Construction

The anti-graft act is a sub-law of criminal law. Therefore, the anti-graft act ontology reuses the elements of criminal law ontology and defines the elements used only in this law. Figure 5 shows the anti-graft act ontology. The lower layers are components of the anti-graft act ontology, which are constructed by reusing the elements of the upper, legal-core, criminal law ontology as super domains.

Crime or Penalty Action concept (same as class of ontology) in criminal law ontology is an upper concept of Improper Solicitation Action and Graft Action in the anti-graft act. Public Official indicates a subject of Legal Action in the anti-graft act and is a lower concept of Legal Person. In addition, Case Artifact is applied to express an object for requisites of Legal Action such as in the form of food and drink, congratulatory or condolence money, gift, etc. Case Artifact such as a gift can have a value that used in the numerical condition. Legal Case (situation) represents a set of various actions, for example, a combination action that a public official receives gifts and is treated to a meal simultaneously. In the anti-graft act ontology, principal entities are an

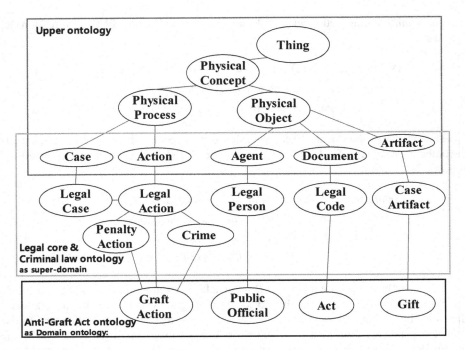

Fig. 5. Layers of ontologies illustrated by relations between some typical concepts

action, a subject, an object, and a value of the object. And a variety of rules can be expressed by the combination of these entities.

Figure 6 briefly expresses a hierarchical structure of Action Classes. The *ReceivingGift* class is an action that has at least one person with *hasReceiver* and *hasProvider* and at least one Gift with *hasObject*.

$$ReceivingGift \equiv Action \land \exists\, hasProvider.Person\land$$
$$\exists hasReceiver.Person \land \exists hasObjectGift$$

A *hasReceiver* or *hasProvider* is a sub predicate of *hasSubject*, and the actions that are restricted by this act are two subjects, the person giving (or asking) and the person receiving (or listening to) a something (or the request).

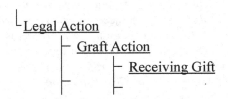

Fig. 6. A brief hierarchy of graft action class

5.2   Rules on Anti-graft Act Domain Ontology

The Korean anti-graft act has two main parts, which are the improper solicitation and graft parts. And the act has an additional section, which regulates external lectures of public officials. Furthermore, it describes various computational cases with numerical limitation. Therefore, numerical calculation rules are needed. As shown Table 4, this law allows for certain activities (such as giving food, general gifts, gifts for wedding and funerals) to be less than a certain amount.

Table 4. Acceptable limits for foods, general gifts, and weddings & funerals gifts (Article 17 of the Enforcement Decree)

Graft action	Details	Limited money
Food	Meals, dessert, alcoholic beverages, drink, etc. which the provider and public officials, etc. share	KRW 30,000
General gifts	Money and other valuables except for food	KRW 50,000
Gifts for weddings and funerals	Congratulatory or condolence money, flowers or other equivalents	KRW 100,000

When other sub-laws of criminal law require numerical calculation rules for money and age, the rules must be designed to that law. However, the most important thing in any rule design is accurate legal analysis. The numbers of rules in the anti-graft act ontology are given in Table 5.

Table 5. Number of SWRL rule per category

Category	# of SWRL rule
Graft	174
Improper solicitation	7
External lecture	9
Graft-numerical calculation	38
Total	228

Some of the designed rules for the improper solicitation action and the graft action are shown in Table 6. The first rule describes the case that a stakeholder improperly solicits a public official through a third party; it is against the anti-graft act without an exception. In this situation, the stakeholder is charged a fine (up to 10,000,000 KRW) for negligence, and disciplinary and criminal punishments (not more than two years or an administrative fine not exceeding 20,000,000 KRW) are imposed on the public official.

Table 6. The SWRL rule examples in the anti-graft act ontology

An example of the improper solicitation action rule

$Action(?a) \wedge IllegalSolicitation(?is) \wedge hasIllegalSolicitation(?a,?is)$
$\wedge\ hasSubject(?a,?p2) \wedge hasObject(?a,?p1)$
$\wedge\ through(?a,?p3) \wedge Person(?p3) \wedge PublicOfficial(?p1)$
$\wedge\ NonPublicOfficial(?p2) \wedge connected(?p1,?p3)$
$\wedge\ connected(?p2,?p3)$
$\rightarrow\ PenaltyAction(?a)$
$\wedge\ hasDisciplinary(?p1, public\ official\ disciplinary)$
$\wedge\ hasPenalty(?p1, article_{22\_2}\ penalty)$
$\wedge\ hasMaxFine(?p2, 10,000,000\ )$

An example of the graft action rule

$ReceivingGifts(?a) \wedge hasProvider(?a,?p) \wedge hasReceiver(?a,?r)$
$\wedge\ PublicOfficial(?r) \wedge hasDutyRelation(?p,?r)$
$\wedge\ hasObject(?a,?gift) \wedge hasValue(?gift,?v)$
$\wedge\ greaterThan(?v,\ 50,000)$
$\rightarrow\ PenaltyAction(?a)$
$\wedge\ hasDisciplinary(?r, public\ official\ disciplinary)$
$\wedge\ hasPenalty(?p, article_{22\_1}\ penalty)$
$\wedge\ hasMinFine(?r,?v \times 2\ ) \wedge hasMaxFine(?r,?v \times 5)$

The second rule explains the graft-numerical calculator rule. When a public official receives a present exceeding 50,000 KRW from a private person, a disciplinary punishment and a fine (2 to 5 times the price of the present) are imposed on the public official and the private person receives a criminal punishment (not more than three years or an administrative fine not exceeding 30,000,000 KRW).

Figure 7 describes a fictive example to demonstrate the graft-numerical calculation. A public official "Person A" is instantiated as a subject for a gift action as a receiver. The Receiving-Gifts has another subject "Person B" as a provider and has a gift object with a value of more than 60,000 KRW. The receiver "Person A" has a relation to the provider "Person B" regarding his or her duties. In this example, it is inferred that the gift action is a penalty action when the rule for the graft-numerical calculation is applied.

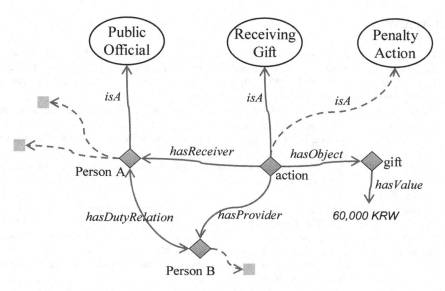

Fig. 7. Reasoning on the anti-graft act ontology

6 Conclusion and Future Work

This paper has presented ontology design and make decision rules for criminal law. These ontologies and rules were created for the legal argument, which should be demonstrated on a clear logical basis. This paper proposed the design of the super-domain ontology based criminal law ontology, which is composed of common elements of the laws in criminal law category. Criminal law ontology was added to the existing European law ontology model (LKIF). This extended legal ontology model enables to reuse the common characteristics of criminal law when construct domain ontologies of the laws in criminal law. Also, this paper introduced the judgment rules of criminal law, which were constructed with the general characteristics of criminal law. Finally, this paper applied the proposed ontology structure and judgment rules to Korea's the anti-graft act, which is one of criminal law.

As a future work, we will extend the usage of the super-domain ontology concept to other law types such as civil law, administrative law, industrial law, customs law, etc. To apply the super-domain concept, careful analysis is required to extract common features of the target law as presented in criminal law ontology design. We also research on ontology learning, ontology population, and automatic judgment rule design to construct domain or application ontology auto or semi automatically from legal texts.

References

1. Benjamins, V.Richard, Casanovas, P., Breuker, J., Gangemi, A.: Law and the semantic web, an introduction. In: Benjamins, V.Richard, Casanovas, P., Breuker, J., Gangemi, A. (eds.) Law and the Semantic Web. LNCS (LNAI), vol. 3369, pp. 1–17. Springer, Heidelberg (2005). https://doi.org/10.1007/978-3-540-32253-5_1
2. Aguiló-Regla, J.: Introduction: legal informatics and the conceptions of the law. In: Benjamins, V.Richard, Casanovas, P., Breuker, J., Gangemi, A. (eds.) Law and the Semantic Web. LNCS (LNAI), vol. 3369, pp. 18–24. Springer, Heidelberg (2005). https://doi.org/10.1007/978-3-540-32253-5_2
3. Breuker, J.: The construction and use of ontologies of criminal law in the eCourt European project. In: Proceedings of Means of Electronic Communication in Court Administration, pp. 15–40 (2003)
4. Bezzazi, E.-H.: Building an ontology that helps identify criminal law articles that apply to a cybercrime case. In: ICSOFT (PL/DPS/KE/MUSE), pp. 179–185. INSTICC Press (2009)
5. Bak, J., Jedrzejek, C.: Application of an ontology-based model to a selected fraudulent disbursement economic crime. In: Casanovas, P., Pagallo, U., Sartor, G., Ajani, G. (eds.) AICOL -2009. LNCS (LNAI), vol. 6237, pp. 113–132. Springer, Heidelberg (2010). https://doi.org/10.1007/978-3-642-16524-5_8
6. Gordon, T.F.: Constructing legal arguments with rules in the legal knowledge interchange format (LKIF). In: Casanovas, P., Sartor, G., Casellas, N., Rubino, R. (eds.) Computable Models of the Law. LNCS (LNAI), vol. 4884, pp. 162–184. Springer, Heidelberg (2008). https://doi.org/10.1007/978-3-540-85569-9_11
7. Contissa, G.: Rulebase Technology and Legal Knowledge Representation. In: Casanovas, P., Sartor, G., Casellas, N., Rubino, R. (eds.) Computable Models of the Law. LNCS (LNAI), vol. 4884, pp. 254–262. Springer, Heidelberg (2008). https://doi.org/10.1007/978-3-540-85569-9_16
8. Governatori, G., Hashmi, M., Lam, H.-P., Villata, S., Palmirani, M.: Semantic business process regulatory compliance checking using LegalRuleML. In: Blomqvist, E., Ciancarini, P., Poggi, F., Vitali, F. (eds.) EKAW 2016. LNCS (LNAI), vol. 10024, pp. 746–761. Springer, Cham (2016). https://doi.org/10.1007/978-3-319-49004-5_48
9. Biagioli, C., Francesconi, E., Passerini, A., Montemagni, S., Soria, C.: Automatic semantics extraction in law documents. In: Proceedings of the 10th International Conference on Artificial Intelligence and Law, pp. 133–140. ACM, New York (2005)
10. Soria, C., Bartolini, R., Lenci, A., Montemagni, S., Pirrelli, V.: Automatic extraction of semantics in law documents. In: Proceedings of the V Legislative XML Workshop, pp. 253–266 (2007)
11. Dragoni, M., Governatori, G., Villata, S.: Automated rules generation from natural language legal texts. In: Workshop on Automated Detection, Extraction and Analysis of Semantic Information in Legal Texts, San Diego, USA, pp. 1–6 (2015)
12. Dragoni, M., Villata, S., Rizzi, W., Governatori, G.: Combining NLP approaches for rule extraction from legal documents. In: Proceedings of the Workshop on 'MIning and REasoning with Legal texts' collocated at the 29th International Conference on Legal Knowledge and Information Systems (2016)
13. Saias, J., Quaresma, P.: A methodology to create legal ontologies in a logic programming information retrieval system. In: Benjamins, V.R., Casanovas, P., Breuker, J., Gangemi, A. (eds.) Law and the Semantic Web. LNCS (LNAI), vol. 3369, pp. 185–200. Springer, Heidelberg (2005). https://doi.org/10.1007/978-3-540-32253-5_12

14. Lenci, A., Montemagni, S., Pirrelli, V., Venturi, G.: NLP-based ontology learning from legal texts. a case study. In: LOAIT, pp. 113–129. CEUR-WS.org (2008)
15. Völker, J., Fernandez Langa, S., Sure, Y.: Supporting the construction of Spanish legal ontologies with Text2Onto. In: Casanovas, P., Sartor, G., Casellas, N., Rubino, R. (eds.) Computable Models of the Law. LNCS (LNAI), vol. 4884, pp. 105–112. Springer, Heidelberg (2008). https://doi.org/10.1007/978-3-540-85569-9_7
16. Saias, J., Quaresma, P.: Using NLP techniques to create legal ontologies in a logic programming based web information retrieval system (2003)
17. Hoekstra, R., Breuker, J., Di Bello, M., Boer, A., et al.: The LKIF core ontology of basic legal concepts. In: LOAIT, pp. 43–63 (2007)

ContrattiPubblici.org, a Semantic Knowledge Graph on Public Procurement Information

Giuseppe Futia[1(✉)], Federico Morando[2], Alessio Melandri[2], Lorenzo Canova[1], and Francesco Ruggiero[1]

[1] Department of Control and Computer Engineering,
Nexa Center for Internet and Society, Politecnico di Torino, Turin, Italy
{giuseppe.futia,lorenzo.canova,francesco.ruggiero}@polito.it
[2] Synapta Srl, Turin, Italy
{federico.morando,alessio.melandri}@synapta.it,
https://nexa.polito.it, https://synapta.it/

Abstract. The Italian anti-corruption Act (law n. 190/2012) requires all public administrations to spread procurement information as open data. Each body is obliged to yearly release standardized XML files, on its public website, containing data that describes all issued public contracts. Though this information is currently available on a machine-readable format, the data is fragmented and published in different files on different websites, without a unified and human-readable view of the information. The ContrattiPubblici.org project aims at developing a semantic knowledge graph based on linked data principles in order to overcome the fragmentation of existent datasets, to allow easy analysis, and to enable the reuse of information. The objectives are to increase public awareness about public spending, to improve transparency on the public procurement chain, and to help companies to retrieve useful knowledge for their business activities.

Keywords: Public procurement · Linked data · Knowledge graph

1 Introduction

In recent years the amount and variety of open data released by public bodies has been factually growing[1], simultaneously with the increase of political awareness on the topic[2]. Public Sector Information (PSI)[3], in the form of open

---

[1] See the Tracking the state of open government data report available at: http://index.okfn.org/. Last visited July 2016.

[2] See national roadmaps and technical guidelines, as well the revised of the EU Directive on Public Sector Information reuse in 2013 guidelines.

[3] Public Sector Information includes "any content whatever its medium (written on paper or stored in electronic form or as a sound, visual or audiovisual recording)" when produced by a public sector body within its mandate. See more details on Directive 2003/98/EC: http://eur-lex.europa.eu/LexUriServ/LexUriServ.do?uri=OJ:L:2003:345:0090:0096:EN:PDF.

© Springer Nature Switzerland AG 2018
U. Pagallo et al. (Eds.): AICOL VI–X 2015–2017, LNAI 10791, pp. 380–393, 2018.
https://doi.org/10.1007/978-3-030-00178-0_26

data, leads to a noticeable value for diverse actors and for different purposes, from transparency on public spending to useful knowledge for business activities. Open data is therefore a toolbox to improve relationships among governments, citizens and companies by directly enabling informed decisions. Nevertheless, access and reuse of data to build useful knowledge is extremely limited, mainly because of the fragmentation in different data sources and websites, which currently characterizes the publication of PSI.

As defined by a World Wide Web Consortium (W3C) issue proposed by Berners Lee [2] on the publication of government data, linked data principles can be a modular and scalable solution to overthrow the fragmentation of information: "Linked data can be combined (mashed-up) with any other piece of linked data. For example, government data on health care expenditures for a given geographical area can be combined with other data about the characteristics of the population of that region in order to assess effectiveness of the government programs. No advance planning is required to integrate these data sources as long as they both use linked data standards." As stressed by Berners Lee, according to these precepts linked data serves to: (1) increase citizen awareness of government functions to enable greater accountability; (2) contribute valuable information about the world; and (3) enable the government, the country, and the world to function more efficiently.

Public procurement is an area of the PSI that could largely benefit from linked data technologies. As argued by Svátek [10], an interesting aspect of public contracts from the point of view of linked data is the fact that "they unify two different spheres: that of *public* needs and that of *commercial* offers. They thus represent an ideal meeting place for data models, methodologies and information sources that have been (often) independently designed within the two sectors." At the same time, linked data is beneficial in the public contracts domain since it gives ample space for applying diverse methods of data analytics, performing complex alignments of entities in a knowledge graph and developing data driven applications.

The contribution is structured as follows. Section 2 presents related works in the field of public procurement and spending information published according to linked data principles. Section 3 describes the Italian context and gives an overall view of public procurement data spread by public sector bodies. Section 4 illustrates the data processing pipeline to improve the quality of data source and to create the ContrattiPubblici.org knowledge graph. Section 5 shows results and potential use of the information structured in the graph. The last section describes conclusions and future advancements of the work.

2   Related Works

In this section, we report contributions in which public procurement and spending data is transformed and published as knowledge graphs, following the linked data principles.

Public procurement domain has already been addressed by several works and projects developed in the linked data field. One of the most notable is the LOD2 project, since it systematically addressed many phases of procurement linked data processing [10]. Such project exploits the Public Procurement Ontology PPROC[4].

There are several other initiatives: the TWC Data-Gov Corpus [4], Public-spending.gr [8], The FTS (Financial Transparency System) project [7], Linked Spending [6], LOTED [11] and MOLDEAS [1].

In particular, the TWC Data-Gov Corpus gathers linked government data on US financial transactions from the Data.gov project[5]. This project exploits a semantic-based approach, in order to incrementally generate data, supporting low-cost and extensible publishing processes, and adopting technologies to incrementally enhance such data via crowdsourcing. Publicspending.gr has the objective of interconnecting and visualizing Greek public expenditure with linked data to promote clarity and increase citizen awareness through easily-consumed visualization diagrams. The FTS (Financial Transparency System) project of the European Commission contains information about grants for EU projects starting from 2007 to 2011, and publishes such data according to the RDF[6] data model. Exploring such dataset, users are able to get an overview on EU funding, including data on beneficiaries as well as the amount and type of expenditure. Linked Spending is a project for the RDF conversion of data published by the OpenSpending.org, an open platform that releases public finance information from governments around the world. The project uses the RDF DataCube vocabulary[7] to model data in order to represent multidimensional statistical observations. LOTED[8] is focused on extracting data from procurement acts, aggregating it over a SPARQL[9] endpoint. Finally, MOLDEAS, between the other things, presents some methods to expand user queries to retrieve public procurement notices in the e-Procurement sector using linked open data.

3   Context and Data Source

The Italian Legislative Decree n. 33/2013 (DL33/2013) of March 14th, 2013[10] re-ordered obligations of disclosure, transparency and dissemination of information by public administrations. According to specific requirements defined by the decree (clause no.9 - DL33/2013), each body is required to create a specific section on its website called "Amministrazione Trasparente" (Transparent

---

[4] More details on Public Procurement Ontology PPROC available at: http://contsem. unizar.es/def/sector-publico/pproc.html.

[5] Data.gov project website: https://www.data.gov/.

[6] RDF (Resource Description Framework) is a standard model for data interchange on the Web. It represents a common format to achieve and create linked data.

[7] DataCube vocabulary information: https://www.w3.org/TR/vocab-data-cube/.

[8] LOTED project website: http://www.loted.eu/.

[9] SPARQL (SPARQL Protocol and RDF Query Language) is a semantic query language for databases, able to retrieve and manipulate data stored in RDF format.

[10] http://www.decretotrasparenza.it/wp-content/uploads/2013/04/D.Lgs_.-n.-332013.pdf. Last visit on July 2017.

Administration). In this section, public administrations provide details related to public procurement, with particular emphasis on procedures for the award and execution of public works, services and supplies (clause no. 37 - DL33/2013). Such data is published on the basis of a precise XML Schema Definition[11] (XSD) provided by *ANAC - Autorità Nazionale Anticorruzione* (the Italian National Anti-Corruption Authority)[12], which has supervisory duties. After the publication on their websites, administrations transmit information on public contracts, in a digital format, to ANAC. ANAC then performs a preliminary check and releases an index file containing details related to the availability of data[13].

Public bodies can publish and transmit to ANAC two types of XML files. The first type contains the actual data on contracts until the publication date (January 31st of each year). As mentioned before, in order to facilitate the consistency of publications and the comparison of information, the structure of the document is defined by a precise XSD Schema[14]. The main structure of the XML file includes a section with the metadata of the dataset, reported in Fig. 1, and a section containing multiple contracts. The metadata section lists diverse information including the first publication date and the last dataset update, the business name of the public body that spreads the dataset, the url of the dataset and the license. The section containing data on contracts includes: the identification code of the tender notice (CIG that stands for Codice Identificativo Gara), the description of the tender identified by the CIG, the procedure type for the selection of the contractor, the identification code (VAT number) and the business name of bidders (tender participants), the identification code and the business name of the tender notice beneficiary, the award amount, the amount paid, the date of commencement and completion of works (for more details of each field see Figs. 2 and 3). In Sect. 3.2 we describe the ontology used to map those fields in the linked data domain to build the semantic knowledge graph of ContrattiPubblici.org.

The second type of XML is an index that collects links to other XML files containing actual public procurement data (Fig. 4)[15]. This data is available in machine-readable format according to a well-defined schema; a semantic layer to interconnect such data is necessary for the assessment of transparency, it is effective to raise awareness about public spending, and to provide useful information for enterprises.

---

[11] XSD is a W3C recommendation that specifies how to formally describe an XML document.

[12] http://www.anticorruzione.it/.

[13] The index is available at https://dati.anticorruzione.it/#/l190, clicking on the "Esporta" (Export) button.

[14] The full representation of the XSD schema is available at http://dati.anticorruzione.it/schema/datasetAppaltiL190.xsd.

[15] A more clear representation of the XSD schema is available at http://dati.anticorruzione.it/schema/datasetIndiceAppaltiL190.xsd.

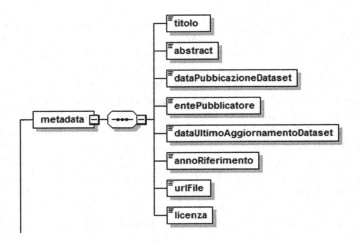

Fig. 1. XSD Schema of metadata

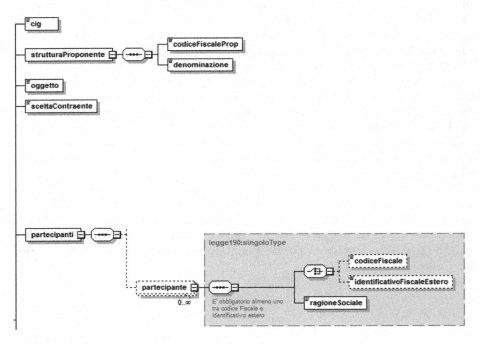

Fig. 2. XSD Schema of public procurement data - Part 1

3.1   Data Quality Issues

The quality of public contracts data is one of the most important issues to be tackled in order to reduce fragmentation and build a semantic knowledge graph.

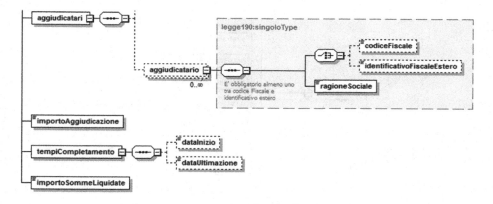

Fig. 3. XSD Schema of public procurement data - Part 2

Let's consider, for example, a company that has participated in two calls for tender proposed by two different bodies. VAT number and business name of this company reported in the two XML files should be identical. However, some data errors may occur due to management processes and software: this prevents to generate a unique entity (the company itself) within the knowledge graph. For example, a VAT number can present a wrong character (*accuracy* issue), or even the field itself could be absent (*completeness* issue)[16]. Analyzing the VAT number issues, we have observed that 62,466 contracts (1.08% of the total) present accuracy problems like wrong characters, and 60,731 contracts (1.05% of the total) do not present the VAT number field in the data (completeness problems).

For this reasons, different checks must be implemented with the aim of correcting, where possible, the wrong data [12]. Section 4 describes the process we have implemented to tackle data quality issues in order to build a semantic graph upon public contracts data.

3.2 Ontology

In order to model the data source to build the ContrattiPubblici.org knowledge graph, we decided to use the Public Contracts Ontology (PCO) developed by the Czech OpenData.cz initiative[17]. The authors of this ontology are modeling "information which is available in existing systems on the Web" and "which will be usable for matching public contracts with potential suppliers" [5]. Therefore, the goal is to model a public contract as a whole, but without going into details of the public procurement domain.

---

[16] Such data quality metrics are defined by the International Organization for Standardization: ISO/IEC 2501.

[17] The Public Contracts Ontology is available on GitHub platform at: https://github.com/opendatacz/public-contracts-ontology.

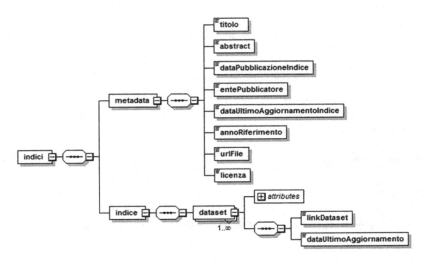

Fig. 4. XSD Schema of public procurement dataset index

In the PCO, a contract notice is a call for tenders, which may be submitted for the award of a public procurement contract. Therefore, we are able to map XML fields described in Sect. 3 into entities, classes and relations provided by the PCO. Figure 5 shows precisely the data model adopted for building the ContrattiPubblici.org knowledge graph. Although there is a significant degree of overlap between the XSD that describes the data model of Italian public contracts and the PCO, we had to introduce measures to better describe our domain. For instance, the concept of tender was not fully expressed in the data model adopted in XML files, since there are only information about participants (inclusive of VAT numbers and company names), but not information related to offering services and prices. Nevertheless, the tender is one of the most important entity in the PCO to link the bidders to the public contract. For these reasons, during the conversion to linked data (Sect. 4), we decided to create tender entities in our knowledge graph using as identifier the VAT number of the participant and the CIG of the contract.

4   Data Processing

When data derives from legacy databases, the publication of linked data is not always immediate [9]; data frequently comes from different sources and it needs to be gathered in a single file before proceeding with the conversion/translation into RDF triples (the so-called triplification) [3]. In the following section we show the process we used to obtain linked data as final result (Fig. 6).

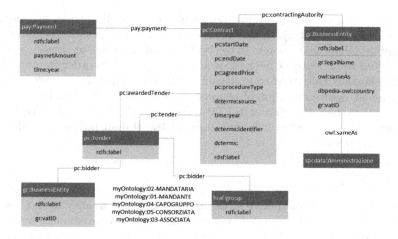

Fig. 5. A scheme of the data model used to build the ContrattiPubblici.org knowledge graph

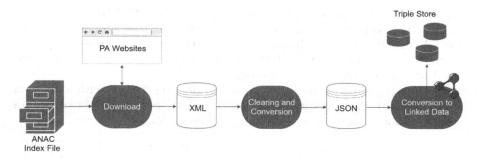

Fig. 6. Linked data conversion pipeline

4.1 Harvesting

As explained in Sect. 3, ANAC releases an index file that provides URLs of available XMLs, which are published on public administrations websites. Based on such index, the Download component tries to fetch data distinguishing between two different cases. In the first case, the component downloads and locally stores the XML containing public contracts data, with additional metadata related to the download outcome. In the second case, if fetched XMLs are indexes to files containing real data, the component is able to cross the links chain[18] and apply the download process shown in the first case. When the component is not able to recognize the expected schema of an XML with data or an XML index, it saves the file apart for a later manual check. In most cases, this means that either the

---

[18] In some cases an index points to another index that finally might point to a file, or to another index.

URLs are wrong or the resource is not published according to an accepted format (e.g., it is a PDF file). In the worst cases, XML indexes are recursive, since they contain URLs that references to the XML index itself. For these reasons, we implemented some features in the Download component in order to manage this critical issue that threatens to undermine the entire pipeline. Moreover, during the download operation a lot of servers do not reply, for several reasons. We collected more than 10 different HTTP responses, which reveal how the quality of service over the 15000+ infrastructures of the Italian public administration might not be reliable.

4.2   Cleaning

By analysing the collected XMLs, we noticed that the quality of data is fragmented: different people with different systems led to inconsistencies and errors, as the example shown in Sect. 3.1. Therefore, we implemented a Cleaning and Conversion module that tries to guess potential errors for each field and attempts to correct data and define a standard format. In particular:

– dates are converted into the ISO 8601 format (YYYY-MM-DD);
– a digit check is performed on the CIGs (identifiers for each procurement) and on VAT numbers for detecting errors and verifying the syntactical correctness;
– agreed prices and payments, which are intended to be euro values, are casted to float number with two decimal digits;
– procedure types, which are fixed text categories, are checked with a function that calculates the similarity between strings. Such function tries to attribute unconventional values to one of those predefined categories.

Every value is analyzed and pushed in a result file serialized in JSON. If a value is modified by the Cleaning and Conversion component, both values, the original one and the guessed one, will be stored in this result file. Furthermore, a reference to the original XML file (the authoritative data) is included in such file.

4.3   Conversion to Linked Data

After the Cleaning stage, we are able to convert the data into RDF using the N-Triples serialization[19]. During this conversion procedure, a component matches each field of the JSON file with the respective property (or relation) and data type from the Public Contract Ontology. When necessary, it also creates the needed entities (see the example of tender entities explained in Sect. 3.2).

One issue we faced during the graph creation is the companies' labels management. While merging data from heterogeneous XML files, it is frequent to find different labels referring to the same company[20]. The creation of the labels

---

[19] More information available at: https://www.w3.org/TR/n-triples/.
[20] The differences may be minimal, as in presence of spelling errors, or even considerable.

triples is therefore handled by an algorithm that chooses the most common label referring to a company.

The last step in the conversion procedure is the so-called *interlinking*. Interlinking means declaring that an entity is *same as* another entity in another dataset, by adding new links to external resources and generating the so called knowledge graph. For this purpose, we chose the SPCData database[21], provided by the *Agenzia per l'Italia Digitale*, that contains the index of Italian public administrations. The knowledge graph is thus created by matching the VAT numbers of the original graph with the ones in the SPCData database.

After this procedure, the completed RDF file is pushed into a Triple Store that exposes data via a SPARQL endpoint.

5   Results

The semantic knowledge graph of ContrattiPubblici.org is published using the Virtuoso Triple Store[22], one of the most adopted technological solution to process and spread linked data. By using the SPARQL endpoint provided by Virtuoso, advanced users and robots are able to satisfy complex information needs. Table 1 details the total amount of RDF triples, entities, contracts, public bodies, companies, and external links to other datasets.

Table 1. Amount of public procurement information available on July 2017

RDF triples	168,961,163
Entities	22,436,784
Contracts	5,783,968
Public bodies	16,593
Companies	652,121
Links to external datasets	13,486

Due to data quality issues illustrated in Sect. 3.1, the number of companies presented in Table 1 is slightly overestimated. As explained in the next session, some future work will be dedicated to implementing further checks and expedients to merge different instances of the same company in a well-defined entity within the knowledge graph.

Despite these problems, in the context of transparency and open spending, it is possible to identify cases of public contracts with anomalies that require more investigation. With the following SPARQL query[23], for instance, advanced

---

[21] More information available at: http://spcdata.digitpa.gov.it/index.html.

[22] More information available at: https://virtuoso.openlinksw.com/.

[23] The endpoint to perform the query is available at: https://contrattipubblici.org/sparql.

users and robots are able to get a list of 100 contracts in which the payment by
the public body is more than doubled of the agreed price.

```
PREFIX pc: <http://purl.org/procurement/public-contracts#>
PREFIX payment: <http://reference.data.gov.uk/def/payment#>
SELECT ?contract ?amount ?agreedPrice WHERE {
    ?contract pc:agreedPrice ?agreedPrice.
    ?contract payment:payment ?payment.
    ?payment payment:netAmount ?amount.
    FILTER (?amount > 2*?agreedPrice)
} LIMIT 100
```

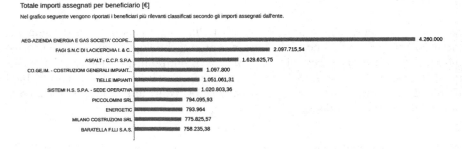

Fig. 7. Total amount of money (in Euros) assigned to a single beneficiary

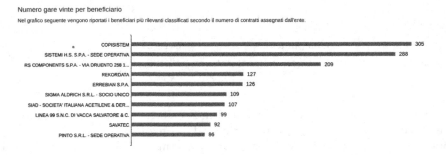

Fig. 8. Number of call for tenders won by a single beneficiary

In addition to data analysis via SPARQL queries, users can exploit features of a human-consumption interface. For these reasons, we have developed
a Web application that is available at: http://public-contracts.nexacenter.org/.
Through a dedicated search form, users can enter the VAT number of a public
administration, obtaining a visualization that shows different information. For
example, a ranking of the top 10 beneficiaries on the basis of the total-allocated

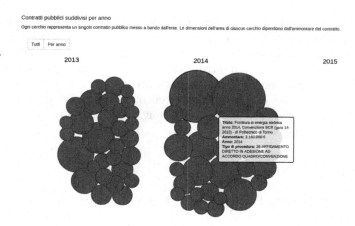

Contratti pubblici suddivisi per anno

Ogni cerchio rappresenta un singolo contratto pubblico messo a bando dall'ente. Le dimensioni dell'area di ciascun cerchio dipendono dall'ammontare del contratto.

Fig. 9. Extent (in Euros) of the public call for tenders divided by year

amounts (Fig. 7), or a ranking on the basis of the total number of contracts (Fig. 8) by means of histograms. Or even a view on contracts by means of a bubble diagram, allowing to compare very clearly the size of contracts put out to tender by the body (Fig. 9). Through this kind of visualizations, an interested company could obtain an overview of tenders and contracts size, acquiring an increased knowledge on how to allocate its investments. Other features on the Web interface, including the search for individual contracts on the basis of keywords and new types of visualization, will be developed in the future.

6   Conclusions and Future Work

This contribution outlines opportunities in building a semantic knowledge graph based on linked data principles in the context of the Italian public procurement data. Despite the difficulties to tackle issues related to coverage and quality of open data sources, handling public contracts information in linked data enables novel avenues to evaluate the transparency of public administration and to create new business opportunities.

As shown in the Results Sect. 3.1, ContrattiPubblici.org semantic graph fosters the extraction of useful knowledge in different ways, ranging from SPARQL queries for complex analyses on data to rich and interactive visualizations. Furthermore, linked data principles lead to an enhanced interoperability across various data formats and Web applications, unleashing the full value of PSI.

Future work on ContrattiPubblici.org will most likely concentrate on the interlinking of the knowledge graph with more external datasets. To support this task, on the one hand, we plan to develop a component to automatize the process of Entity Identification, in particular for business entities. On the other hand, we will include metadata from DCAT-AP_IT[24] ontology to increase the semantic expressiveness of contracts data. Moreover, PCO described in Sect. 3.2 will be extended with more details respect to the period of time of the contract, considering, for example, any interruption of the works, and the provenance of data. Further improvements for the research project are related to the addition of new data quality tests on procurement information, involving legal experts to control and validate the data after the cleaning process, and the development of new human-consumption interfaces.

References

1. Álvarez, J.M., Labra, J.E., Calmeau, R., Marín, Á., Marín, J.L.: Query expansion methods and performance evaluation for reusing linking open data of the European public procurement notices. In: Lozano, J.A., Gámez, J.A., Moreno, J.A. (eds.) CAEPIA 2011. LNCS (LNAI), vol. 7023, pp. 494–503. Springer, Heidelberg (2011). https://doi.org/10.1007/978-3-642-25274-7_50
2. Berners-Lee, T.: Putting government data online (2009)
3. Canova, L., Basso, S., Iemma, R., Morando, F.: Collaborative open data versioning: a pragmatic approach using linked data. In: CeDEM15 - Conference for E-Democracy and Open Governement, pp. 171–183. Edition Donau-Universität Krems, Krems (2015). http://porto.polito.it/2617308/
4. Ding, L., et al.: TWC data-gov corpus: incrementally generating linked government data from data.gov. In: WWW (2010)
5. Distinto, I., dAquin, M., Motta, E.: Loted2: an ontology of European public procurement notices. Semant. Web 7(3), 267–293 (2016)
6. Höffner, K., Martin, M., Lehmann, J.: LinkedSpending: openspending becomes linked open data. Semant. Web J. (2015). http://www.semantic-web-journal.net/system/files/swj923.pdf
7. Martin, M., Stadler, C., Frischmuth, P., Lehmann, J.: Increasing the financial transparency of European commission project funding. Seman. Web J. Spec. Call Linked Dataset Descr. 5(2), 157–164 (2013). http://www.semantic-web-journal.net/system/files/swj435_0.pdf
8. Vafolopoulos, M., et al.: Publicspending. gr: interconnecting and visualizing Greek public expenditure following linked open data directives, July 2012. http://www.w3.org/2012/06/pmod/pmod2012_submission_32.pdf
9. Rowe, M., Ciravegna, F.: Data. dcs: Converting legacy data into linked data. In: LDOW, p. 628 (2010)
10. Svátek, V., Mynarz, J., Węcel, K., Klímek, J., Knap, T., Nečaský, M.: Linked open data for public procurement. In: Auer, S., Bryl, V., Tramp, S. (eds.) Linked Open Data – Creating Knowledge Out of Interlinked Data. LNCS, vol. 8661, pp. 196–213. Springer, Cham (2014). https://doi.org/10.1007/978-3-319-09846-3_10

---

[24] More information on the Italian profile of the DCAT-AP defined in the context of ISA (Interoperability solutions for public administrations, businesses and citizens) program of the European Commission is available at: https://www.dati.gov.it/content/dcat-ap-it-v10-profilo-italiano-dcat-ap-0.

11. Valle, F., dAquin, M., Di Noia, T., Motta, E.: Loted: exploiting linked data in analyzing European procurement notices. In: Proceedings of the 1st Workshop on Knowledge Injection into and Extraction from Linked Data - KIELD 2010 (2010). http://sisinflab.poliba.it/sisinflab/publications/2010/VDDM10

12. Vetró, A., Canova, L., Torchiano, M., Minotas, C.O., Iemma, R., Morando, F.: Open data quality measurement framework: definition and application to open government data. Gov. Inf. Q. **33**(2), 325–337 (2016). http://www.sciencedirect.com/science/article/pii/S0740624X16300132

Application of Ontology Modularization for Building a Criminal Domain Ontology

Mirna El Ghosh[1(✉)], Hala Naja[2], Habib Abdulrab[1],
and Mohamad Khalil[3]

[1] LITIS, INSA, Rouen, France
{mirna.elghosh, habib.abdulrab}@insa-rouen.fr
[2] Faculty of Sciences, Lebanese University, Tripoli, Lebanon
hala.naja70@gmail.com
[3] Faculty of Engineering, CRSI Research Center,
Lebanese University, Tripoli, Lebanon
mohamad.khalil@ul.edu.lb

Abstract. The Ontology modularization is an essential field in the ontology engineering domain helping to reduce the complexity and the difficulties of building, reusing, managing and reasoning on domain ontologies either by applying partitioning or composition approaches. This paper carries out a survey on ontology modularization and presents a modular approach to build criminal modular domain ontology (CriMOnto) for modelling the legal norms of the Lebanese criminal system. CriMOnto, which will be used later for a legal reasoning system, is composed of four independent modules. The modules will be combined together to compose the whole ontology.

Keywords: Ontology modularization · Modular ontology
Ontology composition · Ontology integration · Ontology reuse
Criminal domain · CriMOnto

1 Introduction

It is commonly known that ontologies aim to capture consensual knowledge of a given domain in a generic and formal way, to be reused and shared across applications and by groups of people [1]. The number of available ontologies has increased considerably in various domains such as bioinformatics, genetics, medicine and law, among many others, but they are also becoming larger and more complex to manage and reuse [2]. In this context, interest in modularization techniques, as an ontology engineering principle, has increased to resolve the problems of reusability, scalability and maintenance of ontologies [3]. In addition to this, since the main use of ontologies is making the intended meaning of a given domain available to all agents, an ontology conceptual architecture is required to represent this meaning. According to [4], there is a need to modularize the conceptual architecture to represent this intended meaning dealing with the complexity of the domain such as heterogeneous knowledge with different levels of detail of that knowledge. Therefore, the resulted designed ontologies are obtained with a high quality.

© Springer Nature Switzerland AG 2018
U. Pagallo et al. (Eds.): AICOL VI-X 2015–2017, LNAI 10791, pp. 394–409, 2018.
https://doi.org/10.1007/978-3-030-00178-0_27

Our motivation is to build a legal ontology-based system that performs reasoning tasks in order to support the lawyers and judges in their decisions, specifically, in the criminal domain. Such a system needs a legal domain ontology for modelling the legal norms in order to improve the efficiency of reasoning that requires the representation of the whole semantics of the criminal domain, including well-known properties such as axioms [5]. In order to reduce the complexity of the building process of the criminal domain ontology, to make it as much as possible reusable and able to perform efficient reasoning, we propose to modularize it. According to [6], a modular ontology usually contains a set of modules (component theories), implemented in same or different languages, and a set of semantic relations among those modules.

These semantic relations are obtained by applying an integration process in order to link the ontology modules together. At the end, a criminal modular ontology, named CriMOnto, is obtained. Therefore, the resulting structure of CriMOnto is a *Modular Conceptual Architecture*. The domain application of this research is the Lebanese criminal system and the Lebanese criminal code is considered as the main textual resource since it contains the legal norms of the criminal domain. The main goals of this study are: survey the domain of ontology modularization for a better understanding of this domain and then provide a modular conceptual architecture of CriMOnto as well as the modular construction process. The global view of this architecture is seen as an integration of different ontology modules developed independently.

The remainder of this paper is organized as follows: In Sect. 2, the ontology modularization challenges are outlined. In Sect. 3, the motivation of the study is introduced. In Sect. 4 the ontology modularization concept and approaches are investigated. Section 5 defines the modular architecture of CriMOnto as well as the integration process. The work is evaluated in Sect. 6. Finally, Sect. 7 concludes the paper.

2 Ontology Modularization Challenges

Ontology modularization and the problem of formally characterizing a modular representation for ontologies are great challenges in the ontological engineering domain. Actually, this domain suffers from lack of the modularization theory which uncovers number of unanswered questions [7, 8]:

- How complex ontologies can be built up from parts?
- In what ways can those parts be related (mapping, integration)?
- How the structure of a modular ontology can be represented?
- to create an ontology module with a certain purpose or use-case in mind:
  - Which modularity type of module is defined?

These questions declare various aspects such as: define a modularization approach, precise the modules types and define an integration process for combining modules. By giving answers to these questions, a modular architecture for CriMOnto is introduced.

3 Study Motivation

According to [3], most of the existent ontologies, even if they implicitly relate several sub-domains, are not structured in a modular way. In the other hand, several works tend to combine different ontologies together, such as [9, 10], implicitly without the explicit definition of ontology modularization concept. For [11], in any realistic application, it is often desirable to integrate different ontologies, developed independently, into a single, reconciled ontology. This would allow for the modular design of large ontologies and would facilitate knowledge reuse tasks. Thus, there is no universal way to modularize ontologies and that the choice of a particular technique should be guided by the requirements of the considered application [3]. Therefore, an approach aims at designing a modular architecture as well as an incremental process allowing a collaborative building of CriMOnto. The main features of CriMOnto are: it is composed of four independently developed ontology modules. These modules are obtained from different and heterogeneous sources (partial reuse of existent ontologies and semi-automatic extraction mechanisms from textual resources). CriMOnto is empowered with an integration process to combine the different modules.

4 Ontology Modularization

The main idea of modularization originates from the general notion of modular software in the area of software engineering [12]. In software engineering domain, the modularity is a well-established notion where it refers to a way of designing software in a clear, well-structured way that supports maintenance and reusability [13]. However, in the ontology engineering domain, the notion of modularization and the problem of formally characterizing a modular representation for ontologies are not as well understood [14], which causes suffer in the existing work and prevents further development [3]. Despite this vagueness, ontology modularization is considered as a major topic in the field of formal ontology developments and a way to facilitate and simplify the ontology engineering process [7]. Moreover, ontology modularization has several benefits where modular representations are easier to understand, reason with, extend and reuse [13]. Therefore, using these representations tends to reduce the complexity of designing and to facilitate the ontology reasoning, development, and integration.

4.1 What Is an Ontology Module?

Generally speaking, a module is a part of a complex system that functions independently from this system [15]. In contrast to the software engineering domain, the notion of ontology module is not clear or understood in the domain of ontological engineering [16]. There is a need to formalize and define an ontology module, particularly in terms of its requirements [17]. For [18], ontology module is considered as extractable part that can be reused outside the context of the general ontology. More clearly, an ontology module is defined by [16] as "*An ontology module is a reusable component of a larger or more complex ontology, which is self-contained but bears a definite relationship to other ontology modules including the original ontology*". This definition implies that ontology modules can be reused either as they are, or by extending them with new concepts, and relationships. Each ontology module is considered as ontology itself since it can be extended with new concepts and relationships. Thereby, ontology modules are themselves ontologies [12].

4.2 Ontology Module Criteria

The criteria of ontology modules generally aim at characterizing modular ontologies in order to evaluate the quality of modules [4]. Generally, inspired by the software engineering domain, three main criteria a module should fulfill: *self-contained*, *loose coupling* and *high cohesion* [19, 20]. Therefore, in the ontological engineering domain, some studies, such as [21–23], believe that modularization criteria should be defined in terms of the applications for which the modules are created. They defined some ontology module criteria such as: Encapsulation, Independence and Domain coverage.

4.3 Ontology Module Classifications

In the literature, the authors of [24] proposed to analyze modules by taking as central the following question: modules for what? Based on this question, various classifications of ontology modules are proposed such as [8, 25–27]. Meanwhile, the most useful classification of ontology modules is based on their content where the ontologies are classified into five main categories [28–30]:

- *Generic*, or *top-level*, ontologies: describe generic concepts independently of a particular domain or problem.
- *Core* ontologies: in contrast to generic ontologies that span across many fields, core ontologies describe the basic categories within a domain such as law.
- *Domain* ontologies: specialize a subset of generic ontologies in a domain or sub-domain, e.g. criminal law.
- *Application* or *domain-specific* ontologies: developed for a specific application.

4.4 Approaches of Ontology Modularization

Generally, modularization denotes the possibility to perceive a large knowledge repository as a set of modules, i.e. smaller repositories that, in some way, are parts of and compose the whole knowledge [31]. Therefore, an ontological modularization process is seen as a call for organizing ontologies into modules which could then be reused and combined in novel ways [7]. In the literature, three different approaches of ontology modularization are found [3, 12, 17]: ontology composition, ontology decomposition and module extraction. In this work, the ontology composition approach is used. Ontology composition aims to develop independently a set of ontology modules and assemble them coherently and uniformly, by means of integrating and mapping, to form a wider ontology. Examples of ontology composition approaches are, among others, [32–35].

5   Application of Ontology Modularization in the Legal Domain: CriMOnto

CriMOnto is a criminal modular domain ontology for modelling the norms of the Lebanese criminal system as a domain application for this study. In previous work [36], a middle-out approach is proposed for building CriMOnto where the ontology modularization techniques are discussed implicitly. In this work, the approach is enhanced and explicit modularization techniques are applied for this purpose. The aim of this approach is to show how ontology modularization can simplify and reduce the complexity of ontology building processes. Therefore, a modular architecture of the ontology is outlined by identifying the main modules, their number, type and criteria, as well as the knowledge to be represented in each module. Moreover, ontology reuse process, which is now one of the important research issues in the ontology field [37], is recommended as a key factor to develop cost effective and high quality ontologies. Actually, ontology reuse reduces the cost and the time required for building ontologies from scratch [38–40]. Moreover, by reusing validated ontology components, the quality of the newly implemented ontologies is increased. According to [41], there are two main reuse processes: *merge* and *integration*. Merge is the process of building an ontology in one subject reusing two or more different ontologies on that subject. Meanwhile, integration is the process of building an ontology in one subject reusing one or more ontologies in different subjects that are maybe related. In the current work, the proposed conceptual architecture of CriMOnto is grounded on four different level concepts: Upper ontology module (UOM), Core ontology module (COM), Domain ontology module (DOM) and Domain-specific ontology module (DSOM). The proposed approach is defined by developing the modules independently by using top-down and bottom-up strategies and then combining them together to compose the whole CriMOnto (see Fig. 1) [36]. From this perspective, the different modules are in different subjects since they are in different conceptual levels. Therefore, an integration process is performed to combine them. Inspired by the integration methodology of [37], there are list of activities that precede the integration of modules into the resulting ontology such as identify the knowledge to be represented in the different modules as well as the candidate ontologies to be reused. Therefore, an analyzing and selection process will take place in order to define the existent ontologies to be reused. In the following, these activities are outlined.

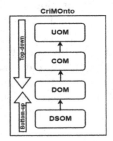

Fig. 1. Middle-out approach for building CriMOnto.

5.1 Upper Ontology Module

The UOM consists of abstract concepts and relations which are effectively independent of any specific domain. For a well-founded building of this module, a partial reuse of existent foundational, or top-level, ontologies can help. These ontologies are theoretically well-founded domain independent systems of categories that have been successfully used to improve the quality of conceptual models and semantic interoperability [42]. In addition to this, partial reuse of foundational ontologies can facilitate and speeding up the ontology development process by preventing to reinvent the wheel concerning basic categories [43]. In the literature, several works seek for reusing concepts from foundational ontologies in order to support in maintaining a well-structured construction of domain ontologies that could serve as a future reusable artifact [44]. Various foundational ontologies exist for reuse such as DOLCE [45] and UFO [46]. In this context, a selection for an appropriate foundational ontology is a crucial and difficult step since it depends on different elements such as: the purpose of building the ontology and the applicability domain. Therefore, after studying the main concepts of these foundational ontologies, UFO is the most convenient.

The unified foundational ontology UFO is a foundational ontology initially proposed by Guizzardi and Wagner [47]. UFO is developed to support the activities of both conceptual and organizational modeling [48]. Therefore, UFO permits the building of an ontology reusing some generic concepts such as *category, kind, subkind, relator, role* and *role mixin* where the ontologist does not need to rebuild these concepts. UFO is divided into three layered sets: (1) UFO-A, ontology of objects, defines terms related to endurants such as *universal, relator, role, intrinsic moment*; (2) UFO-B, ontology of events, defines terms related to perdurants such as *event, state, atomic event, complex event*; (3) UFO-C defines terms related to intentional and social entities including linguistic aspects such as *social agent, social object, social role* and *normative description* [49]. In the current work, UFO-B and UFO-C are needed to ground the criminal domain ontology for building UOM since they define some basic concepts for the criminal domain such as *Agent, Intentional_Moment, Action, Event*, and *Normative_Description*. In order to make possible the activity of conceptual modeling via UFO, a conceptual modeling language, named OntoUML [50], was proposed. OntoUML uses the ontological constraints of UFO as modeling primitives and is specified above the UML 2.0 meta-model [51]. To build, evaluate and implements OntoUML models, a model-based environment is needed such as the standalone tool OLED (OntoUML Lightweight Editor) [52] or the extension of UML production-grade tool Enterprise Architect [53].

Reusing Concepts from UFO-C. There is list of essential concepts in UFO-C to reuse for building the upper module, mainly those related to social entities such as *Agents* and *Objects* [54] (see Fig. 2a). *Agents* can be physical (e.g. *Person*) or social (e.g. *Organization*). *Objects* are also categorized in physical (e.g. book) and social objects (e.g. normative description). *Normative_Description* defines one or more rules/norms recognized by at least one *Social_Agent*. Regulations and constitutions are examples of normative description. In Fig. 2a, a fragment of the conceptual model of the upper module, which is represented in OntoUML language, is depicted.

(a)   (b)

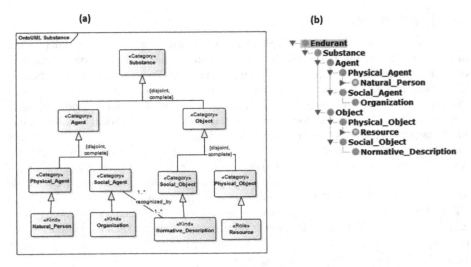

Fig. 2. Fragment of the upper module in OntoUML (a) and Protégé (b).

Therefore, for knowledge representation and reasoning capabilities, there is a need to transform the conceptual model of the upper module represented in OntoUML language to a computational ontology language such as OWL. For this purpose, OLED features defined automatic transformations of the OntoUML models to OWL files [55] that can be managed using ontology editors such as Protégé (see Fig. 2b).

Reusing Concepts from UFO-B. The ontology of perdurants UFO-B defines *Event*, which is a basic concept in the criminal domain (e.g. crime is an event), as a main category [54]. In UFO-B, events can be atomic or complex [56] and an *Action* or *Participation* (Fig. 3). Actions are performed by agents and considered as intentional events caused by intentions [54]. Participation can be for agents and objects. Therefore, participation of an agent can be intentional or unintentional.

5.2   Core Ontology Module

The COM consists of concepts and relations that are common across the domains of law and can provide the basis for specialization into domain and domain-specific concepts. The same perspective can be applied, as for upper module, for reusing existent legal core ontology to build this module. Thus, it is not easy to define appropriate legal core ontology among the existent (LKIF-Core, LRI-Core, and FOLAW). Actually, LKIF-Core [57] is the most recent legal-core ontology and contains essential legal concepts such as *Medium*, *Document*, *Legal_Source*, *Legal_Document*, and *Code* (see Fig. 4).

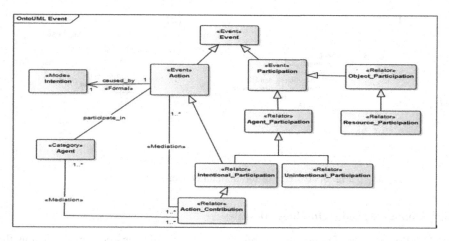

Fig. 3. Fragment of the upper module in OntoUML.

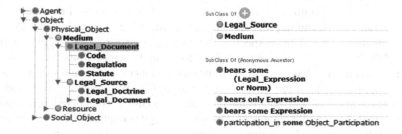

Fig. 4. Excerpt of core concepts reused from LKIF-Core.

5.3   Domain Ontology Module

The DOM is composed of categories that are related mainly to the criminal domain in general such as *Criminal_Act*, *Penalty*, *Misdemeanor*, *Violation*, etc. In order to build this module, two main strategies are applied: (1) specialize the concepts and relations of the core module; (2) extract the knowledge from textual resources. The strategy of specializing the concepts and relations of the core module is applied. Therefore, concepts of the core module such as: *Creation*, *Public_Act*, *Act_Of_Law*, and *Reaction* are specialized in domain concepts such as: *Criminal_Act*, *Punishments* and *Defence* (see Fig. 5a). For the strategy of extracting the knowledge from textual resources, a bottom-up approach is applied as an ontology learning process, with the support of NLP techniques, for extracting the main elements of the domain ontology module from the English version of the Lebanese criminal code (for more details refer to [58]). Examples of extracted concepts are shown in the figure such as *Defender*, *Offender*, *Accessory*, *Accomplice*, *Instigator*, *Perpetrator* and *victim* (see Fig. 5b).

(a)   (b)

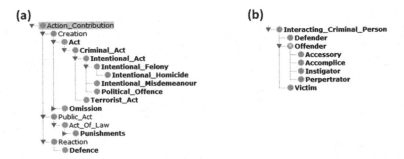

Fig. 5. Excerpt of the domain concepts in Protégé.

5.4   Domain-Specific Ontology Module

The DSOM consists of concepts and relations of a specific subject domain such as the Lebanese criminal system. Domain-specific ontologies are useful in systems involved with reasoning. Thus, they should be at higher level of expressivity, in other words, rich in axioms. To build this module, since it is related directly to the Lebanese criminal system, an ontology learning process is applied on the criminal code in order to extract semi-automatically the domain-specific ontology and part of the domain ontology module [58]. The bottom-up strategy helped to generate semi-automatically an OWL ontology including the basic elements: concepts, instances, taxonomies, relations and axioms. Unfortunately, some of the generated results were inexpressive and thus insufficient for practical use. The resulted ontology module is considered as lightweight or semi-formal. Meanwhile, a more expressive ontology is required. For this reason and inspired by the work of [59], a reengineering process is applied to correct, prune and enrich the extracted ontology and make it more expressive by transforming it to heavyweight or axiom-based ontology. In the Fig. 6, a fragment of the domain-specific module concepts are depicted such as *Fine_Contravention_Penalty* and *Imprisonment_Contravention_penalty*, which are specific concepts in the Lebanese criminal code, are considered as sub-concepts of the *Contravention_Penalty* concept of the domain module.

Fig. 6. Excerpt of the domain-specific ontology module represented in Protégé.

5.5 Evaluation and Integration of Ontology Modules

After building the ontology modules (upper, core, domain and domain-specific), there is a need to evaluate them according to the modules criteria in order to compose the resulting ontology CriMOnto. Actually, the independent building of the modules makes them self-contained and enhances the encapsulation where any changes that affect a module will not affect the others. Moreover, the independency leads to make them reusable as well. Additionally, each module covers an adequate level of the given domain where their integration will create a complete coverage of the Lebanese criminal system. Furthermore, an integration process will be applied to aggregate, combine, and assemble the modules. Subsequently, in the resulting ontology, regions that were taken from the integrated modules can be identified. Moreover, it is essential to consider heterogeneity resolution and related ontology matching or mapping strategies to be an internal part of ontology integration [39]. In this context, list of semantic mappings will be created among concepts of the different modules. Generally, the *mapping* concept is defined by [60] as a morphism. Meanwhile, in this study a more loosely definition is used based on some works in the literature such as [61] and claims such as "simple mappings methods are sufficient and outperform more complex methods" [62]. For ontology mappings, several studies, such as [63, 64], have proposed a number of specialized semantics. Meanwhile, for other studies, such as [65], ontology mappings are represented as OWL2 axioms of the form *subClassOf*, *EquivalentClass* and *DisjointClass* [66]. In CriMOnto, the modules are located on vertical conceptual levels from general (upper module) to specific (domain-specific module). For this reason, the mappings will be based mainly on a parent-child, or subsumption, hierar-chical relationship [67] and established manually as structural axiom of the form *subClassOf*. Thus, the hierarchical relationship is established among the concepts of modules. For this purpose, a linguistic-based matcher, such as WordNet, is used to deal with ontology mapping for calculating the similarity values between concepts [68]. Then a domain expert, knowledgeable about the semantics of legal concepts, validates the proposed mappings. Given two concepts C_i and C_j from the modules UOM and COM respectively, if C_j is considered as a subclass of C_i, then the *subClassOf* axiom is added between the two concepts in the resulting ontology. In CriMOnto, *Event* is a general concept from the upper module UOM and *Legal_Event* is a legal concept from the core module COM. *Legal_Event* is considered as a subclass of *Event*. Thus, the *subClassOf* axiom is added between them (see Fig. 7).

Fig. 7. Hierarchical mapping in Protégé.

6 Evaluation

After building CriMOnto, there is a need to evaluate the characteristics and the validity of the resulting ontology. According to [69], evaluation is required during the whole life-cycle of an ontology in order to guarantee that what is built meets the requirements.

In the literature, various approaches to the evaluation of ontologies have been considered [75]. They are classified mainly in different levels according to ontology quality metrics [76]: lexical and concept/data [77], taxonomic and semantic relations [78], context-level [79], application-based [80] and data-driven [81]. The kind and the purpose of the ontology define the evaluation level. Generally, evaluation methods consist of two parts: *verification* that ensures the ontology is constructed correctly, and *validation* that ensures the ontology represents the real world [70]. For the *verification*, Ontology taxonomy evaluation method is applied manually by domain experts while integrating the ontology modules and by using a logic reasoner that checks the consistency of the ontology such as Pellet. For the *validation*, the application-based method is applied [71] by adding list of concrete individuals to the ontology. Actually, CriMOnto is intended to be used for building a rule-based reasoning system composed of set of formal logic rules. The output of this system will depend mainly on the quality of CriMOnto.

7 Conclusion

In this work, a modular approach is described to build a criminal domain ontology (CriMOnto). In the literature, several works applied implicitly the ontology modularization such as [72] for the automation domain, [73] for ill-defined domains and [74] for the enterprise architecture domain. To the best of our knowledge, there is no works in the legal domain that deal explicitly with the ontology modularization for building legal domain ontologies. For this purpose, this direction is tracked. The aim of this study is to prove how ontology modularization can simplify the development of well-founded legal domain ontologies with the support of ontology reuse and integration. Furthermore, a modular architecture of CriMOnto is outlined. The architecture is composed of four independent ontology modules. The upper and core modules are developed by reusing existent foundational and legal core ontologies. Meanwhile, the domain and domain-specific are constructed with the support of ontology learning process from legal texts. Furthermore, an integration process, based on simple hierarchical mappings, is applied to combine the modules in order to compose the whole CriMOnto. Finally, this approach is considered as useful track for the ontologists who seek to build domain ontologies based on existent valid ontologies and not totally from scratch.

Acknowledgements. This work has been supported by the European Union with the European Regional Development Fund (ERDF) under Grant Agreement no. HN0002134 in the project CLASSE 2 ("Les Corridors Logistiques: Application a la Vallée de la Seine et son Environnement"), Lebanese University and the National Support from the National Council for Scientific Research in Lebanon (CNRS).

References

1. Corcho, O., Fernández-López, M., Gómez-Pérez, A.: Ontological engineering: what are ontologies and how can we build them? In: Jorge, C. (ed.) Semantic Web Services: Theory, Tools and Applications, pp. 44–70. IGI Global, Hershey (2007)
2. Pathak, J., Johnson, T.M., Chute, C.G.: Modular ontology techniques and their applications in the biomedical domain. Integr. Comput. Aid. Eng. 16(3), 225–242 (2009)
3. d'Aquin, M., Schlicht, A., Stuckenschmidt, H., Sabou, M.: Ontology modularization for knowledge selection: experiments and evaluations. In: Wagner, R., Revell, N., Pernul, G. (eds.) DEXA 2007. LNCS, vol. 4653, pp. 874–883. Springer, Heidelberg (2007). https://doi.org/10.1007/978-3-540-74469-6_85
4. Gangemi, A., Catenacci, C., Battaglia, M.: Inflammation ontology design pattern: an exercise in building a core biomedical ontology with descriptions and situations. Stud. Health Technol. Inform. 102, 64–80 (2004)
5. Fürst, F., Trichet, F.: Integrating domain ontologies into knowledge-based systems. In: FLAIRS Conference, pp. 826–827 (2005)
6. Wang, Y., Bao, J., Haase, P., Qi, G.: Evaluating formalisms for modular ontologies in distributed information systems. In: marchiori, m, Pan, Jeff Z., Marie, C. (eds.) RR 2007. LNCS, vol. 4524, pp. 178–193. Springer, Heidelberg (2007). https://doi.org/10.1007/978-3-540-72982-2_13
7. Hois, J., Bhatt, M., Kutz, O.: Modular ontologies for architectural design. In: FOMI-09, Frontiers in Artificial Intelligence and Applications, vol. 198. IOS Press, Vicenza (2009)
8. Khan, Z.C., Keet, C.M.: Toward a framework for ontology modularity. In: The 2015 Annual Research Conference on South African Institute of Computer Scientists and Information Technologists. SAICSIT 2015, Article No. 24 (2015)
9. Francesconi, E., Montemagni, S., Peters, W., Tiscornia, D.: Integrating a bottom–up and top–down methodology for building semantic resources for the multilingual legal domain. In: Francesconi, E., Montemagni, S., Peters, W., Tiscornia, D. (eds.) Semantic Processing of Legal Texts. LNCS (LNAI), vol. 6036, pp. 95–121. Springer, Heidelberg (2010). https://doi.org/10.1007/978-3-642-12837-0_6
10. Saias, J., Quaresma, P.: A methodology to create legal ontologies in a logic programming information retrieval system. In: Benjamins, V.Richard, Casanovas, P., Breuker, J., Gangemi, A. (eds.) Law and the Semantic Web. LNCS (LNAI), vol. 3369, pp. 185–200. Springer, Heidelberg (2005). https://doi.org/10.1007/978-3-540-32253-5_12
11. Turlapati, V.K.C., Puligundla, S.K.: Efficient module extraction for large ontologies. In: Klinov, P., Mouromtsev, D. (eds.) KESW 2013. CCIS, vol. 394, pp. 162–176. Springer, Heidelberg (2013). https://doi.org/10.1007/978-3-642-41360-5_13
12. Abbes, S.B., Scheuermann, A., Meilender, T., d'Aquin, M.: Characterizing modular ontologies. In: 7th International Conference on Formal Ontologies in Information Systems (FOIS), pp. 13–25 (2012)
13. Grau, B.C., Horrocks, I., Kazakov, Y., Sattler, U.: A logical framework for modularity of ontologies. In: IJCAI 2007, pp. 298–303. AAAI Press (2007)
14. Grau, B.C., Kutz, O.: Modular ontology languages revisited. In: The IJCAI-2007 Workshop on Semantic Web for Collaborative Knowledge Acquisition (2007)
15. Konev, B., Lutz, C., Walther, D., Wolter, F.: Formal properties of modularisation. In: Stuckenschmidt, H., Parent, C., Spaccapietra, S. (eds.) Modular Ontologies. LNCS, vol. 5445, pp. 25–66. Springer, Heidelberg (2009). https://doi.org/10.1007/978-3-642-01907-4_3
16. Doran, P.: Ontology reuse via ontology modularization. In: Proceedings of Knowledge Web Ph.D. Symposium, pp. 1–6 (2006)

17. Bezerra, C., Freitas, F., Zimmermann, A., Euzenat, J.: ModOnto: a tool for modularizing ontologies. In: WONTO-08, vol. 427 (2008). ceur-ws.org

18. Grau, B.C., Parsia, B., Sirin, E., Kalyanpur, A.: Modularity and web ontologies. In: KR, pp. 198–209 (2006)

19. Stuckenschmidt, H., Klein, M.: Reasoning and change management in modular ontologies. Data Knowl. Eng. **63**(2), 200–223 (2007)

20. Stuckenschmidt, H., Klein, M.: Integrity and change in modular ontologies. In: 18th International Joint Conference on Artificial Intelligence, pp. 900–905 (2003)

21. d'Aquin, M., Schlicht, A., Stuckenschmidt, H., Sabou, M.: Criteria and evaluation for ontology modularization techniques. In: Stuckenschmidt, H., Parent, C., Spaccapietra, S. (eds.) Modular Ontologies. LNCS, vol. 5445, pp. 67–89. Springer, Heidelberg (2009). https://doi.org/10.1007/978-3-642-01907-4_4

22. Del Vescovo, C., Parsia, B., Sattler, U., Schneider, T.: The modular structure of an ontology: an empirical study. Technical report, University of Manchester. http://www.cs.man.ac.uk/% 7Eschneidt/publ/modstrucreport.pdf

23. Del Vescovo, C., Parsia, B., Sattler, U., Schneider, T.: The modular structure of an ontology: an empirical study. In: Haarslev, V, Toman, D., Weddell, G. (eds.), DL 2010, vol. 573 (2010). ceur-ws.org

24. Borgo, S.: Goals of modularity: a voice from the foundational viewpoint. In: Kutz, O., Schneider, T. (eds.) Fifth International Workshop on Modular Ontologies, Frontiers in Artificial Intelligence and Applications, vol. 230, pp. 1–6. IOS Press (2011)

25. Studer, T.: Privacy preserving modules for ontologies. In: Pnueli, A., Virbitskaite, I., Voronkov, A. (eds.) PSI 2009. LNCS, vol. 5947, pp. 380–387. Springer, Heidelberg (2010). https://doi.org/10.1007/978-3-642-11486-1_32

26. Del Vescovo, C., et al.: The modular structure of an ontology: atomic decomposition. In: IJCAI Proceedings-International Joint Conference on Artificial Intelligence, vol. 22 (2011)

27. Cuenca Grau, B., Halaschek-Wiener, C., Kazakov, Y.: History matters: incremental ontology reasoning using modules. In: Aberer, K., et al. (eds.) ASWC/ISWC -2007. LNCS, vol. 4825, pp. 183–196. Springer, Heidelberg (2007). https://doi.org/10.1007/978-3-540-76298-0_14

28. Guarino, N., Carrara, Giaretta, P.: An ontology of meta-level categories. In: Doyle, J., Sandewall, E., Torasso, P. (eds.) Principles of Knowledge Representation and Reasoning: Proceedings of KR94. Morgan Kaufmann, San Mateo (1994)

29. Guarino, N.: Understanding, building, and using ontologies. Int. J. Hum. Comput. Stud. **46** (2–3), 293–310 (1997)

30. Van Heijst, G., Schreiber, A., Th Wielinga, B.G.: Using explicit ontologies in KBS development. Int. J. Hum. Comput. Stud. **46**, 2–3 (1997)

31. Stuckenschmidt, H., Christine, P., Spaccapietra, S.: Modular Ontologies: Concepts, Theories and Techniques for Knowledge Modularization. Springer, Berlin (2009). https://doi.org/10.1007/978-3-642-01907-4

32. Ben Mustapha, N., Baazaoui-Zghal, H., Moreno, A., Ben Ghezala, H.: A dynamic composition of ontology modules approach: application to web query reformulation. Int. J. Metadata Semant. Ontol. **8**(4), 309–321 (2013)

33. Bezerra, C., Freitas, F., Euzenat, J., Zimmermann, A.: An approach for ontology modularization (2008)

34. Dmitrieva, J., Verbeek, F.J.: Creating a New Ontology: A Modular Approach. arXiv preprint arXiv:1012.1658 (2010)

35. Steve, G., Gangemi, A., Pisanelli, D.: Integrating medical terminologies with onions methodology (1998)

36. El Ghosh, M., Naja, H., Abdulrab, H., Khalil, M.: Towards a middle-out approach for building legal domain reference ontology. Int. J. Knowl. Eng. 2(3), 109–114 (2016)
37. Pinto, H., Martins, J.: Ontology integration: how to perform the process. In: The International Joint Conference on Artificial Intelligence, pp. 71–80 (2001)
38. Bontas, E.P., Mochol, M., Tolksdorf, R.: Case studies on ontology reuse. In: IKNOW05 International Conference on Knowledge Management, vol. 74 (2005)
39. Caldarola, E.G., Picariello, A., Rinaldim A.M.: An approach to ontology integration for ontology reuse in knowledge based digital ecosystems. In: 7th International Conference on Management of computational and Collective intElligence in Digital EcoSystems, pp. 1–8. ACM (2015)
40. Modoni, G., Caldarola, E., Terkaj, W., Sacco, M.: The knowledge reuse in an industrial scenario: a case study. In: The Seventh International Conference on Information, Process, and Knowledge Management eKNOW 2015, pp. 66–71 (2015)
41. Pinto, S.H., Gomez-Perez, A., Martins, J.P.: Some issues on ontology integration. In: IJCAI99's Workshop on Ontologies and Problem Solving Methods: Lessons Learned and Future Trends (1999)
42. Guizzardi, G.: The role of foundational ontology for conceptual modeling and domain ontology representation. In: 7th International Baltic Conference on Databases and Information Systems, pp. 17–25 (2006)
43. Keet, M.: The use of foundational ontologies in ontology development: an empirical assessment. In: 8th Extended Semantic Web Conference, Greece, vol. 6643, pp. 321–335 (2011)
44. Rosa, D.E., Carbonera, J.L., Torres, G.M., Abel, M.: Using events from UFO-B in an ontology collaborative construction environment. CEUR-WSX 938, 278–283 (2012)
45. Masolo, C., Borgo, S., Gangemi, A., Guarino, N., Oltramari, A.: Wonderweb deliverable D18 (ver. 1.0). Ontology Library (2003)
46. Guizzardi, G., Wagner, G.: A unified foundational ontology and some applications of it in business modeling. In: CAiSE Workshops, vol. 3, pp. 129–143 (2004)
47. Guizzardi, G., Wagner, G.: Using UFO as a foundation for general conceptual modeling languages. In: Poli, R., Healy, M., Kameas, A. (eds.) Theory and Applications of Ontology: Computer Applications, pp. 175–196. Springer, Dordrecht (2010). https://doi.org/10.1007/978-90-481-8847-5_8
48. Melo, S., Almeida, M.B.: Applying foundational ontologies in conceptual modeling: a case study in a Brazilian public company. In: Meersman, R. (ed.) On the Move to Meaningful Internet Systems: OTM 2014 Workshops, pp. 577–586. Springer, Heidelberg (2014). https://doi.org/10.1007/978-3-662-45550-0_59
49. Guizzardi, G., Wagner, G.: Towards ontological foundations for agent modelling concepts using the unified fundational ontology (UFO). In: Bresciani, P., Giorgini, P., Henderson-Sellers, B., Low, G., Winikoff, M. (eds.) AOIS -2004. LNCS (LNAI), vol. 3508, pp. 110–124. Springer, Heidelberg (2005). https://doi.org/10.1007/11426714_8
50. Guizzardi, G.: Ontological foundations for structural conceptual models. Ph.D. thesis. Enschede, Telematica Institut, The Netherlands (2005)
51. Guerson, J., Sales, T.P., Guizzardi, G., Almeida, J.P.A.: OntoUML lightweight editor: a model-based environment to build, evaluate and implement reference ontologies. In: IEEE 19th International Enterprise Distributed Object Computing Workshop (EDOCW), pp. 144–147 (2015)
52. http://code.google.com/p/ontouml-lightweight-editor/
53. http://www.sparxsystems.com/products/ea/

54. Guizzardi, G., Falbo, R. A., Guizzardi, R.S.S.: Grounding software domain ontologies in the unified foundational ontology (UFO): the case of the ODE software process ontology. In: Proceedings of the Ibero American Workshop on Requirements Engineering and Software Environments, pp. 244–251 (2008)
55. Barcelos, P.P.F., dos Santos, V.A., Silva, F.B., Monteiro, M.E., Garcia, A.S.: An automated transformation from OntoUML to OWL and SWRL. In: ONTOBRAS 2013. CEUR Workshop Proceedings, vol. 1041, CEUR-WS.org, pp. 130–141 (2013)
56. Guizzardi, G., Wagner, G., Falbo, A., Guizzardi, R.S.S., Almeida, J.P.A.: Towards ontological foundations for the conceptual modeling of events. In: 32th International Conference, ER 2013, pp. 327–341 (2013)
57. Hoekstra, R., Breuker, J., Bello, M.D., Boer, A.: The LKIF core ontology of basic legal concepts. In: Workshop on Legal Ontologies and Artificial Intelligence Techniques, CEUR Workshop Proceedings, vol. 321, pp. 43–63 (2007)
58. El Ghosh, M., Naja, H., Abdulrab, H., Khalil, M.: Ontology learning process as a bottom-up strategy for building domain-specific ontology from legal texts. In: The 9th International Conference on Agents and Artificial Intelligence, ICAART, vol. 2, pp. 473–480 (2017)
59. Gómez-Pérez, A., Rojas-Amaya, M.D.: Ontological reengineering for reuse. In: Fensel, D., Studer, R. (eds.) EKAW 1999. LNCS (LNAI), vol. 1621, pp. 139–156. Springer, Heidelberg (1999). https://doi.org/10.1007/3-540-48775-1_9
60. Kalfoglou, Y., Schorlemmer, W.M.: Ontology mapping: the state of the art. In: Semantic Interoperability and Integration (2005)
61. Dmitrieva, J., Verbeek, F.: Modular approach for a new ontology. In: 5th International Workshop on Modular Ontologies WoMO (2011)
62. Ghazvinian, A., Noy, N.F., Musen, M.A.: Creating mappings for ontologies in biomedicine: simple methods work. In: AMIA 2009 Symposium Proceedings (2009)
63. Euzenat, J.: Semantic precision and recall for ontology alignment evaluation. In: IJCAI, pp. 348–353 (2007)
64. Borgida, A., Serani, L.: Distributed description logics: assimilating information from peer sources. J. Data Semant. 1, 153–184 (2003)
65. Jimenez-Ruiz, E., Cuenca Grau, B., Horrocks, I., Berlanga, R.: Ontology integration using mappings: towards getting the right logical consequences. Technical report, Universitat Jaume, University of Oxford (2008)
66. Cuenca Grau, B., Horrocks, I., Motik, B., Parsia, B., Patel-Schneider, P., Sattler, U.: OWL 2: the next step for OWL. J. Web Semant. 6(4), 309–322 (2008)
67. Wang, Y., Liu, W., Bell, D.: A concept hierarchy based ontology mapping approach. In: KSEM, pp. 101–113 (2010)
68. Miller, G.A.: WordNet: a lexical database for English. Commun. ACM 38, 39–41 (1995)
69. Hartmann, J., et al.: Methods for ontology evaluation. In: Knowledge Web Deliverable D1.2.3 (2004)
70. Gómez-Pérez, A., Fernandez-Lopez, A., Corcho, O.: Ontological Engineering. Springer, London (2004). https://doi.org/10.1007/b97353
71. Gómez-Pérez, A.: Evaluation of ontologies. Int. J. Intell. Syst. 16, 391–409 (2011)
72. Legat, C.: Semantics to the shop floor: towards ontology modularization and reuse in the automation domain. In: World Congress (2014)
73. Thakker, D., Dimitrova, V., Lau, L., Denaux, R., Karanasios, S., Yang Turner, F.: A priori ontology modularisation in ill-defined domains. In: 7th International Conference on Semantic Systems, I-Semantics 2011, pp. 167–170 (2011)
74. Bakhshandeh, M., Antunes, G., Mayer, R., Borbinha, J., Caetano, A.: A modular ontology for the enterprise architecture domain. In: 17th IEEE International Enterprise Distributed Object Computing Conference Workshops, EDOCW 2013, pp. 5–12 (2013)

75. Brank, J., Grobelnik, M., Mladenic, D.: A survey of ontology evaluation techniques. In: Conference on Data Mining and Data Warehouses (SiKDD) (2005)
76. Gangemi, A., Catenacci, C., Ciaramita, M., Lehmann, J.: Modelling ontology evaluation and validation. In: Sure, Y., Domingue, J. (eds.) ESWC 2006. LNCS, vol. 4011, pp. 140–154. Springer, Heidelberg (2006). https://doi.org/10.1007/11762256_13
77. Maedche, A., Staab, S.: Measuring similarity between ontologies. In: Gómez-Pérez, A., Benjamins, V.Richard (eds.) EKAW 2002. LNCS (LNAI), vol. 2473, pp. 251–263. Springer, Heidelberg (2002). https://doi.org/10.1007/3-540-45810-7_24
78. Brewster, C., Alani, H., Dasmahapatra, S., Wilks, Y.: Data driven ontology evaluation. In: International Conference on Language Resources and Evaluation, Lisbon (2004)
79. Ding, L., et al.: Swoogle: a search and metadata engine for the semantic web. In: CIKM, pp. 652–659 (2004)
80. Porzel, R., Malaka, R.: A task-based approach for ontology evaluation. In: ECAI 2004 Workshop Ontology Learning and Population, Valencia, Spain, pp. 1–6 (2004)
81. Patel, C., Supekar, K., Lee, Y., Park, E.: OntoKhoj: a semantic web portal for ontology searching, ranking and classification. In: Proceedings of the 5th ACM International Workshop on Web Information and Data Management. ACM (2004)

A Linked Data Terminology for Copyright Based on Ontolex-Lemon

Víctor Rodriguez-Doncel[1(✉)] ®, Cristiana Santos[2],
Pompeu Casanovas[2,3]®, Asunción Gómez-Pérez[1]®,
and Jorge Gracia[1]®

[1] Ontology Engineering Group, Universidad Politécnica de Madrid,
Madrid, Spain
vrodriguez@delicias.fi.upm.es
[2] Institute of Law and Technology, Autonomous University of Barcelona,
Barcelona, Spain
[3] La Trobe University, Melbourne, Australia

Abstract. Ontolex-lemon is the de facto standard to represent lexica relative to ontologies and it can be used to encode term banks as RDF. A multi-lingual, multi-jurisdictional term bank of copyright-related concepts has been published as linked data based on the ontolex-lemon model. The terminology links information from WIPO (concepts and definitions), IATE (multilingual terms, usage notes) and other sources as Creative Commons (multilingual definitions) or DBpedia (general concepts). The terms have been hierarchically arranged, spanning multiple languages and targeting different jurisdictions. The term bank has been published as a TBX dump file and is publicly accessible as linked data. The term bank has been used to annotate common licenses in the RDFLicense dataset.

Keywords: Term bank · Linked data · Copyright · Legal localization
Multilingualism

1 Introduction

Legal translations, namely the *translations of texts within the field of law*, are among the most difficult types of translations. The legal system referred by the source text may be different from the legal system referred by the target text, and the translation of the parts with a specific legal significance must be particularly precise at ensuring the correspondence of concepts at both sides. The mistranslation of a clause in a contract can lead to lawsuits or loss of money.

A *term bank* (also known as *term base* or more informally as *terminology*) is a database of concepts and terminological data related to a particular field. Terminologies help keeping translations consistent and help choosing the most adequate term when precision is required. Further, the *localization* of legal texts require of specialized terminologies where the exact concept in a legal system must be invoked.

The work presented in this paper describes a terminology created in a half-automated process, where terms and their definitions have been extracted and integrated from different lexical sources and mapped in a supervised process.

© Springer Nature Switzerland AG 2018
U. Pagallo et al. (Eds.): AICOL VI-X 2015–2017, LNAI 10791, pp. 410–423, 2018.
https://doi.org/10.1007/978-3-030-00178-0_28

The resulting terminology has been published[1] in the TBX format – ISO 30042 [1] – which is the standard for the exchange of terminologies; and it has also been published in Resource Description Format (RDF)[2], according to the schema described by Cimiano et al. [4]. The RDF version is especially suitable for establishing links with other resources (like DBpedia[3]) and with other terminologies. IATE[4], the inter-institutional database of the European Union (EU), has been taken as the external reference for some of the extracted terms.

Plain texts can be annotated, makin-g reference to concepts or terms in a term bank. This work also presents the text of a license that has been annotated with the terms in the copyright terminology here presented.

The use of a terminology of legal terms found in licenses is not exhausted with the mere translation or localization. Once in a digital format, it can alleviate the task of identifying the key elements in new licenses as in [5] or can help the study of comparative law.

The paper is organized as follows. Section 1 describes the motivation for having a term bank of copyright-related terms published as linked data. Details on the followed methodology and publication are given in Sects. 2 and 3 provides the related work and finally Sect. 4 contains the conclusions and future work.

2   Motivation: Legal Term Banks as Linked Data

The representation of copyright and related rights constitutes a part of legal knowledge currently at the limelight of European policy. Progress has been made in delivering copyright-related actions identified in the Digital Agenda[5], the Intellectual Property Strategy[6] and in the "Licences for Europe"[7] . The European Commission has presented legislative proposals to make sure that consumers and creators can make the most of the digital world: the reviewed EU copyright rules consists of a regulation[8] and a directive[9] on copyright in the Digital Single Market.

---

[1] The copyright terminology is online at: http://copyrighttermbank.linkeddata.es

[2] http://www.w3.org/RDF/

[3] http://dbpedia.org/

[4] http://iate.europa.eu/

[5] Communication on content in Digital Single Market (COM(2012) 789 final)

[6] In order to modernise the EU copyright legislative framework, "*A Single Market for Intellectual Property Rights*" (COM(2011) 287 final) was announced, which proposed series of measures to promote an efficient copyright framework for the Digital Single Market that include short and long-term key policy actions in various areas: patents, trademarks, geographical indications, multi-territorial copyright licensing, digital libraries, IPR violations, and IPR enforcement by customs

[7] As a premise for a cultural policy and from a structured stakeholder dialogue, industry-led solutions were put forward by stakeholders as a contribution to improve the availability of copyright-protected content online in the EU. Available at http://eur-lex.europa.eu/legal-content/EN/ALL/?uri=CELEX: 52012DC0789

[8] COM(2016), CELEX:52016PC0594

[9] COM(2016)593, CELEX:52016PC0593

The complexity of the regulatory system in this field, together with the variety of the corpus of copyright (patchwork of international and European sources, such as the *Berne Convention for the Protection of Literary and Artistic Works*, the *WIPO Copyright Treaty*, the *Directive 2001/29/EC*[10] (Copyright Directive), amongst other correlated sources[11]), poses difficulties to search, retrieve and understand the legal information in this domain. Moreover, in a pluralistic legal order [10] the *"[EU] legislation is drafted in several languages and [...] the different language versions are all equally authentic. An interpretation of a provision of [EU] law thus involves a comparison of the different language versions"*[12], in accordance with the principle of linguistic equality[13], which entails a "full multilingualism" [11]. Settled case-law refers that *"the need for a uniform interpretation of [EU] regulations makes it impossible for the text of a provision to be considered in isolation but requires, on the contrary, that it should be interpreted and applied in the light of the versions existing in the other official languages [...] [A]ll the language versions must, (...) be recognised as having the same weight"*.[14]

However, due to the factors that act as constraints in particular judgments, *"limited multilingualism"* seems a more realistic approach [18]. Besides, identifiable hindrances prevent cross-border access to legal information:

- Disclosure of open data makes difficult to retrieve relevant and useful information due to its overload and oversupply (large assortments of data);
- Legal documents are published as plain text without hyperlinks to the official legal resources, averting navigation and reasoning among documents; national and EU websites are sometimes poorly interconnected or they use different identification systems;
- Data is not always published in machine readable formats like XML or RDF for Linked Open Data, but in heterogeneous, non standard formats;
- Ambiguity and polysemy of legal terms [6]: the terminological misalignment and the conceptual misalignment [9] between the terminology used at the EU level from that of the national level, even when implementing EU directives [7];

---

[10] The purpose of Directive 2001/29/EC of the European Parliament and of the Council of 22 May 2001 on the harmonisation of certain aspects of copyright and related rights in the information society (Copyright Directive 83), is to implement theWIPO Copyright Treaty and to harmonise aspects of copyright law across Europe, such as copyright exceptions

[11] Connected legal instruments: the Directive 2009/24/EC of the European Parliament and of the Council of 23 April 2009 on the legal protection of computer programs, the Directive 96/9/EC of the European Parliament and of the Council of 11 March 1996 on the legal protection of databases, the WTO's Agreement on Trade-Related Aspects of Intellectual Property Rights (TRIPS)

[12] Case 283/81 *CILFIT e.a.* [1982] ECR 3415, paragraph 18

[13] See EEC Council: Regulation No 1 determining the languages to be used by the European Economic Community, [1958] OJ L 17/385

[14] See Case C-257/00 *Givane and Others* [2003] ECR I-345, para. 36 and C-152/01 *Kyocera* [2003] ECR I – 13833, para. 32

- Context-specificity of legal terms: the meaning of terms is related to the context of the legislation defining it (several context-specific definitions of legal terms with a common thread)[15];
- Cultural-specificity of legal terms: the meaning of terms is related to the context of the legal and political culture to which these terms belong to (think not only of the classical distinction between Common and Civil law countries, but of cultures with ideographic languages such as Chinese and Japanese) [8].

The need for cross-border multilingual access to legislation is required for legal practitioners, such as judges, lawyers, translators, legal drafters and scholars, but also to other decision-makers, amongst enterprises, public administrations and citizens, subject to regulatory compliance (even outside their own area of expertise and also jurisdiction), in order to: (i) exploit legal (open) data and therefore produce new innovative services for the legal information provision market; (ii) to predict the impact of implementing the EU legislature in each member state by enriching [7] structurally the documents (with navigable references along legal texts) and semantically (with concepts from ontologies and annotations); (iii) enhance information retrieval, automatic translation, automated reasoning; (iv) ensure the principle of legal certainty; (v) possibly strengthening the textual (or literal interpretation), and teleological interpretation upon which the European Court of Justice (ECJ)'s reasoning primarily rests.

Our work integrates the Linked Open Legal Data [12] momentum that illustrates *"the accessibility and semantic interoperability of legal sources"*[16]. Some of the advantages for rendering multi-lingual, multi-jurisdictional legal term banks published as linked data are:

- Clear separation and identification of concepts and terms, as data fits a formalized model and every resource is identifiable in a permanent manner.
- Easy browsing from a term in one language to an equivalent term in another language, although this makes only full sense when a preferred term is specified[17].
- Easy browsing among general terms and the jurisdiction-specific terms, as concepts can be hierarchically organized. This clarity helps towards the harmonization of copyright terms in the EU, an explicit goal in the EU copyright roadmap[18].
- Easy comparative analysis, as multiple sources are provided.
- Improved discovery and unequivocal identification of concepts and corresponding terms at both European and national levels.
- Better organization of conceptual domain knowledge and its availability of inter-related data sets on the Web in standard formats.

---

[15] This point is illustrated by the ruling of the ECJ Case 283/81 *CILFIT e.a.* [1982] ECR 3415, paragraph 19

[16] European Council, Draft Strategy on European e-justice 2014–2018, 2013 (2013/C 376/06)

[17] For example, IATE defines *preferred term* as: *"a term which should be used instead of any other (equally correct) synonym(s) present, for harmonisation purposes"*.

[18] For a explicit mention, see the "Draft Report on the implementation of Directive 2001/29/EC of the European Parliament and of the Council of 22 May 2001 on the harmonisation of certain aspects of copyright and related rights in the information society (2014/2256(INI))"

3 Linked Resources and Methodology

3.1 Publication Format

In order to build the present linked term bank, several resources have been considered.

(a) **WIPO** (World Intellectual Property Organization) publishes documents which include glossaries on copyright-related terms[19]. WIPO is an especially authoritative source as the custodian of the treaties on copyright signed by almost every country. Given their almost-universal validity, the definitions provided by WIPO are attributed thus to the most general concepts.

(b) **IATE** (Inter-Active Terminology for Europe) is the current EU's inter-institutional terminology resource database, created from several preexisting databases like EURODICAUTOM (Commission), TIS (Council) and EUTERPE (Parliament), among others. IATE is managed by representatives from different institutions including the authoritative entities like the ECJ or the Translation Centre for the Bodies of the European Union. IATE contains more than 8 million terms in all official 24 EU languages. It has been recently published as a linked data resource [4].

(c) **Creative commons licenses** are text documents published along with the referred work, and usually symbolized by icons, summaries or hyperlink references. Creative Commons licenses, massively adopted by the internet culture, have been published in versions tweaked for up to 60 different jurisdictions and different languages. These licenses commence with the definition of the key terms, which typically address the ones used in the target jurisdiction. From version 4.0[20], Creative Commons aimed at a neutral text, capable of fitting every legal system. Consequently, these definitions have been added to the general concepts and not to the jurisdiction-specific concepts.

(d) **Other resources**. Finally, the term bank can be linked to other linked resources to make it a highly connected linked data resource. In particular, the term bank of copyright-related resources has been linked to DBpedia, the linked data version of Wikipedia, and Lexvo.org[21], a dataset of entities about language. The use of these resources was possible as they had been published under open licensing modalities.

The methodology followed to create the term bank has been the following:

1. **Collection of top concepts**. Key copyright-related concepts have been extracted along with a general definition from the WIPO glossaries.
2. **Mapping to IATE**. The linked data version of IATE version was systematically queried in search of direct matches. From the different sources of IATE, the legal

---

one was preferred over others when more than one term matched. The resulting links were verified and completed manually by inspecting the official IATE place[22].

3. **Addition Creative Commons terms**. Over 100 creative commons terms have been defined, including the different versions, different jurisdiction ports and different languages. These resources are well classified in the RDFLicense dataset[23] [3], which also provides the links between license identifiers and legal texts. Creative Commons issued versions of the same license adapted to different jurisdictions before their version 4.0. Definitions from version 4.0 were added to the general concepts. The publication style of Creative Common licenses favors its automatic parsing and the formatting codes can be easily removed.

The publication of the dataset was made according to the linked data publication guidelines[24] and those specific for term bases [4].

3.2   The Copyright Term Bank

The information in term banks is usually arranged as depicted in Fig. 1, following the principle of strict separation between abstract concepts and the terms referring to them. More than one term is possible for the same concept, even in the same language.

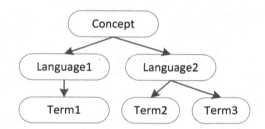

Fig. 1. Concepts and terms in terminology databases.

Concepts are typically accompanied by definitions, whereas terms are sometimes provided with additional information like the source, reliability, domain, additional notes, comments and the context of use.

In order to build our term bank, the structure has been extended to tackle the multi-jurisdiction information that is provided, and jurisdiction-specific concepts have been arranged as subspecies of general concepts (Fig. 2).

---

[22] http://iate.europa.eu/

[23] http://rdflicense.appspot.com/

[24] http://www.w3.org/TR/ld-bp/

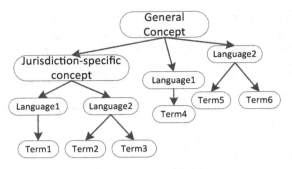

Fig. 2. Concepts in a legal terminology database.

3.3 Publication Format

TermBaseeXchange (TBX) is the industry XML standard language used to represent terminology data, sometimes used as native format, sometimes as interchange format. It is published by ISO as standard ISO30042 and by the Localization Industry Standards Association (LISA). The following excerpt shows an example of the published terminology in TBX:

```
<termEntry id="Derivativework (ES)>
 <langSetxml:lang="es">
  <tig>
   <term>obra derivada</term>
   <termNote type="termType">fullForm</termNote>
   <descrip type="reliabilityCode">3</descrip>
  </tig>
 </langSet>
 <langSetxml:lang="ca">
  <tig>
   <term>obra derivada</term>
   <termNote type="termType">fullForm</termNote>
   <descrip type="reliabilityCode">3</descrip>
  </tig>
 </langSet>
</termEntry>
```

Code excerpt 1. Fragment of a term bank in the industry-standard TBX format (ISO30042)

For an advanced format where linking to other resources is made more straight-forward, the RDF data structure as in [4] has been chosen. In order to represent the linguistic information, we have adopted the *ontolex-lemon* model [2, 3], whose representative schema is shown in Fig. 3. OntoLex is based on the ISO Lexical Markup Framework (LMF) and is an extension of the lemon model (LExicon Model for ONtologies). The specification of *ontolex-lemon* is currently under finalization by the W3C Ontolex Community Group[25] but it is already a *de facto* standard to represent ontology lexica.

---

[25] https://www.w3.org/community/ontolex/wiki/Final_Model_Specification

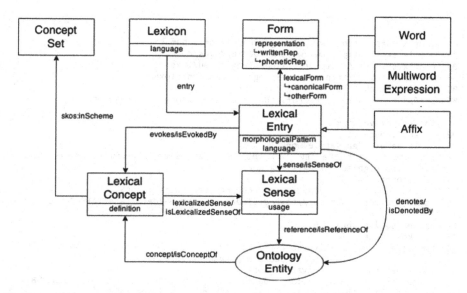

Fig. 3. The Ontolex-lemon model. Boxes denote OWL classes. The upper part of the boxes contains the class name and the lower part contains the name of datatype properties. Black arrows denote object properties, the white arrow denotes derivation and the symbol ↳ denotes a subproperty relationship.

The example in the excerpt that follows shows two concepts: the universal concept of "derivative work" (lines 7–13) and the concept of "derivative work" in particular in the Spanish jurisdiction (lines 14–20). "Derivative work" is a general concept (skos: Concept) that can be linked to the corresponding IATE concept (74645) and even to a DBpedia resource ("Derivative_work"). "Derivative work (ES)" is an abstract concept enshrined in 5 terms in 5 languages (Spanish, Catalan, Galician, Basque, Aranese) for which the creative commons licenses have a translation of the Spanish port. One of these terms is shown in lines 21–25, "obra derivada" in Galician language. The convention of using uppercase for denoting the country code of a jurisdiction has been used, as well as using lowercase to denote the language code.

```
01 @prefix rdfs:<http://www.w3.org/2000/01/rdf-schema#> .
02 @prefix skos:<http://www.w3.org/2004/02/skos/core#> .
03 @prefix tbx:<http://tbx2rdf.lider-project.eu/tbx#> .
04 @prefix ontolex:<http://www.w3.org/ns/lemon/ontolex#> .
05 @prefix dct:<http://purl.org/dc/terms/> .
06 @prefix ctb:< http://tbx2rdf.lider-project.eu/converter/resource/cc/> .

07 ctb:derivative work
08    a skos:Concept;
09    rdfs:label "derivative work";
10    skos:definition "a new work that translates or transforms one or more
 original copyrighted pre-existing works"@en;
11    dct:source "WIPO";
12    owl:sameAs <http://dbpedia.org/resource/Derivative_work> ;
13    skos:closeMatch <http://tbx2rdf.lider-project.eu/data/iate/IATE-74645> .

14 ctb:derivative work (ES)
15    a skos:Concept;
16    rdfs:label "derivative work (ES)";
17    cc:jurisdiction <http://dbpedia.org/resource/Spain> ;
18    skos:narrower ctb:derivative_work ;
19    ontolex:isDenotedBy ctb:obra_derivada_gl, ctb:lan_eratorri_eu, ctb:%C3%B2b
ra_derivada_oci, ctb:obras_derivadas_es, ctb:obra_derivada_ca ;
20    skos:definition "e. Consideraranse obras derivadas aquelas obras creadas a
 partir da licenciada, como por exemplo: as traducións e adaptacións; as revisi
óns, actualizacións e anotacións; os compendios, resumos e extractos; os arranx
os musicais e, en xeral, calquera transformación dunha obra literaria, artístic
a ou científica. Para evitar a dúbida, se a obra consiste nunha composición mus
ical ou gravación de sons, a sincronización temporal da obra cunha imaxe en mov
emento (synching) será considerada como unha obra derivada para os efectos dest
a licenza."@gl .

21 ctb:obra derivada gl
22    a ontolex:LexicalEntry;
23    ontolex:lexicalForm [ontolex:writtenRep "obra derivada"@gl ] ;
24    dct:source <http://creativecommons.org/licenses/by/3.0/es/legalcode.gl>;
25    tbx:reliabilityCode "3" .
```

Code excerpt 2. RDF Turtle serialization of one general concept (Derivative work), its derived concept for the Spanish legislation (Derivative_work (ES)) and one of its lexical entries ("obra derivada") in the galician language. To improve the legibility, the chars '%20' in the namespaced URIs have been replaced by a blankspace. Equivalently, parentheses have been introduced.

4   Qualified Translations

The above RDF representation based on *lemon* supports the modeling of copyright and related rights from a multilingual perspective. In this way, translations among different lexical representations of terms, expressed in different natural languages, can be inferred by traversing the RDF graph through their ontolex:LexicalSense. For instance one can translate "obra derivada" from Galician into Spanish by pivoting on their common sense[26] in the above example. However, the meta-operational relationship between legal reference and coreference has to be worked out.

---

[26] http://tbx2rdf.lider-project.eu/converter/resource/cc/derivative%20work%20%28ES%29

However, this method does not account for the specific type of linguistic translation that is taken place (e.g. literal translation, cultural equivalence, etc.). There exist, however, an extension of the *lemon* model, the so called *lemon translation module*[27], that reifies the translation relation and allows associating additional information to it, such as type of translation, confidence degree, provenance, and even the directionality of the relation [17]. This module has been integrated in the new Ontolex-lemon model as part of the new *vartrans* module.

In the case of the copyright term bank, using such mechanism to represent translations allows distinguishing between term descriptions that are a literal translation one from the other (for instance "obra derivada" in the previous example) from other situations in which the translated description has been adapted to the cultural or jurisdictional specificities of the target language or legal system. This might be beneficial for future semantic-aware applications in the legal domain. For instance, when legal terminology has to be compared across language, it can be done within the same jurisdictional domain, thus being a *literal translations* acceptable, or across jurisdictions, in which *legal equivalents* (rather than literal translations) have to be found.

The use of the *vartrans* module is exemplified in the following code excerpt. The lexical entries have two senses, which related by means of the reference to a common concept. The translation is reified and can be qualified as `trdcat:directEquiv-alent` or similar.

```
01 @prefix vartrans: <http://www.w3.org/ns/lemon/vartrans#> .
02 @prefix trcat: <http://purl.org/net/translation-categories#>

03 ctb:derivative_work (ES)
04   a skos:Concept;
05   rdfs:label "derivative work"@en ;
06   cc:jurisdiction <http://dbpedia.org/resource/Spain> .

07 ctb:lan_eratorri_eu
08   a ontolex:LexicalEntry;
09   ontolex:lexicalForm [ontolex:writtenRep "lan eratorri"@eu ] ;
10   ontolex:sense <http://example.org/sense_1> .

11 ctb:obra%20derivada_gl
12   a ontolex:LexicalEntry;
13   ontolex:lexicalForm [ontolex:writtenRep "obra derivada"@gl ];
14   ontolex:sense <http://example.org/sense_2> .

15 <http://example.org/sense_1> ontolex:reference ctb:derivative_work_(ES) .
16 <http://example.org/sense_2> ontolex:reference ctb:derivate_work_(ES) .
17 <http://example.org/sense_1-sense_2-trans> a vartrans:Translation ;
18   vartrans:relates <http://example.org/sense_1> ;
19   vartrans:relates <http://example.org/sense_2> ;
20   vartrans:category trcat:directEquivalent .
```

Code excerpt 3. Example of use of the ontolex-lemon vartrans module. Prefixes from Code excerpt 1 also apply.

---

[27] http://purl.org/net/translation

5 Related Work

In the literature, different methods exist for approaching the multilingual complexity of European law, for example controlled vocabularies, implemented in terminology database (such as IATE run by all the main EU Institutions that we have resort to in our work), thesauri (as EUROVOC), semantic lexicons or lightweight ontologies(as WordNet, EuroWordNet and, in the legal domain, JurWordNet) that we evoke here. EuroVoc Thesaurus[28] is the most important multilingual, multidisciplinary standardized thesaurus created by the EU, covering the activities of the EU. EuroVoc is managed by the Publications Office, which moved forward to ontology-based thesaurus management and semantic web technologies conformant to W3C recommendations as well as latest trends in thesaurus standards. However, EuroVoc represents a wide-coverage and faceted thesaurus built specifically for processing the documentary information of the EU institutions: the legal terminology is quite poor and limited to the legal fields belonging to the competence of EU.

The CELLAR repository provides semantic indexing, advanced search and data retrieval for multilingual resources to the information system of the Publications Office of the European Union information system. Resources and their Functional Requirements for Bibliographic Records (FRBR) embrace both the web of data perspective and the library or "bibliographic" data perspective [16]. Its new ontology development assumes that "the FRBR classes are collectors of resource metadata at their specific taxonomy level", thus, allowing a direct constant access to the FRBR levels [16, p. 35]. This represents certainly an improvement over the existing model, as it enhances the accessibility of the OP multilingual documents. However, its scope is also limited to the vocabulary of EU documents.

The Legal Taxonomy Syllabus [6] is a multilevel, multilingual ontology that takes a comparative law perspective to the modeling of legal terms and concepts from EU Directives, helping to increase European terminological consistency. Syllabus is an open-access database linking European terms with national transposition law and also linking terms horizontally (i.e., between national legal orders).

LexALP [14] uses a technique defined for general lexical databases to achieve cross language interoperability between languages of the Alpine Convention. This multilingual legal information system combines three main components, (i) a terminology data base, (ii) a multilingual corpus, and (iii) the relative bibliographic database. In this way the manually revised, elaborated and validated (harmonised) quadrilingual information on the legal terminology (i.e. complete terminological entries) will be closely interacting with a facility to dynamically search for additional contexts in a relevant set of legal texts in all languages and for all main legal systems involved.

The multilingual lexical database version of WordNet, EuroWordNet [13], compounds wordnets expressing lexica of 8 European languages. The wordnets are structured in terms of synsets (sets of synonymous words). Each synset in the

---

[28] http://eurovoc.europa.eu/drupal/

monolingual WordNets is linked to the others by cross-lingual equivalence relations to the English synsets recorded by the Inter-Lingual-Index (ILI). The database can be used for monolingual and cross-lingual information retrieval. The LOIS [13] database is compatible with the EuroWordNet architecture, and forms an extension of the EWN semantic coverage into the legal domain. Within this framework, LOIS contributes to the creation of a European Legal WordNet.

6   Conclusions and Future Work

We have perceived a particular European policy deference towards rendering the copyright and related rights domain more accurate. We have framed some of the advantages for yielding a multi-lingual, multi-jurisdictional legal term bank published as linked data in this domain. Therefore our work presents an effort to achieve a technical and semantic interoperability among linguistic domain concepts.

However, creating a term bank of legal terms is a time-consuming task where expertise in the law of different countries is needed and even domain-specific terminologies require a considerable effort. Legal terminologies, legal concepts and legal knowledge are not synonymous.

Several problems might be raised: (i) ISO standards secure the exchange of terminologies but do not manage the *legal value* of such terminologies, (ii) as said, Version 4.0 of Creative Commons aims at a neutral text, capable of fitting every legal system, but nothing prevents legal operators (e.g. judges) to offer different interpretations of general concepts at the jurisdiction-specific level; (iii) the term "bank" related to other linked resources such as *DBpedia* or *Lexvo.org* entails a more careful examination of this kind of relationship, as the *valence* (i.e. the number of edges incident to the vertex) of resources might not be equivalent, and in fact they are not.

Defining `owl:sameAs` relationships requires a more careful examination of the functional entrenchment of legal sources [15], a more extended comparative work of both legal and cultural systems [16] and and a closer attention to limited multilingualism in EU and national Courts [18]. This work will be completed in the next future with the annotations of a complete dataset of existing licenses.

By taking advantage of the fact that a *lemon*-based linguistic representation is available, other possibilities beyond direct matching (*owl:sameAs*) can be explored when mapping to IATE in order to make correspondences effective at the linguistic level [19], and more sophisticated automatic mapping processes implemented [20].

Acknowledgements. This work is supported by the EU FP7 LIDER project (FP7 – 610782), by DER2012-39492-C02-01 CROWDSOURCING, by Ministerio de Economía y Competitividad (Juan de la Cierva Incorpora) and by the fellowship 520250-1-2011-1-IT-ERASMUNDUS EMJD.

References

1. ISO 30042:2008. Systems to manage terminology, knowledge and content – TermBase eXchange (2008)
2. McCrae, J., et al.: Interchanging lexical resources on the semantic web. Lang. Resour. Eval. **46**, 701–719 (2012)
3. Rodriguez-Doncel, V., Villata, S., Gomez-Perez, A.: A dataset of RDF licenses. In: Hoekstra, R. (ed.) Proceedings of the 27th International Conference on Legal Knowledge and Information System, p. 189 (2014)
4. Cimiano, P., McCrae, J., Rodriguez-Doncel, V., Gornostay, A., Gomez-Perez, A., Simoneit, B.: Linked terminology: applying linked data principles to terminological resources. In: Kozem, S. et al. (eds.) Proceedings of the 4th Biennial Conference on Electronic Lexicography, pp. 504–517 (2014)
5. Cabrio, E., Palmero Aprosio, A., Villata, S.: These are your rights. In: Presutti, V., d'Amato, C., Gandon, F., d'Aquin, M., Staab, S., Tordai, A. (eds.) ESWC 2014. LNCS, vol. 8465, pp. 255–269. Springer, Cham (2014). https://doi.org/10.1007/978-3-319-07443-6_18
6. Ajani, G., Boella, G., Lesmo, L., Mazzei, A., Rossi, P.: Terminological and ontological analysis of European directives: multilinguism in law. In: 11th International Conference on Artificial Intelligence and Law (ICAIL), pp. 43–48 (2007)
7. Ajani, G., Boella, G., Martin, M., Mazzei, A., Radicioni D., Rossi, P.: Legal taxonomy syllabus 2.0. In: 3rd Workshop on Legal Ontologies and Artificial Intelligence Techniques Joint with 2nd Workshop on Semantic Processing of Legal Texts (2009)
8. Nakamura, M., Ogawa, Y., Toyama, K.: Extraction of legal definitions and their explanations with accessible citations. In: Casanovas, P., Pagallo, U., Palmirani, M., Sartor, G. (eds.) AICOL -2013. LNCS (LNAI), vol. 8929, pp. 157–171. Springer, Heidelberg (2014). https://doi.org/10.1007/978-3-662-45960-7_12
9. Lesmo, L., Boella, G., Mazzei, A.: Multilingual conceptual dictionaries based on ontologies: analytical tools and case studies. In: Proceedings of V Legislative XML Workshop, pp. 1–14 (2006)
10. Maduro, P.P.: Interpreting European law: judicial adjudication in a context of constitutional pluralism. Eur. J. Legal Stud. **1**, 137 (2007)
11. Hanf, D., Muir, E.: Le droit de l'Union européenne et le multilinguisme. In: Hanf, D.E., Malacek, M.K. (eds.) Langue et Construction Européenne (2010)
12. Casellas, N.: Linked legal data: a SKOS vocabulary for the code of federal regulations. http://www.semantic-web-journal.net/system/files/swj311_2.pdf (2012)
13. Peters, W., Sagri, M.T., Tiscornia, D.: The structuring of legal knowledge in LOIS. Artif. Intell. Law **15**, 117–135 (2007)
14. Lyding, V. et al.: The LexALP information system: term bank and corpus for multilingual legal terminology consolidated. In: Proceedings of the Workshop on Multilingual Language Resources and Interoperability, pp. 25–31 (2006)
15. Casanovas, P., Casellas, N., Vallbé, J.J.: Empirically grounded developments of legal ontologies: a socio-legal perspective. In: Casanovas, P., et al. (eds.) Approaches to Legal Ontologies, pp. 49–67. Springer, Dordrecht (2011). https://doi.org/10.1007/978-94-007-0120-5_3
16. Francesconi, E., Küster, Marc W., Gratz, P., Thelen, S.: The ontology-based approach of the publications office of the eu for document accessibility and open data services. In: Kő, A., Francesconi, E. (eds.) EGOVIS 2015. LNCS, vol. 9265, pp. 29–39. Springer, Cham (2015). https://doi.org/10.1007/978-3-319-22389-6_3

17. Gracia, J., Montiel-Ponsoda, E., Vila-Suero, D., Aguado-de Cea, G.: Enabling language resources to expose translations as linked data on the web. In: Proceedings of 9th Language Resources and Evaluation Conference. European Language Resources Association, pp. 409–413 (2014)
18. Derlén, M.: Multilingual Interpretation of European Union Law. Kluwer Law International, Dordrecht (2009)
19. Gracia, J., Montiel-Ponsoda, E., Cimiano, P., Gómez-Pérez, A., Buitelaar, P., McCrae, J.: Challenges for the multilingual web of data. J. Web Semant. 11, 63–71 (2012)
20. Euzenat, J., Shvaiko, P.: Ontology Matching. Springer, Berlin (2007). https://doi.org/10.1007/978-3-540-49612-0

Legal Argumentation

Anything You Say May Be Used Against You in a Court of Law
Abstract Agent Argumentation (Triple-A)

Ryuta Arisaka[1]($\boxtimes$), Ken Satoh[2], and Leendert van der Torre[3]

[1] University of Perugia, Perugia, Italy
`ryutaarisaka@gmail.com`
[2] National Institute of Informatics, Tokyo, Japan
[3] University of Luxembourg, Luxembourg City, Luxembourg

Abstract. *Triple-A* is an abstract argumentation model, distinguishing the global argumentation of judges from the local argumentation of accused, prosecutors, witnesses, lawyers, and experts. In Triple-A, agents have partial knowledge of the arguments and attacks of other agents, and they decide autonomously whether to accept or reject their own arguments, and whether to bring their arguments forward in court. The arguments accepted by the judge are based on a game-theoretic equilibrium among the argumentation of the other agents. The Triple-A theory can be used to distinguish various direct and indirect ways in which the arguments of an agent can be used against his or her other arguments.

1 Introduction

There has been a long and fruitful interaction between formal argumentation and legal reasoning. Legal reasoning has inspired the development of formal argumentation techniques, and formal argumentation is frequently used as a methodology in the legal domain. Whereas legal applications are typically based on structured argumentation theories, following the work of Dung [16], also more abstract argumentation theories are considered in the law [7,9,13,18,24]. For example, formal argumentation has been applied to modelling doctrines in common law of contract [17], to US Trade Secrets Law [1], and to hypothetical, evidential and abductive reasoning [8,10,11].

In this paper we introduce *Triple-A*, which stands for *Abstract Agent Argumentation*. We are interested in argumentation of agents such as judges, accused, prosecutors, witnesses, lawyers, and experts in court. In particular, in this paper we address the following questions using Triple-A:

This work was partially supported by JSPS KAKENHI Grant Number 17H06103. Moreover, the third author has received funding from the European Union's Horizon 2020 research and innovation programme under the Marie Skodowska-Curie grant agreement No 690974 for the project MIREL: MIning and REasoning with Legal texts.

U. Pagallo et al. (Eds.): AICOL VI–X 2015–2017, LNAI 10791, pp. 427–442, 2018.
https://doi.org/10.1007/978-3-030-00178-0_29

1. How is the argumentation of judges related to the argumentation of the other agents?
2. How can the arguments an agent puts forward, be used against him?

To answer the first question, we use abstract Dung style semantics, but with a twist. Whereas in Dung style argumentation, an agent presents a set of accepted arguments, called an extension, in our approach an agent presents a sub-framework of his or her argumentation framework. We can still recover the extensions from these sub-frameworks, but the sub-frameworks contain more information. This additional information can be exploited by the global argumentation of the judge. In particular, since the argumentation of each agent may depend on the argumentation of the other agents, we define the argumentation of the judge as a game-theoretic equilibrium among the argumentation of the other agents.

The second question refers to the title, which in turn refers to the so-called Miranda warning, also referred to as the Miranda rights. This is a right to silence warning given by police in the United States to criminal suspects in police custody before they are interrogated to preserve the admissibility of their statements against them in criminal proceedings. Every U.S. jurisdiction has its own regulations regarding what, precisely, must be said to a person arrested or placed in a custodial situation. The typical warning states:

- You have the right to remain silent and refuse to answer questions.
- Anything you say may be used against you in a court of law.
- You have the right to consult an attorney before speaking to the police and to have an attorney present during questioning now or in the future.
- *Etc.*

For formal argumentation, this raises the question how an agent's arguments can be used against him or her. In this paper, we use the Triple-A theory to study different ways in which this can happen. An argument of an agent can be used directly against him, for example if he contradicts himself. However, more interestingly, the arguments of an agent can be used against him indirectly, via the argumentation of other agents. We associate with every agent the set of arguments and attacks of other agents he is aware of. Moreover, we assume that the agent takes these arguments and attacks into account when deciding which arguments to accept.

This paper combines former research of the authors, in particular the work on coalitional argumentation of the first two authors [3] and the work on multi-sorted and input/output argumentation of the third author [5,28].

The layout of this paper is as follows. In Sect. 2 we give an overview of abstract argumentation, including the sub-framework variant of Dung's abstract argumentation semantics we need for agents taking the arguments of other agents into account. In Sect. 3 we introduce Triple-A and we explain how the argumentation of judges is related to the argumentation of the other agents. In Sect. 4 we discuss how arguments of an agent can be used against his or her other arguments.

2   Sub-framework Semantics

A sub-framework semantics called AFRA semantics was introduced by Baroni *et al.* [6]. In this section we introduce our version of sub-framework semantics.

We first recall Dung's extension-based semantics. In this paper we consider only stable semantics.

Definition 1 (Stable semantics). *Let $\mathscr{F} = (\mathscr{A}, \mathscr{R})$ be a graph called an argumentation framework, where the elements of $\mathscr{A}$ are called* arguments *and the binary relation $\mathscr{R}$ is called* attack. *A set of arguments $B \subseteq \mathscr{A}$ is a* stable extension *if and only if it does not contain two arguments a_1 and a_2 such that a_1 attacks a_2, and for all arguments a_2 not in B, there is an argument a_1 in B such that a_1 attacks a_2. We write $stb(\mathscr{F})$ for the set of all stable extensions of $\mathscr{F}$.*

We now consider sub-framework semantics. Close-minded stable semantics returns exactly the stable extensions, and no attacks. Attack-minded stable semantics returns all arguments, and all attacks except the ones on arguments in the stable extension. This semantics was introduced as attack semantics by Villata *et al.* [31]. Open-minded semantics returns the attack-minded semantics, as well as attacks from arguments on arguments in the grounded extension. The grounded extension is defined as usual as the fixed point of the characteristic function, that returns all arguments defended by a set of arguments. Max-minded semantics returns all sub-frameworks that have exactly one of the stable extensions of the framework, and that are maximal in the sense that its super-frameworks do not return this stable extension. Also other sub-framework semantics can be defined, but we do not consider them in this paper.

Definition 2 (X-minded stable semantics). *Let f be the defence (or characteristic) function $f(S) = \{a \in \mathscr{A} \mid \forall b \in \mathscr{A} : \mathscr{R}(b, a) \exists c \in S : \mathscr{R}(c, b)\}$, and f^* be the fixed point $f(\ldots(f(\emptyset)))$. Close-minded stable semantics C, attack-minded stable semantics A, open-minded stable semantics O, and max-minded stable semantics M are given by*

- $C(\mathscr{A}, \mathscr{R}) = \{(E, \emptyset) \mid E \in stb((\mathscr{A}, \mathscr{R}))\}$,
- $A(\mathscr{A}, \mathscr{R}) = \{(\mathscr{A}, \mathscr{R} \setminus (\mathscr{A} \times E)) \mid E \in stb((\mathscr{A}, \mathscr{R}))\}$,
- $O(\mathscr{A}, \mathscr{R}) = \{(\mathscr{A}, \mathscr{R} \setminus (\mathscr{A} \times (E \setminus f^*))) \mid E \in stb((\mathscr{A}, \mathscr{R}))\}$,
- $M(\mathscr{A}, \mathscr{R}) = \{(\mathscr{A}, \mathscr{R}') \mid stb((\mathscr{A}, \mathscr{R}')) = \{E\} \subseteq stb((\mathscr{A}, \mathscr{R})), \text{ if } \mathscr{R} \supseteq \mathscr{R}'' \supset \mathscr{R}' \text{ then } stb((\mathscr{A}, \mathscr{R}'')) \neq \{E\}\}$.

Sub-framework semantics can be used as a model of dynamic argumentation, because open-minded agents may on the one hand accept an argument a when also the arguments of other agents are considered, while on the other hand rejecting this argument a when only their own arguments are considered. For example, consider an argument framework $\mathscr{F}$ where argument b attacks argument a. The open-minded sub-framework is $\mathscr{F}$ and expresses the extension b. However, if later argument b is removed, then argument a is accepted. The close-minded single argument framework contains only argument b. Once b is removed, no argument is accepted at all.

Attack-minded and open-minded stable semantics satisfy the property that the stable extensions coincide with the stable extensions of the sub-frameworks. Close-minded and max-minded stable semantics satisfy the same property trivially.

Proposition 1 (Relation). $\cup\{stb(\mathscr{F}') \mid \mathscr{F}' \in X(\mathscr{F})\} = stb(\mathscr{F})$ *for* $X \in \{C, A, O, M\}$.

Proof. Vacuous for $X \in \{C, M\}$. Consider $X = A$, we note that every member $(\mathscr{A}, \mathscr{R}\backslash(\mathscr{A} \times E))$ of $A(\mathscr{A}, \mathscr{R})$ removes from $(\mathscr{A}, \mathscr{R})$ all attacks on members of E. Hence it is not possible that $stb((\mathscr{A}, \mathscr{R}\backslash(\mathscr{A} \times E)))$ does not contain members of E. For $X = O$, note that every member $(\mathscr{A}, \mathscr{R}\backslash(\mathscr{A} \times (E\backslash f^*)))$ of $A(\mathscr{A}, \mathscr{R})$ removes from $(\mathscr{A}, \mathscr{R})$ all attacks on members of E except when the members of E belong to the grounded extension. Let us denote the set of all such members of E by A_g. However, as the arguments attacking any member of A_g cannot be in a member of $stb((\mathscr{A}, \mathscr{R}))$ by the definition of the grounded extension, and, further, that all attacks on those attacking arguments will be preserved in $(\mathscr{A}, \mathscr{R}\backslash(\mathscr{A} \times (E\backslash f^*)))$, we see that A_g continue to be in $stb((\mathscr{A}, \mathscr{R}\backslash(\mathscr{A} \times (E\backslash f^*))))$, which, moreover, is $\{E\}$. □

Sub-framework stable semantics is illustrated in Example 1 below.

Example 1 (X-minded stable semantics). In Fig. 1, we find an argumentation framework $\mathscr{F}_1$, as shown in (A). It consists of three arguments a_1, a_2, a_3, and the following attacks: $(a_1, a_2), (a_2, a_3), (a_3, a_2), (a_3, a_1)$. We have $stb(\mathscr{F}_1) = \{a_3\}$. Hence $C(\mathscr{F}_1) = \{(a_3, \emptyset)\}$. To obtain $A(\mathscr{F}_1)$, we compute $\mathscr{R}\backslash(\mathscr{A} \times E)$. We have that $\mathscr{A} \times E = \{(a_1, a_3), (a_2, a_3), (a_3, a_3)\}$. Therefore the result of computation is $\{(a_1, a_2), (a_3, a_2), (a_3, a_1)\}$. Consequently, $A(\mathscr{F}_1)$ has the argumentation framework shown in Fig. 1 as its sole member. In this example, $E\backslash f^* = E\backslash\{\} = E$, and $O(\mathscr{F}_1) = A(\mathscr{F}_1)$. Finally, there being only one stable extension $\{a_3\}$ for $\mathscr{F}_1$, we have $M(\mathscr{F}_1) = \mathscr{F}_1$. Any sub-framework of $\mathscr{F}_1$ having $\{a_3\}$ as its stable extension cannot belong to M because $\mathscr{F}_1$ as a larger sub-framework has the same extension.

To show that $A \neq O$, consider $\mathscr{F}_2$ in (B) of Fig. 1. Here $f^*(\mathscr{F}_2)$, i.e. the grounded extension of $\mathscr{F}_2$, is not empty and a_2 (not in $stb(\mathscr{F}_2)$) attacks a_3 (in $f^*(\mathscr{F}_2)$), thus (a_2, a_3) remains in $O(\mathscr{F}_2)$. $A(\mathscr{F}_2)$ can be compared to it.

Proposition 2. *We write* $(\mathscr{A}, \mathscr{R}) \subseteq (\mathscr{A}', \mathscr{R}')$ *for* $(\mathscr{A} \subseteq \mathscr{A}')$ *and* $(\mathscr{R} \subseteq \mathscr{R}')$. *Let* $\sqsubseteq: X \times X$, $X \in \{C, A, O, M\}$, *be a predicate such that* $X_1 \sqsubseteq X_2$ *iff, for each (finite) argumentation framework* $\mathscr{F}$ *and for each* $\mathscr{F}_2 \in X_2(\mathscr{F})$, *there exists some* $\mathscr{F}_1 \in X_1(\mathscr{F})$ *such that* $\mathscr{F}_1 \subseteq \mathscr{F}_2$ *and that* $stb(\mathscr{F}_2) = stb(\mathscr{F}_1)$.[1] *Then* $C \sqsubseteq A \sqsubseteq O \sqsubseteq M$.

---

[1] The other direction (i.e. for each $\mathscr{F}_1 \in X_1(\mathscr{F})$) is redundant by Proposition 1.

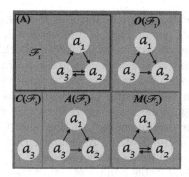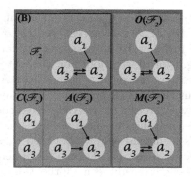

Fig. 1. (A) An argumentation framework $\mathscr{F}_1$ with the only one member of: $C(\mathscr{F}_1)$ (close-minded semantics); $A(\mathscr{F}_1)$ (attack-minded semantics); $O(\mathscr{F}_1)$; and $M(\mathscr{F}_1)$ (max-minded semantics). (B) An argumentation framework $\mathscr{F}_2$ with the only member of: $C(\mathscr{F}_2)$; $A(\mathscr{F}_2)$; $O(\mathscr{F}_2)$; and $M(\mathscr{F}_2)$.

Proof.

$C \sqsubseteq A$: Immediate from $E \subseteq \mathscr{A}$.

$A \sqsubseteq O$: Follows from $\mathscr{R} \backslash (\mathscr{A} \times E) \subseteq \mathscr{R} \backslash (\mathscr{A} \times (E \backslash f^*))$ (also see in Example 1).

$O \sqsubseteq M$: It is vacuous from the definition of M that for each member $(\mathscr{A}, \mathscr{R}')$ of $M(\mathscr{A}, \mathscr{R})$ there does not exist any larger $\mathscr{R}''$ than $\mathscr{R}'$ such that $(\mathscr{A}, \mathscr{R}'')$ has the same stable extension E as $(\mathscr{A}, \mathscr{R}')$ for each such E. Hence it suffices to show that $O(\mathscr{A}, \mathscr{R})$ contains an element $(\mathscr{A}, \mathscr{R} \backslash (\mathscr{A} \times (E \backslash f^*)))$ for each such E, which, however, follows vacuously from the definition of O. $\qquad\square$

An *argumentation framework with input* consists of an argumentation framework $\mathscr{F} = (\mathscr{A}, \mathscr{R})$, a set of external input arguments $\mathscr{I}$, an input extension $E_\mathscr{I}$ of $\mathscr{I}$ and an attack relation $R_\mathscr{I}$ from $\mathscr{I}$ to $\mathscr{A}$. Given an argumentation framework with input, a *local function* returns a corresponding set of sub-frameworks of $\mathscr{F}$. This is a sub-framework version of the local functions defined by Baroni *et al.* [5], returning a corresponding set of extensions of $\mathscr{F}$. Since they define their local acceptance functions for all Dung semantics, not only for stable semantics, their definitions are more general than ours. Similar notions are defined also by Liao [21]. We refer to these papers for further explanations and examples about local functions.

Definition 3 (Local stable semantics). *We write $2^\mathscr{F}$ for $\{\mathscr{F}' \mid \mathscr{F}' \subseteq \mathscr{F}\}$. For a set of arguments $\mathscr{B} \subseteq \mathscr{A}$, we write $(\mathscr{A}, \mathscr{R})_\mathscr{B}$ for $(\mathscr{B}, \mathscr{R} \cap (\mathscr{B} \times \mathscr{B}))$, and for a set of frameworks S, we write $S_\mathscr{B}$ for $\{\mathscr{F}_\mathscr{B} \mid \mathscr{F} \in S\}$.*

An argumentation framework with input is a tuple $(\mathscr{F}, \mathscr{I}, E_\mathscr{I}, R_\mathscr{I})$, including an argumentation framework $\mathscr{F} = (\mathscr{A}, \mathscr{R})$, a set of arguments $\mathscr{I}$ such that $\mathscr{I} \cap \mathscr{A} = \emptyset$, an input extension $E_\mathscr{I} \subseteq \mathscr{I}$ and a relation $R_\mathscr{I} \subseteq \mathscr{I} \times \mathscr{A}$. A local function assigns to any argumentation framework with input a (possibly empty) set of sub-frameworks of $\mathscr{F}$, i.e. $f(\mathscr{F}, \mathscr{I}, E_\mathscr{I}, R_\mathscr{I}) \subseteq 2^\mathscr{F}$.

Local X-minded stable semantics is defined by $f_X((\mathscr{A}, \mathscr{R}), \mathscr{I}, E_\mathscr{I}, R_\mathscr{I}) = X(\mathscr{A} \cup E_\mathscr{I}, \mathscr{R} \cup (R_\mathscr{I} \cap (E_\mathscr{I} \times \mathscr{A})))_\mathscr{A}$ for $X \in \{C, A, O, M\}$.

Example 2 (Continued). From a point of view, X-mindedness in local stable semantics of $\mathscr{F}$ can be regarded as controlling the amount of information about $stb(\mathscr{F})$ to be revealed. Let us consider the simple argumentation framework $\mathscr{F}_2$ in Fig. 1 for illustration. For the context, suppose there was a murder, and that the scene of murder was Laboratory A. A man is being suspected. Another man reasons that the suspect could not have been able to enter Laboratory A, as the facility enforces a very strict access control (argument a_3). He reflects that with an ID card, the suspect could have been there (argument a_2). At this point there occurs a mutual conflict between a_3 and a_2. However, he remembers that the suspect had lost his ID card (argument a_1), dismissing a_2 thereupon.

As can be easily seen, all the X-minded local stable semantics return the same Dung stable semantics: that a_1 (the suspect had lost his ID card) and a_3 (the suspect could not enter Laboratory A) but not a_2 are in the extension. However, the man could be as liberal as giving away all the reasoning as conducted in his mind or, on the other hand, could choose just to state concisely what he thinks are acceptable.

$X = C$ represents the latter, under which he merely reveals a_1 and a_3, which does not necessarily make clear the link between the suspect's possession of an ID card and access to Laboratory A. In this example, $X \in \{O, M\}$ represents the former, revealing his reasoning precisely. Sitting between the two attitudes is $X = A$ under which he nuances his reasoning, that, although the suspect could have been in Laboratory A with an ID card, such a thought should be dismissed because the suspect had lost his ID card and could not get in there.

In the rest, we will focus on C and O.

3   Argumentation of Judge vs Argumentation of Others

An AAA framework is an argumentation framework together with a set of agents and an assignment of the arguments to the agents. We call the agents also the *sources* of the arguments. Rienstra *et al.* [28] call it a multi-sorted argumentation framework.

Definition 4 (Agents). *An abstract agent argumentation (or AAA, or Triple-A) framework is a tuple $\mathscr{F} = (\mathscr{A}, \mathscr{R}, Ag, Src)$ where $\mathscr{A}$ is a non-empty set (of arguments), $\mathscr{R} \subseteq \mathscr{A} \times \mathscr{A}$ is a binary relation over arguments (expressing attack), Ag is a set (of agents) and $Src : \mathscr{A} \to Ag$ is a function mapping each argument to the agent that put it forward (also known as its source). For agent $A \in Ag$, we write $\mathscr{A}_A$ for $\{a \in \mathscr{A} \mid Src(a) = A\}$ and $(\mathscr{A}, \mathscr{R})_A$ for $(\mathscr{A}_A, \mathscr{R} \cap (\mathscr{A}_A \times \mathscr{A}_A))$, and for a set of frameworks S, we write S_A for $\{\mathscr{F}_A \mid \mathscr{F} \in S\}$.*

To illustrate Triple-A, we introduce a legal running example, based on two witnesses.

Example 3. The following scenario is inspired by an example from Okuno and Takahashi [22]. Suppose there occurred a murder, and that there are two persons individually reasoning over the case. One of them, say Wit 1, thinks firmly that the suspect killed the victim at Laboratory C at around 7 pm (argument a_2). All material evidence imply that only the suspect could have killed the victim. However, there is one remaining counter-evidence: the suspect had lost his ID card which is required to enter the laboratory (argument a_1). Thus Wit 1 is unable to prove a_2 beyond doubt. Meanwhile, the other witness Wit 2 has heard from the suspect that he was at restaurant until 7:10 pm (argument a_4). Wit 2 wants to trust the suspect's words. Just at a corner of Wit 2's mind, a doubt lingers: that the suspect could have been at the laboratory, because the security system of the building was faulty and no ID card was needed on the day (argument a_3).

Let us suppose that the overall argumentation $\mathscr{F}_x$ is as shown in Fig. 2. There $Src(a_1) = Src(a_2) = $ Wit 1 and $Src(a_3) = Src(a_4) = $ Wit 2. However, for both Wit 1 and Wit 2, the conclusion that they would draw could be very different if they communicated or otherwise. If Wit 1 learns of a_3, for Wit 1, there will be no longer any doubt that a_2 holds, and if Wit 2 learns of a_2, Wit 2 would reason that a_4 was a lie by the suspect after all. On the other hand, if Wit 1 (Wit 2) is unaware of a_3 (a_2), Wit 1 (Wit 2) would remain inconclusive of his/her decision.

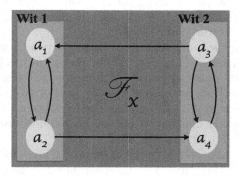

Fig. 2. An argumentation framework $\mathscr{F}_x$ with two agents: Wit 1 and Wit 2, who each has two arguments.

Epistemic Triple-A extends Triple-A with the knowledge of the agents, which reflects the arguments and attacks the agents are aware of. As two extreme cases, we consider so-called *aware agents* that know all the arguments and attacks of other agents, and so-called *unaware agents* that only know their own arguments and the attacks among them.

Definition 5 (Aware and unaware agents). *Epistemic Abstract Agent Argumentation (or EAAA, or Epistemic Triple-A) framework* $\mathscr{F} = \langle \mathscr{A}, \mathscr{R}, Ag, Src, K \rangle$ *extends a Triple-A framework with the agent knowledge K, a function $K_A(\mathscr{F}) \subseteq \mathscr{F}$ that maps agent $A \in Ag$ to a sub-framework of $\mathscr{F}$, representing the arguments and attacks the agent knows. We assume $\mathscr{F}_A \subseteq K_A(\mathscr{F})$, representing that agents know their own arguments and the attacks among them. An agent A is called aware if $K_A(\mathscr{F}) = \mathscr{F}$ and unaware if $K_A(\mathscr{F}) = \mathscr{F}_A$.*

Agent semantics is a local function with respect to the agent input, where the knowledge of the agents is used to define the input of the agents.

Definition 6 (Agent stable semantics). *Let $\mathscr{F} = \langle \mathscr{A}, \mathscr{R}, Ag, Src, K \rangle$ be an Epistemic Triple-A framework, $A \in Ag$ be an agent and $K_A(\mathscr{F}) = (\mathscr{A}', \mathscr{R}')$ be agent A's knowledge. The input of A is $I_A = \{a_1 \in \mathscr{A}' \mid (a_1, a_2) \in \mathscr{R}' \cap ((\mathscr{A} \setminus \mathscr{A}_A) \times \mathscr{A}_A)\}$, and the conditioning relation of A is $R_{I_A} = \mathscr{R}' \cap (I_A \times \mathscr{A}_A)$,*

Given a sub-framework stable semantics $S \in \{C, O\}$, agent stable semantics is local function $f_S(\mathscr{F}, I_A, E_{I_A}, R_{I_A}) = S(\mathscr{A} \cup E_{\mathscr{F}}, \mathscr{R} \cup (R_{\mathscr{F}} \cap (E_{\mathscr{F}} \times \mathscr{A})))_A$.

The running witnesses example illustrates the local agent argumentation semantics of the witnesses.

Example 4 (Continued). We look at C and O for both aware and unaware agents. Let us consider open-minded semantics to begin with ((A)-(B2) in Fig. 3). Suppose Wit 1 is aware, then $\mathscr{F}_A$ (Cf. (A) of Fig. 3) is considered for local agent semantics. When argument a_3, the input argument, is in the input extension, Wit 1's local agent semantics, $f_O(\mathscr{F}_{\text{Wit1}}, \{a_3\}, \{a_3\}, \{(a_3, a_1)\})$, must be the set of sub-argumentation frameworks of $\mathscr{F}_{\text{Wit1}}$ whose Dung stable extension is $\{a_2\}$, and which have all arguments that appear in $\mathscr{F}_{\text{Wit1}}$. $\mathscr{F}(1a)$ as shown in (A1) of Fig. 3 is the only one possibility. Intuitive meaning of this semantics is that, when Wit 2 presumes a_3 acceptable, Wit 1 will presume a_2 acceptable and a_1 unacceptable as his/her response.

When a_3 is not in the input extension, there are two Dung stable extensions for $\mathscr{F}_{\text{Wit1}}$, i.e. $stb(\mathscr{F}_{\text{Wit1}}) = \{\{a_1\}, \{a_2\}\}$. $f_O(\mathscr{F}_{\text{Wit1}}, \{a_3\}, \emptyset, \{(a_3, a_1)\})$, Wit 1's local agent semantics, must therefore be the set of sub-argumentation frameworks of $\mathscr{F}_{\text{Wit1}}$ whose Dung extension is either $\{a_1\}$ or $\{a_2\}$, and which have all arguments that appear in $\mathscr{F}_{\text{Wit1}}$. We consequently obtain $\{\mathscr{F}(1a), \mathscr{F}(1b)\}$ (Cf. (B) of Fig. 3). In a similar manner, we obtain open-minded local agent semantics for aware Wit 2 (Cf. (B)-(B2) of Fig. 3).

Now, suppose that Wit 1 is unaware. Then we consider $\mathscr{F}_{\text{Wit1}}$ (Cf. (C) of Fig. 3). Unaware Wit 1's open-minded local agent semantics $f_O(\mathscr{F}_{\text{Wit1}}, \{a_3\}, \emptyset, \{(a_3, a_1)\})$ is $\{\mathscr{F}(1a), \mathscr{F}(1b)\}$, as shown in (b) of Fig. 3. As expected, this case is the same as for aware Wit 1 when a_3 is not in the input extension. In a similar manner, we obtain open-minded local agent semantics for unaware Wit 2 ((D1) of Fig. 3).

For close-minded semantics ((A2), (B2), (C2), (D2) in Fig. 3), we obtain only arguments for agents local semantics without attack arrows.

We now give the central definition of our multi-agent interaction. Since the local semantics is expressed as sub-frameworks, but the input is expressed as an extension, we represent the equilibria by pairs of an argumentation framework and an extension.[2]

---

[2] We can define multiagent semantics also as a set of arguments only, as follows: A stable MAS extension E is a subset of $\mathscr{A}$ such that there exists a sub-framework $\mathscr{F}'$ of $\mathscr{F}$ such that .... As suggested by Massiliano Giacomin, there seems to be no loss of information using just extensions. We did not do so, because the resulting definition seems to become more difficult to read.

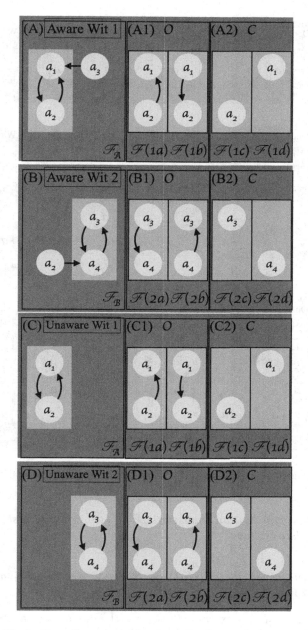

Fig. 3. Illustration of agent stable semantics for aware/unaware agents.

Definition 7 (Multi-agent semantics). *Let* $\mathscr{F} = \langle \mathscr{A}, \mathscr{R}, Ag, Src, K \rangle$ *be an Epistemic Triple-A framework, and for each agent* $A \in Ag$, *let* $S_A \in \{C, O\}$ *be an agent stable semantics for agent* A. *The semantics of a triple-A framework* $\mathscr{F}$

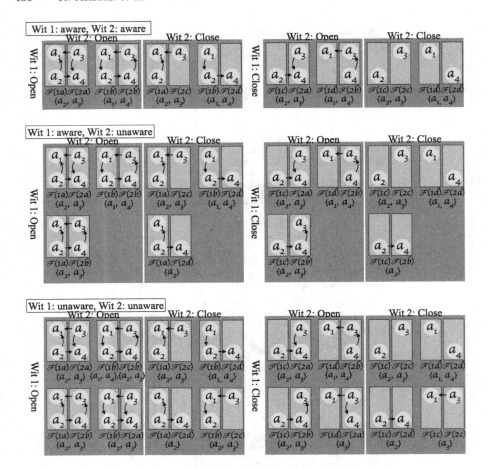

Fig. 4. Multi-agent semantics of Wit 1's and Wit 2's local agent stable semantics.

is a pair of an argumentation framework $\mathscr{F}' = (\mathscr{A}', \mathscr{R}')$ and a stable extension E of $\mathscr{F}'$ such that we have

1. $\mathscr{F}'_A \in S(\mathscr{F}_A, I_A, E \cap I_A, R_{I_A})_A$, and
2. for all (a_1, a_2) such that $Src(a_1) \neq Src(a_2)$, we have $(a_1, a_2) \in \mathscr{R}'$ iff $(a_1, a_2) \in \mathscr{R} \cap (\mathscr{A}' \times \mathscr{A}')$.

The running witnesses example illustrates the global argumentation semantics of the judge.

Example 5 (Continued). Consider $\mathscr{F}_x$ (Cf. Fig. 2) once again. We saw open-minded and close-minded local agent stable semantics for Wit 1 and Wit 2 in Example 4. Figure 4 lists all combinations of open/close-minded and aware/unaware agents and their multi-agent semantics, except for (Wit 1:

unaware, Wit 2: aware) case, as it is symmetric to (Wit 1: aware, Wit 2: unaware) case.

Notice that, even when local agent Wit 1 in its local agent stable semantics accepts a_1 ($\mathscr{F}(1c)$), a_1 may not be accepted in multi-agent stable semantics (see the combination $\mathscr{F}(1b)\mathscr{F}(2a)$ when both Wit 1 and Wit 2 are unaware). As such, the multi-agent semantics reflects judge's viewpoint who must evaluate all arguments provided by involved agents to deliver fair judgement.

For comparisons of open-minded and close-minded semantics, notice that we could gain a set-theoretically smaller extension with close-minded agents than with open-minded agents. As Fig. 4 shows, if, for unaware agents, open-minded Wit 1's $\mathscr{F}(1b)$ is combined with close-minded Wit 2's $\mathscr{F}(2c)$, we obtain $\{a_2, a_3\}$ as the extension for the multi-agent semantics, whereas with close-minded Wit 1's $\mathscr{F}(1d)$ and close-minded Wit 2's $\mathscr{F}(2c)$, we obtain $\{a_3\}$ as the extension, even though Dung stable extensions for $\mathscr{F}(1b)$ and $\mathscr{F}(1d)$ are the same. The rationale is that open-minded witnesses may provide more information for the judge to evaluate.

4   Argument Against the Agent

In this section we illustrate ways in which agent's arguments may be used against him/her. We use a variation of the running example with an accused, a witness, a prosecutor and finally a judge who globally evaluates these arguments.

Example 6. There occurred a murder at Facility C. Acc is being accused. There is a witness Wit and a prosecutor Prc. Acc has in mind two arguments:

a_1 that he was at Facility A on the day of the murder. (This is a fact known to Acc)
a_2 that he is innocent. (This is Acc's claim)

Prc entertains:

a_6 that only Acc could have killed the victim. (This is Prc's claim)

Meanwhile, Wit believes certain information. He has three arguments:

a_3 Acc stayed at home on the day of the murder, having previously lost his ID card. (This Wit originally believes to be a fact)
a_4 Acc could enter any facility provided he is with his ID card. (This is a fact known to Wit)
a_5 Acc could not have been at Facility C at the time of the murder. (This is Wit's claim)

Further, the relation between the three arguments is such that a_3 attacks a_4 which attacks a_5. Altogether, these arguments by the three agents form the argumentation framework in Fig. 5.

Each of Acc, Prc and Wit reveals his/her internal argumentation, partially or elaborately, for the judge to evaluate. But since an agent may come to learn

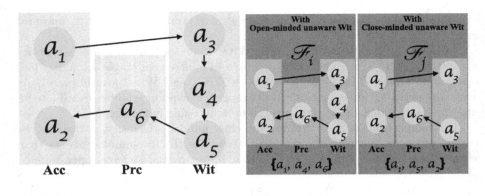

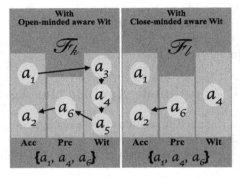

Fig. 5. Left: Argumentation by an accused (marked Acc), by a witness (marked Wit), and by a prosecutor (marked Prc). Right: multi-agent semantics with open-minded unaware Wit ($\mathscr{F}_i$), with close-minded unaware Wit ($\mathscr{F}_j$), with open-minded aware Wit ($\mathscr{F}_k$), and with close-minded aware Wit ($\mathscr{F}_l$).

arguments by other agents when, say, they are expressed before he/she presented his/her own, it is possible that he/she take the additional information into account in delivering his/her decision.

In this example, both Prc and Acc have the trait of our unaware agents, for Prc has no reason to drop his/her argument a_6; neither does Acc, seeing no benefit in admitting to a_6. However, how Wit responds to the fact known to Acc (a_1) can prove crucial for him to be judged innocent or guilty.

Case A. Suppose Wit is unaware and open-minded. Wit presents what he believes, namely his local argumentation framework (see $\mathscr{F}_i$ in Fig. 5). She locally accepts a_3 and a_5. The judge evaluates all arguments, concluding that a_2 is not acceptable, i.e. Acc is guilty. The judge starts his inference with Acc's acceptable a_1, to reject a_2. The two arguments a_3 and a_5 accepted by Wit are not accepted by the judge. This illustrates indirect use of an argument against Acc.

Case B. Suppose Wit is unaware and close-minded. Wit, instead of presenting all reasoning as he did to develop his local argumentation, states the key points concisely: that Acc stayed at home on the day of the murder, and that Acc could not have been at Facility C (see $\mathscr{F}_j$). The omission of the fact known to Wit (a_4), which Wit perhaps considers irrelevant to the criminal case, changes judge's decision completely. In $\mathscr{F}_j$, a_5 is an argument that is globally acceptable, which rejects a_6 in favour of a_2.

Case C. Suppose Wit learns a_1 beforehand. Wit realises that a_3 which she thought was a fact is not factual. She no longer claims a_5 in her local argumentation, although she discloses her argumentation entirely (see $\mathscr{F}_k$). Her decision that a_4 is acceptable agrees with the judge's, and the latter concludes that a_2 shall be rejected.

Case D. Suppose again Wit learns a_1 beforehand, but that she mentions the key arguments concisely. She states that entry to any facility requires an ID card (see $\mathscr{F}_l$). Here again, the judge has no objection to the evidence that might have been provided by Proc. a_6 is accepted, to prove Acc guilty. This illustrates a direct use of an argument by Wit against Acc.

As we highlighted, agents attributes influence global judgement. Further, an argument may be used against an agent directly or indirectly.

5   Related Work

Argumentation by autonomous agents have been studied mostly in the context of strategic argumentation games [2,20,23,25,26,29]. Negotiation dialogues [2] characterise changes in the set of arguments acceptable to an agent in accordance to new arguments another agent introduces into his/her local scope, which, as ours, respects agents locality. Compared to the existing studies, however, the focus of our work is more on analysis of how derivation of local semantics by local agents influences global arguments' acceptance. As we observed, multi-agent semantics for open-minded agents may not be the same as for close-minded agents, even when they accept the same sets of arguments. We observed also that locally accepted arguments may not belong to globally acceptable arguments. Agents attributes: open-minded vs close-minded and aware vs unaware, play a role in the interaction of local agent semantics. There are other agents attributes [23]. While many studies on game-theoretic strategic argumentation games have presupposed complete information (see [19]), realistic legal examples often involve uncertainty of the belief state of other agents', and a theory that adapts to incomplete information is highly relevant. In our framework, local agents may be uncertain of acceptability statuses of the arguments that could be attacking their arguments (the input arguments). As such, they consider their best response to each possible scenario for dealing with the element of uncertainty based on their agents attributes.

Rahwan and Larson [27] contemplate (re)construction of an argumentation framework from the arguments in a given argumentation framework that are distributed across agents. In the construction process, the agents may or may not reveal their arguments, and the global outcome to be obtained varies with their decisions. Concerning this, we saw that even if all involved agents are open-minded and revealing all arguments in their local space, the global outcome may still differ.

Judgement aggregation [4,12,14,30] to determine acceptable arguments based on social choice theory or aggregation of argumentation frameworks [15] are being studied. While they are not the main focus of this paper, such studies become important when we deal with agents perception of other agents' local argumentation. We aim to extend our theory for that kind of a situation in future work.

6 Conclusion

Triple-A is an agent abstract argumentation model, distinguishing the global argumentation of judges from the local argumentation of accused, prosecutors, witnesses, lawyers, experts and so on. In Triple-A, the agents decide autonomously whether to trust the other agents in the sense of taking some of their arguments into account. Moreover, they decide autonomously whether to accept or reject their own arguments, and whether to bring their arguments forward in court. The globally accepted arguments by the judge are defined using a game theoretic equilibrium definition.

Triple-A framework distinguishes various direct and indirect ways in which the arguments of an agent can be used against his other arguments.

Acknowledgement. We thank Massimiliano Giacomin for insightful feedback on an earlier version of this paper.

References

1. Al-abdulkarim, L., Atkinson, K., Bench-Capon, T.: ANGELIC secrets: bridging from factors to facts in US trade secrets. In: JURIX, pp. 113–118 (2016)
2. Amgoud, L., Vesic, S.: A formal analyis of the role of argumentation in negotiation dialogues. J. Log. Comput. 5, 957–978 (2012)
3. Arisaka, R., Satoh, K.: Coalition formability semantics with conflict-eliminable sets of arguments (Extended Abstracts). In: AAMAS, pp. 1469–1471 (2017)
4. Awad, E., Booth, R., Tohmé, F., Rahwan, I.: Judgement aggregation in multi-agent argumentation. J. Log. Comput. 27(1), 227–259 (2017)
5. Baroni, P., Boella, G., Cerutti, F., Giacomin, M., van der Torre, L.W.N., Villata, S.: On the input/output behavior of argumentation frameworks. Artif. Intell. 217, 144–197 (2014)
6. Baroni, P., Cerutti, F., Giacomin, M., Guida, G.: AFRA: argumentation framework with recursive attacks. Int. J. Approx. Reason. 52(1), 19–37 (2011)

7. Bench-Capon, T.: Representation of case law as an argumentation framework. In: JURIX, pp. 53–62 (2002)
8. Bench-Capon, T., Prakken, H.: Using argument schemes for hypothetical reasoning in law. Artif. Intell. Law **18**(2), 153–174 (2010)
9. Bench-Capon, T., Sartor, G.: A model of legal reasoning with cases incorporating theories and values. Artif. Intell. **150**, 97–143 (2003)
10. Bex, F., Bench-Capon, T., Atkinson, K.: Did he jump or was he pushed? Abductive practical reasoning. Artif. Intell. Law **17**(2), 79–99 (2009)
11. Bex, F., Prakken, H., Reed, C., Walton, D.: Towards a formal account of reasoning about evidence: argumentation schemes and generalisations. Artif. Intell. Law **11**(2), 125–165 (2003)
12. Bodanza, G.A., Auday, M.R.: Social argument justification: some mechanisms and conditions for their coincidence. In: Sossai, C., Chemello, G. (eds.) ECSQARU 2009. LNCS (LNAI), vol. 5590, pp. 95–106. Springer, Heidelberg (2009). https://doi.org/10.1007/978-3-642-02906-6_10
13. Brewka, G., Strass, H., Ellmauthaer, S., Wallner, J., Woltran, S.: Abstract dialectical frameworks revisited. In: IJCAI (2010)
14. Caminada, M., Pigozzi, G.: On judgement aggregation in abstract argumentation. Auton. Agents Multi-Agent Syst. **22**(1), 64–102 (2011)
15. Coste-Marquis, S., Devred, C., Konieczny, S.: On the merging of dung's argumentation systems. Artif. Intell. **171**(10–15), 730–753 (2007)
16. Dung, P.M.: On the acceptability of arguments and its fundamental role in nonmonotonic reasoning, logic programming, and n-person games. Artif. Intell. **77**(2), 321–357 (1995)
17. Dung, P.M., Thang, P.M.: Modular argumentation for modelling legal doctrines in common law of contract. Artif. Intell. Law **17**, 167–182 (2008)
18. Gordon, T., Prakken, H., Walton, D.: The carneades model of argument and burden of proof. Artif. Intell. **171**, 875–896 (2007)
19. Governatori, G., Olivieri, F., Rotolo, A., Scannapieco, S., Sartor, G.: Two faces of strategic argumentation in the law. In: JURIX, pp. 81–90 (2014)
20. Grossi, D., van der Hoek, W.: Audience-based uncertainty in abstract argument games. In: IJCAI, pp. 143–149 (2013)
21. Liao, B.: Toward incremental computation of argumentation semantics: a decomposition-based approach. Ann. Math. Artif. Intell. **67**(3–4), 319–358 (2013)
22. Okuno, K., Takahashi, K.: Argumentation system with changes of an agent's knowledge base. In: IJCAI vol. 09, pp. 226–232 (2009)
23. Parsons, S., Sklar, E.: How agents alter their beliefs after an argumentation-based dialogue. In: Parsons, S., Maudet, N., Moraitis, P., Rahwan, I. (eds.) ArgMAS 2005. LNCS (LNAI), vol. 4049, pp. 297–312. Springer, Heidelberg (2006). https://doi.org/10.1007/11794578_19
24. Prakken, H., Sartor, G.: A dialectical model of assessing conflicting arguments in legal reasoning. Artif. Intell. Law **4**, 331–368 (1996)
25. Procaccia, A., Rosenschein, J.: Extensive-form argumentation games. In: EUMAS, pp. 312–322 (2005)
26. Rahwan, I., Larson, K.: Argumentation and game theory. In: Simari, G., Rahwan, I. (eds.) Argumentation in Artificial Intelligence, pp. 321–339. Springer, Heidelberg (2009). https://doi.org/10.1007/978-0-387-98197-0_16
27. Rahwan, I., Larson, K.: Mechanism design for abstract argumentation. In: AAMAS, pp. 1031–1038 (2008)

28. Rienstra, T., Perotti, A., Villata, S., Gabbay, D.M., van der Torre, L.: Multi-sorted argumentation. In: Modgil, S., Oren, N., Toni, F. (eds.) TAFA 2011. LNCS (LNAI), vol. 7132, pp. 215–231. Springer, Heidelberg (2012). https://doi.org/10.1007/978-3-642-29184-5_14

29. Riveret, R., Prakken, H.: Heuristics in argumentation: a game theory investigation. In: COMMA, pp. 324–335 (2008)

30. Tohmé, F.A., Bodanza, G.A., Simari, G.R.: Aggregation of attack relations: a social-choice theoretical analysis of defeasibility criteria. In: Hartmann, S., Kern-Isberner, G. (eds.) FoIKS 2008. LNCS, vol. 4932, pp. 8–23. Springer, Heidelberg (2008). https://doi.org/10.1007/978-3-540-77684-0_4

31. Villata, S., Boella, G., van der Torre, L.: Attack semantics for abstract argumentation. In: IJCAI 2011, Proceedings of the 22nd International Joint Conference on Artificial Intelligence, Barcelona, Catalonia, Spain, 16–22 July 2011, pp. 406–413 (2011)

A Machine Learning Approach to Argument Mining in Legal Documents

Prakash Poudyal[(✉)] [iD]

Department of Informatics, University of Évora, Évora, Portugal
prakashpoudyal@gmail.com

Abstract. This study aims to analyze and evaluate the natural language arguments present in legal documents. The research is divided into three modules or stages: an Argument Element Identifier Module identifying argumentative and non-argumentative sentences in legal texts; an Argument Builder Module handling clustering of argument's components; and an Argument Structurer Module distinguishing argument's components (premises and conclusion). The corpus selected for this research was the set of Case-Laws issued by the European Court of Human Rights (ECHR) annotated by Mochales-Palau and Moens [8]. The preliminary results of the Argument Element Identifier Module are presented, including its main features. The performance of two machine learning algorithms (Support Vector Machine Algorithm and Random Forest Algorithm) is also measured.

Keywords: Legal argument · Natural language analysis
Machine learning

1 Introduction

An argument combines a premise or a set of premises and a conclusion. Historically, Dialectics and Philosophy are the ancient roots of the discipline of argumentation. Arguments have always been considered an important branch of Philosophy and, with the passage of time and advancement in technology, its relevance has grown exponentially in other fields such as Literature, Logic, Law, and also in Mass Communication and Artificial Intelligence. Arguments are the fundamental tools for human beings to argue and reach their objectives. During debates, the conclusion of an argument is the focal point of the discussion. Premises are the vehicle that supports the conclusion's reasoning and approval. There are premises that reinforce other premises and as such add strength to the conclusion. During a discussion, facts, figures and further evidence as well as logic are provided to support, attack and/or refute the opponent's arguments. At a time when social media is one of the most important discussion platforms available, the number of users expressing their opinion has grown exponentially. Usually, such opinions are expressed through an array of premises that generate ideas and claims. Considering the relevance of argumentation in everyday life and its ubiquity in the

© Springer Nature Switzerland AG 2018
U. Pagallo et al. (Eds.): AICOL VI-X 2015–2017, LNAI 10791, pp. 443–450, 2018.
https://doi.org/10.1007/978-3-030-00178-0_30

judiciary, this study was made to analyse and evaluate the natural language used in argumentative legal documents. To automatically identify the argument in an unstructured text, a system was developed in three stages or modules. The first stage or module is the Argument Element Identifier, henceforth referred to by its acronym AEI. In this module, the main aim was to identify the argumentative and non-argumentative sentences in a corpus of legal documents. The structuring of arguments is addressed in the second stage or the Argument Builder Module, henceforth referred to as AB. In the third stage, the Argument Structurer Module (henceforth referred to as AS), the system will distinguish the arguments' components (premise and conclusion). The corpus selected for this study was the Case-Law issued by the European Court of Human Rights (ECHR) annotated by Mochales-Palau and Moens [8]. Details of the corpus are described in [11].

Mochales-Palau and her colleagues [6–10,13] have published several papers identifying and extracting arguments from both the ECHR Corpus and the Araucaria Corpus[1]. Moens et al. [9] used features such as n-gram, verb nodes, word couples, and punctuation and their average accuracy results was close to 74% in various types of text but dropped slightly to 68% in the legal corpus. Mochales-Palau and Moens [8] added more features such as modal auxiliary, keywords, negative/positive words, text statistics, punctuation keywords, same words in both the previous as well as the following sentence, and first and last words in the next sentence and reported accuracy results of 90%. Mochales-Palau and Moens [10] also defined the argument boundaries i.e. the beginning as well as the end of an argument. Since components of the argument can be found scattered throughout the text, the authors suggest using semantic distance to solve this issue and argue for the use of context-free grammars (CFG) to detect the argument structure and claim to have reached and accuracy of 60%. The technique presented by these authors is applied only to a very limited number of Case-Laws.

Stab et al. [15,16] analysed argumentative writings from a discourse structure perspective. They used structural, lexical, syntactic and contextual features to determine argumentative discourse structures in persuasive essays. Their experiment succeeded in establishing the f-measure for identifying argument components at 0.726. They focused on word indicators and lexical features that highlight an argumentative sentence. Doddington et al. [4] described four challenges and identified five types and 24 subtypes of relations. The "Role" type of relation, which refers to the part a person plays in an organization, can be subtyped as Manager, General Staff, Member, Owner, Founder, Client, Affiliate-Partner, Citizen-of or Other. The "Part" type of the relation can be subtyped as Subsidiary, Part-of or Other. The "Near" type identifies relative locations. The "Social" type can be subtyped as Parent, Sibling, Spouse, Grandparent, Other-Relative, Other-Personal, Associate, or Other-Professional.

Bunescu and Mooney [2] presented a novel approach to extract the relation between entities by presenting a new kernel for the relation extraction, based on the shortest path between the two relation entities in a dependency graph. They

---

[1] http://araucaria.computing.dundee.ac.uk/doku.php.

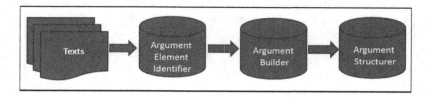

Fig. 1. Proposed Architecture of the System

deployed an "Automatic Content Extraction" on a corpus of newspaper articles and were able to show significant improvements over a recent dependency tree kernel. Biran and Rambow [1] also aimed to identify argumentative relations while Cabrio and Villata *et al.* [3] used a combination of textual entailment framework and bipolar abstract argumentation approach to evaluate argument texts and find the relation between the arguments. Florou *et al.* [5] used a grammatical approach of future and conditional tenses and moods. They highlight the impact of illustration, justification, and rebuttal wording in the argument. Poudyal and Quaresma [12] have found that the Support Vector Machine is the best machine learning algorithm in identifying name entity relation.

2 Proposed Approach

The system we propose consists of three sequential modules or phases as illustrated by Fig. 1.

1. Argument Element Identifier (AEI): identifies argumentative and non - argumentative sentences in legal texts;
2. Argument Builder (AB): handles arguments' components' clustering;
3. Argument Structurer (AS): distinguishes arguments components (premise and conclusion).

During the Argument Element Identifier (AEI) phase, our main task was to find an optimal machine learning algorithm with appropriate features to distinguish an argumentative from a non-argumentative sentence in legal documents. We conducted several experiments with various machine learning algorithms and classified them according to the type of features used. Figure 2 presents an overview of the AEI phase. After identifying the argumentative sentences in a legal text, it is necessary to organize these sentences into argumentative clusters composed by a set of argumentative sentences interconnected or related to each other. Detecting the boundaries of an argument is a very challenging task mainly due to the fact that its components (premise and conclusion) may be connected or related to other arguments. To cluster such sentences, we deployed a fuzzy clustering algorithm (FCA) that provides a membership value ranging from 0 to 1 for each sentence cluster. The membership values are the key assets of the FCA, which allows us to associate each sentence to more than one argument cluster. The performance of the algorithm depends on the type of features

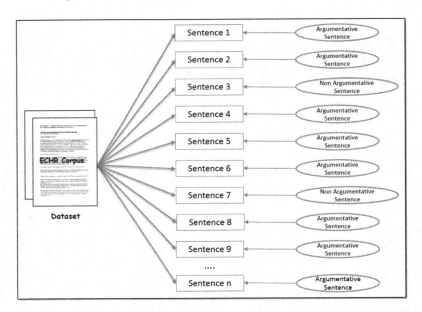

Fig. 2. Overview of the Argument Element Identifier Module (AEI)

selected. In this study, we focus on the following features: 'N-gram', 'Word2vec', and 'Sentence Position'. Figure 3 offers an overview of this phase. On the AS phase, argument components (premise and conclusion) are identified as having a premise or a conclusion basis. The sentences identified as having a premise basis are outright premises or consist of a premise clause. The sentences identified as having a conclusion basis are obvious conclusions or point towards one. Many sentences that have a premise basis and are tagged as such may also include a conclusion clause and the same happens to the sentences labeled as displaying a conclusion basis. To accomplish this task, we deployed indicator features. Indicator features play an important role in identifying argument's premises and conclusions. Words such as "finally," "therefore," "concluding," and "thus" clearly introduce a conclusion and play an important role in the process of identifying argument's conclusions. It is also highly probable that sentences containing words like "should," "could," "almost," "must be," "because," "seems," and "would like," are premises. A major limitation in the AS phase is that each sentence may have one or several premises but only one conclusion, and also the system's accuracy rate will diminish whenever the classifier is not able to identify the sentence's conclusion, or identifies more than one conclusion in a single argument.

3   AEI Preliminary Results

The main goal of the AEI phase was to select the algorithm with the most appropriate parameters. We aimed to develop a system that will automatically

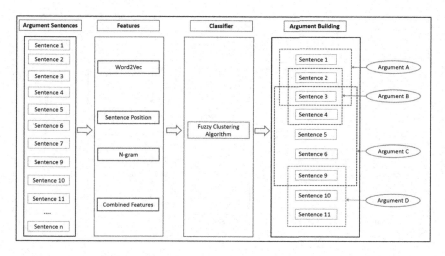

Fig. 3. Overview of the Argument Builder (AB) Module

identify the argumentative sentences on an unstructured textual document. As Fig. 4 illustrates, the AEI system's architecture follows several steps. Initially, the corpus needs to be refined. Once the features are extracted, the classifier can then be built and its performance evaluated.

The words that form a document must be mapped in accordance to a predetermined token and TF-IDF in order to normalise the length of each unit. In our experiment, this procedure created 11374 features. The TF-IDF [11] function was calculated as:

$$tf - idf(w_i, d) = tf(w_i, d)ln\frac{N}{df(w_i)} \tag{1}$$

where $tf(w_i d)$ is the frequency word w_i in document d and $df(w_i)$ is the number of documents where w_i appears and N is the number of documents in the corpus. To measure performance we used precision, recall and f-measure [14] methods. We ran several experiments with the machine learning algorithms Support Vector Machine (SVM) and Random Forest (RF) to determine their performance in identifying argumentative sentences in accordance with the features provided. We selected the top-n informative features (using the gain ratio measures) with $n \in \{100, 200, 500, 1000, 2000, 5000, 11374\}$ and tested the polynomial kernel SVM with various values for the complexity parameter ($C \in \{0.001, 0.01, 0.1, 1, 10,$ and $100\}$). Similar experiments were conducted deploying the Random Forest algorithm using several trees ($nt \in \{7, 11, 17, 50, 100\}$).

Figures 5 and 6 show the graph of f-measure vs. Support Vector Machine (SVM) algorithm and f-measure vs. Random Forest Algorithm respectively. In the SVM chart (Fig. 5), as the number of features increases, the performance of f-measure increases, up to 2000 features. The highest f-measure value of 0.595 was achieved with c = 0.1 and 2000 features in the SVM algorithm experiment.

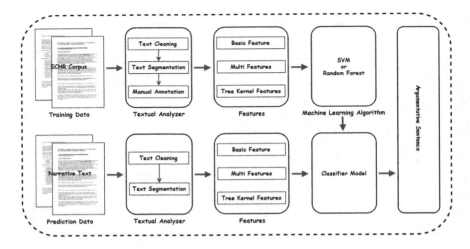

Fig. 4. Architecture of argument element identifier (AEI) Module

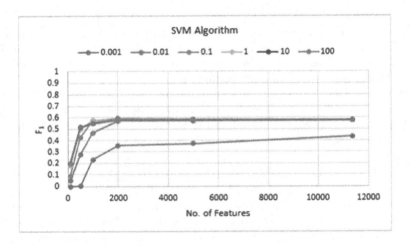

Fig. 5. F-Measure of SVM algorithm

In case of the graph of f-measure obtained from the Random Forest Algorithm chart, (Fig. 6) as the number of features increases, a peak f-measure of 0.52 was reached with 1000 features and 100 trees. Then, the f-measure value decreases up to 2000 and remains constant till 11681 features. We can therefore conclude that the SVM algorithm produced better results than the RF algorithm. Overall, the results achieved are quite promising and support our proposal for the creation of a new argument mining framework.

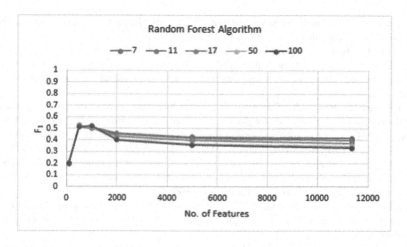

Fig. 6. F-Measure of RF algorithm

4 Conclusion and Future Works

We are proposing a new approach to automatically identify arguments in legal documents which is phased in three modules: Argument Element Identifier (AEI), Argument Builder (AB) and Argument Structurer (AS). The preliminary results of the AEI are extremely promising and support to the development of a new argument mining framework. Further research must be done on the use of string kernel as well as other alternative representation models, including linguistic features such as POS tags, Parse trees and Tree Kernel.

Acknowledgment. The current work is funded by EMMA-WEST in the framework of the EU Erasmus Mundus Action 2.

References

1. Biran, O., Rambow, O.: Identifying justifications in written dialogs by classifying text as argumentative. Int. J. Semant. Comput. **5**(04), 363–381 (2011). https://doi.org/10.1142/S1793351X11001328
2. Bunescu, R.C., Mooney, R.J.: A shortest path dependency kernel for relation extraction. In: Proceedings of the Human Language Technology Conference and Conference Empirical methods in Natural Language Processing (HLT/EMNLP-05), pp. 724–731. Association for Computational Linguistics, Stroudsburg (2005). https://doi.org/10.3115/1220575.1220666
3. Cabrio, E., Villata, S.: Towards a benchmark of natural language arguments. In: Proceedings of the 15th International Workshop on Non-Monotonic Reasoning (NMR 2014), Vienna (2014)
4. Doddington, G., Mitchell, A., Przybocki, M., Ramshaw, L., Strassel, S., Weischedel, R.: The automatic content extraction (ace) program-tasks, data, and

evaluation. In: Proceedings of the Fourth International Conference on Language Resources and Evaluation, vol. 2, pp. 837–840 (2004)

5. Florou, E., Konstantopoulos, S., Koukourikos, A., Karampiperis, P.: Argument extraction for supporting public policy formulation. In: Proceedings of the 7th Workshop on Language Technology for Cultural Heritage, Social Sciences, and Humanities, pp. 49–54 (2013)

6. Mochales, R., Ieven, A.: Creating an argumentation corpus: do theories apply to real arguments?: a case study on the legal argumentation of the ECHR. In: Proceedings of the 12th International Conference on Artificial Intelligence and Law, pp. 21–30. ACM, New York (2009). https://doi.org/10.1145/1568234.1568238

7. Mochales, R., Moens, M.F.: Study on the structure of argumentation in case law. In: Proceedings of the 2008 Conference on Legal Knowledge and Information Systems, pp. 11–20. IOS Press, Amsterdam (2008)

8. Mochales-Palau, R., Moens, M.F.: Study on sentence relations in the automatic detection of argumentation in legal cases. Front. Artif. Intell. Appl. **165**, 89–98 (2007)

9. Moens, M.F., Boiy, E., Palau, R.M., Reed, C.: Automatic detection of arguments in legal texts. In: Proceedings of the 11th International Conference on Artificial Intelligence and Law, pp. 225–230. ACM (2007)

10. Palau, R.M., Moens, M.F.: Argumentation mining: the detection, classification and structure of arguments in text. In: Proceedings of the 12th International Conference on Artificial Intelligence and Law, pp. 98–107. ACM (2009). https://doi.org/10.1145/1568234.1568246

11. Poudyal, P., Goncalves, T., Quaresma, P.: Experiments on identification of argumentative sentences. In: Proceeding of 10th International Conference on Software, Knowledge, Information Management & Applications (SKIMA), pp. 398–403. IEEE (2016). https://doi.org/10.1109/SKIMA.2016.7916254

12. Poudyal, P., Quaresma, P.: An hybrid approach for legal information extraction. Front. Artif. Intell. Appl. (JURIX) **250**, 115–118 (2012). https://doi.org/10.3233/978-1-61499-167-0-115

13. Reed, C., Palau, R.M., Rowe, G., Moens, M.F.: Language resources for studying argument. In: Proceedings of the Sixth International Conference on Language Resources and Evaluation (LREC 2008), Marrakech, Morocco, pp. 91–100 (2008)

14. Salton, G., Wong, A., Yang, C.S.: A vector space model for automatic indexing. Commun. ACM **18**(11), 613–620 (1975). https://doi.org/10.1145/361219.361220

15. Stab, C., Gurevych, I.: Identifying argumentative discourse structures in persuasive essays. In: Proceedings of the Conference on Empirical Methods in Natural Language Processing (EMNLP), pp. 46–56 (2014). https://doi.org/10.3115/v1/D14-1006

16. Stab, C., Kirschner, C., Eckle-Kohler, J., Gurevych, I.: Argumentation mining in persuasive essays and scientific articles from the discourse structure perspective. In: Proceedings with the Workshop on Frontiers and Connections between Argumentation Theory and Natural Language Processing, Bertinoro, Italy, pp. 40–49 (2014)

Answering Complex Queries on Legal Networks: A Direct and a Structured IR Approaches

Nada Mimouni[1]([✉]), Adeline Nazarenko[2], and Sylvie Salotti[2]

[1] Chair Governance Analytics, Université Paris Dauphine – PSL,
75016 Paris, France
nada.mimouni@dauphine.fr
[2] LIPN (UMR 7030), Université Paris 13 – Sorbonne Paris Cité & CNRS,
93430 Villetaneuse, France
{adeline.nazarenko,sylvie.salotti}@lipn.univ-paris13.fr

Abstract. This paper highlights the benefit of semantic information retrieval in legal networks. User queries get more complex when they combine constraints on semantic content and intertextual links between documents. Comparing two methods of search in legal collection networks, we present new functionalities of search and browsing. Relying on a structured representation of the collection graph, the first approach allows for approximate answers and knowledge discovery. The second one supports richer semantics and scalability but offers fewer search functionalities. We indicate how those approaches could be combined to get the best of both.

Keywords: Semantic information retrieval · Legal collection graphs
Exact answers · Approximate search · Knowledge discovery

1 Introduction

Legal practitioners are permanently in the need to search legal collections in order to assess regulatory texts applicable to a specific case. Needs analysis with legal experts and partners of the Légilocal project [1] showed that users express their needs in the form of complex queries that address both the semantic content and intertextual links between documents. For instance, when drafting an order, municipal clerks typically have to identify the legislation to refer to as well as former orders published on the same topic, especially those that have been appealed. They would enter queries like *"Which local acts concerning rural roads have been appealed and were canceled by court decision?"*.

Legal information retrieval (IR) systems widely used by both citizens and practitioners are not able to handle such complex queries. They return documents based on the keyword they contain or are associated to as metadata and not on intertextual grounds. Answers are returned as a list of documents without taking into account the graphs to which those documents belong (esp. references

© Springer Nature Switzerland AG 2018
U. Pagallo et al. (Eds.): AICOL VI-X 2015–2017, LNAI 10791, pp. 451–464, 2018.
https://doi.org/10.1007/978-3-030-00178-0_31

to other texts). To build the context of a given document, a step of exploratory search – starting from one returned result and going through its hypertextual links – is required. In legal collections, where numerous and various types of links exist between legal sources, users get easily lost.

Moreover, legal IR systems operate as logical search systems since a user needs to get all texts related to his query and not only the most relevant ones. Answers are returned when documents match exactly the sent queries. When no exact answer is found or when too few or too many answers are returned, users are not satisfied with the results and must continue to query the system until they get a relevant response.

In an earlier research, we have proposed an approach towards semantic and graph-based search in networks of legal documents [5] and demonstrated the potentialities that a graph-based semantic IR approach could offer to legal content management systems. In this approach, the intertextual information is taken into account at the querying level to that it is possible to answer complex queries like *"What are the legal decisions that cite Article 1382 of the Civil Code?"*, *"I am looking for decisions that were canceled by the Court of Cassation."* or *"What are the code articles that have been confirmed and which are cited by the municipal orders dealing with rural roads?"*.

In this work, we propose to extend that logical approach with advanced search and discovery functionalities, by returning approximate answers when no exact one is found, by allowing to restrict or enlarge the answers set when too many or too few are found and by discovering new knowledge not easily detected by hypertextual navigation from the list of results. Needs analysis showed that such functionalities are increasingly expected. For instance, legal practitioners may need to understand what laws cited by a given text are talking about or what articles citing a given law are dealing with.

We implemented graph-based search using two different approaches: a structured and a direct one. The first approach creates a semantic hierarchical and relational structure on the top of the collection thus allowing for advanced search functionalities but it is limited to sub-collections[1]. The second approach can handle larger collections but supports only exact querying.

We present our experimental data on Sect. 2 and our methods of graph-based IR in Sect. 3. Exact search and browsing functionalities are discussed respectively in Sects. 4 and 5. Section 6 introduces related works addressing the problem of modeling and querying graphs of legal collections.

2   Experimental Data

We test and evaluate our approaches on three collections of documents:

- The *Noise corpus* was used as an illustrative example in Légilocal. It is composed of 10 documents annotated with 10 attributes related to noise and a

---

[1] The target scale is a few hundred documents, but we must further optimize the code for it (solutions exist, it is an implementation issue).

single reference relation. Documents are of different types: local acts (orders) making reference to legislative texts (decree, law, code, ordinance).

- The *Légilocal corpus* is a richer collection extracted from the Légilocal base for demonstration purposes: it is composed of 25 documents and 30 legal articles, various types of documents are represented (local decisions, legislative texts, judgements and editorial documents) – sometimes with different versions of the same document –, as well as various types of links (application, composition, decision either confirmation or cancelation, modification) [5].
- The *ILO corpus* is the largest collection with almost 400 documents collected from the International Labour Office (ILO)[2]. Documents are conventions and recommendations, linked by an implementation relation.

These collections have served us as a primary base to test the proposed approaches. The documents are analyzed to identify their types and extract their structure, they are annotated with semantic descriptors and the intertextual citations are themselves identified and semantically typed. Semantic descriptors annotating documents correspond to concepts extracted from semantic resources dealing with the texts domains. Real scale collections are to be created and documents analyzed by partners of the project.

Needs analysis realized with collaboration of Légilocal legal experts shows that practitioners' spontaneous queries naturally combine content and intertextual criteria. We built a list of queries which are formally different from each other but which covers a wide range of practitioners' queries. We created a set of queries on both ILO and Légilocal (LEGI) corpus along with their relevant answers to test and evaluate our search approaches, the quality of a method being related to the variety of query types that it supports.

- ILO1: "Which convention implements Recommendation 113 on collective bargaining?"
- ILO2: "Which convention implements the recommendation talking about seafarers occupational accidents?"
- ILO3: "What are the recommendations implemented by conventions dealing with air pollution?"
- LEGI1: "What are the legal decisions that cite Article 1382 of the Civil Code?"
- LEGI2: "What are the articles of the Environment Code that deal with motor vehicles and rural roads?"
- LEGI3: "I am looking for the decision that is the subject of the judgment A of the Court of Cassation."
- LEGI4: "I am looking for decisions that were canceled by the Court of Cassation."
- LEGI5: "I wonder if this judgement of the Court of Appeal was itself the subject of an appeal."
- LEGI6: "I would like to see municipal orders regarding rural roads that have been appealed and were canceled by decision of jurisprudence."

---

[2] www.ilo.org.

- LEGI7: "What are the code articles which are cited by the municipal orders dealing with rural roads that have been confirmed?"
- LEGI8: "What are the decisions prior to decision D?"
- LEGI9: "I wonder if the texts referred by municipal orders dealing with rural roads are also cited by those concerning the motor vehicles."
- LEGI10: "What are municipal orders that have been the subject of two appeals?"
- LEGI11: "I wonder if the texts referred by the municipal order 97-17 of Champigné have been modified, and if so, what are the new versions of these texts and the source texts of the amendment."

3   Modeling Legal Collections as Graphs

The document collection is modeled as a graph of documents, which can be exploited directly using semantic technologies (direct approach) or which can be further structured into a hierarchical and relational conceptual structure, that itself supports search and browsing (structured approach).

3.1   Direct Approach

The direct approach models the collection as an RDF graph where the objects (nodes) are document and descriptor identifiers and where properties (edges) are intertextual links (between documents) or annotations (between documents and descriptors). Document descriptors are organized into hierarchies allowing to exploit the links of specialization/generalization in order to adjust the precision of queries. Document types (law, decree, etc.) are also organized into a highly structured hierarchy, which is a feature of the legal domain. The document structure (sections, paragraphs, etc.) is represented rather the whole document. The article is considered as the basic documentary unit, it can be directly cited and has its own life cycle (may be amended, codified, etc.). Intertextual links between documents are represented as direct relations between two documentary units (as for citation, visas, application) or as document operations modeling relations involving more documentary units: source, target and result (as for modification, codification).

Taking into account the history of the different versions of a legal document led to distinguish several levels of representation of documentary objects: the master document, the work, and the various versions that are given, expressions. This involves specifying at what level the intertextual relations are introduced and allows to factorize some document properties on the work avoiding to duplicate them on each of its expressions.

An OWL document ontology controls the semantics of the RDF graph. It provides for fine-grained descriptions of legal collections, taking any type of features into account: semantic metadata, document structure, document types and intertextual relationships. User queries are expressed in SPARQL and are directly matched against the RDF graph.

An example of an instance graph is given in Fig. 1 showing the codification of article $L362-1$ of the Environment Code by the Ordinance $n2000-914$.

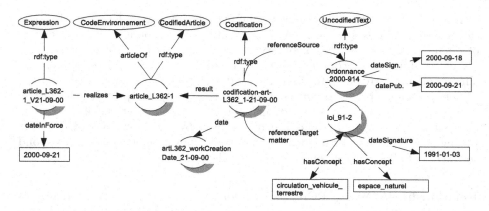

Fig. 1. Codification of article $L362 - 1$ of the environment code by the ordinance n°$2000 - 914$

3.2 Structured Approach

Relying on FCA/RCA, the structured approach [6] models the collection as a set of interlinked hierarchical structures which organizes documents into classes on the basis of their semantic content and their interrelationships (Fig. 2).

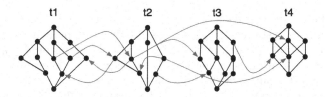

Fig. 2. Example of relational lattice family with relations among the formal concepts of the set of lattices.

The approach is composed of four main steps. The document collection is first structured into formal concept lattices based on the semantic descriptors associated with the documents (Semantic content modeling). The formal concepts are clusters of documents (Extent) sharing a set of semantic and relational attributes (Intent). Those lattices are then enriched with intertextuality (relational information: relational attributes are added to the extents of formal concepts) which produces a relational lattice family (Intertextuality modeling). User queries, possibly combining semantic descriptors and cross-references constraints, are matched against the relational lattice family, which allow for returning graphs of documents as answers (Direct querying). The lattice structure can be further exploited to retrieve approximate results as an alternative or in addition to direct ones (Browsing).

Semantic Content. The semantic content of documents is first modeled as a set of formal contexts using FCA. Each context corresponds to a specific type of documents and describes a binary relation between a set of objects and a set of attributes *(object × attributes)*. The objects correspond to documents. The attributes correspond to the semantic descriptors characterizing the content of these documents. In an information retrieval (IR) perspective, the lattice built by FCA on formal contexts gathers all possible combinations of documents attributes. These combinations are represented by the intensions of concepts having as extensions all the documents sharing these properties and correspond to the set of all satisfiable queries on the collection.

Relationships. We use RCA, the relational extension of FCA, to take into account the intertextual information while modeling the collection. The approach creates a family of relational contexts from binary contexts *(documents × semantic descriptors)* and relations represented separately in new contexts, each of which defines one type of relation between documents *(documents × documents)*. This family of contexts forms the starting point for the creation of corresponding conceptual structures called Relational Lattice Family (RLF).

3.3   Comparaison

Figure 3 compares these approaches. We can notice that modeling and encoding the collection (first and second steps on Fig. 3, bottom side) are more sophisticated with the direct approach: ontological model and RDF triples (the figure shows the graph of instances). This allows the direct approach to express more complex query graphs (fourth step of Fig. 3). In the structured approach (top side on Fig. 3) the initial modeling step is simpler: the collection is modeled as a set of objects/attributes tables, but there is an additional structuring phase (third step) creating a structure that can be further exploited for browsing.

In information retrieval, structuring a document collection as a lattice pre-computes the answers to all queries that are satisfiable on that collection. In addition, browsing the structure provides approximate answers as it allows for generalizing or restricting queries. In the direct approach, answers are calculated on the fly when the SPARQL query is sent to the system. This approach is more flexible (when the model of the collection or the collection itself evolves), is not limited by the collection size and allows to express richer queries. On the contrary, the structured approach performs well on small collections or local perspectives over large collections and allows browsing and visualizing, but it cannot answer complex queries like LEGI11. We have developed a prototype to visualize the answer graphs from the structured approach displaying the objects of the answer along with all their attributes even if they are not mentioned in the initial query.

The choice to use one or the other approach depends tightly on the application requirements (user interfaces, number of documents, granularity of document description or the evolution of the collection).

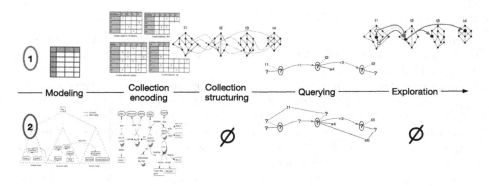

Fig. 3. Structured vs. direct approaches. The first approach (top) relies on FCA/RCA to build a semantic structure over the graph of documents. Queries are answered based on that structure. The second approach (bottom) exploits semantic technologies (OWL/RDF/SPARQL) to model the collection as a graph. Query answers are directly extracted from that graph. Compared with the structured approach, the direct one supports richer semantic graphs but offers no exploration facility.

4 Exact Search in Collection Graphs

As presented in [5], document collections and queries are formalized as graphs. The proposed approaches enable answering different types of elementary and complex queries. We tested 14 types having or not a focus and with or without constraints. For instance, Fig. 4 shows two examples of query graphs: q_a corresponds to an elementary query and q_b to a relational one. The query q_a looks for documents of type t_2 annotated with semantic attributes s_4 and s_5. The query q_b looks for documents of type t_1 annotated with s_1 having the link r_1 with documents of type t_2 annotated with s_4.

$$q_a = Type(x, t_2) \wedge Att(x, s_4) \wedge Att(x, s_5)$$

$$q_b = (x, y) : Type(x, t_1) \wedge Att(x, s_1) \wedge Type(y, t_2) \wedge Att(y, s_4) \wedge Rel(x, r_1, y)$$

Fig. 4. Examples of query graphs: q_a represents an elementary query and q_b a relational query, which is represented with a focus in the formula.

On exact search and for elementary as well as for relational queries, both approaches perform well. All the selected queries are properly answered, with a list of documents or document graphs that exactly match the query or no answer if the query is not satisfiable. We show below some examples of queries, testing the direct and the structured approaches on our three test corpus: Noise, ILO and Légilocal corpus.

4.1   Structured Approach

Once structured as a family of relational lattices, the collection can be exploited to answer elementary and relational queries. We tested this approach on both Noise and ILO corpus.

Let's consider an example of a relational query on the Noise corpus: *"Which orders talk about sound level (nvs) and make reference (rf) to decrees about noisy activities (ab)?"*. Figure 5 shows the structure built for the collection. The query is modeled as an attributed graph, which nodes are virtual objects (variables) created for each unidentified document (Q_o for orders and Q_d for decrees), which attributes are semantic descriptors (*nvs* for node Q_o and *ab* for Q_d) and the link is the intertextual relation (*rf*). An iterative search process calculates relevant answers [6], it instantiates Q_o and Q_d respectively by documents *AS* (Strasbourg order) and *O45* (ordinance 45). It returns the following answer graph (the query has no focus, so answers are presented as graphs): $\mathcal{G}_a = Type(AS, order) \land Att(AS, nvs) \land Type(O45, decree) \land Att(O45, ab) \land Rel(AS, rf, 045)$.

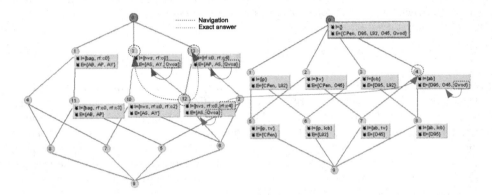

Fig. 5. Exact and approximate search in a relational lattice family.

We tested the approach on the ILO corpus. Two lattices are build: a convention lattice and a recommendation lattice. Created concepts are classes of documents (either conventions or recommendations) sharing a given set of attributes (semantic descriptors). All the collected queries returned the expected relevant answers. We detail hereafter two examples: ILO1 and ILO2.

ILO1: this query contains an identified document $R113$ (recommendation 113), we create the variable $QueryConv$ corresponding to the searched one that we insert in the recommendation lattice. We locate $R113$ on the recommendation lattice, check that it is actually associated with the formal attribute **collective bargaining** and search for the related convention (we check relational attributes). The query graph is:

$$\mathcal{G}_q = Type(QueryConv, convention) \land Type(R113, recommendation) \land$$
$$Att(R113, collective\_bargaining) \land Rel(QueryConv, impl, R113)$$

The search returns convention $C144$. The answer graph is depicted on Fig. 6, with the dashed line surrounding the exact answer.

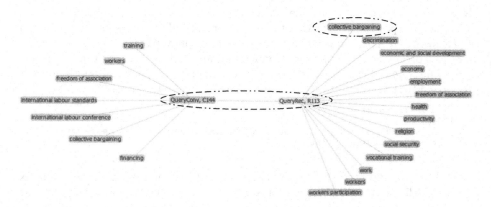

Fig. 6. Answer graph for query ILO1.

ILO2: the query graph contains two variables, two attributes and one relation. The query graph is:

$$\mathcal{G}_q = Type(QueryConv, convention) \wedge Type(QueryRec, recommendation) \wedge$$
$$Att(QueryRec, occupational\_accidents) \wedge Att(QueryRec, seafarers) \wedge$$
$$Rel(QueryConv, impl, QueryRec)$$

The search process instantiates variables $QueryConv$ and $QueryRec$ respectively with documents $C164$ and $R142$. The visualisation of the answer graph is given in Fig. 7. The central part of the graph (surrounded by the dashed line) corresponds to the exact answer having the attributes of the query.

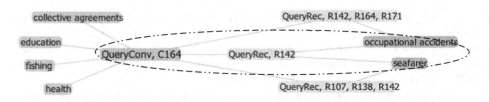

Fig. 7. Exact and approximate answer graphs for query ILO2.

4.2 Direct Approach

As the direct approach allows to model the collection in a more fine-grained manner and is more naturally prepared to process large volume of data, it was more interesting to test it on the Légilocal collection. Nevertheless, we have tested it on the ILO corpus in the aim of comparing the approaches.

In the ILO2 query, we search for objects of the class `Convention` having the relation `implement` with `Recommandation` objects described by semantic concepts `occupational accidents` and `seafarer`. The query is translated in the following SPARQL query (note that the relation `implement` is translated as an object property `ilo:implement` which domain is class `Convention` and range is class `Recommandation`, attributes are attached to documents via the object property `ilo:hasConcept`). It returns documents $C164$ and $R142$.

```
1 SELECT ?conv ?recom
2 WHERE {
3 ?recom ilo:hasConcept ilo:occupationalaccidents , ilo:seafarer .
4 ?conv ilo:implement ?recom .
5 }
```

The expressivity of the query langage enables composing more complex queries dealing with versions and fragments of documents, or with relations with more than two arguments. For instance, the query LEGI11 is translated as follows:

```
1 SELECT ?text ?newversion ?oldversion ?source
2 WHERE {
3 ?visa rdf:type lido:VisaCitation .
4 ?visa lido:citationSource :ArreteChampigne97-17 .
5 ?visa lido:citationTarget ?text .
6 ?modification rdf:type lido:Modification .
7 ?modification lido:referenceTarget ?oldversion .
8 ?modification lido:referenceSource ?source .
9 ?modification metalex:result ?newversion .
10 ?text metalex:realizedBy ?oldversion .
11 }
```

5 Browsing for Approximate Search and Knowledge Discovery

5.1 Exploration Facilities

When a query doesn't have any exact answer, it is interesting to return an approximate answer to the user instead of an empty set of results. Also, when the user gets too few or too many answers to his query, he/she should be able to broaden or narrow his/her search by removing or adding constraints to the initial query.

This could be done by exploring the collection space and selecting documents that are more or less close to the position of the (possibly empty) exact answer variable, *i.e.* documents with less or more semantic or relational properties. The exploration process could be automated and remain transparent to the user (approximate results are calculated by the system and returned), or manual with suitable user interfaces to visualize the data space and navigate within it.

For the time being, this functionality is provided by the structured app-roach thanks to the structure it builds on the top of the collection, and not by the semantic approach [6]. Structuring the collection has the advantage of pre-computing the answers to all the satisfiable queries, either elementary or relational, which allows to find approximate answers to users' queries and discover new knowledge, relying on the strategy of [11] without extra calculation. Some exploration facilities are given in Fig. 8.

Such lattice navigation functionalities cannot be implemented on large collections, but is a track that we explore in the idea of simulating the relevant browsing strategies using SPARQL. We can actually propose some navigation scenarios, in the form of automatically generated sequences of SPARQL queries that would simulate the desired navigation strategies. For instance, the following method corresponds to a query relaxation procedure:

1. Starting from the initial query, relax one or more constraints (RDF triples) in the query graph.
2. Instantiate the relaxed SPARQL queries on the graphs of the collection.
3. Propose the obtained results to the user as an alternative or complement to the exact answer.

5.2 Approximate Search: Examples

Noise Corpus. Let's consider the example presented above (Sect. 4.1) on the noise corpus. It is possible to explore the order lattice by relaxing a semantic constraint or by dropping a relational constraint ending up with an elementary query (as described in Fig. 8). For instance, on the structure of Fig. 5, if we relax a semantic constraint by removing the descriptor nvs, we search for orders making reference to laws and decrees about noisy activities (ab), which are grouped in concept $c13$. A relaxed answer-graph $\mathcal{G}_r$ is given by the document AP linked to the document $D95$:

$$\mathcal{G}_r = Type(AP, order) \wedge Type(D95, decree) \wedge Att(D95, ab) \wedge Rel(AP, rf, D95)$$

ILO Corpus. On Fig. 7, the right side of the graph contains, in addition to the exact answer, several approximate answers that have only one of the query attributes: seafarer for $R107$, $R138$ and occupational accidents for $R164$ and $R171$. They are obtained by upward navigating the conceptual structure which accounts for query generalization.

This can be simulated by the following sequence of relaxed SPARQL queries:

```
1 SELECT ?conv ?recom
2 WHERE {
3 ?recom ilo:hasConcept ilo:seafarer .
4 ?conv ilo:implement ?recom .
5 }
```

```
1 SELECT ?conv ?recom
2 WHERE {
3 ?recom ilo:hasConcept ilo:occupationalaccidents .
4 ?conv ilo:implement ?recom .
5 }
```

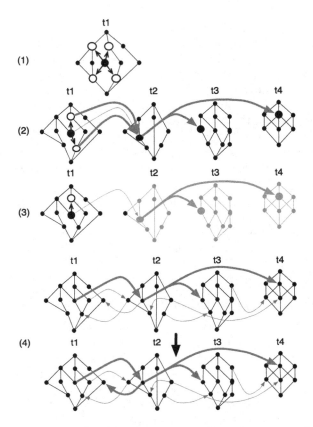

Fig. 8. Exploring facilities offered by the conceptual structure: query broadening and restricting for an elementary query (diagram 1) or a relational query (diagram 2), suppressing a relational attribute (diagrams 3), adding a relational attribute (diagram 4)

5.3   Knowledge Discovery: Examples

On Fig. 7, the left side of the graph represents the convention which implements the recommendation $R142$. The visualisation module presents all the attributes (semantic descriptors) of the convention $C164$ on the result graph. This enables the user to extend the search, looking for conventions that talk about similar topics, *i.e.* which are annotated with a subset of its attributes. This corresponds to the function of search by example [11] where the user has initially a sample, one document or a set of documents, and looks for similar ones (typically the case of a municipal clerk having to draft a local act and who starts by looking for similar ones in neighboring municipalities). We can at this stage (without navigation interface) present directly to the user the similar objects, by performing a simple search (elementary query with the attributes of $C164$) on the initial conceptual structure of conventions.

In addition, visualizing the conceptual structure built on the top of a given collection, allows for discovering clusters of objects that share the same properties (semantic or relational) without having to formulate queries. These clusters have served as a basis for the design and restructuring of domain ontologies [4].

6   Related Work

Many works have studied the intertextuality between legal sources and acknowledged that network analysis is a powerful way to model legal collections [2,7,10]. However, as in citation and social network analysis [8], focus has been put on the network level to identify the most strongly connected sub-collections or the most influential law sources. Less attention has been paid to the detailed analysis of intertextuality and the semantics of intertextual links.

In major legal access systems, intertextuality is presented as hypertextual links between texts or as a metadata that could be queried (*e.g.* Legifrance[3]). New approaches [3,9] try to enrich legal access systems with contextual networks based on link analysis methods. Their proposals consist mainly on the exploration and visualization of the citations network. They do not take intertextuality into account at the query level as we propose to do in exact and approximate search.

7   Conclusion

This paper shows that legal practitioners' complex queries could be handled through modeling and querying legal collections as semantic networks. Network nodes (documents) are associated with semantic attributes and connected to each other by various types of semantic links. Queries are themselves modeled as graphs, which are matched against the collection graph so as to return exact or approximate answers to the user. We proposed two methods – direct vs. structured methods –, which have different advantages and drawbacks. Using one model or the other depends tightly on the application: the granularity of the description required for the collection, the complexity of queries, the size of the collection, the relevance of restricted search perspective. Both proposed approaches are logical ones, they are not evaluated in terms of precision and recall. Most important criteria are the expressivity of the query language (which types of queries could be answered) and performance (collection size, processing time).

Future steps include the implementation of exploration scenarios as sequences of SPARQL queries, the design of adequate interfaces to help users create complex relational queries and analyze the returned results and the test and validation of the direct approach on large scale collections.

Acknowledgments. This work has been partially funded by French Single Inter-Ministry Fund (FUI-9, 2010–2013) and is supported by the Labex EFL supported by the French National Research Agency (ANR-10-LABX-0083).

---

[3] http://www.legifrance.gouv.fr/.

References

1. Amardeilh, F., et al.: The légilocal project: the local law simply shared. In: Legal Knowledge and Information Systems - JURIX 2013: The Twenty-Sixth Annual Conference, University of Bologna, Italy, 11–13 December 2013, pp. 11–14 (2013)
2. Fowler, J.H., Johnson, T.R., Spriggs, J.F., Jeon, S., Wahlbeck, P.J.: Network analysis and the law: measuring the legal importance of precedents at the U.S. supreme court. Polit. Anal. **15**, 324–346 (2007)
3. Gultemen, D., van Engers, T.: Graph-based linking and visualization for legislation documents (GLVD). In: Network Analysis in Law Workshop (NAiL2013@ICAIL) associated with ICAIL 2013, Rome, Italy, June 2013
4. Rouane-Hacene, M., Valtchev, P., Nkambou, R.: Supporting ontology design through large-scale FCA-based ontology restructuring. In: Andrews, S., Polovina, S., Hill, R., Akhgar, B. (eds.) ICCS 2011. LNCS (LNAI), vol. 6828, pp. 257–269. Springer, Heidelberg (2011). https://doi.org/10.1007/978-3-642-22688-5_19
5. Mimouni, N., Nazarenko, A., Paul, É., Salotti, S.: Towards graph-based and semantic search in legal information access systems. In: Legal Knowledge and Information Systems - JURIX 2014, Krakow, Poland. Frontiers in Artificial Intelligence and Applications, vol. 271, pp. 163–168. IOS Press (2014)
6. Mimouni, N., Nazarenko, A., Salotti, S.: A conceptual approach for relational IR: application to legal collections. In: Baixeries, J., Sacarea, C., Ojeda-Aciego, M. (eds.) ICFCA 2015. LNCS (LNAI), vol. 9113, pp. 303–318. Springer, Cham (2015). https://doi.org/10.1007/978-3-319-19545-2_19
7. Boulet, R., Mazzega, P., Bourcier, D.: A network approach to the French system of legal codes- part i: analysis of a dense network. J. Artif. Intell. Law **19**, 333–355 (2011)
8. Rubin, R.: Foundations of Library and Information Science. Neal-Schuman Publishers, Chicago (2010)
9. Winkels, R., Boer, A., Plantevin, I.: Creating context networks in Dutch legislation. In: Legal Knowledge and Information Systems - JURIX 2013, Italy. Frontiers in Artificial Intelligence and Applications, vol. 259, pp. 155–164. IOS Press (2013)
10. Winkels, R., de Ruyter, J.: Survival of the fittest: network analysis of dutch supreme court cases. In: Palmirani, M., Pagallo, U., Casanovas, P., Sartor, G. (eds.) AICOL 2011. LNCS (LNAI), vol. 7639, pp. 106–115. Springer, Heidelberg (2012). https://doi.org/10.1007/978-3-642-35731-2_7
11. Wray, T., Eklund, P.: Exploring the information space of cultural collections using formal concept analysis. In: Valtchev, P., Jäschke, R. (eds.) ICFCA 2011. LNCS (LNAI), vol. 6628, pp. 251–266. Springer, Heidelberg (2011). https://doi.org/10.1007/978-3-642-20514-9_19

Inducing Predictive Models for Decision Support in Administrative Adjudication

L. Karl Branting(✉)(iD), Alexander Yeh, Brandy Weiss, Elizabeth Merkhofer,
and Bradford Brown

The MITRE Corporation, 7515 Colshire Dr, McLean, VA 22102, USA
{lbranting,asy,bweiss,emerkhofer,bcbrown}@mitre.org

Abstract. Administrative adjudications are the most common form of
legal decisions in many countries, so improving the efficiency, accuracy,
and consistency of administrative processes could significantly benefit
agencies and citizens alike. We explore the hypothesis that predictive
models induced from previous administrative decisions can improve subsequent decision-making processes. This paper describes three datasets
for exploring this hypothesis: motion-rulings, Board of Veterans Appeals
(BVA) decisions; and World Intellectual Property Organization (WIPO)
domain name dispute decisions. Three different approaches for prediction in these domains were tested: maximum entropy over token n-grams;
SVM over token n-grams; and a Hierarchical Attention Network (HAN)
applied to the full text. Each approach was capable of predicting outcomes, with the simpler WIPO cases appearing to be much more predictable than BVA or motion-ruling cases. We explore several approaches
to using predictive models to identify salient phrases in the predictive
texts (i.e., motion or contentions and factual background) and propose
a design for incorporating this information into a decision-support tool.

1 Introduction

In many countries, the majority of legal adjudications are administrative, typ-
ified by routine licensing, permitting, immigration, and benefits decisions. The
high volume of these administrative adjudications can lead to backlogs, inconsistencies, high resource loads for agencies, and uncertainty for citizens, notwithstanding the simplicity and uniformity that often characterizes such cases.

This paper presents the hypothesis that predictive models induced from
previous administrative decisions can improve subsequent decision-making processes. The first step in establishing this hypothesis is to show the feasibility of
creating models that predict the outcomes of routine administrative cases. The
second step is to demonstrate how such predictive models can be used to improve
decision processes. Our focus is on assisting individual decision makers by using
predictive models to (1) identify the aspects of the instant case that are most
relevant to its outcome and (2) determine the prior cases that share the most
relevant similarities to the instant case. A promising alternative approach to
decision-process improvement not addressed in this paper consists of improved

© Springer Nature Switzerland AG 2018
U. Pagallo et al. (Eds.): AICOL VI-X 2015–2017, LNAI 10791, pp. 465–477, 2018.
https://doi.org/10.1007/978-3-030-00178-0_32

case routing and triage, e.g., assigning cases to specialized decision processes based on likely outcome and duration or apparent complexity. Since this app-roach depends heavily on the details of a given agency's decision processes, we leave it to future work.

2 Prediction in Law

Predictability is a fundamental property of legitimate legal systems. In tra-ditional jurisprudence, prediction is based on weighing the relative strengths of arguments formulated by attorneys for and against a given proposition. In practice, however, attorneys often depend upon intuitive predictions about the outcome of cases developed from lengthy experience with judges, juries, and opposing attorneys in prior cases. Insurance companies have long used statisti-cal models to estimate the settlement value of claims, and in the 1980s expert systems were developed to model human expertise at this task [12].

More recently, the development of corpus-based techniques for text analysis together with the increased availability of large legal text corpora has made feasible induction of models directly from the texts of case records and decisions [4]. Predictable aspects of cases include such factors as the following:

- The likelihood of success of a given motion (e.g., for dismissal or for extension of time) or claim (e.g., for veterans disability benefits)
- The expected award amount for a claim, e.g., the amount of a veteran's disability award
- The expected return on civil claim, i.e., expected judgment minus expected litigation cost
- Expected litigation duration
- Recidivism probability

Predictive models of such aspects of legal cases have the potential to improve access to justice and the efficiency and consistency of case management. How-ever, such models can be both opaque and susceptible to bias [14]. The work described in this paper is intended to mitigate these risks by focusing on pre-dictive models as aids for improving human decision making rather than as stand-alone substitutes for human discretion.

3 Datasets

In the United States, the agencies responsible for administrative claims, such as for veterans benefits, Social Security disability, immigration status, and Medi-care appeals, all suffer from significant backlogs resulting from the inability of the agencies to handle their growing case loads with the available resources. As a first step in engagement with these agencies, whose data have privacy and sen-sitivity issues, we are developing prototypes on less sensitive, but representative, datasets.

- **Motion Rulings**
  Our first dataset consists of 6,866 motion/order pairs drawn from the docket of a United States federal district court.[1] Motions may be granted, denied, or granted in part and denied in part, and a single order may rule on multiple motions, potentially granting some and denying others. To obviate these procedural complexities, our initial dataset is restricted to orders that either rule on a single motion or that have rulings of the same type for multiple motions, i.e., all granted or all denied. Each training instance consists of the text of the motion, which may contain OCR errors (the original filings were in PDF format), together with a classification as either "granted" or "denied".
- **Board of Veterans Appeals Decisions**
  Adjudicative bodies vary in the extent to which case facts and decisions are published. Many adjudicative bodies publish only decisions but not the factual record on which each decision is based. In many agencies, the original decisions are not published, but only appellate decisions. The absence of published case records can create a cart-and-horse problem in which agencies are unwilling to share sensitive data for an unproven decision-support tool, but the decision-support tool can't be demonstrated because there is no access to the data on which it must be trained.

  A method of finessing this problem exploits the convention that decisions generally contain statements of the fact of the case. Decisions with clear sections can be segmented, with the statement of facts treated as a summary of the actual case record, and the decision treated as the classification of those facts in terms of legal outcome. This "bootstrapping" approach was used to demonstrate the feasibility of predicting decisions of the European Court of Human Rights in [1]. Of course, decision drafters routinely exclude facts that are irrelevant to the decision and often tailor statements of relevant facts to fit the intended conclusions. As a result, bootstrapping is merely a proxy for the actual task of predicting decisions from raw case facts. However, demonstrating that decisions can be predicted from statements of fact, even if those statements are filtered, is an essential first step in demonstrating the feasibility of prediction in more realistic settings.

  Board of Veterans Appeals (BVA) cases[2] have clear sections: Issues, Introduction, Findings, Conclusions, and Reasons. The Issues and Introduction sections contain only facts and contentions, and the decision on each issue is set forth in the Conclusions section. BVA cases often involve multiple issues, but issues are consistently numbered in Issues, Findings, and Conclusions sections. We therefore split each published BVA opinion with n issues into n instances, one for each issue, in which the facts consist of an issue and the entire Introduction, and the classification is extracted (using regular expressions) from the numbered paragraph of Conclusion that corresponds to the

---

[1] Document filings in US federal courts are "semi-public" in that they are publicly accessible through PACER (https://www.pacer.gov/login.html), but per-page charges and primitive indexing impede wholesale document mining.

[2] https://www.index.va.gov/search/va/bva_search.jsp.

Issue (i.e., that has the same numbering). The possible decisions on each issue are (1) the requirements for benefits have been met, (2) the requirements have not been met, (3) the case must be remanded for additional hearings, and (4) the case must be reopened. Conversion of all published BVA cases in this fashion yields 3,844 4-class instances or 1605 2-class (met or unmet) instances. Unfortunately, the Findings section of BVA cases sometimes contain conclusions about facts not discussed in the Issues and Introduction section, so these sections are an incomplete proxy for the actual case record. This incompleteness makes it impossible in principle to predict the outcome of all BVA cases from just the Issues and Introduction.

- **WIPO Domain Name Dispute Decisions**
  The World Intellectual Property Organization (WIPO) publishes decisions resolving complaints brought against the holder of a domain name that "is identical or confusingly similar" to a trademark belonging to the complainant.[3] WIPO cases have only two possible outcomes: the domain name is transferred to the complainant or it is not. WIPO cases are clearly segmented into seven sections: Parties, Domain Name, History, Background, Contentions, Findings, and Decision. The facts of each instance consist of the concatenation of the first 5 sections, and the classification is "transferred" or "not transferred". The WIPO dataset consists of 5,587 instances with a roughly 10-to-1 class skew in favor of "transferred".

4 Prediction

The first step in confirming the hypothesis that predictive models induced from previous administrative decisions can improve subsequent decision-making processes is to demonstrate that decision outcomes can be predicted. We experimented with 3 predictive techniques: hierarchical attention networks, support vector machines (SVM), and maximum entropy classification.

4.1 Hierarchical Attention Networks

In our first approach, we extended the hierarchical neural network model presented in Yang et al. [15] to predict the outcome of legal cases from free-text sections of their case records. The original model takes as input a sequence of sentences. A sentence representation is built for each sentence with a bidirectional gated recurrent unit (GRU) layer over word embeddings. An attention mechanism determines the weight of each time-step's contribution to a sentence vector. Then, a second GRU layer operates over the sentence vectors, an attention mechanism is applied, and the weighted sentence representations are summed to form a hidden document representation. In prior work the document representation was used to predict the ratings of Yelp and movie reviews.

The hierarchical model was extended to account for the deeper structure of legal case documents. With the intuition that human decisions are informed by

---

[3] http://www.wipo.int/amc/en/domains/decisionsx/index-gtld.html.

some combination of the text in each section, we adapted the model architecture to the structure of cases in the two datasets to which the Hierarchical Attention Network was applied: WIPO and BVA cases. Input for WIPO cases consisted of three sections: history, background and contentions. We fed each section separately into Yang et al.'s document model, sharing weights. The resulting section representations were combined to create the case representation. The architecture used for BVA cases, shown in Fig. 1, took as input two sections: the issue and the introduction. The issue is nearly always only one sentence, so was treated as a single sequence of words. The introduction may be tens of sentences long and is passed through the hierarchical architecture described in the paper. The case representation is a learned transformation of the issue and introduction sections.

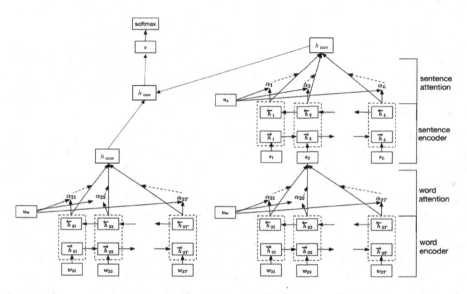

Fig. 1. Hierarchical neural model architecture for Board of Veterans Appeals cases. h_case is a learned function of h_issue, built from the words in the issue section, and h_intro, built from a hierarchical combination of the words-in-sentences and sentences in the case's introduction section.

In our experiments, a fully-connected layer appeared to better combine sections' hidden representations than a recurrent layer. We therefore used a hidden layer size of 50 for the WIPO cases and 64 for the BVA cases. We pre-trained word embeddings using the word2vec algorithm of [9]. For the WIPO cases, we pre-trained on only the WIPO dataset; for the BVA cases, we used a separate dataset of approximately 50,000 appeals. We applied 30% dropout to delay overfitting these small datasets and used the Adam optimizer. Our models were trained on 80% of data, developed with an additional 10%, and the remaining 10% was reserved for testing.

L. K. Branting et al.

The BVA model achieved a mean F1 of .738 and overall accuracy of 74.7%. The architecture reached a mean F1 of .944 on the WIPO cases, with an F1 of .64 for the 10-times-less frequent negative class and overall accuracy of 94.4%.

4.2 Support Vector Machine

The second approach to decision prediction was Support Vector Machine (SVM) learning. For the WIPO and BVA datasets, text was converted into n-gram frequency vectors for $n = 1 - 4$, with only those n-grams retained that occurred at least 8 times. The result was converted into sparse arff format,[4] loaded into WEKA [7], and evaluated in 10-fold cross-validation using WEKA's implementation of Platt's algorithm for sequential minimal optimization [8,13]. Because of memory issues, the WEKA SVM was run against only a subset of the entire WIPO dataset consisting of 649 instances from each category.

In 10-fold cross validation the SVM approach achieved a mean F1 of 0.731 on the BVA dataset, with an overall accuracy of 73%. A mean F1 of 0.950 was achieved on the WIPO dataset, yielding an overall accuracy of 90.5%.

4.3 Maximum Entropy Classification

The third approach to decision prediction that we explored was Maximum Entropy (Maxent) classification [3] (often termed *logistic regression*). We used the jCarafe[5] implementation of Maxent, which adds regularization to mitigate overfitting, to build a model to predict whether a motion will be granted. Our features consisted of the party filing the motion, the judge ruling on the motion, the sub-type of motion, and the sequences of 1 to 4 tokens (alphanumeric character sequences having non-alphanumeric characters on both the left and right sequence borders) that occur in the text of the motion.

We observed that the motions contain many tokens that appear only in one motion and seem to be the result of OCR errors (as noted above, the documents were filed in PDF format, and some were created by scanning images to PDF). To remove these artifacts, any token that only appeared in only one motion in the collection was removed.

There are many different sub-types of motions, e.g., for extension of time to file, for summary judgment, etc. We found that better accuracy was obtained by training separate models for motion subtypes rather than training a single model for all subtypes. Accordingly, we split the motions into the following 3 large classes of sub-types and built a separate prediction model for each class:

- Extension-type motions, such as a motion to extend a filing due date, which tend to have higher grant rates than motions in general
- Motions of the letter sub-type, which tend to have a slightly lower grant rate than motions in general

---

[4] http://www.cs.waikato.ac.nz/ml/weka/arff.html.
[5] https://github.com/wellner/jcarafe.

– Motions not included in either of the 2 classes above

We used 10-fold cross validation to build and test separate models for each of the 3 large classes above and then combined the results. The combined results had an accuracy of 75%, and the recall, precision and balanced F-score for "granted" were 54%, 66% and 59% respectively.

The predictive results for the three experiments are summarized in Table 1 below:

Table 1. Frequency-weighted mean F1 for predictive algorithms applied to three decision datasets. Note that the SVM (Support Vector Machine) result on the WIPO (World Intellectual Property Organization) dataset is on a balanced subset, rather than the entire WIPO collection, whereas the hierarchical attention network was applied to the entire skewed set.

	Maximum entropy	SVM	Hierarchical attn. network
Motion-rulings	0.742	0.757	
BVA		0.731	0.738
WIPO		0.950	0.944

5 Decision Support

The results of the prediction experiments indicate that routine adjudications and orders are predictable to some extent from models trained from text representing the facts of the case (in the WIPO and BVA datasets) or the motion text (for the order-prediction dataset). Since this approach does not perform argumentation mining and has no explicit model of the applicable legal issues and rules, there is a limit to the predictive accuracy that this approach can achieve except in highly routine and predictable domains, such as WIPO decisions. However, our objective isn't replacement of human discretion, but rather support for human decision making. Our hypothesis is that predictive models can assist human decision makers by identifying the portions of the predictive text, e.g., statements of case facts or motion texts, that are most predictive of the outcome. We hypothesize that a decision maker may benefit from having the predictive text identified even when the decision disagrees with the models prediction. This hypothesis is based on the observation that one of the challenges of decision making is sifting through irrelevant portions of the case record to locate the most important facts.

We distinguish two uses of predictive text:

– Highlighting the parts of a document most relevant outcome, e.g., granting or denying a motion, or accepting or rejecting a claim for benefits, so that the decision maker can quickly identify the facts determinative of the outcome.
– Highlighting the parts of one document most relevant to assessing the similarity or difference between the cases. The Common Law doctrine of *stare*

decisis, under which a decision in one case is binding on subsequent similar cases, is generally inapplicable to administrative adjudications, even in countries with Common Law legal systems. Nevertheless, we hypothesize that enabling decision makers to compare the current case to the most similar prior cases could make decision making faster and more consistent.

We therefore turn to the issue of how predictive texts can be identified. In the context of algorithms for prediction based on text, identification of the most predictive text is a special case of the more general problem of feature selection [6]. We first discuss methods that are independent of the predictive model, then turn to those that are derived from the predictive model.

5.1   Salient Fact Detection

Information-Theoretic Relevance Measures. A particularly straightforward approach to predicting relevance is *mutual information* (sometimes termed "average mutual information"), which is a measure of how much knowledge of the value of one variable reduces uncertainty about the value of another variable [5]:

$$I(X,Y) = \sum_x \sum_y P(X = x, Y = y) \log \frac{P(X = x, Y = y)}{P(X = x)P(Y = y)}$$

For example, in the WIPO domain, the phrases "Complainant has failed to" and "did not reply" are among the highest information n-grams, that is, occurrence counts of those phrases are more predictive of the case decision than occurrence counts of most other variables (i.e., phrases). Mutual information in itself doesn't distinguish phrases like "Complainant has failed to", which is associated with successful complainant from phrases like "did not reply", which are associated with unsuccessful complaints.

Point-wise mutual information (PMI) (sometimes termed "mutual information") [5] measures the extent to which each particular value of a variable is predictive of a particular value of another variable:

$$PMI(x,y) = \log \frac{P(x,y)}{P(x)P(y)}$$

PMI can be either positive or negative, depending on whether the presence of one value makes the other more or less likely. Thus, the PMI between "Complainant has failed to" = true and "transferred" = true is positive, whereas the PMI between "did not reply" = true and "transferred" = true is negative.

Neural Network Attention. Attention mechanisms for neural networks allow weights to be learned as part of its feature representation. [2] introduced neural attention for natural language processing, learning a soft alignment for machine translation such that certain input words contribute most to output words. In the context of text classification, the attention mechanism determines relative contributions of words in the input sequence to the prediction. This hierarchical model has attention over the words in each sentence and over the sentences that make up each section. The attention operates on output from a bidirectional recurrent layer, meaning that each time-step folds in context from surrounding words or sentences but is most responsive to the word or sentence at that time-step.

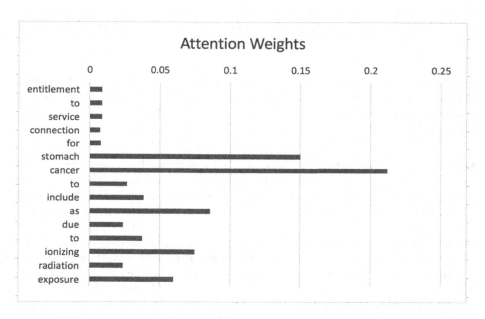

Fig. 2. Attention weights for words in a representative sentence in the introduction of a BVA case. These weights reflect the relative importance of the words in determining the label assigned by the hierarchical attention network to the case.

Extracting the attention weights enables analysis of the model's predictions. Figure 2 illustrates the word-level weights of a representative sentence from a BVA case, showing that words related to the veteran's medical condition had a disproportionate weight in the neural network's prediction.

The use of attention weights to identify the texts most salient to a decision maker is illustrated in Fig. 3, which shows an excerpt from a BVA decision in which the highest-attention sentences are highlighted in color. The sentence in blue received 74% of the attention weight, and the next most important, shown in yellow, received 9% of the attention weight. The sentence in blue is, in fact, highly relevant in that it recharacterizes the issue from being moot into something that can be granted.

While the accuracy of the hierarchical attention network is similar to the other learning models, it has the significant advantage that attention weights are

Issue: Entitlement to a total disability rating based on individual unemployability due to service connected disabilities (TDIU) from May 15 2002 to June [redacted] 2008 for the purposes of accrued benefits.

Intro: The Veteran had active service from March 1971 to February 1973. He died in June 2008 and the appellant is his surviving spouse. This matter comes before the Board of Veterans' Appeals (Board) from February 2012 and November 2013 rating decision of the Department of Veterans Affairs (VA) Regional Office (RO) in Philadelphia Pennsylvania. The issue of entitlement to a TDIU had previously been listed as being from March 15 2002. Since service connection was not in effect for any disabilities prior to May 15 2002 the issue has been reclassified as being from May 15 2002. This appeal has been advanced on the Board's docket pursuant to 38 C.F.R. § 20.900(c). 38 U.S.C.A. § 7107(a)(2) (West 2002).

Fig. 3. A portion of a BVA case. The sentence with the highest proportion of attention weight, 74%, is shown in blue, and the sentence with the next highest weight, 9%, is shown in yellow.

specific to token instances rather than, as in the case of linear model weights, global. A phrase that is insignificant in one context can be very significant in a different context; this distinction can be identified by hierarchical attention networks but not by models that produce global weights.

Linear Model Weights. An alternative approach to using a predictive model to identify the most salient case facts makes use of the feature weights learned during model training. In linear models, such as maximum entropy and SVM with linear kernels, feature weights are indicative of relevance of features to the model's predictions [10], which in our application consists of predicted case decisions. These feature weights are similar to point-wise mutual information (PMI) (discussed above), with features increasing the chances of a positive prediction tending to have positive weights and features decreasing the chances tending to have negative weights. One difference between PMI and the feature weights for logistic regression with regularization is that a regression feature weight differs when a feature either occurs only infrequently (weight magnitude is diminished) or is correlated with other features in the model (weight is adjusted for the effects of correlated features on the model).

For example, when maximum entropy/logistic regression (with regularization) is applied to the domain of motions for an extension of time, phrases having a relatively large positive feature weight for "granted = true" include "to dismiss" (feature weight of 0.319), "dismiss" (0.310) and "with the consent" (0.285), whereas phrases with relatively large negative feature weights include "a stipulation" (-0.385) and "stipulation" (-0.735).

5.2   User Interface for Decision Support

The data derived from the predictive models is intended to be displayed to administrative claimants and decision makers using a Graphical User Interface (GUI). The complexity of the displayed content along with a need to prevent user error necessitates a usable interface. We are therefore exploring interface designs to present this information in a manner that best facilitates its use, that is, to present data in a manner that improves a decider's speed and accuracy [11].

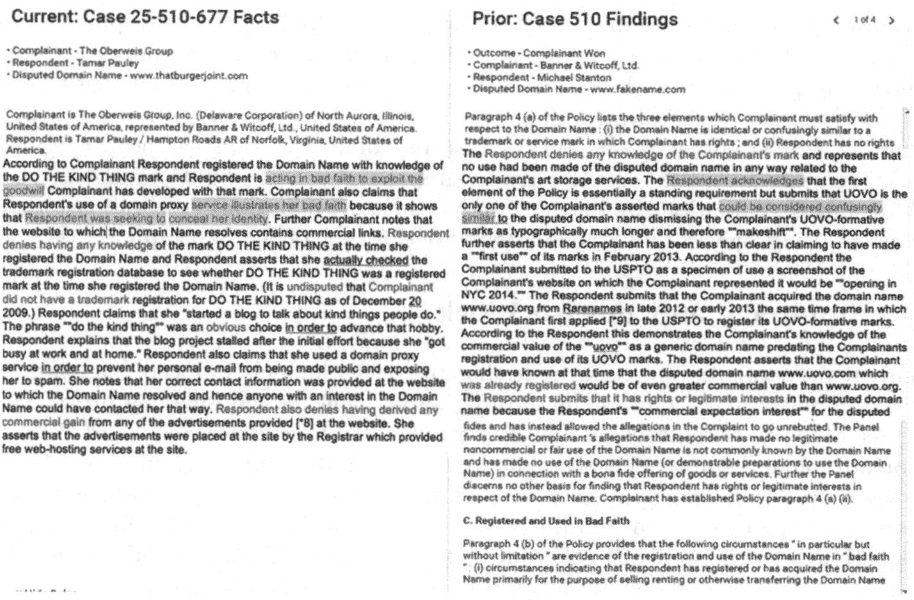

Current: Case 25-510-677 Facts

- Complainant - The Oberweis Group
- Respondent - Tamar Pauley
- Disputed Domain Name - www.thatburgerjoint.com

Complainant is The Oberweis Group, Inc. (Delaware Corporation) of North Aurora, Illinois, United States of America, represented by Banner & Witcoff, Ltd., United States of America. Respondent is Tamar Pauley / Hampton Roads AR of Norfolk, Virginia, United States of America. According to Complainant Respondent registered the Domain Name with knowledge of the DO THE KIND THING mark and Respondent is acting in bad faith to exploit the goodwill Complainant has developed with that mark. Complainant also claims that Respondent's use of a domain proxy service illustrates her bad faith because it shows that Respondent was seeking to conceal her identity. Further Complainant notes that the website to which the Domain Name resolves contains commercial links. Respondent denies having any knowledge of the mark DO THE KIND THING at the time she registered the Domain Name and Respondent asserts that she actually checked the trademark registration database to see whether DO THE KIND THING was a registered mark at the time she registered the Domain Name. (It is undisputed that Complainant did not have a trademark registration for DO THE KIND THING as of December 20 2009.) Respondent claims that she "started a blog to talk about kind things people do." The phrase "'do the kind thing'" was an obvious choice in order to advance that hobby. Respondent explains that the blog project stalled after the initial effort because she "got busy at work and at home." Respondent also claims that she used a domain proxy service in order to prevent her personal e-mail from being made public and exposing her to spam. She notes that her correct contact information was provided at the website to which the Domain Name resolved and hence anyone with an interest in the Domain Name could have contacted her that way. Respondent also denies having derived any commercial gain from any of the advertisements provided [*8] at the website. She asserts that the advertisements were placed at the site by the Registrar which provided free web-hosting services at the site.

Prior: Case 510 Findings   < 1 of 4 >

- Outcome - Complainant Won
- Complainant - Banner & Witcoff, Ltd.
- Respondent - Michael Stanton
- Disputed Domain Name - www.fakename.com

Paragraph 4 (a) of the Policy lists the three elements which Complainant must satisfy with respect to the Domain Name : (i) the Domain Name is identical or confusingly similar to a trademark or service mark in which Complainant has rights ; and (ii) Respondent has no rights The Respondent denies any knowledge of the Complainant's mark and represents that no use had been made of the disputed domain name in any way related to the Complainant's art storage services. The Respondent acknowledges that the first element of the Policy is essentially a standing requirement but submits that UOVO is the only one of the Complainant's asserted marks that could be considered confusingly similar to the disputed domain name dismissing the Complainant's UOVO-formative marks as typographically much longer and therefore "'makeshift'". The Respondent further asserts that the Complainant has been less than clear in claiming to have made a "'first use'" of its marks in February 2013. According to the Respondent the Complainant submitted to the USPTO as a specimen of use a screenshot of the Complainant's website on which the Complainant represented it would be "'opening in NYC 2014.'" The Respondent submits that the Complainant acquired the domain name www.uovo.org from Rarenames in late 2012 or early 2013 the same time frame in which the Complainant first applied [*9] to the USPTO to register its UOVO-formative marks. According to the Respondent this demonstrates the Complainant's knowledge of the commercial value of the "'uovo'" as a generic domain name predating the Complainants registration and use of its UOVO marks. The Respondent asserts that the Complainant would have known at that time that the disputed domain name www.uovo.com which was already registered would be of even greater commercial value than www.uovo.org. The Respondent submits that it has rights or legitimate interests in the disputed domain name because the Respondent's "'commercial expectation interest'" for the disputed fides and has instead allowed the allegations in the Complaint to go unrebutted. The Panel finds credible Complainant 's allegations that Respondent has made no legitimate noncommercial or fair use of the Domain Name is not commonly known by the Domain Name and has made no use of the Domain Name (or demonstrable preparations to use the Domain Name) in connection with a bona fide offering of goods or services. Further the Panel discerns no other basis for finding that Respondent has rights or legitimate interests in respect of the Domain Name. Complainant has established Policy paragraph 4 (a) (ii).

C. Registered and Used in Bad Faith

Paragraph 4 (b) of the Policy provides that the following circumstances " in particular but without limitation " are evidence of the registration and use of the Domain Name in " bad faith " : (i) circumstances indicating that Respondent has registered or has acquired the Domain Name primarily for the purpose of selling renting or otherwise transferring the Domain Name

Fig. 4. A prototype decision-support interface design illustrating how the most salient case facts can by highlighted to assist with analysis of the case record and comparison between cases. Phrases highlighted in yellow are associated with rulings in favor of complainants, whereas phrases highlighted in red are associated with rulings in favor of respondents.

The preliminary design concept shown in Fig. 4 contains several features that we hypothesize will assist users with deciding on cases efficiently and accurately. One feature of this design concept allows a user to view the most relevant cases in multiple ways (i.e., multi-case comparison, high-level comparison, in depth comparison). Providing multiple formats for case comparison allows a user the flexibility to decide how in-depth they would like to view the current case and previous case information. Another design feature provides the user with convenient access to relevant information (e.g., the rules) during the review process. This design concept leverages the pattern of open/close panels, which allow the user the ability to customize their view as they go through the evaluation process. In order to support efficient comparison, this design also provides a highlighting feature that is intended to allow a user to compare the similarities between current and previous cases. A future evaluation of this design concept will provide the information needed to iterate on the design patterns and features. The overall goal is to provide a satisfactory user experience while also assisting the decision maker to make quick and accurate assessments of cases.

We plan on conducting an initial experimental evaluation to assess the overall ability of the combined predictive model and user interface to facilitate improved speed and accuracy in decision making. We hypothesize that the speed and accuracy of decision making can be improved by highlighting the phrases in cases with facts having the greatest weight under a predictive model and by retrieving prior cases with the strongest similarity to the current case in terms of the highest weight phrases. The initial evaluation will be performed using non-lawyers as subjects and WIPO case outcome detection as the predictive task, since WIPO cases have relatively simple and predictable facts and issues. After initial evaluation, we plan to conduct future evaluations that validate this concept using lawyers and other end-users of this type of decision support system.

6   Summary and Future Work

This paper explores the hypothesis that predictive models induced from previous administrative decisions can improve subsequent decision-making processes. Three datasets were developed: motion-rulings, BVA issue decisions, and WIPO domain name dispute decisions. The ability to predict outcomes in these three domains was demonstrated using three different approaches for prediction: maximum entropy over token n-grams, SVM over token n-grams, and a hierarchical attention network applied to the full text. This initial evaluation did not establish the superiority of one approach over another, but rather indicated that the outcome of routine decisions is predictable using any of various alternative models trained on the text alone and that predictive accuracy varies depending on the domain and the nature of the predictive texts.

We propose use of feature weights or network attention weights from these predictive models to identify salient phrases in motions or contentions and case facts. We have developed an interface design for presenting this information to improve decision making, and we propose an experimental evaluation to measure the extent to which speed and accuracy in decision making can be enhanced by enhancing the salience of phrases based on their weight in the decision model.

The ultimate objective of this work is to improve the efficiency, accuracy, and consistency of administrative decision making–the form of adjudication that has the greatest impact on most citizens–by integrating automated decision models into the human decision process. This work represents an initial step towards this objective.

Acknowledgments. The MITRE Corporation is a not-for-profit company, chartered in the public interest, that operates multiple federally funded research and development centers. This document is approved for Public Release; Distribution Unlimited. Case Number 17-2336. ©2017 The MITRE Corporation. All rights reserved.

References

1. Aletras, N., Tsarapatsanis, D., Preotiuc-Pietro, D., Lampos, V.: Predicting judicial decisions of the European Court of Human Rights: a natural language processing perspective. PeerJ Comput. Sci. (2016). https://peerj.com/articles/cs-93/
2. Bahdanau, D., Cho, K., Bengio, Y.: Neural machine translation by jointly learning to align and translate. arXiv preprint arXiv:1409.0473 (2014)

3. Berger, A.L., Pietra, V.J.D., Pietra, S.A.D.: A maximum entropy approach to natural language processing. Comput. Linguist. **22**(1), 39–71 (1996). http://dl.acm.org/citation.cfm?id=234285.234289

4. Branting, L.K.: Data-centric and logic-based models for automated legal problem solving. Artif. Intell. Law **25**(1), 5–27 (2017). https://doi.org/10.1007/s10506-017-9193-x

5. Gallager, R.G.: Information Theory and Reliable Communication. Wiley, New York (1968)

6. Guyon, I., Elisseeff, A.: An introduction to variable and feature selection. J. Mach. Learn. Res. **3**, 1157–1182 (2003). http://dl.acm.org/citation.cfm?id=944919.944968

7. Hall, M., Frank, E., Holmes, G., Pfahringer, B., Reutemann, P., Witten, I.H.: The WEKA data mining software: an update. SIGKDD Explor. **11**(1), 10–18 (2009)

8. Keerthi, S., Shevade, S., Bhattacharyya, C., Murthy, K.: Improvements to Platt's SMO algorithm for SVM classifier design. Neural Comput. **13**(3), 637–649 (2001)

9. Mikolov, T., Chen, K., Corrado, G., Dean, J.: Efficient estimation of word representations in vector space. CoRR abs/1301.3781 (2013). http://arxiv.org/abs/1301.3781

10. Mladenić, D., Brank, J., Grobelnik, M., Milic-Frayling, N.: Feature selection using linear classifier weights: interaction with classification models. In: Proceedings of the 27th Annual International ACM SIGIR Conference on Research and Development in Information Retrieval, SIGIR 2004, pp. 234–241. ACM, New York (2004). https://doi.org/10.1145/1008992.1009034

11. Nielsen, J.: Usability Engineering. Morgan Kaufmann Publishers Inc., San Francisco (1993)

12. Peterson, M., Waterman, D.: Rule-based models of legal expertise. In: Walters, C. (ed.) Computing Power and Legal Reasoning, pp. 627–659. West Publishing Company, Minneapolis (1985)

13. Platt, J.C.: Fast training of support vector machines using sequential minimal optimization. In: Schölkopf, B., Burges, C.J.C., Smola, A.J. (eds.) Advances in Kernel Methods, pp. 185–208. MIT Press, Cambridge (1999). http://dl.acm.org/citation.cfm?id=299094.299105

14. Sidhu, D.: Moneyball sentencing. Boston Coll. Law Rev. **56**(2), 672–731 (2015)

15. Yang, Z., Yang, D., Dyer, C., He, X., Smola, A., Hovy, E.: Hierarchical attention networks for document classification. In: Proceedings of NAACL-HLT, pp. 1480–1489 (2016)

Arguments on the Interpretation of Sources of Law

Robert van Doesburg[(✉)] and Tom van Engers

Leibniz Center for Law, University of Amsterdam, Amsterdam, The Netherlands
robertvandoesburg@uva.nl

Abstract. Many researchers have worked on formalizing legal reasoning and the representation of law. Particularly in the last decade progress has been made in creating formal models of argumentation. We aim to develop an approach that is not only formally correct, but also can be used and understood by common legal practitioners and IT-staff members. The approach should provide an instrument that can be used to inform legal experts on relevant issues when finding a solution to a case at hand. In this paper, we present a real-time case that is in discussion within the Dutch Tax Administration, the Ministry of Finance, in court as well as in Parliament. By making a structured interpretation of sources of norms relevant for the case, and argument schemes to make differences of opinion explicit, we aim to demonstrate the FLINT method for the interpretation of norms, and support a process of redesign of administrative procedures.

Keywords: AI and Law · Knowledge acquisition
Legal knowledge-based systems · E-government · Argumentation

1 Introduction

While formalizing law goes back for over decades, one may even argue back to Leibniz' days, we still haven't managed to develop a method that results in a knowledge representation that can be used in applications that fulfill the demands of normal software engineering. It is not that there is a lack of examples of legal knowledge-based systems that are build using some formal representation of law [1, 2]. The problem is the coder-dependency of the suggested approaches, which limits scalability and has not yet resulted in knowledge engineering to replace the 'art-of-the-expert' that is currently used to acquire knowledge from sources of law in natural language [3].

In our work, we focus on the analysis based on the original sources of norms in natural language, in the legal practice. In previous publications, we have described our approach, which is based upon a revised model introduced by Hohfeld [11]. This approach has been applied to different legal domains, including migration law, tax law and labor law. We have developed a first version of a tool supporting modelers and legal experts [7]. While we see large-scale implementation of legal knowledge-based systems as a huge challenge, knowledge-based systems seem to have become somewhat a side issue in the AI and Law community.

© Springer Nature Switzerland AG 2018
U. Pagallo et al. (Eds.): AICOL VI-X 2015–2017, LNAI 10791, pp. 478–492, 2018.
https://doi.org/10.1007/978-3-030-00178-0_33

Not only scholars with a background in law, but also many AI and Law researchers, seem to be more interested in conflicts and the use of arguments, rather than the formalization of mainstream massive legal case handling that is typical for administrative processes. Designing and executing administrative processes also includes the need for argumentation on the interpretation of the applicable sources of law for general application. It is in that sense we are interested in argumentation. This means we are not using argumentation to argue about claims in a specific case, but we are using argumentation for arguing about an explicit interpretation of sources of law. The question whether interested parties in a legal argument share the interpretation of the meaning of sources of law, is assessed separate from arguments about the facts in a specific case. This type of argumentation serves a specific purpose. One that is not so commonly addressed in AI and Law literature, namely it should support us in coming to decisions rather than understanding a decision that is already been made.

In this paper, we present a case study that is the subject of an ongoing debate in the Dutch Tax Administration, the Dutch Ministry of Finance and the Dutch Parliament. We will show how we support the interpretation of sources of norms that are relevant for the case, and the analysis of arguments about those interpretations. Doing so, we will comment on statements of the State Secretary for Finance concerning the procedures to deal with objections to decisions of the Tax Administration. We also intend to fuel the ongoing debate on the need for adjustment of the policy guidelines regulating those procedures.

In this paper, we focus on interpretations of sources of norms to be used in real-time legal disputes among lawyers, policy advisors and politicians. The representations used should be comprehensible for experts from the domain of law, public administration and politics. Therefore, our focus is not on the formalization of the models used, but on the ability for domain experts to validate the presented knowledge and use it to argue about cases, to interpret laws and statues, to make decisions about instructions and support by IT systems.

2 Method

An important aspect of understanding and settling a legal dispute is the legal qualification of acts. In our work, acts play a central role. In earlier papers, we have shown our formalized version of the Hohfeldian concepts [11], our work is based upon [5–7]. In [6] we discussed the differences between rule-based, case-based, logic based and frame-based approaches to legal knowledge engineering [16] and the differences between the FLINT frame-based method in relation to earlier frame-based methods [4, 12]. The quintessence of the frame-based approach is the transformation of a source of law in natural language into a (semi-) formal interpretation.

In [7], we presented how this approach can be applied on legal sources using an example from Dutch Immigration Law, resulting in executable knowledge models expressed in a domain specific language (DSL): FLINT (Formal Language for the Interpretation of Normative Theories). This DSL is specific in so far that it is targeted towards the specific way we express norms.

FLINT differs from earlier frame-based methods because it focuses on the specifics of the legal domain, and the validation of the results of the analysis by legal experts. Were earlier frame-based models [4, 12] aim at transforming natural language into a frame-based model, FLINT aims at making a transcription between sources of norms, and a formal computational model. Van Kralingen explicitly chose not to pay attention to problems associated with the interpretation of legal knowledge. Breaux focuses on requirement engineering [6].

In this paper, we will present interpretations of sources of norms as institutional acts with a precondition and an effect (postcondition). Furthermore, we use argument schemes to discuss the validity of the presented interpretations. The computational aspects of the resulting model are not discussed in this paper.

2.1   Interpreting Sources of Norms

The FLINT frame for interpreting sources of norms is presented in Tables 1 and 2. Table 1 contains the frame for an institutional act, Table 2 contains the frame for a duty.

Table 1. The institutional act frame

Institutional act	Definition
≪Identifier≫	Description of the institutional act
Action	A type of action that causes the transition of an object
Actor	An agent that performs an act
Object	The thing that makes a transition as a result of an action
Recipient	An agent that receives the result of an action by an actor
Precondition	Condition that must be fulfilled to allow an act. The precondition consists of [institutional facts] and Boolean relations between these [facts]
Postcondition	The description of the transition of the object caused by the act, consisting of the creation and termination of institutional facts or duties
References to sources	References to sources

An act is the description of the transformation of an object caused by an act performed by an acting agent (actor). The result of the act is received by a receiving agent (recipient).

An act can be legally qualified as 'allowed' if that act is described in a source of norms, and if the precondition for allowing the act, as described in those same sources, is met. The result of the act, the transition, is specified in the postcondition. In this paper, the institutional act frames will be shown next to their sources in natural language. In our interpretations, we use the original fragments from sources of norms and put them in a frame structure to specify the conditions that allows the performance of an acts, and the results of that performance.

A duty is the obligation of an agent to perform an act in the future. It also requires an agent that has a claim right on the performance of this future act. A duty can only

Table 2. The frame of a duty

Duty	Definition
<Identifier>	Description of the duty
Duty holder	The agent holding the obligation to perform an institutional act in the future
Claimant	The agent holding the right to claim the termination of the duty
Creating institutional act	The institutional act that, if performed, creates the duty
Termination institutional act	The institutional act that, if performed, terminates the duty
References to sources	References to sources

come to existence if it is created by an institutional act, therefore: no duty can exist without the institutional act that creates it. The creation of a duty implies there is an institutional act that results in terminating, or fulfilling, the duty. The frame of the duty is presented in Table 2.

2.2   Argument Schemes for Normative Systems

In this paper, a set of statements of the Dutch State Secretary for Finance is analyzed. The statements contain interpretations of sources of norms. Disputes on the correctness of the interpretations of these sources are presented using argument schemes, see Table 3.

Table 3. Elements of argument scheme

Elements	Definition
Claim	The issue in an argumentative discourse
Reasons	Facts that support the Claim
Rebuttal	Attack on the claim that defeats the claim (the claim is false)
Undercutter	Attack on the claim that defeats the relation between reasons and claim (it is unclear whether the claim is true or false)

These argument schemes are based on the Toulmin's model of argumentation [8, 15]. The statements analyzed in this paper are considered to be claims, based on reasons. If a claim is attacked successfully, the attack will defeat the claim. This type of attack is called a rebuttal. If the relation between a claim and the reasons that support that claim is successfully attacked, that is called a undercutter [13]. So, a successful rebuttal results in the claim being false, and a successful undercutter results in uncertainty whether the claim is true or false. Formalization of argument schemes, using in tools such as ARAUCARIA and ArguMed [10, 14], lies outside the scope of this paper.

3 Case Study

The case study presented in this paper, is the subject of a Parliamentary debate on the quality of instructions used by the Dutch Tax Administration to process the withdrawal of objections to their decisions based on oral announcements during a telephone conversation. After receiving an objection, the Tax Administration calls the submitter of an objection within 3 days to discuss the objection, aiming to set peace. Explaining the reasons that support the decision can convince the taxpayer that the Tax Administration took the right decision and that insisting on reconsidering the objected decision is a waste of time and resources. In such cases the taxpayer may want to withdraw his/her objection. Roughly 20.000 of the annual 400.000 objections received by the Tax Administration are withdrawn after telephonic contact.

In January 2016, the withdrawal of one specific objection was disputed in a court of law. Following the publication of the verdict the State Secretary for Finance received a request to disclose all instructions and correspondence on policies concerning the withdrawal of objections based on telephone conversations. The disclosed documents raised questions by Parliamentarians. During the Parliamentary debate, the State Secretary announced that the procedures for dealing with objections would be revised. The analysis presented in this paper, is made to support the redesign of the procedures to deal with objections.

3.1 Setting the Scene

In the case at hand, Ms. Jones lodges an objection to a decision of the Tax Administration. The relevant acts in the case are the following.

1. In the beginning of January 2016 Ms. Jones lodges an objection against an order of the Tax Administration.
2. A tax inspector calls Mr. Jones, the husband of Ms. Jones, within 3 days to discuss the contents of the objection and the continuation of the procedure. During the telephone call Mr. Jones orally states he wants to withdraw the objection of Ms. Jones.
3. On January 22, 2016, the tax inspector sends a letter to Ms. Jones that her objection is withdrawn following a telephone conversation with her husband.
4. Ms. Jones lodges an appeal to the administrative court against the withdrawal of her objection.
5. On March 10, 2016, a lawyer of the Tax Administration sends the administrative court a letter that it considers the appeal inadmissible because the objection is withdrawn.
6. On April 12, 2016, the administrative court rules that the written confirmation that the objection is withdrawn, can be seen as a written refusal by the Tax Administration to make an order. The court orders the Tax Administration to decide on the objection within 6 weeks. The verdict is published on July 6, 2016.

7. On July 29, 2016, the Tax Administration receives a request for disclosure of instructions regarding the withdrawal of objections based on telephone conversations and internal correspondence on this subject. On September 27, 2016, the dossier is disclosed.
8. On October 20, 2016, Members of Parliament ask the State Secretary for Finance questions on the quality of policy guidelines for the withdrawal objections to decisions of the Tax Administration.
9. On November 3, 2016, the State Secretary for Finance sends his reply to Parliament.
10. On December 15, 2016, the State Secretary for Finance announces that the procedures for dealing with objections will be reconsidered.

From the questions posed to the State Secretary we selected the two main questions for analysis:

1. Can an objection only be withdrawn in writing, or orally during a hearing?
2. Is the Instruction 'Call in Case of an Objection' contra legem?

In the following subsections, we will demonstrate how our method can be used to create interpretations of sources of norms. Furthermore, we use argument schemes to comment the answers given by the State Secretary. The results of our analysis are presented such that they can be used to support the redesign of the administrative procedures for the reconsideration of objected decisions.

For the analysis, we will use English versions of the statues which are unofficial translations made by the authors in absence of an official version, and the official English version of the General Administrative Law Act (GALA) [9].

3.2 Can an Objection Only Be Withdrawn in Writing, or Orally During a Hearing?

The Reply of the State Secretary. In the opinion of the State Secretary, according article 6:21 GALA and case law, the only way to withdraw an objection, is in writing or orally during a hearing.

Relevant Sources of Law. The withdrawal of an objection to a decision made by an administrative authority, e.g. the Tax Administration, is described in article 6:21 GALA. The article is explicitly mentioned in both the question, and in the answer of the State Secretary.

Article 1:5, paragraph 1, GALA, is added because it contains the definition of an objection and the fact that an objection should be lodged with the administrative authority that took the objected decision. Case law, e.g. the verdict in the case of Ms. Jones, explicitly states that only the person that submits an objection, has the power to withdraw it. These sources where added because the frame of the institutional act is not complete without an actor and a recipient. The agent roles are not mentioned in article 6:21 GALA.

As a result of a search for sources that describe the requirements to make an oral withdrawal undisputable, article 7:7 GALA was included. This article is about the duty to make a report of a hearing. Additionally, the Memorandum of Explanation GALA states that the oral withdrawal of the objection should be mentioned in the report of the hearing.

The files that were made public by the State Secretary also refer to case law that does allow for withdrawal that is not in writing, or orally at a hearing. It concerns the withdrawal during a telephone conversation that is not a hearing. This source is not discussed in the answers of the State Secretary, nor in the Parliamentary debates that from those answers.

The Interpretation of Sources of Law. Table 4 shows the institutional act of withdrawing an objection in writing. It shows the action of 'withdrawing in writing' of the *objection* by the *person that lodged the objection*. The recipient of the result of the act is the *administrative authority that took a decision*. There are no additional conditions for performing this act. As long as there is an *objection*, the *person that lodged the objection* can withdraw it in writing by sending a *withdrawal in writing* to the *administrative authority that took a decision*. As a result of this act, the *objection* is terminated.

Table 4. Interpreting sources of law on the withdrawal of objections in writing

Sources of Law	Interpretation of sources of law
Article 1:5 Section 1 GALA "'Lodging an objection' means exercising the right conferred by law to request the administrative authority that took a decision to reconsider it" *Article 6:21 GALA* "An objection or appeal may be withdrawn in writing It may also be withdrawn orally at a hearing" *Case law* *ECLI:NL:RBDHA:2016:6098* "The power to withdraw an objection lies exclusively with the person that lodged the objection"	≪*withdraw objection in writing*≫ *Action:* [withdraw in writing] *Object:* [objection] *Actor:* [person that lodged the objection] *Recipient:* [administrative authority that took a decision] *Precondition:* (-) *Creating postcondition:* [withdrawal in writing] *Terminating postcondition:* [objection]

The oral withdrawal of an objection during a hearing is described separately in Table 5, because it concerns a different act, with different pre- and postcondition. The oral withdrawal of an *objection* at a hearing can be performed by the *person that lodged the objection* towards the *administrative authority that took decision*. The precondition of this act is that a hearing concerning the objection is taking place. The act can only be performed during a hearing, whereas the written withdrawal can be performed any time.

The postcondition of the oral withdrawal is the creation of a duty to <mention the withdrawal in the report of the hearing>. The *administrative authority that took decision* is the holder of this duty, and the *person that lodged the objection* is the claimant. The duty can be created by the act ≪withdraw objection orally at a

Table 5. Interpreting sources of law on the oral withdrawal of objections during a hearing

Sources of Law	Interpretation of sources of law
Article 1:5 Section 1 GALA "'Lodging an objection' means exercising the right conferred by law to request the administrative authority that took a decision to reconsider it" *Article 6:21 GALA* "An objection or appeal may be withdrawn in writing. It may also be withdrawn orally at a hearing" *Article 7:7 GALA* "A record shall be drawn up of the hearing" *Case law* *ECLI:NL:RBDHA:2016:6098* "The power to withdraw an objection lies exclusively with the person that lodged the objection" *Memorandum of Explanation GALA* Withdrawal of an objection or appeal during the session [hearing] is also possible. (...). In that case it is required that the withdrawal becomes sufficiently indisputable. It should therefore be mentioned in the report of the hearing	≪*withdraw objection orally at a hearing*≫ Act: [withdraw orally at a hearing] *Object:* [objection] *Actor:* [person that lodged the objection] *Recipient:* [administrative authority that took a decision] *Precondition:* [hearing] *Creating postcondition:* <mention the withdrawal in the report of the hearing> *Terminating postcondition:* (-)

hearing≫. It can be terminated by mentioning of the withdrawal in the report of the hearing. There may be possibilities for the claimant to terminate the duty by waiving the claim right, but those possibilities lay outside the scope of this case study.

The institutional act ≪withdraw objection orally at a hearing≫ does not have a terminating postcondition. The *objection* is not considered to be withdrawn at the moment that the withdrawal is uttered during a hearing, but only after the report of the hearing, that contains the mentioning of the withdrawal, has been established, and can no longer be disputed.

Table 6 shows the institutional act ≪withdraw objection orally during a telephone conversation≫. The source that enables this possibility is a lawsuit against the Tax Administration. The relevant fragment of the court order is included in the sources of norms of Table 5. The act to withdraw an *objection* orally by telephone can be performed by the *person that lodged the objection*, also referred to as the *submitter*. The recipient of the act is the *administrative authority that took decision*. The action must be performed during a telephone conversation. The result of the act is the creation of the duty to <send a written confirmation of the withdrawal>. We assume that the *objection* is only terminated after the moment the duty to <send a written confirmation of the withdrawal> is terminated.

Argumentation. The argumentation scheme below shows that State Secretary is wrong. There is a possibility to orally withdraw an objection in a telephone conversation that is not a hearing. Although the withdrawal legally lies within the scope of

Table 6. Case law on the withdrawal of objections by telephone

Sources of law	Interpretation of sources of law
Article 1:5 Section 1 GALA "'Lodging an objection' means exercising the right conferred by law to request the administrative authority that took a decision to reconsider it" *Article 6:21 GALA* "An objection or appeal may be withdrawn in writing. It may also be withdrawn orally at a hearing" *Case law* *ECLI:NL:RBDHA:2016:6098* "The power to withdraw an objection lies exclusively with the person that lodged the objection" ECLI:NL:GHSGR:2009:BI4839 "It must be assumed that a withdrawal of an objection made by telephone [in a conversation that is not a hearing], lies within the scope of Article 6:21, paragraph 2, GALA, provided the administrative authority sends a written confirmation to the submitter, the submitter agrees and the procedure is sufficiently carefully performed" *Memorandum of Explanation GALA* "Withdrawal of an objection or appeal during the session [hearing] is also possible. (…). In that case it is required that the withdrawal becomes sufficiently indisputable. It should therefore be mentioned in the report of the hearing"	≪*withdraw objection orally during a telephone conversation*≫ *Action:* [withdraw orally by telephone] *Object:* [objection] *Actor:* [person that lodged the objection| submitter] *Recipient:* [administrative authority that took decision] *Precondition:* [telephone conversation] *Creating postcondition:* <send a written confirmation of the withdrawal> *Terminating postcondition:* (-)

Article 6:21, paragraph 2, GALA, the act that causes the withdrawal is not performed during a hearing. The reply of the State Secretary is false.

Claim   An objection can only be withdrawn in writing, or orally during a hearing.

Data   Article 6:21 GALA: An objection or appeal may be withdrawn in writing (1). It may also be withdrawn orally at a hearing (2).

Rebuttal An objection can be withdrawn during a telephone conversation that does not qualify as a hearing, provided the administrative authority sends written confirmation of the withdrawal and the submitter agrees with the written confirmation

3.3   Is the Instruction 'Call in Case of an Objection' Contra Legem?

The Reply of the State Secretary. The State Secretary claims the instruction 'Call in Case of an Objection' is contra legem, i.e. contrary to law. No arguments are given for this claim, other than the claim that an objection can only be withdrawn in writing, or orally during a hearing.

Relevant Sources of Law. On page 4 and 5 of the instruction 'Call in Case of an Objection', version 4 of April 26, 2011, the procedure to withdraw an objection based on a telephone conversation is described. The instruction contains no references to other sources of norms.

The Interpretation of Sources of Norms. The fact that an objection can be withdrawn orally in a setting that is not a hearing, as is shown in Sect. 3.2, does not necessarily lead to the conclusion that the instruction 'Call in case of an objection' is not contra legem. In Table 6 the interpretation of the instruction 'Call in Case of an Objection' is presented.

Table 7 shows the institutional act ≪withdraw objection orally during a telephone conversation≫. The act to withdraw an *objection* orally during a telephone conversation can be performed by the *submitter*. The recipient of the act is the *tax inspector*. The act must be performed during a [telephone conversation]. The result of the act is the creation of the duty to <consider the objection not to be withdrawn in case the withdrawer expresses regrets concerning the withdrawal>. We assume that the *objection* is terminated at the time the speech act is performed. If at some point in time the withdrawer expresses regrets concerning the withdrawal, the *tax inspector* is assumed to reverse the withdrawal and to reconsider the objected decision under the regular procedure.

Table 7. Case law on the withdrawal of objections by telephone

Sources of Law	Interpretation of sources of law
Instruction making a telephone call in case of an objection "Following the telephone call the citizen/entrepreneur can withdraw the objection. The call is confirmed by a letter of the tax inspector, upon request of the submitter of the objection" "Note: In the letter, the withdrawer is given a 14-day period to express regrets related to the withdrawal. This 14-day period has an internal meaning only. If someone expresses regrets concerning the withdrawal after the 14-day period, the tax administration will consider the objection to be not withdrawn, and will reconsider the objected decision under the regular procedure"	≪*withdraw objection orally during a telephone conversation*≫ *Action:* [withdraw orally by telephone] *Object:* [objection] *Actor:* [submitter] *Recipient:* [tax inspector] *Precondition:* [telephone conversation] *Creating postcondition:* <consider the objection not to be withdrawn in case the withdrawer expresses regrets concerning the withdrawal> *Terminating postcondition:* [objection]

Argumentation. The instruction 'Call in Case of an Objection' allows the Tax Administration to refrain from sending a written confirmation of the withdrawal. Case law only allows for the withdrawal by telephone if a written confirmation of the withdrawal is send to the submitter of the objection.

Claim   The instruction 'Call in Case of an Objection' is contra legem.
Data   Based on the instruction 'Call in Case of an Objection' an objection can
               be orally withdrawal without written confirmation if the withdrawer
               does not request written confirmation
Undercutter   The objection is considered not to be withdrawn, in case the withdrawer
               expresses regrets concerning the withdrawal

The claim that the instruction 'Call in Case of an Objection' is contra legem is based on
the fact that the instruction made the written confirmation of the oral withdrawal during
a telephone conversation only required if the withdrawer explicitly requests one. The
written confirmation is necessary to make the withdrawal sufficiently indisputable.
Since the objection is reversible by the expression of regret by the withdrawer, the
absence of a written confirmation is no longer a valid support for the claim.

3.4   Reasons for Policy Change

The central matter in this case study is not the case of Ms. Jones, but the fact that the
debate that was sparked by this case lead to the announcement of the State Secretary for
Finance to reconsider the procedures for dealing with objections. The files that were
made public in before and during the Parliamentary debate on this matter, showed
disagreements on legal interpretations within the Tax Administration and the Ministry
of Finance. In the documentation concerning the case, and in the Parliamentary debates
on this matter, these disagreements are not properly addressed. We have used the
FLINT method to make an explicit representation of the positions in the case. Now we
will assess the case of Ms. Jones, using these interpretations, and use the results of that
assessment to deduce aspects that should be addressed during the procedures to propose policy changes.

What Caused the Conflict in the Case of Ms. Jones? It was not the unlawfulness of
the instruction 'Call in Case of an Objection' that caused the Tax Administration to lose
the lawsuit against Ms. Jones. It was the fact that the tax inspector spoke not to Ms.
Jones about her objection and the withdrawal thereof, but to her husband. The
importance of speaking directly to the submitter of the objection is undisputed, and is
mentioned in the instruction.

Additionally, when Ms. Jones lodged an appeal against the withdrawal of the
objection, this was not interpreted as expressing regrets concerning the withdrawal of
the rejection. The case of Ms. Jones is not about improper instructions, but on not
following instructions. It was the publication of the instructions of the Tax Administration that sparked a Parliamentary debate on the lawfulness of these instructions.

The only reason to include the case of Ms. Jones in the assessment of the policy
guidelines for dealing with objections is to find out why instructions were not followed
in the case of Ms. Jones.

The Right to Regret a Withdrawal by Telephone Was Kept a Secret. The
instruction to make a telephone call in case of an objection, was not made public. As a
result of that, taxpayers did not know they had the right to regret the oral withdrawal of

an objection during a telephone conversation. Also, the tax inspector that dealt with the appeal of Ms. Jones, was unaware of the possibility to regret a withdrawal if it (the withdrawal) was withdrawn orally during a telephone conversation. Instead of reversing the withdrawal he decided to declare the appeal of Ms. Jones inadmissible. If citizens are granted rights, whether by law or some other source of norms, the existence of these rights should be publicly announced.

Why Is a Written Confirmation of an Objection so Important? The withdrawal of an objection cannot be reversed. It is for that reason that the Memorandum of Explanation GALA requires administrative organizations to make it sufficiently indisputable that the submitter of an objection performed the act of withdrawing it. The reason to claim that the instruction 'Call in case of an objection' is contra legem, is that the possibility to withdraw an objection, without written confirmation, can harm the legal position of the submitter. Since, according to the instruction, the submitter can express regret concerning the withdrawal indefinitely, and the expression of regret is supposed to be followed by a reconsideration of the objected decision under the regular procedure, the legal position of the submitter of an objection is not harmed because of the instruction itself. The possibility to reverse an objection, should be properly addressed during the redesign of the procedures for dealing with objections.

Is it Desirable to Allow for a Reversal of the Withdrawal Indefinitely? The reason to limit the period that objections can be made regarding decisions of an administrative authority, is the desire to make legal decision incontestable after a fixed period of time, usually 2–6 weeks. By allowing regrets to the withdrawal of objections indefinitely, the objected decision remains contestable forever. When a policy change is proposed, the period in which the withdrawal of an objection can be revoked, should be addressed. At present, written withdrawals cannot be reversed. The oral withdrawal during a hearing becomes definitive if the submitter does not dispute the report of the hearing within several weeks.

Legal Protection by procedures Versus the Accessibility of those Procedures for Everyone. The instruction 'Call in case of an objection' is a derivative of the policy notes "Pleasant relations with the Government" and "Professional Handling of Objections", published by the Ministry of the Interior, and the Ministry of Justice in 2011 and 2014. The goal of these policy notes was to give guidelines for informal procedures to the assessment applications, objections, and complaints by government agencies. The notes describe the margins for deviating from formal procedures. A proposal for redesign of the procedures for dealing with objections should address the tradeoff between the value of legal protection by formal procedures and the need for informal conversations to give laymen access to their rights.

4   Conclusion

In this paper, we show how the FLINT representation formalism that we developed for creating explicit interpretations of legal sources can be used to create an explicit representation of the data of a case study, e.g. on the redesign of procedures for the withdrawal of objections. The representation is superior to the representation in natural text as normally used in legal disputes, because the frameworks enforces completeness and by doing so making relations between different sources of norms explicit. The method to represent institutional acts resulted in adding relevant sources. Sources that were included in the disclosed dossier of instructions regarding the withdrawal of objections based on telephone conversations and internal correspondence on this subject, but were not used in arguments by the State Secretary in his correspondence with Parliament.

The case study presented in this paper, was originally assessed by legal experts of the Tax Administration and the Ministry of Finance. This resulted in two legal statements that are successfully attacked in our representation. These attacks were not made during the parliamentary debates about the case.

The claim that the withdrawal of an objection can only be withdrawn in writing, or orally during a hearing, is successfully attacked by a rebuttal. The claim is false, an objection can, under specific conditions, also be withdrawn orally during a telephone conversation that is not a hearing.

The claim that the instruction 'Call in case of an objection' is contra legem is attacked by an undercutter. Because the objection is considered not to be withdrawn in case the withdrawer expresses regrets concerning the withdrawal, the ground for the requirement to send a written confirmation is defeated. But since the right to reverse a withdrawal was kept a secret, it is unclear whether the claim that the instruction is contra legem is true or false.

The representation presented in this paper also resulted in three specific aspects to be discussed in the coming reconsideration of the procedures for dealing with objections and the withdrawal thereof: regulating possibilities to reverse the withdrawal of objections made by telephone by expressing regrets (1), regulating the period in which a withdrawal can be reversed (2), the public announcement of rights granted to citizens (3).

Furthermore, the explicit representation of the reasons to support and attack the claims in the case study, makes them open for critical questions.

5 Future Work

In our ongoing research on developing a formal method that enables automated legal reasoning, we have developed a domain specific language, FLINT, to express the frames as described in this paper. The FLINT expressions are close enough to the natural language of the sources of law, allowing legal experts to validate these interpretations. FLINT furthermore enables automated reasoning about the consequences of such interpretations. Validating the genericity and testing scalability of the DSL and specification and execution environment are currently done in various projects. In those projects, we are also working on instruments to support the transition of sources of norms into a formalized representation.

Our approach puts much more focus on the correct interpretation of the sources of law compared to traditional knowledge based systems approaches. With our approach, the debate on the correctness of an interpretation consists of separate debates on the correct selection of sources of norms (1), and the correct mapping of concepts retrieved from those norms onto the elements in the institutional act frame, or the duty frame (2). Furthermore disputes on interpretations of sources of law are separated from disputes on the correct application of rules in a specific case.

The frame-based approach presented here, has been tested with experts in the Dutch government, but, as stated before, broader validation is planned. The development of tool support for our method is ongoing and we aim to further develop our method and supporting tools in collaboration with practitioners and academics in the years to come. As we strive for large scale application of our method and supporting tools we will also focus on the knowledge acquisition aspects that come with our formal models. This includes knowledge capturing using natural language processing techniques, and visualizations that are understood by a broader audience, may be even laymen. Interpreting sources of law may not be the easiest task, but being able to present interpretations in a clear way is in the interest of all.

References

1. Bench-Capon, T., et al.: A history of AI and Law in 50 papers: 25 years of the international conference on AI and Law. Artif. Intell. Law **20**(3), 215–319 (2012)
2. Bench-Capon, T., Sartor, G.: A model of legal reasoning with cases incorporating theories and values. Artif. Intell. **150**(1–2), 97–143 (2003)
3. Boella, G., et. al.: A critical analysis of legal requirements: engineering from the perspective of legal practice. In: IEEE 7th International Workshop on Requirements Engineering and Law (RELAW), Karlskrona, Sweden, pp. 14–21 (2014)
4. Breaux, T.D.: Legal requirements acquisition for the specification of legally compliant information systems. Ph.D. thesis, North Carolina State University, Raleigh (NC) (2009)
5. van Doesburg, R., et. al.: Towards a method for a formal analysis of law. In: Study case Report ICT with Industry Workshop 2015, NWO (2016). http://www.nwo.nl/over-nwo/organisatie/nwo-onderdelen/ew/bijeenkomsten/ict+with+industry+workshop/proceedings. Accessed 28 Apr 2017
6. van Doesburg, R., van Engers, T.: Perspectives on the formal representation of the interpretation of norms. In: JURIX 2016, pp. 183–186. IOS Press Amsterdam (2016)
7. van Doesburg, R., van Engers, T., van der Storm, T.: Calculemus: towards a formal language for the interpretation of normative systems. Artif. Intell. Justice **1**, 73 (2016)
8. van Eemeren, F.H., et al.: Handbook of Argumentation Theory. Springer, Dordrecht (2014)
9. General Administrative Law Act from Dutch National Government. http://archief06.archiefweb.eu/archives/archiefweb/20180224072222/https://www.rijksoverheid.nl/binaries/rijksoverheid/documenten/besluiten/2009/10/01/general-administrative-law-act-text-per-1-october-2009/gala18-11-09.pdf. Accessed 30 Sep 2018
10. Hitchcock, D., Verheij, B.: Arguing on the Toulmin Model: New Essays in Argument Analysis and Evaluation, 1st edn. Springer, Berlin (2010). https://doi.org/10.1007/978-1-4020-4938-5
11. Hohfeld, W.N., Cook, W.W.: Fundamental Legal Conceptions as Applied in Judicial Reasoning, and Other Legal Essays. Yale University Press, New Haven (1919)
12. van Kralingen, R.W.: Frame-Based Conceptual Models of Statute Law. Kluwer, Dordrecht (1995)

13. Pollock, J.: Defeasible reasoning. Cognit. Sci. **11**(4), 481–518 (1987)
14. Reed, C., Rowe, G.: ARAUCARIA: software for argument analysis, diagramming and representation. Int. J. Artif. Intell. Tools **13**, 961 (2004)
15. Toulmin, S.E.: The Uses of Argument. Cambridge University Press, Cambridge (1958)
16. Valente, A.: Legal Knowledge Engineering: A Modeling Approach. IOS Press, Amsterdam (1995)

Courts, Adjudication and Dispute Resolution

Dynamics of the Judicial Process
by Defeater Activation

Martín O. Moguillansky$^{(\boxtimes)}$ and Guillermo R. Simari

Institute for Computer Science and Engineering (ICIC) – CONICET,
Universidad Nacional del Sur (UNS), Bahía Blanca, Argentina
{mom,grs}@cs.uns.edu.ar

Abstract. We present a novel activating approach to Argument Theory
Change (ATC) for the study of the dynamics of the judicial process. ATC
applies belief change concepts to dialectical argumentation for altering
trees upon which the semantics for reasoning are defined. The activating
approach to ATC considers the incorporation of arguments to define a
revision operator for studying how to provoke change to the semantics'
outcome. Our objective is to contribute to the discussion of how to deal
with circumstances of the judicial process like hypothetical reasoning for
conducting investigations of a legal case, and for handling the dynamics
of the judicial process. We finally observe the behavior of our proposal
upon the sentences of two different real criminal procedures.

1 Introduction and Motivation

Argumentation provides a theoretic framework for modeling paraconsistent reasoning, a subject of utmost relevance in areas of research like medicine and law.
For instance, legal reasoning can be seen as the intellectual process by which
judges draw conclusions ensuring the rationality of legal doctrines, legal codes,
binding prior decisions like jurisprudence, and the particularities of a deciding
case. This definition can be broaden to include the act of making laws. Observe
that the evolution of a normative system –for modeling promulgation of laws–
would imply the removal/incorporation of norms for ensuring some specific purpose but keeping most conflicts from the original framework unaffected. As an
example, we briefly refer to the Argentinean broadcasting media law reformed
during 2009. The previous media law, promulgated by the latter de facto regime,
empowered the government to regulate the different media allowing total control
of news. When democracy was restituted, the regulation of media was extended
to private investment groups. As years went by, these groups took over majorities
of types of media, conforming monopolies in some cases. This brought excessive
power to groups with partial interests, allowing them to manipulate the social
opinion about the actual government, and even to condition politicians, thus
striking to national sovereignty. Article 161 of the new media law became one of
the most controversial points, since it forces monopolistic enterprises to get rid
of part of their assets in a maximun period of 1 year. Some enterprises warned

© Springer Nature Switzerland AG 2018
U. Pagallo et al. (Eds.): AICOL VI-X 2015–2017, LNAI 10791, pp. 495–512, 2018.
https://doi.org/10.1007/978-3-030-00178-0_34

that they would be forced to sell off their assets at very low prices. This opposes to article 17 of the National Constitution which speaks about private property rights. Moreover, some members of the Supreme Court think that article 161 recalls the control over the media exercised by totalitarian regimes, which would violate article 1 of the National Constitution. In fact, such situation could evolve to a distrust state on the principle of legal security. Hence, an informal analysis of the case imply working with conflicts among arguments in a sense like: $\langle art\ 17 \rangle$ counter-argues $\langle art\ 161 \rangle$, $\langle \langle art\ 1 \rangle$ and $\langle principle\ of\ legal\ security \rangle \rangle$ counter-argues $\langle art\ 161 \rangle$, and so on. (The new media law keeps being discussed in Argentina nowadays.) Consequently, the objective of this article is to study the bridge between the dynamics of the legal reasoning and the dynamics of argumentation. To that end, we rely upon abstract argumentation for constructing a theory of argumentation dynamics, and afterwards we study the dynamics of real legal procedures by analyzing the behavior of the theory upon the legal case's argumentation. However, the arguments that follow from a legal sentence are constructed in an informal manner, since argument mining from legal texts is an independent area that lies beyond the scope of this article.

Argument Theory Change (ATC) [18–20] relies upon the theory of belief revision [3,16] to define models of argumentation change which are devoted to the alteration of *dialectical trees* pursuing *warrant* of a particular argument. Dialectical trees are constructed from a graph of arguments where nodes stand for arguments and arcs for the attack relation between pairs of arguments. The root of a dialectical tree is the argument standing for the main issue in dispute of the reasoning process. The dialectical argumentation semantics analyzes the dialectical tree and as a result, the root argument may end up warranted, proposing a reason to believe that the issue in dispute should prevail. This form of argumentation reasoning brings a theoretical perspective that adapts well for modeling the dynamics of the judicial process. The dynamic abstract argumentation framework [21] extends Dung's framework [14] in order to consider (1) subarguments (internal, necessary parts of an argument that are arguments by themselves), and (2) a set of active arguments (those enabled to be used in the reasoning process). The main contribution provided by ATC is a revision operator that revises a theory by an argument seeking its warrant. For achieving warrant, a revision operator can be defined through deactivation of arguments [20]: the reasoning process disconsiders some arguments for ensuring warrant of the argument at issue. A complementary approach to such revision operation involves only activation of arguments [18]. This approach complements the one based on deactivation because sometimes it is either not feasible to deactivate arguments or the activation of another provokes less change. For instance, studying change in a normative system may imply the derogation of norms through the incorporation of a derogative norm. In this case, the model for derogation is achieved through the activation of an argument standing for a derogative norm in contrast to the proposal of the deactivating approach in which the old norm could only be disconsidered or removed from the system. The activating approach increases the amount of active arguments to achieve warrant. However, since defeaters might be unavailable to be activated, the revision could be not always successful. Moreover, it will be clear that each activation of an argument results in the possible activation of more arguments, thus provoking preexistent arguments to play additional roles.

In this article we present an original model of ATC referred as *global activating approach* which develops the objective of the activating ATC presented in [18] in a different perspective more related to the deactivating model for logic-based argumentation presented in [19]. The advantage of the global activating model includes reducing the theoretical complexity towards an appropriate axiomatic characterization. Our main objective is to contribute to the discussion of virtues and shortcomings of the activating approach as a theoretical resource for analyzing the current epistemic state of a judicial procedure under the presumption that such a legal practice is dynamic by nature. This means that in order to consider dialectical argumentation as a theoretic model of judicial procedures we necessarily must rely upon a theory with capabilities for handling dynamics of arguments. It is important to mention that we will only concentrate on the particularities related to the argumentation dynamics and not on legal concepts –like burden or standard of proof– related to the specific court to which a judicial procedure corresponds (see [6]). However, in Sect. 3, we analyze the sentences of two different real legal cases: a Supreme Court's for analyzing the dynamics throughout appellate instances of the judicial process, and secondly, the argumentation related to a process of a criminal court. To that end, we build the corresponding arguments and show that the judicial process, either from the judge's or from the lawyer's viewpoint, is dynamic by nature by applying the global model of argumentation dynamics presented here. However, we firstly present the change operation from an abstract perspective (Sect. 2), following a practical take on this matter. There, the usual principles of change from belief revision are considered. The axiomatization of the proposed operator should conform to postulates adapted to dialectical argumentation (see [19]) by following such principles. This part of the work is underway.

2   A Model of Abstract Argumentation Dynamics

2.1   Fundamentals for the Argumentation Framework

Arguments, in the usual sense, are interpreted as a reason for a certain claim from a set of premises. In abstract argumentation [14], these features are abstracted away; hence we will work with arguments as "black boxes of knowledge" which may be divided in several smaller arguments, referred to as *subarguments*. In the dynamic framework used here we assume a *universal set* of arguments holding every conceivable argument that could be used by the inference machinery, from which a subset of *active arguments* can be distinguished. These arguments represent the current state of the world and are the only ones to be considered to compute warrant. Therefore, at a given moment, those arguments that are inactive represent reasons that, though valid, cannot be taken into consideration due to the current context. For instance, the presentation of an appeal outside the acceptable period of time would render this argument inactive. That is, although the appeal constitutes a valid reason, it is incompatible with the current state of the world. A similar concept to inactive arguments is given in [23] to *inadmissible arguments*. Another configuration for inactiveness can be explained in the context of legal reasoning when some norm can be inferred from multilateral treaties and therefore, although it can be considered to be part of the normative system, its application depends on the decision of the Supreme Court for establishing jurisprudence regarding its applicability. An example in this sense is developed in Sect. 3.1. In this section, we will abstract away from any comprehensive mechanism for activating arguments. Afterwards, the ATC's activating global model will handle activation of arguments in a proper manner, seeking for a concrete objective. These changes will be performed at a theoretical level, *i.e.*, any inactive argument could be eventually activated. Nonetheless, a practical implementation for legal reasoning should restrict which inactive arguments are currently available to be activated according to interpretation of norms, which lies beyond the scope of this article. The abstract dynamic framework is defined next.

Definition 1 (DAF). *A **dynamic abstract argumentation framework** (DAF) is a tuple $\langle \mathbb{U}, \hookrightarrow, \sqsubseteq \rangle[\mathbb{A}]$, where $\mathbb{U}$ is a finite set of arguments called **universal**, $\mathbb{A} \subseteq \mathbb{U}$ is called the **set of active arguments**, $\hookrightarrow \subseteq \mathbb{U} \times \mathbb{U}$ denotes the **attack relation**, and $\sqsubseteq \subseteq \mathbb{U} \times \mathbb{U}$ denotes the **subargument relation**.*

As said before, an argument $\mathcal{B} \in \mathbb{U}$ may be composed by other arguments. Since an argument is considered a subargument of itself, it holds that $\mathcal{B} \sqsubseteq \mathcal{B}$, and therefore an argument always has at least one subargument. To illustrate the use of arguments and subarguments, consider for instance an argument $\mathcal{B}$: *"the fact that Steven did not turn in the report indicates that he is irresponsible; since Steven is irresponsible, he should be fired"*. There we can identify two subarguments, $\mathcal{B}_1$: *"failing in turning in reports suggests irresponsibility"* and $\mathcal{B}_2$: *"irresponsible people should be fired"*.

The subset of *inactive arguments* is identified as $\mathbb{I} = \mathbb{U} \setminus \mathbb{A}$. This set contains the remainder of arguments (within the universal set) that is not considered by the argumentative process at a specific moment. The principle characterizing argument activation is:

(Activeness Propagation) $\mathcal{B} \in \mathbb{A}$ iff $\mathcal{B}' \in \mathbb{A}$ for any $\mathcal{B}' \sqsubseteq \mathcal{B}$.

A set of active arguments determines that an argument containing them and only them is also active. Furthermore, an argument becoming active makes all of its subarguments to become active. An operator $C_{ap} : \mathcal{P}(\mathbb{U}) \to \mathcal{P}(\mathbb{U})$ is assumed to implement the *closure under activeness propagation*. Thus, $\langle \mathbb{U}, \hookrightarrow, \sqsubseteq \rangle[\mathbb{A}]$ is closed iff $\mathbb{A} = C_{ap}(\mathbb{A})$. To represent change over the set of active arguments we assume an *activation operator* $\oplus : \mathcal{P}(\mathbb{U}) \times \mathcal{P}(\mathbb{U}) \to \mathcal{P}(\mathbb{U})$ such that $\Psi_1 \oplus \Psi_2 = C_{ap}(\Psi_1 \cup \Psi_2)$, with $\Psi_1, \Psi_2 \subseteq \mathbb{U}$.

Usually, the acceptability analysis over an argumentation framework is made over the graph of arguments implicit from the framework. In this article, we build and evaluate a *dialectical tree* rooted in the argument under study in order to determine whether it is warranted. This approach allows us to analyze only the relevant portion of the arguments graph since we are evaluating the warrant status of a single argument. A dialectical tree is conformed by a set of *argumentation lines*; each of which is a non-empty sequence λ of arguments from a DAF, where each argument in λ attacks its predecessor in the line. The first argument is called the *root*, and the last one, the *leaf* of λ. We refer to a DAF as a *dynamic argumentation theory* (DAT) if it is closed under activeness propagation and whose argumentation lines are built according to the *dialectical constraints* (DCs) [15]: different restrictions on the construction of argumentation lines which ensure every line is finally *acceptable*. We assume DCs to avoid constructing circular argumentation lines. The domain of all acceptable argumentation lines in a DAT T, is noted as $\mathfrak{Lines}_\mathsf{T}^\mathbb{U}$, while $\mathfrak{Lines}_\mathsf{T}^\mathbb{A} \subseteq \mathfrak{Lines}_\mathsf{T}^\mathbb{U}$ will be the domain enclosing every acceptable line containing only active arguments. The root argument of a line λ from a DAT T will be identified through the function $\mathsf{root} : \mathfrak{Lines}_\mathsf{T}^\mathbb{U} \to \mathbb{U}$, while the leaf of λ through a function $\mathsf{leaf} : \mathfrak{Lines}_\mathsf{T}^\mathbb{U} \to \mathbb{U}$. From now on, given a DAT T, to refer to an argument $\mathcal{A}$ belonging to a line $\lambda \in \mathfrak{Lines}_\mathsf{T}^\mathbb{A}$, we will overload the membership symbol and write "$\mathcal{A} \in \lambda$", and will refer to λ simply as argumentation line (or just line) assuming it is acceptable. Since argumentation lines are an exchange of opposing arguments, conceptually we could think of it as *two parties engaged in a discussion*: one standing by the root argument and the other arguing against it. Consequently, given a line λ, we identify the *set of pro (resp, con) arguments* containing all arguments placed on odd (resp, even) positions in λ, noted as λ^+ (resp, λ^-).

Definition 2 (Upper Segment). *Given a DAT T and a line $\lambda \in \mathfrak{Lines}_\mathsf{T}^\mathbb{U}$ such that $\lambda = [\mathcal{B}_1, \ldots, \mathcal{B}_n]$, the **upper segment** of λ wrt. $\mathcal{B}_i$ $(1 \le i \le n)$ is defined as $\lambda^\uparrow[\mathcal{B}_i] = [\mathcal{B}_1, \ldots, \mathcal{B}_i]$. The **proper upper segment** of λ wrt. $\mathcal{B}_i$ $(i \ne 1)$ is $\lambda^\uparrow(\mathcal{B}_i) = [\mathcal{B}_1, \ldots, \mathcal{B}_{i-1}]$.*

We refer to both proper and non-proper upper segments simply as "upper segment" and either usage will be distinguishable through its notation (round or square brackets respectively). As stated next, the upper segment of an argument in a line constitutes a (non-exhaustive) argumentation line by itself. (Proofs are omitted due to space reasons.)

Proposition 3. *For any $\lambda \in \mathfrak{Lines}_\mathsf{T}^\mathbb{U}$, if $\mathcal{B} \in \lambda$ then $\lambda^\uparrow[\mathcal{B}] \in \mathfrak{Lines}_\mathsf{T}^\mathbb{U}$.*

As said before, the warrant status of an argument will be determined by analyzing the dialectical tree rooted in it. On the other hand, a dialectical tree rooted in an argument $\mathcal{A}$ will be built from a set of argumentation lines rooted in $\mathcal{A}$.

Definition 4 (Dialectical Tree). *Given a DAT T, a **dialectical tree** $\mathcal{T}_\mathsf{T}(\mathcal{A})$ rooted in $\mathcal{A}$ is built by a set $X \subseteq \mathfrak{Lines}_\mathsf{T}^\mathbb{U}$ of lines rooted in $\mathcal{A}$, such that an argument $\mathcal{C}$ in $\mathcal{T}_\mathsf{T}(\mathcal{A})$ is: (1) a **node** iff $\mathcal{C} \in \lambda$, for any $\lambda \in X$; (2) a **child** of a node $\mathcal{B}$ in $\mathcal{T}_\mathsf{T}(\mathcal{A})$ iff $\mathcal{C} \in \lambda$, $\mathcal{B} \in \lambda'$, for any $\{\lambda, \lambda'\} \subseteq X$, and $\lambda'^\uparrow[\mathcal{B}] = \lambda^\uparrow(\mathcal{C})$. A leaf of any line in X is a **leaf** in $\mathcal{T}_\mathsf{T}(\mathcal{A})$.*

However, the acceptability of a dialectical tree will depend on the set X of lines used to build such tree. Hence, an *acceptable dialectical tree* will be constructed from a *bundle set* $\mathcal{S}_\mathsf{T}(\mathcal{A})$ which –given a DAT T– contains all the acceptable and exhaustive argumentation lines from $\mathfrak{Lines}_\mathsf{T}^\mathbb{A}$ rooted in $\mathcal{A}$. (We refer to a line as exhaustive when no more arguments can be added to it.) Thus, following Definition 4, $\mathcal{T}_\mathsf{T}(\mathcal{A})$ is acceptable if it is built from a set $X = \mathcal{S}_\mathsf{T}(\mathcal{A})$. The domain of all acceptable dialectical trees from T is noted as $\mathfrak{Trees}_\mathsf{T}$. We will refer to acceptable dialectical trees simply as dialectical trees (or trees), unless the contrary is explicitly stated. Besides, we will overload the membership symbol and write "$\lambda \in \mathcal{T}_\mathsf{T}(\mathcal{A})$" when the line λ belongs to the bundle set $\mathcal{S}_\mathsf{T}(\mathcal{A})$ associated to the tree $\mathcal{T}_\mathsf{T}(\mathcal{A}) \in \mathfrak{Trees}_\mathsf{T}$.

Dialectical trees allow to determine whether the root node of the tree is warranted or not. This evaluation will weigh all the information present in the tree through a *marking criterion* to evaluate each argument in the tree by assigning them a mark within the domain $\{D, U\}$, where U (resp., D) denotes an undefeated (resp., defeated) argument. We adopt a skeptical marking criterion: (1) all leaves are marked U; and (2) every inner node $\mathcal{B}$ is marked U iff every child of $\mathcal{B}$ is marked D, otherwise, $\mathcal{B}$ is marked D. This marking has been also used to implement DeLP [15], a rule-based argumentation formalism. Using this particular criterion reduces the conceptual complexity of the approach presented here, allowing us to focus exclusively on the change mechanism. Finally, warrant is specified through a *marking function* $\mathsf{Mark} : \mathfrak{Trees}_\mathsf{T} \rightarrow \{D, U\}$ returning the mark of the root. Thus, given a DAT T, an active argument $\mathcal{A} \in \mathbb{A}$ is *warranted* iff $\mathsf{Mark}(\mathcal{T}_\mathsf{T}(\mathcal{A})) = U$. Whenever $\mathcal{A}$ is warranted, the dialectical tree $\mathcal{T}_\mathsf{T}(\mathcal{A})$ is called *warranting tree*; otherwise, it is called *non-warranting tree*.

The digraph depicted in figure (a) describes a DAT, where triangles are arguments and arcs denote attack. The sets $\mathbb{A}$ of active and $\mathbb{I}$ of inactive arguments (dashed triangles) compose the universal set $\mathbb{U}$. Subarguments were drawn inside their superarguments. $\mathcal{A}$'s superargument is inactive because it contains an inactive subargument. Figure (b) shows a dialectical tree spanning the graph from $\mathcal{A}$. Note that inactive arguments are not considered in the tree, which is non-warranting. This status would change by activating, for instance, a defeater for the root's left defeater.

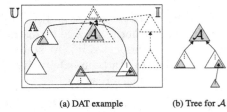

(a) DAT example   (b) Tree for $\mathcal{A}$

2.2   A Global Activating Approach

ATC defines a change operator that revises a DAT by an argument, making the necessary modifications to the theory to warrant that argument, by analyzing the dialectical tree rooted in it. The core of the change machinery involves the *alteration* of some lines in such dialectical tree when it happens to be non-warranting. Therefore, the objective of altering lines is to change the topology of the tree containing them in order to turn it to warranting. Alteration of lines comes from changes applied to the set of active arguments in the theory; that is, arguments cannot be simply removed/added to/from the tree. Hence, since an argument could appear in different positions in several lines in a tree, an alteration of a line could result in collateral alterations of other lines. In this activating approach, by alteration we refer to the addition of an argument (*i.e.*, a defeater) into a line. This may end up extending the line and even incorporating new lines to the domain. Next, we introduce the notion of *attacking lines* [19]: argumentation lines that are somehow "responsible for a non-warranting dialectical tree".

Definition 5 (Attacking Line). *Given a tree $\mathcal{T}_\mathsf{T}(\mathcal{A})$; a line $\lambda \in \mathcal{T}_\mathsf{T}(\mathcal{A})$ is referred as* **attacking** *iff every $\mathcal{B} \in \lambda^+$ (resp., $\mathcal{B} \in \lambda^-$) is marked D (resp., U).*

We refer as *attacking set* of $\mathcal{T}_\mathsf{T}(\mathcal{A})$ to the set $Att(\mathcal{T}_\mathsf{T}(\mathcal{A})) \subseteq \mathfrak{Lines}_\mathsf{T}^\mathsf{U}$ containing all the attacking lines from $\mathcal{T}_\mathsf{T}(\mathcal{A})$. Note that a tree without attacking lines is warranting.

Theorem 6. *A tree $\mathcal{T}_\mathsf{T}(\mathcal{A})$ is warranting iff $Att(\mathcal{T}_\mathsf{T}(\mathcal{A})) = \emptyset$.*

In order to achieve warrant for an argument $\mathcal{A}$, we would need to *alter* the tree $\mathcal{T}_\mathsf{T}(\mathcal{A})$ by altering every attacking line in it, with the objective of obtaining a new tree free of attacking lines. The following example shows the importance of identifying the precise argument –in a line to be altered– for which a defeater needs to be activated. Trees are drawn with gray/white triangles denoting defeated/undefeated arguments.

Example 7. Consider a DAT T yielding the tree $\mathcal{T}_\mathsf{T}(\mathcal{A})$ on the right with lines $\lambda_1 = [\mathcal{A}, \mathcal{B}_1, \mathcal{B}_3]$ and $\lambda_2 = [\mathcal{A}, \mathcal{B}_2, \mathcal{B}_4, \mathcal{B}_5]$. There is a single attacking line within the attacking set $Att(\mathcal{T}_\mathsf{T}(\mathcal{A})) = \{\lambda_2\}$. If we activate a defeater for $\mathcal{B}_2$ in T, we would generate a new line within a new tree having no attacking lines. If we instead add a defeater for $\mathcal{B}_5$, the line that was attacking is "extended" and again, in the resulting tree, there would be no attacking lines. On the other hand, if we activate a defeater for $\mathcal{B}_4$, we would generate another attacking line.

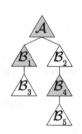

We call *effective alteration* to the alteration of an attacking line that turns it to non-attacking. In the ATC deactivating approach, an effective alteration is achieved by deactivating a con argument in the given line, thus truncating the line. Thus, deactivating a con argument in a line leaves a pro argument as the leaf of the new line. However, in the ATC activating approach presented here, the alteration of a given attacking line is done by activating a defeater $\mathcal{D}$ for a con argument $\mathcal{B}$ in the line. This would imply $\mathcal{B}$ to end up marked as defeated since a new line will sprout activating the undefeated argument $\mathcal{D}$ as its leaf. Afterwards, the resulting altered line would not be attacking. Note that, *any effective alteration of an attacking line has necessarily to be done upon a con argument in the line.* To that end, we identify the set of inactive defeaters associated to each argument in order to choose appropriate activations.

Definition 8 (Set of Inactive Defeaters). *Given a DAT* $\mathsf{T} = \langle \mathbb{U}, \hookrightarrow, \sqsubseteq \rangle [\mathbb{A}]$, *the* ***set of inactive defeaters*** *of an argument* $\mathcal{B} \in \lambda$, *is a function* $\mathsf{idefs}_\mathsf{T}$: $\mathbb{A} \times \mathfrak{Lines}_\mathsf{T}^\mathbb{A} \to \mathcal{P}(\mathbb{I})$:

$$\mathsf{idefs}_\mathsf{T}(\mathcal{B}, \lambda) = \{\mathcal{D} \in \mathbb{I} \mid exists\ \lambda' \in \mathfrak{Lines}_\mathsf{T}^\mathbb{U}\ such\ that\ \mathcal{D} \in \lambda'\ and\ \lambda^\uparrow[\mathcal{B}] = \lambda'^\uparrow(\mathcal{D})\}$$

Each inactive defeater $\mathcal{D}$ of $\mathcal{B} \in \lambda$ belongs to a line $\lambda' \in \mathfrak{Lines}_\mathsf{T}^\mathbb{U}$ which means that λ' is acceptable but contains inactive arguments. Requiring $\lambda'^\uparrow(\mathcal{D})$ to coincide with $\lambda^\uparrow[\mathcal{B}]$ implies not only the segments from the root to $\mathcal{B}$ in both λ and λ' to be equal, but also $\mathcal{D} \hookrightarrow \mathcal{B}$. The following notion allows to anticipate the effect of changes over a DAT T by identifying a *hypothetical tree* $\mathcal{H}_\mathsf{T}(\mathcal{A}, \Psi)$, as the tree rooted in $\mathcal{A}$ that would result from T by the hypothetical activation of the arguments in a set $\Psi \subseteq \mathbb{U}$. We refer to these trees as hypothetical given that they do not appear within the domain $\mathfrak{Trees}_\mathsf{T}$.

Definition 9 (Hypothetical Tree). *Given a DAT* $\mathsf{T} = \langle \mathbb{U}, \hookrightarrow, \sqsubseteq \rangle [\mathbb{A}]$, $\mathcal{A} \in \mathbb{A}$, *and a set* $\Psi \subseteq \mathbb{U}$; *the* ***hypothetical tree*** $\mathcal{H}_\mathsf{T}(\mathcal{A}, \Psi)$ *is the tree built from the set of lines:*

$$\{\lambda^\uparrow[\mathcal{B}] \mid \forall \lambda \in \mathfrak{Lines}_\mathsf{T}^\mathbb{U}, \forall \mathcal{C} \in \lambda^\uparrow[\mathcal{B}] : \mathcal{C} \in (\mathbb{A} \oplus \Psi)\ holds,\ where\ \mathsf{root}(\lambda) = \mathcal{A}\ and$$
$$either\ (\mathsf{leaf}(\lambda) = \mathcal{B})\ or\ (\exists \mathcal{D} \in \lambda : \lambda^\uparrow(\mathcal{D}) = \lambda^\uparrow[\mathcal{B}]\ and\ \mathcal{D} \notin (\mathbb{A} \oplus \Psi))\}$$

The activation of defeaters may bring new shortcomings towards an effective alteration of lines. The addition of a defeater $\mathcal{D}$ in a line λ provokes a *line extension*: if $\mathcal{D}$ attacks the leaf of λ, the whole line ends up extended; but if $\mathcal{D}$ attacks an argument placed strictly above that leaf, a new argumentation line arises by extending an upper segment of λ. The activation of $\mathcal{D}$ not only attaches $\mathcal{D}$ to λ, but also includes the addition of $\mathcal{D}$'s (active) defeaters, and these defeaters bring their (active) defeaters, and so on. An entire subtree rooted in $\mathcal{D}$ sprouts from the activation of $\mathcal{D}$. This subtree could contain arguments that were already active, as well as arguments that are activated by virtue of activeness propagation. For instance, an argumentation line $\lambda = [\mathcal{A}, \mathcal{B}_1, \ldots, \mathcal{D}, \ldots, \mathcal{B}_n]$ may have all its arguments active excepting for $\mathcal{D}$. Thus, a tree rooted in $\mathcal{A}$ would have a line $\lambda^\uparrow(\mathcal{D})$. Afterwards, if we activate $\mathcal{D}$, the resulting hypothetical tree would have the complete line λ. Hence, an effective alteration in the activating approach requires ensuring that the new line appearing from an alteration ends up as non-attacking, or equivalently, ensuring that the new defeater $\mathcal{D}$ ends up undefeated within the resulting tree for ensuring that the selected con argument (attacked by $\mathcal{D}$) finally ends up defeated. Moreover, the activation of a defeater may involve activating other argument/s which may extend other argumentation line/s in the evaluated tree. These shortcomings describes different alternatives of what we have called *collateral alterations*. A fortuitous case results from the collateral alteration of an attacking line which turns the line into non-attacking by chance. However, it may also happen to have a non-attacking line which ends up collaterally altered and turned into attacking, or even to have an effectively altered line which turns into attacking once again due to some collateral alteration occurring above the argument from which the original effective alteration has been done. The following example clarifies this matter.

Example 10. We have two attacking lines $\lambda_1 = [\mathcal{A}, \mathcal{B}_1, \mathcal{B}_3, \mathcal{B}_5]$ and $\lambda_2 = [\mathcal{A}, \mathcal{B}_2, \mathcal{B}_4, \mathcal{B}_6]$ from the tree depicted on the right, warranting $\mathcal{A}$ implies two effective alterations, one per attacking line. Line λ_1 can be altered upon $\mathcal{B}_5$ by activating a defeater $\mathcal{D}_1 \in \mathsf{idefs_T}(\mathcal{B}_5, \lambda_1)$. However, assuming that $\mathcal{C}_1 \sqsubseteq \mathcal{D}_1$ is also inactive then $\mathbb{A} \oplus \{\mathcal{D}_1\}$ will also activate $\mathcal{C}_1$. Afterwards, if it is the case that $\mathcal{C}_1 \hookrightarrow \mathcal{B}_4$, then the effective alteration of λ_1 produces a collateral alteration over λ_2. This situation impose a condition for achieving an effective

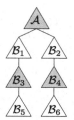

alteration of λ_2. For instance, in figure (a), by activating $\mathcal{D}_2 \in \mathsf{idefs_T}(\mathcal{B}_6, \lambda_2)$, the line is intended to be altered below a collaterality which will affect the current alteration through the activation of $\mathcal{D}_2$, avoiding its effectiveness. The inconvenience is that the collateral alteration extends the segment $\lambda_2^{\uparrow}[\mathcal{B}_4]$, incorporating an attacking line $[\mathcal{A}, \mathcal{B}_2, \mathcal{B}_4, \mathcal{C}_1]$ to the tree, leaving ineffective the alteration of λ_2. This shows the importance of avoiding collateral alterations occurring above the specific alteration in the line. In other words, the only safe collateral alterations are those taking place below the selected con argument in the same line. In this case, the alternative will be either to change the alteration of λ_1 to avoid the collaterality over λ_2, or to change the alteration of λ_2 forcing it to occur above the collaterality, *i.e.*, upon the con argument $\mathcal{B}_2$. The latter case is illustrated in figure (b). Assuming $\mathcal{D}_3 \in \mathsf{idefs_T}(\mathcal{B}_2, \lambda_2)$, the resulting tree ends up warranting its root argument $\mathcal{A}$, given that all the attacking lines would be effectively altered.

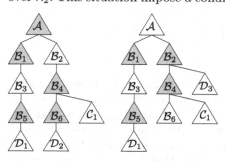

(a) Bad collaterality   (b) Safe collaterality

From the example above, if no inactive defeater for a con argument provides an effective alteration then a different con argument should be *selected* in order to obtain an appropriate inactive defeater for it, ensuring the effective alteration in a different part of the line. Such dynamics allows to overcome from bad collateralitites. The *global defeating function* triggers a set of inactive defeaters which would effectively alter the necessary lines, controlling collateralities, and ensuring a resulting warranting tree through the analysis over hypothetical trees free of attacking lines. However, when no (appropriate) defeater is available for any con argument in the same line, the revision operation will not succeed, and the global defeating will trigger the empty set.

Definition 11 (Global Defeating). *Given a DAT* $\mathsf{T} = \langle \mathbb{U}, \hookrightarrow, \sqsubseteq \rangle [\mathbb{A}]$ *and a tree* $\mathcal{T_T}(\mathcal{A}) \in \mathfrak{Trees_T}$; *the function* $\sigma : \mathfrak{Trees_T} \to \mathcal{P}(\mathbb{I})$ *is a* ***global defeating function*** *iff it holds:*

1. *$\sigma(\mathcal{T_T}(\mathcal{A})) = \emptyset$ iff $(Att(\mathcal{T_T}(\mathcal{A})) = \emptyset$, or there is no non-empty global defeating).*
2. *if $\sigma(\mathcal{T_T}(\mathcal{A})) \neq \emptyset$ then $\mathcal{H_T}(\mathcal{A}, \sigma(\mathcal{T_T}(\mathcal{A})))$ has no attacking lines.*
3. *if $\mathcal{D} \in \sigma(\mathcal{T_T}(\mathcal{A}))$ then the following conditions simultaneously hold*
   (a) there is some attacking $\lambda \in \mathcal{H_T}(\mathcal{A}, \sigma(\mathcal{T_T}(\mathcal{A})) \setminus \{\mathcal{D}\})$,

(b) *there is some $\mathcal{B} \in \lambda^-$ such that $\mathcal{D} \in \mathsf{idefs_T}(\mathcal{B}, \lambda)$,*

(c) *for any $\mathcal{D}' \in \mathsf{idefs_T}(\mathcal{B}, \lambda)$, if $\mathcal{D}' \sqsubseteq \mathcal{D}$ then $\mathcal{D}' = \mathcal{D}$,*

(d) *there is some non-attacking $\lambda' \in \mathcal{H_T}(\mathcal{A}, \sigma(\mathcal{T_T}(\mathcal{A})))$ such that $\lambda^{\uparrow}[\mathcal{B}] = \lambda'^{\uparrow}(\mathcal{D})$,*

(e) *if the following conditions simultaneously hold*
  i. *there is some $\lambda'' \in \mathcal{H_T}(\mathcal{A}, \sigma(\mathcal{T_T}(\mathcal{A})))$,*
  ii. *some $\mathcal{C} \in \lambda''$ such that $\mathcal{C} \notin \mathbb{A} \oplus \sigma(\mathcal{T_T}(\mathcal{A})) \setminus \{\mathcal{D}\}$,*
  iii. *some $\mathcal{D}'' \in \sigma(\mathcal{T_T}(\mathcal{A}))$,*
  iv. *some $\lambda''' \in \mathcal{H_T}(\mathcal{A}, \sigma(\mathcal{T_T}(\mathcal{A})) \setminus \{\mathcal{D}''\})$,*
  v. *some $\mathcal{B}' \in \lambda'''$ such that $\mathcal{D}'' \in \mathsf{idefs_T}(\mathcal{B}', \lambda''')$, and*
  vi. *some $\mathcal{B}'' \in \lambda'''$ such that $\lambda'''^{\uparrow}[\mathcal{B}''] = \lambda''^{\uparrow}(\mathcal{C})$*
  then $\mathcal{B}' \in \lambda'''^{\uparrow}(\mathcal{B}'')$.

The defeating function is the fundamental key of the global activating model, its three conditions are necessary and sufficient for ensuring that it is impossible (resp. of, possible) to turn the non-warranting tree into an altered warranting one, in which case, the function triggers an empty (resp. of, non-empty) set. On the contrary, whenever the original tree is warranting, the defeating function would also trigger an empty-set for ensuring that no unnecessary change will be made. This is controlled by condition (1). Condition (2) states that if the defeating function is non-empty then the activation of the arguments that it maps would result in a tree with no attacking lines. Condition (3) controls the behavior of the function when the revision is possible. It states that the activation of each $\mathcal{D} \in \sigma(\mathcal{T_T}(\mathcal{A}))$ alters a specific line that otherwise would be attacking (cond. (3a). The alteration is done over some selected con argument $\mathcal{B}$ for which an inactive defeater $\mathcal{D}$ is available (cond. 3b), ensuring that $\mathcal{D}$ does not contain any strict subargument that would serve for such a purpose (cond. 3c) –this is necessary for avoiding activations that could trigger unnecessary collateralities. Through condition 3d, it is ensured that the alteration is effective. This is done by identifying the new line λ' that appears as a result of the alteration of λ. And finally, condition 3e takes care of collateralitites, ensuring that when they occur, they never will take place above the selected argument for altering the line. We will see in detail this case, by referring to Example 10, figure (a): λ –from Definition 11– is instantiated with λ_1, $\mathcal{D}$ with $\mathcal{D}_1$, $\mathcal{B}$ with $\mathcal{B}_5$, λ' with the alteration of line λ_1, *i.e.*, with the extended line $[\mathcal{A}, \mathcal{B}_1, \mathcal{B}_3, \mathcal{B}_5, \mathcal{D}_1]$ (which ends up effectively altered satisfying cond. 3d), λ'' with the extended line $[\mathcal{A}, \mathcal{B}_2, \mathcal{B}_4, \mathcal{C}_1]$ which appears from the collaterality that activates $\mathcal{C}$ (instantiated with $\mathcal{C}_1$) from the activation of $\mathcal{D}$ (instantiated with $\mathcal{D}_1$) (cond. 3(e)i and 3(e)ii). Then, $\mathcal{D}''$ is instantiated with $\mathcal{D}_2$, λ''' with λ_2, and $\mathcal{B}'$ with $\mathcal{B}_6$ which is the con argument that would be defeated by $\mathcal{D}''$ in λ''' (cond. 3(e)iii, 3(e)iv, and 3(e)v). Finally, cond. 3(e)vi identifies $\mathcal{B}''$ (instantiated with $\mathcal{B}_4$) as the argument that was defeated by the collaterality $\mathcal{C}$ (instantiated with $\mathcal{C}_1$). This will allow to verify if $\mathcal{B}'$ is above $\mathcal{B}''$ in λ''', which is violated in Fig. (a) since it would require $\mathcal{B}_6$ to be above $\mathcal{B}_4$ for ensuring that the alteration of λ_2 occurs above the collaterality produced by the alteration of λ_1. Observe that the case of Fig. (b) satisfies the conditions of the global defeating function, which will map to a set $\{\mathcal{D}_1, \mathcal{D}_3\}$. Note that Fig. (1) depicted on the right, shows a special case of that presented in Example 10, Fig. (a), where the bad collaterality is produced by the alteration of the same line. The analysis of Definition 11 can be similarly done, where λ'' will coincide with λ', $\mathcal{D}''$ with $\mathcal{D}$, λ''' with λ, and $\mathcal{B}'$ with $\mathcal{B}$. On the other hand, the case presented in Fig. (2) shows a different anomaly: the activation of $\mathcal{D}_2$ brings its own active defeater $\mathcal{C}_2$ to extend the segment $[\mathcal{A}, \mathcal{B}_2]$. In this spe-

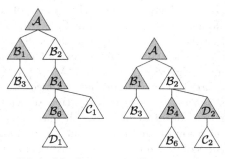

1) Bad collaterality   2) Hidden active defeaters

cific case, the new line $[\mathcal{A}, \mathcal{B}_2, \mathcal{D}_2, \mathcal{C}_2]$ will be attacking and thus the alteration does not change the mark of the selected con argument $\mathcal{B}_2$. This situation will violate condition 3d from Definition 11.

When selecting a con argument from a line $\lambda \in \mathcal{T}_\mathsf{T}(\mathcal{A})$, a *selection criterion* could lead the mapping to an argument $\mathcal{B} \in \lambda^-$ by assuming an ordering among arguments. Moreover, deciding among several alternatives for activating inactive defeaters would also require some specific *activation criterion* which, once again, could be founded upon some ordering among arguments. Both criteria are a necessary condition for determinism. We avoid going further into this subject, abstracting away from specific criteria. Next, we define the condition for a *warranting defeating function*, as a defeating whose outcome ensures a successful revision. This will depend on the availability of all the necessary inactive defeaters for warranting the tree.

Definition 12 (Warranting Defeating). *A defeating function "σ" is said to be **warranting** for $\mathcal{T}_\mathsf{T}(\mathcal{A})$ iff $(\sigma(\mathcal{T}_\mathsf{T}(\mathcal{A})) = \emptyset$ iff $Att(\mathcal{T}_\mathsf{T}(\mathcal{A})) = \emptyset)$.*

The *activating argument revision* is defined upon a warranting defeating. Whenever no such warranting function exists, the revision operation ends up undefined.

Definition 13 (Argument Revision). *Given a DAT $\mathsf{T} = \langle \mathbb{U}, \hookrightarrow, \sqsubseteq \rangle[\mathbb{A}]$ and $\mathcal{A} \in \mathbb{U}$; the operator "$*$" stands for an **activating argument revision** of T by $\mathcal{A}$ iff*

$$\mathsf{T} * \mathcal{A} = \langle \mathbb{U}, \hookrightarrow, \sqsubseteq \rangle[\mathbb{A}' \oplus \sigma(\mathcal{T}_{\mathsf{T}'}(\mathcal{A}))]$$

where $\mathsf{T}' = \langle \mathbb{U}, \hookrightarrow, \sqsubseteq \rangle[\mathbb{A}']$ with $\mathbb{A}' = \mathbb{A} \oplus \{\mathcal{A}\}$, and the global defeating function σ is warranting for $\mathcal{T}_{\mathsf{T}'}(\mathcal{A})$.

Example 14. Consider a DAT $\mathsf{T} = \langle \mathbb{U}, \hookrightarrow, \sqsubseteq \rangle[\mathbb{A}]$, where $\mathbb{A} = \{\mathcal{B}_1, \mathcal{B}_2, \mathcal{B}_3, \mathcal{B}_4, \mathcal{B}_5\}$ and $\hookrightarrow = \{(\mathcal{B}_3, \mathcal{B}_1), (\mathcal{B}_4, \mathcal{B}_2), (\mathcal{B}_5, \mathcal{B}_4)\}$, and assume we need to revise T by an inactive argument $\mathcal{A} \in \mathbb{I}$. The revision operator will analyze the construction of a global defeating function upon the DAT $\mathsf{T}' = \langle \mathbb{U}, \hookrightarrow, \sqsubseteq \rangle[\mathbb{A} \oplus \{\mathcal{A}\}]$, whose resulting dialectical tree $\mathcal{T}_{\mathsf{T}'}(\mathcal{A})$ coincides with the one depicted in Example 7. Assuming the selection over $\lambda_2 = [\mathcal{A}, \mathcal{B}_2, \mathcal{B}_4, \mathcal{B}_5]$ is the con argument $\mathcal{B}_2$, and

$\mathcal{D}_1 \in \text{idefs}_{\mathsf{T}'}(\mathcal{B}_2, \lambda_2)$; the mark of $\mathcal{B}_2$ turns to D. Nonetheless, by assuming $\mathcal{C}_1 \in \mathbb{A} \oplus \{\mathcal{D}_1\}$ and $\mathcal{C}_1 \hookrightarrow \mathcal{B}_3$, line $\lambda_1 = [\mathcal{A}, \mathcal{B}_1, \mathcal{B}_3]$ is collaterally altered, and even more, such collateral alteration turns the line to attacking (triggering a new line $\lambda_3 = [\mathcal{A}, \mathcal{B}_1, \mathcal{B}_3, \mathcal{C}_1]$) in the context of the hypothetical tree $\mathcal{H}_{\mathsf{T}'}(\mathcal{A}, \{\mathcal{D}_1\})$. This situation forces the alteration of λ_3 in order to turn it to non-attacking. Recall that this will require the selection of a con argument placed above the point of

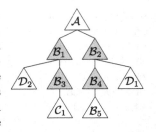

the collaterality, *i.e.*, an argument placed above $\mathcal{C}_1$. The only alternative is $\mathcal{B}_1$. Afterwards, assuming $\mathcal{D}_2 \in \text{idefs}_{\mathsf{T}'}(\mathcal{B}_1, \lambda_3)$, we obtain a hypothetical tree $\mathcal{H}_{\mathsf{T}'}(\mathcal{A}, \sigma(\mathcal{T}_{\mathsf{T}'}(\mathcal{A})))$ free of attacking lines, where $\sigma(\mathcal{T}_{\mathsf{T}'}(\mathcal{A})) = \{\mathcal{D}_1, \mathcal{D}_2\}$. Finally, since σ is a warranting defeating for $\mathcal{T}_{\mathsf{T}'}(\mathcal{A})$, the revision ends up as $\mathsf{T} * \mathcal{A} = \langle \mathbb{U}, \hookrightarrow, \sqsubseteq \rangle[\mathbb{A} \oplus \{\mathcal{A}, \mathcal{D}_1, \mathcal{D}_2\}]$.

Theorem 15. *If* $\mathsf{T} * \mathcal{A}$ *relies on a warranting defeating function then* $\mathsf{T} * \mathcal{A}$ *warrants* $\mathcal{A}$.

3 Dynamics of Judicial Procedures

3.1 An Example of Dynamics Through Appellate Instances

Under certain circumstances a court can let a criminal defendant off on probation[1]. However, this special benefit may not be given to a defendant involved in a gender-based violence case, since probation may end up dismissing the criminal case and thus, no fair nor effective legal procedure would be granted for the woman, contradicting multilateral treaties on the matter like the *Vienna Convention on the law of treaties* (or *Vienna*, for short) and the *Convention of Belem do Pará on the prevention, punishment, and eradication of violence against women* (or *BdP*, for short). Such exceptional case was not considered by the Argentinean Law until the Supreme Court dictated the definitive sentence on *Gongora's case*, on April 23rd, 2013 [11]. In this example, we analyze such a sentence which revoked the prior sentence dictated by the previous appellate instance, referred as *Cámara Federal de Casación Penal*, from now on, *Casación*. In short, Casación's sentence referred to the Penal Code (PC) for conceding the benefit of probation for the case, despite the state of affairs included gender violence evidence as shown in the lowest appellate instance. We will resume the case, by including only the argumentation provided by the Supreme Court, without the specific details of the argumentation given by Casación in the previous appellate instance. We assume $\mathsf{T} = \langle \mathbb{U}, \hookrightarrow, \sqsubseteq \rangle[\mathbb{A}]$ with arguments $\mathcal{B}, \mathcal{B}_1, \mathcal{B}_2, \mathcal{B}'$ in $\mathbb{A}$, where $\mathcal{B}_1 \sqsubseteq \mathcal{B}$ and $\mathcal{B}_2 \sqsubseteq \mathcal{B}$, such that:

$\mathcal{B}$: *Probation for Gongora is ordered according to arguments* $\mathcal{B}_1$ *and* $\mathcal{B}_2$.
$\mathcal{B}_1$: *Article 76 bis (PC), grants probation for sentences of under 3 years mandatory prison time.*

---

[1] Humanitarian effort to give second-chance to minor offenders instead of serving time in prison.

$\mathcal{B}_2$: *A mandatory sentence for Gongora's should not be over 3 years prison time.*
$\mathcal{B}'$: *Evidence of gender violence.*

The argumentation presented through the sentence dictated by the Supreme Court relies mainly upon Vienna and BdP treaties, specifically:

Article 31(1) (Vienna). *"A treaty shall be interpreted in good faith in accordance with the ordinary meaning to be given to the terms of the treaty in their context and in the light of its object and purpose."*
Article 7.b (BdP). *"Apply due diligence to prevent, investigate and impose penalties for violence against women."*
Article 7.f (BdP). *"Establish fair and effective legal procedures for women who have been subjected to violence which include, among others, protective measures, a timely hearing and effective access to such procedures."*

The Supreme Court's argumentation includes the following arguments:

$\mathcal{A}_1$: *Interpreting BdP (due to Vienna, Art. 31(1)) in the light of its objective and purpose (to eradicate violence against women); for gender violence cases, a legal procedure should be ensured (Art. 7.f) without delay (Art. 7.b), discarding any possibility of granting probation.*
$\mathcal{A}$: *According to $\mathcal{A}_1$ and $\mathcal{B}'$, probation cannot be granted for Gongora's.*

The consideration of Supreme Court's arguments can be understood as a dynamic process in which the legal system evolves towards restricting probation grant under the exceptional circumstance of gender violence. We can identify such a dynamic situation by referring to a framework $\mathsf{T}*\mathcal{A}$, whose intermediate stage is defined through a framework $\mathsf{T}' = \langle \mathbb{U}, \hookrightarrow, \sqsubseteq \rangle[\mathbb{A}']$, where $\mathbb{A}' = \mathbb{A} \oplus \{\mathcal{A}\}$. Observe that as a consequence, from activeness propagation, $\mathcal{A}_1$ ends up contained in $\mathbb{A}'$. Note however, that $\mathcal{A}$ would not be warranted given that Casación's sentence (argument $\mathcal{B}$) would appear as a counterargument of $\mathcal{A}$. At this stage, the theory of ATC, through the evaluation of the dialectical tree $\mathcal{T}_{\mathsf{T}'}(\mathcal{A}) \in \mathfrak{Trees}_{\mathsf{T}'}$ built with the unique argumentation line $\lambda = [\mathcal{A}, \mathcal{B}]$ (which is an attacking line), is indicating that although argument $\mathcal{A}$ is a valid supporter against probation for Gongora's, we still need to defeat Casación's previous sentence. Afterwards, the unique selection will be $\mathcal{B} \in \lambda^-$ and therefore, the theory indicates that a defeater $\mathcal{D}$, such that $\mathsf{idefs}_{\mathsf{T}}(\mathcal{B}, \lambda) \supseteq \{\mathcal{D}\}$ (see Definition 8), should be activated looking for a warranting hypothetical tree $\mathcal{H}_{\mathsf{T}'}(\mathcal{A}, \{\mathcal{D}\})$ (see Definition 9). The activation of argument $\mathcal{D}$ seems to be identified by the Supreme Court, which develops a second part of the sentence, providing an appropriate justification for their decision exposed through argument $\mathcal{A}$. Recall that the activation of $\mathcal{D}$ would imply activating each of its subarguments, where $\mathcal{D}' \sqsubseteq \mathcal{D}$, $\mathcal{D}_1 \sqsubseteq \mathcal{D}'$, $\mathcal{D}_2 \sqsubseteq \mathcal{D}'$, $\mathcal{A}_1 \sqsubseteq \mathcal{D}_2$, $\mathcal{D}_{2.1} \sqsubseteq \mathcal{D}_2$, $\mathcal{D}_{2.2} \sqsubseteq \mathcal{D}_2$, and $\mathcal{D}'_{2.2} \sqsubseteq \mathcal{D}_{2.2}$:

$\mathcal{D}$: *The application of Art. 76 bis (PC) is restricted under evidence of gender violence.*

$\mathcal{D}_1$: *Principles of the legal doctrine like* law as integrity *and* coherence *posse obligations for considering the complete legal system, including international treaties, and the ability to reinterpret the law in order to avoid contrary decisions.*

$\mathcal{D}'_{2.2}$: *Article 75(22) (NC) incorporates the international treaties to the constitutional block.*

$\mathcal{D}_{2.2}$: *From $\mathcal{D}'_{2.2}$, both Vienna and BdP have constitutional hierarchy.*

$\mathcal{D}_{2.1}$: *Art. 31 (NC) establishes the supremacy of the National Constitution.*

$\mathcal{D}_2$: *From $\mathcal{D}_{2.1}$ and $\mathcal{D}_{2.2}$, $\mathcal{A}_1$ is over Art. 76 bis (PC).*

$\mathcal{D}'$: *According to $\mathcal{D}_1$ and $\mathcal{D}_2$, Art. 76 bis (PC) should be reinterpreted in the light of $\mathcal{A}_1$.*

Finally, $\mathsf{T} * \mathcal{A} = \langle \mathbb{U}, \hookrightarrow, \sqsubseteq \rangle [\mathbb{A} \oplus \{\mathcal{A}, \mathcal{D}\}]$ ends up warranting the Supreme Court's argument $\mathcal{A}$ since $\mathcal{T}_{(\mathsf{T}*\mathcal{A})}(\mathcal{A})$ is a warranting tree with a unique non-attacking argumentation line $[\mathcal{A}, \mathcal{B}, \mathcal{D}]$. From the viewpoint of law, the case is interesting given that argument $\mathcal{D}$ can be seen as an instance of creation of law by an administrative operator of the judicial organ, which in the Argentinean Law is an exceptional case normally reserved for the legislature. From a different theoretical perspective, when creation of law is not admitted for judges, argument $\mathcal{D}$ can be seen as a case of law discovery, by assuming that the norm was already in the system, but it simply has never been applied before. In this case, the activation of $\mathcal{D}$ can be understood as a case of jurisprudence [8].

3.2   An Example of Dynamics on a Criminal Procedure

We analyze a small part of a criminal case sentenced on April, 16th 2007 by the *Tribunal en lo Criminal No. 1* (Bahía Blanca) [22]. This was a resonant case due to the great astonishment it caused in society. In short, the prosecutor claims guilt by attempting to prove that Cuchán had killed and burned his girlfriend, Lucy, in a grill at his house, whereas the defense's case is that the girl died from a cocaine overdose and was afterwards burned by the man in a state of despair. In order to make a practical example, we have extracted a small but representative amount of allegations, *i.e.*, arguments, and organized them within a dialectical tree. The tree's root is the initial argument posed by the defense, which ends up defeated, and then we will apply ATC's logical machinery to bring arguments that turn the root argument into a warrant. In this way, ATC proves to be a useful tool to perform hypothetical reasoning. We will assume a DAT $\mathsf{T} = \langle \mathbb{U}, \hookrightarrow, \sqsubseteq \rangle [\mathbb{A}]$, where the set $\mathbb{U}$ will include the following arguments:

$\mathcal{A}$: *Lucy died of cocaine overdose, so Cuchán did not kill her.*

$\mathcal{B}_1$: *Cuchán burned Lucy's remains; the burning objective was to hide the homicide.*

$\mathcal{B}_2$: *According to friends, Lucy never did drugs and she was afraid of cocaine.*

$\mathcal{B}_3$: *No traces of violence were found at the crime scene.*

$\mathcal{B}_4$: *No records of previous incidents between Cuchán and Lucy implies no motive for a homicide.*

$\mathcal{B}_5$: *An overdose might happen the first time a person consumes cocaine.*

$\mathcal{B}_6$: *Threads of hair belonging to Lucy were found nearby the crime scene implying violence.*

$\mathcal{B}_7$: *Psychological and psychiatric studies discovered Cuchán's psychopathic features.*

$\mathcal{D}_1$: *From the autopsy report, no cause of death could be determined.*

$\mathcal{D}_2$: *If the cause of death cannot be determined, there is no proof for a homicide.*

$\mathcal{D}_3$: *If the cause of death cannot be determined, there is no proof for an overdose.*

$\mathcal{D}_4$: *Recorded phone calls suggest Lucy's friends were threatened to declare in her favor.*

We will assume that every argument is active, except for $\mathcal{D}_1$ and $\mathcal{D}_4$. Let also consider two more inactive arguments: $\mathcal{D}$ and $\mathcal{D}'$, where $\mathcal{D}_1 \sqsubseteq \mathcal{D}$ and $\mathcal{D}_2 \sqsubseteq \mathcal{D}$; $\mathcal{D}_1 \sqsubseteq \mathcal{D}'$ and $\mathcal{D}_3 \sqsubseteq \mathcal{D}'$. The attack relation among active arguments is depicted on the right. Additionally, we have that $\mathcal{D} \hookrightarrow \mathcal{B}_1$, $\mathcal{D}' \hookrightarrow \mathcal{B}_5$ and $\mathcal{D}_4 \hookrightarrow \mathcal{B}_2$. Note that, in each argumentation line, arguments placed at odd positions are those posed by the defense, whereas the ones in even positions correspond to the prosecution. Now suppose the defense accounts with this infor-

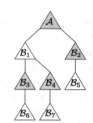

Dialectical tree defeating the defense's argument.

mation –representing the current state of the trial– and wishes to know how to proceed to change the outcome, *i.e.,* which allegations it should present. In order to warrant the defense's initial argument, we need to effectively alter the attacking lines $\lambda_1 = [\mathcal{A}, \mathcal{B}_1, \mathcal{B}_3, \mathcal{B}_6]$ and $\lambda_2 = [\mathcal{A}, \mathcal{B}_1, \mathcal{B}_4, \mathcal{B}_7]$.

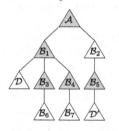

Activation of defeater $\mathcal{D}$ for $\mathcal{B}_1$

We select $\mathcal{B}_1$ as the con argument in λ_1, then, a defeater $\mathcal{D} \in \mathsf{idefs}_\mathsf{T}(\mathcal{B}_1, \lambda_1)$ appears. The activation of $\mathcal{D}$ requires to activate $\mathcal{D}_1$ (since $\mathcal{D}_2$ is already active). Note that, $\mathcal{D}$ itself is interpreted as a collaterally activated defeater for $\mathcal{B}_1$ but in λ_2. Thus, the global defeating function restricts the selection in λ_2 to occur in the segment $\lambda_2^\uparrow[\mathcal{B}_1]$. This will provoke the selection of con arguments in both λ_1 and λ_2 to coincide, triggering $\mathcal{B}_1$ in both cases. Hence, the activation of $\mathcal{D}$ turns both attacking lines into non-attacking, as depicted on the right.

Nonetheless, the revision is not complete, since an undesirable side-effect has occurred: the activation of $\mathcal{D}_1$ has also activated argument $\mathcal{D}'$, which attacks $\mathcal{B}_5$, since it dismisses $\mathcal{B}_5$'s overdose hypothesis. This collateral activation is controlled by the global defeating function in its condition 3e. Afterwards, the collateral alteration provokes λ_3 to turn into a new attacking line $\lambda' = [\mathcal{A}, \mathcal{B}_2, \mathcal{B}_5, \mathcal{D}']$ in the context of the hypothetical tree $\mathcal{H}_\mathsf{T}(\mathcal{A}, \{\mathcal{D}\})$. From cond. 3a in Definition 11, the new extended line λ' is effectively altered through

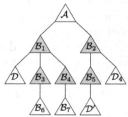

Dialectical tree for $\mathcal{A}$ resulting from $\mathsf{T} * \mathcal{A}$

the activation of the inactive defeater $\mathcal{D}_4 \in \mathsf{idefs}_\mathsf{T}(\mathcal{B}_2, \lambda')$ for the selected con argument $\mathcal{B}_2$, turning the line into non-attacking. The figure depicted on the right shows that $\mathcal{A}$ ends up warranted from the revision operation $\mathsf{T} * \mathcal{A} = \langle \mathbb{U}, \hookrightarrow, \sqsubseteq \rangle [\mathbb{A} \oplus \{\mathcal{A}, \mathcal{D}, \mathcal{D}', \mathcal{D}_4\}]$.

4   Conclusions, Related and Future Work

We have presented an approach for studying dynamics of the judicial process through an operator of argument revision which considers activation (incorporation) of arguments. This approach is comprehended within Argument Theory Change [18,20] and provides another standpoint to change the status of warrant of an argument in dialectical trees. The method is particularly interesting in the context of legal reasoning given that it could bring the theoretical foundations for recommender systems for the study of a legal case prior to the corresponding judicial procedure. This would render different critical points in the legal argumentation of the case for which further investigations could be directed towards discovering implicit norms that have not been applied before (judge's viewpoint), or towards discovering new pieces of evidence (lawyer's viewpoint).

Several recent articles (like [5,7,9,10,12,13]) deal with the dynamics of arguments. Some consider change by removing attacks between arguments, others by enriching logics with dynamic features. However, our perspective of change pursued here is different: we provoke change upon the morphology of arguments' graph for studying dynamics. In this sense, [17] is more similar since it studies dynamics upon graphs. However, the main difference is that the argumentation semantics that we follow in this article is necessarily the one derived from dialectical trees, since they probably constitute the most appropriate argumentation model for the analysis of the judicial process.

Regarding future work, the activating approach is the stepping stone towards the definition of a *hybrid revision* for deciding between the activation or deactivation in order to choose the most appropriate of both. This choice could apply activation in some attacking lines and deactivation in others. From the standpoint of the legal domain, the hybrid method would bring a theoretic model for studying promulgation of laws. A process of promulgation may involve the derogation of invalid norms (by disuse) that break the coherence of the legal ordering when considering the new law. Additionally, it may be the case that some articles of the new law should be modified for avoiding it to be declared inconstitutional due to contradictions –for instance, with some principles of the doctrine. A hybrid operator could model such a situation by activating arguments standing for derogative norms and deactivating arguments standing for conflicting articles of the new law. This would render a recommender system for identifying which previous norms should be derogated and which parts of the new law should be reformulated towards a successful process of promulgation.

References

1. KR 2014, Vienna, Austria, 2014. AAAI Press (2014)
2. IJCAI 2015, Buenos Aires, Argentina, 2015. AAAI Press (2015)
3. Alchourrón, C., Gärdenfors, P., Makinson, D.: On the logic of theory change: partial meet contraction and revision functions. J. Symb. Logic **50**, 510–530 (1985)
4. Baroni, P., Cerutti, F., Giacomin, M., Simari, G.R. (eds.): Computational Models of Argument. In: Proceedings of COMMA 2010. IOS Press, Amsterdam (2010)
5. Baumann, R., Brewka, G.: AGM meets abstract argumentation: expansion and revision for dung frameworks. In: IJCAI 2015, Buenos Aires, Argentina, 2015 [2], pp. 2734–2740
6. Bex, F., Verheij, B.: Legal shifts in the process of proof. In: Ashley, K.D., van Engers, T.M. (eds.) ICAIL 2011, Pittsburgh, PA, USA, pp. 11–20. ACM (2011)
7. Booth, R., Kaci, S., Rienstra, T., van der Torre, L.: A logical theory about dynamics in abstract argumentation. In: Liu, W., Subrahmanian, V.S., Wijsen, J. (eds.) SUM 2013. LNCS (LNAI), vol. 8078, pp. 148–161. Springer, Heidelberg (2013). https://doi.org/10.1007/978-3-642-40381-1_12
8. Bulygin, E.: Sentencia Judicial y Creación de Derecho. La Ley **124**, 355–369 (1966)
9. Coste-Marquis, S., Konieczny, S., Mailly, J.-G., Marquis, P.: A translation-based approach for revision of argumentation frameworks. In: Fermé, E., Leite, J. (eds.) JELIA 2014. LNCS (LNAI), vol. 8761, pp. 397–411. Springer, Cham (2014). https://doi.org/10.1007/978-3-319-11558-0_28
10. Coste-Marquis, S., Konieczny, S., Mailly, J., Marquis, P.: On the revision of argumentation systems: minimal change of arguments statuses. In: KR 2014, Vienna, Austria, 2014 [1]
11. CSJN: Góngora, Gabriel Arnaldo s/causa No. 14092 (2013). http://riom.jusbaires.gob.ar/sites/default/files/gongora_csjn.pdf
12. Diller, M., Haret, A., Linsbichler, T., Rümmele, S., Woltran, S.: An extension-based approach to belief revision in abstract argumentation. In: IJCAI 2015, Buenos Aires, Argentina, 2015 [2], pp. 2926–2932
13. Doutre, S., Herzig, A., Perrussel, L.: A dynamic logic framework for abstract argumentation. In: KR 2014, Vienna, Austria, 2014 [1]
14. Dung, P.M.: On the acceptability of arguments and its fundamental role in non-monotonic reasoning and logic programming and n-person games. AIJ **77**, 321–357 (1995)
15. García, A.J., Simari, G.R.: Defeasible logic programming: an argumentative approach. TPLP **4**(1–2), 95–138 (2004)
16. Hansson, S.O.: A Textbook of Belief Dynamics: Theory Change and Database Updating. Springer, Dordrecht (1999)
17. Moguillansky, M.O.: A study of argument acceptability dynamics through core and remainder sets. In: Gyssens, M., Simari, G. (eds.) FoIKS 2016. LNCS, vol. 9616, pp. 3–23. Springer, Cham (2016). https://doi.org/10.1007/978-3-319-30024-5_1
18. Moguillansky, M.O., Rotstein, N.D., Falappa, M.A., García, A.J., Simari, G.R.: Argument theory change through defeater activation. In: Baroni et al. [4], pp. 359–366
19. Moguillansky, M.O., Wassermann, R., Falappa, M.A.: Inconsistent-tolerant base revision through argument theory change. Logic J. IGPL **20**(1), 154–186 (2012)
20. Rotstein, N., Moguillansky, M., Falappa, M., García, A., Simari, G.: Argument theory change: revision upon warrant. In: COMMA, pp. 336–347 (2008)

21. Rotstein, N.D., Moguillansky, M.O., García, A.J., Simari, G.R.: A dynamic argumentation framework. In: Baroni et al. [4], pp. 427–438
22. SCBA: Cuchán, Pablo Victor (2007). http://www.scba.gov.ar/prensa/Noticias/17-07-07/Mat%F3.htm
23. Wyner, A., Bench-Capon, T.: Modelling judicial context in argumentation frameworks. In: COMMA, pp. 417–428 (2008)

Claim Detection in Judgments of the EU Court of Justice

Marco Lippi[1]([✉]), Francesca Lagioia[2], Giuseppe Contissa[2,3],
Giovanni Sartor[2,3], and Paolo Torroni[4]

[1] DISMI, Università degli Studi di Modena e Reggio Emilia, Reggio Emilia, Italy
marco.lippi@unimore.it
[2] EUI – European University Institute, Fiesole, Italy
{francesca.lagioia,giovanni.sartor}@eui.eu
[3] CIRSFID, Università degli Studi di Bologna, Bologna, Italy
giuseppe.contissa@unibo.it
[4] DISI, Università degli Studi di Bologna, Bologna, Italy
paolo.torroni@unibo.it

Abstract. Mining arguments from text has recently become a hot topic in Artificial Intelligence. The legal domain offers an ideal scenario to apply novel techniques coming from machine learning and natural language processing, addressing this challenging task. Following recent approaches to argumentation mining in juridical documents, this paper presents two distinct contributions. The first one is a novel annotated corpus for argumentation mining in the legal domain, together with a set of annotation guidelines. The second one is the empirical evaluation of a recent machine learning method for claim detection in judgments. The method, which is based on Tree Kernels, has been applied to context-independent claim detection in other genres such as Wikipedia articles and essays. Here we show that this method also provides a useful instrument in the legal domain, especially when used in combination with domain-specific information.

Keywords: Claim detection · Argumentation mining
Legal arguments

1 Introduction

One of the most traditional yet lively research sub-areas at the intersection of Artificial Intelligence and Law is the study of argumentation in the legal context [5,6]. Argumentation is a wide research field that spans across several different areas, having its roots in logic, philosophy, and linguistics, as it basically studies how different theses and opinions are proposed, debated and evaluated, taking into account their relations and inter-dependencies. The legal domain

This work was done while Marco Lippi was at DISI – University of Bologna and Francesca Lagioia was at CIRSFID – University of Bologna.

© Springer Nature Switzerland AG 2018
U. Pagallo et al. (Eds.): AICOL VI-X 2015–2017, LNAI 10791, pp. 513–527, 2018.
https://doi.org/10.1007/978-3-030-00178-0_35

thus offers a natural scenario for the application of different argument models, in order to perform legal reasoning [26], to build specific ontologies [2], or to support the teaching of jurisprudence [3,10].

From the Artificial Intelligence viewpoint, many contributions have been made in the context of building computational and logic models for legal arguments [26,27], in case-based reasoning [1,7], in the full semantic interpretation of judicial opinions [20], in yielding the syntactic structure of sentences using a rule-based parser in order to detect legal modifications [8], and also in the automatic extraction of arguments (or part thereof) from legal documents, as an application of the recent discipline of *argumentation mining* [21,22]. Some recent works [36] are focused on the discovery and analysis of the internal structure of an arguments, the identification of its premises and the conclusions, and the internal syntactical and grammatical structure of each statement.

Building tools capable of automatically detecting arguments in legal texts would produce a dramatic impact on many disciplines related to Law, providing invaluable instruments for the retrieval of legal arguments from large corpora, for the summarization and classification of legal texts, and finally for the development of expert systems supporting lawyers and judges. Mochales Palau and Moens [22] gave an influential contribution in this domain, providing the first system for mining arguments from legal documents. Their system, specifically designed by experts in the legal domain, combines highly engineered feature construction, machine learning approaches, and a hand-crafted context-free grammar to infer links between arguments. Their results are yet hard to reproduce, since the dataset they used, made up of documents extracted from legal texts of the European Court of Human Rights (ECHR) and from the AraucariaDB, is currently not available, whereas their methodology exploits plenty of context-dependent information that was specifically extracted from that corpus.

In this work, we aim to contribute to the budding field of argumentation mining in legal documents by moving in two different directions. First, we present a novel, freely available, annotated corpus for argumentation mining in the legal context, accompanied by a set of guidelines that have been followed during the document labeling process. Second, we consider a machine learning approach for the extraction of claims from legal documents that has recently been applied to context-independent argument mining [18], and we evaluate it in this new genre. Our preliminary results show that context-independent claim detection is also helpful in the legal domain, thus providing a powerful framework that can be used in combination with domain-specific information.

2 Background

Argumentation mining is concerned with the automatic extraction of arguments from generic textual corpora. This has a self-evident application potential in a variety of domains. IBM recently funded a multi-million cognitive computing project called *Debater*, whose core technology is argumentation mining, and which aims to retrieve pro and con arguments concerning a given controversial topic.[1] If we consider user-generated content available on the Web, argumentation mining can be seen as the evolution of sentiment analysis: its goal is to detect not only opinions, but also the reasons behind them [15].

One of the pioneering applications of argumentation mining was in the legal domain. Building on Teufel's work on argumentation zoning [30], Hachey and Grover proposed a system for legal document summarization [16]. Mochales Palau and Moens [22] proposed the first argumentation mining system, focussing on the extraction of claims and their supporting premises from a collection of structured legal documents. They worked on two datasets: the European Court of Human Rights (ECHR) [21] and AraucariaDB, a collection maintained by the University of Dundee.[2] More recently, the Vaccine/Injury Project (V/IP) [4] was carried out, with the goal of extracting arguments from a set of judicial decisions involving vaccine regulations.

Although the general idea of argumentation mining is clear, a precise definition of the problem is difficult to obtain, because the problem is complex in itself (there are many sub-tasks that can be identified), and the very notion of argument is still a matter for discussion, and is somehow genre-dependent. An argument in law is different from an argument in an online discussion, although they do share commonalities.

A simple and intuitive characterization of an argument is given by Walton as a set of statements consisting of three parts: a conclusion, a set of premises, and an inference from the premises to the conclusion [33]. Aside from this basic premise/conclusion argument model, there are other noteworthy models are due to Toulmin [31] and Freeman [14]. A rather comprehensive account of argumentation models from an argument analysis perspective is given by Peldszus and Stede [25]. To add to the terminological complexity, in the literature conclusions are sometimes referred to as *claims*, premises are often called *evidence* or *reasons*, and the link between the two, i.e., the inference, is sometimes called the *argument* itself. The task of detecting the premises and conclusion of an argument, as found in a text of discourse, is typically referred to as *detection* or *identification* [33]. More specific sub-tasks are *claim detection* and *evidence detection* [17,18,28].

Even the targets of argumentation mining vary widely. Some research aims at extracting the arguments from generic unstructured documents, which is a fundamental step in practical applications [17], whereas other research starts from a given set of arguments and focuses on aspects such as the identification of attack/support [11] or entailment [9] relations between them, or on the classification of argument schemes [13] in the sense of Walton et al. [34]. The aforementioned approach by Mochales Palau and Moens [22] represents, to date, one of the few works whose goal was to implement a full-fledged argumentation mining system, albeit specific to a single genre.

---

[1] More about IBM Debating Technologies at http://researcher.watson.ibm.com/researcher/view_group.php?id=5443.

[2] http://corpora.aifdb.org/.

Diverse methodologies have been developed which involve aspects of natural language processing and understanding, information extraction, feature discovery and discourse analysis. In general, all the argument mining frameworks proposed so far can be described as multi-stage pipeline systems [19], whose input consists of natural, free text documents, and whose output is a marked-up document, where arguments (or parts of arguments, such as claims) are marked up. Each stage addresses a sub-task of the whole argumentation mining problem, by employing one or more machine learning and natural language processing methodologies and techniques.

A first stage usually consists in detecting which sentences in the input document are argumentative, which means that they contain an argument, or part thereof. Once argumentative sentences are singled out, one needs to detect the boundaries between the various argument components. Finally, a last stage in the pipeline considers these components in order to predict links between them and/or between the arguments they are part of. For an overview of the state of the art in argumentation mining, the reader can refer to [19]. In this work, we focus on the first stage of the pipeline, considering *concluding claims* as the target. By the concluding claim of an argument we mean its conclusion, namely, the proposition that is affirmed on the basis of the argument's premises. The concluding claims affirmed in the opinion conclusions are crucial for its understanding, as they highlight the core legal grounds supporting the judgment.

We choose to focus on judicial opinions since they are highly structured legal texts, in which an account of the arguments by different parties is first presented, and then the justification for the judge's decision is provided. Both aspects are extensively developed in the opinions of the European judges.

3 Corpus

The source corpus consists of fifteen relevant European Court of Justice (ECJ) decisions from 2001 to 2014 extracted from the EUR-LEX database, all related to data protection. These documents were manually labeled following a procedure that we describe in detail in the following subsections. These annotations will represent the *ground truth* for our claim detection system.

3.1 Data Collection

This source was selected because: (a) ECJ decisions contain different types of legal arguments by different actors (e.g. arguments appealing to statues, principles or precedents, according to different interpretive canons, e.g. arguments by the parties, the Advocate General or the judges); (b) ECJ decisions have a standard (although not fixed) structure, in which the complex and highly variable structure of arguments is embedded; (c) the selected decisions come from the same domain (data protection), in which the annotators have some expertise. ECJ decision usually include the following sections:

1. preamble: information on the parties and the main object of the judgment;
2. legal context: listing of all the legal instruments used in the judgment;

3. background of the case: the procedural history of the case and the question referred to the court;
4. consideration on the question(s) referred: the observations submitted to the court by the parties and other actors such as the Governments of Member States, plus the responses of the Court;
5. costs: the attribution of costs;
6. ruling: the final decision and the orders to the parties.

3.2 Annotation Guidelines

In analyzing the ECJ decisions, we did not consider Sects. 1 (preamble), 2 (legal context) and 3 (background of the case), because they contain only legal and factual information, but no arguments are put forward. The most interesting part for our aims is Sect. 4 (consideration on the question(s) referred), which contains all argumentative steps leading to the final ruling. Section 5 (costs) was taken in to account. We did not consider Sect. 6 (ruling), since it usually repeats the top claims of Sect. 4, completed with orders to the parties. The text is divided into numbered paragraphs. In selecting arguments we proceeded as follows: for each paragraph, if arguments were present, we considered the chaining of arguments [32], identified the top-level argument, that is, the ultimate argument in the chain, and we annotated the claim corresponding to its conclusion, as well as the keywords signaling or introducing such argument. Highlighting keywords and markers in the text was useful for the purpose of keeping the annotations uniform.

In order to detect an argument we first considered the grammatical and syntactical structure of the text, looking for occurrences of conclusion indicators [12] such as "as a result", "therefore", "consequently", "thus", "for this reason". Nevertheless, sometimes the grammatical and the syntactical structures were not sufficient to detect arguments, and it was necessary to take into account the semantics and the legal context. For instance, consider the following statements taken from judgment C-301/06, paragraphs 28 and 38, respectively:

*Ireland submits that **the choice of Article 95 EC as the legal basis for Directive 2006/24 is a fundamental error**.*

Article 4 of Directive 2006/24 provides that the conditions for access to and processing of retained data must be defined by the Member States subject to the legal provisions of the Union and international law.

We can say that the first statement introduces a claim that can be evaluated as the conclusion of an argument, while the second simply repeats the content of a legal provision and it is not part of an argumentative claim.

The contextual analysis also helped us to distinguish two uses of precedents and other legal sources: (1) an argumentative use, where the court refers to a precedent or source in order to reinforce and bolster its arguments supporting the decision; (2) a non-argumentative way, in which the court incidentally mentions a previous decision or an argument of other parties, as a contextual element. Only in the first case did we annotate the sentence as containing a claim. As an example, consider the following statements of the Court from judgment C-275/06, paragraph 36 and 62:

> *It should be recalled that **it is solely for the national court before which the dispute has been brought, and which must assume responsibility for the subsequent judicial decision, to determine in the light of the particular circumstances of the case both the need for a preliminary ruling in order to enable it to deliver judgment and the relevance of the questions which it submits to the Court** (Case C 217/05 Confederación Española de Empresarios de Estaciones de Servicio [2006] ECR I 11987, paragraph 16 and the case-law cited).*

> *It should be recalled that the fundamental right to property and the fundamental right to effective judicial protection constitute general principles of Community law (see respectively, to that effect, Joined Cases C 154/04 and C 155/04 Alliance for Natural Health and Others [2005] ECR I 6451, paragraph 126 and the case-law cited, and Case C 432/05 Unibet [2007] ECR I 2271, paragraph 37 and the case-law cited).*

This first statement is an example of how the Court refers to a previous ruling to strengthen its argument, while the second one refers to a contextual element.

When a paragraph includes two or more top-level arguments, we highlighted the conclusions of both arguments and also marked the keywords or the expressions linking the arguments, such as "moreover", "furthermore", "additionally", "it should be added that", etc. As an example, consider the following two statements taken from judgment C-131/12, paragraph 22 in which we marked both the top-level claims, highlighted in bold in the text:

> *According to Google Spain and Google Inc., **the activity of search engines cannot be regarded as processing of the data which appear on third parties web pages displayed in the list of search results.***

> *Furthermore, even if that activity must be classified as "data processing", **the operator of a search engine cannot be regarded as a "controller" in respect of that processing since it has no knowledge of those data and does not exercise control over the data.***

When contiguous arguments are chained together, so that the preceeding ones are only meant to provide the premises for the last one, we have marked only the last argument (highlighted in bold in the text). Look at the following example:

As regards Article 12(b) of Directive 95/46, the application of which is subject to the condition that the processing of personal data be incompatible with the directive, it should be recalled that, as has been noted in paragraph 72 of the present judgment, such incompatibility may result not only from the fact that such data are inaccurate but, in particular, also from the fact that they are inadequate, irrelevant or excessive in relation to the purposes of the processing, that they are not kept up to date, or that they are kept for longer than is necessary unless they are required to be kept for historical, statistical or scientific purposes.

It follows from those requirements, laid down in Article 6(1)(c) to (e) of Directive 95/46, that even initially lawful processing of accurate data may, in the course of time, become incompatible with the directive where those data are no longer necessary in the light of the purposes for which they were collected or processed. That is so in particular where they appear to be inadequate, irrelevant or no longer relevant, or excessive in relation to those purposes and in the light of the time that has elapsed.

*Therefore, if it is found, following a request by the data subject pursuant to Article 12(b) of Directive 95/46, that the inclusion in the list of results displayed following a search made on the basis of his name of the links to web pages published lawfully by third parties and containing true information relating to him personally is, at this point in time, incompatible with Article 6(1)(c) to (e) of the directive because that information appears, having regard to all the circumstances of the case, to be inadequate, irrelevant or no longer relevant, or excessive in relation to the purposes of the processing at issue carried out by the operator of the search engine, **the information and links concerned in the list of results must be erased.***

When a party in the case mentions an argument by another to endorse that argument, we considered the conclusion of the argument as a claim by the party. As an example, look at the structure of the following statement, taken from judgment C-101/01, paragraph 31:

*The Swedish Government submits that, when Directive 95/46 was implemented in national law, the Swedish legislature took the view that **processing of personal data by a natural person which consisted in publishing those data to an indeterminate number of people, for example through the internet, could not be described as "a purely personal or household activity" within the meaning of the second indent of Article 3(2) of Directive 95/46.** However, that Government does not rule out that the exception provided for in the first indent of that paragraph might cover cases in which a natural person publishes personal data on an internet page solely in the exercise of his freedom of expression and without any connection with a professional or commercial activity.*

In this example, the claim put forward by the Swedish legislature, introduced by the expression "took the view that", is endorsed by the Swedish Government, an endorsement expressed by the locution "submits that".

The annotated corpus is available at http://argumentationmining.disi.unibo.it/aicol2015.html.

4 Methods

In this work, we focus on the first stage of the pipeline sketched in Sect. 2, i.e., on argumentative sentence classification, and in particular on claim detection. Our goal is thus to detect sentences that contain a claim.

The most common approaches to this task typically employ machine learning systems, whose aim is to construct a classifier that is capable of associating a given sentence x with a label y that indicates whether or not the sentence contains a claim. There is a wide variety of methods for building such a classifier. They differ by their chosen machine learning algorithm and by how they represent sentences. Some techniques simply represent the sentence with the well-known bag-of-words model, in which a sentence x is just represented by the set of its words, regardless of their order, encoded into a linear vector. Advanced variants of that model also consider bigrams and trigrams of words. The most common existing approaches to claim detection rely on large sets of sophisticated features, that are very often domain-dependent and designed by hand to address the task of interest. While simple machine learning algorithms are typically used as off-the-shelf tools [19], a lot of effort is dedicated in these approaches to the development of such highly engineered features. This is the case, for example, in the work by Mochales Palau and Moens [22] on judicial decision, the works by the IBM Haifa research team in the context of the Debater project [17,28], and the approach presented by Stab and Gurevych on persuasive essays [29]. Such works use, for example, the following inputs: pre-determined lists of special keywords that are usually highly indicative of the presence of an argument; the output of external classifiers that compute the sentiment or the subjectivity score of a sentence; semantic information coming from thesauri and ontologies like WordNet.

A recent work by Lippi and Torroni [18] has shown that the structure of a sentence is very often highly informative on the presence of argumentative components, such as claims. The key idea is that information coming from natural language processing, as in the case of parse trees, can be employed to measure similarity between sentences, and thus to detect fragments and structures that typically encode claims. As an example, consider the following two sentences:

The Netherlands Government submits that **Directive 95/46 does not preclude Member States from providing for greater protection in certain areas.**

The Parliament also argues that **reliance on Article 95 EC as the legal basis is not invalidated by the importance attributed to combating crime.**

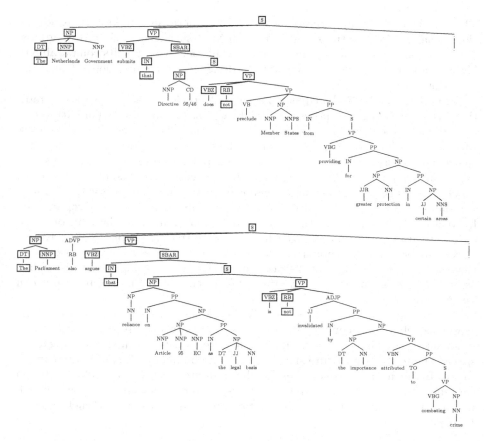

Fig. 1. Constituency trees for two sentences containing claims. Boxed nodes highlight the common structure of a subordinate introduced by a third-person verb (VBZ) and the *that* preposition (IN). Examples are taken from judgments collected in our corpus

The first sentence is taken from judgment C-101/01 (paragraph 93), while the second one is taken from judgment C-301/06 (paragraph 37) and they have both been labeled as containing a claim (highlighted in bold) in our corpus. The parse trees for these sentences are shown in Fig. 1, where boxed nodes highlight the common structures, in this case consisting of a subordinate introduced by a third-person verb (VBZ) and the preposition "that". The two verbs introducing such subordinates (submit, argue) are also indicative of the presence of an argument. Other patterns are frequently observed in sentences containing claims.

The structure of a sentence is thus highly indicative of the presence of a claim, and constituency parse trees represent a very powerful instrument to capture such information. Based on this observation, Lippi and Torroni [18] built a claim detection system that employs a Support Vector Machine (SVM) classifier capturing similarities between parse trees through Tree Kernels [23].

The Tree Kernel approach has been shown to outperform competitors exploiting classic, handcrafted features, widely used in NLP, such as bag-of-words, bigrams, trigrams, part-of-speech tags and lemmas, while achieving results comparable to highly sophisticated systems, specifically designed for context-dependent claim detection.

Kernel methods, and in particular Tree Kernels, have a quite long tradition in natural language processing applications, including relation extraction, named entity recognition, or question classification [24]. A kernel machine classifier learns a function $f : \mathcal{X} \to \mathcal{Y}$ where $\mathcal{X}$ is the input space, usually a vector space representing features, and $\mathcal{Y}$ is the output space representing the set of labels, or categories, to be distinguished (in our case, claim vs. other). To learn function f, a loss function is minimized over a set of N given observations, which is a dataset $\mathcal{D} = \{(x_i, y_i)\}_{i=1}^{N}$. Examples $x_i \in \mathcal{X}$ are not necessarily represented by vectors of features, but they can also exploit structured data, in order to encode relational information, as it happens with trees or graphs. A Tree Kernel (TK) can be basically thought of as a *similarity measure* between two trees, that evaluates the number of their common substructures, sometimes also called *fragments*. According to the definition of fragments, different TK functions can be constructed.

For example, one could consider only complete subtrees as allowed fragments, as well as define more complex fragment structures. Intuitively, each possible tree fragment is associated with a different feature in a high-dimensional vectorial space, where the j-th feature simply counts the number of occurrences of the j-th tree fragment: the TK can therefore be computed as the dot product between two such representations of different trees. A kernel machine is then defined, which exploits the structured information encoded by the tree kernel function $K(x, z)$:

$$f(x) = \sum_{i=1}^{N} \alpha_i y_i \phi(x_i) \cdot \phi(x) = \sum_{i=1}^{N} \alpha_i y_i K(x_i, x) \qquad (1)$$

where ϕ is the feature mapping induced by the tree kernel K, and N is the number of support vectors. In general, the kernel between two trees T_x and T_z can be computed as:

$$K(T_x, T_z) = \sum_{n_x \in N_{T_x}} \sum_{n_z \in N_{T_z}} \Delta(n_x, n_z) \qquad (2)$$

where N_{T_x} and N_{T_z} are the set of nodes of the two trees, and $\Delta(\cdot, \cdot)$ measures the score between two nodes, according to the definition of the considered fragments.

In this work we consider the Partial Tree Kernel (PTK) [23], which allows the most general set of fragments (called Partial Trees), being any possible portion of subtree at the considered node. The higher the number of common fragments, the higher the score Δ between two nodes.

The representation power behind tree kernels is evident. Basically, a kernel-like PTK is capable of automatically generating a very rich feature set, that captures structured representations without the need of a costly, hand-crafted feature engineering process. Nevertheless, it is very interesting to notice that the TK framework allows us to include in the representation of each example also a plain vector of features, which can enrich the description of the considered instance given by the parse tree. In this case, the final kernel would be computed as the combination between a classic kernel between feature vectors K_V and the kernel between trees K_T, e.g., with a weighted sum or product of the two contributions. Also note that the use of a TK by itself does not take into account information about the context of the considered documents, which, in our case, is the legal domain, nor the whole structure of the document. For this reason, context-dependent information could be appended to the feature vector to be combined with the TK, thus exploiting both context-dependent and context-independent information, whereas relational learning algorithms could be applied in order to capture the relations across different sentences.

5   Results

For our experiments, we employed the new corpus of judgments of the ECJ related to data protection described in Sect. 3. We employed a leave-one-out procedure (LOO), as customary in machine learning experimental evaluation. The procedure dictates that in turn, each judgment be considered as a test case, while all the other documents constitute the training and validation sets. With N documents, training and testing are thus independently performed N times, and results are finally averaged across all the runs.

We used the Stanford CoreNLP suite[3] both to split each document into sentences, and to compute the parse tree for each sentence. We obtained in this way a total of 1,096 sentences, of which 435 were labeled as positive (i.e., containing a claim) and the remaining 661 as negative (i.e., not containing any claim). Aside from computing the parse trees, we also extracted from each sentence a vector of features, that have been extensively used in a variety of Natural Language Processing applications: bag-of-words, bag-of-bigrams and bag-of-trigrams for words, stems and part-of-speech tags.

We thus trained three distinct classifiers: (1) an SVM based on the PTK described in Sect. 4 as the kernel computed over the parse trees (we exploited a combination of both stemmed and not-stemmed constituency parse trees); (2) an SVM trained with a linear kernel over the vector of features only; (3) an SVM combining (summing) the PTK and the linear kernel over the feature vector. We will refer to these three classifiers as PTK, FV, and PTK+FV. For all classifiers, we selected the SVM regularization parameter C by employing three documents as a validation set. We relied on default values for the other PTK parameters.

Table 1 shows the results obtained by the three classifiers with the LOO procedure, macro-averaged on the 15 test documents, and also the results obtained with a random baseline classifier. Since our problem is a binary classification task (with two classes only), we define as True Positives (TP) the correctly detected elements of the positive class, as False Positives (FP) the negative examples that

---

[3] http://nlp.stanford.edu/software/corenlp.shtml.

Table 1. Results obtained on our ECJ corpus, macro-averaged over the 15 documents.

Classifier	P	R	F_1
Random	39.5	39.5	39.5
FV	40.0	63.1	47.9
PTK	39.7	80.5	52.4
PTK + FV	44.3	78.3	55.4

are wrongly classified as positives, and as False Negatives (FN) the positive cases that are not retrieved. Standard classification measurements for these kind of tasks include Precision ($P = \frac{TP}{TP+FP}$), Recall ($R = \frac{TP}{TP+FN}$), and $F_1 = \frac{2PR}{P+R}$, i.e., the harmonic mean between Precision and Recall.

The results show that all approaches perform much better than a random predictor, even with a relatively small training set. It is interesting to note that the combination of PTK and FV achieves the best performance, thus indicating that the information exploited by the two distinct approaches is somehow complementary, and that PTK could be conveniently used also in combination with more context-dependent information. In order to assess the statistical significance of these results, we run a Wilcoxon paired test [35] on the F_1 values obtained on each document, which produced a p-value < 0.01 for the PTK+FV classifier with respect to FV.

Finally, consider also that the approaches used here do not take into account the whole document structure, which is instead a crucial piece of knowledge for retrieving the concluding claims, as explained by the guidelines illustrated in Sect. 3. Therefore, it is clear that there is a large margin of improvement for the considered task, especially if including in the model contextual and relational information.

6 Conclusion

The ECJ decisions related to data protection are a small-sized but novel annotated corpus for argumentation mining in the legal domain. We are actively working on its extension. Nevertheless, we hope that it can represent a useful benchmark for future work in this domain. We have demonstrated that a context-independent methods such as the Tree Kernel-based classifier proposed in [18] could be a valuable asset for claim detection in this genre, especially when used in combination with domain-specific information. We are aware that this is only a first step, and there is certainly room for improvement. In the future, we plan to expand our corpus, and to extend the analysis to the labeling and prediction of premises, the labeling and prediction of support/attack links, and the extraction of argument maps directly from text. One important remark is that labeling was made using a considerable amount of information from the document and discourse structure. Not only ECJ decisions are structured in well-defined sections, only some of which contain argumentative content, but the structure itself of the argumentation within each section was analyzed and captured by the used labeling (top-level claims, embedded arguments, arguments referring to other arguments, such as strengthening arguments or repeated arguments, etc.). Often, the labeler is able to correctly identify a concluding claim thanks to the structure of the argumentation. By contrast, our classifier—which is nevertheless able to provide acceptable results—does not use this structure. This opens an avenue for further work that should go in the direction of exploiting the discourse structure. Statistical relational learning could thus represent a perfectly suitable framework for exploiting relational information across sentences. Another key contribution could also come from deep learning, which has recently achieved breakthrough results in a variety of tasks related to natural language processing.

In future work, we will also compare our approach with other classifiers and in particular with a simple rule-based one, that implements basic pattern recognition rules. We expect that our system and the classifier using pattern recognition rules will deliver similar outcomes with regard to small source corpora, but that our approach will deliver better results when applied to larger sets of documents.

References

1. Aleven, V.: Using background knowledge in case-based legal reasoning: a computational model and an intelligent learning environment. Artif. Intell. **150**(1), 183–237 (2003)
2. Alexander, B.: LKIF core: principled ontology development for the legal domain. In: Law, Ontologies and the Semantic Web: Channelling the Legal Information Flood, vol. 188, p. 21 (2009)
3. Ashley, K.D., Desai, R., Levine, J.M.: Teaching case-based argumentation concepts using dialectic arguments vs. didactic explanations. In: Cerri, S.A., Gouardères, G., Paraguaçu, F. (eds.) ITS 2002. LNCS, vol. 2363, pp. 585–595. Springer, Heidelberg (2002). https://doi.org/10.1007/3-540-47987-2_60
4. Ashley, K.D., Walker, V.R.: Toward constructing evidence-based legal arguments using legal decision documents and machine learning. In: Francesconi, E., Verheij, B. (eds.) ICAIL 2012, Rome, Italy, pp. 176–180. ACM (2013)
5. Bench-Capon, T., Freeman, J.B., Hohmann, H., Prakken, H.: Computational models, argumentation theories and legal practice. In: Machines, A. (ed.) Reed C, Norman TJ. Argumentation Library, vol. 9, pp. 85–120. Springer, Dordrecht (2003). https://doi.org/10.1007/978-94-017-0431-1_4
6. Bench-Capon, T., Prakken, H., Sartor, G.: Argumentation in legal reasoning. In: Simari, G., Rahwan, I. (eds.) Argumentation in Artificial Intelligence, pp. 363–382. Springer, Boston (2009). https://doi.org/10.1007/978-0-387-98197-0_18
7. Bench-Capon, T., Sartor, G.: A model of legal reasoning with cases incorporating theories and values. Artif. Intell. **150**(1), 97–143 (2003)
8. Brighi, R., Lesmo, L., Mazzei, A., Palmirani, M., Radicioni, D.P.: Towards semantic interpretation of legal modifications through deep syntactic analysis. In: Proceedings of the 2008 conference on Legal Knowledge and Information Systems: JURIX 2008: The Twenty-First Annual Conference, pp. 202–206. IOS Press (2008)
9. Cabrio, E., Villata, S.: A natural language bipolar argumentation approach to support users in online debate interactions. Argum. Comput. **4**(3), 209–230 (2013)

10. Carr, C.S.: Using computer supported argument visualization to teach legal argumentation. In: Kirschner, P.A., Buckingham Shum, S.J., Carr, C.S. (eds.) Visualizing Argumentation. Computer Supported Cooperative Work, pp. 75–96. Springer, London (2003). https://doi.org/10.1007/978-1-4471-0037-9_4

11. Chesñevar, C.I., et al.: Towards an argument interchange format. Knowl. Eng. Rev. **21**(4), 293–316 (2006)

12. Copi, I.M., Cohen, C., McMahon, K.: Introduction to Logic: Pearson New International Edition. Pearson Higher Education (2013)

13. Feng, V.W., Hirst, G.: Classifying arguments by scheme. In: Lin, D., Matsumoto, Y., Mihalcea, R. (eds.) The 49th Annual Meeting of the Association for Computational Linguistics: Human Language Technologies, Proceedings of the Conference, Portland, Oregon, USA, 19–24 June 2011, pp. 987–996. ACL (2011)

14. Freeman, J.B.: Dialectics and the Macrostructure of Arguments: A Theory of Argument Structure, vol. 10. Walter de Gruyter (1991)

15. Habernal, I., Eckle-Kohler, J., Gurevych, I.: Argumentation mining on the web from information seeking perspective. In: Cabrio, E., Villata, S., Wyner, A. (eds.) Proceedings of the Workshop on Frontiers and Connections Between Argumentation Theory and Natural Language Processing. Forlì-Cesena, Italy, 21–25 July 2014. CEUR Workshop Proceedings, vol. 1341. CEUR-WS.org (2014)

16. Hachey, B., Grover, C.: Extractive summarisation of legal texts. Artif. Intell. Law **14**(4), 305–345 (2006)

17. Levy, R., Bilu, Y., Hershcovich, D., Aharoni, E., Slonim, N.: Context dependent claim detection. In: Hajic, J., Tsujii, J. (eds.) COLING 2014, Dublin, Ireland, pp. 1489–1500. ACL (2014)

18. Lippi, M., Torroni, P.: Context-independent claim detection for argument mining. In: Yang, Q., Wooldridge, M. (eds.) Proceedings of the Twenty-Fourth International Joint Conference on Artificial Intelligence, IJCAI 2015, Buenos Aires, Argentina, 25–31 July 2015, pp. 185–191. AAAI Press (2015)

19. Lippi, M., Torroni, P.: Argumentation mining: state of the art and emerging trends. ACM Trans. Internet Technol. **16**(2), 10:1–10:25 (2016)

20. McCarty, L.T.: Deep semantic interpretations of legal texts. In: Proceedings of the 11th International Conference on Artificial Intelligence and Law, pp. 217–224. ACM (2007)

21. Mochales Palau, R., Ieven, A.: Creating an argumentation corpus: do theories apply to real arguments? A case study on the legal argumentation of the ECHR. In: Proceedings of the Twelfth International Conference on Artificial Intelligence and Law (ICAIL 2009), Barcelona, Spain, 8–12 June 2009, pp. 21–30. ACM (2009)

22. Mochales Palau, R., Moens, M.F.: Argumentation mining. Artif. Intell. Law **19**(1), 1–22 (2011)

23. Moschitti, A.: Efficient convolution kernels for dependency and constituent syntactic trees. In: Fürnkranz, J., Scheffer, T., Spiliopoulou, M. (eds.) ECML 2006. LNCS (LNAI), vol. 4212, pp. 318–329. Springer, Heidelberg (2006). https://doi.org/10.1007/11871842_32

24. Moschitti, A.: State-of-the-art kernels for natural language processing. In: Tutorial Abstracts of ACL 2012, ACL 2012, p. 2. Association for Computational Linguistics, Stroudsburg (2012)

25. Peldszus, A., Stede, M.: From argument diagrams to argumentation mining in texts: a survey. Int. J. Cogn. Inf. Nat. Intell. (IJCINI) **7**(1), 1–31 (2013)

26. Prakken, H., Sartor, G.: A dialectical model of assessing conflicting arguments in legal reasoning. In: Prakken, H., Sartor, G. (eds.) Logical Models of Legal Argumentation, pp. 175–211. Springer, Dordrecht (1997). https://doi.org/10.1007/978-94-011-5668-4_6

27. Prakken, H., Sartor, G.: The role of logic in computational models of legal argument: a critical survey. In: Kakas, A.C., Sadri, F. (eds.) Computational Logic: Logic Programming and Beyond. LNCS (LNAI), vol. 2408, pp. 342–381. Springer, Heidelberg (2002). https://doi.org/10.1007/3-540-45632-5_14

28. Rinott, R., Dankin, L., Perez, C.A., Khapra, M.M., Aharoni, E., Slonim, N.: Show me your evidence - an automatic method for context dependent evidence detection. In: Màrquez, L., Callison-Burch, C., Su, J., Pighin, D., Marton, Y. (eds.) Proceedings of the 2015 Conference on Empirical Methods in Natural Language Processing, EMNLP 2015, Lisbon, Portugal, 17–21 September 2015, pp. 440–450. The Association for Computational Linguistics (2015)

29. Stab, C., Gurevych, I.: Identifying argumentative discourse structures in persuasive essays. In: Moschitti, A., Pang, B., Daelemans, W. (eds.) EMNLP 2014, Doha, Qatar, pp. 46–56. ACL (2014)

30. Teufel, S.: Argumentative zoning. Ph.D. Thesis, University of Edinburgh (1999)

31. Toulmin, S.E.: The Uses of Argument. Cambridge University Press, Cambridge (1958)

32. Walton, D.: Fundamentals of Critical Argumentation. Critical Reasoning and Argumentation. Cambridge University Press, Cambridge (2006)

33. Walton, D.: Argumentation theory: a very short introduction. In: Simari, G., Rahwan, I. (eds.) Argumentation in Artificial Intelligence, pp. 1–22. Springer, Boston (2009). https://doi.org/10.1007/978-0-387-98197-0_1

34. Walton, D., Reed, C., Macagno, F.: Argumentation Schemes. Cambridge University Press, Cambridge (2008)

35. Wilcoxon, F.: Individual comparisons by ranking methods. Biom. Bull. 1(6), 80–83 (1945)

36. Wyner, A., van Engers, T.: From argument in natural language to formalised argumentation: components, prospects and problems. In: Proceedings of the Worskhop on Natural Language Engineering of Legal Argumentation, Barcelona, Spain (2009)

A Non-intrusive Approach to Measuring Trust in Opponents in a Negotiation Scenario

Marco Gomes[1]([✉]), John Zeleznikow[2], and Paulo Novais[1]

[1] ALGORITMI Centre, University of Minho, Braga, Portugal
{marcogomes,pjon}@di.uminho.pt
[2] College of Business, Victoria University, Melbourne, Australia
john.zeleznikow@vu.edu.au

Abstract. There is a consensus that trust in one' opponent plays a significant role in promoting parties to engage in the conflict management process. Trust is an important yet complex and little-understood relation among parties in conflict. In general, trust can be seen as a measure of confidence that an entity or entities will behave expectedly. Without trust, the instruments to prevent or manage the conflict, such as negotiation, are handicapped and cannot reach their full potential for promoting an end to or a mitigation of a conflict. Hence, our motivation to examine trust is three-fold. First, the present study aims to address and expand on this line of research by investigating the possibility of measuring trust based on quantifiable behavior. To do so, we provide a brief review of the existing definitions of trust and define trust in the context of a negotiation scenario. Further, we propose a formal definition so that the analysis of trust in this kind of scenarios can be developed. Thus, it is suggested the use of Ambient Intelligence techniques that use a trust data model to collect and evaluate relevant information based on the assumption that observable trust between two entities (parties) results in certain typical behaviors. Third, this work aims to study the particular connection between relational aspects of trust and parties' conflict styles based on two dimensions: cooperativeness and assertiveness. The main contribution of this work is the identification of situations in which trust relationships influences the negotiation performance. To do so, an experiment was set-up in which we tried to streamline all the relevant aspects of the interaction between the parties and its environment that occur in a sensory rich environment, to measure trust. To simulate a conflict situation, a web-based game was developed. It was designed to enable test participants to engage in a conflict experience induced by the presence of Ambient Intelligence systems. Several tests were performed. We then engaged in rigorous assessment, post- processing and analysis of results. We validated the results comparing them with trust measures obtained through the use of a questionnaire (carefully adapted) from social networks.

Keywords: Ambient intelligence · Conflict handling styles
Negotiation · Trust measurement

© Springer Nature Switzerland AG 2018
U. Pagallo et al. (Eds.): AICOL VI-X 2015–2017, LNAI 10791, pp. 528–542, 2018.
https://doi.org/10.1007/978-3-030-00178-0_36

1   Introduction

Trust is understood as a complex phenomenon, and it is widely accepted as playing a significant role in human social relationships. Analysing trust definitions in the main disciplines concerned with trust relationships (psychology, sociology, etc.) lead us to a profusion of interpretations containing different trust types or facets, with different properties, which require different models for analysis. This abundance of meanings leads to a degree of uncertainty about what is meant by trust, creating conceptual and terminological confusion. While trust in the system and your adversaries is vital in negotiating a dispute, it is not clear what trust is, nor how trust can be enhanced. In fact, the most potent concern about trust seems to be when it is absent [1]. Although a variety of definitions of the term *trust* have been suggested, this paper will use the definition proposed by Castelfranchi who saw trust as a rich and complex mental attitude of x towards y as for a given action and goal [2]. This attitude consists of evaluations of y and the situation, and of expectations about y's mind, behaviour and possible results. This includes, of course, the assumption that trust should be understood and interpreted by framing its natural subjectivity and the information needed at a particular time and for a specific context in a computer-based model: an abstraction that has the *power* to represent data in terms of entities and relationships relevant to a domain of inquiry (trust).

Scholars and practitioners agree that trust and trust scarcities play a central role in conflict and conflict resolution [3]. From empirical studies, the absence of trust binds parties to conflict. Further, the presence of trust is stated as a necessary condition for parties engaging in a conflict mitigation process. These considerations can be distinctly observed in a typical conflict scenario (buyer versus seller) in which the need for trust emerges where the eventual outcome is dependent on the actions of both parties and also from strategies within the conflict management process itself. In other words, trust is involved where, to get what you want, you are dependent on the other party not exploiting the situation to your eventual cost. For example, a seller who is faced with a claim by a buyer may realize that to resist the claim would only encourage the buyer leaving the negotiation process for lower-price sellers elsewhere. By agreeing to the claim, this exodus would be (apparently) prevented. With this outcome, both seller and buyer appear to receive some benefit but the seller has to trust that the buyer will not then claim a similar benefit to other sellers. Zeleznikow used his Family Winner system to analyse the Israeli-Palestinian dispute [4]. His results mirrored the outcomes of Oslo accords signed twenty years previously. Arafat, Peres, and Rabin won a Nobel Peace Prize for their efforts. Nevertheless, the accord unravelled. Zeleznikow claimed while a logical, a mutually beneficial solution exists, the proponents will not take it up, because of a lack of trust in each other. Further, every act of violence further increases this distrust.

By investigating this link, one can better understand the potential effects of trust in conflict and be better prepared to prevent conflict from escalating [20,21]. When researchers and practitioners understand which conditions lead to trust, it seems plausible to state that they can follow different avenues toward trust building, and therefore toward conflict mitigation. Furthermore, being able to measure existence, emergence or dissolution of trusting relationships in a conflict situation will give a new set of information that can be used to improve processes and interventions, enabling the characterization of individuals and enhancing negotiation performance. It is also important to understand whose factors of parties' trust relationships can be captured algorithmically to specify the relationship between trust and conflict and to advance significantly the conflict mitigation process. Despite the shared understanding that trust plays a crucial role in conflict, the relation of trust to conflict is poorly studied. This is partly due to the complexity (multi-dimensionality) of the trust. Consequently, there is an evident lack of research on this link (trust-conflict) as well as to a lack of instruments to measure trust in such context.

The multi-dimensionality of trust (meanings that trust is not determined by one single component of the relationship, but by multiple components) makes conflict interventions more complex since they have to meet different conditions. But it also allows more entry points for the interventions. From a computer science perspective, it becomes attractive to adopt an approach that reduces this multidimensionality to something that computer systems can handle. This is a point of view aligned with the dominant tradition in Economics and Game Theory which suggests that trust as a concept is reducible to "subjective probability" (a quantitative and opaque view). Although differences of opinion still exist, there appears to be some agreement that the reduction of trust to a manageable number, quantity or probability is highly satisfactory. This is because, after realizing the difficulty in interpreting the human perception subjectivity of trust prevents us from defining objective evaluation criteria. However, we still need to find a way of evaluating (measuring) trust to guide the research effort in the correct direction. Facing this issue, we must raise a critical question: how to balance the subjective nature of trust with the objectivity-dependent nature of a computer system? In other words, how can a computer system deal intelligently with this kind of subjectivity? Well, some glimpses into the ways that computer systems deal with subjectivity can be found in the "expert" literature. This is exemplified in the work undertaken by Rosalind Picard in which she stressed that this endeavour is challenging but achievable [5]. Afterwards, she outlined a strategy for computer systems to cope with subjectivity issues. Specifically, it is proposed a three-fold approach: that they [computer systems] will need to (1) share some of the common sense of the user, (2) observe and model the user's actions, and (3) learn from these interactions. To summarize, this approach suggests that subjectivity is expressed as the user interacts with the system during a succession of queries. These involving inputs of the user can be tracked, modelled, and use to retrieve data consistent with changing requests. In resume, this strategy seems to be suitable to be applied, so we planned to follow it in our work in ways to overcome the further issue.

We describe, in the remainder of this article, the progress we have made towards achieving these goals. The rest of the article is organized as follows. In the following section, we provide insight into conflict and conflict handling styles along with an explanation of the mathematical model used to classify the parties' conflict style. Then a formal definition of the problem of measuring trust is presented. The conditions of the negotiation game, the main findings, and their analysis are provided next. The final section details the main conclusions drawn from this study.

2   Conflict and Conflict Handling Styles

It is difficult to define and to reach a universally accepted definition of conflict. We define it as a disagreement through which the parties involved perceive a threat to their needs, interests or concerns [6]. Similarly, it can also be seen as an opposition of interests that disrupts or blocks an action or decision-making process [7]. Thus, a conflict may be seen as a process that begins when a party feels that the other parties have or are about to negatively affect their interests. In order to enhance conflict resolution, we believe it is important to: (1) provide the parties and manager with valuable knowledge about the conflict and (2) to assist parties throughout all the process. Having such information can lead to a reduction in the severity of a conflict. Conflicts can develop in stages and consequently may involve many different responses as the conflict proceeds. People involved develop various strategies, solutions or behaviours, to deal with the conflict. In order to classify the conflict style, the proposals must be analysed, namely regarding of their utility. In that sense, in each stage of the negotiation the parties' proposals are analysed according to their utility value and a range

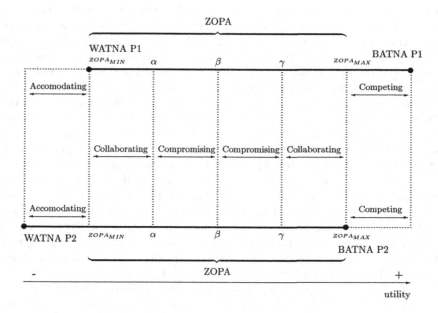

Fig. 1. Relationship between the utility of a proposal and the personal conflict handling style.

of possible outcomes defined by the values of the Worst Alternative to a Negotiated Agreement (WATNA) and Best Alternative to a Negotiated Agreement (BATNA) of each party. Lodder and Zeleznikow provide a detailed account of such approaches [8]. This approach uses a mathematical model [9], which classifies a party's conflict style considering the range of possible outcomes, the values of WATNA and BATNA as boundaries, and the utility of the proposal (Fig. 1). The utility quantifies how good a given outcome is for a party, it is acceptable to argue that a competing party will generally propose solutions that maximize its own utility in expense of that of the other party (the utility of the proposal is higher than the WATNA of the other party), whereas, for example, a compromising party will most likely search for solutions in an intermediary region (the utility of the proposal falls within the range of the zone of possible agreement, the range of overlapped outcomes that would benefit both parties). Essentially, we were able to classify the personal conflict style of a party by constantly analysing the utility of the proposals created. Once the styles are identified, strategies can be implemented that aim to improve the success rate of procedures for resolution and conflict management. This information and other insights about how the individual's conflict style is classified can be found in [9].

3   Measuring Trust Using an Algorithmic Approach

As suggested in [10], trust literature can be categorized based on three criteria: (i) trust information collection, (ii) trust value assessment, and (iii) trust value dissemination. Each in turn can be further classified: trust information gathering from three sources, namely (i) attitudes, (ii) behaviors, and (iii) experiences; trust value assessment according to the data model, namely (i) graph, (ii) interaction, and (iii) hybrid; and trust value dissemination into trust-based recommendation and visualization models. With regard to this work, and taking into account Sherchan's strategy [10], we will highlight the trust definitions, trust types, properties, and measurement models from the perspective of the Computer Science and Economics disciplines. Such approach seeks to focus on some particular aspects of trust measurement, which are simplified, so that these properties can be captured algorithmically. We wish to obtain and/or quantify trust by detecting statistically significant realizations of these trust-like behaviours in computer-based systems. Therefore, the basis for our study is a proposition that trust results in characteristic interaction behaviour patterns that are statistically different from random interactions in a computerized conflict management system. Another important decision was to reduce the study of the *trust domain* to the study of *interpersonal trust*, transforming the challenge of measuring trust to make it slightly more accessible. Furthermore, this type of trust is common in most conflict situations and it plays a key role in conflict dynamics [11].

Facing these challenges, how, from a Computer Science point of view, can trust can be classified? According to [10], in general, it can be divided into two broad categories: "user" and "system". For the scope of this present work, we will consider only the notion of "user" trust is derived from Psychology and

Sociology, with a standard definition as "a subjective expectation an entity has about another's future behavior" [10]. This implies that trust is inherently personalized. In this sense, trust is *relational*. As two individuals interact with each other frequently, their relationship strengthens, and trust evolves based on their experience. Following the Adali proposition [12] related to interpersonal trust, the main type or facet of trust understudy will be the basis for our proposal. Hence, the focus will be on the following proposition: is it possible to observe that trust between two entities A and B and will this result in certain typical behaviours that can be statistically captured. In other words, our aim is to quantitatively measure dyadic trust (trust between two entities) based on observed behaviour in a negotiation process. These behaviours are not only an expression of trust but can also facilitate the development of further trust. The simplest such behaviour is just interaction, in which an action occurs as two or more entities have some kind two-way effect upon one another. Regarding trust evaluation models, our approach to trust computation will be based on an interaction-based trust model. In this case, our interaction-based model evaluates trust based on the interactions performed in a computer-based conflict management system.

Then trust-related information will be captured and assessed following the strategy aforementioned. The sources and the means to assess trust can be resumed to:

- **Source of trust information gathering:** Past Behaviour. Why? Because user behaviour is an important aspect of trust. Another reason is that past behavior is identified by patterns of interactions that can be captured by an algorithm running on a computer system. Therefore, this will be our main source of information gathering. For example, in a negotiation scenario if a party is an extremely active participant and suddenly stops participating, this change in behaviour (the interaction is interrupted) is noticeable and might imply that this party's trust in the other party or with the party with whom he/she has been frequently interacting with has decreased.
- **Trust value assessment:** Regarding the techniques used to measure (compute) trust, they can be broadly classified into statistical and machine learning techniques, heuristics-based techniques, and behaviour-based techniques. In the present work, we will use behaviour-based techniques to assess trust. The reason for this choice lies in the fact that our measure of trust is based on quantifiable behaviour. So it seems obvious to choose assessment techniques based on this proposition.

After we have defined which directions and techniques we will add to measuring trust, let us then formally define our notion based on Adali's approach. This formalization is applied to the context of a negotiation, a process for two (or more) parties to find an acceptable solution to a conflict. Within a negotiation process, each party can make several proposals and exchange an unlimited number of messages. For the context of the interaction in a negotiation, the input is the proposal stream in a negotiation process, specified by a set of *4-tuples*,

$$\langle sender, receiver, message, time \rangle \tag{1}$$

note that we pretend to study the problem of trust purely from the observed interaction statistics, using no semantic information. Meanwhile, in our formalization, in an interaction between parties some semantic aspects (e.g. message) are considered in order to provide posterior semantic analysis. The output considered here is a set T induce from these inputs. The participants of the negotiation are represented by the elements of this set.

There is evidence that parties anticipating an online negotiation expect less trust before the negotiations begin and have less desire for future interaction with the other party [13]. Assuming that, we postulate in this work that the longer and more balanced an interaction is between two parties (meaning that the average number of times that two entities interact within the process), the more likely is less trust each other and, also, the less tightly connected they are. In other words, assuming that parties negotiating electronically are characterized by lower levels of pre-negotiation trust, they will need to interact more to develop trust and so increasing the likelihood that negotiation will proceed in a positive direction. So, the fundamental task is first to identify when two elements of T set are interacting. Let A and B be a pair of users, and let $P = \{t_1, t_2, ..., t_k\}$ be a sorted list of the times when a message was exchanged between A and B. Therefore the average time between messages is defined as $\tau = (t_k - t_1)/k$.

The measure of trust will be based on the interactions in I, obeying the following postulates: (1) Longer interactions imply less trust; (2) More interactions imply less trust; and (3) Balanced participation by A and B implies less trust. We define the relational trust $R_I(A, B)$ as follows:

$$R_I(A, B) = \sum_{i=l}^{l} \|I_i\| \cdot H(I_i) \qquad (2)$$

Where $H(I_i)$ is a measure of the balance in the i interaction contained in I. We use the entropy (measure of the amount of information that is missing in the flow of interaction) function to measure balance:

$$H(I_i) = -p \log p - (1 - p) \log(1 - p), \qquad (3)$$

where $p(Ii)$ is the fraction of messages in the interaction Ii that were performed by A. The complexity of the algorithms for computing relational trust is $\Theta(|D| \log |D|)$, where $|D|$ is the size of the interaction stream.

4   Case-Study: A Negotiation Scenario

A negotiation *scenario* is commonly used to describe the setting of a negotiation. It consists of a *domain*, an *outcome space*, *preference profiles*, and *negotiation styles* (adapted from [14]). A negotiation *scenario* should specify everything we know about the problem being addressed in order to frame the interactions that occur within. The detailed scenario that frames our experiments is presented in the following subsection (Subsect. 4.2). Taking into account the *domain* of the negotiation (which specifies the *issues* that the negotiators need to agree upon), in our case-study, the single issue negotiators need to agree on is the price of the item being sold. The *negotiation space* represents all the outcomes achievable i.e. all possible issue value combinations within the domain. Once again, the negotiation space is restricted following the mathematical model presented in Sect. 2. Moreover, the *negotiation space* represents all the outcomes achievable i.e. all possible issue value combinations with the domain. Once again, the negotiation space is restricted following the mathematical model presented in Sect. 2. Regarding the *negotiation styles* being used in a negotiation process, this refers to how a participant behaves, and how she is expected to behave. And even within the process, negotiating behaviours add a layer of complexity to the negotiation. Again, this issue will be addressed applying the model introduced in Sect. 2.

With this purpose in mind, we adapted a technological framework (presented in Subsect. 4.1) that aims to support the decision-making of the conflict manager by facilitating access to information such as the conflict handling style of the parties or their social context. In this work, we introduce a new module that takes into account the context using trust analysis. The development of such a framework previews a set of services or functionalities that will support the work of the conflict manager. The underlying aim is to release her so that she can have a more informed and effective approach to deal with complex issues such as the improvement of interpersonal communication and relationships.

Moreover, the main objective of this research work is to identify and measure the users' interpersonal trust, to correlate to their negotiation performance and how it can be used in a simple conflict (zero-sum) situation. To demonstrate this, an experiment was set up (See Subsect. 4.2) in which we tried to estimate all the relevant aspects of the interaction between the individual that occur in a sensory rich environment (where contextual modalities were monitored). The participants of the experiment were volunteers socially connected with our lab members. Twenty individuals participated, both female and male, aged between 22 and 36. The first step of the experiment was to ask the volunteers to fill in a small individual questionnaire (depicted in the following section). The following step was the monitoring of the individuals' interaction with the developed web-based negotiation game. During the experiments, the information about the user's context was provided through a monitoring framework, which is customized to collect and treat the interaction data. The participants played the web-based game through computers that allowed the analysis of the described features.

4.1   An Intelligent Conflict Support Environment

An Ambient Intelligent (AmI) system consists of a series of interconnected computing and sensing devices which surround the user pervasively in his environment and are invisible to him. It is clear that when one designs a system with these characteristics there are some challenges that are raised by the heterogeneity and number of devices and technologies present in this kind of environment. Is not just a bunch of devices interconnected but instead a group of devices

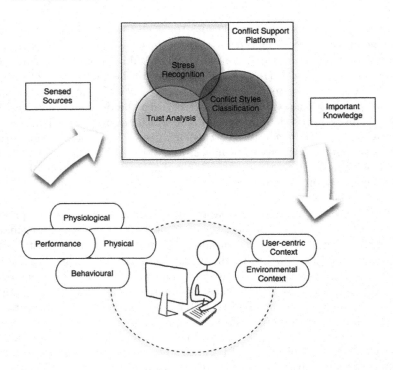

Fig. 2. A conceptual framework to support the decision-making of the conflict manager.

working together and sharing information towards a common goal. To cover it the system must ensure that these devices interact and exchange information, and compatibility must be guaranteed between the different technologies and components. Our aim is to provide a service that is dynamically adapted to the interaction context so that users (parties and the conflict manager) can naturally take advantage of interacting with the system and thus enhance the conflict management process. It can be stated that our underlying intent is to extend the traditional technology-based conflict resolution/management methods, in which a user simply interacts with the system, with a new component, an Intelligent Environment (IE). These environments should be made in a pervasive and transparent way since when people are aware that they are being monitored, they tend to behave differently. Therefore, towards constructing an intelligent conflict support system the following ambient intelligence system was developed (Fig. 2).

The aim of the system is to sense conflict context, acquire knowledge and then make reasoning on the acquired context and thus act on the parties' behalf. To achieve this, the system builds a profile of each party and can link that profile subsequently with the individual performance within the conflict process that is monitored by the system. In other words, while the user conscientiously interacts with the system and takes his/her decisions and actions, a parallel and transparent process takes place in which contextual and behavioural information is sent in a synchronized way to the conflict support platform. Upon converting the sensory information into useful data, the platform allows the conflict manager to obtain a contextualized analysis of the user's data. The contextualized analysis of user's data is critical when the data is from heterogeneous sources of diverse nature like sensors, user profile, and social media and also at different timestamps. To overcome some of these problems, the features are extracted from multiple sensor observations and combined into a single concatenated feature vector that is introduced into different classification modules (conflict styles, trust analysis, etc.). To integrate all the multimodal evidence we used a decision level integration strategy. Examples of decision level fusion methods used in this work include weighted decision methods and machine-learning techniques and are detailed in previous work [15,16].

4.2 Experimental Set-Up

As stated before, to simulate a conflict situation in real-life environments a web-based game was developed. It was designed to enable test participants to have a conflict experience induced by the presence of an Ambient Intelligence system. In that sense, the game simulates a business situation (a conflict) where each party wishes to achieve a desired result in the negotiation or else go bankrupt. The desired outcome was a win/win situation for both parties. A performance-based reward was settled to increased participants' intrinsic motivation. The game starts with the application randomly giving one of the predetermined roles to each party. The instructions to win the game were to negotiate a satisfactory deal and ensure that the party in question didn't go bankrupt. Each party's instructions were presented, visible to them through the application interfaces. The objectives and the persona for each party are depicted as:

- Role A - party A was a piano seller who specialized in selling cheap pianos. He was not the only supplier of this kind of pianos. In order to stay in business, he needed to sell each piano at 1000 Euro or more, knowing that piano prices vary greatly depending on the locale and the particular situation. If A did not achieve this result, she would go bankrupt. Party A was also given the information that Party B needed to make this deal.
- Role B - Party B represented a musician that need a piano urgently. He had recently received a contract to give a concert and needed a piano to play. The contractors were prepared to pay 1200 Euro per concert. If Party B did not manage to negotiate with Party A to buy the piano at 1200 Euro or less, then he would go bankrupt. Party B was told that party A was in a little financial trouble and needed to make the deal to survive.

Regarding the conflict styles analysis, the ZOPA (Zone Of Possible Agreement) was bounded by the BATNA (1000 Euro) and WATNA (1200 Euro) values. The range of possible agreement is 200, but the parties were not aware of this detail. Moreover, it does it in an entirely transparent and non-intrusive way, i.e., rather than relying on traditional self-reporting mechanisms such as questionnaires to infer behaviours, it analyses the actions of the parties, in real-time.

To validate our trust measurements, we will assume that trust phenomenon in some way increases or decrease in magnitude and strength within a relationship. In other words, it is assumed that, at early stages of a relationship, an individual will carefully calculate how the other party is likely to behave in a given situation depending on the rewards for being trustworthy and the deterrents against untrustworthy behaviour [17]. From this perspective, in our study we hypothesised that the degree of a relationship between two individuals could be a suitable measure of their trust relationship. To do so, in this work, we used a social network analysis method to map and measure the experiment's participants relationships. This approach was based on the intuitive notion that these patterns are important aspects of trustworthy relations of the individuals who display them through their interaction, namely in a conflict situation. In this manner, the data was obtained through a questionnaire (carefully adapted) of social networks. Since the interest of the research was to analyse the strength of relationships, we use responses on a 5-point Likert Scale from "not at all" (1) to "very much" (5). With the data obtained, we measured the in-degree centrality scores for each disputant. The in-degree score is an indication of centrality, which measures the number of nominations received by a person. This variable was calculated for all individuals in the Advice, Hindrance and Friendship Network. At the individual level, we can also calculate the position of individuals who may be intermediaries (Betweenness Centrality), influential (Eigenvector Centrality) or conflicting (In-degree Centrality in Hindrance Network). The questionnaire was sent to a network of twenty individuals, the data was collected in binary format and was stored in 20×20 square matrices. We calculated dependent variables with the software program UCINET VI. The meta-analytic techniques used to analyse the data obtained were as follows: Descriptive statistics, both standard deviations, etc.; Correlations between the independent variables (centrality and density) and dependent variables (hindrance); Regressions to test the model. Gender was used as a control variable.

4.3   Results

The data containing the required information was acquired in digital form through the players' monitoring framework, which is customized to collect and treat the interaction data. This data is combined and synchronized to describe several important aspects of the behavior of the user. The participants played the web based game through computers that allowed the analysis of the described features. In the preliminary data analysis, the experimental data is organized into two groups based on the social network analysis. One group contains the collection of data obtained through the application of the questionnaire (measuring the participant's relationships). This enables the establishment of a baseline for comparison with the second group, gathered through the web-based negotiation game (applying the trust measuring algorithm previously presented), which comprises the data gathered from the parties negotiating. To statistically deal with data concerning to the utility values of the parties' proposals, it was necessary to convert data to an arbitrary numeric scale (zero is the least favorable style for the resolution and four the most favorable style). This type of scale ensures that the exact numeric quantity of a particular value has no significance beyond its ability to establish a ranking over a set of data points. Therefore, it was built rank-ordering which describes order, but not the relative size or degree of difference between the items measured. This was a necessary step to make the data suitable for statistical and machine-learning techniques. Further, according to our postulates (see Sect. 3), the basis for this analysis was the assumption that if A and B have a strong relationship then $R_I(A, B)$ value (the *relational trust*) is below the median of the calculated trust for all the pairs within the interactions data set. In other words, this implies that if one pair of participants has a high degree of relationship then the same pair of participants, during the game, will perform fewer interactions than the median of total interactions per game. At this point, it should be highlighted that to apply non-parametric statistical analysis the raw data was firstly pre-processed and secondly, it was subjected to tests. The outcomes were compared using the Mann-Whitney U test (compares the central tendencies of two independent samples), given the fact that most of the distributions are not normal. The null hypothesis is thus: $H_0 =$ The medians of the two distributions are different. For each pair of distributions compared, the test returns a p-value, with a small p-value suggesting that it is unlikely that H_0 is true. For each parameter (a pair of participants), data from both samples is compared. In all the tests, a value of $\alpha = 0.05$ is used. Thus, for every Mann-Whitney test whose p-value $< \alpha$, the difference is considered to be statistically insignificant, i.e., H_0 is rejected. Consequently, the results have shown that no (statistically) important difference between data from the two samples were found. In other words, it means that our assumptions were valid. So it is possible to infer that trust measurements using our algorithmic approach are valid to a certain extent.

To analyse if trust relationships influence the negotiation performance, in the preliminary data analysis, the experimental data is organized into two groups based on the analysis of the trust measurements. One group contains the collection of experimental data about how a user (A) behaves when he/she negotiates with someone (B) in which $R_I(A, B)$ has a low value ($R_I(A, B) <$ median). This approach enables the establishment of a baseline for comparison with the second group, which comprises the data gathered from parties that negotiate with someone that has high R_I values ($R_I \geq$ median). To statistically deal with data concerning the utility values of the parties' proposals, it was necessary to convert the data to an arbitrary numeric scale (0 is the least favourable style for the resolution and four the most favourable style). This type of scale means that the exact numeric quantity of a particular value has no significance beyond its ability to establish a ranking over a set of data points. It was constructed using in rank-ordering (which describes order), but not the relative size or degree of difference between the items measured. This was a necessary step to make the data suitable for statistical and machine-learning techniques.

From the data analysis regarding the evolution of the conflict handling styles evidenced by the parties, we concluded that the conflict style is on average more favourable (mutually beneficial) when the parties have a lower value of R_I than average. The final value of the negotiation process occurs when R_I is lower, the parties reaches mutually satisfactory solutions, i.e., solutions that are closer to the optimum result. Also interesting is the conclusion that participants who have a high R_I value need more rounds and exchange longer messages to achieve a successful outcome. This outcome is aligned with our postulates, in which we have hypothesized that more interaction implies less trust in a conflict situation. However, it can be assumed that when the trust relationship is weak, the development of trust between the opponents need more steps than otherwise. Indeed, events at the beginning and end of a negotiation sequence play a major role in building and maintaining trust [18].

Moreover, the analysis shows that there is an apparent difference between the two groups regarding the conflict styles exhibited during the game. One conclusion is that when participants share a significant trust relationship (low R_I value) the frequency of collaborative behaviours is far superior (49%) than otherwise (24%). A conclusion that corroborates the Malhotra and Murnighan study, in which they found in their study that an individual's trust will increase as the number of positive interactions between parties increases [19]. In a similar analysis, but now concerning the roles played by participants, we conclude that the sellers are much more competitive than buyers (57% vs. 29%) while buyers are primarily collaborative. To interpret the significance of these results it is important to recall that participants were asked to negotiate a favourable deal in a competitive and win-lose scenario. Nevertheless, it is shown that when participants have a significant trust relationship they are more likely to transform it into a win/win situation. This is especially visible in the final results of the negotiations. On the one hand, we find that 100% of the agreements made by parties with an important trust relationship accomplished a successful deal, i.e., between the range of solutions that would benefit both. On the other hand, only 50% of negotiations that occurred between untrusted opponents (low R_I value) reached a mutual benefits agreement. It may be that they assumed they had to negotiate and get the best price (win/loose). But that was not the objective. Their objective was to negotiate a deal so they would not go bankrupt (win/win).

The preliminary evidence suggests a basis for expecting a connection between the trust relationship and the use of conflict styles. Despite these results, we still do not know much about how this kind of influence might facilitate (or inhibit) positive conflict outcomes. Therefore, we will perform more and deeper experiments to understand how to collect and analysis relational ties that can influence negotiation performance.

5 Conclusion

The starting point for the development of trust measurements lies in the fact that current computer-based conflict assessment tools do not consider (or are unable to measure it) the underlying trust relations between parties in a particular scenario. Thus, within this work, we aim firstly to identify and apply an algorithm for measuring interpersonal trust; secondly, to validate this app-roach opposing data collected from a questionnaire with data gathered from a web-based negotiation game and to statistically study the correlation between mutual trust and conflict styles. From the experiment outcomes, the findings highlight the potentially quantifiable measurements of trust which further the understanding of conflict dynamics. They indicated relationships between the features being monitored and the participants' relationships elicited through a small questionnaire. These findings have the potential to enable the characteriza-tion of individuals and enhance negotiation performance. The main contribution of this work is thus the identification of trust relations between opponents in a negotiation scenario.

These results are preliminary in the sense that there is more information that one can retrieve from the collected data namely through a deeper semantic anal-ysis. This type of analysis could considerably enhance the trust measurements. Furthermore, due to the small sample size used in the current study, some cau-tion must be taken when interpreting the results of the statistical analysis pre-sented and underpinning the conclusions. In that sense, additional limitations of the current research must be pointed out. First, the participants were recruited from a particular population (that are socially related to our lab members)- a population that may limit the generalizability of the results. Admittedly, the participants of the experiment may not be representative of conflict parties in general. Consequently, we are unable to demonstrate the causality of the vari-ables conclusively. Moreover, it is possible that individual differences (i.e., per-sonalities) might have influenced the impact of the results. Another drawback of our study was that we tested all of the variables at the individual level. This limited us from conducting global level analysis, which could provide us more variance of the data. Also, the data was collected through self-reported surveys at one time, which is subject to common method variance problem. Finally, the computational facet of this work should provide an understanding of the diffi-culties in algorithmically capturing and computing interpersonal trust. A more comprehensive and in-depth study to provide theoretical advances, as well as implement technological solutions, is yet to be developed.

Acknowledgements. This work has been supported by COMPETE: POCI-01-0145-FEDER-007043 and FCT - Fundação para a Ciência e a Tecnologia (Portuguese Foun-dation for Science and Technology) within the Project Scope UID/CEC/00319/2013.

References

1. Fells, R.E.: Developing trust in negotiation. Empl. Relat. **15**(1), 33–45 (1993)
2. Castelfranchi, C., Falcone, R.: Trust is much more than subjective probability: mental components and sources of trust. In: Proceedings of the 33rd Hawaii Inter-national Conference on System Sciences, Washington, DC, USA, HICSS 2000, vol. 6, p. 6008. IEEE Computer Society (2000)
3. Kappmeier, M.: Its all about trust how to assess the trust relationship between conflict parties. In Proceedings of the IACM 24th Annual Conference Paper (2011)

4. Zeleznikow, J.: Comparing the Israel–Palestinian Dispute to Australian Family Mediation. Group Decis. Negot. **23**(6), 1301–1317 (2014)
5. Picard, R.W.: Computer learning of subjectivity. ACM Comput. Surv. **27**(4), 621–623 (1995)
6. Deutsch, M.: The Resolution of Conflict: Constructive and Destructive Processes. Carl Hovland Memorial Lectures. Yale University Press, New Haven (1977)
7. Robbins, S.P.: Organizational Behavior. Prentice Hall, Upper Saddle River (2001)
8. Lodder, A.R., Zeleznikow, J.: Enhanced Dispute Resolution Through the Use of Information Technology. Cambridge University Press, Cambridge (2010)
9. Carneiro, D., Gomes, M., Novais, P., Neves, J.: Developing dynamic conflict resolution models based on the interpretation of personal conflict styles. In: Antunes, L., Pinto, H.S. (eds.) EPIA 2011. LNCS (LNAI), vol. 7026, pp. 44–58. Springer, Heidelberg (2011). https://doi.org/10.1007/978-3-642-24769-9_4
10. Sherchan, W., Nepal, S., Paris, C.: A survey of trust in social networks. ACM Comput. Surv. **45**(4), 47:1–47:33 (2013)
11. Ebner, N.: Online dispute resolution and interpersonal trust. In: ODR: Theory and Practice (2012)
12. Adali, S., et al.: Measuring behavioral trust in social networks. In: 2010 IEEE International Conference on Intelligence and Security Informatics (ISI), pp. 150–152, May 2010
13. Naquin, C.E., Paulson, G.D.: Online bargaining and interpersonal trust. J. Appl. Psychol. **88**(1), 113–120 (2003)
14. Marsa-Maestre, I., Klein, M., Jonker, C.M., Aydoan, R.: From problems to protocols: towards a negotiation handbook. Decis. Support Syst. **60**, 39–54 (2014)
15. Gomes, M., Oliveira, T., Carneiro, D., Novais, P., Neves, J.: Studying the effects of stress on negotiation behavior. Cybern. Syst. **45**(3), 279–291 (2014)
16. Carneiro, D., Novais, P., Andrade, F., Zeleznikow, J., Neves, J.: Online dispute resolution: an artificial intelligence perspective. Artif. Intell. Rev. **41**(2), 211–240 (2012)
17. Lewicki, R., Brinsfield, C.: Measuring trust beliefs and behaviours. In: Lyon, F., Möllering, G., Saunders, M. (eds.) Handbook of Research Methods on Trust, p. 29. Edward Elgar Pub. (2012)
18. Lewicki, R.J., Polin, B.: Trust and negotiation. In: Handbook of Research on Negotiation, chap. 7, p. 161 (2013)
19. Malhotra, D., Murnighan, J.K.: The effects of contracts on interpersonal trust. Adm. Sci. Q. **47**(3), 534–559 (2002). 9
20. Ebner, Noam, Zeleznikow, John: Fairness, trust and security in online dispute resolution. Hamline Univ. Sch. Law's J. Public Law Policy **36**(2), (2015)
21. Han, G., Harms, P.D.: Team identification, trust and conflict: a mediation model. Int. J. Confl. Manag. **21**(1), 20–43 (2010)

Network, Visualization, Analytics. A Tool Allowing Legal Scholars to Experimentally Investigate EU Case Law

Nicola Lettieri[1,3,4](✉), Sebastiano Faro[2], Delfina Malandrino[3], Armando Faggiano[3], and Margherita Vestoso[4]

[1] National Institute for Public Policies Analysis (INAPP), Rome, Italy
n.lettieri@inapp.org
[2] Institute of Legal Information Theory and Techniques (ITTIG-CNR), Florence, Italy
[3] University of Salerno, Fisciano, SA, Italy
[4] University of Sannio, Benevento, Italy

Abstract. Legal Informatics has recently witnessed a growing interest towards the insights offered by the intersection among Network Analysis (NA), visualization techniques and legal science research questions. Also thanks to several seminal works, the field is ready to tackle new challenges at a theoretical and application level. The first is to bring the network approach into "genuinely legal" research questions. The second is to create tools allowing legal scholars without technical skills to exploit NA with two goals: (i) make experiments with NA and push new ideas both in legal and NA science; (ii) use NA and visualization in their daily activities (e.g., legal analysis and information retrieval). Against this backdrop, a truly interdisciplinary approach deeply involving legal experts/scholars is needed. The paper presents an ongoing research project - *EUCaseNet* - dealing with these challenges and aiming to explore the potentialities of NA in supporting the study of EU case law.

Keywords: EU case law · Legal documents' relevance
Network analysis · Visualization · Analytics · On-line laboratory

1 Introduction

As witnessed by a growing literature, Legal Informatics research area has been developing a growing interest towards the insights offered by the intersection among Network Analysis (NA) [1], visualization techniques and legal science research questions (see, i.a., [2,3]). Thanks to its high level of abstraction and ability to support the understanding of both structural and functional features of

© Springer Nature Switzerland AG 2018
U. Pagallo et al. (Eds.): AICOL VI–X 2015–2017, LNAI 10791, pp. 543–555, 2018.
https://doi.org/10.1007/978-3-030-00178-0_37

real networks, NA is spreading in the legal domain focusing on different research priorities:

- Analyze the structural and functional features of more or less wide areas of legal systems (e.g., the level of complexity of legislation, case law, legal literature);
- Determine the relevance of legal documents and sources, according to the different meanings acquired by the concept of "relevance" itself in different legal contexts;
- Study the relations between different expressions - or, in the words of [4] different "legal formants" - of the legal phenomenon (relationship between legislation, case law and legal literature, or between supranational case law and domestic case law, etc.);
- Investigate the evolution of a legal order also in a predictive fashion;
- Design innovative visual analytics tools for better legal information communication and retrieval.

In the following sections we present a research project aiming to find new ways to deal with the above mentioned priorities. The attention is focused, more in detail, on the creation of EuCaseNet [5], an innovative tool enabling experimental use of NA techniques in the study of EU case law. The first part of the paper is devoted to a brief overview of the "NA and Law" research experiences that are somehow inspiring our project, followed by a sketch of the challenges to be faced in this field. In its second part the paper presents and discusses both the domain-related and technical issues of the project, sketching on-going works and future directions.

2   Network Analysis and Law: Current Experiences and Future Challenges

The determination of the relevance of legal sources and documents with NA techniques is one of the most discussed issues in recent times. The study of networks has been frequently used to analyze case law especially in common law countries where precedents have a prominent role (see, i.a., [6–8]). An interesting and seminal work is the one presented in [7], that exploits the HITS algorithm [9] and the patterns in citations networks within and across cases to create importance scores identifying the most legally relevant precedents in the network of US Supreme Court case law. By comparing different centrality measures, the authors show how the HITS algorithm allows to identify, with an higher level of precision than the other centrality measures, those cases in the network that are "influential" (inwardly relevant) or "well founded in law" (outwardly relevant). Another relevant research experience in this area is the one recently described in [10] in which the PageRank algorithm is combined with InDegree and the HITS algorithm to investigate the relevance of the decisions of the EU Court of Justice.

As to the uses of NA to measure structural characteristics of legal systems, such as the complexity of large bodies of law, a paradigmatic example is the research proposed by [11] in a work focusing on the legal complexity of the United States Code that borrows concepts and tools from a range of academic disciplines, including computer science, linguistics, physics, and psychology. By developing a knowledge acquisition protocol that considers structure, language and interdependence of Code's norms as elements contributing to its complexity, authors employ NA methods to test the interdependence level of the norms of the Code, concluding that the more norms are connected, the higher is the amount of energy an individual should expend in order to acquire knowledge regarding the content of the United States Code. The work presented in [12] deals with a somehow similar challenge: the authors try to build the "legal neighborhoods" of Dutch norms aiming to verify if, given the network of an article in focus, other relevant documents could be automatically identified just using "objective" meta-information deriving from the norm graph (in the same direction see [3]). Quantifying the complexity of a given legal system is also close to the goal of a recent research project [13] which aims to explore the interdependence between different kinds of legal documents, such as case law and doctrine, or judgments and norms, presenting a multi-relational network modeling the hierarchy and showing the relationships between different legal sources of the European Union law (Treaties, International agreements, Legislation, Complementary legislation, Preparatory acts, Jurisprudence) in order to shed light on properties and behaviours of its different elements. The different sub-graphs built by the authors have been also employed to realize a temporal analysis of the evolution of the European legislation network, as well as to test the resilience of the entire system, measuring its vulnerability under specific cases that may lead to possible breakdowns. In the same vein, i.e., predicting the future developments of a given legal system, in [7] the network centrality measures are used to forecast which cases will be most cited in the future.

All the mentioned experiences gave a significant contribution in building a bridge between law and NA and in creating the basis for further scientific and application developments. In this scenario, another factor of paramount relevance is represented by the involvement of legal scholars in NA experiments in order to support both the design of research activities and the validation of the obtained results. Legal experts knowledge is essential in identifying mistakes or ambiguities emerging from the legal network analysis performed by non-legal experts compared to the real features of the law. As a matter of fact, there is not necessarily an overlap between the results that can be simply achieved through a naive application of NA measures to legal data and what could be considered relevant for the law. It could happen that some typical network properties, usually measured by computer scientists interested to the computational features of a specific graph (e.g., the resilience), were not usefully applicable to networks in legal context, especially without an expert explaining the legal rationale or meaning of the raw outcomes. From this perspective, it is essential to create tools allowing legal scholars without technical skills to exploit NA in the legal field with two goals: (i) make experiments with NA and, thus, push new ideas both in legal and NA science; (ii) use NA and visualization in their daily activities (e.g., legal analysis and information retrieval).

3   The EuCaseNet Project

EUCaseNet is an interdisciplinary research project aiming to apply data mining and network analysis techniques to the study of EU case law made available in open format by the EU Commission portal EUR-Lex. It aims not only to experiment new ways to analyze legal corpora, but also to create an on-line laboratory freely exploitable by legal scholars to conduct experiments by themselves. The project so far has moved in a twofold direction. The first one consisted in the design of a tool allowing "on the fly" application of NA techniques to the entire corpus of EU case law (judgments, orders, opinions and conclusions of the General Advocate of the Court of Justice and of the General Court, from the date of their creation) in XML format. The basic idea is to enable the exploration of NA techniques by domain (law) experts stimulating an inductive process that encompasses, in a cyclic form, two fundamental steps:

- on the basis of the knowledge of the legal domain and having a basic understanding of NA, it is crucial to choose the measures and the data to consider;
- apply measures, compare the results with those achieved by domain experts through traditional legal analysis methods and establish which combination of data and measures better map knowledge of legal reality.

The second direction aims to devise new measures and algorithms to be validated according to the state of the art of legal literature.

3.1   System Functionalities and Application Workflow

EuCaseNet allows users to make experiments within the network of case law generated from the judgments of the EU Court of Justice. The tool allows to visualize the connections among all the judgments given by the Court until today[1] and make experiments to study relevant phenomena from the legal theory viewpoint. More in detail, the judgments are considered as a network and mapped on a graph: nodes correspond to judgments and edges correspond to citations between them. Therefore, by leveraging NA and visualization techniques we are able to analyze the network.

To perform experiments on the graph of judgments, *EuCaseNet* provides filters and measures of the social network analysis. Specifically, to define the color and the size of the nodes, users can apply several algorithms. Moreover it is possible to filter the judgments on the available attributes, so as to focus

---

[1] We currently consider judgments given until April 2014.

only on a subset of them. The process that allowed us to build the graph can be illustrated as follows.

- *Data retrieving*
  Judgments are freely available from the EUR-Lex portal[2]. We downloaded them in XML format.
- *Judgment Parsing*
  The downloaded XML file includes, for each judgment, a large number of information. We decided to analyze only a subset of them:
  - Title and reference (Celex number) of the judgment;
  - The name of the Advocate-General who delivered its conclusions;
  - Classification according to the EUR-Lex classification schema;
  - Date;
  - Involved EU country;
  - Relationships (expressed in terms of citations) among judgments;
  - List of bibliographic references to comments on judgments published in books and journals (expressed as a number).
- *Graph creation, import and manipulation*
  Given the XML file of the judgments, we allowed users to visualize and manipulate the generated graph through NA metrics (degree, betweenness, closeness, eccentricity), and other well-known algorithms (i.e., PageRank). In Fig. 1 we show a screenshot of *EUCaseNet*. In the center the generated graph of the judgments is shown. On the left side, we show an Interactive Panel in which it is possible to interact with the graph. Specifically, it is possible to:
  - Define the size and the color (in red scale) of the node according to the above-mentioned SNA metrics;
  - Apply filters based on the attributes defined inside the judgments graph and that we considered for our work;
  - Select a data range in order to focus on a portion of the graph.

  When a judgment is selected, all cited judgments and those citing it (graph neighbours) will be highlighted. Moreover, on the right side, an Information Panel will show the attributes of the selected judgment.

3.2 Architecture

Here we briefly describe the technical architecture of EuCaseNet, and how components interact each other. As we can see in Fig. 2, *EUCaseNet* is a client-server architecture. The Server component (*EUCaseNet* Server) is a Java Servlet and manages both the database module (MySQL) accessible with JDBC, and the XML Manager module; the Client component contains a Web Browser module to make requests.

The *EUCaseNet* Server implements the third step of the aforementioned process (Graph creation, import and manipulation), through the Servlet within Apache Tomcat. A generic client can interact with *EUCaseNet* through a simple

---

[2] http://eur-lex.europa.eu/homepage.html.

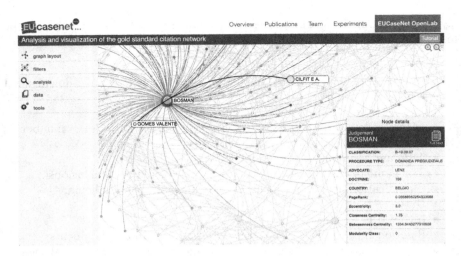

Fig. 1. EuCaseNet: network of the judgments with details about the Bosman case.

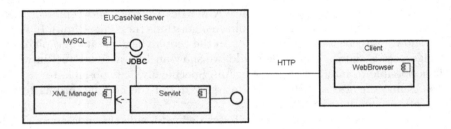

Fig. 2. EuCaseNet architecture: overview.

Web Browser. When a user accesses to *EUCaseNet* an HTTP request is sent to the Server that interacts with XML Manager in order to generate the graph. Once the process has finished a JSON file is produced (with the information about the graph) and is sent to the client through an HTTP response. The Web Browser contains a JavaScript library to render the graphs. Users can interact with them through the operations described in previous section.

3.3 Preliminary Experiments

After a short setup phase, we began testing the tool. First we confirmed that even the EU case law network, like other legal networks, has a scale free topology. As shown in Fig. 3, the degree distribution follows a power law.

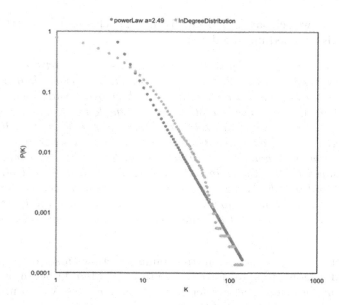

Fig. 3. In-degree distribution of the judgments of the EU Court of Justice. Data are plotted on doubly logarithmic axes via the cumulative distribution.

Hence, we decided to start dealing with the problem of the determination of the relevance of judgments in the specific context of EU case law. Indeed, one cannot ignore the difficulty, especially in legal information retrieval systems, to trace the concept of relevance back to a unitary definition, due to the interplay between different factors. As highlighted in [14], according to Saracevic's theory of multiple "manifestations" of relevance [15], a document cannot be conceived relevant in an absolute sense. The importance of a legal document, in particular, should be measured in relation to the role it takes with regard to the user, the information retrieval system or the legal domain. Therefore, its relevance can be conceived in terms of a match between the information object and a range of elements, such as the query codification (i.e., algorithmic relevance), the subject (i.e., topical relevance), users' information need (i.e., cognitive relevance) or motivations (i.e., situational relevance), as well as the opinion of the domain experts (i.e., domain relevance).

Being aware of the "multi-dimensionality" of the concept of relevance [16] (and of the fact that its different profiles partly overlap and are often indicated by similar clues), we decided to focus on a profile of relevance - substantially traceable to the concept of "domain relevance"- that is well-identified in a recent book edited by two scholars of EU law listing the "classics of the EU law" [17]. The concept is summed up as follows:

> The "classic" judgment in the jurisprudence of a Court are those that survive the passing of time but also those which, even when their concrete legal answer has become obsolete or has even been overturned, have lived on through their multiple effects in other areas of the law. They are judgments of systemic impact, embodying a broader normative lessons about the legal order in which that Court operates. To identify them we must look not only at the particular judgment as such but also at how it has been interpreted and developed by the Court in other cases. We also need to look at the attention paid to it by lawyers, legal scholars and other social actors. The law is also a function of how the judicial decisions are interpreted and challenged by the broader legal and social communities in which a court operates.

Taking cue from this definition, the volume identifies a set of 19 judgments that we used as gold standard for our experiments. More in detail, keeping the cases listed in the volume as a reference, we used *EuCaseNet* to measure the values assumed, for each case, by the typical NA metrics:

- *Degree centrality.* This metric measures the number of links incident upon a node. In graph theory, degree centrality weights the number of ties a given node has, by allowing to identify which nodes are central in the network with regard to information spreading and the ability to influence others in their immediate neighbourhood. Moreover, in directed networks, we can distinguish between in-degree and out-degree centrality, which respectively measure the number of ties directed to the node and the number of ties that the node directs to others.
- *Closeness centrality.* This measure expresses the mean length of all shortest paths from a node to all other nodes in the network (i.e., how many hops on average it takes to reach every other node), making possible to estimate how fast a given node is reached by the other nodes of the network.
- *Betweenness centrality.* Betweenness centrality depends on the relative number of shortest paths that run through a node, by measuring how many times a node works as a bridge along the shortest path between two other nodes. As a result, the higher is the level of betweenness, the more the node is crucial in allowing communication between all couples of nodes.
- *Eccentricity.* In the mathematical field of graph theory, the distance between two nodes in a graph is the number of edges in a shortest path (also called a graph geodesic) connecting them. This is also known as the geodesic distance. Notice that there may be more than one shortest path between two nodes. If there is no path connecting the two nodes, i.e., if they belong to different connected components, then conventionally the distance is defined as infinite.
- *Page-Rank.* PageRank is a link analysis algorithm and it assigns a numerical weighting to each element of a hyperlinked set of documents, such as the World Wide Web, with the purpose of measuring its relative importance

within the set. The algorithm may be applied to any collection of entities with reciprocal quotations and references.

- *Eigenvector centrality*. Grounded on an iterative process similar to Page-Rank, eigenvector centrality allows to estimate the influence of a node in a network, by weighting the connection level of nodes directly linked to it. In other terms, the score assigned by the algorithm to each node depends on scoring level of those connected to it, with high-scoring nodes having an higher impact on target node's eigenvector value then low-scoring nodes. Therefore, the metric is useful in determining which are most "popular" nodes, which are those linked to the most connected nodes.

Our goal was twofold: on the one hand, start testing the functionality of the *EUCaseNet* tool; on the other hand, like other authors do (see, e.g. [10]) explore even if in an initially "rough" way, the performance of each metric in mapping the relevance of the cases belonging to our gold standard.

Table 1 shows the judgments and the values assumed by the above mentioned metrics. Table 2 provides an overview of the performance of each of the parameters taken into account by comparing the relevance assigned to the 19 judgments by the gold standard (in our analysis these judgments can be considered as equally relevant) and the position that the same 19 judgments occupy in a ranking based on NA measures values. In both tables the number of comments published in books or journals that each case received from legal scholars can be found (the values reported are contained in the EUR-Lex XML file).

Table 1. Measures and attributes of the case study judgments.

Judgment	Doctrine	In-degree	Out-degree	Eccentricity	Closeness	Betweenness	PageRank
VAN GEND EN LOOS	46	8	0	0	0	0	0.00049
COSTA	14	23	0	0	0	0	0.00111
INT.HANDELSGESELLSCHAFT	2	19	0	0	0	0	0.00120
COMM./COUNCIL(case 22/70)	20	37	0	0	0	0	0.00121
NOLD	3	13	0	0	0	0	0.00072
DASSONVILLE	9	117	0	0	0	0	0.0020
DEFRENNE	17	48	0	0	0	0	0.0018
SIMMENTHAL	35	49	1	2	1.666	3315.4763	0.00075
REWE-ZENTRAL	23	70	0	0	0	0	0.00194
CILFIT	19	22	1	2	1.5	1506.7138	0.00031
LES VERTS	11	14	2	1	1.0	2921.9004	0.00066
FOTO-FROST	13	20	2	2	1.777	9078.7165	0.00046
WACHAUF	3	20	1	2	1.666	2554.2996	0.00040
ERT	8	42	10	8	3.352	54365.1861	0.00069
FRANCOVICH	74	55	14	7	3.4431	54442.0397	0.00093
BOSMAN	82	140	21	10	4.0945	272540.6123	0.00139
MARTiNEZ SALA	14	36	0	0	0	0	0.00026
COMM./UK(case 466/98)	16	1	12	9	4.8045	0	0.00006
BAUMBAST	10	22	11	12	5.7630	26859.8971	0.00018

Table 2. The cases in which the judgment stands in one of the top 20 positions of the ranking calculated using the measure considered are highlighted in grey

	Judgment ranking						
	Doctrine (max: 52)	In-degree (max: 67)	Out-degree (max: 44)	Eccentricity (max: 22)	Closeness (max: 5301)	Betweenness	PageRank	Eigenvector Centrality
VAN GEND EN LOOS	16	59	44	22	5301	34	939	614
COSTA	39	44	44	22	5301	34	35	203
INT. HANDELSGE-SELLSCHAFT	50	48	44	22	5301	34	33	515
COMM./COUNCIL (case 22/70)	32	30	44	22	5301	34	31	256
NOLD	49	54	44	22	5301	34	443	288
DASSONVILLE	45	2	44	22	5301	34	6	6
DEFRENNE	36	19	44	22	5301	34	12	33
SIMMENTHAL	18	18	43	20	5296	1557	386	44
REWE-ZENTRAL	32	6	44	22	5301	34	10	13
CILFIT	34	45	43	20	33	2265	1360	209
LES VERTS	41	53	42	21	20	1699	551	763
FOTO-FROST	39	47	42	20	18	81	1043	263
WACHAUF	49	47	43	20	5296	1832	1193	234
ERT	44	25	34	14	380	882	502	35
FRANCOVICH	2	12	30	15	415	884	95	15
BOSMAN	1	1	23	12	655	2	23	1
MARTINEZ SALA	39	31	44	22	5301	34	1444	174
COMM./UK (case 466/98)	36	66	32	13	1330	183	614	2679
BAUMBAST	42	45	33	10	3621	1791	1599	395

4   Discussion and Future Work

A brief analysis of the experiments and of the overall experience so far conducted allows us to sketch some considerations. From a legal standpoint, we can say that we have just scratched the surface: there is a long series of challenges to deal with the essential contribution of legal experts in order to better understand how the NA paradigm with its methodological and technical apparatus can shed new light in our understanding of legal phenomena.

As our preliminary results clearly show, when applied to a "simple" citation network, traditional NA measures have poor performances. Incongruences arise, just to give an example, if you consider the rankings assigned by the measures and the parameters listed in Table 2 to Van Gend en Loos: the most relevant precedent in EU case law - according to the Court itself[3] - shows very low value of In-Degree centrality and 0 in all the other measures, although it collects a relevant number of citations from legal literature. A first explanation of this result could be related, among the other reasons, to the problem of "obliteration by incorporation", or OBI [18]. Borrowed from sociology of science and well-known in the literature of citation analysis and sociology of the law, OBI describes the phenomenon that typically occurs when an idea, such as a scientific development, is considered so influential to make unnecessary to explicitly cite

---

[3] http://curia.europa.eu/jcms/jcms/P_95693/.

its contributors. As highlighted by Garfield [18] while explaining the impact of OBI on the usefulness of the explicit citations analysis,

> *In the course of this hypothesized process [obliteration by incorporation], the number of explicit references to the original work declines in the papers and books making use of it. Users and consequently transmitters of that knowledge are so thoroughly familiar with its origins that they assume this to be true of their readers as well.*

The phenomenon is not surprising in the legal field. The "authority" citing [19], i.e., the use of citations to provide an authoritative basis for a statement in the citing work, is common in such field, especially in case-law system, where judges typically cite a case to extend its "authority" to their own decisions. However, it is not unusual that an important legal principle, affirmed by a given judgment, became so commonly accepted that later the precedent expressing it is not cited anymore. Therefore OBI can represent a major issue when the citation analysis is the only method used for identifying the relevance of specific documents over long run, since citations allow to detect only the explicit links (i.e., an express reference), without any consideration for those just implicitly contained in a document (e.g., the case reinterpreted as general principles of law within an argumentative path). It is clear, against this backdrop, the importance to better reflect on the ontology of the phenomenon investigated (e.g., relevance) that is on its concrete expressions (data, relations) and on the algorithms more suitable to identify it. Many aspects have to be deepened and taken into account. Different studies, for example, suggest to combine the research on the citation network of a given set of legal precedents with the network of scholarly opinions, in order to obtain a more detailed picture of which decisions and verdicts should be reckoned as relevant in a given legal system [20,21]. Another study [7] uses legal journals as benchmark of the forecasts made starting from the analysis of the decisions network. The main idea is that the analysis of cross citations between judicial decisions could be inadequate to identify the relevance of a case, so it should be integrated by the evaluations arising from the legal literature.

It is to be noted that there is a huge difference between citations by scholars and by judges, which depends, first of all, on the reasons why both cite a case. As highlighted by [21], judges typically cite other decisions only if they are relevant for the cases that are accidentally brought to their attention. Therefore, it may happen that a landmark case can be undervalued *vis-a-vis* less-relevant decisions which are habitually cited in routine cases. Scholars indeed have a view on legal relevance which is not confined to those decisions relevant for a specific case under scrutiny. To define the relevance of a case they consider many other elements, e.g., the political impact of a given decision or its popularity among the people, usually ignored by the judges in deciding what cases they have to cite. Therefore, the number of citations that a given document has received from legal scholars could be considered just as a clue of its relevance, since it provides no information about the reasons why the document was cited.

Other approaches can be exploited in this respect. Some researchers [22, 23], have proposed to use semantics-based legal citation network for having a better awareness of the arguments surrounding the citation that appears to be fit to deal with the OBI phenomenon. Another approach worthy of attention is represented by the combination of NLP and argument extraction (see, i.a. [24]), a methodology that is opening up new and promising possibilities to support both legal information retrieval and the identification of authoritative sources. These considerations suggest to pay attention to the definition of the research question namely the nature and the features of information to be extracted from the network, in order to achieve a better understanding of the way in which the network itself should be built.

From a technical standpoint, we have realized a freely available online tool[4] that, even with room for improvements, is efficient enough to allow to domain experts to make basic experiments with EU case law data. Regarding the future developments, we will invite domain experts to use the system involving them in the validation of both the tool and the methodology; to this aim, *EuCaseNet* features will be extended in order also to allow the analysis of different legal sources. Moreover, we will work on more refined operational definitions of legal research questions (starting from the concept of relevance) to be addressed by means of NA techniques. On the one hand, we will try to identify other data sources and suitable metrics (e.g., drawing inspiration by the techniques which are being developed in multimodal network analysis area [25,26]); on the other we will implement more advanced techniques for the visualization of complex structures that begin to be used in more other research areas [27,28].

References

1. Easley, D., Kleinberg, J.: Networks, Crowds, and Markets: Reasoning About a Highly Connected World. Cambridge University Press, New York (2010)
2. Lettieri, N., Winkels, R., Faro, S.: Network Analysis in Law. ESI, Naples (2013)
3. Lettieri, N., Altamura, A., Malandrino, D.: The legal macroscope: experimenting with visual legal analytics. Inf. Vis. **16**(4), 332–345 (2017)
4. Sacco, R.: Legal formants: a dynamic approach to comparative law (installment I of II). Am. J. Comp. Law **39**(1), 1–31 (1991)
5. Lettieri, N., Altamura, A., Faggiano, A., Malandrino, D.: A computational approach for the experimental study of EU case law: analysis and implementation. Soc. Netw. Anal. Min. **6**(1), 56:1–56:17 (2016)
6. Post, D.G., Eisen, M.B.: How long is the coastline of law? Thoughts on the fractal nature of legal systems. J. Leg. Stud. **29**, 545 (2000)
7. Fowler, J.H., Spriggs, J.F., Jeon, S., Wahlbeck, P.J.: Network analysis and the law: measuring the legal importance of precedents at the US Supreme Court. Polit. Anal. **15**(3), 324–346 (2007)
8. Smith, T.A.: The web of law. San Diego Law Rev. **44**, 309 (2007)
9. Kleinberg, J.M.: Hubs, authorities, and communities. ACM Comput. Surv. (CSUR) **31**(4es), 5 (1999)
10. Malmgren, S.: Towards a theory of jurisprudential relevance ranking. Using link analysis on EU case law, Graduate thesis, Stockholm University (2011)

---

[4] http://www.isislab.it:20080/snam/index.php#one.

11. Katz, D.M., Bommarito II, M.J.: Measuring the complexity of the law: the United States Code. Artif. Intell. Law **22**(4), 337–374 (2014)
12. Winkels, R., Boer, A.: Finding and visualizing context in Dutch legislation. In: Proceedings of NAiL 2013 (2013)
13. Koniaris, M., Anagnostopoulos, I., Vassiliou, Y.: Network Analysis in the Legal Domain: A complex model for European Union Legal Sources. arXiv preprint arXiv:1501.05237 (2015)
14. van Opijnen, M., Cristiana, S.: On the concept of relevance in legal information retrieval. Artif. Intell. Law **25**(1), 65–87 (2017)
15. Saracevic, T.: Relevance reconsidered. In: Information science: Integration in Perspectives. Proceedings of the Second Conference on Conceptions of Library and Information Science, Copenhagen, Denmark, pp. 201–218 (1996)
16. Cosijn, E., Ingwersen, P.: Dimensions of relevance. Inf. Process. Manag. **36**(4), 533–550 (2000)
17. Maduro, M., Azoulai, L.: The Past and Future of EU Law: The Classics of EU Law Revisited on the 50th Anniversary of the Rome Treaty. Bloomsbury Publishing, London (2010)
18. Garfield, E.: Citation Indexing: Its Theory and Application in Science, Technology, and Humanities. ISI Press (1979)
19. Posner, R.A.: The Theory and Practice of Citations Analysis, with Special Reference to Law and Economics. Special Reference to Law and Economics (1999)
20. Agnoloni, T., Pagallo, U.: The power laws of the Italian constitutional court, and their relevance for legal scholars. In: 28th International Conference on Legal Knowledge and Information Systems. JURIX (2015)
21. van Opijnen, M.: Citation analysis and beyond: in search of indicators measuring case law importance. In: JURIX (2012)
22. Zhang, P., Koppaka, L.: Semantics-based legal citation network. In: Proceedings of the 11th International Conference on Artificial Intelligence and Law, ICAIL 2007, pp. 123–130 (2007)
23. Panagis, Y., Sadl, U.: The force of EU case law: a multi-dimensional study of case citations. In: 28th International Conference on Legal Knowledge and Information Systems (JURIX) (2015)
24. Ashley, K.: Applying argument extraction to improve legal information retrieval. In: ArgNLP (2014)
25. Du, N., Wang, H., Faloutsos, C.: Analysis of large multi-modal social networks: patterns and a generator. In: Balcázar, J.L., Bonchi, F., Gionis, A., Sebag, M. (eds.) ECML PKDD 2010. LNCS (LNAI), vol. 6321, pp. 393–408. Springer, Heidelberg (2010). https://doi.org/10.1007/978-3-642-15880-3_31
26. Ghani, S., Kwon, B.C., Lee, S., Yi, J.S., Elmqvist, N.: Visual analytics for multi-modal social network analysis: a design study with social scientists. IEEE Trans. Vis. Comput. Graph. **19**(12), 2032–2041 (2013)
27. Malandrino, D., Pirozzi, D., Zaccagnino, G., Zaccagnino, R.: A color-based visualization approach to understand harmonic structures of musical compositions. In: 19th International Conference on Information Visualisation, IV 2015, Barcelona, Spain, 22–24 July 2015, pp. 56–61 (2015)
28. De Prisco, R., Lettieri, N., Malandrino, D., Pirozzi, D., Zaccagnino, G., Zaccagnino, R.: Visualization of music plagiarism: analysis and evaluation. In: 20th International Conference Information Visualisation, IV 2016, Lisbon, Portugal, 19–22 July 2016, pp. 177–182 (2016)

Electronic Evidence Semantic Structure: Exchanging Evidence Across Europe in a Coherent and Consistent Way

Maria Angela Biasiotti[(✉)], Sara Conti, and Fabrizio Turchi

Institute of Legal Information Theory and Technique, 50127 Florence, Italy
mariangela.biasiotti@ittig.cnr.it
http://www.ittig.cnr.it/en/persone/ricerca/maria-angela-biasiotti

Abstract. In a cross-border dimension considering the specific collaboration among European Union Member States related to criminal investigations and criminal trials, it becomes crucial to have a common and shared understanding of what Electronic Evidence is and how it should be treated in the EU context and in the EU MS. In this context the EVIDENCE project developed a tailor-made categorization of relevant concepts that allow to rely on a common and shared knowledge in this domain. The categorization provides a starting analysis for the exchange of Electronic Evidence and data between judicial actors and LEAs, with a specific focus on issues of the criminal field and criminal procedures. This semantic Structure might represent a good starting point for the alignment of electronic evidence concepts all over Europe in across border dimension. This categorisation is significant as it is one of the few initiatives to identify and classify relevant concepts in a domain, which currently lacks of clear boundaries and touches upon different disciplines.

Keywords: Electronic evidence categorization
Electronic evidence exchange · Judicial cooperation · European Union

1 Introduction

Crime has become global, and almost all crimes involve electronic evidence. A significant problem has become the exchange of data, across jurisdictions and between the domestic participants in the criminal judicial process. Taking this development and the problems into account, the EVIDENCE Project[1] was conceived. The project concluded that the European Union needs to develop a better means to exchange information and evidence relating to crimes quickly

---

[1] European Informatics Data Exchange Framework for Court and Evidence, (funding scheme: CSA (Supporting Action), Call ID FP7-SEC-2013-1; grant agreement no: 608185; duration: 32 months (March 2014 – October 2016); coordinator: Consiglio Nazionale delle Ricerche (CNR-ITTIG), Italy; EU funding: Euro 1,924,589.00); http://www.evidenceproject.eu.

© Springer Nature Switzerland AG 2018
U. Pagallo et al. (Eds.): AICOL VI-X 2015–2017, LNAI 10791, pp. 556–573, 2018.
https://doi.org/10.1007/978-3-030-00178-0_38

from one country to another for the purpose of investigating crime in a timely manner. The exchange becomes crucial in counterterrorism operations and when dealing with global crimes. At the same time, a secure and trusted exchange of information and of electronic evidence relating to crimes is an important element in order to promote judicial cooperation in criminal matters, as well to contribute to an effective and coherent application of EU Mutual Legal Assistance[2] (MLA) and European Investigation Order[3] (EIO) procedures.

In a cross-border dimension considering the specific collaboration among European Union Member States related to criminal investigations and criminal trials, it becomes crucial to have a common and shared understanding of what Electronic Evidence is and how it should be treated in the EU context and in the EU MS.

In this scenario, the categorization has been carried out taking into consideration the "status quo" governing the collection, preservation and exchange of electronic evidence at International and European Union levels.

In fact, Member States in Europe have basically different criminal legal systems and different tradition in the sources of criminal law.

That is, there is a lack of uniformity within Member States criminal legislations, thus a common understanding in the electronic evidence domain is required. The categorization of electronic evidence domain did not rely on a simple comparative analysis and overview of national laws; but it just fostered the building up of a common and shared "language" related to the handling of electronic evidence, with the final aim of highlighting common requirements being able to guarantee a uniform regulation of the use of electronic evidence itself.

The Council of Europe and the European Union are, in this respect, two supranational entities whose actions aim to develop a common legal substrate and implement legislative harmonization between the various EU countries and also with third States. Therefore, the Evidence project team took in due consideration the most important documents and laws related to the criminal field, issued by those entities.

With regard to electronic evidence, the Council of Europe Convention on Cybercrime is highly relevant: although electronic evidence may not necessarily

---

[2] European Convention on Mutual Assistance in Criminal Matters, Strasbourg, 20/04/1959, ETS No. 030; Council of Europe Convention on Laundering, Search, Seizure and Confiscation of the Proceeds from Crime, Strasbourg, 08/11/1990, ETS No. 141; Council of Europe Convention on the Transfer of Sentenced Persons, Strasbourg, 21 March 1983, ETS No. 112; Mutual assistance in criminal matters between Member States, Council Act of 29 May 2000 establishing in accordance with Article 34 of the Treaty on European Union the Convention on Mutual Assistance in Criminal Matters between the Member States of the European Union, 2000/C 197/01, OJ C 197, 12.7.2000; Second Additional Protocol to the European Convention on Mutual Assistance in Criminal Matters, Strasbourg, 8 November 2001, CETS No. 182; Council of Europe Convention on Cybercrime, Budapest, 23 November 2001, ETS 185.

[3] Directive 2014/41/EU.

origin only from cybercrime, this is the main framework for the categorization domain as it offers many provisions to improve investigations where electronic evidence is involved.

Section 1, Chapter II (substantive law issues) of the Convention has been very relevant to the electronic evidence categorization point of view[4]. In particular, this Section deals with the definition of offences, grouped in 4 different categories (offences against the confidentiality, integrity and availability of computer data and system; computer-related offences; content-related offences, finally offences related to infringements of copyright and related rights) related to the use of computer networks and Internet.

For each of the mentioned categories, these offences are defined and described: illegal access, illegal interception, data interference, system interference, misuse of devices, computer-related forgery, computer-related fraud, offences related to child pornography and offences related to copyright and related rights.

The categorization of the Electronic evidence domain based on these distinctions: the different offences have represented a starting point to build up the categorization itself, as the basis for the development of the "legal" classes (in particular, the class Crime and the class Rule).

The categorization classes also based on several initiatives, at EU level, directed to create a common framework to combat crime in general, and also crimes in which electronic evidence is involved, by establishing a cooperation between Member States.

Such as the Convention on mutual assistance in criminal matters[5], which aims at improving the speed and efficiency of judicial cooperation between Member States.

It is worth mentioning the European evidence warrant (EEW), which may be used to obtain any objects, documents and data for use in criminal proceedings for which it may be issued[6], aiming at facilitating speedier cooperation between Member States in criminal proceedings, specifically in the transfer of evidence (and, obviously electronic evidence) [3].

A significant role for the Electronic Evidence categorization has been also played by the Directive 2013/40/EU of the European Parliament and of the Council of 12 August 2013, on "Attacks against information systems"[7], and by the Directive 2014/41 of the Parliament and of the Council of 3 April 2014, on the "European Investigation Order" 4 (EIO)[8].

The Directive 2013/40/EU gives common definitions in the area of attacks against information systems: offences of illegal access to an information system, illegal system interference, illegal data interference and illegal interception. There is the attempt to establish a common framework "of minimum rules concerning

---

[4] Explanatory Report to the Convention on Cybercrime.
[5] Council Act of 29 May 2000.
[6] Council Framework Decision 2008/978/EU.
[7] Directive 2013/40/EU.
[8] Directive 2014/41/EU.

the definition of criminal offences in that area", in which electronic evidence becomes of the utmost importance.

As for the EIO, this order should apply to all investigative measures aimed at gathering evidence (and also, electronic evidence) and it will promote the growth of a uniform and comprehensive system for obtaining evidence, in cases with a cross-border dimension.

Finally, developing a common and shared language on the Electronic Evidence domain has properly been the aim of the categorization team, as a starting point for creating a unanimous framework for a coherent, consistent and uniform application of new technologies in the collection, use and exchange of electronic evidence in the criminal field.

According to this point of view, to make it possible, has been necessary to build the "legal" classes of the categorization complying with the definitions of the Convention on Cybercrime and in general with a specific view to all the EU criminal legislation, as to have a common minimum standard of offences and terms within the Electronic Evidence domain.

In this context the EVIDENCE project developed a tailor-made categorization of relevant concepts that allow to rely on a common and shared knowledge in this domain. The categorization provides a starting analysis for the exchange of Electronic Evidence and data between judicial actors and LEAs, with a specific focus on issues of the criminal field and criminal procedures. Moreover, due consideration is devoted to the impact of harmonized procedures on how police, prosecutors and lawyers in criminal cases, and parties in civil cases, handle Electronic Evidence so as to preserve its integrity.

The proposed categorization offers a common terminology for the electronic evidence domain bearing into account the twofold challenges to be considered according to the Electronic Evidence lifecycle:

- the treatment of evidence/data/information by means of ICT in the context of criminal law, considering the entire evidence lifecycle from the incident on, passing through the investigative phase;
- the exchange of evidence/data/information by means of ICT complying with the issues related to specific requirements and shared procedures.

The process of handling electronic evidence can be broken down under different phases (see Fig. 2), and the exchange process can occur during any of these phases.

When electronic evidence is acquired and exchanged, information about its provenance must be maintained to help establish authenticity and trustworthiness. This information includes the origin of the evidence, its condition, and any unique or distinctive characteristics. Any irregularities in the handling of electronic evidence might spoil the probative value of the evidence, making it not admissible.

All the relevant concepts related to these requirements have been included in the Categorization.

2 Some Electronic Evidence Issues

The very nature of data and information held in electronic form makes it easier to manipulate than traditional forms of data. When acquired and exchanged, the integrity of the data must be maintained and proved, i.e. demonstrated that the electronic evidence has not been altered since the time it was created, stored or transmitted. Legislation on criminal procedures in many European countries was enacted before the use of electronic evidence, although many Member States have amended their legislation to accommodate the new form of evidence. However, some issues remain, and include, but are not limited to, the following:

(i) In certain countries there are defined rules as to admissibility of evidence in legal proceedings, while in other countries admissibility is flexible.
(ii) Legislation and policies may affect an investigation. For example, privacy and data protection laws in some Member States may prevent the collection of evidence, and varied data retention periods across jurisdictions may hinder investigations.
(iii) Legislation may furthermore not sufficiently address the realities of modern investigations, especially when it comes to evolving new technologies[9].

The EVIDENCE Project concluded with the following results:

(i) The categorization of electronic evidence.
(ii) A survey on the legal position in handling and exchanging electronic evidence in Europe.
(iii) A survey on the technical position in handling and exchanging electronic evidence in Europe, along with a proposal for the representation of data and meta data involved in the exchange process.
(iv) A plan for realising a Common European Framework for the Exchange of Electronic Evidence. The plan provides a brief overview of the legal issues; considerations relating to standards; technical aspects; law enforcement requirements; the nature of the market, data protection issues, and the challenges these topics pose. The aim of the Common European Framework Framework for the Exchange of Electronic Evidence is to improve the efficiency of investigations and judicial procedures while maintaining adequate safeguards aimed at protecting relevant fundamental human rights and respecting clear standards of conduct.

3 Preliminary Remarks on the Concept of "Electronic Evidence"

There is such a wide variety of possible evidences that potentially anything may become the evidence of a crime. Moreover, the introduction and the extensive

---

[9] See EVIDENCE Deliverable 3.1 - Overview of existing legal framework in the EU Member States: http://s.evidenceproject.eu/p/e/v/evidence-ga-608185-d3-1-411.pdf and EVIDENCE Deliverable 3.2 - Status quo assessment and analysis of primary challenges and shortcomings: http://s.evidenceproject.eu/p/e/v/evidence-ga-608185-d3-2-412.pdf.

use of ICT has additionally generated new forms of crimes or new ways of perpetrating them, as well as a new type of evidences. This different setting implies that, although all kinds of evidences have to be handled according to criminal law and procedures, the 'new'type of evidences need additional and specific ways of handling. For instance, to give an initial suggestion of some of the new problems that arise, an increasing number of crimes (not only cybercrime) involve geo-distributed Electronic Evidence and therefore an evidence 'location' needs to be re-conceptualized, including issues concerning direct access to extraterritorial data by LEAs (see [1,6,7,11]).

Electronic Evidences, as the traditional ones, have to be acquired and handled following specific procedures that demonstrate their authenticity and integrity. The fulfilment of these principles specifically applied to Electronic Evidence requires the adoption of ad hoc procedures that demonstrate that the Electronic Evidence has not been altered since the time it was created, stored or transmitted. Such procedure has been developed in the field of digital forensics (see [4,5]).

The idea to conceptualize the source of evidence and to outline the transition from generic evidence to digital/Electronic Evidence establishing standards and methods to assure authenticity over time also descends from diplomatics. This field is providing an important contribution in this domain, by stating the principle called "record trustworthiness". This principle has two qualitative dimensions: reliability and authenticity. Reliability means that the record is capable of standing for the facts to which it attests, while authenticity means that the record is what it claims to be. The trustworthiness of records as evidence is of particular interest to EVIDENCE project, where Electronic Evidence is trustworthy being the result of the process of assessing its reliability and authenticity.

One of the main aims of the project was to develop a common and shared understanding on what electronic evidence is, together with the relevant concepts (digital forensics, criminal law, criminal procedure, criminal international cooperation) as well as to draft a proposed 'standard process' occurring when a crime occurs.

A definition of electronic evidence needs to be is broad enough to include all kinds of evidence regardless of their origin. This was a particularly important for the aim of the EVIDENCE Project, which focused on the exchange, as well as on the harmonized handling of electronic evidence within a common European framework. Based on these premises, the following definition is proposed:

> *Electronic Evidence is any data resulting from the output of an analogue device and/or a digital device of potential probative value that are generated by, processed by, stored on or transmitted by any electronic device. Digital evidence is that Electronic Evidence which is generated or converted to a numerical format.*

The term data includes any analogical or digital item, because these items may be the output of analogue devices or data in digital form.

In particular, it has been chosen to use the term data to include any analogical and/or digital item specifying that these items may be the output of analogue devices or data in digital form. With respect to this notion it must be considered that Electronic data cover every method by which data are made available: over the internet, stored on a computer, a smartphone, a separate hard disk, a CD-ROM, a USB stick. There is no distinction to be made between data created in analogue or digitized forms and the ones born digitally. Therefore scanned images are also to be included in this term.

More specifically a print-out is merely a secondary evidence of the original (or primary) digital version. A scanned version of a paper document is a secondary item of evidence because it is a copy. And it remains a copy, even if the original is destroyed. A distinction relevant to the project categorization relates to primary and secondary evidence (see [8, 10]), also in relationship with physical and Electronic Evidence. "In physical word the distinction between primary and secondary evidence lies on the difference between the production of an original document to prove a content and the submission of inferior evidence, such as a copy of document termed, secondary evidence". The primary evidence of a document in electronic form is different from the primary evidence of a physical object and this difference is significant for the EVIDENCE categorization. The concept of primary or original in the electronic dimension is related to the hardware or storage media where the file is kept. Then the print out of the document on paper represents the secondary evidence in a human readable format. Mason underlines that "even if the hard drive or storage device is correctly identified as primary evidence, the physical items is of no value unless a person testifies to its relevance and qualities that make it pertinent". For this reason courts rely on the production of the output of electronic data in a human-readable format, printed on paper, which can be considered as a secondary evidence of Electronic Evidence.

The term potential indicates that it has been considered the entire Electronic Evidence lifecycle from the very start of the investigation process (the occurrence of a criminal incident) to the handling and presentation in Courts. This allows us to take in due consideration the exchange/transmission of Electronic Evidence that may occur in any phase after the incident.

The term probative value highlights the aspect of relevance of the Electronic Evidence (not its admissibility in courts that depends on the different jurisdictions as well as on the adjudicator evaluation) and also indicates the fact-finding process that transforms potential Electronic Evidence into an Electronic Evidence.

Moreover, coherently with the inclusion of all forms of Evidence, the definition stresses on information that is manipulated, generated through, stored on or communicated by any electronic device, thus including any type of computers and/or information systems. Therefore, in the current definition, any physical and analogue evidence, which has once been digitized (e.g. image sent by fax and then printed again) is considered Electronic Evidence. These three dimensions of the Electronic Evidence as conceived by the EVIDENCE Categorisation structure takes in due consideration the basic distinction between evidence which was born digital (e.g. data on a hard drive) and evidence which has been digitized only later (see Fig. 1).

Categorization perspective considers:

– Digital evidence: the evidence that is originally born digital as created by any digital device (computer or computer like-device);
– Analogical Evidence: the evidence originally in analogue format that enters into the digitization process acquiring the digital status;
– Digitalized Physical evidences: the evidence that is born physical and entered into the digitization process acquiring the electronic status.

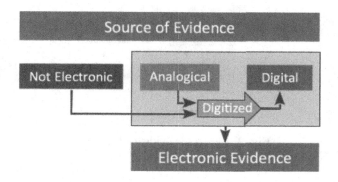

Fig. 1. From source of evidence to electronic evidence

4   The Electronic Evidence Life Cycle

The process of handling electronic evidence can be divided in several phases. The first phase includes the identification, collection and anti-contamination precautions (searching the scene, collecting the evidence, packaging and labelling and creating documents reporting the activities performed at every step) of electronic evidence. In the second phase, the acquisition of the source of evidence takes place, determining which items are most likely to serve the purposes of the investigation, which are the most time sensitive, which are most at risk of being lost or corrupted, including the identification of similar issues. During the third phase, the findings are evaluated and interpreted. The fourth phase includes the presentation of the results in a report, which should include factual findings, interpretation, and expert opinion. The report and presentation are essential steps in the electronic evidence lifecycle, because the court will examine the report that should contain all relevant findings as well as technical and non-technical explanations of the case and its issues. During each of the phases involved in handling electronic evidence, it is essential to guarantee the preservation of the evidence: every precaution must be taken when collecting evidence, because any break in the process or improper handling of a procedure could spoil the probative value of the evidence, potentially making it inadmissible. The same principle applies to documenting procedures. Everything must be documented: how the evidence was found, its condition, model and serial numbers, markings, etc. The exchange may happen in different phases of the electronic evidence lifecycle. Figure 2 illustrates the different phases of electronic evidence.

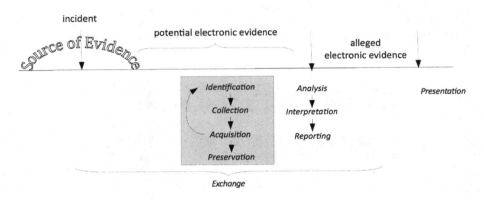

Fig. 2. Electronic evidence life cycle

On the basis of the life-cycle outlined above, eight different concepts have been identified by the EVIDENCE Project. The concepts have been organized and classified as follows:

(i) Crime is an act, default or conduct prejudicial to the community, for which the person responsible may, by law, be punished by a fine or imprisonment.

(ii) Sources of electronic evidence: comprise any physical, analogical and digital device (computer or computer like device) capable of creating information that may have a probative value in legal proceedings.

(iii) A process is a series of actions or steps taken in order to achieve a particular end within the electronic evidence lifecycle.

(iv) Electronic evidence is any information (comprising the output of analogue devices or data in digital form) of potential probative value that is manipulated, generated through, stored on or communicated by any electronic device.

(v) A requirement represents principles or rules related both to legal rules and handling procedures that are necessary, indispensable, or unavoidable to make potential electronic evidence admissible in legal proceedings.

(vi) A 'stakeholder' (interested party) includes people or organizations having a concern in or playing a specific role in the electronic evidence lifecycle.

(vii) A rule contains a set of explicit or understood regulations or principles governing conduct or procedures for the identification, collection, preservation, analysis, exchange and presentation of electronic evidence in a cross border and national dimension.

(viii) Digital forensics is the application of forensic science to electronic evidence in a legal matter.

These main classes have been hierarchically structured in sub-classes that may be easily updated and maintained. The concepts are directly linked to the class they refer to according to the EVIDENCE Project conceptual model developed from the perspective of the life-cycle of electronic evidence.

5   EVIDENCE Semantic Structure: An Overview

Figure 3 shows the classes of the categorization reporting their main relationships at a high level of detail. The core of the categorization is the class Electronic Evidence that is connected with all the other classes. The Electronic Evidence class is related with the class *Source of Evidence* (see also Fig. 4), through the relation *"is contained in"*, is managed applying specific processes and is validated according to legal and technical Requirements, generally studied in the different disciplines of *Digital Forensics*; it concerns different types of crimes. Different types of *Stakeholders* are concerned with the *Electronic Evidence*, who apply specific rules, such as standards, soft and hard laws to examine it.

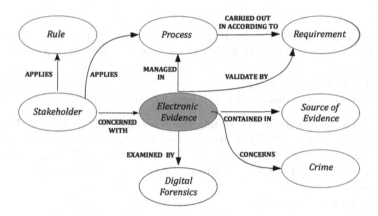

Fig. 3. EVIDENCE project categorization - main relationships at high level

6   EVIDENCE Semantic Structure Development: Methodology

The following activities were carried out to develop the categorization:

1. Identification of information sources;

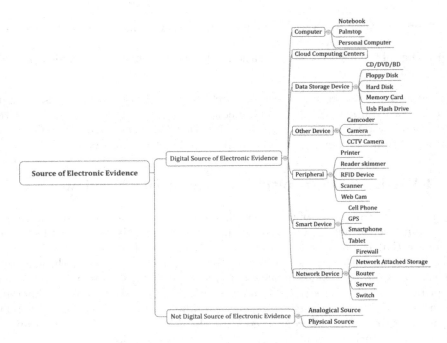

Fig. 4. Class source of electronic evidence, hierarchical view of main items

2. Extraction of relevant concepts, using bottom-up and top-down strategies;
3. Choice of a standard way to represent and support the categorization activities;
4. Structuring relevant concepts;
5. Review of the conceptual model/categorization internally.

The first step consisted in building the relevant bibliography on Electronic Evidence domain, identifying sources of information relevant to the domain. The sources were also collected in full text, mainly in PDF format, and then transformed in text format for the automatic treatment foreseen later on by the adopted methodology[10].

The sources are divided in:

- academic papers and monographs (45)
- guidelines (30 sources)
- report (13 sources)

---

[10] Copyright note: documents included in the corpus have been downloaded using (a) biblioproxy.cnr.it, the internal web platform of Italian National Research Council to access commercial bibliographic resources, (b) downloaded from the Web if freely accessible. Please note that the full text collected during the categorization building-up activities had only research purposes and excluded any commercial use of resources.

– project reports (16 sources)
– legislative code of practice and regulation commentaries (16 sources)
– recommendation and policy document (8 sources).

6.1   Extraction of Relevant Concepts

In this phase relevant concepts of the Electronic Evidence semantic structure
were identified combining a top-down approach with a bottom-up approach.
This double strategy allowed to build up the EVIDENCE Categorisation on two
different layers: an upper layer made of relevant and abstract concepts identified
as "classes" and a lower layer populated by concepts of the Electronic Evidence
concrete reality, identified as "instance". The connection between the two layers
is made through sub-classes partly extracted from the top-down strategy and
partly coming from the bottom-up extraction, as shown in Fig. 5.

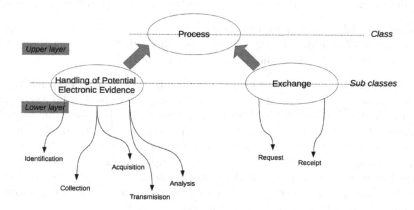

Fig. 5. Top-down method, building up of classes, sub classes and instances

The Top-down approach allowed to extract relevant concepts from a subset of
the collected sources using a manual method. The selection of the most relevant
documents was carried out on the basis of following criteria:

– the relevance of the author;
– the relevance of the organization responsible for the publication: for example
  the Association of Chief Police Officers (ACPO), the Council of Europe, the
  National Institute for Standard and Technology, the National Institute of
  Justice (US), the International Standard Organization;
– a direct evaluation of the document relevance within the scientific literature
  of the domain.

The top-down method consisted in reading the selected set of documents
and identifying the most relevant concepts for each source and for the domain

of interest. This resulted in a first list of concepts. The different lists and results were compared and this cross evaluation phase allowed to create a shared and common list of relevant concepts as well as to assign to each concept a specific weight.

The most common concepts, identified in this phase, have been included in the Categorization (http://www.evidenceproject.eu/categorization).

Then some main classes have been identified and many concepts, already selected, were assigned to those classes as subclasses or instances. In order to verify whether the terms selected in the top down approach were those generally used in the specialist domain a bottom-up strategy was implemented. This allowed also to verify the set of concepts manually collected and increase the number of terms to be taken into consideration.

The bottom-up phase adopted a semi-automatic concept extraction using a Natural Language Processing basic technique. This parallel activity was performed on a subset of documents gathered by all project partners, specifically on 91 documents out of the previously collected 128 for the following reasons:

- Documents 122 to 128 were too technical;
- Documents 35, 36, 37, 45, 86, 118 were not in English;
- Documents 22, 26, 39 had no pdf full version available.

The automatic extraction relied on a lemmatization process determining the lemma for each word found in the documents corpus. In particular the extraction process has exploited the *WordNet Lemmatizer* that uses the WordNet Database[11] to lookup lemmas[12]. Also a stop word list has been developed in order to eliminate articles, prepositions, etc. The result of this step was the identification of a list containing the main concepts of the Electronic Evidence domain based on the relevance of the concepts identified as well as the context where the concepts were extracted. In this phase a collection of definitions of the relevant concepts were also gathered and analysed.

Automatic systems are based on statistical methods that generally require a high number of documents to perform a meaningful linguistic analysis. Even if our corpora was not so large, it was sufficient to determine the most relevant terms in the collection, using an information retrieval technique. For this aim it has been used the *Term Frequency-Inverse Document Frequency* (*TF-IDF*) formula to discover which terms were more relevant for the Electronic Evidence domain. TF-IDF weight is a method often used in information retrieval and text mining. This weight is a statistical measure used to evaluate how important a word is within a document or in a collection or corpus. The importance increases proportionally to the number of times a word occurs in the document but it is offset by the frequency of the word in the corpus.

---

[11] http://wordnet.princeton.edu/.

[12] A lemma is a canonical form of the word that may appear in several inflected forms. For example, in English, the verb 'to investigate' may appear as 'investigate', 'investigated', 'investigates', 'investigating'. The base form, 'investigate', that one might look up in a dictionary, is called the lemma for the word.

On the basis of the previous considerations, concerning the reliability of the automatic methods, all lemmas automatically extracted (more than 21.000 terms) were reduced to about 16.000 lemmas. They were then manually examined in order to detect the terms not included in the top-down methods and also to distinguish and select concepts belonging to the specific language domain. Moreover terms belonging to common language were also eliminated. The resulting list of terms was refined and then merged with the previous concepts, obtaining a list of about 220 terms, setting A few of the new terms selected during the bottom-up process are shown in Table 1.

Table 1. Terms selected during the bottom-up process

Lemma	Occurrences
Cybercrime	3.341
Requirement	905
Seize	854
Integrity	636
Preservation	630
Fraud (online fraud)	450
Judge	448
Prosecutor	435
Label (labeling)	293
Authenticity	268
Police officer	134
Phishing	127
Encase (encase forensics)	122

Finally, to exploit the statistical data gathered by the bottom-up method, it has been extracted the occurrences of the main syntagms identified during the top-down strategy.

In other words the syntagms have been extracted in a manual way and later each item of the list has been used for an automatic processing in order to establish the related frequency.

Table 2 shows the result of this processing.

6.2   Choice of a Standard Way to Represent and Support The categorization Activities

In order to represent the categorization, it has been chosen SKOS (Simple Knowledge Organization System)[13] that "provides a model for expressing the

---

[13] SKOS Simple Knowledge Organization System Primer, W3C Working Group Note 18 August 2009, http://www.w3.org/TR/skos-primer.

Table 2. Occurrences of syntagms from EVIDENCE project corpus

Syntagm	Occurrences
Digital evidence	1.933
Electronic Evidence	1.076
Digital forensic(s)	926
Child pornography	806
Computer forensic(s)	613
Chain of custody	196
Incident response	176
Forensic(s) examiner	165
Law enforcement agency(ies)	161
Best practice(s)	146
Hash value	138
Police officer(s)	134
Personal computer	109
Cyber crime(s)	61
Expert witness	54
Digital evidence specialist(s)	53

basic structure and content of concept schemes such as thesauri, classification schemes, subject heading lists, taxonomies, 'folksonomies', other types of controlled vocabulary, and also concept schemes embedded in glossaries and terminologies". SKOS has the advantage of expressing knowledge organization systems in a machine-understandable way within the framework of the Semantic Web. It was introduced by the W3C and has become a W3C recommendation, based on other Semantic Web standards such as RDF and OWL. The main element of the SKOS vocabulary is the concept. "Concepts are the units of thought—ideas, meanings, or (categories of) objects and events—which underlie many knowledge organization systems. As such, concepts exist in the mind as abstract entities which are independent of the terms used to label them[14]". Moreover, "concepts can be identified using URIs, labelled with lexical strings in one or more natural languages, assigned notations (lexical codes), documented with various types of note, linked to other concepts and organized into informal hierarchies and association networks, aggregated into concepts schemes, grouped not labelled and/or ordered collections, and mapped to concepts in other schemes" [15]. To implement the categorization with SKOS, it has been used, *iQvoc* a vocabulary management tool[16] that combines easy-to-use human interfaces with Semantic Web interoperability.

---

[14] http://semanticweb.com/introduction-to-skos_b33086.
[15] http://www.w3.org/TR/skos-primer.
[16] http://iqvoc.net/.

According to the knowledge management system chosen, for each identified term the following features were provided:

- A Label: SKOS allows the use of multiple labels, one single preferable and multiple alternatives, nevertheless this feature has been used only for a limited set of concepts;
- A singular Definition, even though SKOS allows the use of multiple definitions for the same concept;
- Structuring concepts in classes and sub classes using hierarchical relationships
- An Editorial Note where all reliable sources, are specified to determine the single definition of the concept. In particular it has been used:
  - "team definition" to specify definition set by the team that worked on the categorization task;
  - "Definition based on..." to indicate that an original source was adopted with minor changes and/or adapted to the domain;
  - "E. Casey (see [2]) etc." to indicate that it has been cited exactly the definition provided in the source.
- Scope Note that explains and clarifies the meaning of the term and describes its intended use as a subject heading.
- a Relation term that explains the type of association between the defined term and other terms belonging to other classes and subclasses of the categorisation. The type of relation is specified for each association. When relationships are transitive, associations are reported accordingly both in related and relating class (i.e. Forensic examiner uses Digital forensic tool; Digital forensic tool is used by Forensic examiner).
- an Historic Note in order to handle the changes of the concepts definitions and to keep track of all changes affecting the definition or scope of that specific concept during the entire Project lifecycle.

The EVIDENCE project does not take into consideration a multilingual version of the proposed categorization due time scheduling allocation. Moreover a linguistic alignment of concepts in different languages would require not only a translation of terms but also the compliance with specific legal and judicial order as well as with the specific context in which those concepts are placed (legislation, case law, European, domestic, etc.). Every concept identified has been represented using, at minimum, the following data model:
Description/Preferred label (obligatory, unique): the name of the concept;
Definition of the concept (one is obligatory, more are optional);
Scope Notes an extended explanation of the concept and its context of use (optional, one or more).
An example of the data model is given in Table 3:

Table 3. Example of concept acquisition in SKOS

Description	Acquisition
Definition	The process of creating a copy of data within a defined set
Scope note	The Digital Evidence First Responder should adopt a suitable acquisition method based on the situation, cost and time, and document the decision for using a particular method or tool appropriately. Digital evidence, by its very nature, is fragile and can be altered, damaged or destroyed by improper handling or examination. Examination is best conducted on a copy of the original evidence. The original evidence should be acquired in a manner that protects and preserves the integrity of the evidence. (ISO 27037)
Editorial note	Definition based on the ISO/IEC 27037:2012

7   Conclusions

This semantic Structure might represent a good starting point for the alignment of electronic evidence concepts all over Europe in a cross border dimension. This categorisation is significant as it is one of the few initiatives to identify and classify relevant concepts in a domain, which currently lacks of clear boundaries and touches upon different disciplines. When the activities of the EVIDENCE Project started, the knowledge on this domain and the awareness about it were very limited and a few persons were able to speak about it in a comprehensive way. Even actors directly involved in the treatment of electronic evidence by default (public prosecutors, LEAs and judges) demonstrated real important gaps and challenges in their knowledge and training.

The Categorization has been mainly exploited for the Evidence project activities in order to determine a common terminology over the different work packages. The future steps would consist of turning this first result into an ontology fruitful to the digital forensic community. This entails to compare to other European projects related to the digital forensics domain and the electronic evidence exchange among the involved/interested stakeholders.

Furthermore it will be essential to take into account the differences in national legislation within the EU member States, and the evidence rules amongst countries with similar legal tradition, an issue that would primarily find a solution through legislative and/or policy action. Policy makers should define an efficient regulation for the treatment and exchange of electronic evidence.

Another essential feature is to meet the need to develop definitions that are future-proof in order not to be affected by technological developments.

The status quo at the beginning of the EVIDENCE project was *"I know electronic evidence exists, I know I cannot make it without but I don't know how to deal with it and treat and handle it without compromising it..."*.

Now that the cornerstone has been put in place the future work to be done will be to migrate this simple categorization into a more sophisticated way of managing concepts and their semantic relationship such as the ontological ones and to match this semantic structure with others already existing in complementary domain such as digital forensics (see [9,12]).

References

1. Association of Chief Police Officers UK. Good Practice Guide for Digital Evidence (2012). http://www.digital-detective.net/digital-forensics-documents/ACPO_Good_Practice_Guide_for_Digital_Evidence_v5.pdf
2. Casey, E.: Digital Evidence and Computer Crime. Forensic Science, Computers, and the Internet, vol. XXVII, 3rd edn, p. 807. Elsevier, Amsterdam (2011). ISBN 9780123742681
3. Murphy, C.C.: The European evidence warrant: mutual recognition. In: Eckes, C., Konstadinides, T. (eds.) Crime Within the Area of Freedom Security and Justice: A European Public Order. Cambridge University Press, Cambridge (2011)
4. Ćosić, J., Ćosić, Z.: An ontological approach to study and manage digital chain of custody of digital evidence. J. Inf. Organ. Sci. **35**(1), 1–13 (2011)
5. Ćosić, J., Ćosić, Z.: The necessity of developing a digital evidence ontology. In: Proceedings of the 23rd Central European Conference on Information and Intelligent Systems, pp. 325–230. University of Zagreb (2012)
6. Council of Europe: Electronic Evidence Guide. A basic guide for police officers, prosecutors and judges (2014)
7. ISO/IEC 27037: Guidelines for identification, collection, acquisition, and preservation of digital evidence (2012)
8. Mason, S.: Electronic Evidence, p. 934. LexisNexis-Butterworths, London (2012). ISBN 9781405779876
9. Park, H., Cho, S.H., Kwon, H.-C.: Cyber forensics ontology for cyber criminal investigation. In: Sorell, M. (ed.) e-Forensics 2009. LNICST, vol. 8, pp. 160–165. Springer, Heidelberg (2009). https://doi.org/10.1007/978-3-642-02312-5_18
10. Schafer, B., Mason, S.: The characteristics of digital evidence. In: Mason, S. (ed.) Electronic Evidence, p. 25. LexisNexis Butterworths, London (2012)
11. SWGDE: Digital evidence: standards and principles, forensic science communications, vol. 2, no. 2, p. 2 (2000). www.swgde.org
12. Talib, A.M., Alomary, F.O.: Toward a comprehensive ontology based-investigation for digital forensics cybercrime. Int. J. Commun. Antenna Propag. **5**(5), 263–268 (2015)

Author Index

Printed in the United States
By Bookmasters